THE LEGIONARY FORTRESS AT WROXETER

Excavations by Graham Webster
1955–1985

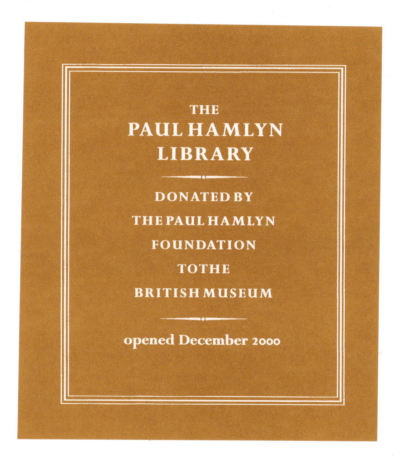

THE LEGIONARY FORTRESS AT WROXETER

Excavations by Graham Webster
1955–85

by Graham Webster
edited by John Chadderton

with contributions by
D Bailey, F Ball, N Ball, R J Brickstock, P J Casey, H E M Cool,
G Dannell, M J Darling, B Dickinson, M Henig,
D Mackreth, B A Noddle, T O'Connor, and J Price

ENGLISH HERITAGE

2002

ARCHAEOLOGICAL REPORT 19

Copyright © English Heritage 2002

First published 2002 by
English Heritage, 23 Savile Row, London W1S 2ET

Printed by Latimer Trend & Company Ltd

ISBN 1 85074 685 0
Product code 50081

Editors: Blaise Vyner and Julie Gardiner
Layout design: Multiplex Techniques Ltd
Print Production Manager: Richard Jones, Publications and Design, English Heritage
Brought to press by Karen Dorn and Andrew McLaren, Publications and Design, English Heritage,
Chris Evans, Graphics Artist, English Heritage, and Peter Ellis

Contents

Illustrations

Tables

Acknowledgements

The excavation of Wroxeter was originally planned, in collaboration with the Ministry of Public Buildings and Works, as a training school organised by the Department of Extra-Mural Studies of the University of Birmingham. The school was initiated in 1955 by the Head of the Department, Donald Dudley, and my gratitude goes first to him, and thereafter to his successors, for maintaining the school with its high academic standard and subsequent reputation. I must also thank a succession of Chief and Area Ancient Monument Inspectors in the Ministry of Public Buildings and Works and its successor bodies the Department of the Environment and English Heritage, from Brian O'Neil onwards, who established the on-site arrangements which proved to be very satisfactory. More recently, I have been particularly indebted to Beric Morley and to Gill Chitty for their support and encouragement during the post-excavation stage of the project, undertaken since 1985.

During the 30-year period of excavations over 2000 students took part and there were many site and technical assistants, all of whom deserve my gratitude. In particular I would wish to single out Charles Daniels and Peter Gelling in the early years, and, later, Donald Mackreth and Tim Strickland, each of whom did much to elucidate the complicated stratigraphical sequence. A particular debt of gratitude must go to Frank and Nancy Ball, who started as students and continued as site assistants. They have been an enormous help over the years, both during the excavations and later with the difficult and detailed post-excavation resolution of the building sequence.

In the process of setting up the excavation archive and checking the stratigraphic evidence, we have constantly been surprised by the quality of the site records. This is especially gratifying since a great deal of the work was done by students. It is not possible to name all those who have made valuable contributions; I am grateful to them all, but I must especially mention Julie Sanders in the early years: my wife Diana, for her site work and the drawings: Jane Faiers, both for her work on site, and later with the finds: and Barrie and Shirley Ecclestone, who drew many of the sections and plans.

At the end of the season in 1985 a small post-excavation team was set up at Wroxeter to prepare an archive and process the records, to enable a full stratigraphical appreciation of the structural sequences and occupation deposits to be prepared for the publication. I must express gratitude to Susan Reynolds, Colin Wallace, and Cameron Moffet, who all did excellent work in this difficult task, and to Andrew Skitt for his work as a draughtsman and in organising the photographic records.

I would like to thank all the authors of the specialist reports who have contributed so much to this volume, and am most grateful to Dr Martin Henig for his search of parallels for the nymph. Most of the published plans, including all the sections, were drawn by Barrie Ecclestone, and additional plans were drawn by Candi Stevens of Warwick Museum. Barrie Ecclestone also drew the decorated samian, while Bevis Sale drew the glass vessels and objects, and my wife, Diana, drew the brooches and small finds. The plates have come primarily from the site archive, but I must mention Robert Wilkins, who took the photographs of the dioscurus and the intaglio, and Arnold Baker, who provided the air photographs, while Donald Mackreth is grateful to Lady Pauline Richmond-Brown for kindly allowing him to study the Hildyard Collection.

Finally, I must thank my editor, John Chadderton, who has assembled, organised, and painstakingly checked all the material for this volume.

Chesterton
Warwickshire
March 1992

Summary

The Roman legionary fortress and civilian town of *Viroconium Cornoviorum*, modern Wroxeter in Shropshire, is situated on a strategic crossing-point on the River Severn. The major series of excavations reported on here began in 1955 within one of the central *insulae* of the Roman town. This is the first of two volumes on the town, and presents the evidence for the military activity on the site.

The military association of the site was indicated by the discovery in the eigtheenth century of tombstones of soldiers of *Legio* XIV, although the nature of the site was previously known because of the presence of visible upstanding ruins. It is thought likely that the site was first occupied by an auxiliary fort established in the mid-first century AD at the point where Watling Street crossed the Severn, but little evidence of this phase of occupation was recovered in the excavated area. In around AD 60 a legionary fortress was established to house *Legio* XIV. Evidence for two of the barrack blocks and part of the centurial quarters were recovered during excavation and further information was revealed in air photographs taken in the dry summer of 1975.

After about five years or so *Legio* XIV was apparently posted elsewhere. The fortress was reorganised, and was substantially rebuilt for occupation by *Legio* XX, at least in the area excavated. The site appears to have continued as a military base until the late 70s AD. The fortress was then apparently downgraded to the status of a depot and a legionary barracks was demolished to make way for a workshop. It is possible that the site may have retained legionary status until around AD 81. After this there is evidence that the site retained its military function until AD 90, although possibly only as a storage depot.

The excavations produced extensive evidence for the method of survey and construction of the legionary timber defences, as well as considerable quantities of coins, metalwork, pottery, and glass. Those artefacts recovered from the military phases of the site are published here; the evidence for the civilian history of the site is to be found in *The Roman Baths and* Macellum *at Wroxeter* (Ellis 2000).

Résumé

La place forte qui abritait la légion romaine et la cité civile de *Viroconium Cornoviorum* se trouvent sur un lieu de passage stratégique sur la rivière Severn. Cet endroit porte maintenant le nom de Wroxeter (dans le comté de Shropshire).

L'importante campagne de fouilles qui fait l'objet de ce rapport a commencé en 1955 dans une des *insulae* centrales de la ville romaine. Nous avons ici le premier de deux volumes et on y présente les témoignages relatifs aux activités militaires sur le site. C'est la découverte, au XVIIIᵉ siècle, de tombes de soldats de la *Legio* XIV qui mit en évidence l'existence de liens entre le site et l'armée, bien qu'on ait déjà su qu'il existait des vestiges romains sur le site en raison de la présence de ruines en surface.

On pense que le site fut d'abord occupé par un fort auxiliaire établi au milieu du premier siècle ap. J.-C. à l'endroit où Watling Street traversait la rivière Severn, mais on n'a retrouvé que peu de témoignages de cette phase d'occupation dans la partie qui a été fouillée. Vers 60 ap. J.-C. une place forte fut construite pour héberger la *Legio* XIV. Des témoignages relatifs à deux casernes et à une partie des quartiers des centurions ont été retrouvés au cours des fouilles, de plus des photos aériennes prises au cours de l'été sec de 1975 ont révélé des renseignements supplémentaires.

Après cinq ans environ la *Legio* XIV fut apparemment postée ailleurs, la place forte fut réorganisée et, au moins dans la partie fouillée, fut en grande partie reconstruite pour accueillir la *Legio* XX. Le site semble avoir continué à servir de base militaire jusqu'à la fin des années 70 ap. J.-C. Apparemment la place forte fut à ce moment là rabaissée au statut de dépôt et une des casernes de la légion fut démolie pour faire place à un atelier. Il se peut que le site ait gardé son statut de "légionnaire" jusqu'aux alentours de 81 ap. J.-C., nous avons des preuves qu'après cela le site a continué à jouer son rôle militaire, bien que peut-être seulement en tant qu'entrepôt, jusqu'en 90 ap. J.-C.

Les fouilles ont produit un grand nombre de témoignages concernant les méthodes utilisées par les légions pour planifier et construire les défenses en bois, ainsi qu'une quantité considérable de pièces de monnaie, d'objets en métal, poterie et verre. Ceux de ces objets façonnés qui ont été mis à jour parmi les phases militaires du site sont examinés ici, tous les témoignages liés à l'histoire civile du site se trouvent dans *The Roman Baths and* Macellum *at Wroxeter* (Ellis 2000).

Zusammenfassung

Die römische Legionslager und Zivilstadt *Viroconium Cornoviorum* mit dem modernen Namen Wroxeter liegt in Shropshire an einem strategischen Kreuzungspunkt am Fluß Severn in den 'Welsh Marches'. Die hier angeführte, bedeutende Reihe von Ausgrabungen begann 1955 innerhalb der zentral gelegenen *insula* in der römischen Stadt. Dieses Buch ist der erste von zwei Bänden und liefert das Beweismaterial für das militärische Besetzung auf diesem Gelände.

Obwohl man anhand der bestehenden Ruinen über die Existenz von römischen Überresten auf diesem Gelände wußte, wurde auf die militärische Bedeutung dieses Geländes erst im achtzehnten Jahrhundert bei der Entdeckung der Grabmäler von Soldaten des *Legio* XIV hingewiesen.

Es ist sehr wahrscheinlich, daß das Gelände anfangs von einer Auxiliarlager eingenommen wurde und in der Mitte des ersten Jahrhunderts AD gegründet worden war, an der Stelle, wo die Watling Street den Fluß Severn überquert. Jedoch wurden bei den Ausgrabungsarbeiten wenige Beweise aus dieser Zeit über die Besetzung dieser Fläche geliefert. Um AD 60 wurde eine Legionslager gegründet, um den *Legio* XIV unterzubringen. Beweismaterial über das Bestehen von zwei Kasernen und einen Teil der Kopfbau für den Centurio wurde während der Ausgrabungsarbeiten gefunden, und weitere Hinweise wurden bei den Flugaufnahmen im trockenen Sommer in 1975 erkennbar.

Nach umgefähr fünf Jahren wurde *Legio* XIV woanders hinversetzt und die Festung umorganisiert, zumindest auf der ausgegrabenen Fläche umgebaut, um *Legio* XX unterzubringen. Allem Anschein nach wurde das Gelände bis in die 70er Jahre AD als Militärstützpunkt benützt. Es scheint, daß dann das Lager an Status verlor und als Depot benützt wurde. Die Legionärkasernen wurden demoliert, um einer Werkstätte Platz zu machen. Es ist aber auch möglich, daß das Gelände bis um AD 81 den Legionärstatus hielt; es gibt Beweise danach, daß das Gelände die militärische Funktion als Ablagerungsdepot behielt, jedoch möglicherweise nur bis AD 90.

Die Ausgrabungen ergaben nicht nur weitgehende Beweise für Messungsmethoden und die Holzbefestigungen der Legionslager, sondern auch Funde beträchtlicher Mengen von Münzen, Metallarbeiten, Keramik und Glas. Die auf diesem Gelände gefundenen Artefakten aus diesen militärischen Zeiten sind in diesem Buch angeführt, die Beweise für die Zivilgeschichte des Geländes könnten im *The Roman Baths and* Macellum *at Wroxeter* (Ellis 2000).

1 The discovery of the legionary fortress at Wroxeter

Introduction

In 1945 the University of Birmingham created an Extra-Mural Department and appointed as its first Director Donald Dudley, a distinguished classical scholar with a deep interest in archaeology. He saw in local fieldwork and excavation an opportunity for development as a subject in his new department. It was, he felt, one of the few subjects in which amateurs could play a significant role. But first it was necessary to organise training opportunities. In 1952 he invited Kathleen Kenyon to direct a two-week course at Wroxeter and asked me to be one of her assistants. At the time I was Curator of the Grosvenor Museum, Chester, and had been assisting Ian Richmond on an excavation there in 1948–49. It is possible that Ian recommended me to Donald. The two seasons at Wroxeter were devoted to excavating a house revealed by air photographs in the field south of the baths. This experience, and the great enthusiasm shown by the students, convinced Donald of the need for a permanent summer school at Wroxeter, especially with the nearby presence of the fine residential accommodation at Attingham Park, almost within walking distance, under its remarkable warden, George Trevelyan. Fortunately, the Chief Inspector of Ancient Monuments was at that time Bryan O'Neil, who was well disposed towards such a project on a Guardianship site. From this time and throughout the excavations, all subsequent Chief Inspectors and their staff have been most cordial and exceptionally helpful, and this contributed materially to the success of the school.

The training school began in 1955 and continued until 1980, when with my retirement as Tutor in Archaeology to the Extra-Mural Department the school was transferred to Philip Barker's excavations on the bath's palaestral basilica and the area to the east, which he had begun in 1966. However, the work I had started continued with a voluntary workforce until the close of excavations in 1985.

The fortress at Wroxeter

The Roman fortress and city of Wroxeter, Shropshire, is situated on a low flat plateau overlooking the river Severn (SJ 570090). The importance of this part of the Severn Valley must have been appreciated at an early stage as a base for forces advancing along the river into Wales, a point discussed in more detail below. This was also a good location from which to monitor possible incursions from the Welsh valleys and to control the ancient north–south route linking the Dee and Severn estuaries (Fig 1.1). A more precise indication of the presence of a large military base in the vicinity of *Viroconium* comes from the Roman road, Watling Street, which cuts across the landscape towards Wroxeter from the east. Watling Street appears originally to have been constructed as a military supply road for an advancing army and its bases, and the road's alignment suggests a possible fortress somewhere between modern Shrewsbury and the village of Cressage (Fig 1.2). The existence of a legionary base close to Wroxeter could also be deduced from the discovery of three tombstones of soldiers belonging to *Legio XIV* (*Roman Inscriptions of Britain* (*RIB*) 292, 294, and 296) found close to the Roman city between 1752 and 1861 (Fig 1.3). Another tombstone (*RIB* 294), found in 1752, is that of a *beneficiarius* of *Legio XX*, but the precise location of the fortress remained unclear until 1975 (Webster 1988, 123).

Before the 1955–85 excavations there had been four campaigns of archaeological investigation on the site. The earliest, the excavations of Thomas Wright, took place in the years 1859–60, and again in 1867. These were instigated by the local Member of Parliament, Boriah Botfield, and funds were provided by public subscription (Wright 1872, I–II). The day-to-day organisation and running of the site was left to Dr Henry Johnson, secretary of the Shropshire and North Wales Natural History and Antiquarian Society. The excavations began in February 1859 and ceased at the beginning of 1860; the work focused on the upstanding piece of masonry, the Old Work, in Near Old Works field. Much of the activity was directed at the baths, which were almost completely cleared, while the basilical hall was only trenched. This campaign was followed in 1867 by a limited excavation, directed by Johnson, on the latrine area at the north end of the range of buildings fronting Watling Street. This was timed to coincide with the British Association visit to Shrewsbury. The published accounts of Wright's excavations are to be found in many journals and are extremely repetitive. An edition of and commentary on Wright's texts by Donald Mackreth is published elsewhere (Ellis 2000, 347–75).

A second campaign was undertaken by George Fox in 1894 and 1896, the impetus for the excavations coming from a meeting of the Royal Archaeological Institute at Shrewsbury in 1894. Fox's work was largely concerned with elucidating Wright's account, with excavation being limited to the *frigidarium* and its cold plunge pools.

In 1930–31 limited excavations were undertaken by John Morris and Francis Jackson. Excavation took place in the two rooms at the north end of the west range and in the latrine, and was carried eastward along the south side of the basilical hall. The work was principally confined to clearing backfill.

The fourth campaign of excavation was that of Kathleen Kenyon in 1936 and 1937. The work occupied a five-week period in 1936 and seven weeks in 1937, although by no means all of this time was occupied in excavating the baths, as three trenches

Fig 1.1 Britain in the first century AD

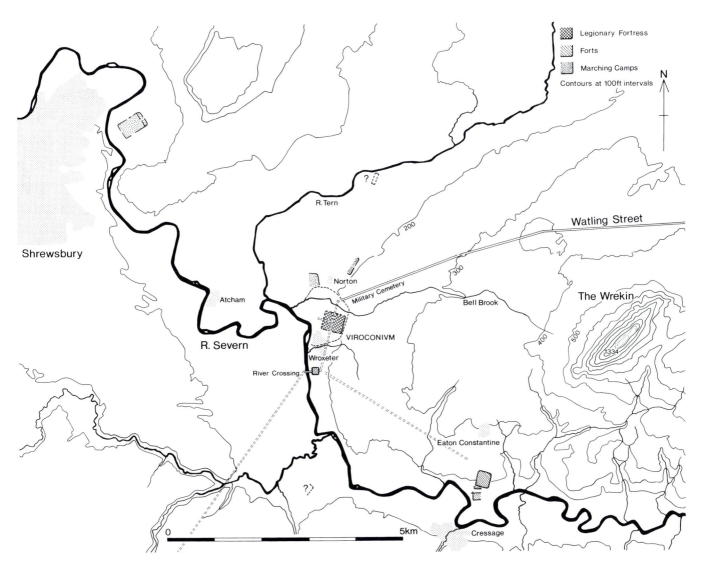

Fig 1.2 The site of the Roman town in relation to modern settlement and other known Roman military sites

were also cut across the defences (Kenyon 1940, 175–6). Her work on the baths was concentrated on two areas; the *tepidarium* and eastern baths suite, and the basilical hall (Fig 1.8). Later work has shown that her principal conclusions with regard to the buildings were mistaken.

With a few exceptions, none of these excavations penetrated military levels. A trench by Wright across the courtyard, and his clearance of the northernmost room in the west range, reached the military destruction levels, while a long trench cut by Kenyon to the east of the baths is likely to have cut into military deposits there, but to date no detail of earlier excavation into the fort levels is known. The excavations undertaken prior to 1955, however, had a major impact on the post-military archaeology of *Insula* 5, and these are therefore discussed in detail in the volume dealing with the later work on the baths and *macellum* (Ellis 2000), and in the report on the basilical hall excavations (Barker 1997).

In 1948 a programme of clearance and consolidation was initiated by the Ministry of Public Buildings and Works, the intention being to expose the foundations of

all the buildings within the *insula*. Consolidation began before 1955, when excavation restarted, and the two operations ran in tandem for much of the 1960s. However, repair work on the structures did not affect military levels.

The subsoil at Wroxeter, and over much of this part of the Severn Valley, is a typical glacial deposit of sand, gravel, and clay. The well-drained conditions are ideal for the development of differential crop growth in dry seasons and in consequence it has been possible to take remarkable photographs from the air, which show buildings with stone foundations and defences in fine detail. This has prompted several important aerial studies of Wroxeter and its environs, especially by Professor J K S St Joseph and Arnold Baker (St Joseph 1949 *et seq*; Frere and St Joseph 1983; Baker 1969/70; 1971). These resulted in the discovery of several Roman military installations. Between 1945 and 1947 J K St Joseph discovered and identified a 2.3ha (5.7 acre) fort, 0.5km to the south of the Roman town (Figs 1.2 and 1.4, St Joseph 1953b). This fort, with its commanding position on the east bank of the Severn, could keep watch on the territory west of the river and was no

Fig 1.3 Legionary tombstones of Legio XIV *from Wroxeter*

doubt placed there to guard the important crossing point. Later aerial reconnaissance discovered a fort of 2.29ha (5.66 acres) at Eye Farm, Eaton Constantine (St Joseph 1973, 234–5), with indications of at least two temporary marching camps (Fig 1.2). Further marching camps were also identified north of Wroxeter, at Norton, as well as a large temporary camp close to Shrewsbury, on the east bank of the Severn (Fig 1.2). It was thus clear that this was an area of considerable military activity, but none of these sites was identified as large enough, or of the correct type, to represent a permanent legionary base.

Many of the aerial surveys focused on the remains of *Viroconium* itself and the photographs have prompted several detailed studies of the Roman town (Fig 1.5) based on the high quality of information (Webster and Stanley 1964; Wilson 1984; Barker 1985). The evidence included military features which appear when not covered by later buildings, although their significance was not at first understood. The location of a military site under the later town had not been confirmed when the excavations started on the baths *insula* in 1955 (Fig 1.5, G), but these eventually revealed evidence for early timber buildings between the main bath house and the *macellum*. These buildings showed indications of military type, with walls constructed of timbers set vertically in trenches, and subsequent study of their plan showed that they were

Fig 1.4 Cropmark of the auxiliary fort south of Wroxeter; view south-east

barrack blocks. However, what kind of military site had been uncovered still remained unclear, as did the position of the defences.

It was not until 1975 that the line of the northern defences of the fortress was discovered from the air by Arnold Baker (National Monuments Record (NMR) Air Photography Library, SJ 5608 242/4). First photographed in the late 1960s, a dark linear feature, evidence of a buried ditch, was eventually traced for some 350m across the north-east quarter of the Roman town (Figs 1.5, A and 1.6). This was presumed to represent some form of boundary or defensive perimeter, but by 1975 it did not fit comfortably into the growing understanding of Wroxeter's urban morphology. It was noted that the ditch was remarkably straight compared to the polygonal alignment of the other urban defensive ditches. It was then realised that this rigid feature was probably of military origin, and that it most probably formed part of the defences of a large military site, built on the favourable ground to the south of the Bell Brook. Furthermore, careful examination of the photographs revealed a gap in the ditch alignment at the west end, which was presumed to indicate the existence of a gate.

Further aerial investigation showed that the ditch could not be traced beyond the later town ditch (Fig 1.5, C): it was concluded that the alignment of the eastern defences of the proposed fortress probably

coincided with that of the urban defences. The attempt to establish the eastern side of the fortress resulted in a reappraisal of Kathleen Kenyon's excavations of 1936–37 (Figs 1.5, B and Fig 1.7). These had involved an investigation of the civil defences, including a section of the eastern line which revealed a pair of ditches of an earlier period (Kenyon 1940, 176, pls 68 and 70). These were quite flat in profile and had a slot in the bottom. Kenyon also recognised a turf rampart associated with the ditches, and recovered some pottery from it, together with a coin of Claudius I. The pottery then was dated to AD 90–120. The conclusion drawn was that these defences 'presumably dated from the first layout of the town after *Viroconium* ceased to be a military camp' (Kenyon 1940, 177, fig 16, no 6). Of the pottery, a hooked rim mortarium 'in a orange-buff ware', dated here to the period of Trajan, is of a type appearing in Claudian contexts at *Camulodunum* (Hawkes and Hull 1947, 254), and Longthorpe (Frere and St Joseph 1974, 111, fig 56, nos 143 and 144). When Arnold Baker's north alignment was plotted it became evident that Kathleen Kenyon had, in fact, cut through the eastern alignment of the fortress, but she had been misled by the pottery dating, as an insufficient number of well-dated examples had been published at that time. Kenyon may well have had in mind the early civil defences of *Verulamium*, which had recently been investigated (Wheeler and Wheeler 1936). These have since been reviewed in the light of further excavation evidence which demonstrates the existence of a conquest period fort (Frere 1983, 33–7). An area adjacent to the Kenyon section was reopened by Dr Stephen Johnson in 1975 (Fig 1.7), when the turf revetment at the front of the rampart was clearly visible (Johnson 1976, 17; 1977, 20–1).

In this remarkable year of 1975 the training school excavations on the baths *insula* (Fig 1.5, G) included the emptying of a deep delve in the north-west corner of the *macellum*. When the bottom of the hole was carefully cleared it was seen that the Victorian excavator had reached the top of the reduced legionary rampart without recognising it. This was the first evidence for the presence of the western side of the fortress below the west portico of the *macellum*, and it was then possible, from analogies with Gloucester, Inchtuthil and elsewhere (Hurst 1976; Richmond 1959), to extrapolate a complete plan (Fig 1.7).

With the position of the western and eastern defences established, it was noted that the gateway represented by the gap in the north ditch was not central to the northern defences, but offset towards the west side of the fortress. It was concluded that this gateway must be the *porta principalis dextra*, the north gate of the *via principalis*, which ran across the full width of the fortress, but not through the centre, as this ground was usually occupied by the *principia*, or headquarters building. At Wroxeter it would therefore appear that the *via principalis* ran along the west side of the *principia*, and this accordingly dictated the position of the *via praetoria*,

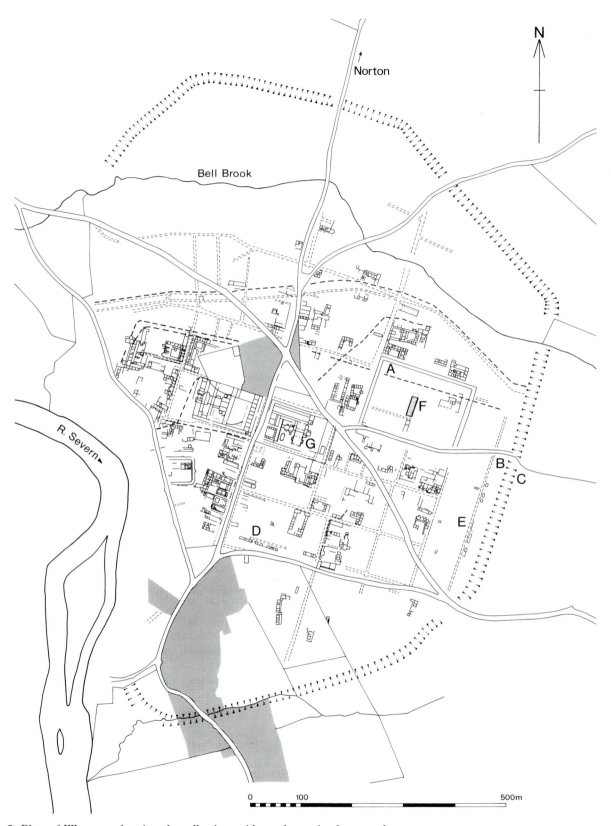

Fig 1.5 Plan of Wroxeter showing the collective evidence from air photographs

which always joined the *via principalis* at right-angles, to form a T-junction in front of the headquarters building. The *via praetoria* would have led to the main gate, the *porta praetoria*, which at Wroxeter would have been located in the centre of the western defences. The position of this gateway was to be confirmed by the excavations.

As the excavations continued, further discoveries were made which, when assessed alongside evidence that already existed on air photographs, allowed more of the fortress plan to be established or confirmed. The existence of a narrow stone building built along the back of the rampart drew attention to parch marks revealing the presence of rows of similar stone

Fig 1.6 Air photograph of the northern legionary defences and the granary; view south

buildings in other parts of the town (Fig 1.5, E and D). On the east side there may be as many as six visible (Fig 1.5, E), located along the back of the east rampart and closely associated with a road (Fig 1.7), presumably the *intervallum* road. Another row of parchmarks to the south (Fig 1.5, D), indicating the presence of more buildings of the same type, suggests the likely location of the southern defences. The short length of east–west road just to the north of these buildings may again be evidence of the *intervallum* road. It was noted that this road did not fit comfortably into the civil street grid, and that it was out of alignment with the later roads.

Further excavation will be required to confirm the postulated position of the defences, but if the above is accepted, the dimensions of the fortress at *Viroconium*, measured from the front of the rampart, may be c 462m east to west and c 402m north to south, an enclosed area of c 19ha (46 acres). In comparison, Inchtuthil is larger, 472 by 460m, 21.74ha (55.73 acres), and was presumably designed to hold more troops, probably auxiliaries (Pitts and St Joseph 1985, 58–9).

Once the location of the fortress defences was established, the air photographs were re-examined in an attempt to identify some of the internal buildings. However, only one possible military structure could be isolated from the mass of cropmarks. This was a large stone building located behind the northern defences (Figs 1.5, F and 1.7, F). The long narrow plan of the structure, the thick buttressed walls, and the closely set rows of numerous pillars which would have supported a raised floor, are all characteristic of the many examples of military granaries (*horrea*) known from other fortresses in Britain and Germany (Rickman 1971). The north end of the granary appeared to face onto the *intervallum* road, behind the northern defences, a location which would have been preferred for access and loading. It is interesting to note that in terms of the fortress layout the Wroxeter granary occupies a position similar to that of two granaries discovered at Inchtuthil (Pitts and St Joseph 1985, 117).

The incomplete plan of another large stone building, also identified from the air, appeared not to conform with those of other civil buildings. The building occupied a position just to the south of where the fortress *principia* would have been, and a row of columns was noted along the west side of the structure, apparently facing on to the *via principalis*. If this stone building was military, it may have been a bathhouse, but only excavation will ascertain its function and date.

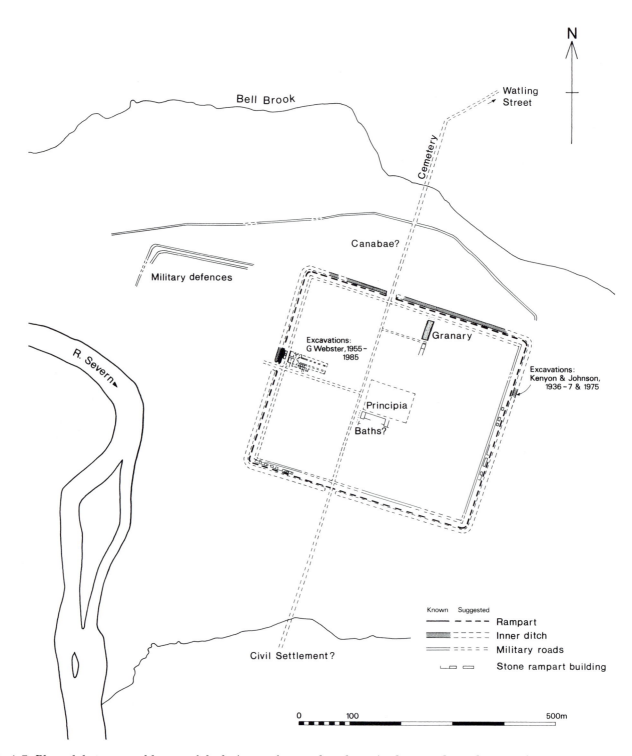

Fig 1.7 Plan of the presumed layout of the legionary fortress, based on air photographs and excavations

The historical background

It is very fortunate that there is a historical account of events in first century AD Britain in the *Annals* (Jackson 1951) and *Agricola* (Moore 1925) of the Roman historian, Tacitus, but these include no direct evidence for the existence of a military base at Wroxeter, since the information given by Tacitus is almost completely lacking in geographical detail. There

is therefore little in his account to help to identify the location of any particular military base. However, it seems clear that the Roman military establishments along the river Severn played significant roles in the first century, when the Roman army was engaged in a series of campaigns in Wales and the borderland. To understand this, it is necessary to appreciate the importance of the area in terms of the military strategy of this period against the historical background.

The campaign against Caratacus

The Roman invasion of Britain took place in AD 43 and its purpose may have been to subdue the tribes and create a province of that part of Britain south of a line from the Humber to the Severn estuary, marked by the rivers Trent, Avon, and lower Severn (Fig 1.1). It seems possible that Rome had no intention of extending the conquest further, but sought to protect the frontiers with the aid of friendly rulers willing to become client kings and queens. This was successfully achieved in the north, where a large confederation of the tribes of *Brigantia* was united under Queen Cartimandua. Efforts were probably made to find suitable rulers to protect their western flank, but they were thwarted by Caratacus. This prince of the Trinovantes had assumed the role of the defender of British freedom, but realising that his forces could not face the Roman army in open combat in the southern lowlands, he persuaded the tribes of Wales, in particular the Silures, to unite under his banner. Doubtless he was encouraged and supported by the powerful Druids, now concentrated in their sanctuary on Anglesey. He launched an attack across the lower Severn in the winter of AD 47–8, taking the Romans by surprise. The first governor, Aulus Plautius, had departed and Caratacus planned his attack to take place before the succeeding governor, Ostorius Scapula, had arrived. This swift and surprise action may also have been linked with the hostile Durotriges, still smarting from their subjugation by Vespasian.

These unexpected events forced the new governor to bring his troops out of their winter quarters to drive the Britons back across the Severn. He was then obliged to reassess his western frontier. Clearly Caratacus could not be allowed to attack at any point in its considerable and vulnerable length, so Scapula decided to seek out and destroy the British prince, knowing full well that he had no authority to extend the province, nor had he the troops to do it. It was for this latter reason that Scapula first stripped the rearward areas of troops. The maintenance of the peace was made the responsibility of two client kingdoms under Prasutagus of the Iceni and Cogidubnus of the Regni; Tacitus suggests (Moore 1925: *Agricola* 14) that the latter was also given control of other areas (Fig 1.1). Scapula then carried out a swift campaign of terror, by searching for hidden arms, against those tribes of doubtful loyalty to Rome, according to one translation of *Agricola* (Bradley 1883). Once they had been stunned into submission, he calculated that they could be left with a much reduced garrison. Yet this savage act of military expediency was to sow the bitter harvest to be reaped in AD 60.

The river Severn, the vital strategic line providing water-borne communication, had crossing-places which could be held in strength, but first reconnaissance was needed to supply the information lacking about the topography of the region, especially the central and northern sectors, since the friendly Dobunni could tell Scapula only about the southern stretch of the river (Fig 1.1). Tacitus tells us that a task force effectively crushed the Deceangli of Flintshire, and made contact with the Irish Sea (Jackson 1951: *Annals* 12, 32), which makes it clear that this was a reconnaissance in strength. Scapula may also have felt the need to seal off any possibility of Brigantian dissidents attempting to join Caratacus. This created trouble which is dismissed by Tacitus in diplomatic language (the word is *discordia*, a low-key term), but it warned Scapula of the need for caution in any move which might appear to threaten Brigantian territory. The Roman raiding party would have swept through the Cornovii, the tribe which presumably occupied the modern county of Shropshire and probably adjacent areas (Webster 1975, 26). The strategic importance of this part of Shropshire, where the Severn emerges from the heartland of Wales and turns to the south, would not have escaped the Romans.

Legio XX was moved from *Camulodunum* to Gloucester (Fig 1.1) to prevent any further crossing of the lower Severn and to supply Scapula's main forces for an advance beyond the river. The first plan may have been to advance up the Wye and attempt to encircle Caratacus within Silurian territory, but the wily Briton escaped from such a trap by moving his forces into central Wales, thus bringing more tribal levies into his army and incidentally blocking the route to the Druid sanctuary on Anglesey. Caratacus chose the place to resist the Roman advance with great care, so that, if overrun, his forces could escape into the woods and hills, and foil the usual Roman cavalry pursuit and kill tactics.

The great battle, so vividly but all too briefly described by Tacitus, may have occurred in the upper reaches of the Severn where the ancient trackway over the hills joins the river, probably in a narrow valley near Newtown, and it need not necessarily have been an existing hillfort; it was in fact fortified at a low level. The attack proceeded as Caratacus had planned. The legionaries, forced to cross the river, fought their way up a steep slope defended by banks to the top, only to find that the British chief and the bulk of his forces had escaped.

Caratacus then tried to involve Cartimandua in the struggle against Rome, but she refused to change sides, and trapped and handed him and his family over to Rome as captives. Scapula had every reason to feel greatly aggrieved, deprived both of a great victory and the capture of his arch-enemy on the battlefield. He allowed his turbulent emotions to sway his reason, and swore to exterminate the whole of the tribe of the Silures. Nothing could have enraged the tribe more. Now they had nothing to lose and could only continue the struggle to postpone their elimination as long as possible. The Britons began a vigorous guerrilla war against the Roman units as they were trying to establish their posts in the frontier zone, designed to block up the exits from the hills into the Severn Valley. Tacitus skilfully disguised the serious Roman losses (Jackson 1951: *Annals* 12, 38–9), but it is quite evident that the army was now engaged in a difficult campaign in a terrain of hills, woods, and marshes familiar to the natives. The frustrated and embittered Scapula became overwrought, his health deteriorated rapidly, and he expired, to the jubilation of the Silures. They continued to fight in increasing numbers, and the Roman losses mounted.

The Britons' success brought more tribes under their banner, encouraged by the offer of spoils and captives. In the interval between the sudden death of Scapula and the advent of a new governor, a legion was defeated in the field. This clearly demonstrated that the Britons were now numerous and confident enough to fight in the open.

The Scapulan frontier

Any attempt to reconstruct the frontier, with its network of forts, is possible only if evidence is present on the ground. However, a starting-point in this quest is an appreciation of the limitations under which Scapula was forced to operate. He had no authority from Rome to advance into and conquer Wales, but only to punish those who had attacked the province by defeating them in battle, and then to deploy his forces to protect it from the possibility of further attacks. The account of Tacitus suggests that Scapula was concentrating his efforts towards establishing a frontier zone, rather than the subjugation of the tribes, but at the same time he was forced to engage the Silures in a running series of surprise attacks mounted by them across the new frontier under construction. The Roman units would have been dispersed for the construction work, and this may have allowed the Britons to achieve some successes. Once the network of forts was complete, it would have severely impeded the movement of any large war parties, and insured against any serious invasion.

Had Scapula been a cautious man, he could more easily have fallen back to the Severn and used this river as his main barrier, with all the major crossing-points, like Gloucester and Wroxeter, guarded. However, this might have been seen by Rome as well as by the Britons as a retreat after an unsuccessful campaign. He preferred the forward positions, presumably with the idea that it was possible to block the exits from Wales more easily by stopping up the narrow valleys through which hostile groups would emerge. It was precisely the same solution Agricola applied to the Highlands of Caledonia, since Rome had not provided enough troops to occupy the great Highland massif. Agricola, in the words of Richmond, 'closed all the principal exits from the Highlands by a *cordon militaire*' (Ogilvie and Richmond 1967, 66–9), with a legion at Inchtuthil on the Tay, a central position in the rear, although this suggestion has been challenged (Hanson 1987, 148–9).

How effective this brilliantly conceived defence deployment would have proved was never tested, since Domitian needed more troops elsewhere and Caledonia was abandoned; Rome never had thereafter enough spare troops to return to it. The question is whether Scapula attempted this in a similar way with the large highland zone of Wales. It is a possibility

which could be tested by fieldwork and excavation. Some of the sites are those of known forts, but only a few have produced any dating evidence for this particular phase (Webster 1981, 61–86 and fig 23).

Scapula was succeeded in AD 52 by an elderly but very experienced pro-consul, Aulus Didius Gallus, whom Tacitus dismissed with the contemptuous phrase 'weighed down with age and many honours' (*Agricola* 12), adding that he was content to act through subordinates and to keep the enemy at a distance. But Gallus was probably working on instructions, since Rome must have been gravely concerned with the heavy losses and difficulties into which Scapula had led his forces. This frontier had become a running sore, but no drastic solution was possible while Claudius, in the mental stupor of his declining years, was incapable of making decisions. Gallus was to engage in a holding operation and to seal the frontier, pinning the turbulent Britons in their own territory until a new policy for Britain could be decided.

Since he is at least given the credit of adding a few forts (*Agricola* 14) he evidently made some frontier adjustments. Gallus faced trouble on two fronts, however, since Cartimandua needed assistance following her estrangement from her husband Venutius. A logical solution for Gallus would have been an advance of the northern frontier zone to bring Roman forces nearer to the client kingdom in order to secure the throne for Cartimandua (Webster 1981). This appears to be corroborated by the presence of Neronian pottery at Chesterfield (Courtney 1978) and Templeborough (May 1922). With the completion of the western frontier planned by Scapula, the movements of the Silures and other tribes of Wales were restricted.

When Claudius died in AD 54 Nero's senior advisors in Rome were undecided about the future of Britain. There were three options open to Rome: a total evacuation, a limited withdrawal, or an advance and total annexation of Wales. There is a suggestion from Suetonius (Rolfe 1924: *Nero* 18) that the first option was considered. This appears to be confirmed by Dio (Carey 1914: Dio, lxii 2), who in discussing the causes of the revolt in AD 60 informs us that, quite suddenly and ruthlessly, Seneca recalled substantial loans he had made to the Britons. It may have been that the Britons had confused a money loan with the notion of a gift. As one of the two advisors to the young Nero he would doubtless have been closely involved in any discussions on the future of Britain, and may have had good reasons to anticipate a withdrawal. The lack of mention of Seneca in Tacitus (*Agricola*) might be explained by his use of Fabius Rustius as a source, a man who supported Seneca and who might have excluded unfavourable information (N Reed pers comm). Alternatively, Tacitus might have been above noting spiteful gossip (Squire 1958), and it has also been suggested that, although Dio's comment is not unlikely, Seneca is unlikely to have been the sole offender (Griffin 1984, 226).

Since the Marches frontier was now secure, a limited withdrawal, already rejected by Scapula, was unthinkable. But as those around Nero debated the issue, positive action had been taken to deal with another frontier at the other extremity of the Empire, in Armenia. Here the solution was to send the best available commander, C Domitius Corbulo, and he was highly successful. It may have been this first taste of military glory that aroused in Nero a desire for more; Britain, already on the agenda, furnished the opportunity. Thus the old Claudian policy of a limited conquest, based on the assumption that client kingdoms could be created on the western frontier, was finally abandoned.

However, by now Rome had other problems in Britain, with the first rumblings of the approaching storm. The sudden withdrawal of the loans had been an unpleasant shock to some of the tribal rulers, and the colonists at *Camulodunum* had been treating the Britons with that contempt one often finds in native communities occupied by forces who represent themselves as superior, as with the British in India (Webster 1978, 88). A governor was needed who was not only a competent and experienced commander, but also a skilled diplomat, an unusual combination.

Campaigns in Wales and the north
c AD 57 – *c* 73

The little that is known of Quintus Veranius suggests that he may have been an excellent choice (Birley 1981, 50–4). Unfortunately this was not to be put fully to the test, since he died within a year of taking office. However, his only campaigning season, against the Silures in AD 57–8, appears to have been highly successful, as the tribe is not heard of again as a hostile people. The preparations for the campaign presumably saw great military activity in the lower Severn valley.

The vacant governorship was filled by C Suetonius Paullinus, an experienced general who had won renown in the mountains of Mauretania in AD 42, but lacked diplomacy and had little sympathy for civilians. Paullinus continued the campaign in Wales, but by now it was realised that the anti-Roman activities were emanating from the Druids, and that they were responsible for much of the continuing tribal unrest. The main target became the Druids' sanctuary in Anglesey (Fig 1.1), but after their annihilation Paullinus had rapidly to bring his army back into the province to deal with the great uprising under Boudicca, which may well have been initiated by the Druids to divert the Governor from his objective (Webster 1978). *Legio XIV*, which accompanied Paullinus on these campaigns, covered itself with glory at the great and decisive battle when Boudicca was defeated, and received its title *Martia Victrix*. The army was then involved in numerous pacification duties in the Midlands and East Anglia.

By AD 66 the province appears to have been peaceful and stabilised enough to allow Nero to transfer troops from Britain for his proposed campaign of eastern conquest. The legion he chose to withdraw was the Fourteenth, so renowned for its part in the great victory of AD 60. For several years after this no large-scale military operations appear to have been undertaken in the province. The garrison took little part in the civil war of AD 69, which brought Vespasian to the purple, but the Brigantian chieftain Venutius took the opportunity, while Rome was so preoccupied, to invade and dispossess Cartimandua, who thenceforth vanished from history. The hostile northern frontier now demanded urgent attention, but troops could not be spared until AD 71.

Quintus Petillius Cerialis was then sent to Britain with a new legion, *Legio II Adiutrix*, and numerous auxiliary units, with which, togcther with the existing garrison, he launched a campaign into Brigantia. It involved a two-pronged northerly advance to either side of the Pennines; the *II Adiutrix* along the east side of the Pennines, and *Legio XX* along the western side, under the command of Agricola. Venutius was subsequently defeated, but the difficulty of establishing a secure frontier across the difficult terrain of the Pennines remained. Cerialis and Agricola could have had no conception that this problem would haunt a succession of emperors for the next hundred years.

The problem of the north brought about a shift in emphasis in the province, and there was a gradual redeployment of military resources. This process accelerated as the Midlands and Wales became more consolidated. Cerialis was succeeded by Sextus Julius Frontinus in about AD 73–4, and his task appears to have been to complete the pacification of Wales and establish a northern frontier.

Agricola

Gnaeus Julius Agricola returned to Britain as governor in AD 77–78, to find that the instability of the northern frontier continued. His task was to advance beyond the Pennines, to bring the natives to submission, and find and consolidate on a new, more suitable defensive frontier.

The date of the arrival of Agricola in Britain is a matter of conjecture, and could have been late in AD 77 or early in the following year (Hanson 1987, 40–5). His first campaigning season, in AD 78, was in north Wales, the last time this region appears to have troubled the Romans until the fourth century. The campaign may have involved only a minor revolt as it was settled very quickly. In the following year Agricola turned his attention to the north. Precisely how far this northern policy was to be pursued may not have been fully appreciated by Vespasian and his successor Titus in AD 79, but Agricola knew that he had their support. The choice of the best line along which to form the frontier depended on the geography and on a careful assessment of the potential hostility of the Caledonian tribes to the north. Agricola could only come to any decision, and be able to advise his Emperor, after he had surveyed the terrain and tested the attitude of the northern tribes. These operations would have required large numbers of troops from all over the province.

By AD 80 Agricola had overrun the Lowlands of Scotland and reached the Forth–Clyde Isthmus (Hanson 1987, 107). This was the obvious line on which to establish his frontier, as Tacitus makes clear (*Agricola* 23). However, by now it was probably manifest to Agricola that this frontier would be difficult to hold if the northern tribes made a determined assault as a combined force. Titus had died in AD 81, so Agricola had to call a halt until he had instructions from his successor Domitian, and to advise him that a further advance was necessary to subdue the Caledonians in order to secure a lasting peace. Domitian, however, was planning a war in Germany in AD 83 and withdrew vexillations from all the British legions and probably *auxilia* as well. At the same time he ordered Agricola to launch a campaign, in spite of his depleted strength. Why did Domitian give authority for this? He could have recalled his governor after so successfully completing his four-year term. Had Domitian embarked on an expansionist policy, in which he could seek military glory? Bearing in mind the Emperor's character from later events (according to Tacitus), one might even suspect that his jealous, suspicious mind did not see a possibility for a lack of success for Agricola and glory for himself in Germany. Nevertheless, Agricola gained an outstanding victory, and it may be significant that the Emperor found him

no more employment: he lapsed into 'forgotten' retirement in AD 84. The meaning of *Agricola* 41 and 42 has been speculated upon at length (Dorey 1960, 66–77; Hanson 1987, 180–5): the truth may simply be that Agricola was in poor health, impaired by his long and arduous governorship in a cold climate, which may have accounted for his early death at the age of 53. With the departure of Agricola it was left to his successors to consolidate the frontier, to redeploy the provincial garrison to hold this new permanent defensive line, and to police areas of potential hostility.

The Wroxeter excavations, 1955–85

Detailed information regarding the internal structures of the fortress has been recovered only from the excavations conducted on the baths *insula* between 1955 and 1985. The area of the guardianship site was chosen because the Ancient Monuments Department of the Ministry of Works, as it then was, wanted to expose more of the surviving remains of the Hadrianic baths *insula* for consolidation and public display (Figs 1.5, G and 1.8).

Most of the Hadrianic buildings in this *insula* had been stripped down to floor level by Thomas Wright between 1859 and 1867, and subsequently published in his *Uriconium* (Wright 1872). In 1936–7 further excavations were undertaken by Kathleen Kenyon, but these were limited by the outbreak of war to the palaestral basilica and the north-east area of the main baths block

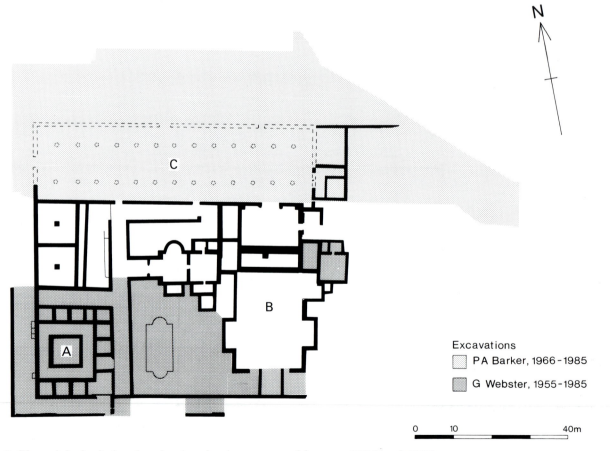

Fig 1.8 *Plan of the baths* insula, *showing the sites excavated between 1955 and 1985*

(Kenyon 1940, 175–227). In 1955 many of the bath's rooms and halls still awaited final clearance, particularly on the eastern and southern sides. The initial seasons, 1955–8, concentrated on this task and also explored various aspects of the bath's structural history.

The early efforts of the training school demonstrated that there had been so much interference in the area of the main structure that there was little archaeological advantage, and even less training facility, in continuing there. The excavations were consequently moved to the open areas, apparently free of Hadrianic remains, to the west and south of the main bath block and to the south of the added western range (Figs 1.8–1.10). One of the accepted techniques of excavation at this time was the grid method developed by Wheeler, who had always insisted on the prime importance of the vertical section (Barker 1993, 37–40). In accordance with this seven boxes, 10 feet (3.05m) square, were laid out on a north-west by south-east axis between the main bath block and the added western range. In subsequent seasons more boxes were systematically excavated on the same alignment (Fig 1.9), and by 1963 most of the area had been explored using 53 separate boxes (Fig 1.10).

However, by then it had become apparent that it was impossible to produce a coherent plan of the military timber buildings and considerable number of pits, which had been revealed at a depth of *c* 2.0m. It was decided to go back to the beginning and strip the whole area, removing all the baulks (Fig 1.10). Box 30 was expanded to re-excavate Boxes 1, 2, 3, 9, and 10 as one area. To the east of the *piscina*, Boxes 12, 13, 33, and 34, were re-excavated as Area 63, and Box 52 was expanded to include the deposits to the south of Box 42. Box 50 and its extension to the south of the piscina was redug as Areas 76 and 75 respectively, and all the boxes located in the main north–south corridor (Boxes 8, 29, 40, 43, 45, and 51) were later included in Area 92. Elsewhere, individual baulks were removed and their contexts and finds assigned to a neighbouring Box or Area. This process not only produced a more coherent plan of the military features, but also succeeded in identifying some features that had not previously been seen in the deposits. There remained, however, a serious limitation in the form of the baths. The Ancient Monuments Department decided that the *piscina*, an open pool in a colonnaded area, should be preserved

Fig 1.9 Air photograph of the baths insula, c *1959, under excavation; view north*

together with its mortar surround, thus creating a large blank area (9.0 by 21.0m) at a crucial point in the junction of the barrack blocks with the centurial quarters. The excavation then continued around this feature and the southern part of the *insula*, using the method of open area rather than box excavation.

The training school continued to clear the areas around the *piscina* until all the deposits immediately west of the main bath block had been exhausted, and the excavations then moved to the *macellum* in the south-west corner of the *insula* (Figs 1.8 and 1.10). Here, however, the presence of the thick Hadrianic walls and the need for safety baulks seriously limited the size of the available area and made the linkage of continuous features difficult (Fig 1.11). The problem was further complicated by the many exploratory holes and trenches dug by nineteenth- and early twentieth-century archaeologists. In some areas these had completely obliterated the archaeological evidence. The west portico did, however, provide an open strip 5.5 by 35m in size (Fig 1.10, Areas 90 and 97, and Fig 2.9), and it was fortunate that this included the rampart front which could be examined in detail. Also, in the centre of the *macellum*, the courtyard, Area 84, allowed relatively unrestricted access to the archaeological deposits over an area *c* 15m square. Its excavation was facilitated by the agreement of the Department of the Environment to the removal of the foundations of the inner courtyard wall of the *macellum* (Fig 1.10), which were in a poor state of preservation. Excavations were completed in 1985, when the available area was exhausted.

The excavation record

From 1958 each Box or Area (both now referred to as Area) was allocated a consecutive number (Fig 1.10, Areas 1 to 98). The Areas excavated prior to this within the Hadrianic baths were allocated letters (a to v) and are not discussed here (see Ellis 2000). Each archaeological layer or context identified within an Area was given a consecutive number in a separate numerical sequence for each Area. Thus each context is identified by two numbers, the number of the Area within which it occurs, and the number of the particular layer or deposit itself. The Area number is always given first; for example, the notation 90/67 refers to Area 90, layer 67. Note that during the excavations, and subsequently in the archive, Area numbers were always designated by a circle around the number.

Layers, or groups of layers, associated with an identifiable archaeological feature, such as a wall or pit, were given a feature number in a sequence covering the whole site. These numbers are always proceeded by F. The use of feature numbers was not begun until the 1970s, but all previously excavated pits, trenches, slots, hearths, and other features were eventually allocated feature numbers. Details of each layer or feature were recorded in site notebooks, which were kept separately for each Area. These form the basis of the primary archive. Plans and sections were drawn in a variety of scales, initially using the Imperial, and later, metric systems. A photographic record was also compiled in both colour and monochrome.

The presentation of the evidence

The excavated evidence and the derived archaeological sequence are presented in chronological order and for the site as a whole. An assessment of the archaeological sequence by each individual Area has not been attempted, as the complicated nature of the stratigraphy and the restricted size of many of the Areas would make it difficult to construct an overall impression of the site. The text is therefore divided into sections dealing with each identified phase of the site. These sections describe the evidence for each phase and a discussion of the interpretation of this evidence. When describing and discussing the excavations, the text normally refers to feature numbers alone, and the Areas within which they occur. However, individual context numbers are referred to in some specific cases. A summary of the military feature numbers, by chronological phase, is given in Appendix 1. Appendix 2 lists, by Area, the military features and the context numbers relevant to them, and other important military layers.

The plans show the location of all relevant archaeological features found and recorded in the excavation. Each phase is accompanied by a feature location plan showing the phased features in relation to the Areas excavated and the later walls of the baths *insula*. An interpretation plan attempts a phased reconstruction of the site sequence from the available evidence. The numbers of features not directly discussed in the report have been omitted for the sake of clarity. The inner wall of the *macellum* courtyard, which was removed during the excavations, has also been omitted from the feature location plans. It should be noted that many features have been truncated and dislocated by the numerous later disturbances, while the need to comply with safety requirements often limited the area available for investigation. Few military buildings could therefore be examined in their entirety, and it has been necessary to extrapolate relationships between many of the features in order to produce an orderly sequence. This was only attempted after alignments and measurements were carefully calculated and checked.

The published sections are intended to supplement the above information and demonstrate the stratigraphic relationships between different layers and features. In most cases the layers and features of the military periods of the site have been extracted from the larger original sections.

The archaeological sequence

The excavations revealed a complicated sequence of buildings and structures beneath the construction levels of the bath house and *macellum* (Figs 1.11 and 2.44).

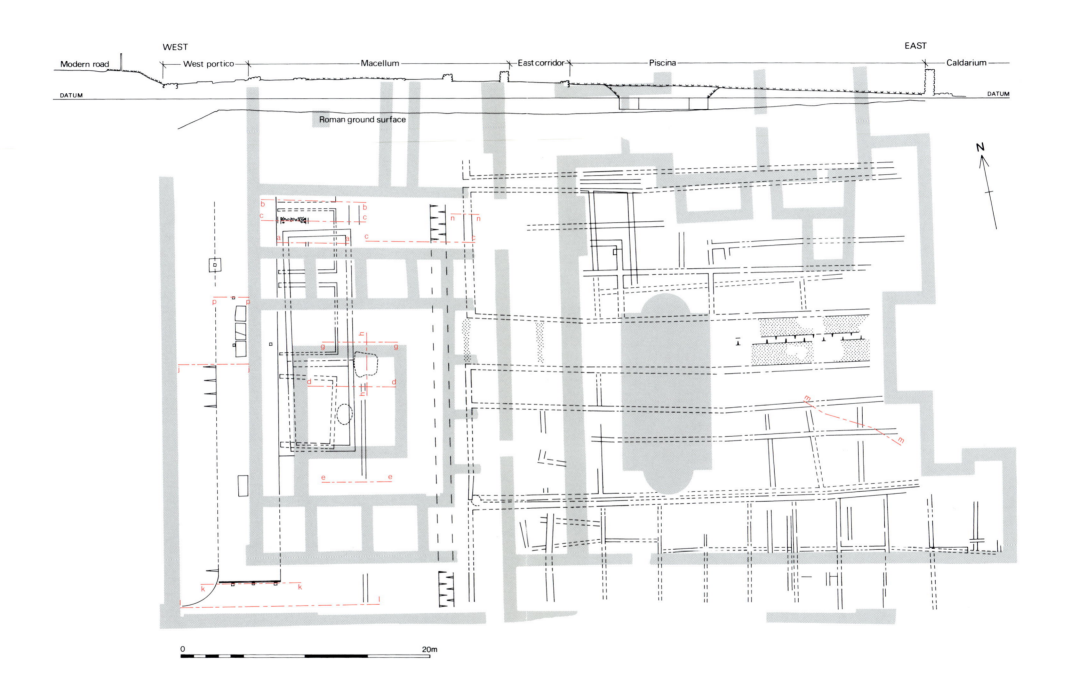

WEST   EAST

Modern road —— West portico —— ———— Macellum ———— —— East corridor —— —— Piscina —— —— Caldarium ——

DATUM   DATUM

Roman ground surface

N

0   20m

Fig 1.11 Plan of the principal military features for phases 1–6 in relation to the walls of the later macellum and bath house, and location of principal sections

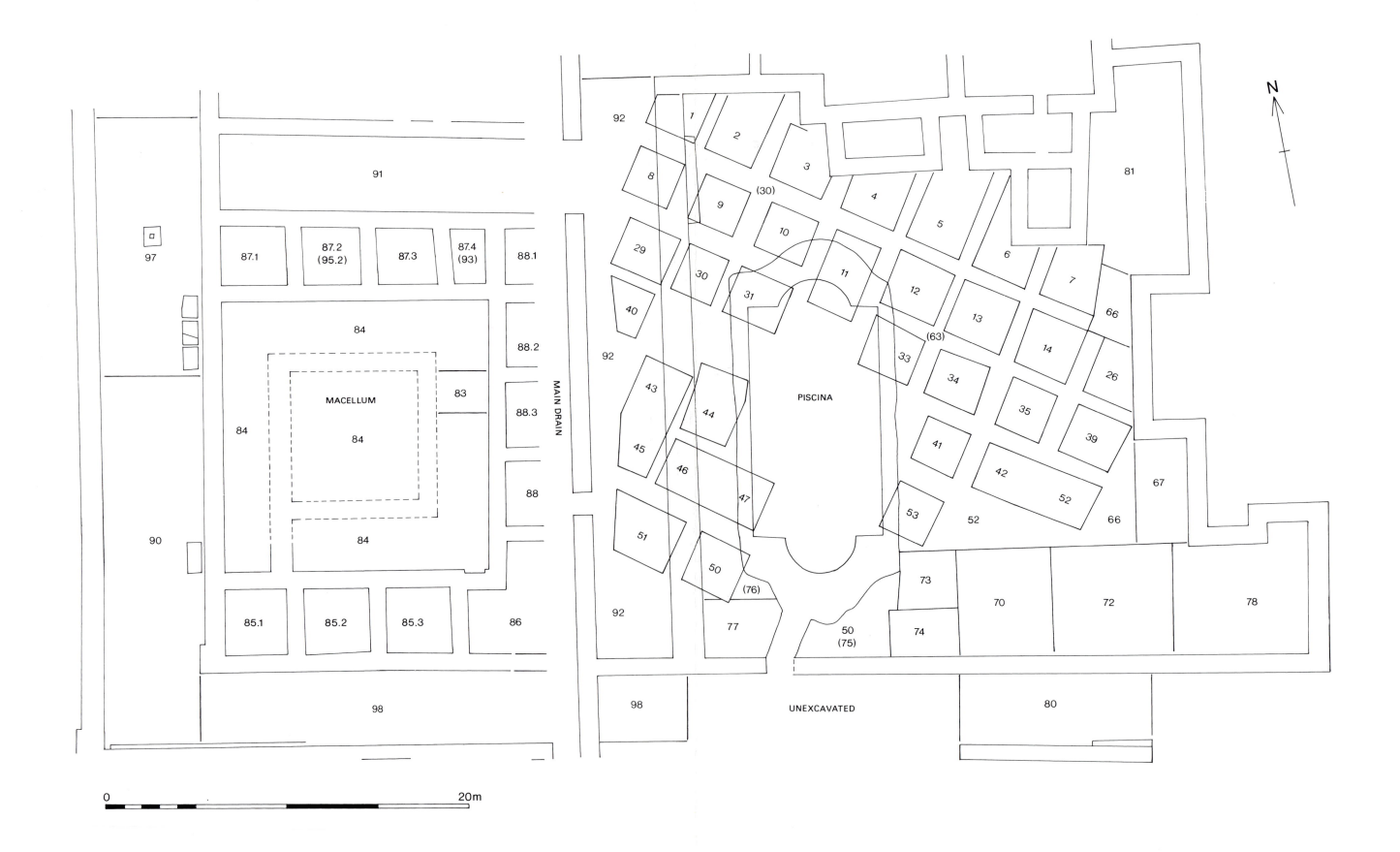

Fig 1.10 Plan showing excavated boxes and areas in relation to the walls of the later macellum *and bath house*

When analysed this sequence was shown to divide into three main periods; a period of activity prior to the construction of the legionary fortress, the period associated with the legionary fortress itself, and a period of apparently post-fortress activity. Subsequent refinement expanded this to four periods, each identifying a major change on the site. These are referred to as the pre-legionary period, first legionary period, second legionary period, and depot period. The pre-legionary period contained only a limited amount of information and has been described under a single period heading. However, the two legionary periods and the depot period are sub-divided into separate phases, 1–7, which represent specific identifiable events in the complicated archaeological record.

The fragmentary nature of the evidence often created difficulties in reconstructing the archaeological sequence in detail, phase by phase. Fortunately, the sequence of *intervallum* roads, each superimposed upon its predecessor, provided a useful base from which to phase the site. Changes to the site, represented by the first six phases, tended to be accompanied by the relaying of the *intervallum*, road surfaces 1–6. Each phase is labelled accordingly: Phase 1, road 1, Phase 2, road 2 etc, with the exception of Phase 4. Because of the nature of the archaeological evidence, and in order to preserve the numerical relationship between the later phases and roads, Phase 4 has been sub-divided into Phase 4a and 4b. By Phase 7 the archaeological events can no longer be linked to a particular *intervallum* road surface and the sequence of timber structures at the end of the depot period proved difficult to disentangle. In view of this, and rather than allocate each minor alteration in these structures with a separate phase, the final sequence has been grouped under Phase 7 but divided, where possible, into four sub-phases, numbered 7i–7iv. The report ends with the final clearance of these structures.

All timber buildings have been allocated an identification number, in chronological order (mess hall/timber building 1–9), with the exception of the two barrack blocks, the *tabernae*, and the large store building, which are given their full titles. The only stone building associated with the military periods of the site is the two-phase stone 'office' which is referred to in the text as stone building A in its first phase, and later as the stone building A/B. All the pits indicated on the plan are allocated with their feature number where appropriate, and the four layers post-dating road 6, deposited above the old *intervallum* road, have been given consecutive numbers (post-road 6, layers 1–4) on the plans.

Wroxeter publication strategy

The 1955–85 excavations are published in three volumes, the first dealing with the basilical hall excavations (Barker 1997), the present volume with the military occupation, and the third volume dealing with the work on the baths and *macellum* (Ellis 2000). In the present volume two approaches have been taken to the publication of the finds: recognisable military finds, including small finds, brooches, pottery lamps, and vessel glass, are dealt with as a group here regardless of their stratigraphic position, and the same treatment is afforded the coins prior to AD 90. However, in the case of other finds, such as glass objects, pottery, and the animal bone assemblage, only the material from stratified military contexts is presented here, although some mention is made of military period material which is residual in civilian contexts. In general the policy has been to publish in this volume all the finds from the military period at Wroxeter while the volume by Ellis considers selected material from key stratigraphic groups in most categories.

Reports for the military volume were prepared first and some were completed before reports on later material. The volume itself, and the finds texts, was completed before detailed stratigraphic work was undertaken for the post-military levels. Initially this volume was to be published without a report on the military pottery, which was to appear with the civilian material in the third volume, but the report on the military phase pottery is now included here.

To facilitate the military pottery report the establishment of a structural sequence for the later periods was extended to the military levels in order to provide a stratigraphic database. Correlating the new sequence with the old has inevitably revealed that in a few instances some items published here and hitherto thought to be from stratified military contexts are not, and, by the same token, some items presented in the third volume are in fact military.

The treatment of the various artefact and ecofact categories is as follows. The coin report was written as a single text cataloguing all the coins from the excavations. The catalogue and text appear in the third volume, while all the coins dating to earlier than AD 90 are repeated from the catalogue and listed here. Unfortunately, a large group of pseudo-Claudian coins, 34 from military and 7 from post-military levels, came to light after the coin report had been completed. In this volume it has been decided to form a single list of coins from both groups showing the relevant cross-references. The pseudo-Claudian coinage is discussed in this volume, but it should be noted that the text is not based on a detailed study of the additional 41 coins, although they have been scanned.

The small finds report here presents the pre-AD 90 military material from all periods. One or two items in the third volume are perhaps also from the fort, and a further group of later military finds from the civilian period is published in that report. The brooch report also deals not only with the stratified material but with all military brooches known from Wroxeter as a whole, except those from the basilical hall excavations. The same applies to the intaglios. Pottery lamps are all grouped in this volume regardless of context. The vessel glass report discusses all the Claudio–Neronian and Flavian glass regardless of context, and includes Flavian to mid-second-century glass when found in the military levels. The glass object report considers only the stratified pieces, although this group, in particular, appears in a number of contexts which are not in fact military.

The pottery report deals with stratified military pottery: residual military pottery is discussed in the Ellis volume. The samian catalogues show only stratified military material here although there is a degree of overlap in the text which appears here and that which can be found in the third volume.

Finally, the animal bone report deals with bone from selected groups from military contexts, and a report on soils and pollens also deals with stratified military contexts.

Some 30 seasons of excavation on a Roman military and urban site with deep stratigraphy produced a huge quantity of material: only the portion relevant to the military occupation of the site is considered here. The quantity of finds involved and the nature of the excavations meant that the long and detailed analysis of the material has not been without its difficulties.

All the catalogue entries refer to site provenance using the *area/context* notation as in the rest of the report. Items without an area/context code are unstratified. A small find number (sf) is quoted where applicable. Where significant, information on the phase of the site in which the item was found, or to which it may be attributed, has also been included.

2 The lifetime of the fortress

The pre-legionary period

Below the levels associated with the construction of the fortress were clear indications of pre-legionary activity on the site. The earliest features appeared to be irregular ditches (F2409, F2735) which may have extended across the whole site on an east–west axis (Fig 2.1). The purpose of these shallow features was not clear, although they may have been for drainage.

Cutting through the western part of these ditches was the defensive ditch of a small enclosure, first identified in Areas 1, 2, 9, 10, and 30 (F2025). A definite turn to the west in the eastern edge of F2025 was noted in the north end of Areas 1 and 2, where the ditch began to form the beginnings of a corner. The ditch was 2.9m wide, with a relatively clean, sandy fill, but undetermined depth. The northern end of F2025 extended beyond the limit of excavations and it was impossible to trace the ditch below the *piscina* since it was necessary to preserve this structural feature. However, a second length, also *c* 3.0m wide and almost at right-angles to F2025, was found to the west of the *piscina* in Area 92 (F3251). The northern edge of another feature, F349, with the same alignment as the northern edge of F3251, was uncovered under the south range of the *macellum* in Area 85.2. F3251 was recorded as being at least 1.5m deep in Area 92. The similarities between these three lengths of ditch strongly suggested that they were part of the same sub-rectangular feature, with the southern and eastern sides meeting under the *piscina* (Fig 2.2). No evidence for any bank was found, although a Roman temporary camp, as this was thought to be, would normally be expected to have possessed one.

Other features found below the south-western area of the *macellum* in Areas 85.1 and 85.2 comprised two hearths (F214 and F285) associated with a clay floor. Apart from the fact that these hearths were clearly earlier than the legionary fortress, there was no stratigraphic link to indicate their relationship with the small enclosure ditch. However, it is suggested that they were later than the ditch, since they occupied the space where an inner bank of the enclosure would have been, and no trace of any bank was found over these features.

There was no evidence of any pre-Roman occupation or prehistoric use of the site. The only pre-Roman pottery was the rim of a Bronze Age burial vessel with stabbed decoration, found in the Hadrianic construction deposit, and this sherd could have been brought to the site with the large quantities of sand deposited at that period. The drainage ditches, small ditched enclosure, and hearths are most likely to belong to pre-fortress activity by the Roman army, possibly associated with a campaign camp, and/or winter *hibernae*. The clean fill of the enclosure ditch would suggest only a short period of use, implying a temporary installation. Such an enclosure might have existed for only a few days, or even hours, the time required for construction and demolition being very short, and this might explain the absence of any evidence for a bank. The upcast from the ditch would have been used to form a loose bank along its interior side, into which soldiers could push stakes to form a rudimentary demarkation or defensive line. Once abandoned, this insubstantial bank could easily have been pushed back into the ditch, leaving little or no archaeological trace of its existence.

The first legionary period, AD 57–66

Phase 1, road 1

The preparation of the ground

Any pre-legionary features still standing appear to have been demolished to clear the ground for the legionary fortress. The evidence for this, in the form of a thin layer of trampled earth, appeared to extend across the whole excavated site, and covered the remains of the hearths and ditches. Since the site had been used as a possible *hiberna* or for temporary camps, parts of it would have already been cleared of vegetation. Soil analysis suggests that, whatever the immediately preceding vegetation cover may have been, the local soils in their natural state would have supported patchy woodland and scrub (Canti 1988). Imprinted into the earth trample over the pre-legionary features were slight but definite marks forming a kind of cross-hatching at an angle to the final fortress alignment (Figs 2.3 and 2.4). This pattern was traced in Area 84 (F444, F1059, F3253–4), Area 85.1 (F176), Area 85.2 (F274), and Area 91 (F3252), and it undoubtedly spread much further, certainly over most of the above areas, and possibly over the whole site. It is significant that at one point (F176) it was found beneath the rampart. The pattern appeared to be of organic origin, and on close study of a projected slide enlargement was identified as a layer of hurdling. This had been carefully placed and may have been pegged down. The spacing of the verticals was *c* 0.20m and the horizontal cross-pieces could be seen as twisted withies. These hurdles must have been laid in sections, or perhaps even rolled out from large bundles, but the evidence was too fragmentary to establish the size of any individual units. The purpose of the layer of hurdling was presumably to provide a firm working surface.

One striking feature of the excavations was the recurrent discovery, at various points under the *macellum*, of a closely layered sequence of several metalled surfaces. These layers, together with their foundation deposits,

18

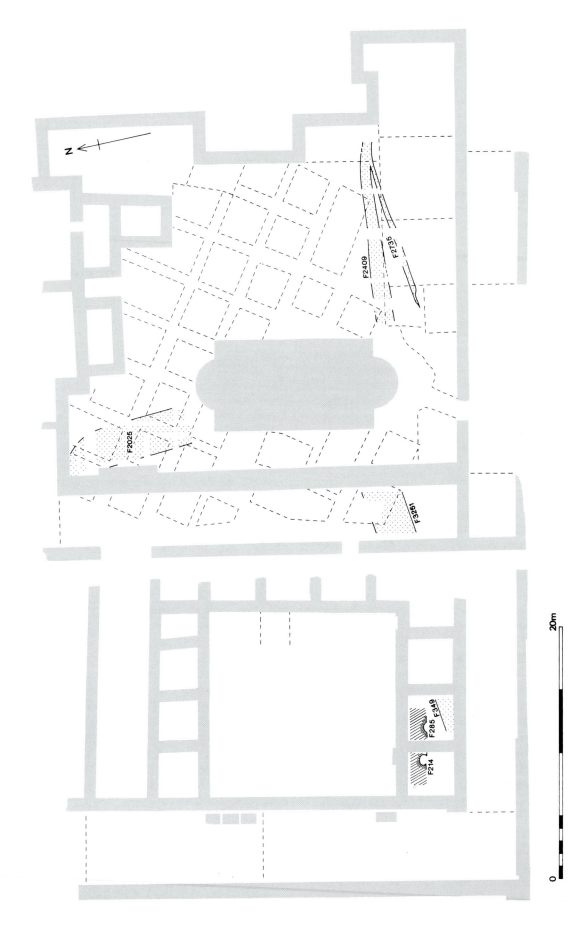

Fig 2.1 Pre-legionary period: feature location plan

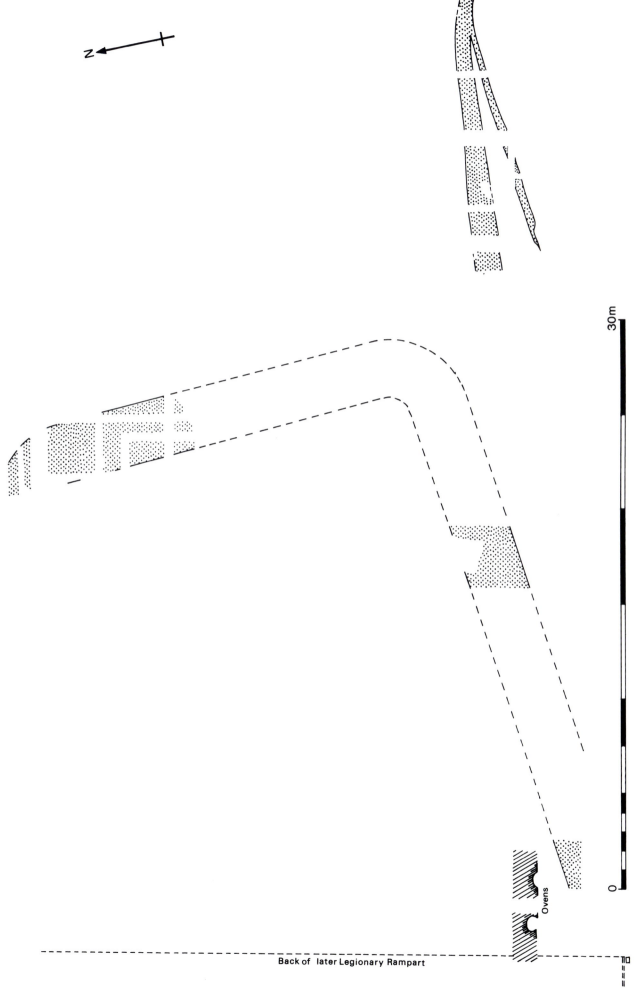

Z

Back of later Legionary Rampart

Ovens

0   30m

Fig 2.2 Pre-legionary period: reconstructed plan

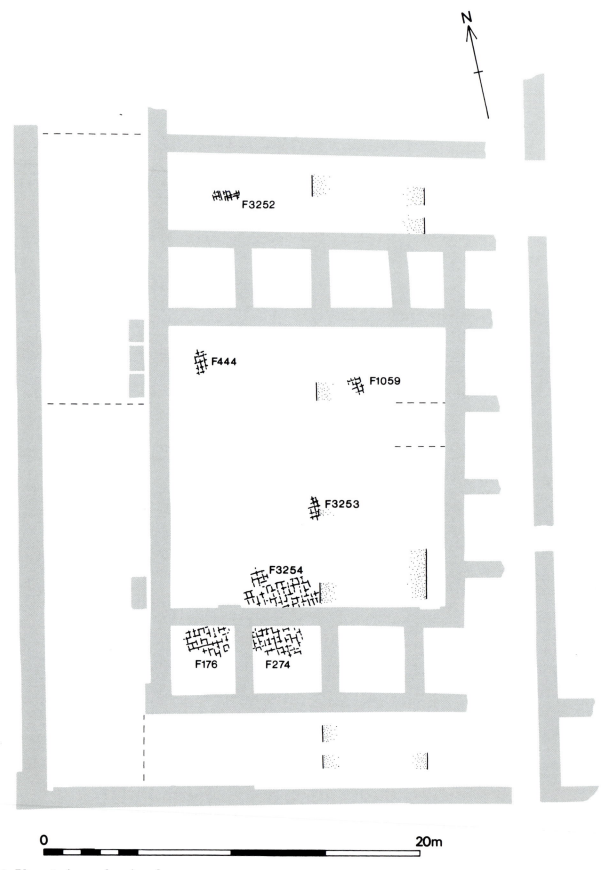

Fig 2.3 Phase 1: feature location plan

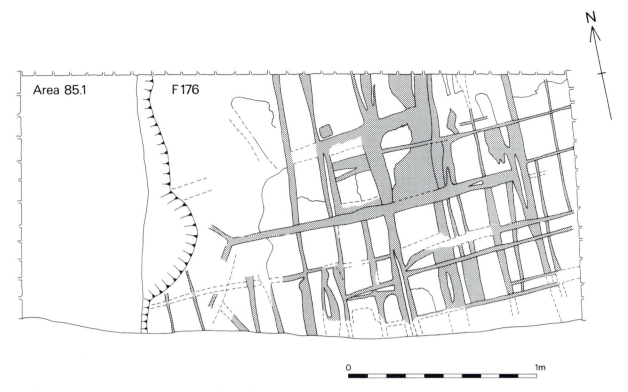

Fig 2.4 Plan showing the construction hurdling, F176, Area 85.1

were particularly clear in the eastern halves of Areas 84, 91, and 98 (Fig 2.5), and it became evident that they continued across the whole site from north to south in a relatively narrow band, approximately 5m in width. There could be little doubt that this was a sequence of roads, and further excavation, supplemented by several carefully placed east–west sections, revealed at least six surfaces (Figs 2.5 and Fig 2.18, section c-c, nos 7–12; see also Figs 2.17, 2.34, and 2.51). The earliest road in the sequence, road 1, belongs to Phase 1. This was a thin spread of gravel forming a rudimentary road surface *c* 4.75m wide, isolated in Areas 84, 91, and 98 (Fig 2.18, section c-c, no 7; Fig 2.51, section g-g; Fig 2.34, section d-d; Fig 2.17, section e-e). Road 1 was shown to have been laid directly onto the hurdling in Area 84 (F1059), although there was slight evidence to suggest that some pre-road levelling had occurred to counter the natural north–south slope of the site. The natural east–west slope appears to have been retained.

These events must represent the preparation of the site before the construction of the fortress, beginning with turf and other ground clearance, indicated by the layer of earth trample, and then consolidation, represented by the laying of the hurdles. Some levelling of the site, possibly associated only with road 1, may have been undertaken at this point. Judging by its insubstantial nature, road 1 may have begun as a temporary construction road, designed to offer better access and grip to the legion's vehicles as they moved around the fortress with building materials (Fig 2.6). As road 1 and its successors ran parallel with the eventual rear of the fortress rampart, they were positively identified as *intervallum* roads. Presumably they continued all the way

around the circuit of the fortress defences, according to the normal plan. The presence of the hearths and clay floor suggests a stopover of at least a day, perhaps suggesting a longer stay, for construction or shelter.

The legionary defences: Phase 2, road 2

Once the ground had been cleared and consolidated, the building of the fortress itself could begin. An early priority would have been the construction of the defences as a protection against sudden attack.

As discussed above, the only evidence of the defences prior to 1975, apart from aerial photographs, came from the excavation on the east side of the fortress by Kathleen Kenyon in 1936–7 (Kenyon 1940, 176, pl 19). This area was re-examined by Stephen Johnson in 1975 and 1976 (Johnson 1976; 1977). It is clear that this was a typically military construction, with a turf-fronted rampart and central slot in the ditches. The published sections of the 1936–7 excavations show two ditches (Kenyon 1940, section C, pl lxx). The inner one was 24 feet (7.3m) wide and 4 feet (1.2m) deep, with a slope of *c* 20° and a wide central shovel slot. The outer ditch was only *c* 15 feet (4.6m) wide and is shown less than 3 feet (0.9m) deep, but has a flat bottom, which may suggest that it was not fully excavated. There is a space of *c* 12 feet (*c* 3.60m) between the ditches. Kenyon's section B shows only one ditch, *c* 8 feet (*c* 2.44m) wide and 4 feet (*c* 1.22m) deep, presumably the inner one, the outer having been cut away by the excavation of the

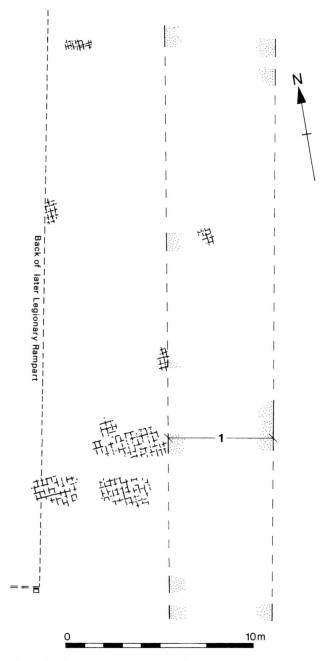

0   10m

Fig 2.5 Phase 1: reconstructed plan

late second-century civil ditch. The inner ditch excavated by Johnson was *c* 4.0m wide and 1.25m deep, which corresponds reasonably well with that found by Kathleen Kenyon.

The exact position and alignment of the western defences under the *macellum* were also established in 1975. The re-excavation of a pit, originally dug by Victorian antiquarians in the western end of Area 91, revealed the lower part of the back of a turf rampart (F511) under the west wall of the *macellum* (Fig 2.7). The individual turves were clearly visible when the bottom of the pit was cleared, and it was realised the back of the fortress rampart had been found.

The presence of the massive *macellum* walls and stylobate base of the west portico prevented a section from being excavated across the full width of the rampart and

ditches. The Kenyon/Johnson sections across the eastern ditches still remain the fullest sample of Wroxeter's defensive system. In the past the majority of Roman military defences have been excavated by cutting sections across them, yet it has frequently been demonstrated that this method will invariably provide only a partial understanding of the presence and structure of linear features. As space was available, it was resolved to excavate as much of the rampart front as possible within the confines of the available area (Areas 90 and 97; Figs 2.7 and 2.8). This resulted in a length of 30m of the rampart being examined, with 10.75m of the rampart front thoroughly excavated, producing details of the rampart's timber construction which might not have been recovered by sections alone.

The rampart and inner ditch

Following the discovery of the back of the rampart in Area 91, excavations proceeded to trace the remainder of the rampart's inner face across Areas 87.1, 84, and 98 (Fig 2.7, F178 and F438). The alignment of the rampart front was confirmed in Areas 90 and 97 (Fig 2.7, F932 and F931). The edge of the inner ditch (F3093) was discovered at the very front of the rampart, leaving no space for a berm (Fig 2.9, section j-j, no 8; Fig 2.10). The small cutting in front of the rampart (Fig 2.9, section j-j, no 1) may have been a surveyor's setting-out trench for the alignment of the rampart. Within the confines of the west portico of the *macellum* (Areas 90 and 97), only the east side of the inner ditch could be examined to a point 3.4m from the rampart front (Fig 2.9), and the full width could not therefore be determined. The slope was *c* 25° and there were traces of a clay lining.

The surviving rampart was 5m wide and *c* 0.90m high, and had been built of ditch spoil with turf layers at intervals and with turf concentrations at the front and back (Fig 2.9). Details of the rampart's internal construction also began to emerge. The base of the rampart was formed of logs placed side by side, at a right-angle to the alignment, to form a timber corduroy (Fig 2.7, F1032 and Fig 2.9, section j-j, no 3). The logs, which were of random length, had been laid horizontally up to and abutting a clay foundation at the rampart front (Fig 2.9, section j-j, no 2). Only traces of this clay foundation were left, as it appeared to have been heavily disturbed along the whole of its exposed length at the time of the systematic demolition of the rampart. In places, enough clay survived to show that this had been a substantial feature, 0.46m wide and originally *c* 0.08m thick, which had been carefully laid with neat, straight edges. Even where the evidence for the foundation had been completely removed, its original presence was confirmed by the corduroy base, since the ends of the logs formed a perfect straight line where they had abutted the eastern edge of the clay base (Figs 2.7–2.9). Above this the spade cuts of the demolition teams were clearly visible cutting into the rampart front (Fig 2.11 and Fig 2.9,

Fig 2.6 The exposed sequence of intervallum *road surfaces in Area 91, Roads 1 to 6*

section j-j, no 7), and these had exposed the western ends of several cross-rampart timbers which survived as a decomposed, crystalline deposit in the rampart material. Eventually 13 of these transverse timbers were uncovered on the same vertical plane in the rampart front and at regular 1.66m intervals (Fig 2.7, F3256–68 and Fig 2.9, section j-j, no 4). Excavations at the rear of the rampart in Areas 84 and 91 succeeded in locating the eastern ends of three of the transverse timbers (F281; F3269; F3270), and these were shown to have been attached to lateral timbers laid along the back of the rampart (F3271; F3272; F1000; Fig 2.9, section j-j, no 5).

One of the transverse beams (F3264) was exceptional in having been replaced. The evidence for this was a trench cut into the rampart while it was still under construction. Another timber, *c* 0.6m long, had been laid at right-angles to this transverse; no satisfactory explanation can be offered.

The careful measurements of the rampart and its timbers were compared with the Roman units of measurement, the *pes Drusianus* (PD) and the *pes Monetales* (PM), with results which are discussed below, at the end of this chapter.

Although the rampart had been demolished and only a height of *c* 1.0m survived, sufficient evidence of its internal timbers had survived for a reconstruction to

be attempted, together with a careful study of the sequence of dismantling the rampart front. A full reconstruction of the rampart is attempted and illustrated at the end of this chapter (Figs 2.60–2.64) together with a possible alternative.

The interval tower

Between two of the transverse timbers (F3260 and F3261) in Area 97, the dark stain of a large vertical post was observed in the body of the rampart (Fig 2.7, F1048; Fig 2.12; Fig 2.13, section p-p, no 2). It had been sawn off at the height of the lowered rampart, leaving the bottom part to decay in position. The post measured 0.20m square and was shown to be located in a large postpit, at least 1.35m square, under the rampart (Fig 2.13, section p-p, no 1). Since the postpit was covered by the log corduroy this post must have been in position before the construction of the rampart (Fig 2.13, section p-p, no 4).

A second post, F1067, was located in Area 97, 4m to the south of the first and on the same north–south alignment (Fig 2.7). This was also 0.20m square, but the close proximity of the later stone steps into the *macellum* prevented a detailed examination of the postpit. A third post, again 0.20m square, was recovered in Area 84 (Fig 2.7, F440), 3.33m to the east of F1067

24

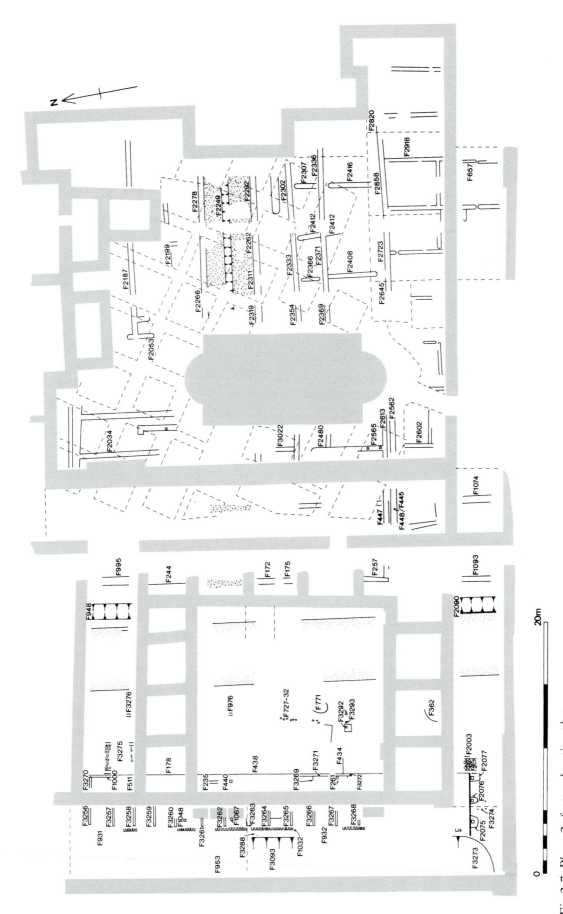

Fig 2.7 Phase 2: feature location plan

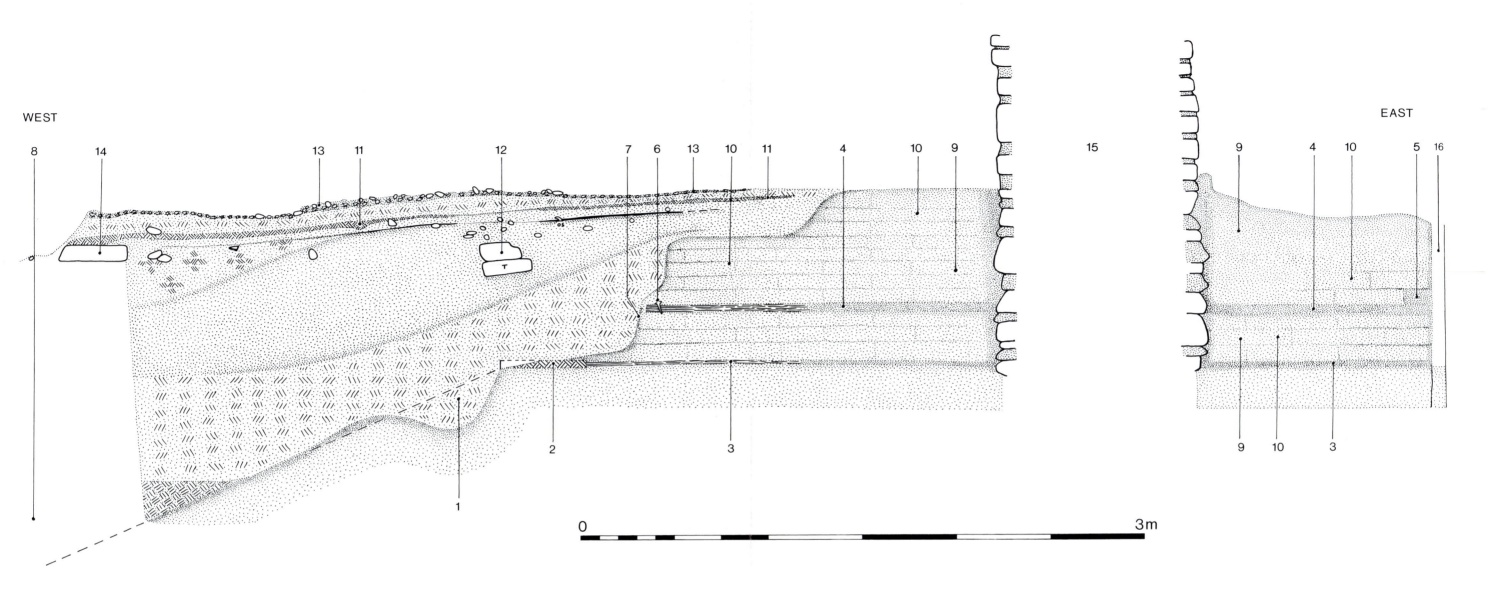

WEST   EAST

Fig 2.9 Section j-j: the legionary fortress inner ditch and reduced turf rampart. Areas 90 and 84 (key for sections on reverse)

1   Lockspit
2   Clay foundation (F3288)
3   Log corduroy (F1072)
4   Transverse timber (F3263)
5   Longitudinal timber (F3271)
6   Nail in transverse timber
7   Spade cut
8   Legionary ditch (F3093)
9   Rampart (F932)
10 Rampart turves
11 Floor of building 9, Phase 7iii
12 Foundation of participation structure in building 9, Phase 7iii (F3283)
13 Second floor of building 9, Phase 7iv
14 West wall foundation of building 9, Phase 7iii and 7iv
15 Macellum west wall
16 Ascensus clay back

0   3m

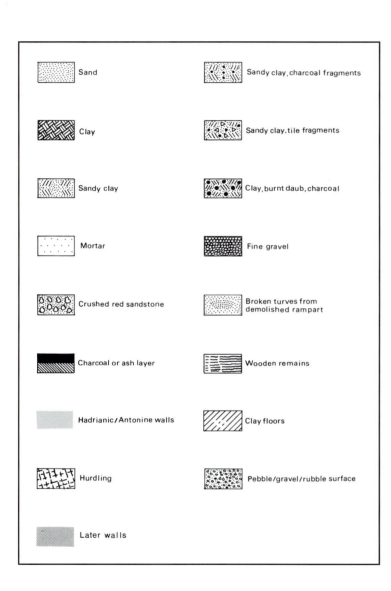

	Sand		Sandy clay, charcoal fragments
	Clay		Sandy clay, tile fragments
	Sandy clay		Clay, burnt daub, charcoal
	Mortar		Fine gravel
	Crushed red sandstone		Broken turves from demolished rampart
	Charcoal or ash layer		Wooden remains
	Hadrianic/Antonine walls		Clay floors
	Hurdling		Pebble/gravel/rubble surface
	Later walls		

Key for sections

Fig 2.8 The front of the legionary defences, Areas 90 and 97, from the south-east

and on the same east–west alignment. Once again, this postpit could not be examined in detail due to the presence of the west wall of the *macellum*.

This structure was a four-post interval tower; the three discovered posts representing its north-west, south-west, and south-east corners. Attempts to find the fourth, north-east, post proved inconclusive. If the tower had been an exact square the north-east post should have been located in Area 87.1, but it could not be identified, despite a detailed examination of the back of the rampart in this area. It was concluded that the posts of the tower had not formed an exact square, and that the north-east post was probably located under the *macellum* wall, south of Area 87.1. Unfortunately, a limited excavation under the wall could not determine its position.

Although the postpits for three of the posts could not be studied in detail, the north-west example showed that the post had been packed into position at an early stage in the construction of the rampart, prior to the laying down of the log corduroy. This was presumed to be the same for the other three posts, and the rampart would then have been built up round them. In Area 84 there was an indication of the removal of a horizontal brace, laid north-south, at the level to which

the rampart had been reduced, between the south-east and north-east posts of the tower (Fig 2.7, F235). This was presumably to make the structure more rigid, and each post could have been braced by a series of similar horizontal connecting timbers.

It may have been intended that the tower would be square, with sides possibly of ten Roman feet (*c* 3.33m). However, if this was the case the north-west post (F1048) was out of alignment by 0.5m to the north, and the failure clearly to establish the position of the north-east post meant that it was difficult to draw any firm conclusions about the exact dimensions. The evidence recorded suggested a tower with a frontage of 12 PD (4.0m) and a depth of 10 PD (3.33m). The reconstructed appearance of this tower is considered below.

Only this one tower is so far known at *Viroconium* and the spacing between the tower and the gate, discovered at the southern end of the site (see below), is much less than at other fortresses. Its measured south side 19.4m (almost a half *actus* PD, see below) from the north face of the gate (Fig 2.23). The distances between the interval towers at other fortresses vary, presumably in accord with the lengths of their sides. The spacing between the face of each tower varied from as much as 60m at *Lambaesis* to *c* 30.40m at Chester (Carrington 1977). The total projected length of the west side of the *Viroconium* fortress is *c* 402m, allowing for a double-towered west gate (similar to Manning and Scott's type V2 (1979, 20, fig 1), and a 30m space to allow for the width of the tower. It could then be suggested on the basis of this known spacing that there were 12 towers, 6 on each side of the gate.

The *porta praetoria*

The discovery of the west gate of the fortress at the mid-point of the west side was anticipated in the south-west corner of the *macellum* portico (Fig 2.7, Areas 90 and 98), once the alignment and length of the west side of the defences, including the two corners, were known and had been plotted from air photographs. Nevertheless, it was only in the very last season of the excavations, in 1985, that the deeper deposits in this area could be examined (Fig 2.14). Time and appalling weather conditions allowed only a limited extension to the south to make contact with other posts of the northern gate tower.

In the south end of Area 90 the inner edge of the fortress ditch (F3273) was observed curving away to the west to form a butt end, and the rampart was found to terminate at this point on an east–west alignment marked by three postpits (Fig 2.7, F2075, F2076, and F2077; Fig 2.15, section k-k, nos 1–3). Of the three posts themselves, only the medial post survived *in situ* (Fig 2.15, section k-k, no 5), and it was shown that this post had been sawn off at the height of the reduced rampart. The 'shadow' of the post created by the decomposition stain was clearly visible, and this allowed a direct measurement of its cross-section, which was 0.20m by 0.15m. This post appears to be smaller than those at the corners, both of which had been completely dug out during demolition, as was evident from the trenches cut into their postpits (Fig 2.15, section k-k, nos 9 and 11). However, the east post had left a ghost impression of its dimensions in the bottom of its postpit (Fig 2.15, section k-k, no 6), which measured 0.20m square, the same dimensions as the interval tower posts.

This three-post structure was undoubtedly the north side of the north tower of the *porta praetoria* gate, which allowed access through the western defences of the fortress. The two corner posts were presumably structurally more important, and therefore larger, than the smaller medial post. The lower part of the medial post was probably left in position to support the vertical rampart face while the gate was being demolished.

A small north–south cut into the standing rampart against the north side of the medial post showed a thin downward sloping line projecting from the external north face of the tower (Fig 2.16). This was interpreted as a trace of the weatherboarding nailed to the three vertical posts. This boarding, which may have consisted of radially split oak boards tapering from 0.05m (2 inches) to 0.065m (2.5 inches), extended slightly beyond the back of the rampart since the tower projected 0.38m behind it (Fig 2.15, section k-k, no 7). An extension to the west would have been necessary to retain the vertical face of the rampart, as the rampart front projected 0.5m beyond the north-west corner post of the tower. However, the evidence of this had been removed by the large trench dug for the removal of the post (Fig 2.15, section k-k, no 9). The posts and the weatherboarding must have been in position before the construction of the rampart, which would have been built against the north face of the northern gate tower. The minimum width of the tower from front to back would have been *c* 3.8m.

A trench was cut to the south along the line of the east face of the gate tower in an effort to make contact with the post or postpit of the next tower post. Although it was possible to excavate a distance of 8 Roman feet (2.66m) from the north-east corner post-pit (F2077) to the south, no evidence of the next post or its post-pit was found. This, at least, proved that there was no medial post in the east face of the tower, and indeed such a post was probably not required, since the medial post on the north face would have been added primarily to support the vertical side of the rampart.

The interior of the tower was only evident on the vertical face of the southern limit of excavation. There was no visible evidence of any recognisable floor or trample layer, except a thin layer of burning (Fig 2.55, section l-l, no 7), which may denote a period of use at the level of the pebble scatter on the west side of the gate (Fig 2.15, section k-k, no 15; Fig 2.55, section l-l, no 3). Associated with this layer were four small peg-holes forming a square of 0.8m, which presumably

indicates the presence of a minor structure (Fig 2.7; Fig 2.15, F3274). It is possible that there were floorboards, but they left no trace in the sections.

In considering the plan of the gate, it is necessary to compare similar plans from contemporary timber fortresses. There are examples from Inchtuthil (Pitts and St Joseph 1985, 71, fig 8), Longthorpe (Frere and St Joseph 1974, 11, figs 8 and 9), and Usk (Manning 1981, 70–5, fig 71). It is immediately evident that the Wroxeter gate is on a much smaller scale than these. On the evidence from these sites the gate tower might be expected to be *c* 20 PD (*c* 6.7m) square, but the north side of the Wroxeter tower appears to have been no more than 4.0m in length, which would allow for a tower only *c* 12 PD square. The tower could, however, have been rectangular in plan, with a 20 PD frontage, the narrow width being in response to the narrowness of the rampart with its vertical front. Even so, both the front and back of the rampart projected beyond the tower, and would have needed the protection of weatherboarding attached to, and projecting beyond, the back and front corner posts.

In the absence of further evidence, however, it must be assumed that the tower was square. Instead of the usual eight or nine post structures the *Viroconium* gate tower appears to have had only four main posts and to have been of a similar size to an interval tower (see below), but the proof of this will only be established by a southern extension of the excavation. Allowing for an identical southern gate tower and a narrow gateway of 10 PD (*c* 3.3m), the smallest possible reconstruction for the Wroxeter gate would be *c* 11m by 4m, consistent with Manning and Scott type IIIa (1979, 20, fig 1).

The *ascensus*

The evidence of the *ascensus* consists only of detached fragments, since it had been thoroughly demolished. At a point 10m (*c* 3.0 PD), north of the north side of the *porta praetoria* in Area 84 were the slight remains of a turf-built structure (Fig 2.7, F434; Fig 2.9, section j-j, no 16; Fig 2.17, section e-e, nos 10 and 11). It had been added to the back face of the rampart, projecting at right-angles to it. This was identified as an *ascensus*, and it was assumed at first that it ran parallel with the rampart towards the gate. However, with the discovery of a first period oven built against the rampart back immediately to the north of the gate tower in Area 98 (Fig 2.7, F2003), this was found to be impossible. The solution came only with the discovery in Area 84 of a single turf, a setting-out stakehole (Fig 2.7, F3293), and two postholes (F3292; Fig 2.17, section e-e, nos 10 and 11); evidence for a probable revetment which indicated that the *ascensus* had been built at right-angles to the rampart towards the *intervallum* road. The distance from the western edge of the *intervallum* road and the rampart back was *c* 22 Roman feet (7.32m). A suggested reconstruction (below, Fig 2.60) shows five sloped steps, which at an angle of *c* 15° would have

Fig 2.10 The front of the reduced and cut back fortress rampart (Area 90, F932), from the south

Fig 2.12 The posthole of the north-west interval tower post (Area 97, F1048), from the west (Area 97)

Fig 2.11 The front of the fortress rampart (Area 90, F932), from the south-west

presented no difficulties for trained foot-soldiers. There was no evidence to indicate the width of the *ascensus*. In the reconstruction it is suggested to have been ten Roman feet (*c* 3.33m).

This appears to be an unusual arrangement, but few *ascensus* are known at the mid-first-century fortresses in Britain (Jones 1975, 89), perhaps partly because there have been few attempts to locate them. At Usk, the excavations were not extended from the gates along the rampart back, but it was assumed that access to the rampart top was by means of timber ladders against the gate towers (Manning 1981, 75 and fig 19). However, ladders would appear to have been much too steep and narrow to give rapid access by a body of troops in an emergency. The problem was considered by Ian Richmond at Hod Hill, where the two gates were carefully studied (Richmond 1968, 73). Two presumed artillery platforms were identified, one at each gate, and *ascensus* built on each side, similar to those at Housesteads (Daniels 1978, 147) and Saalburg (Jacobi 1937). With an arrangement like that at Hod Hill, however, it might have been difficult for the men ascending the *ascensus* rapidly in a body to avoid any interference with the *ballista* crews. It is more likely that these *ascensus* were intended solely for the use of the *ballista* crews.

1   *North-west interval tower post pit*   3   *Turf rampart (F931)*
2   *North-west interval tower post-void*   4   *Log corduroy (F1072)*
     (F1067)   5   *Legionary ditch (F953)*

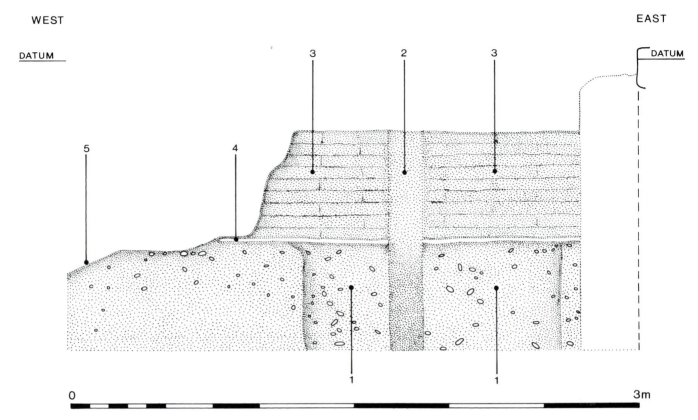

Fig 2.13 Section p-p, Area 97: the north-west interval tower post pit and void

Fig 2.14 The north side of the porta praetoria *gateway (Area 98), from the south-east*

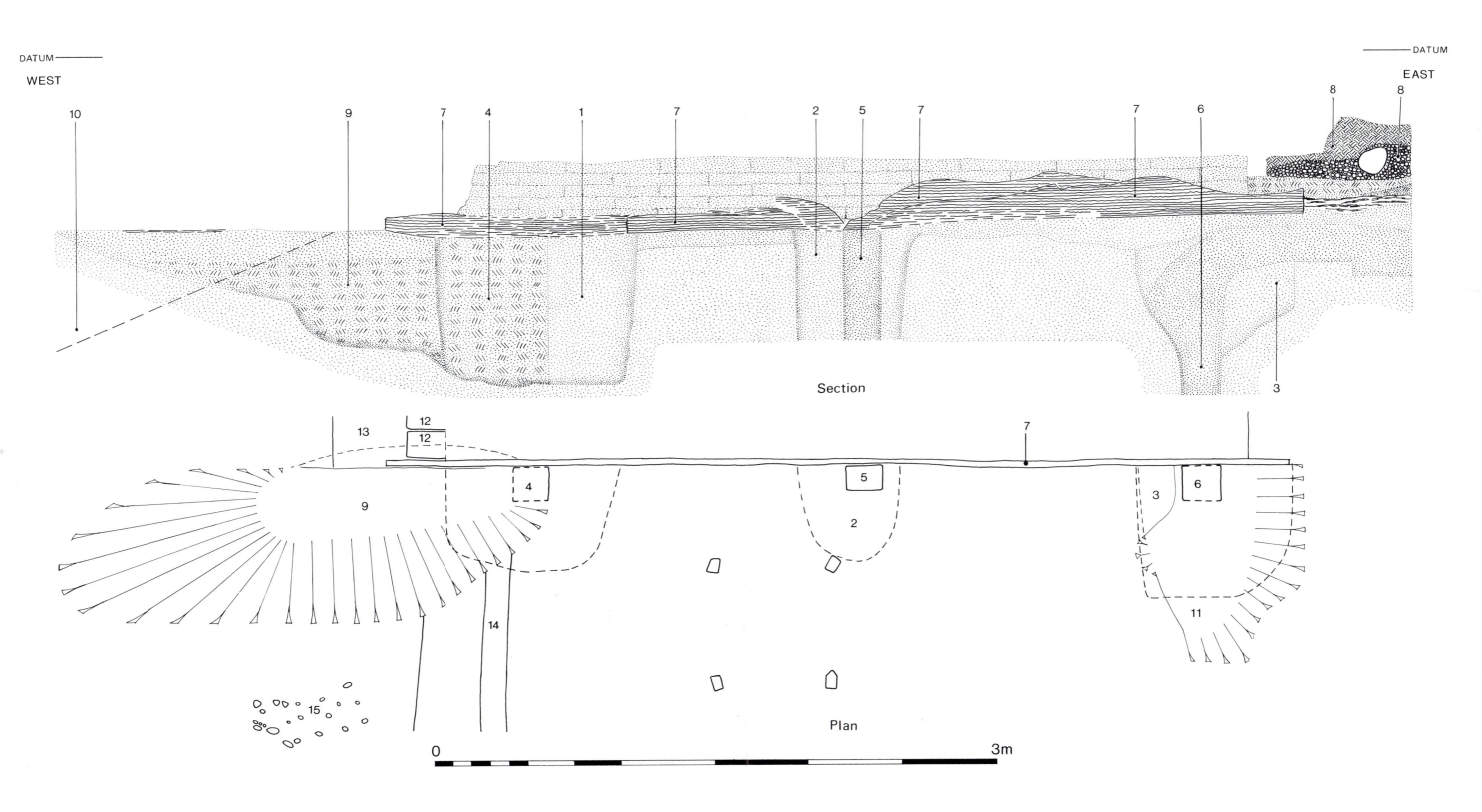

DATUM ——— WEST

DATUM ——— EAST

10   9   7   4   1   7   2   5   7   7   6   8   8

3

Section

13   12   12   7

9   4   5   2   3   6

14   11

15

Plan

0   3m

1 North-west post pit. The north tower, the west gate – porta praetoria (F2075)
2 Medial post pit. The north tower, the west gate – porta praetoria (F2076)
3 North-east post pit. The north tower, the west gate – porta praetoria (F2077)
4 Probable position of north-west post
5 Medial post
6 Position of north-east post
7 Weather-boarding
8 Oven, Phase 2 (F2003)
9 Robber trench of north-west post
10 Line of filled in legionary ditch (F3273)
11 Robber trench of east post
12 Corduroy
13 Clay foundation
14 Horizontal timber, west face of gate
15 Gravel surface

Fig 2.15 Section k-k and plan: the north side of porta praetoria gateway with the three north tower post pits

Fig 2.16 Detail of the exploratory cut into the south end of the rampart

The *Liber de munitionibus castrorum* (Lenoir 1979) makes the point that in hostile terrain the *ascensus* should be *duplex*, which probably means of double width.

The construction of the defences: a summary

After the preparation of the ground, which the legionary surveyors would have chosen with great care, the first stage of the construction would have been to set out the outline of the defences and the main streets with small trenches and wooden pegs or stakes. A close study of the layout of the defences, and also the relative position of the internal buildings and *intervallum* roads described below, strongly suggests that the fortress was laid out on a grid system based on the *pes Drusianus* Roman foot.

The fortress roads appear to have been laid down initially as temporary construction roads, including the first *intervallum* road, road 1. After this the defences would have been built. This began with the at least partial erection of the gates, and the interval and corner towers. When this had been completed the rampart, 15 PD wide, would have been built on its log base with a revetment of turf at the front and back, and binding layers of turf in the main body. At the same time the ditches would have been cut and would have provided spoil for the body of the rampart. The method of moving spoil by the use of small wicker baskets is clearly shown on Trajan's Column. The size of the baskets was carefully gauged for handling by individual soldiers (Richmond 1935, 18, *Cophinus quibus portetur terra*). For moving large amounts of spoil any distance it is presumed that wagons would have been used, although there is no evidence of this on the column.

As the rampart increased in height, the transverse timbers would have been carefully placed in their correct positions in the body of the rampart. When these had been attached to the lateral timbers at the rampart back, and both fixed in position with further turves and spoil, each of the vertical front posts would have been tied to the horizontal beams and secured to a transverse

timber by a brace. Weatherboarding or hurdles could then have been attached to the back of the front verticals to support the rampart front. As more turves and spoil were added to the rampart a second row of transverse timbers would have been laid down and fixed to the front verticals to prevent them from being pushed over into the ditch by the growing weight of earth. Once the required height had been achieved, the patrol track and parapet would have been completed, and the *ascensus* added to the back of the rampart. A discussion on the quantities and types of timber required by the legion for the construction of these defences is included in the description of the reconstruction (below).

Construction of the internal buildings: the ovens and mess halls

Abutting the back of the rampart in Area 91 was a foundation for a substantial oven (Fig 2.7, F3275). This was a massive construction (Fig. 2.18, section c-c, no 17) on a thick foundation of large river cobbles, over which a solid clay base had been laid. The upper part of the structure had been removed by later levelling and construction work, but a thickness of 0.40m survived with the burnt oven floor (Fig 2.18, section c-c, no 18), and part of the oven west wall (Fig 2.18, section c-c, no 19). The position of this oven, in direct contact with the back of the rampart (Fig 2.18, section c-c, no 22), and built at the same level as the rampart base and *intervallum* roads 1 and 2 (Fig 2.18, section c-c, nos 7 and 8), clearly links it with the first period of legionary occupation. The large deposit of ash (Fig 2.18, section c-c, no 24) showed that this oven was in use for a considerable length of time.

Another cobble and clay oven foundation, also built against the back of the rampart, was discovered in Area 98 (Fig 2.7, F2003; Fig 2.20). It was much smaller than F3275, but it was bounded on the east side by a clay wattle wall, the outer face of this wall being 1.50m from the back of the rampart. All remains of it east of this wall had been wholly removed by a later excavation, during the period apparently associated with roads 4 and 5. The west side of the oven foundation appeared to extend up to the east face of the north gate tower of the *porta praetoria* (Fig 2.15, section k-k, no 8), but unfortunately a trench cut to remove the north-west post of the tower during demolition had removed the clay base at this critical point. Although this meant that the oven could not be clearly linked with other structures, the similarity of its cobble and clay construction, and its close location to the back of the rampart, would suggest that it should probably be associated with this phase and the oven in Area 91. The clay and wattle wall suggests that the oven was roofed, and that it could have been fuelled from either the north or the south side.

These ovens were intended to supply the soldiers in the barrack blocks on the eastern side of the *intervallum* road. It is suggested that the smaller oven, built at the north-east corner of the *porta praetoria*, was specifically for the men on guard duty, while the larger oven in Area 91 (F3275) was to satisfy the needs of a legionary century (*c* 80 men). Each century had its own oven, built against the back of the rampart, and further excavation might have uncovered more examples, but it was possible to examine only the single example in Area 91. This was due to the presence of the west courtyard wall of the *macellum*, together with the necessity of leaving a safety baulk, which restricted deep excavations along the rear of the rampart in Area 84.

A tile oven of the second legionary period (Phases 4a and 4b), which was also located close to the back of the rampart in Area 91, was clearly covered by a timber building (Fig 2.30, mess hall 3), and it seemed likely that the cobble and clay oven (F3275) would have also been covered during the first legionary period. A section in Area 91 confirmed the existence of a first period timber wall (Fig 2.19, section a-a, no 3; Fig 2.7, F3276), under the remains of the second period structure (Fig 2.19, section a-a, no 2). Elsewhere, however, the evidence for the remainder of this first period structure was confused by the walls of the second period building, rebuilt in almost precisely the same position, of virtually the same dimensions, and using similar construction techniques. The limited area in which it was possible to excavate made it impossible to attribute many of the stakeholes of the different walls to a particular phase and to complete the plan of the first period building. Only the short length of the east wall, seen in the section, could be confidently associated with Phase 2 (Fig 2.7, F3276).

As this building was associated with the oven it was concluded that this was a century mess hall (Fig 2.23, mess hall 3), of dimensions similar to its better substantiated successor. Further excavations suggested that there were two other mess halls between mess hall 3 and the *ascensus*. As in the case of mess hall 3, there was good evidence for two second period buildings occupying this space in Phase 4a (Fig 2.30, mess halls 1 and 2), and the excavation of these later structures revealed indications of first period mess halls. A section cut across the east wall of mess hall 2 (Fig 2.51, section g-g, nos 2 and 3), showed that the structure was of two periods, and that F976 (Fig 2.7) probably belonged to Phase 2. Numerous postholes identified the east wall of mess hall 1, but it was only after detailed examination that six of these features were isolated and allocated to Phase 2 (Fig 2.7, F727–32).

From what little evidence there was for the three mess halls in Phase 2, the buildings were *c* 4.3m (13 PD) wide from the back of the rampart. In the case of mess hall 3, the foundation of the east wall was of rudimentary character. Lengths of hurdling with long vertical posts had been driven into the ground at regular intervals and clay plastered into both sides from the ground level upwards. It was possible only to suggest the position of the east walls of the three mess halls during Phases 2–3. No evidence was found for any of the other walls, while the existence of the east walls represented a particularly difficult problem. The oven in mess hall 3 (F3275) had been placed directly against the vertical back of the rampart, with no wall between the two that could have supported a roof. It is possible that the slots for such a wall may have been cut into the upper clay superstructure of the oven and that this evidence had been removed with the oven's destruction, but it seems more likely that the mess hall was built directly onto the back of the rampart as a lean-to structure. Mess halls 1 and 2 were presumably of similar character. The complete dimensions of the three mess halls, and their probable positions during Phase 2, are postulated on Figure 2.23, based largely on the evidence derived from their second period successors (Fig 2.30).

In the space between the mess halls and the *intervallum* road were two large pits, found in Areas 84 and 85.2 (Fig 2.7, F771 and F362). These were part of a sequence of pits dug in this area, which may have been for rubbish disposal, or they might possibly have been latrines. Each mess hall may have had its own latrine, and there could have been other latrines in the *intervallum* area. However, the evidence from other fortresses indicates that latrines tended to be grouped together, and it should be noted that latrine pits were usually rectangular, rather than round (Davison 1989, 233–6). F771 appeared to be associated with mess hall 1, and F362, south of the *ascensus*, was perhaps connected with the gateway (Fig 2.23). There may have been other pits within the *intervallum* zone during this phase, but the limitations imposed on the excavation meant that only these two examples were examined. Furthermore the evidence could not clearly demonstrate whether these two pits had functioned contemporaneously, or as separate elements in the sequence of Phase 2 pits.

Road 2

At some point during the construction of the fortress, presumably when the work was at an advanced stage, road 1 was replaced by the much more substantial road 2. The thin gravel spread of the construction road was sealed by a make-up deposit and road 2 laid over it. This raised the level of the *intervallum* road by 0.30m (Fig 2.18, section c-c, no 13; see also Figs 2.34, section d-d, 2.17, section e-e, and 2.51, section g-g). Road 2 was 4.90m wide (*c* 15 Roman feet), and clearly associated with this road surface were two lengths of steep-sided, V-shaped ditch, 1.30m wide and 0.80m deep (Figs 2.21 and 2.23), found cut along its eastern edge in Areas 91 and 98 (Fig 2.7, F948 and F2090 respectively). These two sections of ditch were probably part of the same drainage ditch running parallel with the *intervallum* road across the whole site (Fig 2.23).

The ditch remained in use until the end of the second legionary period (Phase 4b), a timespan which may have covered as much as 20 years (see below). Although there was some evidence of silting in the bottom of the feature, the section (Fig 2.18, section c-c, no 4) clearly shows that the sides of the ditch had retained their shape,

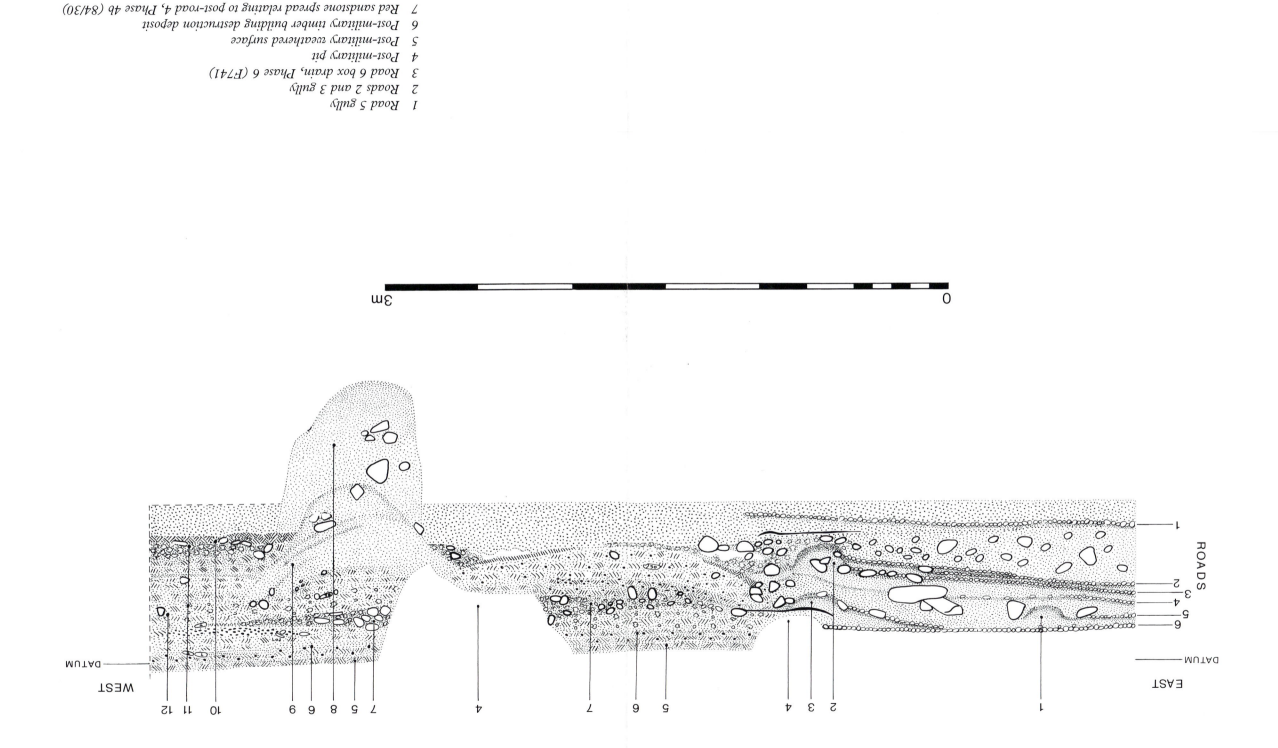

Fig 2.17 Section e-e, Area 84: the sequence of intervallum roads and the remains of the ascensus

1   Road 5 gully
2   Roads 2 and 3 gully
3   Road 6 box drain, Phase 6 (F741)
4   Post-military pit
5   Post-military weathered surface
6   Post-military timber building destruction deposit
7   Red sandstone spread relating to post-road 4, Phase 4b (84/30)
8   Legionary construction pit, Phase 1
9   Pit, unphased
10 Clay turves – ascensus foundations, Phase 2 – 4a (F434)
11 Lower part of the ascensus, Phase 2 – 4a (F434)
12 Ascensus turves

WEST

EAST

DATUM

ROADS

3m

0

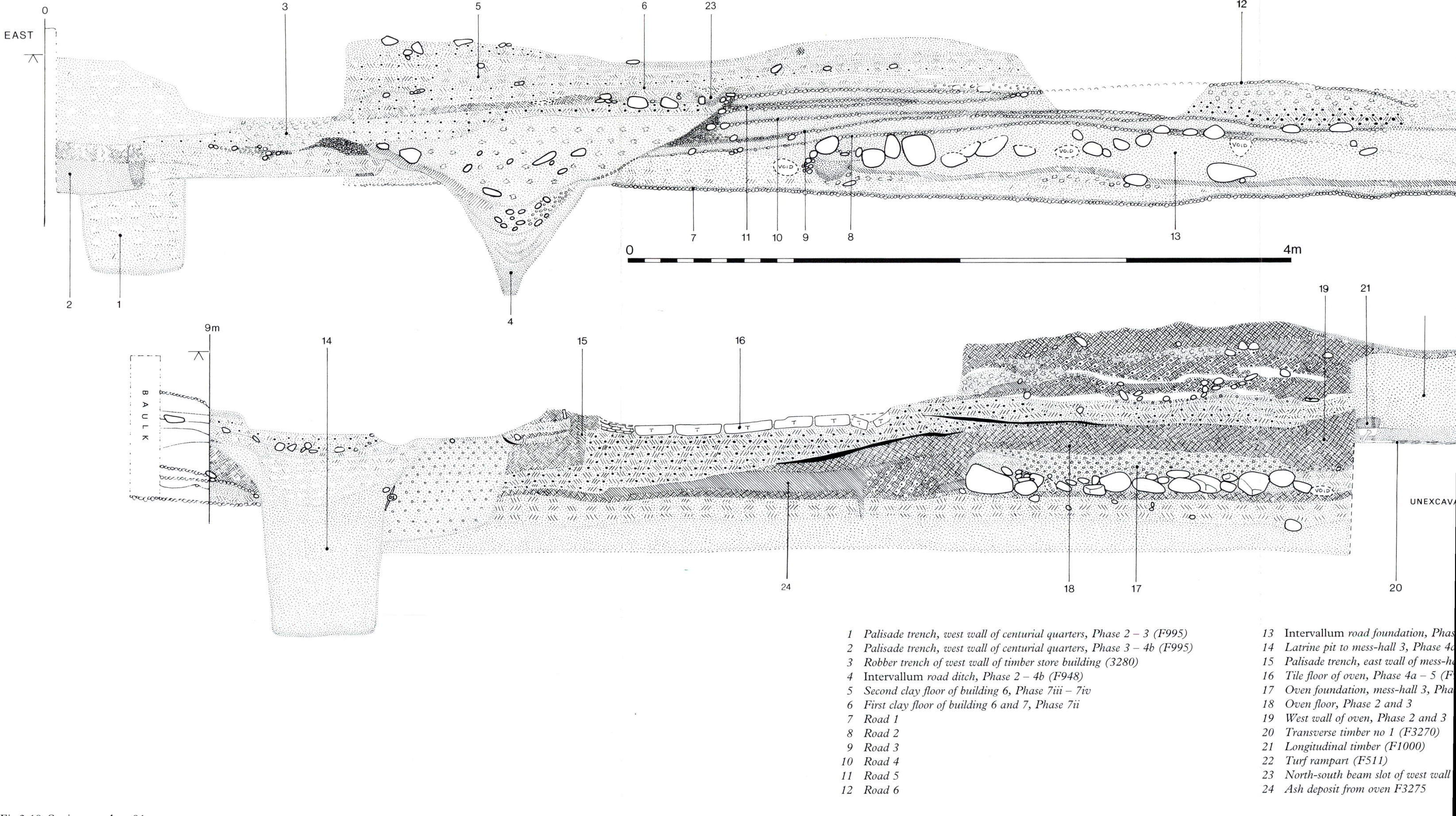

EAST

1   Palisade trench, west wall of centurial quarters, Phase 2 – 3 (F995)
2   Palisade trench, west wall of centurial quarters, Phase 3 – 4b (F995)
3   Robber trench of west wall of timber store building (3280)
4   Intervallum road ditch, Phase 2 – 4b (F948)
5   Second clay floor of building 6, Phase 7iii – 7iv
6   First clay floor of building 6 and 7, Phase 7ii
7   Road 1
8   Road 2
9   Road 3
10   Road 4
11   Road 5
12   Road 6

13   Intervallum road foundation, Phas
14   Latrine pit to mess-hall 3, Phase 4
15   Palisade trench, east wall of mess-h
16   Tile floor of oven, Phase 4a – 5 (F
17   Oven foundation, mess-hall 3, Pha
18   Oven floor, Phase 2 and 3
19   West wall of oven, Phase 2 and 3
20   Transverse timber no 1 (F3270)
21   Longitudinal timber (F1000)
22   Turf rampart (F511)
23   North-south beam slot of west wall
24   Ash deposit from oven F3275

Fig 2.18 Section c-c, Area 91

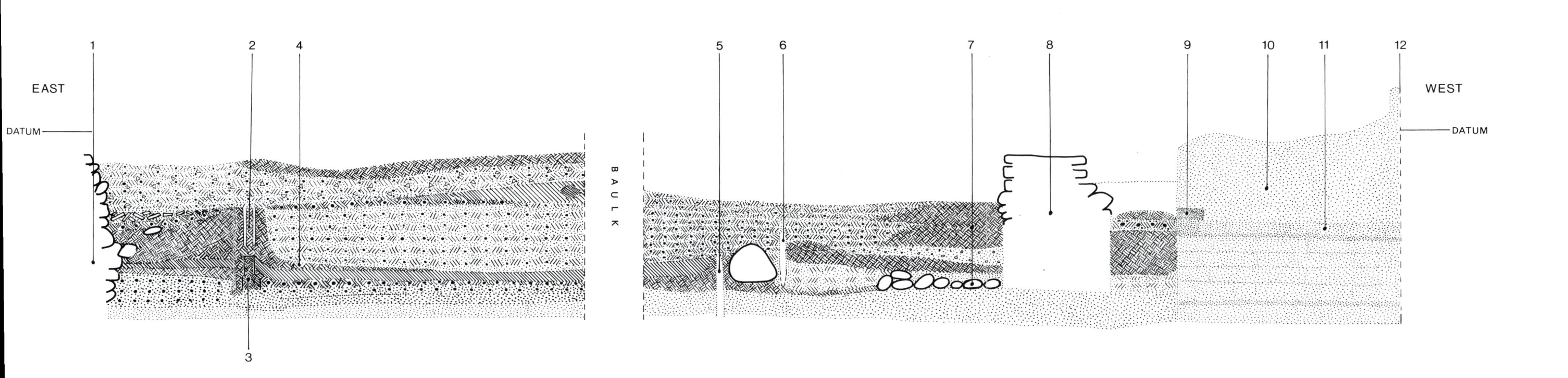

EAST

DATUM

BAULK

WEST

DATUM

1   2   4   3   5   6   7   8   9   10   11   12

0   3m

1   East wall of stone building A/B, Phase 6 – 7iv (F513)
2   East wall of mess-hall 3, Phase 4a, 4b, & 5 (F959)
3   East wall of mess-hall 3 Phase 2 & 3 (F3276)
4   Clay floor of mess-hall 3, Phase 4a, 4b, & 5
5   Wattles of oven wall, Phase 2
6   East wall of oven, Phase 3
7   Foundation and oven bottoms, Phase 2 & 3 (F3275)

8   West wall of stone building A/B, Phase 6 – 7iv (F512)
9   Longitudinal rampart timber nailed to transverse timber
    no 2 (F1000)
10 Reduced turf rampart (F511)
11 Transverse rampart timber no 2 (F3257)
12 Position of east side of west wall of macellum

Fig 2.19 Section a–a, Area 91

Fig 2.20 Clay and cobble oven foundation (Area 98, F2003), from the north

and that there was no obvious evidence of any recutting. This might be seen as remarkable when the apparent long term existence of the feature is considered. It must be assumed, therefore, that the ditch was either very well maintained, or alternatively that it had been protected from the elements in some way. Certainly, some form of covering would have been required across the ditch, adjacent to the alleyways between each barrack block (see below). This would have been essential to allow rapid and safe access from the barracks to the *intervallum*

road and the fortress defences. These crossing-points would have afforded some protection to the ditch underneath, but the lengths of ditch examined did not occur adjacent to a barrack block alleyway, so it is suggested that the whole length of the ditch was covered. This could have taken the form of timber boarding, presumably strong enough for foot traffic. Unfortunately no evidence could be found to support this, although it might be argued that for safety reasons it seems unlikely that a large ditch, next to a principal road such as this, would have been left open.

Construction of the internal buildings: the barrack blocks and centurial quarters

Evidence for early timber buildings in the area east of the *macellum*, and south of the added bath house range (Fig 2.7), was discovered in the early years of the training school excavations. This evidence consisted of foundation trenches, aligned both north–south and east–west across the site. Some measured as much as 0.60m in width (Area 32, F2311), while others, particularly the north–south examples, measured as little as 0.20m (Area 77, F2602), but the majority were around 0.40m wide. When excavated, the bottom of many of these trenches revealed indications of square and round postholes where posts had been set. At this time,

Fig 2.21 The V-shaped intervallum *road ditch (Area 91, F948) and road surfaces, from the north-west*

the position of the rampart and *intervallum* road were not known and the identity of these structures remained unclear, but the method of construction strongly suggested that these were military buildings.

In spite of the difficulties for interpretation afforded by, in the first place, the 'Box' method of excavation and, latterly, by the interference of later features, baulks, and the *piscina* (see Chapter 1) a reasonably coherent picture of the internal buildings emerged (Fig 2.23).

The timber trenches were found to follow a relatively uniform pattern (Fig 2.7). The east–west trenches, such as F2354/F2333/F2302 and F2645/F2723/F2858/F2820, formed long continuous alignments across the area excavated (Fig 2.22). These slots, which were recorded both west and east of the *piscina*, apparently formed the walls of narrow, corridor-like buildings, all orientated on the same east–west axis. The shorter north–south foundation trenches, such as F2408, Area 52 and F2918, Area 72, formed partition walls subdividing the narrow buildings into rows of sub-rectangular rooms. This was especially clear in the southern half of the site, where the rooms where constructed in adjoining north–south pairs. The configuration of the rooms was of particular interest in Areas 39, 41, 42, 52, and 53, where the southern room of each pair was twice the size of its northern neighbour. The northern rooms measured *c* 3.0m by *c* 2.0m and the southern rooms measured *c* 3.0m by *c* 4.3m (for example, see Fig 2.7, the two rooms demarcated by F2333, F2412, F2371, and F2366, and F2371, F2412, F2723, and F2408 respectively). Parallel with the north wall of these asymmetrical pairs of rooms (F2354, F2333, and F2302), was another east–west foundation trench running across Areas 33, 34, 35, 14, and 26 (F2319, F2311, F2262, F2292). This wall created an apparent passageway, *c* 2.6m wide, along the north side of the paired rooms, and it was noted that this was not obstructed by any north–south partitions, except for one example to the west of the *piscina* in Area 44 (F3022).

This arrangement was immediately identified as being typical of military barrack blocks. The asymmetrical pairs of adjoining rooms are characteristic of *contubernia*, each designed to accommodate eight men. The larger room provided the living and sleeping quarters, and the smaller anteroom would have been for equipment storage. The connecting passageway, running along the north side of the *contubernia*, would most likely have been an open verandah, which normally fronted barrack blocks (Davison 1989, 18–19; Webster 1985, 197–9).

Fig 2.22 (left) The northern parts of Areas 72 and 70 under excavation, seen from the east; (right) Area 73, and (partly excavated) Areas 70 and 72, from the west

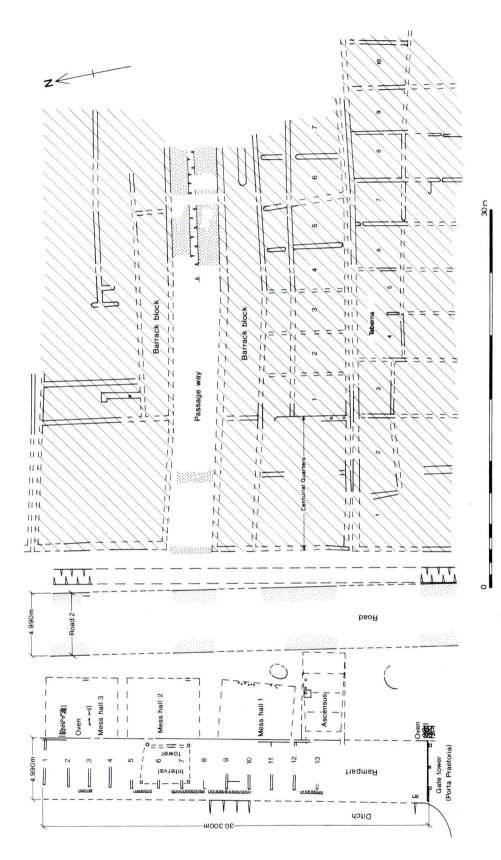

Fig 2.23 Phase 2, First Legionary period: reconstructed plan

Once the basic elements of one barrack block plan had been established, it was possible to attempt a full reconstruction of the excavated buildings, based on numerous analogies from known legionary fortresses elsewhere. However, the limits of the excavation, and the presence of the *piscina*, prevented the recovery of a whole plan for any of the buildings investigated. To the north of the *contubernia* and verandah already discussed, there was evidence for another barrack block, built on the same east–west axis, in the northern half of the site. However, the added baths range had caused considerable disturbance and the foundation trenches were not as clearly defined (Fig 2.7). It was possible to excavate the outer foundation of the verandah of this second barrack block, running east–west through Areas 12, 13, and 7 (F2266 and F2278), but only a short length of the inner verandah/*contubernia* foundation was recorded in Area 6 (F2199). Despite the recovery of various timber foundation trenches belonging to it (eg Area 4, F2053 and Area 5, 2187), no individual *contubernium* could be identified. However, the presence of the verandah at least confirmed that this block, and its neighbour to the south, were constructed as a facing pair, as is normal for legionary fortresses. A gravelled passageway with a central drainage gully (Area 14, F2249) *c* 3.5m wide separated the two buildings. Evidence for this metalled surface was also found west of the *piscina* in Areas 88.2 and 92, strongly suggesting that the passageway connected with the *intervallum* road, which would also have been in keeping with Roman military planning (Fig 2.23).

To the south of this pair of barrack blocks there was clear evidence for a third building, also orientated east–west along the southern limit of excavations. The back wall of this building ran through Areas 92, 50, 76, 73, 70, 72, and 78 (Fig 2.7, F448/445, F2562, F2645, F2723, F2858, and F2820; see also Fig 2.22), where it had been constructed against the back wall of the barrack block to the north. The trenches for the two back walls of these separate buildings were clearly seen, lying parallel to each other in Area 92 (F448/445 and F447), and Area 50 (F2562 and F2613). To the south of this wall, in Areas 50, 76, 77, 75, 73, 74, 70, 72, and 78, was evidence for another row of subrectangular rooms, with indications of an adjoining row of rooms to the south of this, in Area 80. The building appeared to be another barrack block, but its south wall was not recovered, as it occurred beyond the limit of excavations, and the internal partitions show several changes, making it impossible to suggest the original plan. Furthermore, the room examined in Area 80 appeared to be at least as large as its adjoining counterpart in Area 72 (*c* 3.5m by 4.0m), as opposed to the asymmetrical arrangement of the *contubernia* of other barrack blocks.

These inconsistencies were not resolved until the discovery of the *porta praetoria*, in the south-west corner of the site. The principal east–west road of the

fortress, the *via praetoria*, would have extended from the *porta praetoria* along, and just beyond, the southern limit of the excavations. As a result, there was space to construct only this building, which would have stood alone and fronted directly onto the road. This was unusual, as barrack blocks were normally built in facing pairs, so it seems a more likely solution that this building was a *taberna*, used for baggage storage or perhaps as stabling. *Tabernae* were normally open-fronted buildings, and, like their urban counterparts, were built along the main roads of fortresses, presumably to allow easy access. Such buildings are known at Inchtuthil and were described by Ian Richmond as store-rooms for 'pottery and glass, tools, tents and other miscellaneous equipment' (Richmond 1959, 153). This suggestion was supported by the discovery of broken glass and pottery in the gutters outside the *tabernae* at Inchtuthil (Pitts and St Joseph 1985, 180–2), and there are similar buildings at *Carnuntum* and *Vindonissa* (Petrikovits 1975, 51–4, bild 6 and 7).

Having established the north–south limits of two barrack blocks and a probable *taberna*, the next problem was to identify the east–west extent of these buildings, and in particular the location of the centurial quarters which would have been located at one end of each barrack block. This was difficult, because the site available for excavation was bounded on the east side by the main block of the Hadrianic baths, and to the west by the *piscina* and *macellum*. It was not until the discovery of the rampart and *intervallum* road that the western limit of the barrack blocks could be firmly established. Normal Roman practice dictated that the centurial quarters would have been built adjacent to the *intervallum* road at the western end of the barrack blocks. Excavation in Areas 91, 88.1, 88.3, 86, and 98 (Fig 2.7) revealed an intermittent north–south alignment of trench foundations (F995, F244, F172, F175, F257, and F1093), forming a timber building frontage along the east side of the *intervallum* road ditch (Fig 2.18, section c-c, no 1; Fig 2.39, section n-n, no 4). These foundation trenches clearly represented the west wall of the centurial quarters. However, the *piscina*, together with the east walls of the *macellum* and the main north–south drain (Figs 1.10 and 2.7), prevented any examination of the area immediately to the east of these structures and the possibility of recovering the plans of the centurial quarters. The presence of the *piscina*, in particular, prevented any excavation of the junction between the barrack blocks and their centurial quarters. It was therefore not possible to be certain whether there was a gap between the two, or whether they shared a party wall, as was more normal. It has been suggested that the distinction in plan was not a function of chronology but of individual legionary style (Pitts and St Joseph 1985, 155).

However, it was possible to excavate a small area north of the *piscina* (Areas 2, 3, 9, 10, and 30), and a close study of the construction trenches appeared to suggest that the centurial quarters and the barrack blocks were joined, although this was not certain, as has been shown on the plan (Fig 2.23). It is normal in the plans of barrack blocks for the verandah to terminate against the wall of the larger centurial quarters. Area 44, F3022, the only recorded north–south foundation across the verandah of the southern barrack block, may indicate the eastern side of the centurial quarters. It shares the same north–south alignment, with a foundation trench to the south, in Areas 46, 47, and 50 (F2480/F2565), and also to the north, in Areas 9 and 30 (F2034). However, if this alignment represents the east side, the length of the centurial blocks from west to east would have been only *c* 10m (Fig 2.23). This would mean that the Wroxeter centurial quarters would have been less than half the length of most centurial quarters known from other sites, the majority of which are at least 20m in length (Pitts and St Joseph 1985, 173; Table 2.4, below). It is possible that the centurial quarters were of this length, and that the evidence for their east wall had been lost under the *piscina*. In the absence of any other evidence, they have been shown as only 10m long (Fig 2.23).

The presence of the main Hadrianic bath house prevented any extension of the excavation to locate the east end of the barrack blocks. The maximum length excavated from the west end of the centurial block to the eastern edge of the excavation was *c* 35m. If each of the *contubernia* was approximately 3.0m wide, then it is possible to reconstruct seven *contubernia* and a 10m long centurial quarters within the area excavated (Fig 2.23). As most barrack blocks contained not less than ten *contubernia*, the full length of the barrack block, together with the centurial quarters, would have been at least 45m. However, extra rooms were often built to provide additional quarters and storage. The barrack blocks at Inchtuthil, for example, had 14 *contubernia*, and the Wroxeter barrack blocks may thus have been as long as *c* 57m (Webster 1985, fig 41; Petrikovits 1975, 36–43).

The legionary defences: Phase 3, road 3

Subsequently, the *intervallum* road was completely re-surfaced, with road 2 being sealed by a thin foundation layer and a fresh gravel surface (Fig 2.17, section e-e; Fig 2.18, section c-c, no 9; Fig 2.34, section d-d; Fig 2.51, section g-g). Road 3 respected the presence of the road ditch along its eastern edge (Fig 2.24, F948 and F2090), but in Area 91 a short length of U-shaped gully was uncovered, cut along the western edge of the road (F3290). This gully was also noted in sections at several points in Area 84 (F3289), where it was seen to be linked with road 3 (Fig 2.51, section g-g, no 4; Fig 2.17, section e-e, no 2; Fig 2.34, section d-d, no 3). It appears, therefore, that this gully ran most of the length of road 3 and was presumably intended for drainage.

The oven built at the back of the rampart in Area 91 (F3275), appears to have continued operating during Phase 3. The depth of the rake-out (Fig 2.18, section c-c, no 24) suggests a continued period of use, which would support this, and it would appear that the mess hall 3 was retained to protect the oven from the elements. All three mess halls remained in place, but at the end of Phase 3 they were all rebuilt, presumably in accord with the demolition and rebuilding of the barrack blocks and centurial quarters described below.

A large pit (F770) outside mess hall 1 replaced the smaller one of Phase 2 (F771) and continued in use into Phase 4. The Phase 2 pit south of the *ascensus* (Fig 2.7, F362) was replaced, and cut by another pit (Fig 2.24, F347) in the south-east corner of Area 85.2. No other pits belonging to this phase were located in the *intervallum* area. The most dramatic change during Phase 3 occurred east of the *intervallum* road. During the excavation of the barrack blocks and centurial quarters it was noted that there were several foundation trenches that could not be satisfactorily incorporated into the plan of the Phase 2 buildings (eg Fig 2.24, F2067, F2897, and F2721). In some areas, particularly those north of the *piscina*, it was observed that some of these trenches cut those of the Phase 2 centurial quarters and therefore represented later buildings. Furthermore, at least five of the east–west foundation trenches (F2266/F2278; F2319/F2311/F2262/F2292; F2354/F2333/F2302; and F2369/F2371/F2336) which formed the principal walls of the barrack blocks, demonstrated signs of recutting, clearly indicating the replacement of walls at some stage (Fig 2.25, section m-m, nos 1 and 2). This was also apparent in some of the north–south trenches (Fig 2.25, F2307, and Fig 2.26, section m-m, nos 3 and 4). The construction trenches for these second period buildings were *c* 0.50m deep, tending to be slightly shallower than those of the earlier phase, which averaged *c* 0.70m in depth. Excavations in the east end of Area 91 showed that the west wall of the centurial quarters had also been replaced (F995, Fig 2.18, section c-c, no 2; Fig 2.39, section n-n, no 2), and that this had taken place while the *intervallum* road ditch was still functioning.

All this evidence indicated that the barrack blocks and their centurial quarters had been totally dismantled and then rebuilt after the end of Phase 2 and before the end of Phase 4, presumably at some point during Phase 3. They were rebuilt on almost the same alignment, but with some differences in the internal partitioning. The main outline plans remained the same, except that in this second period the *tabernae* and the southern barrack block were built back to back, and the second period centurial quarters appear, from the evidence of the north block, to have been about twice the size of the first period ones. Figure 2.24 shows the location of all the foundation trenches for Phases 2 to 4, and Figure 2.26 demonstrates their phasing.

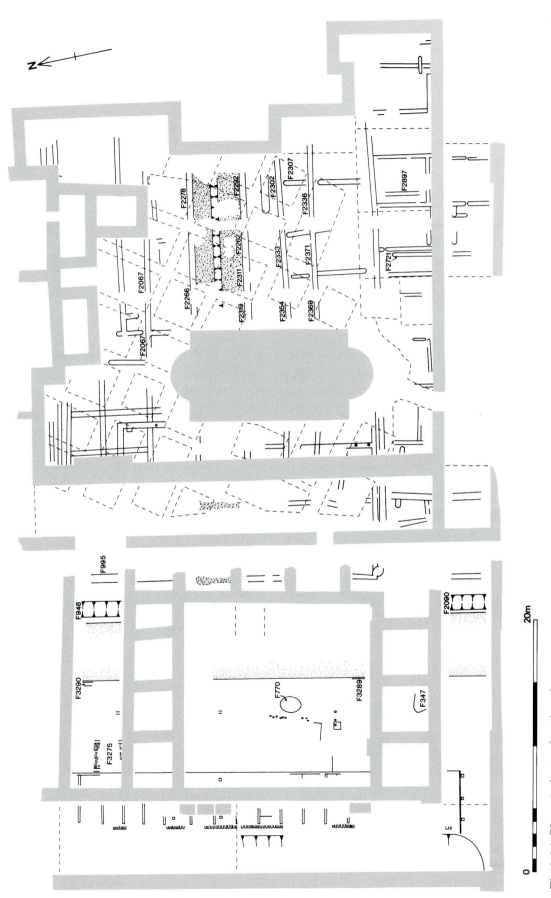

Fig 2.24 Phase 3: feature location plan

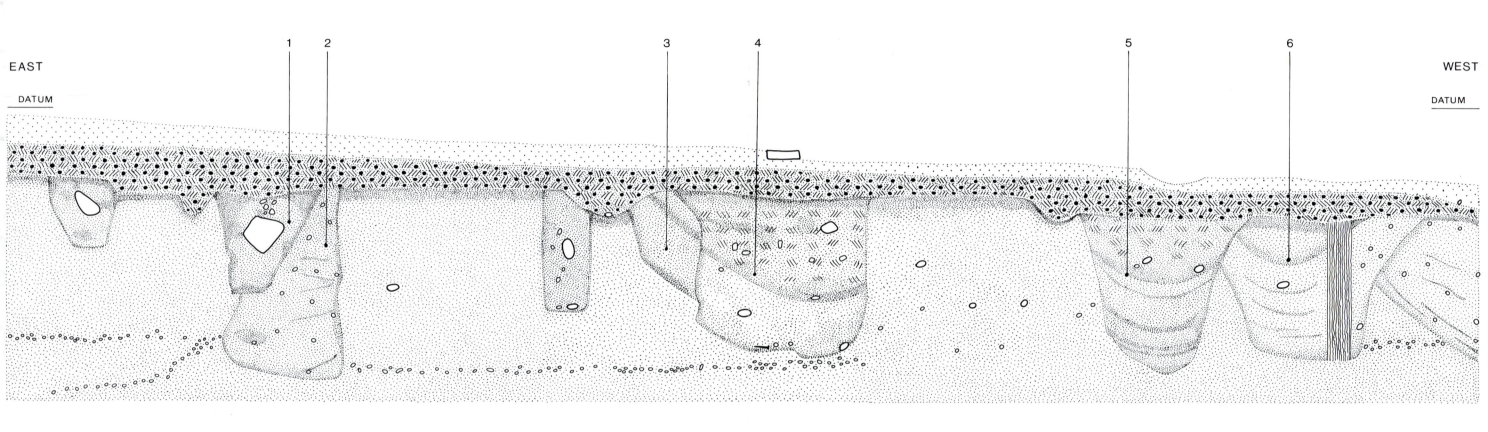

EAST

DATUM

WEST

DATUM

0   3m

1   East-west palisade trench of barrack block no 1, Phase 3 – 4a (F2336)
2   East-west palisade trench of barrack block no 1, Phase 2 – 3 (F2336)
3   North-south palisade trench of barrack block no 1, Phase 2 – 3 (F2307)
4   North-south palisade trench of barrack block no 2, Phase 3 – 4a (F2307)
5   East robber trench of timber store building, Phase 7iv (F2247)
6   East-west palisade trench of barrack block no 2, Phase 3 – 4a (F2333)

Fig 2.25 Section m-m, south-west face of Areas 35 and 39

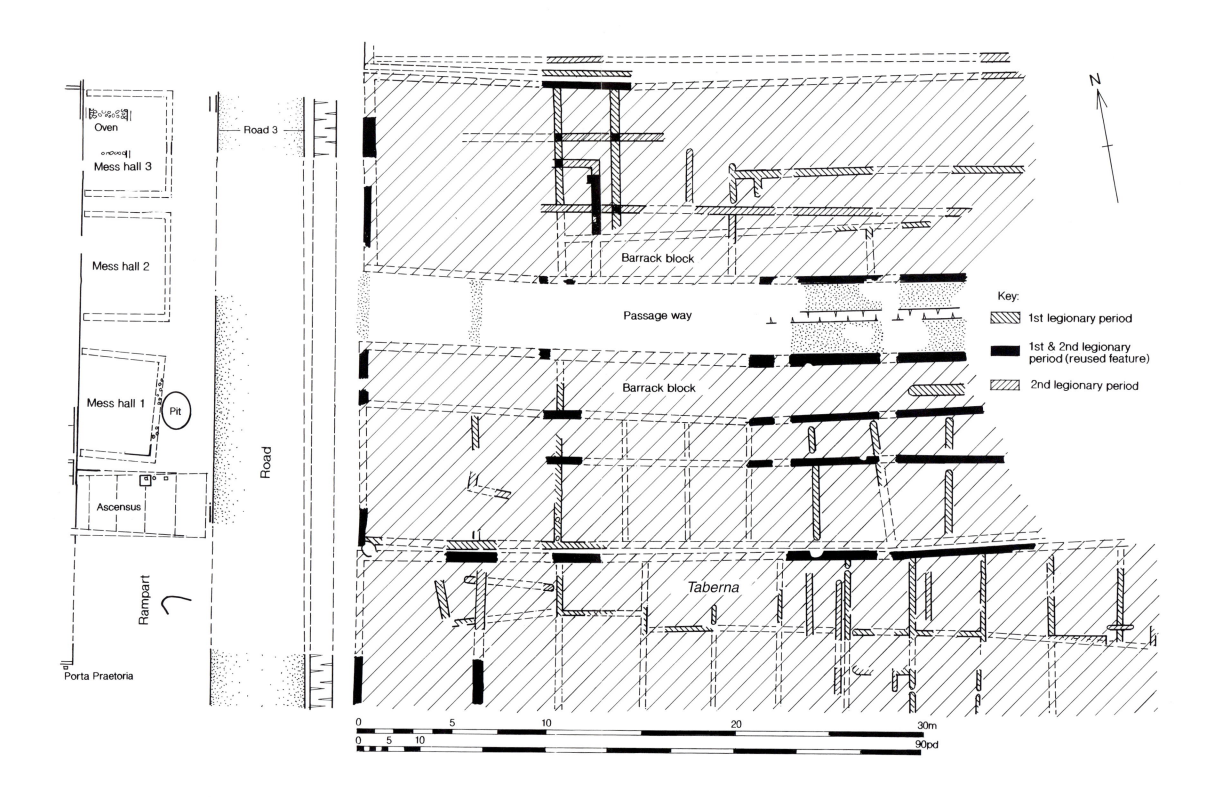

Key:

- ▨ 1st legionary period
- ■ 1st & 2nd legionary period (reused feature)
- ▨ 2nd legionary period

Oven

Mess hall 3

Mess hall 2

Mess hall 1

Pit

Ascensus

Rampart

Porta Praetoria

Road 3

Road

Barrack block

Passage way

Barrack block

Taberna

N

0   5   10   20   30m

0   5   10   90pd

Fig 2.26 Phase 3, First to Second Legionary period: reconstructed plan

The second legionary period, AD 66–79

Phase 4a, road 4

The rebuilt barrack blocks and centurial quarters were certainly in place by Phase 4a, and as this redevelopment appears to represent a major change in the fort's archaeological sequence it has been assigned to the second legionary period. The new barrack blocks were not as well defined as those of the first legionary period, as the presence of the *piscina* and later walls continued to prevent any detailed examination (Fig 2.27). No individual *contubernia* could be isolated, but the main east–west walls of the new buildings continued to occupy the same positions as their predecessors (eg F2369/F2371/F2336). The only exceptions to this were the *taberna* and the southern barrack block, which were built back to back, apparently employing the same back wall (F249/F2562/F2645/F2723/F2858/F2820), rather than the two separate parallel walls used in the first legionary period. This shared wall occupied the same location as the original Phase 2 *taberna* north wall.

A wall in Area 11/12 (Fig 2.27, F2180) appeared to represent a blocking wall at the end of the northern barrack block's verandah. If this marked the east end of the verandah, it must be concluded that the eastern limit of the barrack block had been moved by some 10m to the east from its original Phase 2 position, as described above. This would have allowed an enlargement of the centurial quarters to a total length of almost 20m, which would be in keeping with most examples from other legionary fortresses in the empire. However, the evidence for this interpretation is far from conclusive.

Intervallum road 3 was superseded by road 4, which served the completed second period of barrack blocks and centurial quarters (Fig 2.27; Fig 2.18, section c-c, no 10). Road 4 was 4.82m (14.5 PD) wide, with the ditch along its east side still functioning. The 1.30m wide ditch retained its original profile and probably continued to be covered by a timber walkway. The shallow gully that had followed the west edge of the road in Phase 3 was obliterated, and there was evidence at various points in Area 84 that this was replaced by a stone kerb (Fig 2.34, section d-d, no 15; Fig 2.51, section g-g, no 5). The western side of road 4 was very fragmentary and worn, suggesting a prolonged period of use.

The mess halls were all rebuilt by Phase 4a. Mess hall 3 was replaced with another building of identical construction technique and similar dimensions. The evidence for this rebuilt version of mess hall 3 was more substantial than the first period example, with the north and east walls being identified in Area 91 (Fig 2.27, F970 and F959), and the south-east corner (F186) and most of its south wall foundation (F283/F180) being recorded in Areas 87.2 (95.2) and 87.1. In Area 91 it was possible to see that the first

version of mess hall 3 had been demolished (Fig 2.19, section a-a, no 3), and how the double-staked wall hurdles of the rebuilt east wall (Fig 2.27, F959; Fig 2.19, section a-a, no 2) had been driven directly into the top of the demolition levels of the earlier walls. The west end of the south wall ended at the back of the rampart in Area 87.1, where the foundation trench (F283) terminated as a butt end. As in Phase 2 and 3 there was no evidence for a connecting west wall running along the back of the rampart, and this suggested that the mess halls were built directly on to the back of the rampart.

The oven with its cobble and clay foundation (F3275, Figs 2.7 and 2.24), which had been incorporated into this mess hall during the first legionary period, was also demolished. It was replaced by a large oven (F958) of a very different type (Figs 2.27 and 2.28), which had been built against the wattle and daub wall in the north-east corner of the mess hall, where details of both the mess hall wall (Fig 2.18, section c-c, no 15; Fig 2.52, section b-b, no 8) and the oven itself survived to be studied. The oven was of an irregular plan, *c* 1.5m wide, and with a base that had been constructed of large flat tiles, each *c* 0.35 by 0.25m and 0.045m thick (Fig 2.28; Fig 2.18, section c-c, no 16). The north side of the oven had been cut away by the southern wall trench of the later timber building, associated with Phase 6 (Fig 2.38, F805, mess hall 4), and the stokehole had also been lost on the south side.

In Areas 87.2 (95.2) and 87.1 were the remains of the north wall (F289 and F181) and north-east corner (F184) of mess hall 2, which were closely associated with the south wall of mess hall 3 (Fig 2.27). As in the case of mess hall 3, the western end of the north wall foundation trench terminated in a butt end against the back of the rampart (F289), and there was no evidence for mess hall 2 having had an east wall. To the south, in Area 84, section g-g (Fig 2.51) revealed further evidence for the superimposition of mess hall walls, where the stakes of the east wall of mess hall 2 (F786) had been driven into the top of what may have been the foundation trench (Fig 2.7, F976) for the Phase 2 and 3 building (Fig 2.51, section g-g, nos 2 and 3). A clay floor was found in the south-east corner of the building.

Mess hall 2 also possessed an oven during this phase. Like the tile oven in mess hall 3, it had been built up against the east wall of the building, rather than the back of the rampart, which appeared to have been the normal practice during the first legionary period. However, this oven (F831), was not built of tiles, but retained the first period method of construction, with a clay and cobble foundation (Fig 2.29).

It was possible to define only parts of the east and south walls of mess hall 1. However, the six or nine postholes that had represented the east wall of the mess hall during Phases 2 and 3 were replaced by two square posts (Fig 2.27, F753 and F754), and part of the building's

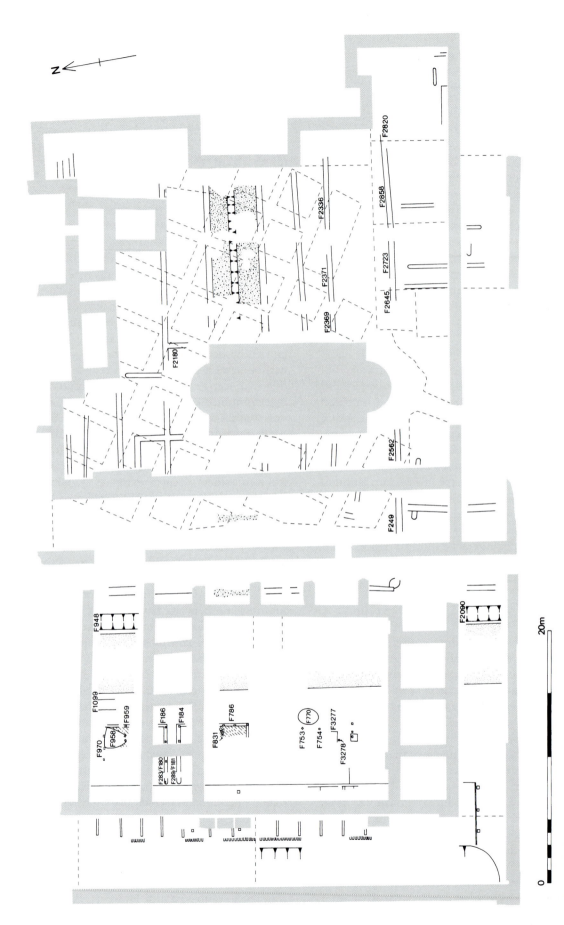

Fig 2.27 Phase 4a: feature location plan

Fig 2.28 The tile oven base, F958

Fig 2.29 Clay and cobble oven foundation, F831

south-east corner was also excavated (F3277), together with a third square post (F3278). There was some evidence to suggest that the walls had been covered in a thin white plaster, rather than the clay daub which had still been used for the rebuilding of mess halls 2 and 3. However, the general construction technique for all three mess halls remained the same post, hurdle, and clay method observed in the east wall of mess hall 3 in Phase 2 (Fig 2.7, F3276). Each mess hall measured c 5.80 by c 4.50m (c 17.5 by 13.5 PD), occupying much the same space as their first legionary period predecessors (Fig 2.30).

The pit (F770) associated with mess hall 1 continued to function, and a new pit (F1099) was excavated in Area 91, between the east wall of mess hall 3 and the *intervallum* road. The square shape of this pit suggested that it was a latrine.

The depot period, AD 79–90

Phase 4b, post-road 4

The end of Phase 4 marks a dramatic change in the character of the site. The second legionary period barrack blocks and their centurial quarters were completely demolished. This operation cleared the area east of the *intervallum* road (Fig 2.31). The drainage ditch, on the east side of the *intervallum* road, was filled in at the same time (Fig 2.18, section c-c, no 4), and road 4 itself appears to have lapsed into poor condition, with evidence of repair work in places. The western edge of the road surface was very fragmentary (Fig 2.34, section d-d; Fig 2.17, section e-e; Fig 2.51, section g-g), which effectively reduced the width of road 4 from 4.82m (14.5 PD) to 3.17m (9.5 PD).

West of the road, in Area 84, the *ascensus* was demolished, leaving little evidence of its existence. In its place a substantial layer of broken red sandstone c 2.5 by 14.5m (*84/340*) was laid, sealing the latest latrine pit associated with mess hall 1 (Fig 2.27, F770), but respecting the presence of the west wall of mess hall 1 (Fig 2.31, F753/F754), which was evidently still

in use. The purpose of this sandstone layer, and why it was considered important enough to demolish the *ascensus* to accommodate it, is not understood. There was no apparent structure associated with it and the layer may have covered much, if not all, of the space between mess hall 1 and the *via praetoria*, as further deposits of red sandstone were recorded to the south in Areas 85 and 98. Due to the interference of the later *macellum* walls no stratigraphic link between these deposits could be identified, but their character and extent made it possible that they all belonged to the same context. It is suggested that the red sandstone layer may have been intended as a hard-standing for vehicles. The three mess halls, built at the back of the rampart, appear to have remained unaltered.

Phase 4b may represent selective demolition prior to a major redevelopment of the fortress (Fig 2.32); at least within the area excavated, where it was heralded by the demolition of the barrack blocks and the centurial quarters. The poor state of road 4 may indicate the high levels of activity associated with this demolition, the deterioration of the surface being due to the movement of men and their vehicles. The removal of the *ascensus* would suggest a change in status of the site, there was no evidence for the dismantling of the rampart, or its associated structures, at this stage. The evidence suggests that this took place later in the archaeological sequence.

Phase 5, road 5

The heavily worn *intervallum* road was resurfaced with road 5, a thin deposit laid down directly over road 4 (Fig 2.18, section c-c, no 11), with evidence of a small gully along its west edge in Area 84 (Fig 2.33, F3279; Fig 2.34, section d-d, no 2; Fig 2.17, section e-e, no 1). Road 5 was only c 3.0m wide at the northern limit of the excavation, and c 4.0m at its southern end, which implied a somewhat irregular construction which might suggest a rapid resurfacing of road 4 to provide what may have been a construction road. This area, occupied by the barrack blocks and centurial quarters, was subsequently redeveloped.

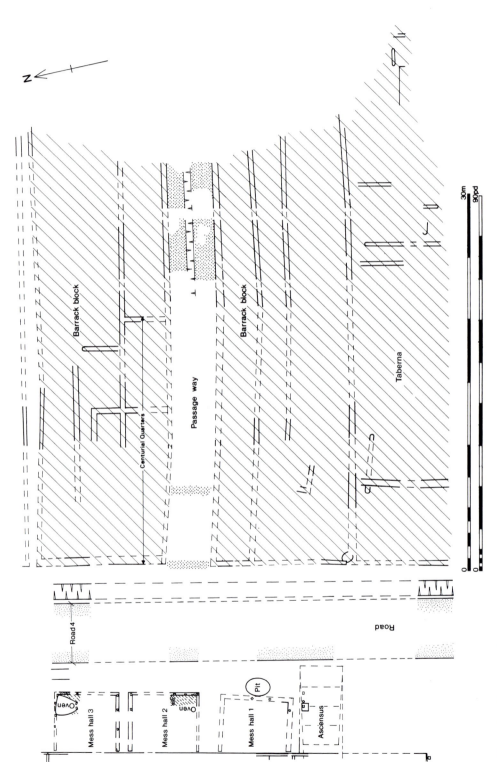

Fig 2.30 Phase 4a, Second legionary period: reconstructed plan

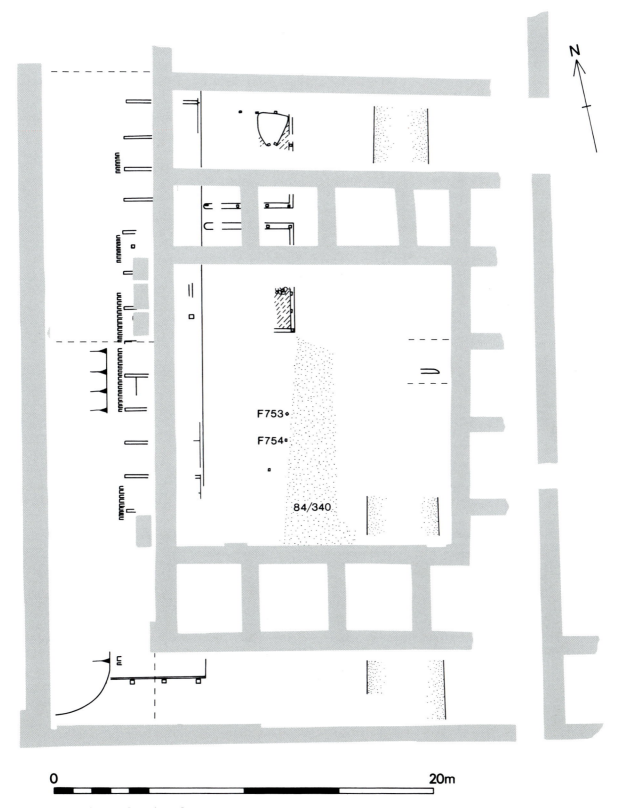

Fig 2.31 Phase 4b: feature location plan

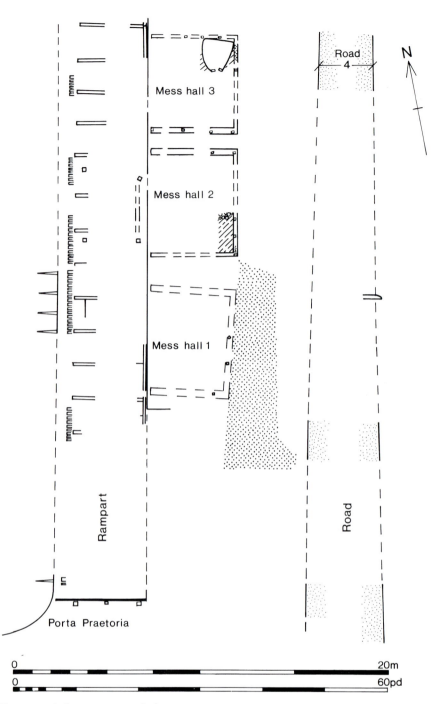

Mess hall 3

Mess hall 2

Mess hall 1

Rampart

Porta Praetoria

Road 4

N

Road

0 _____ 20m

0 _____ 60pd

Fig 2.32 Phase 4b, Depot period: reconstructed plan

During this phase mess hall 1 was demolished and replaced by a stone building, the foundations of which were found in the centre of Area 84, in some places cutting and partially overlapping the red sandstone foundation. The whole of the east wall was uncovered (Fig 2.33, F262; Fig 2.34, section d-d, no 7), along with connecting sections of the north (F277) and south walls (F3294). A short length of the west wall was also identified (F417), although the presence of the required safety baulk at the back of the *macellum* west wall restricted any detailed examination. The structure, stone building A, was built of grey sandstone and measured 7.0m by 5.1m, and its west wall continued to respect the back of

the rampart (Fig 2.33), which was probably still standing. The walls were 0.5m thick and survived to a height of 0.48m, but it was unclear whether they had been built entirely of stone, or whether the building had been partly of timber, with stone footings. The discovery of a fireplace built into the east wall (Fig 2.33, F550; Fig 2.35) indicates that the lower parts of the walls had been of stone, although a timber wall with a stone flue and chimney is a possibility. Stone building A contained no evidence for any specific activity, but the presence of the fireplace suggested that the building was a workplace of some kind, possibly an office, which would have required warmth during periods of cold temperatures.

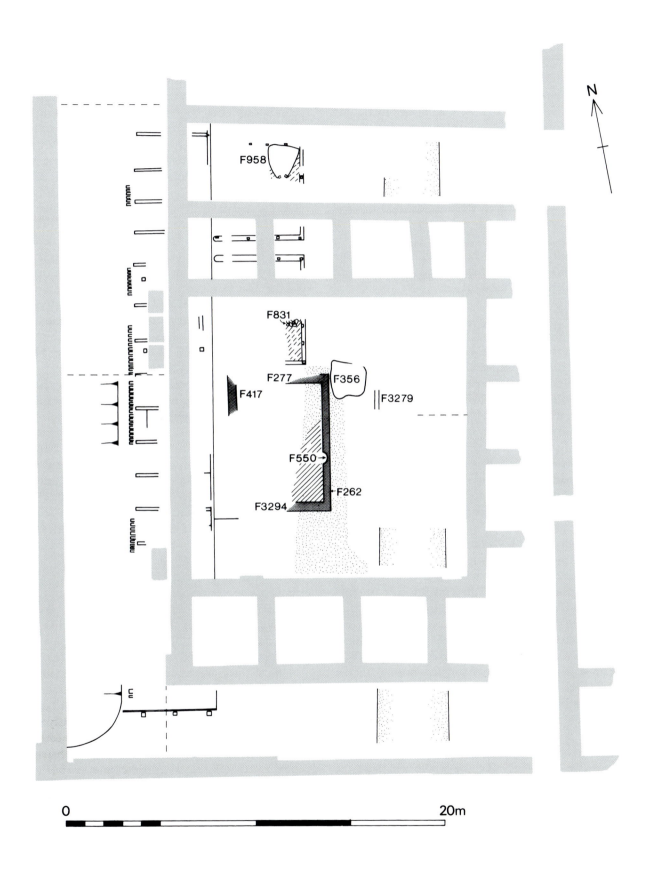

Fig 2.33 Phase 5: feature location plan

At the base of the fireplace were fragments of a broken amphora and traces of a sequence of thin clay floors, which presumably spread over the full width of the building (Fig 2.34, section d-d, no 10; Fig 2.35). Stone building A was also provided with a large external latrine (Fig 2.33, F356) which measured c 1.2 by 1.7m (Fig 2.36, section h-h, no 1).

Mess halls 2 and 3 apparently remained unaltered (Fig 2.33 and 2.37), and seem to have continued functioning along with their ovens (Figs 2.33, F831, F958, and 2.37).

To the east of road 5, in the area now cleared of the barrack blocks and centurial quarters, construction work began on a large timber building. This building could not be accurately associated with any phase, but as there was no evidence of a clearly defined interval between the removal of the barracks and the erection of the building it is assumed that the two events were linked. Construction work began shortly after the demolition of the barracks, presumably during Phase 5, and was completed by Phase 6.

Phase 5–6, the store building

Excavations to the east of the *piscina* revealed a pair of large trenches, running parallel with each other across the site in a north–south direction (Fig 2.38). The western trench (F2056/F2230/F2312/F2349/F2373), and the eastern trench (F2210/F2247/F2713), both clearly post-dated the foundations of the second period barrack blocks and centurial quarters which they cut across (Fig 2.25, section m-m, no 5). The possibility that both these trenches belonged to the same structure was confirmed when they were observed to turn sharply together through 90° to continue their parallel course in a westerly direction; the eastern trench in Area 80 (F661), from where it extended beyond the limits of the excavation and could not be traced any further, and the western trench in Area 73 (F2644), where it continued beneath the south end of the *piscina* (F2511) and through Area 92 (F280), towards the *macellum*. The trenches varied in width from 0.75m to almost 1.0m, and sections cut across them showed variations in their profiles. It could be inferred from a close study of the base of these trenches that they had originally been of the normal timber trench type, but cut through and widened by robbing. Vertical posts would have been extracted more efficiently by individual robbing, as in the case of the corner tower posts of the *porta praetoria*. However, in this case, the width of the robber trenches appeared to indicate much more extensive robbing along the whole length of the walls. This was most probably to extract lateral beams connecting the uprights below ground level, suggesting that these timbers were large enough to be worth the effort of recovery. As there were no indications in the trench filling of any stone or mortar, it must be assumed that this was a construction wholly of timber.

The only evidence for this building were these trenches, and since much of the structure was outside the confines of the excavation its plan was far from complete. However, although the trenches could not be directly linked to other features for this phase, two trenches were identified as probably belonging to the same building. It was clear that the two robber trenches did not extend across the *intervallum* road in Areas 85 or 98. The west wall of the building presumably respected the eastern edge of the *intervallum* road, as the centurial quarters had done in previous phases. Excavations in the east end of Area 91 revealed the bottom of a U-shaped trench (F3280), similar to the robber trenches to the east of the *piscina*. This trench ran north–south and clearly post-dated the foundation trench of the west wall of the second period centurial quarters (Fig 2.18, section c-c, no 3; Fig 2.39, section n-n, no 6), thus placing it on the same archaeological horizon as the other robber trenches. It was concluded that this represented the west wall of the building, which fronted on to the *intervallum* road. Unfortunately this trench could not be traced anywhere else along this line due to disturbance from the east wall of the *macellum* courtyard (Fig 2.38). The north trench was identified in Areas 1 and 2, where a complicated sequence of legionary foundation trenches was finally cut by another U-shaped trench running east–west across the site. This is also assumed to have been a robber trench belonging to this building.

When these elements are plotted the plan is still largely incomplete, but there is enough evidence to suggest a building with an inner square, or courtyard, measuring 24.9 by 22m between the inner edges of F3280 and F2056/F2230/F2312/F2349/F2373. Around this square was an outer surround forming a corridor, 5.0m wide on the eastern side and 6.0m on the south side (Fig 2.38). Only 2.75m of the outer surround on the south side was traced (F661), and excavation c 20m to the west in Area 98 along the projected alignment of this surround revealed no trace of it. No evidence was found for the north side of the outer surround, as this occurred beyond the northern limit of the excavations. If the building was symmetrical then the width of the north corridor may have been c 6.0m, the same as the south corridor (Fig 2.44). No internal features or floors were found; these may have been built at ground level and therefore left no archaeological trace when the building was demolished.

This was a substantial building which may have covered an area at least 29 by 40.4m (Figs 2.40 and 2.41). It was apparently rectangular and bears a distinct resemblance to legionary store buildings known at *Aquincum*, *Bonna*, *Noviomagus* (Nijmegen), and *Lambaesis* (Fig 2.41) (Petrikovits 1975, 82–98); comparison can also be made with an uncompleted building at Corbridge (Daniels 1978, 95). The legions needed a vast amount of stores of various kinds; apart from food kept in the granaries, there were weapons, tools, clothing, equipment, oil, wine, cut timbers, furniture, and other items. The new building might be seen as part of the reordering of the fortress, no longer housing the fighting strength, but converted into a rearward depot for stores,

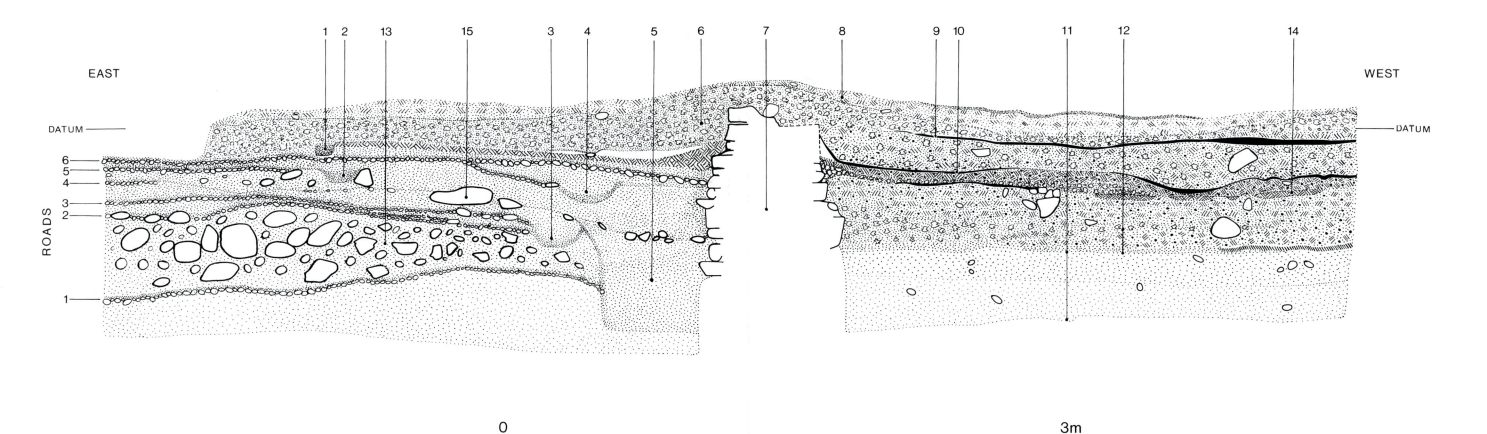

EAST

DATUM —— — DATUM

ROADS

6
5
4
3
2

1

1

0   3m

Fig 2.34 Section d-d, Area 84

1   North-south beam slot, east wall of building 8,
    Phase 7iii and 7iv (F609)
2   Road 5 gully, Phase 5 (F3279)
3   Roads 2 and 3 gully
4   Road 6 box drain, Phase 6 (F741)
5   Possible latrine pit
6   Destruction material associated with the stone
    building A/B, Phase 7iv
7   Stone building A, Phase 5 (F262)
8   Post-military timber building destruction layers
9   Stone building A/B floor, Phase 6 – 7iv
10 Stone building A floor, Phase 5
11 Mess-hall 1 floor, Phase 2 and 3
12 Mess-hall 1 destruction deposit, Phase 3
13 Intervallum road foundation, Phase 2
14 Mess-hall 1 floor, Phase 4a and 4b
15 Stone kerb, Road 4

Fig 2.35 Fireplace (Area 84, F550) in stone building A, from the west

administration, and training. How much this change affected other areas of the fortress remains for future excavations to determine.

Phase 6, road 6

A new surface was laid 4.99m wide (15 PD), restoring the *intervallum* road to its original width (Figs 2.38 and 2.40). This was road 6, which had a 0.5m wide north–south drain down its west edge (Fig 2.38, F741, F357, and F2000; Fig 2.52, section b-b, no 17; Fig 2.34, section d-d, no 4; Fig 2.17, section e-e, no 3; Fig 2.51, section g-g, no 7). This may have been a box drain, as there were occasional slight indications in the gully's profile suggesting that a straight-sided structure had been placed within it. There were also deposits of ash in the gully that may have been derived from the drain's final destruction. If the drain had been open, it might also have acted as an eavesdrip for the stone building A (Fig 2.40).

Timber mess halls 2 and 3 were demolished to clear the ground for a northern extension to stone building A (Fig 2.38). The north wall (Fig 2.33, F277) was demolished and the west and east walls (F417 and F262) were extended to the north. The west wall (F233) continued up to, and under, the north courtyard wall of the *macellum*, crossed Area 87.1 (F18), and was seen to emerge

in Area 91 (F512, Fig 2.19, section a-a, no 8), where it turned through 90° to the east to form the north wall of the extended structure (F512, F513). It was noted that the north-west corner of the building was very close to the back of the rampart. The north wall (F513) continued for some 5.5m before meeting the east wall of the building. In Area 84 the extended east wall was also traced up to the north wall of the *macellum* (Fig 2.38; Fig 2.51, section g-g, no 11), but no stones were recorded in Area 87.2, where the wall had been completely robbed out, leaving only the robber trench. In both Areas 84 and 91 the east wall was seen to respect the western limit of the *intervallum* road and the box drain. The full length of the completed building (stone building A/B) was 17.5m (Figs 2.40 and 2.42).

There was an entrance on the east side at the point of the extension. This gave access into a timber vestibule, the sill beams of which were traceable (F605, F606, F278, F614, and F612), together with a suggestion of internal partitioning. A second fire place (F611) was built against but not cut into the east wall of the extension (Fig 2.43). The clay floor of stone building A (Fig 2.34, section d-d, no 10) was replaced with a new clay floor, which extended along the whole length of stone building A/B (Fig 2.34, section d-d, no 9). This was particularly apparent around the new hearth, and in the north-west corner of the building in Area 91.

46

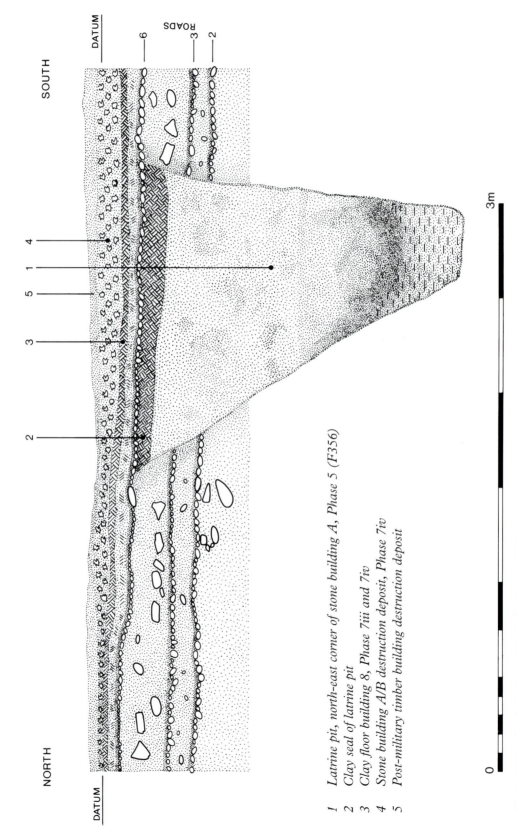

DATUM

SOUTH

ROADS

6
3
2

4

1

5

3

2

NORTH

DATUM

1 Latrine pit, north-east corner of stone building A, Phase 5 (F356)
2 Clay seal of latrine pit
3 Clay floor building 8, Phase 7iii and 7iv
4 Stone building A/B destruction deposit, Phase 7iv
5 Post-military timber building destruction deposit

0   3m

Fig 2.36 Section h–h, Area 84: the latrine pit F356

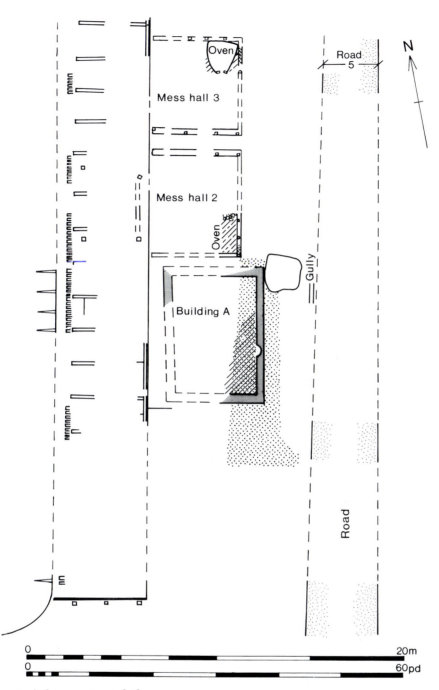

Fig 2.37 Phase 5, Depot period: reconstructed plan

It was noticeable that the building work on the extension of stone building A/B lacked the quality of stone building A. This was especially true of the shallow foundations, which were supported on a clay pad (Fig 2.51, section g-g, no 11). In consequence a problem arose on the east side near to the north-east corner of the building, where a back-filled pit was cut by the building's foundation trenches. This pit, which appeared to be the south end of the mess hall 3 latrine (Phase 4a, F1099), was very narrow and 1.5m deep, and evidently caused the builders some structural difficulties. In consequence the foundations were deepened at this point, but the job lacked the normal standard of

workmanship of the legionaries, and it may be suggested that non-legionary labour had been involved (Fig 2.19, section a-a, no 1).

To the north of the extended stone building A/B there was evidence for another timber building. Although most of this structure occurred beyond the northern limits of the excavation, part of the west wall was seen (Fig 2.38, F806; Fig 2.52, section b-b, no 3), as well as the south-east corner (Fig 2.38, F805; Fig 2.52, section b-b, no 9). Like the other timber buildings, this example had foundation trenches and its walls had been lined with clay. The presence of an oven in the south-west corner of the building (F3281) suggested that this was another

48

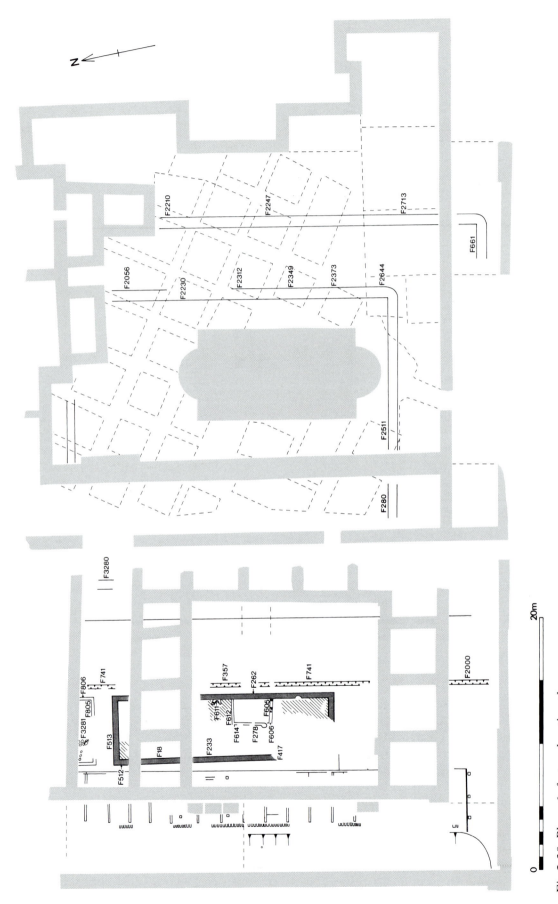

Fig 2.38 Phase 6: feature location plan

0   20m

mess hall (Fig 2.40, mess hall 4). The oven had a clay base (Fig 2.52, section b-b, no 4), over which was laid a cobble foundation (Fig 2.52, section b-b, no 5). This method of construction was very similar to that of the ovens built during the first and second legionary periods. Most of the available evidence for this oven, and for mess hall 4, occurred only in the section on the north side of Area 91 (Fig 2.52, section b-b). However, enough survived to show that the south wall of mess hall 4 ran parallel with the north wall of stone building A/B, forming a passageway 1.3m wide between the two, and that both buildings shared similar widths (c 5.4m), respecting the western edge of road 6 and the back of the rampart (Fig 2.40).

Phase 7 The post-road 6 sequence

Up to and including Phase 6 the archaeological sequence has been based on the succession of the *intervallum* roads. Road 6 represented the last usable *intervallum* surface, since it was subsequently blocked by new structures built over it. Furthermore, the events recorded during Phase 7 were difficult to date precisely and occur within a much disturbed archaeological sequence, due to the insertion of later walls and large pits. The following sequence may be postulated despite the later disturbances. Some of the archaeological features could not be accurately phased, but these have been fitted into the sequence where appropriate gaps and logic dictated. Against this background it would therefore appear more useful to list the final structural sequence under one phase, divided into four suggested sub-phases

(7i–7iv), up to the final military demolition. Figure 2.44 shows the location of all the features associated with Phases 6 to 7iv.

Phase 7i, post-road 6

A short timber slot was discovered connecting the south-east corner of mess hall 4 with the north-east corner of stone building A/B (Fig 2.45, F851). This appeared to block the east–west passageway between the two buildings at its east end. Although this was only a slight alteration, the blocking wall was clearly later than the two Phase 6 buildings and was also shown to have coexisted, at least for a while, with the drain along the west edge of the *intervallum* road (Phase 6, F741). The box drain was subsequently filled in, and the western edge of the original road 6 surface was extended up to the east wall of the extended stone building A/B (Fig 2.51, section g-g, no 8; see also Fig 2.34, section d-d; Fig 2.17, section e-e). The blocking wall (F851) remained in place. The effect of this appeared to be the widening of the *intervallum* road, but excavations in Areas 85.2, 85.3, and 98 suggested that the road was no longer intended to act as an open thoroughfare. In Area 85.3 three features were observed to cut into the old surface of road 6 (Fig 2.45, F123, F75, F121, and F122). F123 was a narrow foundation trench aligned east–west across the *intervallum* road. The west end of this feature terminated in a butt end, associated with a square post (F75) to the north, and what appeared to be the corner of a room to the south (F121 and F122, building 5). The east end of F123 extended under the *macellum* wall, and

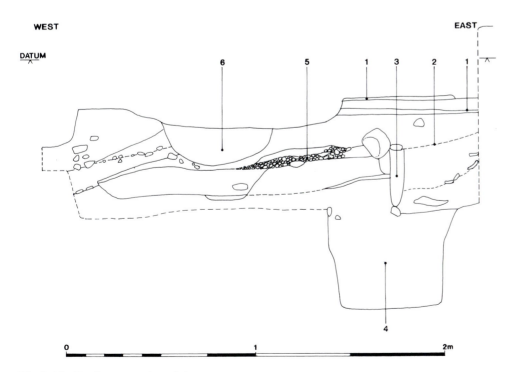

WEST   EAST

DATUM

1   *Clay*

2   *North – south palisade trench of the west wall of the centurial quarters, Phase 3-4b (F995)*

3   *Post-hole, Phase 3 – 4b*

4   *North – south palisade trench of the west wall of the centurial quarters Phase 2 – 3 (F995)*

5   *Gravel to the west of the west wall of the centurial quarters, Phase 3 – 4b*

6   *Truncated north – south robber/foundation trench of the west wall of the timber store building, Phase 6 – 7iv (F3280)*

0   1   2m

Fig 2.39 Section n-n, Area 91

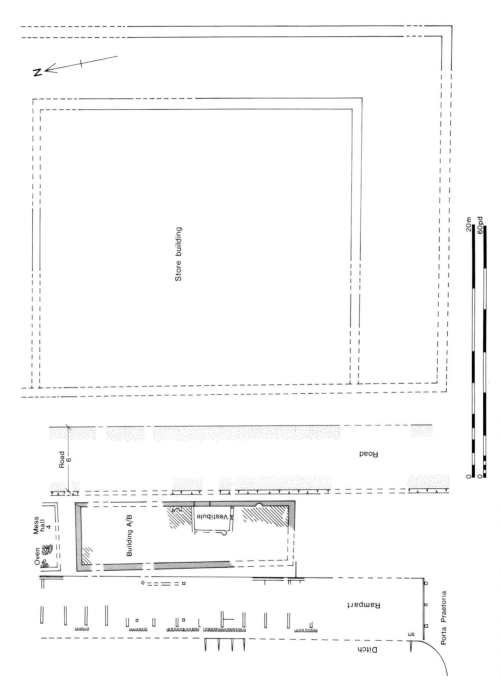

Fig 2.40 Phase 6, Depot period: reconstructed plan

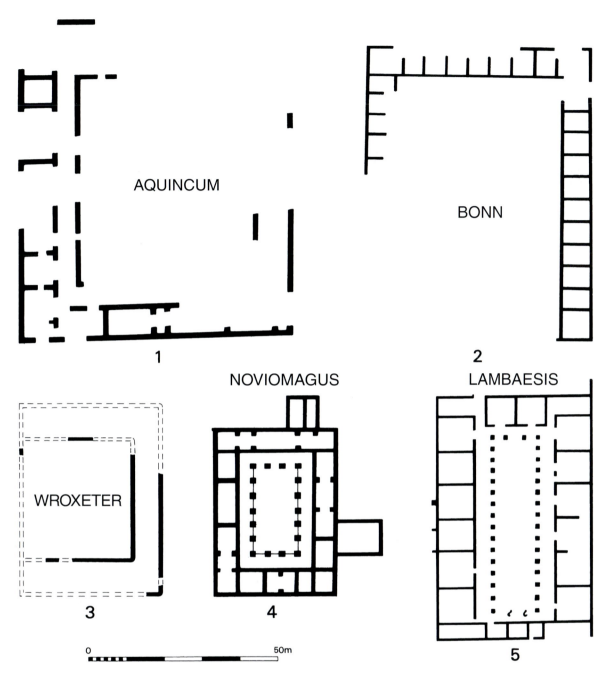

Fig 2.41 Comparison of the large timber store building with other known legionary storehouses: 1 Aquincum, 2 Bonn, 3 Wroxeter, 4 Noviomagus, 5 Lambaesis

presumably continued across Area 86 to link with the west wall of the timber store building (Fig 2.46). However, the disturbance caused by the *macellum* drain in Area 86 had removed any evidence for the continuation of the feature.

Excavations in Area 98 uncovered further evidence for building 5 (Fig 2.45, F1079). The shallow trench with the outlines of the posts of the structure's southern wall and corners were clearly visible (Fig 2.46), cut into the surface of road 6 in the same way as the features in Area 85.3 had been. It was also noted that a new gravel surface (*98/199*) had been laid inside the building, and also outside it, around the south-west corner of the structure. The position of the west wall was established in Area 85.2 (F195), with the new gravel surface along its west side

(*85.2/242*). The postholes and part of the foundation trench of this wall were clearly visible, again cut into the surface of road 6. It was noted that the west wall of building 5 (F195) extended beyond the structure's north wall (F121), and appeared to continue towards the north. In Area 84 only the east edge of this foundation trench could be recorded (F3282), continuing the same north–south alignment as F195 in Area 85.2. No evidence was found for any postholes and the west edge of the foundation trench could not be clearly identified. However, the new gravel surface recorded in Areas 98 and 85.2 was also uncovered in Area 84, where it had continued up to the south wall of stone building A/B (*84/253*). This surface was seen to form a straight line along its east side, where it had been laid up to a

Fig 2.42 Building A/B, Area 84, from the north-west

Fig 2.43 The fireplace added to the east wall of the stone building A/B (Area 84, F611), from the west

north–south obstruction, presumably the west side of F3282. It was clear that this feature had linked the north-west corner of building 5 with the south-east corner of stone building A/B, presumably forming some kind of fence. An interesting aspect of this fence was its junction with the corner of stone building A/B. Instead of abutting the corner, it appeared that the fence had been attached flush with the outer face of the stone building's east wall. A similar example of this type of construction was also used in a later building (building 6).

These structures effectively blocked the *intervallum* road at its southern junction with the *via praetoria* (Fig 2.47). Access from one road to the other was apparently now limited to the small, *c* 1.0m wide gap between the north-east corner of building 5 and F75. This has been interpreted as a controlled entry point, for the use of pedestrians. The features extending to the north (F195 and F3282) and east (F123) of building 5 were presumably fences, blocking all the other available routes onto the *intervallum* road from the south. Building 5 itself measured just 3.5 by 2.5m from the outer edges of its timber trenches; this is interpreted as a small room, from which the narrow gap could be guarded.

Phase 7ii

After the extension of road 6 and the demolition of the box drain, the blocking wall in Area 91 (Fig 2.45, F851) between mess hall 4 and stone building A/B, was removed. The passageway between the two buildings was surfaced with a pebble layer. Halfway along it, and central to the passageway, there was a single posthole (Fig 2.48, F724), which may indicate the presence of a gate to control entry. Cutting the remains of the south end of the blocking wall, against the north wall of stone building A/B, was evidence of a timber wall, apparently extending from the outer face of the stone wall in a manner similar to that employed to join F3282 to the south-east corner of the stone building in Area 84. Further excavations in Area 91 showed that the new wall (F666, F665, F382) had been built across the

intervallum road, using the timber trench construction method, and that it extended towards the west wall of the timber store building (F3280), although a direct link could not be established. As there was a clay floor associated with it to the south (Figs 2.48 and 2.18, section c-c, no 6) this was interpreted as the north wall of a building (Figs 2.48 and 2.49, building 6) which was presumably roofed. The outer north wall of the *macellum* had removed the evidence for the southern wall of building 6, as the clay floor did not extend south of this later feature. However, Fig 2.49 shows this south wall in the most southerly alignment it could possibly have occupied in relation to the area disturbed by the Hadrianic builders. Placing the wall in this position would give building 6 a width of 2.5m (7.5 PD), thus conforming with the neighbouring building 7 and the later building 8, both of which were also 2.5m wide. The north wall of building 6 contained a threshold which was 1.25m wide at its western end by the north-east corner of the stone building A/B. It consisted of a carefully laid clay base, possibly for a stone threshold, between the first of the wall timbers and the wall of the stone building A/B (F666).

Towards the eastern end of building 6 there was a north–south partition wall (F715) set into the clay floor 2.5m (7.5 PD) west of the timber store building (Fig 2.18, section c-c, no 23), and running parallel with it (Fig 2.48). This wall extended to the south forming a possible verandah (building 7) along the west side of the store building for a distance of at least 7.5m from the north wall of building 6. At this point, in the north-east corner of Area 84, there was an east–west slot at right-angles (F3283), apparently connecting the west wall of building 7 with the west wall of the store building. This east–west slot may only have been an internal partition, rather than an end wall, and it is possible that building 7 may have formed a longer verandah along the side of the store building, although no evidence was found to support a further projection to the south (Fig 2.49).

The area of *intervallum* road between the stone building A/B and the timber store building was now completely enclosed, forming a small 'courtyard' (Fig 2.49).

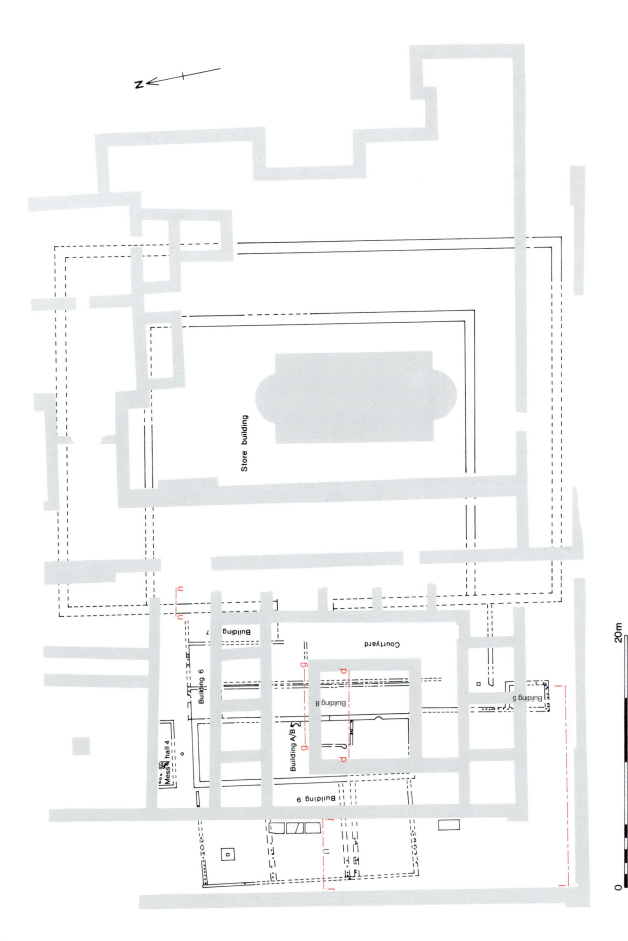

Fig 2.44 Phases 6–7iv: plan of principal military features and location of sections

Store building

Building 7

Building 6

Courtyard

Mess hall 4

Building 8

Building A/B

Building 9

Building 5

N

0   20m

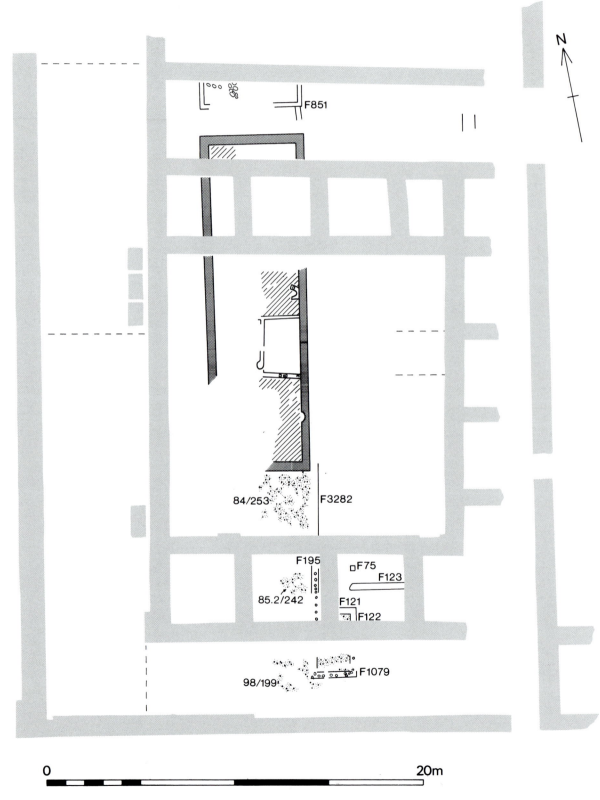

Fig 2.45 *Phase 7i: feature location plan*

Fig 2.46 The shallow palisade trench (Area 98, F1079), with stakeholes marking the southern end of building 5, seen from the north

The old *intervallum* road 6 was still exposed at this time and provided the new courtyard area with a hard surface. A short length of east–west timber slot found in the centre of this area could not be placed in relationship to other structures or sequences. The area to the west of building 5 and the controlled access point were regravelled (*84/251, 85.2/235, 98/189*) and the new surface continued to respect the walls of building 5 and its associated fence.

Phase 7iii

Excavations in Area 91 showed that building 6 continued to stand, retaining its original north wall but with a new clay threshold (Fig 2.50, F666) replacing the one at its western end. A new clay floor was associated with this second threshold (Fig 2.18, section c-c, no 5); it extended up to the west wall of the timber store building (F3280) and clearly sealed the foundation of the west wall of building 7 (Fig 2.48, F715; Fig 2.18, section c-c, no 23) which had partitioned building 6 in Phase 7ii. This foundation had not been renewed and it was concluded that building 7 was demolished during Phase 7iii.

However, another north–south foundation slot (F738) was cut into the second clay floor, partitioning the west end of building 6 in the same manner as building 7 had been divided at its east end in the previous phase. Excavations to the south in Area 87.3 and Area 84 revealed further evidence for this foundation (Fig 2.50, F685, F607, F609, F627), which ran parallel to the east wall of the stone building A/B for its entire length. This structure appeared to form a timber extension, or verandah, along the east side of stone building A/B (Fig 2.53, building 8). The south end of building 8 was closed off by another timber slot (F628) at right angles to the north–south foundation (F627) and adjacent to the south-east corner of stone building A/B. It was noted that the west end of F628 did not terminate directly against the east wall of the stone building and that there was a distinct gap where the wall had presumably abutted the north–south fence (F3282) associated

with building 5. Both the sill beams of building 8 rested on the top of the old road 6 surface (Fig 2.34, section d-d, no 1; Fig 2.52, section g-g, no 10). The building was 2.5m (7.5 PD) across, the same width as building 7. It had a clay floor (Fig 2.51, section g-g, no 9) over which were found flecks of a fine white plaster which had presumably covered the walls. An intermittent shallow depression (F742 and F740), running parallel with the east wall of building 8 in Areas 84 and 87.3, was probably an eavesdrip gully.

The gap between F628 and the east wall of stone building A/B indicated that the fence (F3282) associated with building 5 was still in position during this phase. This was confirmed by the second renewal of the gravel surface around and inside the controlled access (*84/247, 85.1/138, 85.2/230, 85.3/54, 98/175*), which continued to respect the foundation trenches of building 5 and its fences (F195, F1079, F121, F122, F123). The old *intervallum* area between the store building and stone building A/B therefore continued to be isolated as a courtyard from the rest of the site. At some point, probably during this phase, a pebble surface (Fig 2.50, *84/248*), together with its make-up layer (*84/249*), was laid in the enclosed courtyard area, sealing the original road 6 metalling. However, the limits of this pebble surface, and its stratigraphic relationship to surrounding features, could not be established due to later disturbances.

During this phase, or possibly at an earlier stage, a timber addition was made to the west side of the stone building A/B, built over, and cut into, the top of the demolished rampart and backfilled ditches. This confirmed that the defences were no longer in place by Phase 7iii: the implications of this are discussed below. A section across the ditch (Fig 2.9, section j-j) clearly indicated that the legionary ditch fill had compacted and subsided, and that it was necessary to level the space before any building could be erected. This extra filling had a maximum depth of 0.35m and indicated that time must have elapsed since the demolition of the defences to allow for the consolidation of the original ditch fill.

Building 9 was of timber trench construction, 8.0m by 17m, and its north and south walls (F803/F509 and F919–29/F3284) abutted the corners of the stone building A/B (Fig 2.50). Two internal partition walls (F939 and F1058) divided it into three rooms of similar dimensions; each room had a clay floor. There was no evidence of sinkage into the legionary ditch (Fig 2.9, section j-j, no 11). In the central room there were traces of an internal structure supported on a large piece of red sandstone and a reused tile (Fig 2.50, F3285; Fig 2.9, section j-j, no 12). However, the purpose of this foundation could not be established.

The west wall of building 9 (Fig 2.50, F867 and F814; Fig 2.9, section j-j, no 14) appears to have marked a new western boundary line, respected by subsequent structures, which in the later civil period was to form the east edge of the main north–south street of the city.

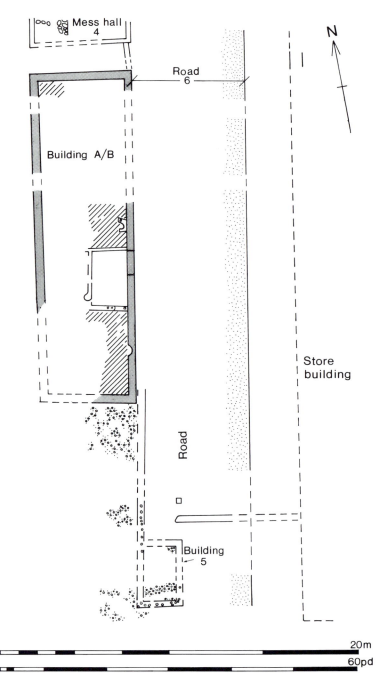

Fig 2.47 Phase 7i, Depot period: reconstructed plan

The demolition of the fortress defences

No firm evidence was recovered to establish precisely when the legionary defences were demolished in the archaeological sequence. Certainly, the rampart had been reduced and the ditches filled in by Phase 7iii, when building 9 was constructed over them. The evidence of levelling-up on top of the ditch fill and the lack of any signs of sinkage in the floor of building 9 would suggest that the ditch fill had time to consolidate and that there may have been a considerable pause between the filling of the ditches and the erection of building 9.

The earliest likely time for the demolition of the defences would logically accompany the removal of the

rampart *ascensus* during Phase 4b and the demolition of the barrack blocks and *taberna*. This would be in keeping with an apparent change in status of the fortress and the assumed withdrawal of the full legionary fighting strength. It should also be noted that the builders of the extension to the stone building A/B in Phase 6 might have found it difficult to complete the north-west corner of the building in the cramped space available, had the rampart still been standing to its full height. However, there are obvious dangers in drawing conclusions about the status of the fortress as a whole from excavations of a very small percentage of its total area. The replacement of the barrack blocks with the storehouse may not have been repeated elsewhere in

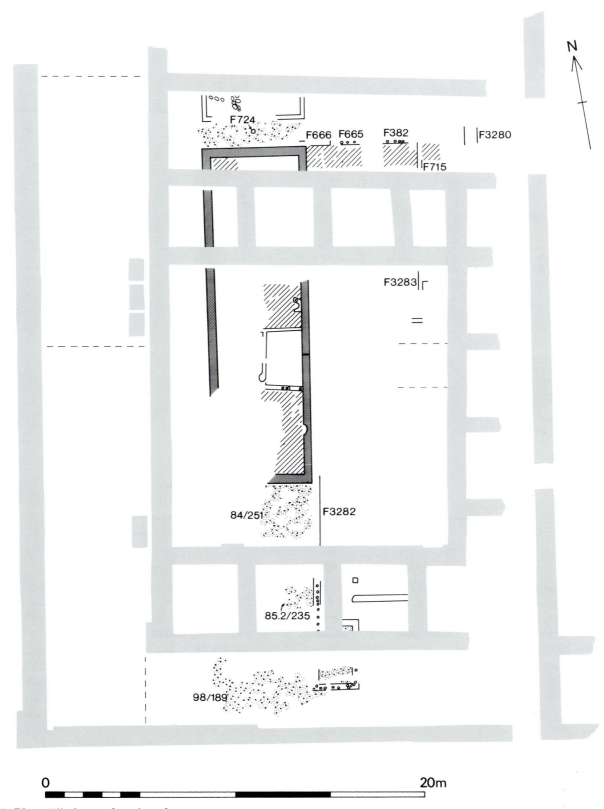

Fig 2.48 Phase 7ii: feature location plan

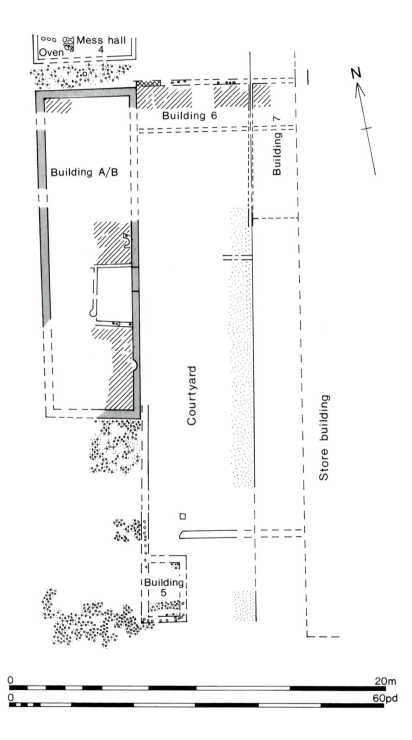

Fig 2.49 Phase 7ii, Depot period: reconstructed plan, Phase 7ii

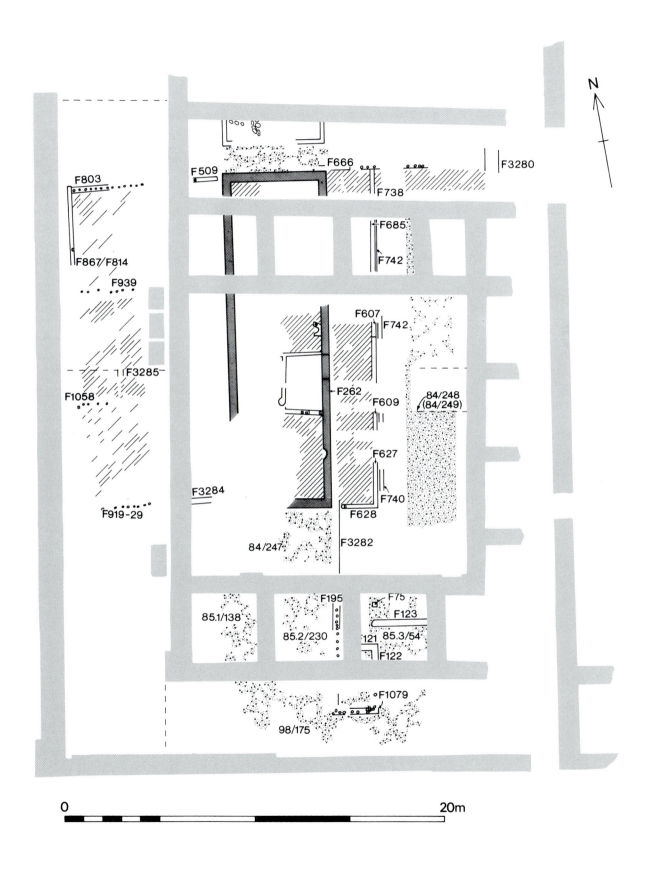

Fig 2.50 Phase 7iii: feature location plan

the fortress, and the demolition of one *ascensus* does not necessarily indicate the reduction of the rest of the defences. Arguably, the west wall of mess hall 4, constructed in Phase 6 along with the extension to the stone building, seems still to respect the alignment of the rampart back.

There is little stratigraphic evidence for the demolition of the rampart. Ideally it should have been possible to identify demolition deposits from the rampart, and link these to the sequence of structures in the fortress interior. However, most of the turf spoil was presumably deposited to the west, into the inner ditch, which had no archaeological relationship with any of the phased structures to the east of the rampart. Some deposits of broken turves were recorded in Area 98 over the remains of the *porta praetoria* (Fig 2.55, section l-l, no 14), but these deposits were isolated from other events in the sequence. Only at one point did turf material appear in a context that could be approximately phased. A scatter of what was apparently turf was recorded in the passageway between the extended stone building A/B and mess hall 4. Neither building appeared to cut or disturb this material, which was subsequently sealed by the later gravelling of the passageway. If this turf material was derived from the rampart, and represents the rampart's reduction, then the demolition of the defences might be placed some time after the end of Phase 6 (after the construction of the stone building extension and mess hall 4), and before Phase 7ii (the gravelling of the passageway). As already suggested above, the erection of timber structures to limit access to the *intervallum* area west of the timber storehouse during Phases 7i and 7ii may have been in response to the de-restriction of the area caused by the concurrent demolition of the defences. However, the evidence is far from certain and the two possible options, that the defences may have been demolished in Phase 4b or during Phases 7i–7ii, are offered as equally viable alternatives.

As already discussed, the demolition of the rampart may have been necessary to recover the larger reusable timbers. The rampart walkway, merlons, and other features on the top of the rampart would have been removed first, and the body of the rampart then lowered by between 2.0m and 2.4m, down to the level of the upper transverse timbers and diagonal braces supporting the main vertical posts at the front. As the rampart was reduced, the weatherboards attached to the back of the front verticals would have been removed as they were exposed to enable the spoil to be shovelled into the inner ditch without hindrance. Once the proposed upper level of transverse timbers had been reached the demolition teams could remove them and detach the upper braces from the front verticals. It is suggested that these upper transverse timbers and braces were close to the final level of the top of the reduced rampart. To extract the front verticals, and the beams

on which they rested, the rampart front had to be cut back in order to free the lower braces. The spade cuts to enable the horizontal beams to be freed from their clay base were clearly visible at the base of the rampart front (Fig 2.9, section j-j, no 7). When this had been completed the rampart had been reduced to *c* 0.9m of its original height. The gradual rise in the fortress occupation level by Phase 7i was such that the top of the reduced rampart would have been level with the general ground surface. To the south-west, the principal timbers at least of the *porta praetoria* appeared to have remained standing until after the demolition of the rampart and the filling of the ditches, since the trench dug to extract the north-west post of the northern gate tower cut through the fill of the inner ditch (Fig 2.15, section k-k, nos 9 and 10). However, it was noted that a trench apparently cut for gate dismantling (Fig 2.55, section l-l, no 5) was sealed by broken turf material, presumably derived from the rampart (Fig 2.55, section l-l, no 14).

Phase 7iv

To the north of the stone building A/B mess hall 4 was demolished, and with it the central post which may have regulated movement between the two buildings (Fig 2.54), but the gravel pathway associated with the now de-restricted passage was renewed. The pebble surface in the courtyard area may also have been replaced (*84/245* post-road 6, layer 3), together with a fourth layer of gravel laid around building 5 and the controlled access point, suggesting continued heavy usage (*84/237*; *85.2/226*; *98/124*). In building 9 both the internal partition walls were renewed (Fig 2.50, F939 and F1058). A beam slot wall base replaced the northern partition on the same alignment (F939), but the southern partition was moved *c* 1.0m to the south and retained its timber trench construction (F938). This increased the dimensions of the central room and decreased the size of the room to the south. All three rooms were given new clay floors.

At the end of Phase 7iv the whole area was cleared of all buildings. The timber store building was finally demolished, together with the stone building A/B and its timber additions (Fig 2.56, buildings 5, 6, 8, and 9). The final pebble surface to the west of the store building was strewn with a considerable scatter of pottery, mainly amphorae, which had apparently been trampled into the surface and probably represented unwanted stores from the store building (Fig 2.54, *84/244*, post-road 6, layer 4; Fig 2.57). Fragments of samian, including decorated forms, indicated a date of *c* AD 90 for this operation, which must represent the final demolition of the military buildings. All subsequent building work employed noticeably different construction techniques and has therefore been interpreted as belonging to the early town.

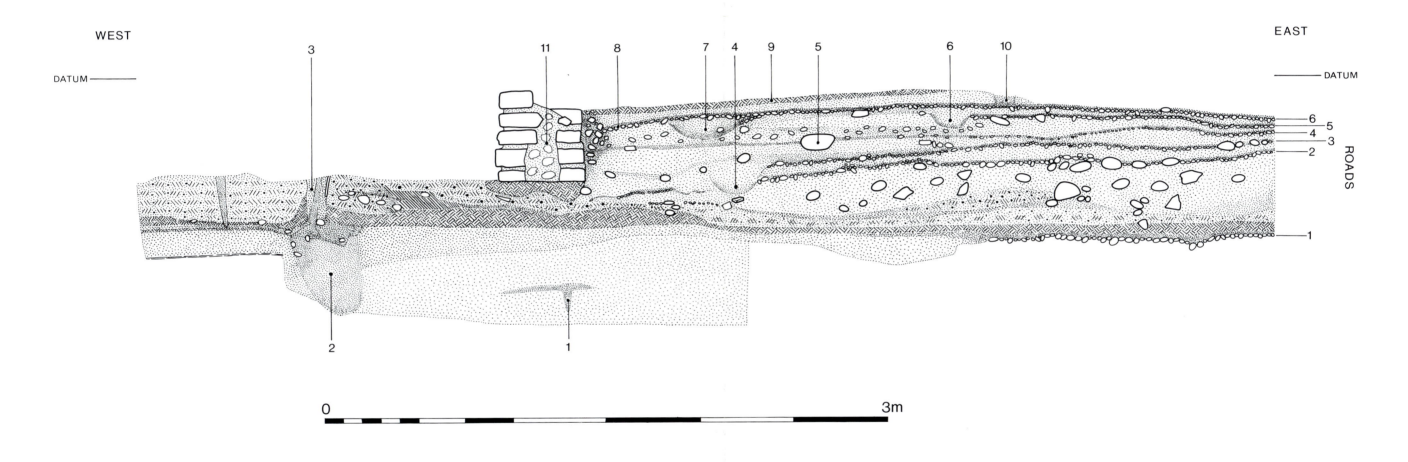

WEST

EAST

DATUM

DATUM

ROADS

3

11 8 7 4 9 5 6 10

6
5
4
3
2

1

2

1

0 3m

1   Setting-out stakehole no 3, Phase 1
2   Palisade trench, east wall of mess-hall 2, Phase 2 – 3 (F976)
3   Palisade trench, east wall of mess-hall 2, Phase 4a – 5 (F786)
4   Road 2 and Road 3 gully
5   Stone kerb, Road 4
6   Road 5 gully, Phase 5 (F3279)
7   Road 6 box drain, Phase 6 (F357)
8   Road 6 extension to the east wall of the stone building A/B, Phase 7i
9   Floor of building 8, Phase 7iii – 7iv
10   North-south beam slot for east wall of building 8, Phase 7iii – 7iv (F607)
11   East wall of stone building A/B, Phase 6 – 7iv (F262)

Fig 2.51 Section g-g, Area 84

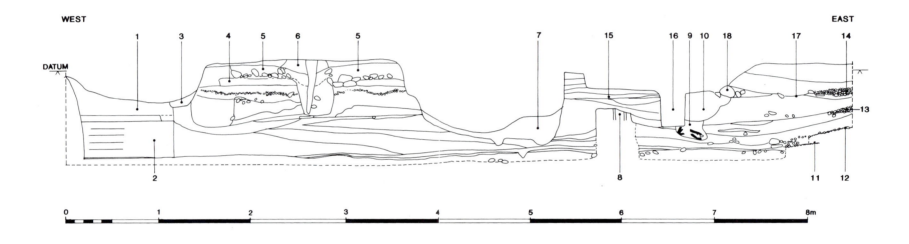

WEST
EAST

DATUM

1   3   4   5   6   5   7   15   16 9 10 18   17   14

2

0   1   2   3   4   5   6   7   8m

1   Back of turf rampart (F511)
2   Corduroy
3   Base of west wall palisade trench of mess-hall 4, Phase 6 – 7iii
4   Clay oven base, mess-hall 4, Phase 6 – 7iii
5   Oven foundation, Phase 6 – 7iii (F3281)
6   Post-military – early civil building, east wall
7   Post-military pit
8   East wall of mess-hall 3, Phase 4a, 4b, and 5 (F959)
9   First phase, east wall palisade trench of mess-hall 4, Phase 6 – 7iii? (F806)
10   Second phase, east wall palisade trench of mess-hall 4, Phase 6 – 7iii? (F806)
11   Road 1
12   Road 2
13   Road 4
14   Road 6
15   Oven rake-out, mess-hall 4
16   Post-military building trench
17   Road 6 box drain, Phase 6 (F741)
18   Extension to Road 6, Phase 7i

Fig 2.52 Section b-b (schematic), Area 91

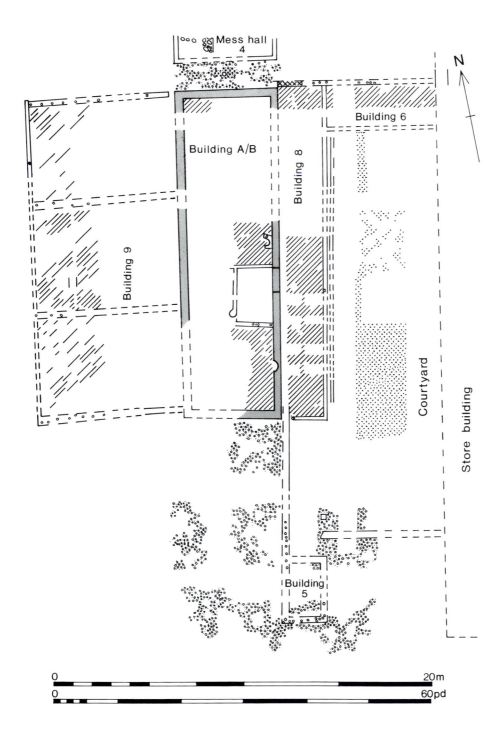

Fig 2.53 Phase 7iii, Depot period: reconstructed plan

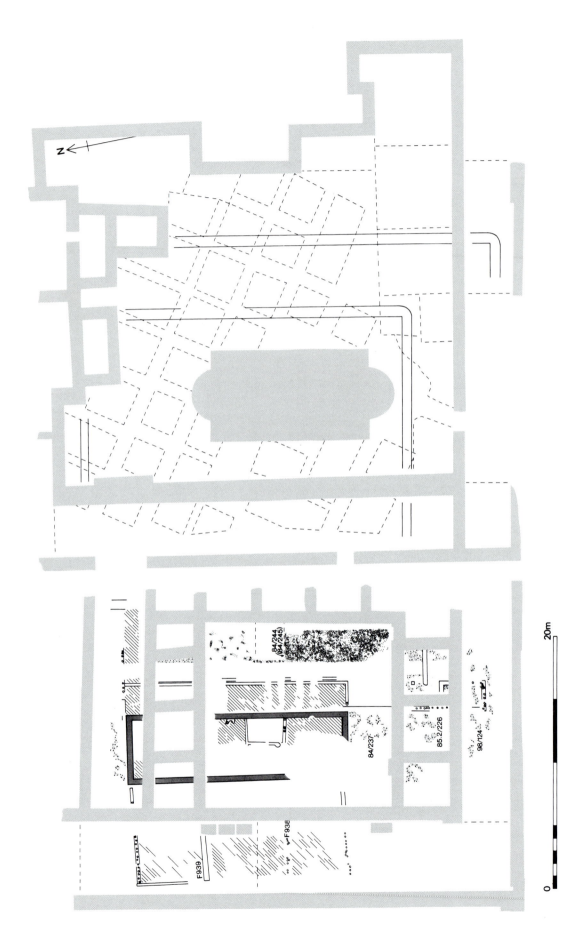

Fig 2.54 Phase 7iv: feature location plan

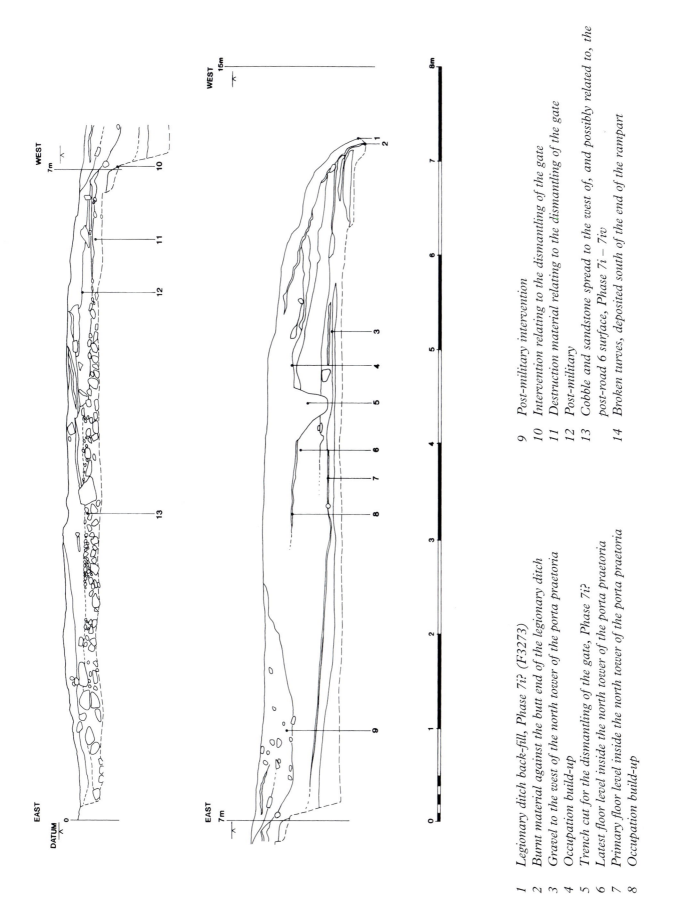

EAST   WEST

DATUM   7m

1 Legionary ditch back-fill, Phase 7i? (F3273)
2 Burnt material against the butt end of the legionary ditch
3 Gravel to the west of the north tower of the porta praetoria
4 Occupation build-up
5 Trench cut for the dismantling of the gate, Phase 7i?
6 Latest floor level inside the north tower of the porta praetoria
7 Primary floor level inside the north tower of the porta praetoria
8 Occupation build-up

9   Post-military intervention
10 Intervention relating to the dismantling of the gate
11 Destruction material relating to the dismantling of the gate
12 Post-military
13 Cobble and sandstone spread to the west of, and possibly related to, the
    post-road 6 surface, Phase 7i – 7iv
14 Broken turves, deposited south of the end of the rampart

Fig 2.55 Section l-l (schematic), Areas 90 and 98

The use of the *pes Drusianus* in setting out the fortress at Wroxeter

by F Ball and N Ball

The excavation of part of the fortress at Wroxeter afforded the opportunity to study its initial setting out in some detail and to identify which unit of Roman foot, the *pes Monetalis* (PM) or the *pes Drusianus* (PD), had been employed.

There are instances in Britain where both units of measurement have been stated to have been used on the same military site, even in the same phase, but these interpretations have usually been based on published small-scale drawings which rarely include actual dimensions or, at the most, show dimensions which have been rounded up or down (Walthew 1981, 16). In the case of Wroxeter, when this problem was recognised, dimensions were included on all field drawings, the acceptable error being limited to ±0.01m. This narrow limit was adopted in order to reduce the margin of error, the difference between the PM and the PD being merely 0.036m. In all instances the PM and PD measurements have been converted to the nearest 0.0001m.

Both the *pes Monetalis* and the *pes Drusianus* were considered, the value of the former, the standard Roman foot, being taken as 0.2957m (Dilke 1987, 26), and the *pes Drusianus*, one-eighth longer, as 0.3326m. The four decimal places were preferred in order to reduce the accumulation of error over dimensions greater than one *actus* and to overcome the problems of rounding three decimal places up or down. In some instances the PM produced a round number of Roman feet, but these failed to relate directly to the proportions of the *actus* PM of 120 feet, whereas by applying the *actus* PD of 120 feet and its proportions of an eighth, a quarter or a half, it became clear that this was the basis for the initial setting out of the interval tower, rampart, *ascensus*, *intervallum* space, and road. The discovery of four original setting-out stakeholes also served to support the evidence of the *pes Drusianus* being the chosen unit of measurement (Fig 2.58 and Table 2.1).

The unexcavated area occupied by the Hadrianic *piscina* prevented the full extent of the centurial quarters and barrack blocks from being recovered. There was, however, sufficient archaeological evidence to project the missing elements within the *contubernia*. The overall widths of the centurial quarters and barrack blocks relate to the proportions of the *actus* PD as shown (Fig 2.59).

Setting-out stakeholes

During excavation four primary stakeholes were discovered which were recognised as representing the setting out of the interval tower, the *ascensus*, and the original fortress construction road. The stakeholes were set out at regular intervals of approximately 30 PD on a north–south axis (Fig 2.58, 1–4). The eastern and western edges of the construction road are marked on the plan by stakeholes 1 (F1076) and 4 (F1057) respectively. Stakehole 2 (F3293) relates to the north side of the *ascensus*, 30 PD from the north side of the northern tower of the *porta praetoria* and 12.5 PD from the back of the rampart. Stakehole 3 (F3296) lines up precisely with the south-east post of the interval tower, 20 PD to the west. The distance between stakeholes 1 and 3 and between 2 and 4 is 60 PD, a half *actus* PD. A further point projected to the south from stakehole 2 and based on the above spacing of 60 PD indicates the position of the south side of the south tower of the *porta praetoria*.

The specific method adopted for surveying and setting out a permanent fortress is unrecorded in the surviving ancient accounts, as Polybius and Hyginus record only campaign camps. If the method they propose is followed, ie to place the *groma* at a central point on the *via principalis* and then set out the *via praetoria* at right-angles to the *via principalis*, the north–south dimensions at Wroxeter would relate to a line projected down the centre of the *via praetoria*. Unfortunately this road and the gate are in the unexcavated area.

The major gate posts excavated on the north side of the northern gate tower were only 0.20m square and would have been quite inadequate for supporting the rampart walkway over the *porta praetoria* had the centre of the road been 60 PD from stakehole 2. This distance would have meant that the overall dimension of the gate, including the two towers, would have been 60 PD. The gate proposed on plan represents the minimum configuration based on the small amount of evidence available.

The interval tower

The position of the four posts related to this timber structure suggested that the tower measured 12 PD north–south and 10 PD east–west (Table 2.1). If the interval towers were all of equal size and the same distance apart there would be room for seven between the north side of the north tower of the *porta praetoria* and the north-west corner tower. This calculation is based on overall measurements of the fortress obtained from the aerial photograph plot (Webster 1988, 124). The towers would be closer together than those postulated for Exeter (Henderson 1988, 107) or Usk (Manning 1981).

The rampart

Evidence for the use of the PD unit of measurement in setting out the fortress was also obtained when plotting the transverse timbers within the rampart. These timbers, of which 13 were plotted, with diagonal braces nailed to them, helped to support the main vertical timbers at the rampart front and were held in place at the rampart back by nails through the longitudinal timber.

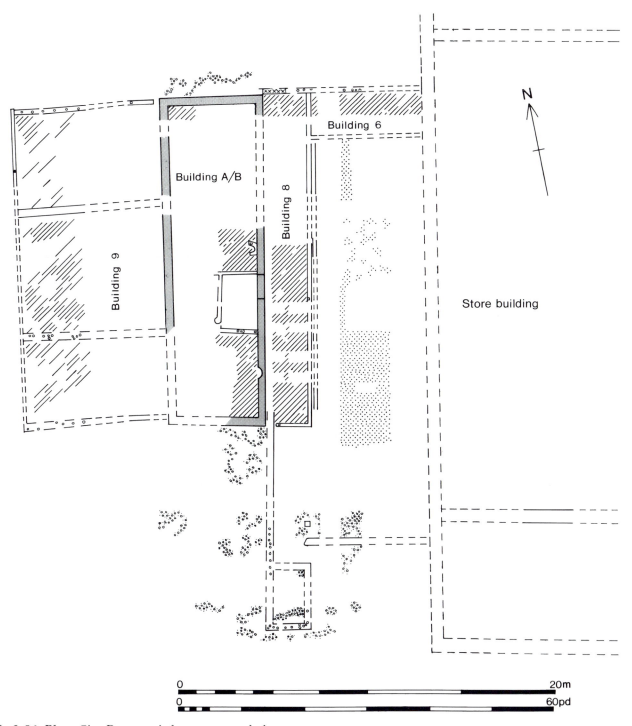

Fig 2.56 Phase 7iv, Depot period: reconstructed plan

The transverse timbers were set out by the use of a 5 PD rod (1 *passus*) for measuring the distance between each one, the preferred dimension for 5 PD being 1.663m. The average width of the timbers was 0.121m. The west wall of the stone-built Hadrianic *macellum* cut through the centre of the rampart, but it was still possible to determine its full width of 15 PD.

Table 2.2 lists the timbers, numbered from north to south. This indicates some slight discrepancies, including a space between timbers 8 and 9 apparently caused by timber 9 being replaced by digging a small trench and inserting a T-shaped timber. Other factors to be taken into account are slight movements during the rampart construction (Figs 2.61 and 2.62), a potentially uneven ground surface, any instability of the ground, and original error. The overall measurements show that the PD *passus* of 1.663m was employed, and comparison with the results of applying the PM *passus* in Table 2.2 appears to confirm this.

The *intervallum* area

The *intervallum* area was 20 PD wide and contained within it mess halls 1–3 and the *ascensus* with its setting-out

Fig 2.57 The military destruction amphora and samian dump (Area 84, F244), from the east

stakehole (F3293). The reconstruction of the *ascensus* and its relationship to the rampart are shown on Figure 2.60.

Mess halls

The overall plan of the three timber mess halls was incomplete, as only the south and east walls of the first phase of mess hall 1 were recovered. However, enough survived of the first phase mess halls 2 and 3 to demonstrate that they were roughly square structures (Table 2.3).

Centurial quarters and barrack blocks: first legionary period

The presence of the Hadrianic *piscina* prevented the recovery of a complete plan of the centurial quarters and their *contubernia*, but sufficient evidence was available to demonstrate the relationship of these buildings to the proportions of the *actus* PD (Fig 2.59). Tables 2.4–2.6 contain the detailed analysis of the metric dimensions, with the PD and PM equivalents. Although the missing structural elements have been projected on to the plan, the tables include only those dimensions for which direct measurement was obtainable. In all instances the metric dimensions have been taken from between the palisade trenches and beam slots. The average width of these trenches and slots is approximately 0.230m, which corresponds closely with the Romano-British spade widths at *Verulamium*, illustrated in Corder (1943, 224–31). These trenches and slots represent the approximate thickness of the walls themselves. Elsewhere on the site, sections a-a and c-c (Figs 2.19 and 2.18) suggest that a wall width of *c* 0.20m may be inferred.

Although the individual metric dimensions are variable, resulting in an average error of 2.01% for the individual PD within the *contubernia* and *taberna*, the overall east–west dimension of the ten rooms of the *taberna* is precisely 1 *actus* PD.

Centurial quarters and barrack blocks: second legionary period

The archaeological evidence for the second phase of barrack building was very fragmentary. Most of the main construction trenches were in precisely the same position as those of the first legionary period, but the centurial quarters of the second legionary period barrack 3 had been extended from 30 PD east–west to 60 PD east–west.

Taberna 1, together with the centurial quarters and barrack 2, share a common back wall with only one known internal division in barrack 2, but with internal divisions, represented by palisade trenches, in *taberna* 1. The configuration of the second period centurial quarters and barracks can be seen on Figure 2.30.

The street between the *contubernia*

The measurements of the street between the barrack blocks relate to the latest surface, which may differ from the street first laid down at the time of setting out the fortress. The dimensions (Fig 2.59) vary slightly, but the average width of 3.750m converts to

Table 2.1 *Pes Drusianus*: defences and *intervallum* space

Description	metric	pD	proportion of actus	% error	pM	proportion of actus	% error
Rampart	4.990	15.003	1/8th	0.02	16.875		0.735
preferred dimension		15			17		
Intervallum space	6.655	20.009	1/6th	0.045	22.505		0.022
preferred dimension		20			22.5		
Road	4.990	15.003	1/8th	0.02	16.875		0.735
preferred dimension		15			17		
Eastern edge of road to centurial quarters	3.350	10.072	1/12th	0.72	11.329	1/10th	5.591
preferred dimension		10			12		
Front of rampart to end of centurial quarters	19.985	60.087	1/2	0.145	67.585	9/16ths	0.125
preferred dimension		60			67.5		

11.274 PD or 12.681 PM. This includes a central gully approximately 0.50m (1.5 PD or 1.69 PM) wide, leaving a walkway of roughly 5 PD on either side. As the buildings have been demonstrated as having been laid out using the PD unit, it seems reasonable to accept this was also used for the setting out of the original street which went with the first phase of buildings.

Conclusions

Although the excavated area represents only a small proportion of the fortress, there is no doubt that the plan of the defences and *intervallum* space here was based on the PD unit of measurement. The widths of the two centurial quarters and barrack blocks of the first period buildings also form a proportion of the *actus* PD.

Where instances of the possible use of the *pes Monetalis* occur, analysis invariably produces a balance in favour of PD based on either the proportion of the *actus* or the comparative percentage of error. In view of the difference of one-eighth between PM and PD it is inevitable that some dimensions will convert to either, and this was considered when carrying out the analysis. It is also noted that there is even less difference between the 2.5 PD unit (0.831m) and the megalithic unit of length of 2.72 feet (0.829m), postulated by Thom (1962, 243). The difference is merely 0.002m or 0.24%. It is not suggested, however, that Wroxeter is an example of the adaptation of a native unit to Roman measurement.

The plans and tables, based on metric measurement, demonstrate the degree of accuracy achieved by the Roman military surveyors engaged in the overall setting out of the fortress. This accuracy is not reflected in the setting out of the *contubernia* east of the west end of the centurial quarters of the centurial quarters of barrack block 2. The plan illustrates irregularities which result in an accumulation of error, although this regulates itself over a distance of 1 *actus* PD measured from the west end of the centurial quarters. Where apparent discrepancies occur these could be the result of the need to accommodate buildings with specific functions within the area available. The dimensions of structures such as mess halls and barrack blocks, which relate to the accommodation of people, require further analysis.

Wroxeter is, perhaps, unusual in that the overall setting out of the first period employed only the *pes Drusianus*. Excavations at the smaller military sites of Hod Hill (Richmond 1968), Longthorpe (Frere and St Joseph 1974), and Baginton (Hobley 1975), have produced evidence for the use of both PD and PM, and there is the possibility that analysis of later phases of military buildings at Wroxeter may identify the use of PM also.

The results of the PD and PM analysis can be complemented by a study of the proportional relationships of the various structures on the site, as suggested by the authors

(1988, 294–301). This may provide a further insight into the methods of setting out not only the military buildings but also the civil buildings in Roman Britain.

The reconstruction of the fortress defences
by F Ball and N Ball

Introduction
by Graham Webster

The rampart had a vertical timber front, held in position by a system of internal braces and transverse timbers. Although none of the frontal timber elements had survived, the evidence of the demolition team's spademarks strongly suggests that the front of the rampart had been cut back for the removal of large structural timbers. Vertical timber fronts are not unusual (Jones 1975, 78–89), but what makes the *Viroconium* rampart remarkable is the presence of the clay foundation at the base of the rampart front, rather than a trench into which the vertical front posts would have been packed, as at Lincoln (Jones 1988; Webster 1949). It is suggested that this clay foundation supported a line of large horizontal timber beams, into which the vertical front posts were tenon-jointed. The great care with which the clay foundation had been placed, and its considerable size, would support the theory that it had an important function and was capable of supporting large timbers (see below). The heavily disturbed remains of the foundation seem to confirm the conjectured existence of the lower beams, the clay presumably adhering to them as they were removed.

As the front vertical posts had not been anchored in a slot, or in individual post-pits, they could not have retained the full weight of the rampart without internal bracing. This would explain the presence of the transverse timbers discovered within the rampart body. Once the horizontal beams on their clay foundation and the timber corduroy were in position, construction of the rampart body would have begun with layers of turf. Analysis of the rampart soils suggests that their coarse texture would have required the inclusion of turf in order to maintain the stability of the structure (Canti 1988). Excavation showed that when the rampart reached a height of around one Roman foot (*c* 0.30m) above the log corduroy base, transverse timbers were laid at right angles to the rampart front (Fig 2.7, section j-j, no 4; Fig 2.9), presumably behind each vertical front post. These were at five Roman feet (PD) intervals (1.66m), so exactly that one end of a five foot rod must have been placed at right angles to the side of each timber and the next placed at the end of the rod, so that the timbers were laid precisely five *pes Drusiani* apart. At the back of the rampart these timbers were connected by the line of horizontal longitudinal timbers laid over

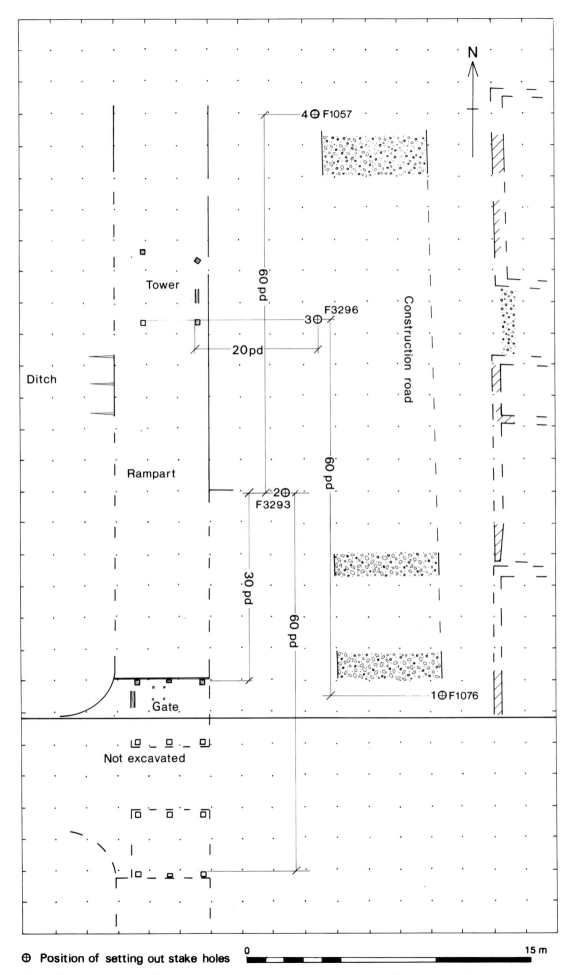

⊕ **Position of setting out stake holes**

Fig 2.58 Partial plan of intervallum *area superimposed on a* pedes Drusiani *grid*

69

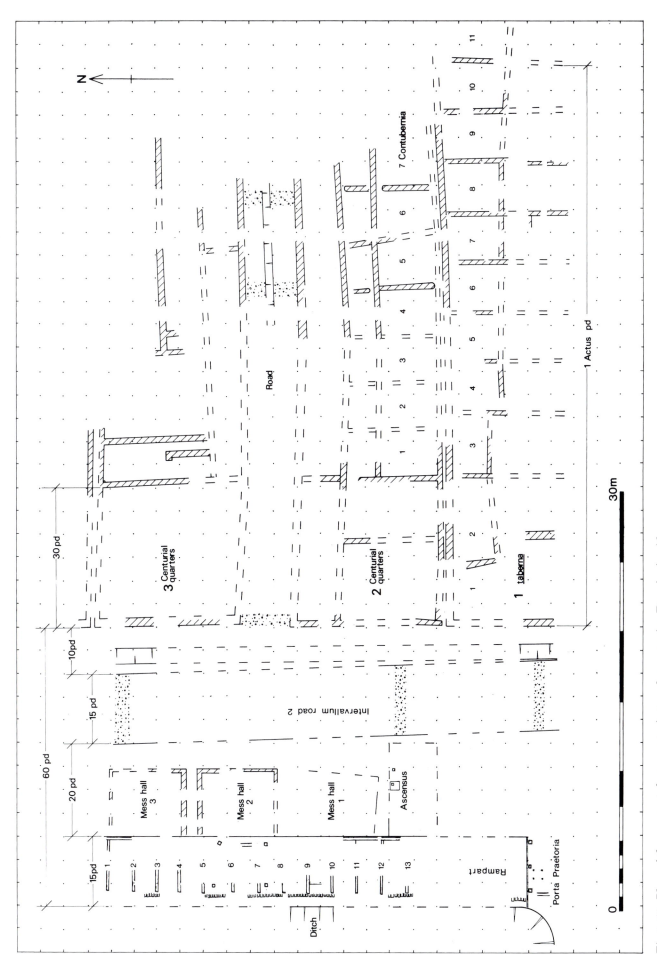

Fig 2.59 Plan of the excavated area superimposed on a pedes Drusiani grid

Table 2.2 *Pes Drusianus:* spaces between rampart timbers

Between timbers	metric	pD	% error	pM	% error
Nos 1 and 2	1.660	4.990	0.2	5.613	12.26
Nos 2 and 3	1.665	5.006	0.12	5.630	12.6
Nos 3 and 4	1.485	4.464	10.72	5.021	0.42
Nos 4 and 5	1.640	4.930	1.4	5.546	10.92
Nos 5 and 6	1.740	5.231	4.62	5.884	17.68
Nos 6 and 7	1.635	4.915	1.7	5.529	10.58
Nos 7 and 8	1.664	5.003	0.06	5.627	12.54
Nos 8 and 9	1.820	5.472	9.44	6.154	23.08
Nos 9 and 10	1.640	4.930	1.4	5.546	10.92
Nos 10 and 11	1.660	4.990	0.2	5.613	12.26
Nos 11 and 12	1.665	5.006	0.12	5.630	12.6
Nos 12 and 13	1.663	5.000	0.00	5.623	12.46

Table 2.3 *Pes Drusianus:* mess halls

Description	metric	pD	proportion of actus	% error	pM	proportion of actus	% error
Mess hall 2							
external, east-west	4.900	14.732	1/8th	1.78	16.570	17/120ths	2.529
preferred dimension		15			17		
internal, north-south	5.050	15.183	1/8th	1.22	17.078		0.458
preferred dimension		15			17		
Mess hall 3							
external, east-west	4.900	14.732	1/8th	1.78	16.570		2.529
preferred dimension		15			17		
internal, north-south	4.950	14.882	1/8th	0.78	16.739		1.535
preferred dimension		15			17		

Table 2.4 *Pes Drusianus*: centurial quarters

Description	metric	pD	proportion of actus	% error	pM	proportion of actus	% error
2. east-west	10.000	30.066	1/4	0.22	33.818		3.377
preferred dimension		30			35		
2. north-south	9.960	29.945	1/4	0.18	33.682		3.765
preferred dimension		30			35		
3. east-west	9.550	28.713	1/4	4.29	32.296		7.725
preferred dimension		30			35		
3. north-south	9.950	29.915	1/4	0.28	33.648		3.862
preferred dimension		30			35		

and nailed into them (Fig 2.7; Fig 2.9, section j-j, no 5). The function of these longitudinal timbers along the back face of the rampart was to hold the transverse timbers in position. They were buried in the rampart and did not support a back revetment. The vertical posts at the rampart front could then have been placed in position, tenon-jointed into the horizontal beams on their clay foundation at the base of the rampart, and jointed into a transverse timber to hold them in position. However, it was noted that the transverse timbers did not connect directly with the vertical posts, as they were shown to terminate *c* 0.75m east of the edge of the ditch (Fig 2.9). A nail was recorded in one of these timber ends (F3264, Fig 2.9, section j-j, no 6) and it seems probable that each

transverse timber was connected by a bird's beak joint to a short diagonal brace which was then attached to a front vertical (see below). The system of diagonal bracing closely resembles that used to support the rear timber wall of the second period box rampart of the fort of Valkenburg at the mouth of the old Rhine (van Giffen 1948). The rampart could then have been built up against the front verticals. Hurdling or weatherboarding attached to the inner face of the front verticals may have been intended to prevent any of the rampart from weathering and spilling into the ditch.

As the rampart body was under construction, its weight would have helped hold the front vertical posts in position, but at least another diagonal brace would

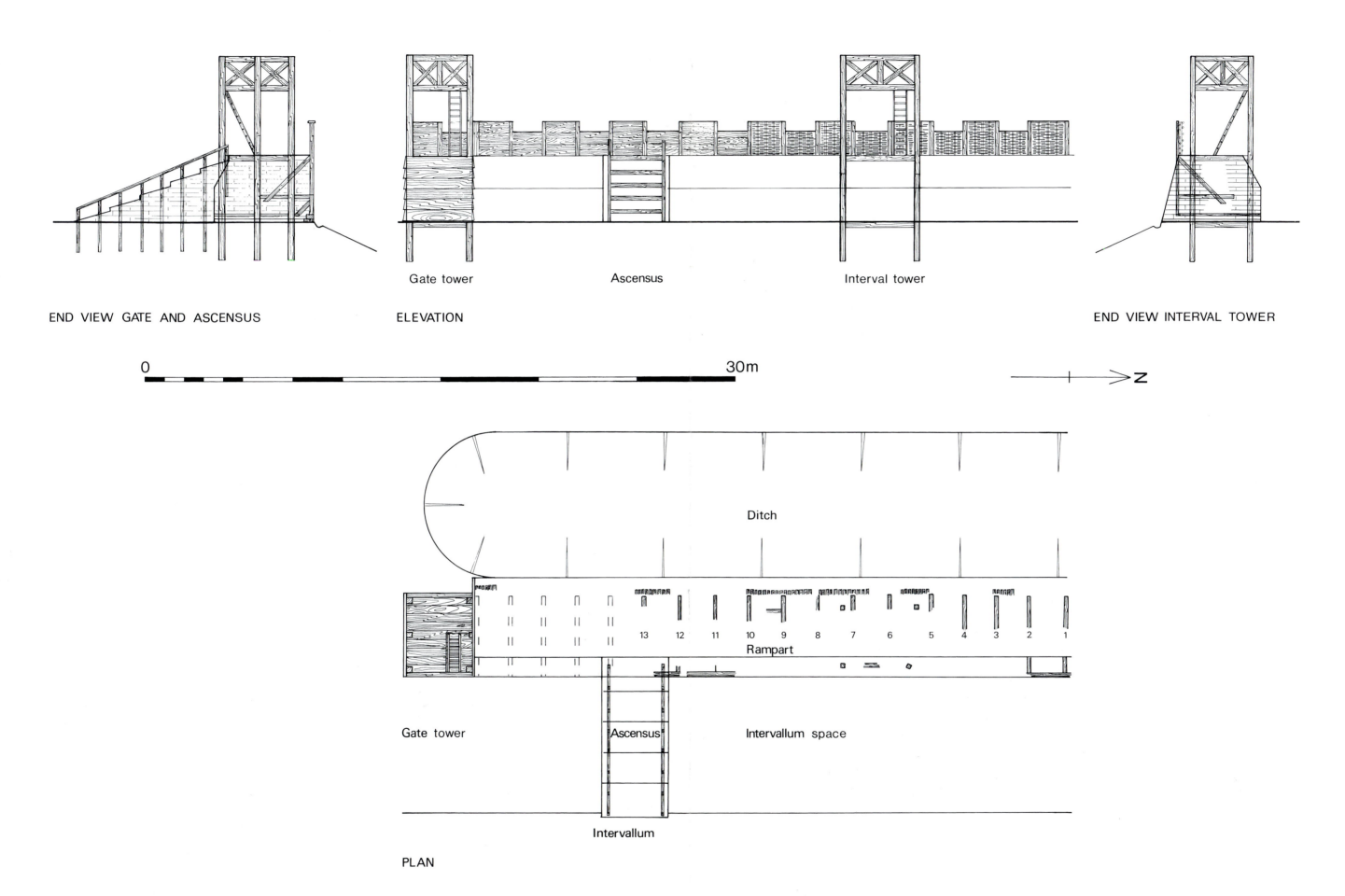

END VIEW GATE AND ASCENSUS

Gate tower   Ascensus   Interval tower

ELEVATION

END VIEW INTERVAL TOWER

0   30m

N

Ditch

13 12 11 10 9 8 7 6 5 4 3 2 1

Rampart

Gate tower   Ascensus   Intervallum space

Intervallum

PLAN

Fig 2.60 Plan and elevations of the reconstructed gate tower, interval tower, ascensus, *rampart and ditch*

Gate tower

Interval tower

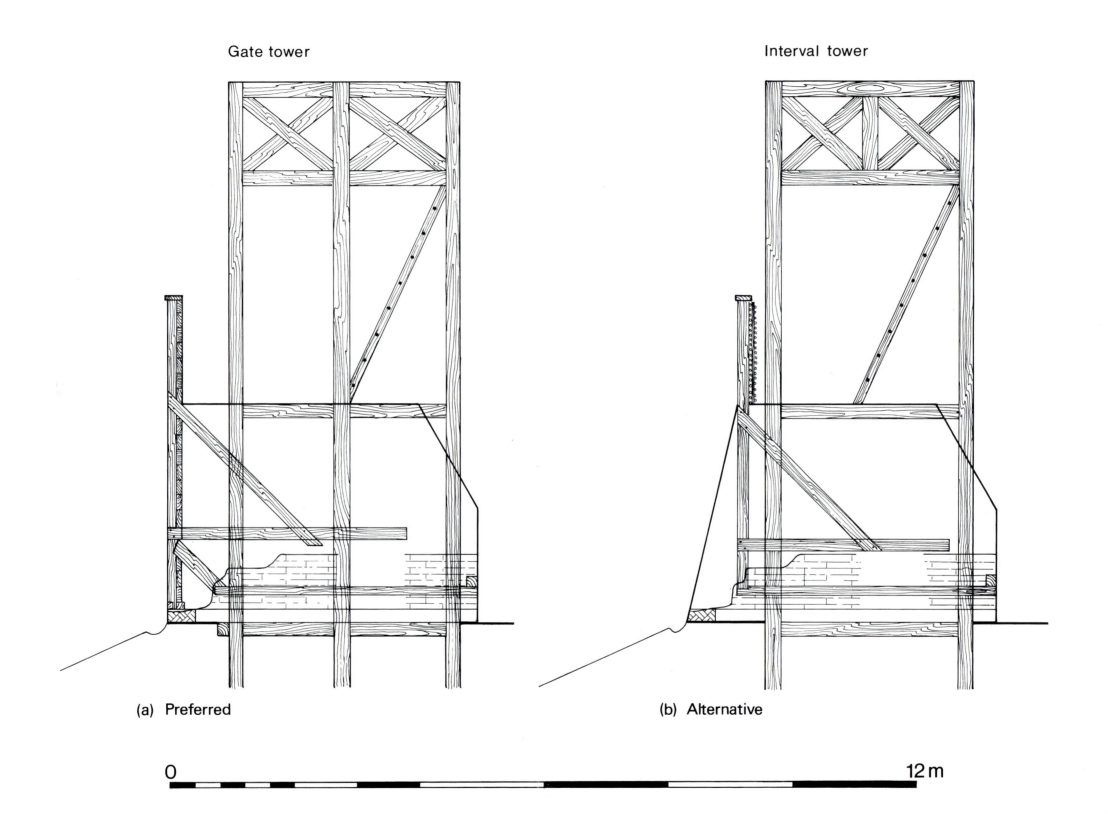

(a) Preferred

(b) Alternative

0   12 m

Fig 2.61 Section through the reconstructed gate and interval towers: a) preferred reconstruction; b) alternative version

have been required. This was probably inserted after the addition of another two Roman feet above the lower transverse timbers, which was the height to which the rampart seems to have been demolished, perhaps specifically for the extraction of this second layer of timbers buried in the rampart. This would have enabled the postulated diagonal brace to be removed in order to free the front verticals. Similarly, the cutting back of the rampart front, illustrated by the evidence of spade cuts, would have allowed the lower diagonal braces to be freed from the transverse timbers.

The surviving height of the vertical back of the rampart was 0.98m. The need for a vertical face was apparent from the surviving remains of clay ovens packed against it (see above). In the reconstruction described below it is assumed that five Roman feet (c 1.6m) would have been a reasonable height for the back of the rampart. Although Vitruvius suggests enough width was required on urban defences for two armed men to pass comfortably (Granger 1983, 49), much more space was needed for hurling projectiles, and for stacking them. A width of ten Roman feet (c 3.33m) has been allowed for the patrol track, and this would

involve a slope down to the top of the vertical back of c 45°. The total height of the rampart from corduroy base to patrol track would have been around 3.5m.

The reconstruction

Certain fundamental considerations had to be made when producing the reconstruction drawings of the gate, interval tower, rampart, ditch, and *ascensus* (Fig 2.60), which are based on the surviving archaeological evidence. These were the availability of suitable local materials, and the essential craft skills. It is assumed there was a ready supply of suitable material within a reasonable distance from the site. The use of wattles to provide hurdles, placed on the ground to form a firm surface after the removal of the turf during the construction phase, serves as an example of forest and woodland management in the vicinity, with coppicing already well established; otherwise branchwood laid on the ground would have been adequate for wheeled vehicles. Calculations of the quantity of timber required for a legionary fortress are discussed by Hanson (1978, 297–8), and Webster (1982, 47).

Table 2.5 *Pes Drusianus*: taberna

Description	metric	pD	proportion of actus	% error	pM	proportion of actus	% error
Room 1. east-west preferred dimension	4.000	12.026 12	1/10th	0.21	13.572 12	1/10th	12.75
Room 2. east-west preferred dimension	5.820	17.498 17.5	1/7th	0.01	19.682 20.000	1/6th	1.59
Room 2. north-south preferred dimension	3.100	9.320 10	1/12th	6.8	10.483 10	1/12th	4.83
Room 3. east-west preferred dimension	4.125	12.402 12	1/10th	3.35	13.949 15	1/8th	7.00
Room 3. north-south preferred dimension	2.5	7.516 7.5	1/16th	0.21	8.454 7.5	1/16th	12.72
Room 4. east-west preferred dimension	3.400	10.222 10	1/12th	2.22	11.498 12	1/10th	4.183
Room 4. north-south preferred dimension	3.400	10.222 10	1/12th	2.22	11.498 12	1/10th	4.183
Room 5. east-west preferred dimension	3.350	10.072 10	1/12th	0.72	11.329 12	1/10th	5.59
Room 5. north-south preferred dimension	3.400	10.222 10	1/12th	2.22	11.498 12	1/10th	4.18
Room 6. east-west preferred dimension	3.350	10.072 10	1/12th	0.72	11.329 12	1/10th	5.59
Room 6. north-south preferred dimension	3.400	10.222 10	1/12th	2.22	11.498 12	1/10th	4.18
Room 7. east-west preferred dimension	3.200	9.621 10	1/12th	3.79	10.821 10	1/12th	8.21
Room 7. north-south preferred dimension	3.800	11.425 12	1/10th	4.79	12.850 12	1/10th	7.08
Room 8. east-west preferred dimension	3.400	10.222 10	1/12th	2.22	11.498 12	1/10th	4.18
Room 8. north-south preferred dimension	4.000	12.026 12	1/10th	0.21	13.527 12	1/10th	12.75
Room 9. east-west preferred dimension	3.250	9.771 10	1/12th	2.29	10.990 10	1/12th	9.9
Room 9. north-south preferred dimension	4.100	12.327 12	1/10th	2.72	13.865 12	1/10th	15.54
Room 10. east-west preferred dimension	3.320	9.981 10	1/12th	0.19	11.227 12	1/10th	6.44

According to Josephus the legion would provide the necessary manpower and expertise, and the requisite tools would also have been available (Thackeray and Marcus 1960). With the knowledge that all skilled people work with economy of effort, material, and time, it is obvious that the construction work would proceed quickly and competently, although it is necessary to remember the physical limitations of people when engaged on construction work on a large scale.

The timbers and construction methods are discussed in some detail as it is necessary to have an understanding of the potential of the materials involved, particularly timber, about which there are many misconceptions, and the methods employed to produce the three-dimensional structures upon which any reconstruction is based.

A turf and timber rampart is preferred for Wroxeter, although the surviving archaeology would also support the suggestion of a turf rampart of the type referred to for *Britannia* by Lepper and Frere (1988, 264) when discussing the reliefs on Trajan's Column. This alternative is illustrated with the interval tower in Figure 2.61 and also in Figure 2.62.

Structure and construction

Assuming an average unseasoned hardwood with a moisture content of 24%±4% and a weight between 50 and 60 lbs per cubic foot (22.68kg and 27.22kg per 0.028 cubic metre), the reconstruction is based on the minimum dimensions for timbers structurally capable of withstanding the optimum 'dead' and 'live' loading. The term 'structure' is used to refer to the arrangement of the various elements. The detail of the structure is based on the archaeological evidence, and the visual reconstruction is derived from a broad interpretation of the reliefs on Trajan's Column. The term 'construction' refers to the methods used to join the various elements together. This incorporates the simplest of jointing systems, with a large proportion of the work capable of being carried out by the skilful use of the hand-axe.

The fundamental principles related to timber construction methods are listed below but it must be noted that in the majority of instances of 'simple jointing', a combination of basic principles would be involved.

Location joint: This usually takes the form of a notch and positions the element within the total structure, but contributes only marginally to the strength of the completed structure. Often used in sub-assembly and nailed for additional strength.

Lap joint: Positions the element within the structure and, if shouldered and halved, gives the structure diagonal strength, particularly when secured with either wooden pegs or iron nails. If used in conjunction with a mortise, the shouldered and halved lap joint becomes a 'barefaced' tenon.

Locking joint: This is a more complex jointing system than either of the above and may not have been used in the structures under consideration. It positions the

Table 2.6 *Pes Drusianus:* barrack block 2 (*contubernia*)

Description	metric	pD	proportion of actus	% error	pM	proportion of actus	% error
Rear rooms 1 2 3 4. east-west	13.350	40.138	1/3rd	0.34	45.147	3/8th	2.60
preferred dimension		40			45		
Rear room 1. east-west	4.000	12.026	1/10th	0.21	13.572	1/10th	12.75
preferred dimension		12			12		
Rear room 5. east-west	3.250	9.771	1/12th	2.29	10.990	1/12th	9.9
prferred dimension		10			10		
Rear room 5. north-south	4.000	12.026	1/10th	0.21	13.572	1/10th	12.75
preferred dimension		12			12		
Rear room 6. east-west	3.100	9.320	1/12th	6.8	10.483	1/12th	4.83
preferred dimension		10			10		
Rear room 6. north-south	4.000	12.026	1/10th	0.21	13.572	1/10th	12.75
preferred dimension		12			12		
Front rooms 1 2 3 4. east-west	13.200	39.687	1/3rd	0.78	44.639	3/8th	1.45
preferred dimension		40			45		
Front rooms 1 and 4 north-south	1.995	5.998	1/20th	0.03	6.746	1/20th	12.43
preferred dimension		6			6		
Front room 5. east-west	3.150	9.470	1/12th	5.3	10.652	1/12th	6.52
preferred dimension		10			10		
Front room 5. north-south	2.000	6.013	1/20th	0.21	6.763	1/20th	12.71
preferred dimension		6			6		
Front room 6. east-west	3.500	10.523	1/12th	5.23	11.836	1/10th	1.36
preferred dimension		10			12		
Front room 6. north-south	2.100	6.313	1/20th	5.21	7.101	1/16th	5.32
preferred dimension		6			7.5		
Verandah north-south (mean)	2.500	7.516	1/16th	0.21	8.454	1/16th	12.72
preferred dimension		7.5			7.5		
Barrack block 3							
Verandah north-south (mean)	2.500	7.516	1/16th	0.21	8.454	1/16th	12.72
preferred dimension		7.5			7.5		

element within the structure and locks it two-dimensionally. Three-dimensional locking and maximum diagonal strength may be achieved by the use of wooden pegs or iron nails to further secure the joint.

Examples of the use of all three systems of jointing are illustrated by Dillon (1989, fig 1, 230).

The gate and interval tower

Based on the archaeological evidence, the probable structure, construction, and method of assembly may be deduced from the relationship of the horizontal crystalline timbers to the associated postholes indicating the position of the verticals (Figs 2.60 and 2.61). On the west side of the gate tower, the position of the horizontal timber adjacent to the north-west posthole is indicative of the lap joint being used. On the east side of the interval tower, the position of the horizontal timber between the north and south postholes suggests the use of mortise and tenon joints. A stakehole (F3296) 6.66m (20 PD) east of the south-east corner post (F440) of the interval tower (Fig 2.58, no 3), indicates the position of a post top, prior to raising to a vertical position.

The structures would require prefabrication prior to sub-assembly on the ground and raising into the vertical position by the use of sheer-legs, as described by Vitruvius (Granger 1985, 279–81), for the final assembly to be carried out. Wood chippings discovered adjacent to the north-east gate tower post (F2077) were probably the product of either adze or axe working necessary for minor adjustments to the construction during final assembly. The minimum gate possible would be type 111a, illustrated by Manning and Scott (1979, fig 1, 20).

The rampart: preferred interpretation

The surviving timbers within the remains of the rampart, and the level to which the rampart had been reduced, provided sufficient information from which to develop the reconstruction (Fig 2.63). Where positive constructional

Table 2.7 Width of intermediate timbers in the rampart

Timber no	feature no	width (m)
1	3256	0.125
2	3257	0.130
3	3258	0.120
4	3259	0.110
5	3260	0.120
6	3261	0.125
7	3262	0.140
8	3263	0.125
9	3264	0.140
10	3265	0.130
11	3266	0.110
12	3267	0.100
13	3268	0.110

evidence is lacking alternatives have been proposed, such as hurdles or cross-boarding for the rampart front, and a gravelled surface or 'duckboards' for the patrol track, either of these being considered more suitable than a log corduroy, although this is not ruled out.

The preferred reconstruction of the rampart front incorporates horizontal timbers laid on the clay foundation and mortised at 5 PD intervals to accommodate the barefaced tenons of the verticals holding the horizontal cladding at the rampart front and forming the parapet of the patrol track. The internal timber structure is the result of analysis based on the minimum necessary structural engineering requirement for stabilising the turf within the rampart and supporting the parapet. The widths of the intermediate timbers, numbered from north to south, are set out in Table 2.7. Their average width is 0.121m with an average thickness of 0.060m and an approximate length of 3.99m (12 PD).

In all instances involving the use of timber, availability of the vast quantities required for the building of a fortress would be the most important factor.

The rampart: alternative interpretation

Previous excavations on the east side of the fortress (Kenyon 1940; Johnson 1976; 1977), together with the *macellum* excavations, have produced sufficient archaeological evidence to propose a turf revetment to the rampart as an alternative to the preferred vertical timber front.

Turves were visible in the reduced rampart at least 2m from the rampart front, and at the back extended to the west wall of the *macellum* (Fig 2.9, section j-j). The width of the rampart at corduroy level was 4.989m (15 PD) (Fig 2.61) and with a reconstructed height of 3.326m (10 PD) would give a batter of 76° to the horizontal, and a walkway of 3m (9 PD) wide, which would be adequate for two people to pass (Granger 1983; 1985: *Vitruvius* 1, 49). To produce an angle of batter within a range of 65 to 75° to the horizontal, as suggested by Jones (1975, 32), would, of necessity, see the rampart reduced by approximately 0.825m to a height of 2.5m (7.5 PD) above ground level, giving a batter of 72.5°. This, together with the breastwork and ditch, would still present a formidable obstacle, both physically and psychologically.

The rampart end at the south was closed by turves for a distance of at least 1.30m to the north. The intermediate timbers buried in the body of the rampart 0.785m from the east edge of the lockspit may have held the vertical timbers forming the breastwork (Fig 2.60 and Fig 2.61).

The ditch

The presence of the Hadrianic stylobate wall prevented excavation of the military ditch for a distance of more than 3.4m to the west, and the archaeology indicated that the bottom had not been reached at that point.

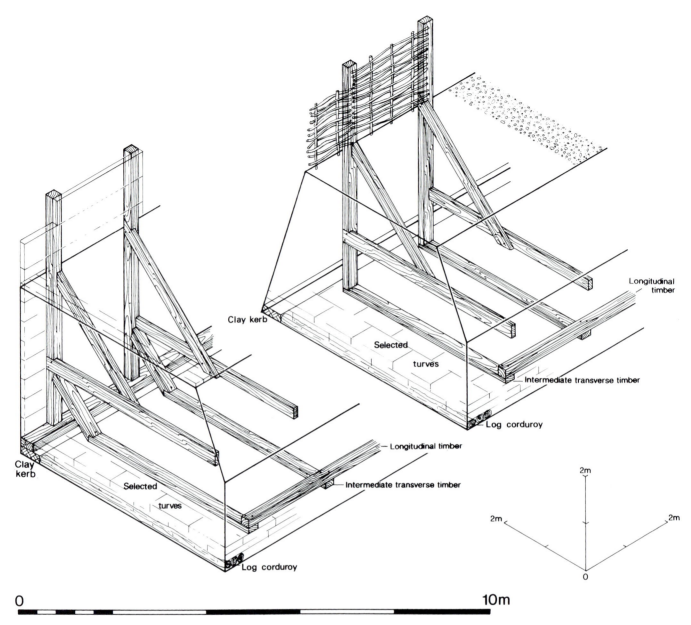

Fig 2.62 Isometric projection of the rampart structure: a) preferred reconstruction; b) alternative version

Calculations based on a regular V-shaped ditch suggest it was wider than 7m and the reconstruction (Fig 2.60) proposes a width of 7.483m (22.5 PD).

The Kenyon excavations of 1936–7 to the east of the fortress produced incomplete first-century ditches, interpreted as early civil. Although there is a common element in the angle of the ditch slope with the military ditch to the west, any other comparison would not be appropriate.

The *ascensus*

Building constrictions meant that the *ascensus* could not be placed adjacent to the *porta praetoria* but was positioned at right-angles to the rear of the rampart, 6.65m (20 PD) north of the gate (Fig 2.60). The reconstruction (Figs 2.60 and 2.64) is based on slight archaeological evidence and the logical calculations of

the optimum dimensions for its purpose. The gradient is very modest at approximately 15°, with each step 1 *passus* wide. The proposed dimensions would allow for quick and easy passage for men and equipment to and from the top of the rampart. The selected turves forming the *ascensus* would have required revetting at the sides with either hurdles or close-boarding, and the posts for retaining the revetment would have supported the handrails on either side of the *ascensus*. Horizontal boards would have formed the steps, and it is proposed that these would have had gravelled surfaces.

Timber

Timber is, by nature, hygroscopic, and the structural properties of different timbers are determined by certain factors, eg the proportion of wood substance

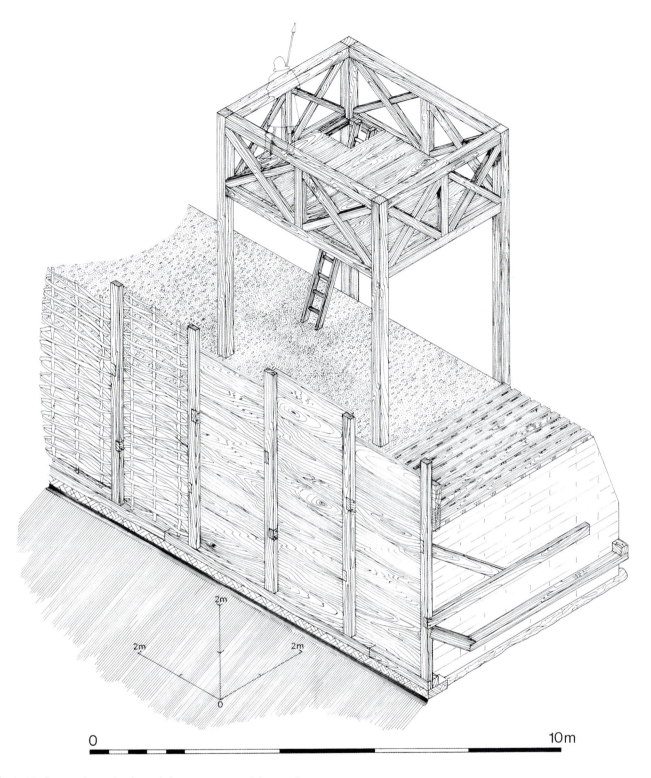

Fig 2.63 Isometric projection of the rampart and interval tower

to air space, and the amount of moisture contained within the cell structure. These properties will decide the suitability of a timber for a particular purpose. The moisture content of timber should be in equilibrium with the atmospheric conditions surrounding it, the moisture content of timber being calculated quite simply as:

$$\frac{\text{wet weight} - \text{dry weight}}{\text{dry weight}} \times 100 = \% \text{ moisture content}$$

Dependent upon the season of the year, freshly felled timber will have a moisture content of approximately 85%, comprising free water in the cell cavities and absorbed water in the cell walls.

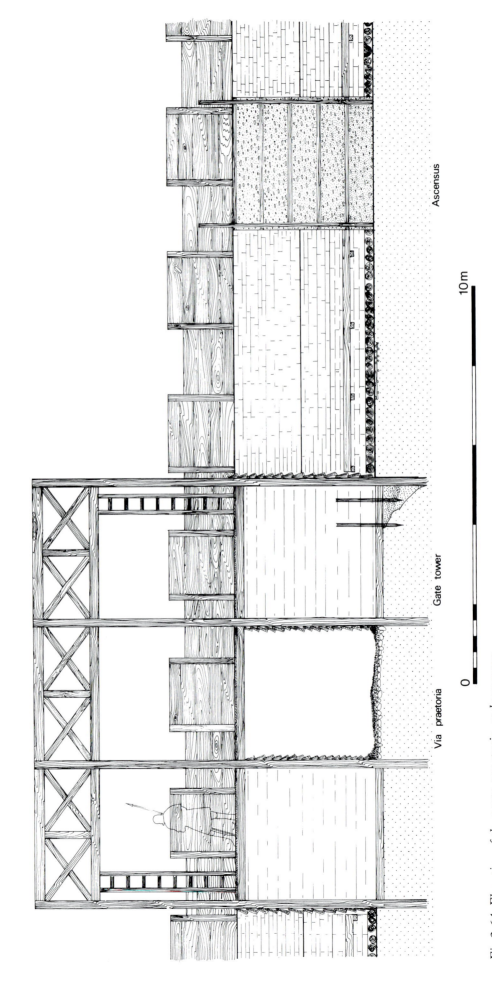

Via praetoria   Gate tower   Ascensus

0   10m

Fig 2.64 Elevation of the porta praetoria *and* ascensus

A moisture content of 30%, or fibre saturation point, is reached when all the free water has evaporated and the time taken for this to occur also depends upon the season of the year and the atmospheric conditions.

Seasoning is ordinarily understood to imply a drying process. This is not quite correct, for in addition to the evaporation of the moisture the partial decomposition of the albuminous substances which occurs renders the timber more permeable, which increases the hardness and stiffness, thus making it more stable for large scale structures. With the outside ambient moisture content in Britain being approximately 21%, it will be appreciated that lengthy periods of seasoning are unnecessary for the construction work under discussion.

The logistics of timber supply for building the fortress defences require consideration. A variety of different species and forms of timber would be required, from wattles for hurdles and branchwood and small diameter logs for the corduroy, to straight, squared timbers approximately $10 \times 0.20 \times 0.20$m for the gate and interval tower posts. Numerous riven boards for the cladding would also be necessary. The dimensions of the timber sections used in the reconstruction have been deduced from the timber sections surviving *in situ*:

Gate and tower posts	0.20×0.20m
Gate and tower horizontal timbers	0.12×0.12m
Rampart transverse timbers	0.12×0.60m
Rampart longitudinal timbers	0.12×0.12m

The dimensions of the additional projected timbers in the reconstruction are based on the assumption that the known dimensions are nominal. Therefore, half 0.20×0.20m would become two pieces each 0.20×0.10m nominal, and half 0.12×0.12m would become two pieces each 0.12×0.06m nominal.

Timber in contact with the ground surface is liable to fungal decay and the durability of different timbers has been established by field tests on timbers of 0.05m square section as shown in Table 2.8. The life of timbers of 0.20m square section, in contact with the ground, would be appreciably longer, but not *pro rata*.

In the absence of a pollen spectrum for the site, precise identification of the timbers was not possible as only small samples were recovered, although these were sufficient to establish the presence of ring-porous

Table 2.8 The timbers

Description	purpose and suitability	height (m)	durability 0.050 m² section
Hardwoods			
Alder (*Alnus glutinosa*)	easily worked: internal timber structure of rampart	10 (30ft)	under 5 years
Ash (*Fraxinus excelsior*)	ladders: horizontal cladding	36 (120 ft)	under 5 years
Birch (*Betula pendula*)	internal timber structure of rampart	18 (60ft)	under 5 years
Elm (*Ulmus procera*)	Horizontal cladding on rampart front: gate posts	36 (120ft)	10-15 years
Hazel (*Corylus avellana*)	wattles for hurdles: rods for revetment	coppice underwood	
Oak (*Quercus robur*)	gate posts	24 (80ft)	20-25 years
Willow (*Salix* sp)	basket work and hurdles	24 (80ft)	under 5 years
Softwood			
Pine (*Pinus sylvestris*)	gate posts etc	30 (100ft)	5-10 years

Compiled with reference to the publications of the Forest Products Research Laboratory (1937; 1941; 1956; 1957; 1960; 1964; 1965)

Table 2.9 Rampart timbers

Description	no	timber size	cubic content: Hoppus feet
Corduroy	50 logs	$14' \times 4'' \times 4''$	77
Intermediate timber	3	$12'9'' \times 4'' \times 2''$	2
Longitudinal timber	1	$16'4'' \times 4'' \times 4''$	1
2nd Horizontal timber	3	$12'9'' \times 4'' \times 4''$	4
Diagonal timber	3	$11'6'' \times 4'' \times 4''$	4
Horizontal sill timber	1	$16'4'' \times 8'' \times 4''$	4
Front vertical timber	3	$15' \times 8'' \times 4''$	10
Close-boarding		$16'4'' \times 15' \times 2''$	40
Total for five metre length of rampart			142

hardwoods such as ash, elm or oak. The common timbers likely to have been available, together with their respective properties, are set out in tabular form. The durability of timber buried within the rampart would be considerably greater than indicated in Table 2.8.

All these timbers can be worked easily in their green state and it is suggested the initial preparation would take place where they were felled, leaving only the usable timber to be transported to the site. This preparatory operation would involve the removal of branchwood for the corduroy and hurdles; the squaring of logs for posts; the riving of logs for the tapered boards for cladding; and the removal of sapwood which contains starch and sugars and is liable to attack by insects.

The limited amount of available information means that any estimate of the quantity of timber required, and the area of woodland necessary to provide sufficient material for the fortress defences, can only be approximate. In *Hoppus's Measurer*, a building trades ready reckoner of around 1750, a foot equals 1.273 cubic feet and is used when calculating the cubic content of standing timber and timber in the round (Hoppus 1750). The amount of waste occurring during conversion to squared timber makes the Hoppus foot equal to one cubic foot of usable timber. The average yield per acre of managed woodland is approximately 1317 Hoppus feet; thus

the area necessary for providing the total timber requirement of 47,002 Hoppus feet for constructing the fortress rampart would be 35.68 acres (14.43 ha) (Table 2.9).

The overall fortress dimensions from the front of the rampart are 462m east–west, and 402m north–south (Webster 1962a; 1988, fig 6.3, 124), giving a total of 1708m for the length of the defences, including the gates.

The distance between the north side of the *porta praetoria* and the south side of the interval tower was established as 19m. If a similarly sized tower, with equal spacing, were considered, there would be sufficient space around the perimeter of the defences for a total of 64 towers, including corner towers. The total amount of timber for the towers could be computed from the quantity required for a single tower (Table 2.10).

Similarly, the timber requirements for all the gates could be calculated on the basis of the quantity necessary for the reconstructed single portal *porta praetoria* (Table 2.11).

Any reconstruction based on archaeological evidence which will support more than one solution will inevitably be subjective. The specialised use of timber technology and the understanding of timber construction have provided a measure of objectivity for the alternatives illustrated.

Table 2.10 Interval tower timbers

Description	no	timber size	cubic content: Hoppus feet
Posts	4	30′ × 8″ × 8″	53
End beams	8	10′ × 8″ × 4″	18
Side beams	8	12′ × 8″ × 4″	21
Diagonal rails	16	6′6″ × 4″ × 2″	6
Floor		12′ × 10′ × 2″	20

Total of 118 *Hoppus* feet = 0.089 acres at 1317 *Hoppus* feet per acre

Table 2.11 Gate, single portal timbers (minimum possible)

Description	no	timber size	cubic content: Hoppus feet
Posts	8	30′ × 8″ × 8″	106
Posts	4	30′ × 6″ × 4″	20
End beams	16	11′6″ × 8″ × 4″	40
Side beams	22	10′ × 8″ × 4″	48
Bridge patrol track		30′ × 10′ × 2″	50
Tower floor		30′ × 10′ × 2″	50
Guard room cladding		80′ × 10′ × 2″	133
Parapet cladding		30′ × 5′ × 2″	25
Diagonal rails	32	6′6″ × 4″ × 2″	11
Gate		10′ × 10′ × 3″	25

Total of 508 *Hoppus* feet = 0.386 acres at 1317 *Hoppus* feet per acre

3 The historical interpretation

A general account of the military history of the years following the Roman conquest of Britain was provided in Chapter 1. This chapter reviews the principal archaeological evidence for the major military campaigns, with particular reference to Wroxeter and its hinterland.

The historical account of Tacitus is highly compressed and lacking in detail, especially geographical, which would have been so helpful in an attempted reconstruction of the events of first-century Roman Britain. Archaeology on the ground and from the air has supplied much information about sites of campaign camps, winter bases, and permanent forts and fortresses. When plotted on a map, however, they tell us little about the actual campaigns and sites of battles. Even with extensive excavation, the date range provided by the pottery and coins is rarely narrow enough to separate one series of events from another within the 34 years (ie c AD 57–90) which form the timespan of this period. It would clearly be desirable to be able to relate the main changes in the archaeological sequence to established historical events, but there is always the danger in making the wrong choice, as has been apparent with Wheeler's identification of Wheathampstead as the *oppidum* of Cassivellaunos in Caesar's campaign in Britain. He may well have made the same mistake with Stanwick as the *oppidum* of Venutius.

The first Roman military intrusion into the Wroxeter hinterland in any strength probably occurred in the reconnaissance raid along the eastern border of the hills of Wales described by Tacitus (*Annals* 12, 35). This campaign would have taken the task force across the territory of the *Cornovii*. If the tribe chose to resist this move, the Roman military objectives would have been their strongholds, such as the Wrekin, the Iron Age citadel overlooking Wroxeter and the River Severn. The discovery of burnt timber buildings on the Wrekin, and the presence of a large fort of c 2.29ha (5.66 acres) and marching camps at Eye Farm in the parish of Eaton Constantine (Fig 1.2), suggest that the force was met with resistance which had to be overcome (St Joseph 1973). The military base at Rhyn Park near Oswestry may also belong to this episode (Goodburn 1978; 1979; Jones 1977), and there is evidence of Roman occupation from around this period from cremation burials at Chester (Stevens 1948; Strickland and Davey 1978; Carrington 1977). This was presumably followed by intense military activity in the middle and upper Severn valley during Scapula's attempts to find and destroy Caratacus and the British forces (Webster 1960). Although it is uncertain whether there was any military occupation at Wroxeter at this time, the importance of the site must have been appreciated at an early stage as a springboard for forces advancing due west into the heartland of Wales along the Severn Valley. The recent suggestion that Llanymynech might be a candidate for the last stand of Caratacus (Jones 1990) does not exclude the possible military use of the Wroxeter location. Moreover, a unit here could block any hostile force emerging from the foothills and control the north–south route from the Dee to the Severn Estuaries. The pre-legionary ditch and drainage features at Wroxeter may belong to this period, but the evidence is inadequate.

After the capture of Caratacus, attention moved to the hostile *Silures* and Rome's attempts to maintain the Scapulan frontier. The crossing of the Severn at Wroxeter was defended at this stage by an auxiliary unit. The 5.66 acre (2.29ha) fort was discovered by Professor St Joseph (Fig 1.4), who sectioned the defences and discovered scraps of mid-first century pottery (St Joseph 1953a; 1953b; 1959). The name of the unit which occupied this bridgehead fort may be indicated by a tombstone (*RIB* no 291), of a trooper of a Thracian *cohors equitata* found at Wroxeter (Fig 3.1). It is unfortunate that the right hand edge is so eroded that the number of the cohort is no longer on the stone. The spacing, however, would preclude more than two digits and this reduces the number of possibilities. Birley has considered the unit to have been *Coh I* (Birley 1939, 212), and this has been accepted by Bogaers on the presumption that it was known to have been serving in Britain at the conquest period before returning to the continent c AD 70 (Bogaers 1974). Perhaps a better case could have been made for *Coh VI*, which is known to have been stationed at Gloucester (RIB 121), since the most likely time for this unit to have been there is the period c AD 43–8, before being replaced by *Legio XX*, which was moved from *Camulodunum* by Scapula.

The Thracian tombstone was found in 1783 at a place 'now the blacksmith's shop' (Page 1908, 245–6; fig 19, no 5), in the central area of the Roman city. It is likely to have been re-used as a building stone in late Roman or later times, after it had been removed from its original position in the military cemetery. The question arises, nevertheless, of what happened to the auxiliary unit's cemetery when the site was needed for the later fortress. There are examples of early burials at Wroxeter; Bushe-Fox found a cremation burial with a melon bead at the lowest level of Site III at the edge of the main north-south street of the city (Bushe-Fox 1913a, 12). This clearly shows a policy of respecting the burial remains which remain safe beneath the ground, and doubtless special ceremonies would have been made to placate the 'Shades'. But the tombstone was removed, and a logical solution would have been to have re-erected it with due ceremony in the new legionary cemetery, where it could have remained until discovered in land clearance at a much later date. This early burial is some distance from the auxiliary fort, although it is not unusual to find cemeteries along a

Fig 3.1 Tombstone of a trooper of the Thracian cohors equitata

road a mile or further from the fort, as was the case at Lincoln (Richmond 1947; Jones 1988, 146), where there remains the possibility of the discovery of further Roman military occupation on the South Common.

The auxiliary fort must have been approached from the south-east from Greensforge by a road which has been subsequently lost. But the route from the north has survived as an extension of the *via principalis* of the legionary fortress, and which was later incorporated into the city street plan. This road continued to the north to join the main road round the north side of the Wrekin. Recent investigations on the east bank of the river have so far failed to reveal any traces of a bridge, but there are indications of a small dock (A W J Houghton, pers comm).

The founding of the fortress under Veranius, AD 56–7

Nero's decision to conquer Wales brought Q Veranius to Britain *c* AD 56–7 to replace Didius Gallus, and this would have instigated a corresponding rise in military activity. It would have been necessary to move a legion nearer the front line in the Severn valley for the proposed campaign, and the legion most available for this forward move was *Legio XIV* at Mancetter, where this redeployment appears to be supported by archaeological evidence, although pottery from the site has been suggested to be somewhat earlier (Scott 1981, 11–12). The legionary fortress at Wroxeter provides the best candidate for the new base of *Legio XIV* (Webster 1981, 105), and the presence of *Legio XIV* at *Viroconium* had been suspected since the discovery of three tombstones of its soldiers (*RIB* 292, 294, and 296) found in 1861, 1752, and before 1789 respectively (Fig 1.3). All three lack the title *Martia Victrix* awarded in AD 60 for the legion's valour in the defeat of Boudicca, and which may have been promulgated by the Emperor sometime afterwards. A fourth military tombstone found in 1752 (*RIB* 294) is that of a *beneficiarius* of *Legio XX* and this also lacks its similar honorific title *Valeria Victrix* (strong and victorious). This legionary was, on retirement, seconded for police or customs duties, and would in all probability have been away from his unit. The inscription is, accordingly, of no assistance in placing this legion at *Viroconium*.

The founding of the legionary fortress presumably post-dates the mid first-century auxiliary fort, as it seems unlikely that they would have co-existed, and the tombstones indicate the presence of *Legio XIV* at *Viroconium* prior to AD 60. This would date the legionary fortress to sometime during the 50s, and Veranius's single campaign in AD 56–7 would seem to be the most likely occasion for the construction of the fortress to have taken place. Unfortunately the dating evidence from the excavations is of little help, since very little pottery was found in the primary construction (Phase 1) deposits. Forts and fortresses were normally kept clean, and 75–80% of the pottery was found in the terminal, demolition deposits.

Legio XIV presumably took part in a combined operation with *Legio XX*, which had established a forward supply base at Usk, where relatively little of the fortress interior has been excavated (Manning 1981), while retaining the Gloucester fortress at Kingsholm (Fig 3.2). The Twentieth may have borne the brunt of the subsequent fighting, while the Fourteenth protected the right flank from any intervention by the *Ordovices*.

The next campaign of *Legio XIV* would have been with C Suetonius Paullinus to destroy the Druids and their sanctuary in Anglesey. This operation had only just been concluded when Paullinus had to return to the Midlands to face Boudicca's revolt (Webster 1978). It was the Wroxeter legion, *Legio XIV*, which covered itself with glory at the great and decisive battle and received its title *Martia Victrix*. While the western frontier was still held, some units were moved into the Midlands and East Anglia to stamp out all surviving traces of the rebels and exact retribution. It is possible that *Legio XIV* was moved nearer to this area of activity, but it would need also to be available for any

Fig 3.2 Legionary dispositions in Britain in the first century AD

troubles developing from Wales, still not completely conquered and occupied. The choice for a new fortress may have been Wall (*Letocetum*) on Watling Street, about 48.25 km (30 miles) to the east of Wroxeter and with good communication to the south and north. The evidence for this is far from conclusive, but there was a large military establishment of at least 12.14 ha (30 acres) there, associated with Neronian pottery (Gould 1967). It may, however, have been a large base for another purpose and there is no certainty that it was occupied by legionary troops, while the evidence of archaeology shows that the fortress at Wroxeter continued to function.

By AD 66 the province had calmed down sufficiently to allow Nero to reduce the garrison. He had developed a military fantasy of a great eastern conquest, and his first thought was of *Legio XIV*, the legion which had brought him so much glory in Britain. This withdrawal prompted a reappraisal of the legionary dispositions (Fig 3.2). As the south-west was now subdued *Legio II Aug* could be moved from Exeter to Gloucester, where the site of the fortress was moved from Kingsholm to the site where the *colonia* was later established (Hurst 1988, 49–55) to become the nucleus of the medieval and modern city. The previous occupants of Gloucester, *Legio XX*, may have been moved north to the now vacant fortress at Wroxeter. It is possible too, that this was the occasion of the transfer of *Legio IX* from Longthorpe to its hill-top position at Lincoln. The arrival of *Legio XX* at Wroxeter may be indicated by the changes observed in Phase 3 of the site. Whether the coming of the Twentieth necessitated a complete redevelopment of the Wroxeter fortress is not certain, but the two barrack-blocks and centurial quarters investigated were completely rebuilt, most probably at this stage.

Legio XX presumably remained at Wroxeter for the next five years or so (Phase 4), conducting normal policing and pacification operations until AD 71, when the worsening situation in the north brought Q Petillius Cerialis to Britain with a large number of military units, and an additional legion, *II Adiutrix*, which he established at Lincoln. He mounted a campaign against *Brigantia* with two legions, *Legio IX* advancing along the eastern flank of the Pennines and *Legio XX*, now under the command of Agricola, along their western side. Venutius was defeated, possibly at Stanwick, where the evidence is lacking at present.

The task of establishing a northern frontier was now that of Sextus Julius Frontinus (AD73/4 to 77). It was soon appreciated that this was difficult without a further advance. The problem was deferred and a temporary solution attempted. There is occupation at Carlisle which appears to support a Roman military presence at this date (Caruana 1992) then, although all that Bushe-Fox's suggestion provides is 'a date before, rather than after AD 80' (Bushe-Fox 1913b, 301), and further confirmation is required; but the presence of an earlier military structure has also been noted (Birley

1961, 137; Wilson 1974, 410; Goodburn 1976, 310; Frere 1977, 376; Goodburn 1978, 421; Jones 1968, 6). What role *Legio XX* played in these developments to the north and what effect this had on its base at Wroxeter is uncertain. Frontinus also appears to have completed the military consolidation of Wales, so Wroxeter would have continued to be an important military base. It is not until the appointment of Agricola as governor that the status of the fortress appears radically to alter.

Agricola and the northern campaigns

The appointment of Gnaeus Julius Agricola as governor of Britannia in AD 77–8 signified a dramatic new Flavian policy for the province. In AD 71 there could have been little doubt in the minds of Cerialis and his able co-adjutor, Agricola, that the unconquered peoples further to the north, some perhaps allies of defeated Venutius, still presented a serious potential threat. They would also have been aware that the terrain, with the central Pennines flanked by broad river plains, effectively prevented the creation of a defensive barrier. Frontinus had presumably only had limited success in establishing such a barrier. The immediate task for the new governor was to advance beyond the Pennines, to bring the natives to submission and consolidate on a suitable defensive line.

Agricola's first campaigning season of AD 78 was in north Wales, and Wroxeter would probably have been part of this operation, but in AD 79 he devoted his whole attention to an advance to the north, with the purpose of establishing a permanent frontier. The real brunt of this advance was to be borne by his old legion, *Legio XX*, with the support of *Legio IX*, now established at York. The maintenance of the security of the west, and any potential trouble from Wales, was to be the task of *Legio II Adiutrix*, which was now established at Chester (Fig 2.66). This move probably took place as early as AD 78, the legion having demolished its Lincoln fortress and transferred its useable timber. At Chester lead water pipes dating to the first half of AD 79 are unlikely to have been laid in the initial stages of the fortress construction (Wright and Richmond 1955, no 199; Wright and Hassall 1971, 2923, no 17).

The implication of this move is that *Legio XX* was to be established in a new base in the north as part of the permanent northern garrison, possibly at Carlisle, from where there is now evidence in the form of a writing tablet bearing the name of a *miles* of *Legio XX* (Tomlin 1992). *Viroconium* was, by this stage, probably outdated as a legionary fortress, and the excavations appear to provide evidence for the downgrading of the site. Dramatic changes took place within the small area investigated, which may, of course, not be true of other parts of the fortress. The pair of barrack blocks and their centurial quarters were totally demolished (Phase 4b), and the site occupied by a large timber building (Phases 5–7). But when precisely this took place in the Agricolan timetable must remain speculative. The rampart appears to have been retained for a while, indicating a continued military presence and this would suggest that Wroxeter had become a military depot, presumably holding stores and military personnel, perhaps with a cohort in training.

The conversion of the fortress to the status of that of a depot eventually led to the reduction of the rampart and filling of the ditches (Phase 6–7), at least along this length of the defensive circuit. The remarkable decision to demolish the defences while the fortress remained in use, even as a depot, appears to be so far unparalleled elsewhere.

It seems illogical that only a short length, or one side of the fortress, would have been chosen. To complete the demolition of the whole circuit, a work force would presumably have been required from the legion, but the question remains when and why? It is here that one ventures into speculation. A possible explanation is that the large amount of useable timber in the rampart was needed elsewhere, perhaps for military works in the north. An occasion which may have provided the need, and the opportunity, was the death of Titus on 13 September AD 81, after which Agricola was required to call a halt to his campaign and await instructions from the new emperor Domitian. By this time, Agricola had reached the Forth-Clyde isthmus and its value as a defence line must have been fully recognised. So it could have been seen from Rome that Agricola had completed the task originally allocated to him, of defining and constructing a suitable northern frontier. He had served almost four years, and it could have been taken as an opportune time to consolidate the frontier and complete his term of office (although the latter was to be extended). As part of this consolidation a suitable place may have been chosen for a new permanent fortress for *Legio XX* in the rear of the frontier system. On the basis of these assumptions (Hanson 1987, 107), the winter of AD 81 could have been the time for the building of this fortress. The stationing of *Legio XX* in a new base in the north would have finally confirmed the loss of Wroxeter's already eroded legionary status. If Wroxeter still retained its defences in AD 81, these events may have signalled their removal.

A suggestion has been made by Mackreth (pers comm) that possibly only the west side of the defences was demolished and the area of the fortress expanded to the river escarpment. This would at least explain the pair of military ditches (Fig 1.7), which if continued, would join the north-west corner of the fortress defences. This pair of ditches turns to the south, and, if extended, would reach the river escarpment. However, no traces have been observed of a corresponding pair for the south-west corner, although the quality of the cropmarks in the southern area is much poorer due to the greater amount of clay in the subsoil. Nor, however, were there any indications of the ditches found by Bushe-Fox in his 1912 excavation in this area (Bushe-Fox 1913a). It would be difficult to explain the expansion of the fortress/depot in terms of historical events.

The end of the military occupation at Wroxeter *c* AD 90

The construction of timber buildings over the reduced rampart (Phase 7iii) clearly indicates that space was available on the site of the defences, but these post-rampart buildings can still be identified as military by the timber trenches used for their foundations and their direct association with the depot buildings. It would therefore seem that the site continued as a military depot after the reduction of the defences and prior to the final clearance of all military structures from the site (Phase 7iv). The dismantling of this part of the Wroxeter fortress/depot can be dated archaeologically from the pottery discarded by the army to *c* AD 90, and the buildings of the new city were erected on the levelled platform prepared by the military demolition party.

The date of AD 90 is significant in terms of events elsewhere in the province and the rest of the empire. In AD 82 Domitian had extended Agricola's term of office and given instructions for a further campaign in the north in which *Legio XX* would have played a prominent part. Wroxeter appears to have continued as a depot throughout these years. Agricola finally departed from Britain in AD 84, and it was probably left to his successor to consolidate the frontier. As part of this, *Legio XX* began the construction of Inchtuthil (Pitts and St Joseph 1985, 264–7), and it seems likely that this was to be the permanent fort of the legion in the new defensive system. For a long time the identification of the legion which built and occupied Inchtuthil has been an open question, but in his study of the section of Ptolemy devoted to this area, Richmond advanced an interesting case for the name of the fortress being Victoria (Ogilvie and Richmond 1967), and this has been accepted by Rivet and Smith (1979, 449). This is based on the implication that the unit there was *Legio* XX *Valeria Victrix*. However, the legion's association with the site was very limited. The excavations of Richmond at Inchtuthil uncovered the realities: a fortress under construction, suddenly dismantled and demolished (Ogilvie and Richmond 1967, 69–74). The absence among other buildings of the *praetorium* and the diminutive size of the *principia* indicate that the commandant and headquarters staff were based elsewhere, either at another fortress or in an adjacent compound.

The abandonment of Inchtuthil has been dated by the presence of mint coins of AD 86 and 87 associated with its demolition deposits. The re-deployment of the legion was made necessary by the withdrawal from Britain of *II Adiutrix* (Hanson 1987, 152). This reduction of the British garrison was required to deal with the growing unrest amongst the Dacians on the Danube. The Roman reaction to a Dacian incursion in AD 85 was an expedition under Oppius Sabinus, which resulted in a serious disaster, with heavy losses, and a second attempt under Cornelius Fuscus fared little better. Preparations were in hand in AD 88 to restore the frontier and avenge the two defeats. This is the most likely occasion for the withdrawal of the *II Adiutrix*, and there is epigraphic evidence for the presence of one of its centurions in the Balkans (*ILS* 1916, 9193). Shortly after this, presumably in AD 89–90, *Legio XX* was moved south from Inchtuthil to occupy the vacant fortress at Chester. The base at Wroxeter does not appear to have survived for very long after these events, falling victim to the rationalisation process imposed on the province at this time. It was now an opportune occasion for a reappraisal of the sites still held by the army in Britain (Fig 3.2).

By AD 90 many fortresses and forts were still under care and maintenance, or, like Wroxeter, converted into depots. Continued military occupation seems to have become a serious deterrent to economic growth and expansion in those areas. The new towns founded under Claudius in the south-east, apart from those destroyed during the Boudiccan revolt, were now well established. Any such development in the west and north was prevented by the continued presence of the redundant military sites, although the civil settlements which had grown round them had by now developed into sizeable communities. Rome's policy of an urban expansion into newly conquered territories was implemented by the creation of new centres, planned on the Roman urban model and with the establishment of markets. The initial result of this new policy was the founding of two *coloniae* for legionary veterans on the old fortress sites at Lincoln and Gloucester, while Wroxeter and Exeter were handed over to the local communities to become the tribal capitals of the *Cornovii* and *Dumnonii* (Webster 1988).

4 Finds of metal, bone and stone

Coins

by R Brickstock and P J Casey

Reference to period in the following discussion is in relation to the currency divisions used in the histograms in the report on the baths and *macellum* (Ellis 2000, 91–108), which follow the methodology laid out by Casey (1994), and not to the structural periods described in the main text of the excavation report. This coin report and appended catalogue represent the first sections of the full report and catalogue which appear in Ellis (2000).

The coins from these excavations (Fig. 4.1) extend in date from issues of the Dobunni to the end of the fourth century and tend to display the well-established period patterning which is characteristic of urban coin assemblages from Roman Britain (Casey 1994). The coins from the military fort are catalogued here as well as those from the later civilian site. It has proved impossible to divorce the coinage from the military phases from consideration in this discussion, since there is an inextricable relationship between the coins of the military phase and the first structural phase following the fort.

Period 1 (AD 43–54)

Despite all structural contexts being post-military, a good deal of coinage is present which derives either from disturbed military contexts or has entered the currency pool of *Viroconium* through the one-time presence of soldiers. Thus there is a certain degree of unreality in any attempt to define civilian and military in the earliest phases of civil life through the medium of the recovered coinage. This is especially true in the present case where the volume of

pseudo-Claudian copper coinage of Period 1 from the baths and *macellum* site, normally closely associated with the Julio-Claudian army, dominates the first-century coin pattern to a marked degree (Fig 4.2). Comparison with the pattern of Period 1 coinage at Wroxeter as a whole (Fig 4.1) demonstrates the extent to which localised deeper archaeological sondage, and the erection of buildings with deep and substantial foundations, has increased the presence of Period 1 coins on the baths and *macellum* site. This is in marked contrast, for instance, with the coinage from the adjacent baths basilica excavations

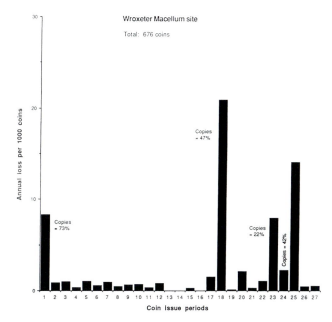

*Fig 4.2 Coins: coin loss per issue period, Wroxeter, *macellum* site*

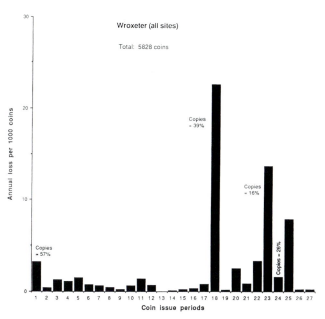

Fig 4.1 Coins: coin loss per issue period, Wroxeter, all sites

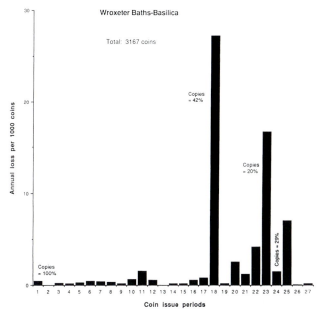

Fig 4.3 Coins: coin loss per issue period, Wroxeter, baths-basilica

85

where pseudo-Claudian coinage (Fig 4.3) is poorly represented, demonstrating the derivation of the coins on this site from significantly later deposits than those under consideration here (Barker 1997). A further degree of uncertainty concerning the economic significance of these coins is introduced by the fact that pseudo-Claudian coins remained in circulation in army contexts for many years after they ceased to be produced. The presence of such coins in the Coventina's Well votive deposit, at Carrawburgh on Hadrian's Wall, shows that these coins were in circulation until at least the middle of the second century (Allason-Jones and MacKay 1985). The Wroxeter deposits present two aspects of residuality; physical in the sense of redeposit, and economic in the sense of persistence in the currency pool.

The pseudo-Claudian coinage

The analysis of the pseudo-Claudian coins does not include a group of 42 from the excavations which came to light after the report was finished, and which are catalogued separately below, with the prefix 'a'. A scan of this group does not suggest alterations to the conclusions here and in the report on the civilian phases (Ellis 2000).

As has been observed, a component of the earliest coinage in Roman Britain consists of copies of the *orichalcum dupondii* and copper *asses* of Claudius. The context for this wave of imitation is well documented. Senatorial condemnation of the Emperor Gaius (Caligula) extended to the melting down of his coinage. The effectiveness of this may be judged by the scarcity of coin in his name carried to Britain by the invading armies of Claudius. An exception was made in the case of the condemned emperor's issues in the name of his grandfather, Agrippa, and his father, Germanicus, which are found in conquest period contexts, including at Wroxeter (coins 16–22). For reasons that are not understood, the coin shortage created by the senatorial decision was exacerbated by Claudius, whose base metal coinage dating after *c* AD 43, bearing the title *Pater Patriae*, is very scarce indeed. In Germany worn currency, which had been withdrawn from use, was re-circulated. Coins had countermarks struck upon them to revalidate their use; these countermarks often re-value very worn coins to a lower denominational value. A *sestertius* of Claudius in the present catalogue (coin 31) bears a countermark PROB(avit), revalidating its use in the reign of Nero. Hence the invasion army was virtually bereft of small denomination currency. Untroubled by the impact of this situation on the emerging economy of the north-western provinces, the imperial authorities issued no base metal coinage at all for the first ten years of the reign of Nero (AD 54–64).

Throughout these two decades of monetary deprivation, copies of the last extant official coin of Claudius circulated throughout the military and passed into the civil sphere. The bulk of these copies comprise imitations, of varying degrees of fidelity, of the *asses* of Claudius with the reverse type of Minerva bearing a

shield and flourishing a spear (RIC 100, e.g. coins 32–35). Claudian copies are normally graded into four categories of deviation from the prototype (Sutherland 1935; Boon 1988; Kenyon 1987).

Grade 1: These are very close approximations of official issues, legends are correct and portraiture and reverse type are skilfully executed in a style distinctively at variance with the products of the imperial die cutters. Weights often fall below the *c* 11g of official issues, varying from full weight to *c* 8.5g.

Grade 2: Copies of this grade represent a further deviation from the stylistic fluency of official issues, and may themselves be copies of Grade 1 coins. Flans are often smaller in diameter than the dies struck on them, and as a result legends are missing from the flan. When present, legends are epigraphically correct. Weights are, on average, lower than the prototype, clustering around the lowest weight of Grade 1 copies.

Grade 3: Copies in this category represent a deviation from the prototype, which is characterised by crude execution of portrait and reverse type, both being rendered in a schematic manner. Weights are normally below the lowest range of Grade 2 copies, falling to 5.5g and less.

Grade 4: Essentially a sub-type of Grade 3, this version of the Claudian coinage is struck from dies which produced a reversal of either, or both, the obverse or reverse designs.

Within these categories there is a good deal of overlap in weights and flan sizes, and the attribution to specific grade in these cases is a subjective matter depending, in the end, on an aesthetic judgement.

Dating the appearance of the various grades of copy is assisted by the appearance of the coins in military sites which can be associated with the advance of the Roman army from the south-east to the north and west. Thus a degree of horizontal stratigraphy is created by the activity of the army itself. At Colchester 76% of the Claudian copies are of Grade 2 and 14% are in the lowest category, indicative of the receipt by the site of a preponderance of copies early in the cycle of production (Kenyon 1987). By contrast, Usk, an undoubted Neronian site with a suggested foundation date of *c* AD 58 and an effective abandonment in the mid-60s (Boon 1982a), has 68% of its pseudo-Claudian coinage in the lowest categories of copies and 26% in Grade 2.

In the Wroxeter assemblage the bulk of the copies is heavily weighted towards the latter end of the production cycle in the Neronian period and is comparable to the picture derived from Usk: Grade 1, 19%; Grade 2, 19%; Grade 3/4, 62%.

Period 2 and onwards

Relative to the coin deposition picture from Wroxeter as a whole (Fig 4.1) the present assemblage demonstrates something of a strength in the coinage of Nero (Period 2), probably reflecting the military context of the site at this time, and a marked fall off of late Flavian issues (Period 4 = Domitian) which is not reflected in the coinage of Wroxeter as a whole. Thereafter the coin finds down to Period 12 (Severus Alexander) conform very closely to the spread normally associated with major urban sites in Britain, and are consonant with the overall numismatic history of the town visible in the 'all site' histogram (Fig 4.1).

Summary catalogue

Each entry contains the following information in the sequence: coin number; issuer; denomination; date; reference; wear; mint; *context*; phase; small find number. A copy or counterfeit of a particular ruler/issuer is denoted thus 'CLAUDIUS I', and by c. in the catalogue reference, thus c. 100 = a copy of RIC100. The use of the word 'of' indicates that a precise catalogue reference has been obtained; 'as' is used, for both official issues and copies, to denote an incompletely catalogued coin. G1–4 indicates the grade of copy.

Denominations: ANT, Antoninianus; AS, As; DEN, Denarius (pl = plated); DP, Dupondius; SEST, Sestertius.

Catalogues (catalogue numbers refer to *Roman Imperial Coinage* (RIC; Mattingly *et al*, 1926; 1984) unless otherwise stated): BMC, Mattingly 1965–8; CR, Crawford 1974; MACK, Mack 1973; VA, van Arsdell 1989.

Mints: LG, Lyons; RM, Rome.

Wear: where recorded, the condition of both the obverse and reverse is denoted by the following abbreviations:

UW Unworn; SW Slightly worn; W Worn; VW Very worn; EW Extremely worn; NSU Not struck up; C Corroded

1 B.SCRIBONIUS; DEN; 154BC; CR201/1; VW/VW; RM; *50/13*, M, sf769

2 L.TITURI L.F.SABINUS; DEN; 89BC; CR344/1c; VW/VW; RM; *22/19*, BP 2.1, sf392

3 C PISO LF FRUGI; DEN; 67BC; CR408/16; VW/VW; *87/u/s*, WR 4, sf 3353

4 MN CORDIUS RUFUS; DEN; 46BC; CR463/1a; W/W; RM; *83/530*, WR 2.3, sf4452

5 M.ANTONIUS; DEN; 32–31BC; CR544/24; W/W; *81/15*, M, sf1766

6 M.ANTONIUS; DEN; 32–31BC; CR544/31; W/VW; *91/266*, M, sf6011

7 M.ANTONIUS; DEN; 32–31BC; CR544/8+; W/VW; *39/20*, M, sf 1237

8 M.ANTONIUS; DEN; 32BC; CR543/1; W/VW; *70/68*, M, sf 1646

9 LATE REPUBLIC/EARLY IMP; DEN; C1BC/AD; C/C; *83/506*, WR 2.3, sf 4344

10 DOBUNNIC SILVER CLASS C; c 20BC-AD10; MACK378a, VA1045–1; ?W/W; *83/68*, M, sf3863

11 DOBUNNIC GOLD PLATED; AD30–60; MACK393, VA1035–1; NSU/SW; *40/9*, C 2.2, sf519

12 AUGUSTUS; DEN; 29–27BC; 264; W/VW; *80/136*, P 3.3, sf4341

13 AUGUSTUS; AS; 15–10BC; 230; C/C; LG; *92/61*, M, sf3555

14 TIBERIUS; DEN; 36–37; 30; SW/SW; LG; *70/78*, M, sf1747

15 TIBERIUS; DEN; 36–37; 30; UW/SW; LG; *85/63*, WR 2.1, sf3172

16 GAIUS; AS; 37–41; 58; W/W; RM; *80/245*, M, sf5226

17 GAIUS; AS; 37–41; 58; C/C; RM; *50/109*, M, sf1737

18 GAIUS; AS; 37–41; 58; SW/SW; RM; *80/191*, M, sf4915

19 GAIUS; AS; 37–41; 58; SW/SW; RM; *77/2*, C 2.2, sf1602

20 GAIUS; AS; 37–41; 58; SW/C; RM; *98/192*, M, sf6200a

21 GAIUS; AS; 37–41; 58; EW/EW; RM; *92/61*, M, sf3592

22 GAIUS; AS; 40–41; 50; VW/VW; RM; *80/189*, M, sf4863

23 'GAIUS'; AS; 41+; c.G2 as 58; W/W; *98/175*, 1.2, sf6274

24 CLAUDIUS I; DP; 41–50; 92; W/W; RM; *98/190*, 1.1, sf6182

25 CLAUDIUS I; DP; 41–50; 92; SW/SW; RM; *7/22*, C 2.2, sf90

26 CLAUDIUS I; DP; 41–50; 92; VW/EW; RM; *80/181*, P 2.1, sf4695

27 CLAUDIUS I; DP; 41–50; 94; SW/W; RM; *88/4*, WR 2.3, sf3352

28 CLAUDIUS I; DP; 41–50; 94; W/W; RM; *29/8*, C 2.3, sf415

29 CLAUDIUS I; AS; 41–50; 95; W/W; RM; *45/3*, C 2.3, sf483

30 CLAUDIUS I; AS; 41–50; 97; SW/SW; RM; *80/189*, M, sf4839

31 CLAUDIUS I; SEST; 41–50; 99; SW/SW; RM; *97/133*, P 2.3, sf5248

32 CLAUDIUS I; AS; 41–50; 100; W/W; RM; *80/179*, P 2.1, sf4718

33 CLAUDIUS I; AS; 41–50; 100; W/W; RM; *u/s*, sf78

34 CLAUDIUS I; AS; 41–50; 100; W/W; RM; *48/u/s*, BP 4, sf590

35 CLAUDIUS I; AS; 41–50; 100; W/W; RM; *29/16*, C 2.2, sf487

36 CLAUDIUS I; AS; 41–50; W/C; *80/201*, M, sf4937

37 CLAUDIUS I; AS; 41–50; W/C; RM; *98/168*, 1.2, sf6060

38 CLAUDIUS I; AS; 41–50; EW/EW; RM; *98/87*, P 2.3, sf5872

39 CLAUDIUS I?; DP; 41–50; C/C; RM; *92/60*, M, sf3795

40   'CLAUDIUS I'; DP; 41+; c.G1 as 92; W/W;
      87/100, WR 2.3, sf4975

41   'CLAUDIUS I'; DP; 41+; c.G1 of 92;
      SW/W; *12/27*, C 2.2, sf51

42   'CLAUDIUS I'; DP; 41+; c.G1 of 92;
      C/SW; *50/92*, M, sf1662

43   'CLAUDIUS I'; DP; 41+; c.G1 as 94;
      SW/W; *85/224*, WR 2.3, sf3208

44   'CLAUDIUS I'; AS; 41+; c.G1 as 97;
      SW/SW; *84/399*, M, sf6254

45   'CLAUDIUS I'; AS; 41+; c.G1 as 100;
      SW/W; *98/192*, M, sf6201b

46   'CLAUDIUS I'; AS; 41+; c.G1 as 100;
      SW/C; *98/192*, M, sf6201a

47   'CLAUDIUS I'; 41+; c.G1 as -; C/C; *98/178*,
      1.3, sf6314

48   'CLAUDIUS I'; DP; 41+; c.G2 as 92; W/W;
      98/152, 1.2, sf6027

49   'CLAUDIUS I' MULE; DP; 41+; c.G2 as
      obv 94, rv 92; VW/VW *85/65*, M, sf3180

50   'CLAUDIUS I'; AS; 41+; c.G2 as 100;
      ?SW/SW; *2/7*, C 3.3, sf137

51   'CLAUDIUS I'; AS; 41+; c.G2 as 100;
      W/VW; *22/13*, BP 2.2, sf331

52   'CLAUDIUS I'; AS; 41+; c.G2 as 100;
      SW/C; *80/191*, M, sf4949

53   'CLAUDIUS I'; AS; 41+; c.G2 as 100;
      SW/SW; *80/201*, M, sf4922

54   'CLAUDIUS I'; AS; 41+; c.G2 as 100;
      SW/W; *98/52*, P 2.3, sf5474

55   'CLAUDIUS I'; DP; 41+; c.G3 as 92; C/C;
      98/192, M, sf6200b

56   'CLAUDIUS I'; DP; 41+; c.G3 as 94;
      VW/VW; *90/198*, 1.3, sf5692

57   'CLAUDIUS I'; AS; 41+; c.G3 as 95; W/W;
      45/3, C 2.3, sf483

58   'CLAUDIUS I'; AS; 41+; c.G3 as 95; C/C;
      98/152, 1.2, sf6027

59   'CLAUDIUS I'; AS; 41+; c.G3 as 100; C/C;
      10/14, M, sf824

60   'CLAUDIUS I'; AS; 41+; c.G3 as 100;
      SW/W; *98/100*, F855, P 3.1, sf5708

61   'CLAUDIUS I'; AS; 41+; c.G3 as 100;
      W/VW; *50/11*, C 2.2, sf602

62   'CLAUDIUS I'; AS; 41+; c.G3 as 100;
      W/W; *90/184*, 1.2, sf5651

63   'CLAUDIUS I'; AS; 41+; c.G3 as 100;
      W/W; *u/s*, sf1125

64   'CLAUDIUS I'; AS; 41+; c.G3 as 100; C/C;
      u/s, sf320

65   'CLAUDIUS I'; AS; 41+; c.G3 as 100;
      W/VW; *91/144*, 1.3, sf4941

66   'CLAUDIUS I'; AS; 41+; c.G3 as 100;
      SW/SW; *9/6*, C 3.2, sf243

67   'CLAUDIUS I'; AS; 41+; c.G3 as -; C/C;
      98/162, 1.1, sf6030

68   'CLAUDIUS I'; AS; 41+; c.G4 as 100; C/C;
      80/181, P 2.1, sf4694

69   'CLAUDIUS I'; AS; 41+; c.G4 as 100; C/C;
      98/178, 1.3, sf6312

70   'CLAUDIUS I'; AS; 41+; c.G4 as 100;
      SW/SW; *51/18*, M, sf763

71   'CLAUDIUS I'; AS; 41+; c.G4 as 100; W/C;
      98/138, P 2.3, sf5982

72   'CLAUDIUS I'; AS; 41+; c.G4 as 100;
      NSU; *84/535*, M, sf5362

73   'CLAUDIUS I'; AS; 41+; c.G4 as 100;
      W/SW; *80/181*, P 2.1, sf4828

74   'CLAUDIUS I'; AS; 41+; c.G4 as 100;
      SW/SW; *u/s*, sf110

75   'CLAUDIUS I'; AS; 41+; c.G4 as 100;
      W/W; *9/22*, M, sf355

76   'CLAUDIUS I'; AS; 41+; c.G4 as 100;
      W/SW; *80/207*, M, sf5118

77   'CLAUDIUS I'; AS; 41+; c.G4 as 100;
      ?VW/VW; *u/s*, sf1852

78   'CLAUDIUS I'; AS; 41+; c.G4 as 100; C/C;
      98/192, M, sf6195

79   'CLAUDIUS I'; AS; 41+; c.G4 as 100; C/C;
      98/178, 1.3, sf6273

80   'CLAUDIUS I'; AS; 41+; c.G4 of 100; C/C;
      42/7, M, 538

81   'CLAUDIUS I'; AS; 41+; c. as -; C/C;
      80/191, M, sf4930

82   'CLAUDIUS I'; 41+; c. as -; C/C; *98/156*,
      1.2, sf6039

83   'CLAUDIUS I'; 41+; c. as -; C/C; *98/211*,
      M, sf6259

84   'CLAUDIUS I'?; 41+; c. as -; C/C; *98/192*,
      M, sf6204

85   NERO; AS; 64–68; C/C; *58/4*, BP 3.2, 778

86   NERO; AS; 64–68; as 300; W/W; *97/164*,
      1.1, sf5563

87   NERO; DP; c 64–67; as 375; UW/UW;
      50/11, C 2.2, sf615

88   NERO; SEST; c 65; 389; UW/UW; LG; *u/s*,
      no sf

89   NERO; AS; c 65; 474; SW/C; LG; *35/48*, M,
      sf1477

90   NERO; AS; c 66; as 542; SW/UW; LG;
      78/15, M, sf1775

91   NERO; AS; c 66–67; 543/5, 605; UW/UW;
      LG; *72/48*, M, sf1667

92   NERO; AS; c 66–67; 543/605; UW/UW;
      LG; *90/247*, M, sf6328

93   JULIO-CLAUDIAN; AS; C1st; C/C; *98/87*,
      P 2.3, sf6064

94   VESPASIAN; AS; 69–70; 399; W/SW; LG;
      90/177, P 2.2, sf5660

95   VESPASIAN; AS; 69–78; EW/EW; *56/2*, BP
      3.3, sf992

96   VESPASIAN; AS; 69–78; C/C; *84/79*, M,
      sf3611

97   VESPASIAN; AS/DP; 69–79; C/C; *57/u/s*,
      BP 4, sf843

98   VESPASIAN; DP; 70–79; as 541; C/SW;
      RM; *57/u/s*, BP 4, sf842

99 VESPASIAN; DP; 71–72; 475/740; VW/VW; *84/48*, WR 3.1, no sf

100 VESPASIAN; AS; 71–79; as 494; ?SW/W; *9/21*, C 2.1, sf343

101 VESPASIAN; AS; 72–73; 528; W/W; RM; *91/158*, 1.3, sf5182

102 VESPASIAN; DP; 72–73; 743; UW/SW; LG; *87/114*, M, sf6301

103 VESPASIAN; AS; 72–78; as 528; C/VW; *85/u/s*, WR 4, no sf

104 VESPASIAN; AS; 73; 747; SW/SW, LG; *97/230*, M, sf5980

105 VESPASIAN; DEN; 74; 73–75; ?W/C; RM; *80/5*, P 3.4B, sf1686

106 VESPASIAN; DP; 77–78; 757c; W/VW; LG; *91/94*, WR 2.3, sf4470

107 VESPASIAN; AS; 77–78; 763; SW/C; LG; *81/15*, M, sf1760

108 VESPASIAN; AS; 77–78; 763; SW/SW; LG; *43/12*, 1.3, sf496

109 DOMITIAN; DP; 84–96; VW/EW; RM; *59/5*, BP 3.2, sf678

110 DOMITIAN; DP; 86; 326a; UW/UW; RM; *30/18*, M , sf1346

111 DOMITIAN; DEN; 89; 146; W/W; RM; *90/209*, F951, P 2.2, sf5927

112 DOMITIAN/HADRIAN?; C/C; AS; 81–117?; *u/s*, sf199

The following coins came to light after the completion of the coin report, and are catalogued here for completeness. Listed by coin number; issuer; type; reference; *context* (where available), phase (M = military). No sf numbers were assigned and some context details are no longer available.

a1 CLAUDIUS I; DP; 94; M7iv

a2 CLAUDIUS I; DP; 94; M7iv

a3 CLAUDIUS I; DP; 94; *78/11, 33, 57*, F2807; M4b

a4 CLAUDIUS I; DP; 94; *72/55, 119, 120*, F2898; M4b

a5 CLAUDIUS I; AS; 100; *72/39*, F2886 M4b

a6 CLAUDIUS I; AS; 100; *78/11, 33, 57*, F2807; M4b

a7 CLAUDIUS I; AS; 100; *78/11, 33, 57*, F2807; M7iv

a8 CLAUDIUS I; AS; *73/24, 31, 32, 45*, F2662; M4b

a9 CLAUDIUS I; AS; 100; *72/50*, F2895; M7iv

a10 CLAUDIUS I; AS; 95; M4b

a11 CLAUDIUS I; AS; 97; M7iv

a12 'CLAUDIUS I'; DP; *c* GI as 94; M7iv; Grade 1

a13 'CLAUDIUS I'; DP; *c* G2 as 92; *78/10*, F2806; M4b; Grade 2

a14 'CLAUDIUS I'; DP; *c* G2 as 92; M1–2; Grade 2

a15 'CLAUDIUS I'; DP; *c* as 92; *78/11, 33, 57*, F2807; M4b

a16 'CLAUDIUS I'; DP; *c* G2 as 92; *78/11, 33, 57*, F2807; M4b; Grade 2

a17 'CLAUDIUS I'; DP; *c* G1 as 92; *78/19*, F2814; M3+; Grade 1

a18 'CLAUDIUS I'; AS; *c* G1 as 100; *78/10*, F2806; M4b; Grade 1

a19 'CLAUDIUS I'; AS; *c* G1 as 100; *73/44*, F2676; M3; Grade 1

a20 'CLAUDIUS I'; AS; *c* G1 as 100; M7iv; Grade 1

a21 'CLAUDIUS I'; AS; *c* G1 as 100; *81/63, 88*, F3069; C4.0; Grade 1

a22 'CLAUDIUS I'; AS; *c* G2 as 100; M7iv; Grade 2

a23 'CLAUDIUS I'; AS; *c* G2 as 100; M7iv; Grade 2

a24 'CLAUDIUS I'; AS; *c* G2 as 100; *73/48*, F2894; M3+; Grade 2

a25 'CLAUDIUS I'; AS; *c* G2 as 100; *72/48*, F2894; M3+; Grade 2

a26 'CLAUDIUS I'; AS; *c* G2 as 100; *72/63, 122*, F2905; M7iv; Grade 2

a27 'CLAUDIUS I'; AS; *c* G2 as 100; u/s

a28 'CLAUDIUS I'; AS; *c* G3 as 100; M7iv

a29 'CLAUDIUS I'; AS; *c* G3 as 100; M7iv

a30 'CLAUDIUS I'; AS; *c* G3 as 100; *75/4, 10*, F2619; C2.4

a31 'CLAUDIUS I'; AS; *c* G3 as 100 C2.2

a32 'CLAUDIUS I'; AS; *c* G3 as 100; *78/11, 33, 57*, F2807; M4b

a33 Prob CLAUDIUS; AS or DP; *73/44*, F2676; M3

a34 Prob CLAUDIUS; AS; *78/11, 33, 57*, F2807; M4b

a35 'CLAUDIUS I'; AS; M7iv (coin lost); *c* as —

a36 Poss CLAUDIUS; AS or DP; *73/27*, F2663; M3+

a37 Poss CLAUDIUS; AS or DP; *72/48*, F2894; M3+

a38 'CLAUDIUS I'; AS; RIC66; C3.1; *c* G1 as 100

a39 'CLAUDIUS I'; AS; *c* RIC66; M7iv; *c* G1 as 100

a40 'CLAUDIUS I'; AS; *c* RIC66; C3.4; *c* G1 as 100

a41 'CLAUDIUS I'; AS; *c* G3 as 100; C4

a42 'CLAUDIUS I'; AS or DP; u/s; *c* as —

Military brooches

by D F Mackreth

Introduction

As the fortress is sealed under the later Roman town, it is unlikely that excavations designed specifically to deal with military matters will ever take place. It is therefore assumed that the material recovered from under the south-eastern part of the baths *insula* will form the only material available for study for some time. The excavation provided only a highly localised and small sample. All items stratigraphically later than the military period, but which can only date to that time, have been extracted and added to those from safely sealed contexts. This has increased the collection, but it is still a small one. In order to explore some of the wider aspects of the study of the brooches, the same kind of material of a similar early date from previous excavations and discoveries in the town has also been added. In practice this means items from Bushe-Fox's and Atkinson's excavations, as well as finds from clearance work carried out by the Department of the Environment, an item from Hattatt's collection, another from the Hildyard Collection, a stray find from outside the northern defences (Brooch 29 below), and finds with no precise provenance in Rowley's House Museum, Shrewsbury, have also been included. Brooches from Philip Barker's excavations on the area north of the Old Work have been excluded.

There are two factors which prevent a simple analysis of the collection so assembled. Firstly, within the fortress it is reasonably certain that its occupancy was of two different characters, and that it was occupied initially by the substantial part of a legion, and later by a very much smaller garrison. Secondly, the whole of the artificially constructed group covers sites which lay both inside and outside the fortress and, while there may have been a great lessening of activity within the defences, this need not have applied outside. Indeed, the history of the settlement after its military use is strongly suggestive of a fairly intense activity at odds with the marked downturn in military involvement for the later stages of the fortress. That being the case, the overall group needs to be carefully dissected so that

whatever it may have to reveal is not encumbered by too broad a division or too minute a discrimination in argument.

Before taking a closer look at the contents of Table 4.1, it would be as well if two further aspects of the site and its collection were to be mentioned. There is a presumed change in the military unit on the site: it should be axiomatic, in the early years of the frontier in this sector, that any unit moved to it had been stationed somewhere else, closer to its point of first entry into Britain. The part of Britain first taken over was one in which the natives wore brooches as a matter of course and used, alongside their own varieties, whatever was fashionable in the nearer parts of the continent (Stead and Rigby 1989). The use of bow brooches was, however, confined only to the lands south-east of the Fosse Way, with an extension to cover the lower reaches of the Severn and much of the south-west. Wroxeter lies well outside this native brooch-wearing area. In seeking new supplies the Roman soldier would have had the choice of buying what was available of continental manufacture, or acquiring what was British, providing he was in an area where native manufacture supported native custom. Once he crossed into lands where the brooch did not have the same general currency, he was faced with only the continental material or what the quick-witted could devise for him, and the distribution of one type suggests just such an initiative (Atkinson 1942, fig 36, H16).

We know very little about the change-over rates for brooch types, and the lack of dated pieces means that we are not likely to learn very much for a long time. The true picture will always be hidden, as there can be no doubt that there was a fairly efficient scrap metal recovery rate, even if it was not as good as it appears to

Table 4.1 The military brooches: Wroxeter

Types, in broad terms	Fortress		Other		Totals	
	no	*%*	*no*	*%*	*no*	*%*
Colchester Derivatives (1–4)	4	12.9	5	12.8	9	12.9
Headstud (5)	1	3.2	–	–	1	1.4
*La Tène II (6–8)	3	9.7	–	–	3	4.3
*Drahtfibel Derivatives (9–10)	2	6.5	2	5.1	4	5.7
*Langton Down (11)	1	3.2	–	–	1	1.4
*'Aucissa' (12–22)	11	35.5	3	7.7	14	20.0
*'Aucissa'/Hod Hill (23)	1	3.2	3	7.7	4	5.7
*Hod Hills (24–26)	3	9.7	15	38.4	18	25.6
Unclassified (27)	1	3.2	1	2.6	2	2.9
Pannonian (28)	1	3.2	1	2.6	2	2.9
*Plate 1 (29)	1	3.2	1	2.6	2	2.9
Plate 2 (30)	1	3.2	–	–	1	1.4
Penannular (31)	1	3.2	–	–	1	1.4
*Harlow –			2	5.1	2	2.9
*Colchester –			1	2.6	1	1.4
Studded Variety –			1	2.6	1	1.4
*Nauheim Derivative Lowbury –			2	5.1	2	2.9
Nauheim Derivative –			2	5.1	2	2.9
TOTALS	31	100	39	100	70	100
* Pre AD 70	22	71.1	29	71.7	51	72.8
* minus Hod Hill types	19	61.4	14	33.3	33	47.2

have been in pre-conquest times. However, a brooch assemblage on a site may occasionally yield a hint of both earlier activities and of other territories.

Discussion

Now we can turn to the collection to see if there is a way in which an initial date for the assemblage can be detected. Two factors come into play here. First, the biases within the imported material, and secondly, the date of the earliest native material obviously derived from the south-east. Looking at the brooches from within the fortress, one feature is remarkable: the proportion of 'Aucissa' types to Hod Hill types is about 4:1. Outside the fortress it falls to 1:5, ignoring the hybrids in each case. On the other hand brooches from the areas outside the fortress, including the unlocated material, yield examples well away from their homelands. They include one Colchester type (Atkinson 1942, 204, fig 36, H32) which belongs to the latest type known to the writer. It is usually diminutive when compared with the bulk of the main sequence and shows in its proportions that its progeny was either on its way, or that some had even come into being. Four other brooches deserve particular notice. Two belong to the Harlow spring-fixing arrangement, in which the spring is fastened to a plate with two holes behind the head of the bow (Rowleys House Museum, B262, B380), and two are Nauheim Derivatives (Rowleys House Museum, 48, B426) of the kind called by the writer the 'Lowbury' because of the number found at Lowbury Hill, Berkshire (Atkinson 1916, 33, pls 7, 4, 6–12, 14–16). It is true that these four, not having a secure provenance, need not have come from the fortress itself, but that point is perhaps not material in this discussion.

All five reflect a movement from the south-east and the Colchester example should point to that movement having taken place significantly before AD 60. The proportion of 'Aucissa' to Hod Hill types definitely from within the fortress not only indicates the same thing, but is distinctly unusual. For instance, at Hod Hill itself, the ratio of 'Aucissa' to Hod Hill types is 1:3.2. Hod Hill dates no later than AD 50 (Richmond 1968, 117–9), before the fortress at Wroxeter seems to have been founded. In terms of the kind of dating available for this part of the first century, c AD 55 is the latest 'early' date which should allow these features to appear, and would also cover the Langton Down, Brooch 11. Even the last may be counted as late, but without knowing the detailed history of what should be at this time the *Legio XIV*, it cannot be asserted that the date must be earlier. If the legion had been stranded for some years in the frontier lands, supplies may have been sparse when compared with those to units stationed in more favoured districts and this may account for the very low proportion of Hod Hill types.

The Harlow system belongs unreservedly to the eastern side of England save for a group generally centred on Cirencester (see Brooch 1). Of the two examples, one is a Harlow proper (Rowleys House Museum, B380), but it is the two Lowbury types which call for particular comment. They are both marked by the distinctive square stamping of the type (eg Frere 1984a, 21, fig 5, 15, 16). The variety was almost certainly established by the conquest and this may account for its main distribution, which is south of the Thames in central southern England in, as it were, Atrebatic territory. To find two at Wroxeter should argue for a specific connection with the homeland, but of what nature is unknown.

When trying to estimate from the pieces themselves when the major military presence had been reduced, we meet a crux in brooch studies. What is at issue here is the date by which the larger part of the *Legio XX* had left. From the spectrum of brooches laid out in Table 4.1 one could hazard the guess that it was between AD 70 and 80, as there appears to be no major component to replace the Hod Hill type, which had virtually passed out of use by the beginning of that range. But we encounter here a major bias in the constructed collection which certainly prevents any force being laid on this point, a lack of knowledge on the detailed dating of Colchester Derivatives. The brooches gathered for Table 4.1 have been screened to eliminate material which could have run on to the end of the first century. Brooches 2 and 3 have been included on typological grounds alone, neither being stratified in definite military contexts, but their inclusion is justified by the undoubted military phasing of Brooch 4.

As an unknown quantity of brooches has had to be excluded from consideration because of a lack of evidence, any argument based on what has survived the process has to be cautious. But it could be that because a group of additional Colchester Derivatives cannot be chosen, they are not actually there and so the following line of enquiry may have greater value than can actually be shown. On Table 4.1 various brooch types have been marked ★. These are more or less guaranteed to be early in the history of the site. Within the fortress, they form 71.1% of the whole, and outside it 71.7%. The ratio of the Hod Hill to the 'Aucissa' tends to obscure the issue and, with these removed, the figures are 61.4% and 33.3% respectively. There is, therefore, a major presence dating to before AD 70, if not AD 65, within the defences. The brooches marking the occupation outside are much more varied and this could be a mark either of a more diverse population or of a different kind of occupation. In general, the figures do not allow a very close analysis, but the feeling arises that the extra-mural sites were active at a high level for a longer time.

To illustrate some of the hypotheses advanced it may be instructive to look at Kingsholm, the main station of *Legio XX* following Colchester. The relevant material has not been published *in extenso*, but the writer has been fortunate in having seen the pieces from the excavations carried out in the 1980s.

Table 4.2 sets out the Kingsholm assemblage in the same format as that from Wroxeter. What is immediately apparent is the very high percentage of Colchester

Table 4.2 The military brooches: Kingsholm

Types, in broad terms	no	%
Colchester Derivatives	10	17.5
Drahtfibel Derivatives	3	5.2
Langton Downs	2	3.4
'Aucissas'	6	10.4
'Aucissas'/Hod Hill	3	5.2
Hod Hills	18	31.0
Plate 1	1	1.7
Plate 2	3	5.2
Harlow-spring	5	8.7
Colchesters	2	3.4
Rosette family	2	3.4
Nauheim Derivative, fe, odd	1	1.7
Augenfibel family	1	1.7
Pannonian family	1	1.7
TOTALS	**58**	**100**
Combined Colchester Derivatives		26.0

Derivatives, a total of 26%. The two Colchester type brooches are instructive: one is actually a hybrid showing the development of the Polden Hill spring-fixing arrangement, the other is an oddity with a separately made foot-knob and atypical wings. Both are obviously late, even very late, in the overall sequence of the type and this has a bearing on the dating of the familiar type. In contrast with Wroxeter, the 'Aucissa'/Hod Hill ratio is more than reversed. Even if the Wroxeter figures are of those of the overall site, Kingsholm has 1:3 to Wroxeter's 0.8:1, and the transitional forms are again omitted. In other words, the ratio reflects the 1:3.2 found at Hod Hill. There seems to be an absence of the four-coil internal-chord spring systems at Kingsholm. While these details have something to suggest about particular areas in the east and south of England, the date of Kingsholm is perhaps more pertinent at this stage, being roughly equivalent to the *Legio XIV*'s occupation of Wroxeter although beginning earlier.

The 'Aucissa'/Hod Hill ratios can be ignored for the moment as the make-up of the group of Colchester Derivatives is more important, as well as the presence of two particular types of continental brooch. To deal with the first, the group is marked by two hybrids and a Rearhook. Hybrids belong to the short transitional period between the Colchester proper and the main families of Derivative forms and, coupled with the hybridised Colchester which is put earlier in the transition than these others, and the distinctly odd Colchester, the manufacturing period of the group belongs at best to *c* AD 40–45. There has to be some uncertainty because of the difference in the quality of dating between pre-Roman and early Roman material, and it may be that the margin at the beginning is more extended than the one at the end. The Rearhook has no good dating for its introduction, but has a very good terminal one: the type is Icenian in every sense of that word and the evidence for the actual end-date points unequivocally to AD 60–65 as the time when it not only ceased to be made but also went out of use. It is concurrent with

what the writer calls the Harlow type (eg France and Gobel 1985, 78, fig 40, 50), which is at home in Catuvellaunian territory and lasts for a longer time.

The two continental types are the Langton Down and the Rosette. Both the Langton Down examples are full-blown and not of the rather spavined style of Brooch 11 at Wroxeter. One is a Nertomarus (see discussion of Brooch 11). The other is damaged and corroded but has all the appearance of the standard reeded type as defined by Wheeler (Wheeler and Wheeler 1932, 74–6). Both must be survivors-in-use. One of the Kingsholm Rosettes is the upper part of a *Léontomorphe* (Feugère 1985, 278–91, *types* 18bl, 19c–e) of a fairly devolved nature, but not yet reduced to an almost meaningless formula like an example from Barton Court Farm, Oxfordshire (Miles 1986, 5:D7, fig 102, 9). The other is the fantail foot of a brooch made in more than one piece. On balance, the Kingsholm collection not only begins before that from Wroxeter, but also finishes well before. In other words, a foundation date of *c* AD 50 and an end at *c* AD 60 would cover all those from Kingsholm, but it is hard to demonstrate a satisfactory pre-*c* AD 55 element in the Wroxeter assemblage.

These dates appear to be uncomfortably precise, but they depend on easily detectable changes in styles which can, in overall terms, be fitted tightly into a chronological framework because of the extraordinary circumstances attending the archaeology of the period. This is exemplified further by the highly regional character of assemblages datable to *c* AD 44–75, which allows reasonable conjecture on the passage of major units of the Roman army across regional boundaries. For instance, the brooch collection at Kingsholm contains so much of what is specific to the south-east and East Anglia that the chances that any other legion than *Legio XX* was involved is very severely reduced. The lack of direct evidence for *Legio XX* has been discussed by Hurst (1985, 122).

If such deductions are valid, what can the Wroxeter evidence suggest? The clue is perhaps supplied by the two Lowbury Nauheim Derivatives. Despite a different timespan and, one assumes, a different detailed history between the units involved at Kingsholm and Wroxeter, the statistics presented in Table 4.2 can be used to point to a marked difference between the two sites, the ratios of Nauheim or *Drahtfibel* Derivatives to Colchester Derivatives. In this case, the one odd Nauheim Derivative at Kingsholm has been ignored as it is too peculiar to have any bearing here. In crude terms, the figures are nearly five Colchester Derivatives to every one *Drahtfibel* Derivative at Kingsholm. Within the fortress at Wroxeter the ratio is 2:1 and 3:1 overall. As both units passed through south-eastern Britain, it would be imagined that each would stand a chance of renewing its brooches at roughly the same rate, and from the same kind of source. Thus each should have some kind of uniform representation of the native types available, and the figures though not particularly close are not widely dissimilar: Wroxeter 32.9%, Kingsholm 34%. But it is the balance within these figures which should be instructive.

The lower ratio between four-coil internal-chord spring brooches and the Colchester and its family need not be a pure aberration. When discussing the brooches from Wroxeter, it was pointed out that two came from an area which could be described as being under Atrebatic influence. Now, a marked feature of the southern part of that district, central southern England between Kent and Dorset, is the strong preference for the four-coil internal-chord spring as opposed to any of the Colchester variants. In fact, Colchester brooches themselves are relatively uncommon. Therefore, it is not beyond the bounds of possibility that a major part of the first unit at Wroxeter would have passed through part of the overall territory marked by the two Lowbury style brooches and, in terms of what is known of Wroxeter's history, that would have been part of *Legio XIV Gemina*.

One other major unit passed through this area and ended up at Exeter. The figures for that site show a marked dissimilarity with both Kingsholm and Wroxeter (Table 4.3). It will be seen that the total for the Colchester and its offspring is 63.6%. Firstly, however, we may note the presence of one late Colchester, two local variants of the studded Wroxeter Brooch (Atkinson 1942, fig 36, H16), a member of the Pannonian family, and an example of the Harlow itself. There is nothing new here when compared with the assemblages already reviewed. There is even one *Drahtfibel* Derivative, but there is no marked Nauheim Derivative element, in fact none recorded or seen by the writer at all. Even if one has been missed by the author, it would not match this element at Wroxeter. There should be no doubt that *Legio II Augusta* passed through Atrebatic lands and, on the face of things, stood as much chance as any other large body of troops of picking up native brooches on the way. Speed of transition may be one reason, but one would think that the other legions would have moved almost as quickly over the equivalent amount of ground. There is one factor which applies to Exeter and its local region which did not apply to either *Legio XX* or *Legio*

XIV: *Legio II Augusta* ended up in an area which already had a brooch-wearing tradition. Colchester Derivatives married to the wrongly named Strip Brooches add up to 57% of the total and are entirely south-western types. The army here could replace from native supplies: further north in the same frontier land, it could not.

This leads to a principal difficulty in the Wroxeter collection. If it is possible to suggest what marks the presence of *Legio XIV*, is there anything present which is characteristic of, or represents in some form, the succeeding *Legio XX*? This is a hard question to answer. There is nothing in the stratified material from the fortress which offers a hint, unless it is the Headstud, Brooch 5, which might well have been excluded from consideration had it occurred in later contexts or in earlier excavations outside the fortress. That being the case, there can be no doubt that other items which had been on the site before, say, AD 80, but whose date-range would run beyond that limit, have had to be excluded on the grounds that there were no specific reasons to include them. The identifiable military items from Usk offer a clue, as it appears that *Legio XX* was stationed there before being moved to Wroxeter.

The writer is indebted to W H Manning for very kindly supplying details in advance of his own publication of the brooches recovered from his excavations. The selection shown in Table 4.4 is as before: those brooches from definite military contexts with the addition of others from later deposits or which were unstratified of the same types or of guaranteed early date. There are few surprises. Colchester Derivatives are in the ascendant and there is one typologically very late Colchester. The Hod Hill types barely outnumber the 'Aucissa' types, a difference of one is neither here nor there. What may be represented here is the passing out of use of the Hod Hill type, the 'Aucissa' types being survivals beyond their time. However, their number is of interest for it shows that, apart from having been made in great numbers, they were also popular.

There is a surprise among the Colchester Derivatives, two Rearhook types and one marked variant of the Polden Hill method of securing the spring. The former are overwhelmingly of Norfolk and Fen edge origin, and the other belongs to the east Midlands.

Table 4.3 The military brooches: Exeter

Types, in broad terms	no	%	
Colchester Derivatives	11	33.3	57.5
Strip	8	24.2	
'Aucissa'	1	2.9	
Hod Hills	8	23.6	
Harlow type	1	2.9	
Pannonian family	1	2.9	
Colchester	1	2.9	
Studded Variety	2	5.9	
Drahtfibel Derivative	1	2.9	
TOTALS	34	100	
Combined Colchester Derivatives		61.8%	

Table 4.4 The military brooches: Usk

Types, in broad terms	no	%
Colchester Derivatives	10	29.4
Drahtfibel Derivative	3	8.8
'Aucissa'	3	8.8
Hod Hill	4	11.8
Plate 1	2	5.9
Penannular	3	8.8
Harlow	2	5.9
Colchester	1	2.9
Nauheim Derivative	4	11.8
Aesica	2	5.9
TOTALS	34	

There are also two Harlow type brooches which belong to the Catuvellaunian lowlands. In all, 5 out of 12 brooches do not belong to the west of England in any form. The Harlow types could have been, but are not necessarily, survivals from the previous station, but the absence from Kingsholm of the Rearhook and the other variety, save for one possible example of the first, may be a hint that part of the unit had returned to the east of England in the wake of the Boudiccan revolt.

The remaining Colchester Derivatives do little to define which varieties in particular should have been used at Wroxeter during its occupation by *Legio XX*. They show, as might be expected, some selection from those in use in the south-west, and this is emphasised by two Aesica types whose spring-fixing system also belongs to the west, mainly the lands to the east of the lower Severn valley. Perhaps the answer to the problem at Wroxeter is that one of the commonest types of Colchester Derivative found in the Marches and generally in the western parts of England, and very well represented at Wroxeter, should be considered to have started earlier than seems to have been the case on present evidence. There is one example without the usual foot-knob from a context which should be earlier than AD 75 at The Lunt (Hobley 1969, 107, fig 19, 1), and there is another with a rudimentary knob from Wroxeter (Shrewsbury, Rowleys House Museum, X 1). The general type, including decorated variants, is generally late first century into the early second, perhaps AD 125–50. If Wroxeter was finally given up by the military between AD 85 and 90, it is inconceivable that some at least had not been made and worn for perhaps up to ten years before then.

One note of caution must be sounded. The early brooches represent the introduction into new areas of the brooch-wearing habits of the south-east. By the time that Wroxeter ceased to be a maintained fortress there was a thriving extra-mural settlement and this should have included craftsmen who had their eyes on the main chance. This was not only to sell the soldiery whatever could be supplied, but also to sell to the local populace. By the time the army withdrew, the wearing of brooches was undoubtedly more frequently to be seen amongst local people. Such a market could be supplied from types developed locally and which were to remain in production for some time, and this must undoubtedly prevent a clear picture from emerging of what is specific to *Legio XX* itself.

While this is a convenient way of explaining away the absence of readily identifiable brooches, there is a disturbingly heavy emphasis on the date-range which suits *Legio XIV* rather than any later period. In other words, if something like 71% of the brooches in Table 4.1 can be assigned to that unit for a period of occupation hardly more than 10 years long, even a doubling of the rest seems very light for a unit which maintained the fortress for something like 20 to 25 years. Although it could be argued that the main part of *Legio XX* was away for long periods, there was at least a minimum of ten years when

it should be expected that the bulk of the legion overwintered at Wroxeter. Yet the numbers of brooches seem to be a poor reflection of this, and the paucity is even more marked if only the collection from inside the fortress is examined. After all, no matter what the civilian population was wearing, the brooch remained a required item for the Roman soldier for scores of years to come.

Catalogue of brooches

Colchester Derivatives

All are of copper alloy unless otherwise stated.

(Fig 4.4)

1 The spring is held by a variant of the Polden Hill method: the axis bar through the spring passes through a pierced plate at the end of each wing. The variation is that the chord is held by a short forward-facing hook. Each wing is plain except for a buried moulding at the end. The bow has a flat back and a curved front. There is a slight step across the top and on the head of the bow is a narrow tapering zone marked by a groove down each side and with a series of cross-cuts down the middle. Just before the two side grooves meet, the zone is stopped by three cross-grooves. The rest of the bow is plain and tapers to a pointed foot. The catch-plate has a piercing the shape of which is reminiscent of a celtic harp.

The immediate associations of this brooch are far from certain. The way in which the ornament is stopped across the bottom by a series of grooves is distinctive and is also found in a small group of almost equally anomalous brooches (eg Rawes 1981, 65, fig 8, 1) found in and around Cirencester. However, these brooches have a plate with two holes behind the head of the bow to which the spring-fixing arrangement is fitted, a system more commonly found in the east of England. The dating of the group is not fixed, but the size of the pieces would suit a date fairly early in the range *c* AD 75–125. However, the forward-facing hook should help to provide some idea of dating, as it is found on a few brooches other than the Colchester such as the early Headstud types (see Brooch 4) but is practically unknown on what is, to all intents and purposes, an ordinary Polden Hill system (but see the discussion after Brooch 3). The date must be early and related to the demise of the parent itself, which had largely passed out of use by AD 55. The present brooch should have been made in the decade AD 50–60 and could have survived in use for another twenty years which would bring its deposition up to *c* AD 70–80. *84/281*, sf5168 Military

2 The spring was held as that in Brooch 1, except the hook is rearward-facing. The end of each wing was bent round to hold the axis bar. Each wing

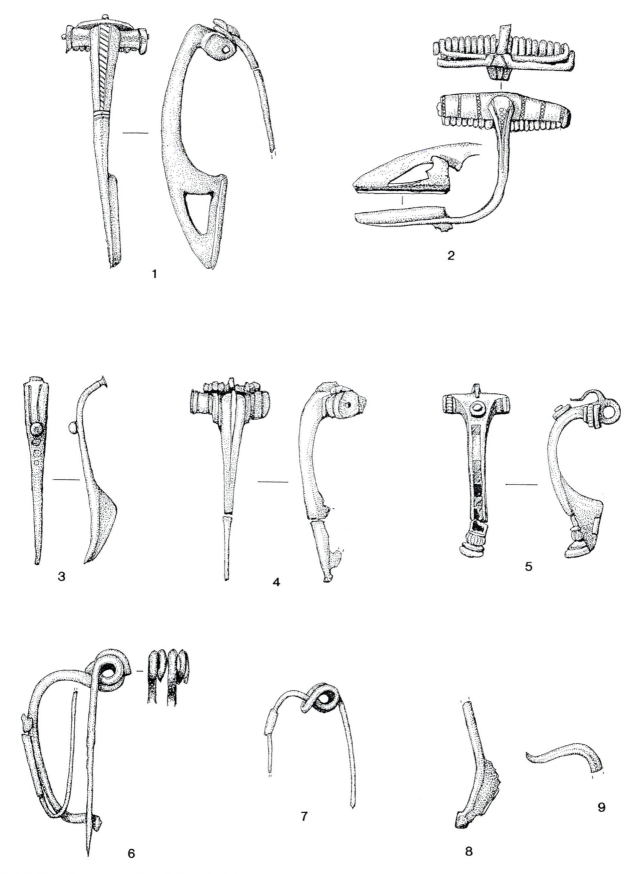

Fig 4.4 Brooches: copper alloy, 1–9; scale 1:1

has three equi-spaced buried bead-rows. The bow is very narrow and tapers to a pointed foot. The only ornament is a short length of sunken bead-row. The head of the bow finishes about halfway up the wings, but its line is continued as a pair of grooves which meet in a point at the end of the wide hook. The catch-plate is damaged, but has a piercing shaped like an asymmetrical heart. *91/86*, sf 3845 Early Civil

3   The wings and the pin-fixing arrangement are missing. The top of the bow has a tenon-like projection whose end has been burred over by beating. This feature once fitted into a separately made set of wings. The profile of the bow has a reflex curve and there is a boss riveted through at the point of inflection. Above the boss is a narrow groove down each side of the bow with a wider one down the centre. The upper bow is flat and thin in section with straight sides, the lower has a rounded front and tapers to what looks like the remains of a peg on which might have been mounted a separately made foot-knob. The catch-plate is solid and has lost its return. *80/61*, sf3843 Not phased

Brooch 2 is typical of a group found in the lower Severn Valley and running along the general zone through which the Fosse Way runs from Alcester to Derby (Mackreth 1985, 281–3, fig 123, 2). The chief characteristic of the design as represented here is the extreme thinness of the bow and the evidence for forging shown by the way in which the wings are bent back and not cast in that position. There would seem to be a relationship with a batch of brooches to which Brooch 3 belongs in which the final item is assembled from separately made components. The evidence that any of the Brooch 2 type had been so made is limited to one found at Alcester (Mackreth 1994, 162–3, fig 75, 4). The style developed into a version of the common Dolphin Brooch found all over western Britain (eg Metchley, Wroxeter, Hildyard Collection 194). Although cast, the very thin sections suggest that the type had evolved out of sheet-metal prototypes and this is to some extent borne out by the very wide and thin hooks for the chord of the spring. Dating for brooches like 2 is difficult. The one from Derby (above) came from a context which was only first or second century, and the rest from potentially useful contexts are, as yet, unpublished (excavations at Cirencester, Beckford, and Lechlade).

However, there are two pointers to an early date. The first is a brooch from Cirencester (unpublished) which is similar to the present piece, but with a wider bow. The wings, however, have the same section and an unbeaded version of the decoration. The hook is also wide, but faces forward like that of Brooch 1 here. The other pointer is a brooch from Baginton which, as far as ornament is concerned, lies between the present style and the full

Dolphin. It came from a context dating to before *c* AD 75 (Hobley 1973, 66, fig 19, 6). The present piece can only be related typologically to these specimens, but the absence of any descendants other than the proto-Dolphin types strongly suggests that Brooch 2 ought to date to before *c* AD 65.

Excluding the sprung-pin, Brooch 3 started out as at least three separate pieces and it may be easier in the first instance to consider the dating of this kind of manufacture rather than take the associations of the design first. A brooch from Oakengates (unpublished) has resemblances with the overall shape of Brooch 2 and its separate wings, hook, and bow were joined by a rivet. On that site, it should date to before *c* AD 75. Another comes from Metchley (to be published) and the same closing date would be appropriate, and a third comes from Broxtowe, another site which would be difficult to carry beyond AD 70–5. But the present specimen looks forward: the recurve, the boss, and the ornament on the straight-sided upper bow occur in a more elaborate form on a brooch from Wall, also made in two pieces (Gould 1967, 15, fig 7, 5) whose context was Hadrianic-Antonine in which it should have been residual. Another design on the same form of brooch was dated AD 60–1 to *c* 150 at Colchester (Crummy 1983, 13, fig 9, 66). Enamelling in red with a reserved metal wavy line typical of the first century occurs on two brooches which may be said to mark the beginning of the main sequence. On these, the boss has been replaced by enamelled spots. They come from Wroxeter, but are old discoveries (Rowleys House Museum, Shrewsbury, X24, X27) and another, also from Wroxeter, shows the development going one way towards the Dolphin (Webster and Daniels 1970, 18–9 fig 4, no 3) while the mainstream was towards a variant of the Trumpet and had come into being by AD 100–20 (Cotton 1947, 145, fig 8, 3). In the present instance it is better to associate this typological stage with a date before *c* AD 75–85 at the latest.

4   The spring is held in the Polden Hill manner (see Brooch 1), the chord being held by a rearward-facing hook. The right wing is covered in corrosion, the left has a buried moulding at each end. Rising from the wings and clasping the head of the bow is a curved moulding. The hook behind the head is carried over the top as a ridge and dies out so that in profile there is a skeuomorph of the Colchester's hook. Under the corrosion can be seen traces of beading on one of the wing mouldings, the right hand masking moulding and the ridge down the bow. The head of the bow is wide, but narrows after a short distance to taper to the pointed foot which has a small forward projection. The catch-plate is incomplete but shows that there had been a single large piercing reminiscent of that on Brooch 1. *92/70*, sf3312 Military

The origins of the design lie in a small group with exceptionally thin wings and bow (eg Mackreth 1986, 221, fig 141, 1) which appear to have derived from a type made in separate pieces and assembled using a rivet (eg Oakengates excavations, D Brown, in prep). The present design belongs basically to the lower Severn Valley and the lands to the immediate west. It does, however, occur on military sites running up through Warwickshire (Alcester, Mackreth 1994, 162–3, fig 75,5 and 6; Metchley to be published; Baginton, The Lunt, Hobley 1973, 66, fig 19, 7) with one outlier at Little Chester, Derby (Mackreth 1985, 281–3, fig 123, 2). Although dating is limited, it is useful, the example from The Lunt is earlier than *c* AD 75 and one from Baginton is dated AD 50–5 (Clifford 1961, 173, fig 31, 5). Another from Nettleton was first century (Wedlake 1982, 123–5, fig 52, 36A). Two come from elsewhere at Wroxeter, one in a Flavian context (Atkinson 1942, 204, fig 36, H105), and the other was a chance find (Hildyard Collection, 194). Both have been included in Table 4.1. This type should be seen as the precursor of the standard Dolphin dating to the later first century and the earlier second (eg in plain form, Mackreth 1985, 283–5, fig 123, 5), and which has lost the piercings in the catch-plate. In the present case there is no difficulty in assigning the brooch to the second half of the military phases at Wroxeter and, in turn, its stratified position within the fortress provides a welcome additional confirmation of the typological development of the whole series.

Headstud

(Fig. 4.4)

5　The spring is missing. It had been mounted on a loop behind the head of the bow by means of a tube of rolled sheet copper alloy through loop and coils, which would have been secured by a wire mounted in each end and carried up to form a loop whose waist was bound by a collar. The chord of the spring passed under the forward-facing hook on the head of the bow. Each wing is curved to seat the spring and each has on the front two narrow mouldings with a broad, rounded one between, all three stepping forward to the bow. On the head of this is a circular stud with a sunken *annulus* on top. The hook just reaches the stud. The bow has a flat front and squared sides. Below the stud is a single recess for enamels. The colours of these are not clear; there could be beds of red, or another colour alternating with a third, giving a two-colour effect. Or, and perhaps more likely, the red itself alternated. The bow tapers slightly to a quadruple moulded foot, the upper pair are separated from the lower, which splay

out, by a flute. The second moulding from the top is beaded. The catch-plate is solid. *84/71*, sf3584 Military

The essential form of the type, although without the stud, had evolved early as two examples from Alcester (Mackreth 1994, 164–5, fig 27, 34) and Catterick (unpublished) show. These have a Colchester spring system, separately made moulded foot-knobs and, more important, the stepped wings to be seen on common Headstud types as well on as the present specimen. Enamelling in a continuous strip is uncommon: the usual early style has a series of rectangular cells and these occur most often with hinged-pins. However, single long recesses occur most often with sprung-pins, as here. Dating evidence is hard to come by, but one from Wall was dated *c* AD 60–85 (Gould 1964, 43, fig 18, 3), and that should apply here as the more common patterns had come into being before the end of the first century. The roots of the design represented by Brooch 5 are in the lands along the Fosse Way and to the south.

La Tène II

(Fig 4.4)

6　The integral spring had four coils and an internal chord. The bow is narrow and has a nearly circular section. The lower part bends back to form the back of the catch-plate with the return and then turned up to run along the front face of the bow to end in a clasp round the bow. *50/12*, sf699 Military

7　The upper bow and spring of a brooch precisely similar to the last; the remains of the clasp are corroded in position. *80/111*, sf3492 Not phased

The writer has noted examples of this type from the following sites: *Ariconium* (Hull and Hawkes 1987, 182, 8717), Chester, two examples (unpublished), Cirencester (Corinium Museum, C200), Colchester (Hawkes and Hull 1947, 308, pl 89, 1), London (British Museum 1958, 95, fig 99), Mildenhall, Suffolk, two examples (Jewry Wall Museum, Leicester, 836 1951; 208), Richborough, three examples, one with pre-Flavian pottery (Bushe-Fox 1949, 107, pl 25, 1 and 2; Cunliffe 1968, 77, pl 26, 1), Sea Mills, Bristol (Nazareth House Museum), Stockton, Wiltshire (Salisbury Museum, 85.46), and *Verulamium* (Wheeler and Wheeler 1936, 203, fig 42). Others in addition were recorded by Hull (Hull and Hawkes 1987, 180–2, pls S2–3), but the only extra site is Caister by Norwich. Most of these sites have an undoubted early Roman presence and many of them are forts. The type, as far as can be seen, comes in with the army and is not in use when the army moves north in the AD 70s. The brooch type belongs to Feugère *type* 3b1 and he assigns its manufacture to the period Tiberius to Vespasian (Feugère 1985, 196). The large number found at Augst gives a good idea of the *floruit*, for, despite the relatively high residual factor in the collections, most run from Augustan–Tiberian to the second half of the first century, and most appear to be entering the ground in Claudian times and the remainder of the first century. So few examples can be dated to the late first and early second century and later that a closing date of *c* AD 75 would be in order, and it may be that this is a little late (Riha 1979, 56–7, Tafn, 1–2, 11–84).

8   Iron. The spring system is as that for Brooches 6 and 7. The lower bow with the catch-plate is missing. The bow has a slightly lenticular section and, at the break, shows signs of bending back. On the top of the bow is a thickening which may be all that is left of the collar to be expected on this type, although it cannot be guaranteed that it does so. The variations in both bow profile and the position of the collar are well illustrated by Hull and Hawkes (1987, pls S2–S3). Though the actual proof that this brooch is of this type is wanting, the balance of probabilities is that it does and on that basis has been included on Table 4.1. *90/125*, sf5132 Not phased

Drahtfibel Derivatives

(Fig 4.4)

9   Two fragments which make up the bow; the upturn at the top once continued into a spring system like those on the previous three brooches. The profile of the round-sectioned bow has a marked reflex so that the foot points forward slightly and carries on it a foot-knob which runs back under the base of the damaged catch-plate. *98/87*, sf5909 Early civil

(Fig 4.5)

10   A brooch very like the last, but without the foot-knob. *60/21*, sf939 Not phased

The distinctive features are the recurve in the profile of the bow and the foot-knob. Two others have been published from Wroxeter, one dated, apparently, by the Claudian pottery found with it (Kenyon 1940, 222, fig 15, 2), the other possibly belonging to the last quarter of the first century (Bushe-Fox 1916, 22, pl 15, 1). None appears at Saalburg or Zugmantel, sites which began in the mid 80s (Böhme 1972, 9–10). One was found at Newstead and should not be much later than AD 80–5 (Curle 1917, 231–2, fig 1, 1). The analysis carried out by Rieckhoff of the brooches from Hüfingen and assemblages from other sites concluded that this style of *Drahtfibel* Derivative had ceased to be made by the early years of Domitian (Rieckhoff 1975, Taf 13). Several appear at Hofheim (Ritterling 1913, Taf 9, 169–75) and this should, in broad terms, point to a date before *c* AD 75 (Schönberger 1969, 152–3). The single specimen illustrated from Augst was found with Claudian pottery (Riha 1979, 61, Taf 3, 127). Perhaps a limit of *c* AD 75 would suit the available information, with one or two carrying on, as the example from Newstead shows.

Langton Down

11   The separately made spring is housed in a sheet metal case formed from flanges cast along the top and bottom edges of the wings. One end plate survives of what had been a completely enclosed cylinder. Along the front is a line of rocker-arm ornament. The bow is thin, mainly straight-sided, but with a slight taper to the foot which is damaged. The front of the bow has three vertical mouldings. The catch-plate is almost a trapezium in shape and has a circular hole. *35/19*, sf1228 Military

Both the profile and the poverty of detail on this brooch show that it is late in the sequence. The type was entering Britain in quantity before the conquest as the numbers in the King Harry Lane cemetery, St Albans, show (Stead and Rigby 1989). Very few of the specimens recorded by the writer are dated, but of the 300 so far gathered, only the following come from sites which seem to have no good pre-Roman occupation: Fishbourne, a Nertomarus, period 1, AD 43–*c* 75 (Cunliffe 1971, 100, fig 38, 28), Kingsholm, one ordinary and one a *Nertomarus, Margidunum* (Todd 1969, 88, fig 37, 4), Richborough, a Nertomarus (Cunliffe 1968, 84, pl 29, 40). All four sites are noted for early Roman activity. It may be significant that three of these brooches belong to the one main type to carry a name and it may be that its manufacturing period lasted almost up to the conquest. The message seems clear: none of the main series was being made by AD 43. Turning to the present example, parallels are few: Bromham, Bedfordshire (Tilson 1973, 56, fig 28, 280), Canterbury (Frere *et al* 1982, 121, fig 59, 6), Piddington, Northamptonshire (excavations, Friendship-Taylor in prep), Wakerley, Northamptonshire (Jackson and Ambrose 1978, 216, fig 56, 1). All four sites have pre-Roman occupation. The Wroxeter brooch should date to after the Conquest as not only is there no pre-Roman occupation known, but the brooch is well outside the normal distribution area of the Langton Down. That said, it should also be obvious that the brooch could only have arrived at Wroxeter in the earliest years of the site.

'Aucissa'/Hod Hill types

All have rolled-over heads for the axis bar of the hinged-pin.

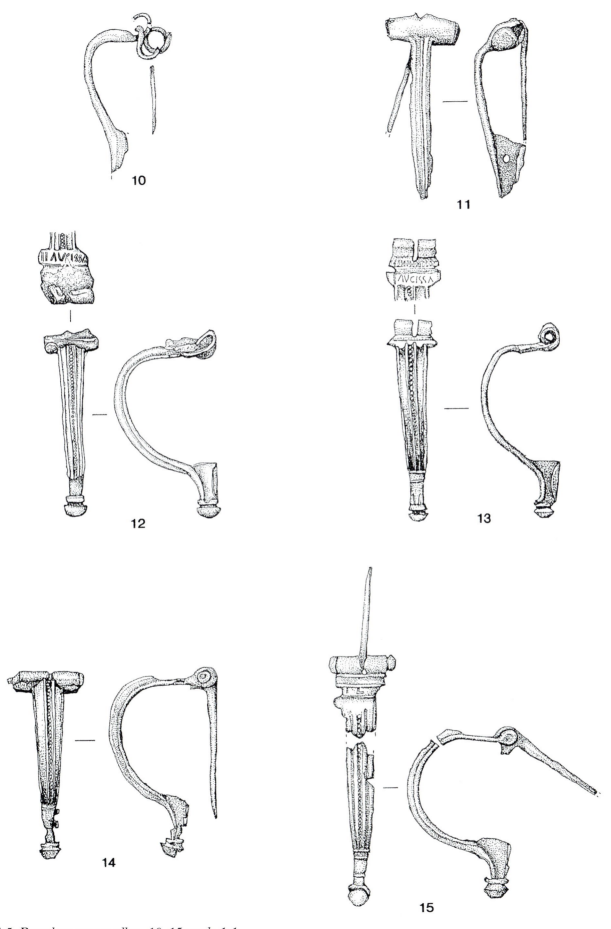

Fig 4.5 Brooches: copper alloy, 10–15; scale 1:1

(Fig 4.5)

12 The head-plate is partially concealed under corrosion products. There is a central flute with a small cut-out at each end. Next to the bow is a panel inscribed AVCISSA preceded by two vertical ridges. The name is intended to be read from the top. The upper, or main part, of the bow has a ridge down each side and a buried bead-row down the middle of the swelled front. The lower bow is chamfered below two cross-grooves at the bottom of the main section. The foot-knob was made separately and then sweated or brazed on, and has a moulding round the top. *91/286*, sf6253 Military

13 As no 12, with the same style of inscription, only this time there is a sunken bead-row next to the rolled-over head. The grooves across the base of the upper bow have moved to form a separate element. *81/15*, sf1753 Military

14 As no 12 with a bead-row next to the rolled-over head and with indistinct traces of a name which is not necessarily 'Aucissa'. The knobs on the ends of the axis bar survive. *84/91*, sf3844 Military

15 Basically complete with pin and knobs on the head, corrosion hides some details, especially of the head which has the usual three-part layout, but with no inscription: the space where it would have been is too narrow. *95/1*, sf3156 Not phased

(Fig 4.6)

16 An uninscribed 'Aucissa'-type brooch whose axis bar in the head still retains the knob at each end. The mouldings on the head are indistinct and the plate itself gets wider towards the pin. The rest is the same as in Brooch 13. *39/20*, sf1235 Military

17 As no 16, including the axis bar knobs of the last but with a better defined head-plate. The part next to the pin has a sunken bead-row and is wider than the part next to the bow. The surface here is covered with corrosion products. *92/74*, sf3878 Military

18 Covered in corrosion and with the lower bow and catch-plate missing, one knob survives and the layout of the head shows that there is no name. *92/18*, sf3252 Baths construction

19 Again covered in corrosion, both knobs are missing, but these were apparently lost in antiquity as one end at least of the axis bar had been bent to prevent it from coming out. The pin is short, possibly due to wear and the profile of the bow is much more rounded than is usual suggesting that it had been bent to accommodate the shortened pin. *95/1*, sf3160 Not phased

20 As no 13, but with no inscription and with indistinct mouldings on the head-plate; there is apparently no other change. *34/37*, sf828 Military

21 Almost precisely like Brooch 13, but with an inscription reading TARRA and with what may be a leaf-stop at each end. *77/9*, sf1712 Military

All nine are standard 'Aucissa' types, except for the one inscribed TARRA which otherwise is the same as the others. The minor differences such as whether there is a name or not, or whether the head is essentially straight-sided as opposed to widening out towards the pin, are unimportant in this context as the collection is consistent enough for the major constraints to apply to all. These are the date range and the distribution. Both are linked: no 'Aucissa' of the latest style, such as these, has yet been published from a pre-conquest context in Britain. They arrive in some numbers with the army and its attendants, and the distribution in Britain shows that they are largely confined to the area south-east of the Fosse Way. It is only military sites of reasonably certain early date in the area between Wales and the Fosse Way that have any. As the descendant of the general 'Aucissa' type, the Hod Hill, arrives in Britain in even greater numbers, it should be taken that the parent types had almost certainly ceased to be made by *c* AD 40. Therefore, those which did arrive in Britain were, in effect, survivors-in-use and a limit of *c* AD 60 would cover most of the specimens found, although Feugère notes one from York (1985, 328, fig 46). One of the oddities of the present assemblage is the fact that most of the 'Aucissa' types were recovered from securely stratified military deposits. The name TARRA has been recorded by the writer only once elsewhere in Britain: Wickford, Essex. Wroxeter has also yielded ATGIVIOS (Atkinson 1942, 199, pl 47, H22), and again this has only been noted once more in the country: Colchester (Niblett 1985, 116, fig 75, 25). These, and other, names serve as a reminder that uninscribed brooches need not have come from the same workshop which used the name AVCISSA. The uniformity which covers all these brooches may hide a host of separate workshops.

(Fig 4.7)

22 A diminutive brooch only 22mm from top to bottom. The form is precisely that of the 'Aucissa' type except for a circular hole through the head-plate next to the bow. The foot-knob is lost and corrosion hides much detail, but it can be seen that the section of the bow is typical of the full-sized 'Aucissa'. *98/188*, sf6303 Early civil

Small brooches are rare and this may reflect the fact that they are more vulnerable to corrosion and less easy to spot during excavation. However, the distinctive feature here is the hole through the head-plate, and this has not been recorded on any other from Britain, and is excessively uncommon on the continent. The hole should not be confused with the open 'eyes' found on some early brooches in the Alesia-'Aucissa' sequence as two examples published by Feugère show. On these, there is a staple mounted in the hole and it would seem that one at least was used to anchor a chain, and this

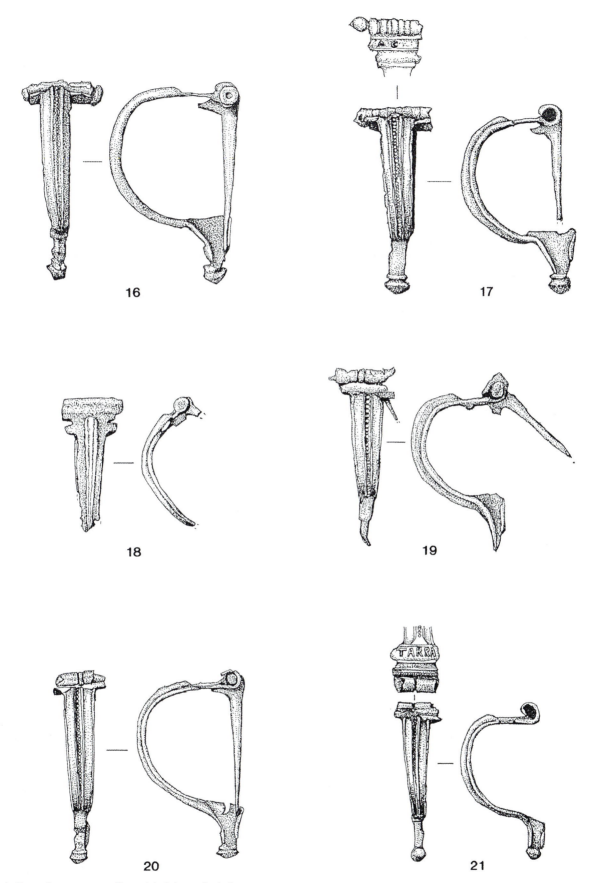

Fig 4.6 Brooches: copper alloy, 16–21; scale 1:1

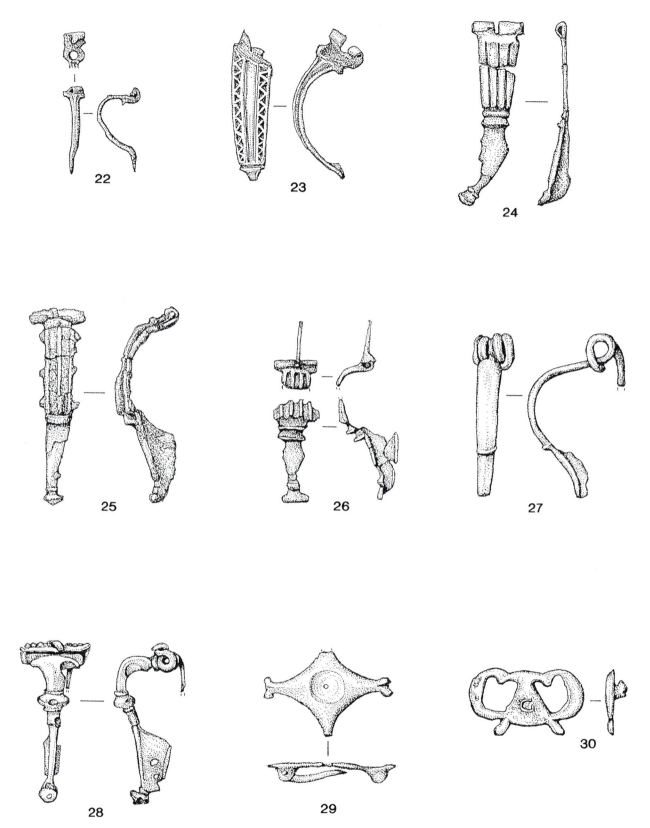

Fig 4.7 Brooches: copper alloy, 22–30; scale 1:1

is probably true of the other, but the drawing shows the chain looped round the bow (Feugère 1985, 313–4, pl 119, 1519, 1524). There is no reason to think that the date range should be different from that of the standard form in Britain: from the conquest to *c* AD 60.

23   The head-plate is reduced to a feature hardly wider than the bow, a slightly concave edge on each side and a ridge at top and bottom. The upper bow has a wide and deep flute down the centre bordered by minor single mouldings. Along each edge of the bow is a series of triangular

recesses which create a reserved chevron effect. At the top of the lower bow is a bridging section, which repeats the head-plate design, to the lower bow which is plain and breaks off before the foot-knob. *98/173*, sf6149 Baths construction

On the face of things, this should be an example of the transition from the 'Aucissa' to the Hod Hill as the central flute is to be found on a main alternative variety of the parent stock, and the simplicity of the head-plate may well show that this is precisely what this brooch is. However, it also shows that the 'Aucissa' was not the only brooch of the family of Alesia Derivatives which had an influence on the early styles of the Hod Hill. Never as numerous as the 'Aucissa'-type bow section, these fluted patterns develop *pari passu* and the same date range can be applied.

24 The head-plate has disappeared. The upper bow has five mouldings separated by flutes, and at its base are two cross-mouldings. The lower bow splays out for a short distance and then tapers to the simple two-part foot-knob leaving a point on each side. No trace survives of the punched-dot ornament generally to be found on the lower bow. *TR AJ L4 (68)* K M Kenyon's excavations 1952–3

25 The upper bow has a pronounced cross-moulding top and bottom. Between is a panel with three vertical mouldings separated by wide flutes. Projecting on each side again are three small pseudo-bosses. The lower bow has a flat front face and tapers to a foot-knob. *98/116*, sf6998 Early civil

26 The upper bow is damaged but displays the remains of five vertical mouldings with the beginning of a wing on one of the lower corners. Beneath this arrangement are two marked cross-mouldings. The lower bow is shaped like that of Brooch 24, but has a median arris and the remains of a silvery finish. The foot-knob has a broad lower member. *85.2/246*, sf3597 Military

The Hod Hill is almost the type *par excellence* of the army of conquest. The numbers found at the eponymous site (Brailsford 1962) are, as the assemblage closes at *c* AD 50 (Richmond 1968, 117–9), enough to show that the type arrived in quantity and fully developed and this should guarantee that the parent types had ceased to be made some years before then. None of these examples displays any particular points of special interest. They all reveal, one way or another, their relationship with the 'Aucissa'. The distribution of the type in Britain is enough to show that the bulk surviving in use were entering the ground between AD 60 and AD 70, very few finding their way into the new lands taken into the province in the early 70s. All should date to before AD 70–5 at the latest. None belongs to the strain which continued to be made on the continent to the end of the first century and was to lead to new types.

Unclassified

(Fig 4.7)

27 The spring arrangement is the same as that on the La Tène II brooches above. The bow is broad and tapers towards the foot, now missing. The profile has a marked recurve with a small cross-moulding at the point of inflection. Above this, the bow has a swelled front, but is flat below. *R/57* Not phased

If it were not for its pin-fixing arrangement, this brooch could be seen as being related to a group of which the Augenfibel is a principal member. This aspect shows in the profile, the cross-moulding at the base of the upper bow, and the generally broad bow in relation to its thickness. Wroxeter has produced one other, this time with a sunken bead-row down the middle of the upper bow, another feature of the group (Rowleys House Museum, Shrewsbury, B330). The writer has not recorded any other example than these two in Britain. None is given by Almgren (1923), Böhme (1972), van Buchem (1941), Dollfus (1975), Ettlinger (1973), Feugère (1985), Haalebos (1986), Jobst (1975), Kovrig (1937), Lerat (1956; 1957), Rieckhoff (1975), Rieckhoff-Pauli (1977), Riha (1979), or Ritterling (1913). With such a background, any detailed comment is inadvisable; if the associations suggested suit the general Augenfibel range, then all that can be said is that both this and the item in Rowleys House Museum should be assigned to the military phase of Wroxeter's history.

Pannonian

(Fig 4.7)

28 The Colchester spring arrangement is mounted behind a plain bar separated from the upper bow by a marked waist. The hook for the chord is short and flat. The upper bow is a flattened trumpet in shape. The knop is made up of three mouldings, the central one being prominent. The lower bow is narrow and tapers to the foot-knob which is below the catch-plate, and fully moulded with a version of the knop, except for the bottom element which is reduced to a boss. The catch-plate has a small circular hole. *16/109*, sf264 Not phased

The Pannonian is a well recognised type, yet is uncommon in Britain. The distribution here is of interest: hardly any occur outside the deepest south-east of England and they are basically unknown in the zone through which the Fosse Way runs. Hildyard (1945) sought to derive the Trumpet type from this, but no further evidence has come forward to suggest that this should be the case. One other example has been assigned to Wroxeter (Hattatt 1985, 64–6, fig 27, 334), but the form of the catch-plate points more towards the continent than any example found in Britain. However that may be, the basic message is that the Pannonian arrived early in small numbers and failed to travel as far as Hod Hill. As Wroxeter is one of the very few assured finds in advance of the Fosse Way, it should have passed out of use in these islands by *c* AD 60, or AD 65 to give a maximum limit.

Plate

(Fig 4.7)

29 The pin is hinged. The plate is flat and shaped as a concave-sided lozenge. The ends of the long axis are bifurcated with a tapering groove between. The ends of the short axis are largely missing, but there is no sign of the dividing groove which suggests that they had been different. In the centre is a sunken circular area with a poorly beaded ridge near the outer edge. In the centre is a hole for a stud, now missing. The front of the brooch has traces of a silvered finish. *Field surface find*, sf2088

30 The pin was hinged. The centre of the plate is flat and formed into a triangle with a curved bottom edge and with a crude pelta on top. On each side is a voided area bounded by an element with slight relief in a rough C form, with an outward-facing tail at the base. *78/57*, sf1870 Military

Brooch 29, although a chance find along with pieces of samian forms 18 and 24/25, is included here as it must have arrived while the fortress was in full occupation. It belongs to a well established family whose traits lead to various diverse forms but whose main connecting features are the bifurcated ends or, more generally, the circular recess with the poorly beaded ridge. Although not frequent, examples are numerous enough for the overall distribution to be a possible guide to its dating. Hardly any occur along the Fosse Way, and Wroxeter and Kingsholm for the present are the only sites in advance of that known to the writer to have produced them. Of the two, Kingsholm should be counted as having formed part of the Fosse system. Hod Hill produced three of the family (Brailsford 1962, 12, fig 11, F2, F3, F5) and this shows that it was firmly established by *c* AD 50 (Richmond 1968, 117–9), and its distribution suggests that it was passing out of use in the following decade and had effectively done so by AD 60–5. Another specimen from Wroxeter was found on the forum site (Atkinson 1942, 208, fig 36, H86) and the present example may have come from the area of the early cemetery.

Brooch 30 does not have such wide associations and, indeed, is hard to relate to any group.

There is a pattern which has a circle in the centre and then loops on each side rather like the present ones which can be interpreted as possibly Dolphin-shaped: Bannaventa (unpublished), and through these to a set of variations (eg Riha 1979, 198, Taf 66, 1700–2, 1706), but there seems to be no adequate dating.

Penannular

(not illus)

31 The ring has a circular section. Each terminal was turned up at right angles to the plane of the ring, possibly as a coil, but the remains are too poorly preserved for this to be certain. *78/10*, sf1795 Military

Little can be said about this specimen: coiled terminals belong to the first century AD and may run back into the first century BC.

Text written 1988

The bronze *dioscurus*
by Martin Henig and Graham Webster

The *dioscurus*, a youthful male figure of Castor or Pollux, totally nude apart from his distinguishing *pileus*, is portrayed with his left leg advanced and his right set well back, the foot just off the ground. His arms are bent at the elbows with his hands across the chest. These are not well preserved but a piercing behind the right hand must have held an attribute. Despite some corrosion and consequent loss of detail, the quality of the workmanship is at once apparent (Fig 4.8 and front and back cover). The modelling of the body is very assured, as can be seen in the naturalism of the chest muscles in front. Furthermore, when the figurine is viewed from the rear, the curving ridge of the spine from the nape of the neck down to the well-rounded buttocks is in total sympathy with the torsion of the body. Facial details lack clarity, largely because of corrosion, but the fringe of hair which projects from below the *pileus* is attractively rendered as a convex ridge extending from temple to temple. The texture of the locks was suggested by means of fine vertical striations. The *pileus* is pierced and a ring with open terminals passes through it, presumably for a length of chain. It is not certain whether the piercing is an original feature and certainly the workmanship of the ring is rather crude. The figure is mounted on a low and narrow base, probably once longer than it now is, but subsequently snapped and on the left side also filed just beyond the foot. This base was originally soldered on to a slightly curving surface, probably also of bronze. Height (including base) 65mm; base length 29 mm; base width 8 mm; base thickness 1.5mm. *178*, sf6309

Fig 4.8 The dioscurus

Further examples are known from Colchester (Colchester Museum Inventory no 4677 1924, unpublished, P Garrard and A Savage pers comm), and Tongeren, Belgium (de Boe 1981). A fourth bronze, from St John's Lane, Canterbury (Henig *et al* 1987) suggests that the *dioscurus* may have been holding a torch, reminding us of a Tarentine terracotta of Hellenistic date showing the *dioskouroi* taking part in a torch race (Petersen 1900, 19 no 28, Abb vii, 2).

We have previously concluded (Henig *et al* 1987) that these bronzes relate to the late Classical–early Hellenistic traditions of central-southern Italy, and this has been supported by authorities in this field (J Boardman and S Haynes pers comm). They are certainly more 'classical' and stylish than the common run of Roman bronzes and, taken by themselves, the possibility of their being heirlooms was suggested. However, we now think it possible, in the light of the fact that four near-identical bronzes have been found in the north-west provinces, that a late Classical bronze was being copied. It was perhaps in Campania, at a later date, during the late first century BC or in the first century AD, that these bronzes found favour with soldiers in the Imperial Army.

We should not be surprised to find the Romans cherishing heirlooms or copies of ancient works of Greek and Etruscan art. Often these were small portable items capable of serving the use for which they were originally intended, such as the Ptolemaic intaglio, also from Wroxeter (below). Others were old objects, perhaps selected for some sentimental reason or to serve as amulets. A full study of Roman uses of, and attitudes to, the past, in domestic situations as

well as in public life, in the provinces as in Rome, would explain a great deal about how and why Roman art developed along the lines it did. It is apposite to note a Roman period figurine, evidently a furniture-mount, from *Piolenc* (Vaucluse) showing a *dioscurus* running beside his horse (Rolland 1965, 71 no 107). Such a bronze is ultimately dependent on classical conceptions such as the bronzes under discussion. More to the point, because certainly provincial, is a bronze mount showing a nude male figure from Trier; although described as *einen treverischen Krieger mit Helm und Lanze* (AdT 1984, 240, no 93), his headgear looks like a *pileus* and it is not impossible that the spear was at least derived from a torch. Did yet another Italo-Greek bronze lie behind this curious little fitting?

Catalogue of military equipment
by Graham Webster

Armour

(Fig 4.9)

1 Fragment of a strip of *lorica segmentata* with two rivets, one edge has a slight curve. *72/19*, sf1933

2 Small fragment of a laminated strip from a *lorica segmentata* with half a bronze hinge. *80/192*, sf5017

3 Slightly tapered and rounded end of a strip from a *lorica segmentata* with two bronze rivets for a buckle and a hook (cf Robinson 1975, figs 176–80). *14/37*, sf1172

4 Small fragment from the end of a strip from a *lorica segmentata* with three bronze studs (cf no 3). *70/33*, sf1854

5 Part of a cuirass-plate with a badly corroded bronze circular rosette decoration (cf no 7 below, Robinson 1975, figs 176 and 178). *73/25*, sf1682

6 Fragment of an iron strip from a *lorica segmentata* with a hook attached (cf Robinson 1975, fig 178). *9/30*, sf1329

7 Rosette mount from a *lorica segmentata* (cf Ulbert 1969, Taf 29, nos 1–7). *83/52*, sf3590

8 Part of a cuirass hinge (for a complete pair see Brailsford 1962, A72, fig 3; cf also Ulbert 1969, Taf 33, no 1; Ulbert 1959, Taf 61, nos 15–20; Crummy 1983, 130, fig 145; Webster 1981, fig 28, no 22; Niblett 1985, fig 64, no 30). *87/101*, sf5048

9 Pair of folded cuirass hinges (cf no 8). *98/100*, sf5713

10 Cuirass hook (cf Ulbert 1969, Taf 34, nos 45–52; Ulbert 1959, Taf 17, nos 1–6, Taf 61, nos 71–73; Richmond 1968, fig 56, nos 13 and 14; Ulbert 1970, Taf 3, nos 71–73; Webster 1981, fig 7; Robinson 1975, fig 183). *50/40*, sf1547

11 Cuirass hook from a *lorica segmentata* (cf no 10). *81/15*, sf1759

12 Cuirass hook from a *lorica segmentata* (cf nos 10 and 11). *3/20*, sf112

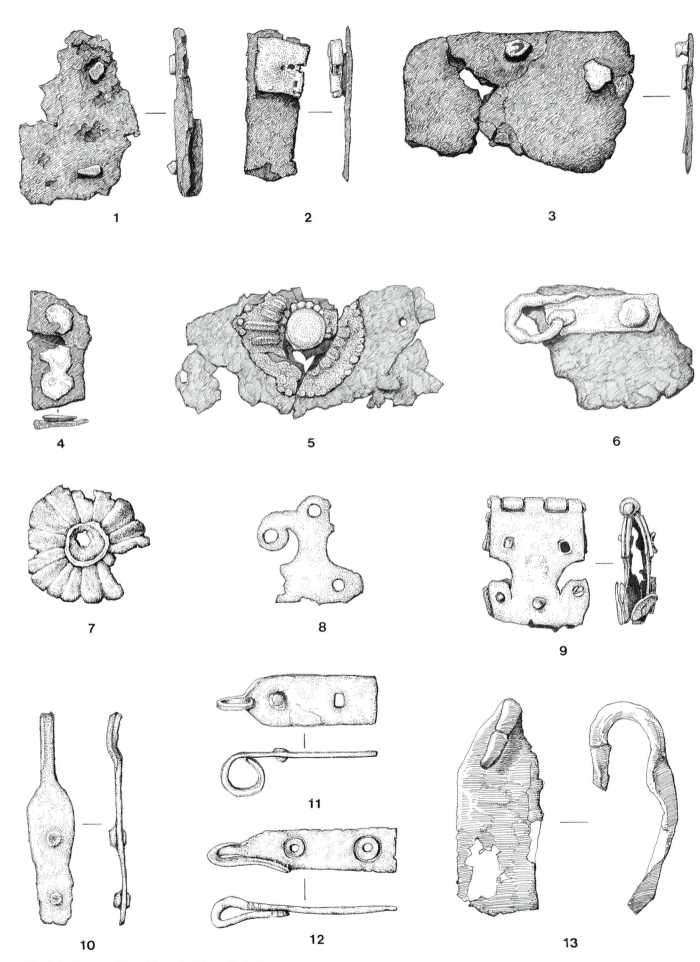

Fig 4.9 Copper alloy objects 1–13; scale 1:1

13 Cuirass hook from a *lorica segmentata* (cf nos 10 and 12). *78/11*, sf1829

(Fig 4.10)

14 Fragment with the shape of a cuirass hook, but attachment rivets missing. *90/87*, sf5379
15 Iron cuirass hook, not uncommon in this metal (cf Ulbert 1969, Taf 52, nos 7–9). *90/125*, sf5132
16 Part of a cuirass hook (cf nos 10–14). *90/56*, sf4829
17 Object with the appearance of a cuirass hook, similar to nos 10–15, but with the hook unusually waisted and flattened out. Possibly an unfinished hook, discarded from the *fabrica*. *78/33*, sf1812

Buckles of copper alloy, iron, and bone

(Fig 4.10)

18 Small strap D-buckle from a *lorica segmentata* of common type (cf Down 1978, no 19, fig 10.30; Webster 1949, no 2, fig 4, Broxstowe (Campion 1938, pl ivd); von Groller 1901, Taf xvii; Ulbert 1959, Taf 17, nos 8–11; Ulbert 1969, Taf 33, nos 23–38; Robinson 1975, fig 188). *83/519*, sf4335
19 Buckle similar to no 18, with hinged strap-plate. *81/42*, sf1819
20 Buckle similar to no 18, with a hinge and attached strap-plates with two large headed-rivets. *26/11*
21 Small thin buckle-strap plate, 12mm wide, with a single rivet (cf Ulbert 1969, Taf 34, no 40. *92/61*, sf3596
22 Cuirass strap buckle-plate with a hinge and rounded end. *6/28*, sf43
23 Cuirass buckle with plate and a small attached hinge strap plate with a single large-headed rivet and a separate asymmetric rivet hole, similar to no 18. *39/11*, sf522
24 Part of a cuirass hinge-plate and D-buckle (cf no 18). *81/15*, sf1752
25 a) Pair of cuirass hinge-plates and D-buckle, from a *lorica segmentata*, cf no 18, (Ulbert 1959, Taf 17, nos 1–144), and Hod Hill (Richmond 1968, fig 56, nos 10–12).
   b) Cuirass hinge-plate, similar to nos 18 and 19. *49/163*, sf2093
26 Buckle plate from a *lorica segmentata* with traces of gilding. *85/42*, sf3020
27 Small D-buckle from a *lorica segmentata* (cf nos 18–20; Ulbert 1969, Taf 33, nos 23–38). *35/14*, sf504
28 Small D-buckle from a *lorica segmentata* (cf nos 18–20). *70/16*, sf1503
29 Cuirass D-buckle, slightly larger than 28 (cf nos 18–20, 27 and 28). *78/10*, sf1835
30 Cuirass D-buckle (cf nos 18, 20–22, 27–29). *6/73*, sf1157
31 Small cuirass buckle-plate, 13 x *c* 25mm, with a fragment of the buckle. It had two rivet heads circumscribed around each of which are two circles. Often the plate has only one rivet head (cf no 21). *80/177*, sf4618
32 Large D-buckle of common form (cf Bushe-Fox 1949, no 71, pl xxxiii; Behrens 1918, no 1, Abb 8; Ulbert 1959, Taf 17, nos 32 and 33; Ulbert 1969, Taf 26, nos 1 and 2. *90/169*, sf5447

(Fig 4.11)

33 Large D-buckle, identical to no 32. *84/91*, sf3852
34 Large D-buckle, similar in form but slightly smaller than nos 32 and 33. *84/379*, sf5797
35 Small D-buckle, similar to nos 27 and 28.
36 Small buckle of the square incurved form with corner knobs and traces of tinning (cf Bushe-Fox 1914, pl xxi, no 5; Cunliffe 1968, pl xxxv, nos 97 and 98; Curle 1911, pl xcii, no 1; Rieckhoff 1975, Taf xi, no 41; Davies and Spratling 1976, 127, fig 4, no 10; Schönberger 1978, Taf 21, nos B138 and B139; for a remarkable example in bone see Crummy 1983, fig 144, no 4176). *22/19*, sf360
37 Small buckle, similar to no 36. *82/503*, sf4334
38 Large and much corroded square buckle with out-turned knobbed terminals, similar to nos 30 and 31. Part of the belt plate is still attached. *90/128*, sf5148
39 Similar buckle to nos 36 and 37, but with an extra pair of knobs.
40 Small bone D-buckle copying the bronze form. These bone objects are quite common on military sites, especially from *Vindonissa* (Stephen Greep has drawn my attention to the unpublished catalogue of material in the Vindonissa Museum, Brugg, by Christoph Unz). There are two forms, the simple bow and the more sophisticated one with curved back ends, of which this is an example. *80/176*, sf4615
41 Bone buckle tongue of *fleur-de-lys* pattern, an elaboration of a normal type in bronze (cf Crummy 1983, fig 144, no 4176; Down 1978, fig 10.30, no 151). *81/15*, sf1796
42 Buckle tongue with medial horn-like projections (cf Ulbert 1969, Taf 26, nos 13–17; Frere 1984a, fig 13, no 96). *41/6*, sf1358
43 Silver decorated buckle tongue from a belt (cf no 37, Ulbert 1969, Taf 26, nos 14–19), one from Mainz was still attached to the buckle (Behrens 1918, Abb 8, no 1). *72/53*, sf1750
44 Tongue of a large buckle. *12/32*, sf304
45 Buckle tongue. *98/93*, sf5859
46 Buckle plate for a thin strap or belt (16mm wide) decorated with concentric circles and slightly raised moulding, and a pair of very finely punched opposed scrolls. There are traces of silvering. It was attached to the leather by four rivets with washers at the back. These plates were usually decorated in niello and this is an unusual, probably early, pattern and has similarities with examples from *Vindonissa* (unpublished). *81/55*, sf1868

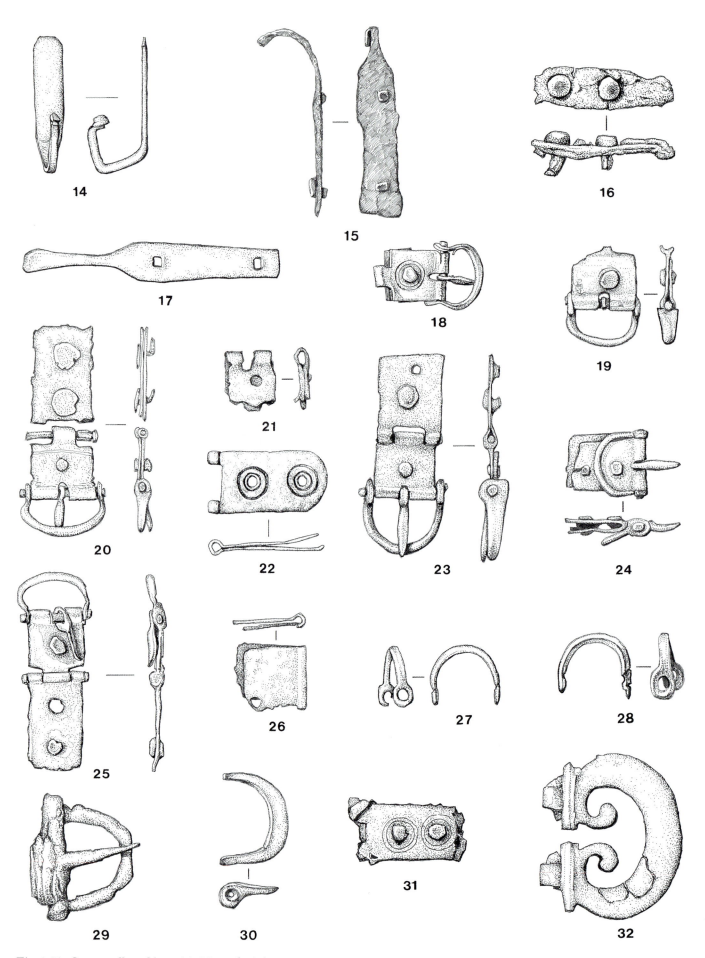

Fig 4.10 Copper alloy objects 14–32; scale 1:1

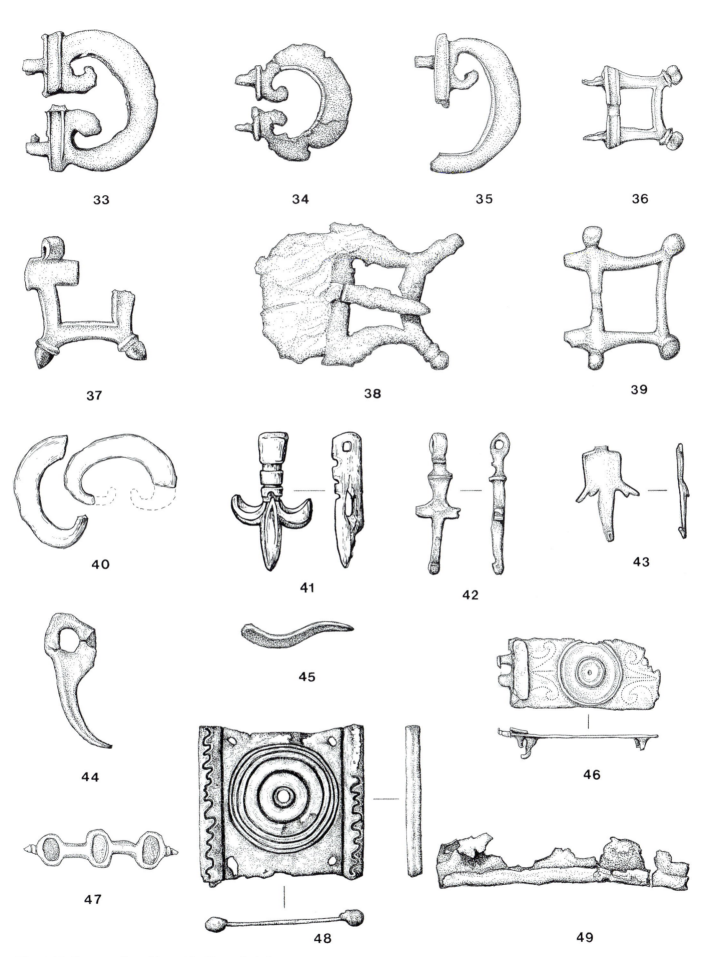

Fig 4.11 Copper alloy objects 33–49; scale 1:1

47 Three small joined oval mounts filled with blue enamel which formed part of the decoration of an officer's belt plate, the surrounding parts are unusually inlaid with millefiori. A complete example has been found at *Carnuntum* (Swoboda 1964, Taf xxiv, 100), and a small one from Osterburken has a bear on a rope in the centre (Schumacher 1929, Taf vi, no 310; Oldenstein 1976, Taf 63, no 813). Other examples include two from Wroxeter (Webster 1960, 98, no 258), and another found by P Barker (inf K Pretty), others from Caerleon (Nash-Williams 1932, fig 33, nos 24, 25, and 39), including a fragment from the *principia* (Boon 1970, 56 and fig 17, no 2) and a complete example at the Caerleon Museum (ibid, fig 17, but unnumbered), from Corbridge (Bishop and Dore 1988, fig 84, no 146), and Newstead (Curle 1911, pl lxxvii, no 8 and pl lxxxix, no 33). The type had a long life, presumably as highly prized objects, and examples are found on Antonine sites, as shown by those published by Oldenstein (1976, Taf 63, 195–6, nos 809–815, and fn 663 with further references). *16/25*, sf25

48 Square belt-plate with a wavy line decoration on each edge and a centre rivet hole for a mount which has been detached, surrounded by incised circles (cf a very similar example in Brailsford 1962, fig 5, A121). *52/5*, sf534

49 Folded edge of a large belt-plate. *41/6*, sf1363

(Fig 4.12)

50 Small apron or belt terminal which appears to be complete, and, although of the normal pattern, is of unusual small size. The surface is slightly corroded but appears to be plain, another unusual feature. It is a little smaller, but very similar to an example from *Cunetio*, Mildenhall, Wiltshire (Annable 1976, 176 and fig 1.1; Griffiths 1982, 53–4, no 9). *98/189*, sf6215

51 Long thin mount from a belt or apron with leaf decoration in niello (cf Ulbert 1970, Taf 23, nos 351 and 353; Ulbert 1959, Taf 62, nos 1–6).

52 Apron mount with a rounded terminal similar to the one from Hod Hill (Richmond 1968, fig 56, no 15). The surface corrosion has removed all traces of decoration. *40/14*, sf556

53 Part of a junction loop with double rivets. Many examples could be quoted (including Hurst 1985, fig 11, no 7; Bushe-Fox 1914, pl xxi, fig 2; Curle 1911, pl lxxii). *80/22*, sf1895

54 Part of a junction loop of unusually small size with traces of niello decoration in the clip.

55 Junction loop with traces of niello decoration on the loop, an unusual feature on this type of equipment, but as on no 54.

56 Junction loop with plain surfaces (cf Ritterling 1913, Taf xiii for the main types). *91/46*, sf3321

57 Broad hook, 12mm wide, with a narrow attachment 5.5mm wide. It is probably from a junction loop (cf nos 55 and 56). *10/25*, sf1328

58 Part of a mount from a junction loop. A similar fragment but with part of the loop still attached has been published from Rheingönheim (Ulbert 1969, Taf 35, no 8). *68/1*, sf1341

59 Part of a junction loop with two rivet holes central to each part (cf Ritterling 1913, Taf xiii, no 11). *90/184*, sf5766

60 Part of a junction loop with two rows of double rivets, similar to examples from Gloucester and elsewhere (Hurst 1985, fig 11, no 7); Wroxeter (Webster 1960, no 247); Newstead (Curle 1911, pl lxxii, nos 1, 2, 5, 6, 7, and 11); Wroxeter (Bushe-Fox 1914, pl xxi, fig 2, no 48). *91/77*, sf3788

61 An unusual type of junction loop with a slightly tapering attachment strip decorated with horizontal moulding, it has a single rivet hole. *78/5*, sf1630

62 Strap terminal with a toggle, the use of which has been demonstrated by Bishop (1988, 101, no 8, and table 10).

63 Small baldric toggle with faint traces of niello inlay and a seating for a detached mount, similar to examples from Hofheim (Ritterling 1913, Taf xiii, nos 16–19), Newstead (Curle 1911, pl lxxiv), *Verulamium* (Webster 1960, no 208), London (ibid, no 150). *80/123*, sf4591

64 Fragment from a hinged fastener from which the decorated disc has become detached. It is similar to examples from Hod Hill (Brailsford 1962, A98), *Camulodunum* (Hawkes and Hull 1947, pl xiii, no 3), and *Vindonissa* (unpublished). It is basically in the form of a cloak fastener, but the hinge suggests it was attached to a belt with the disc or knobs (cf Brailsford 1962, A97), fastening into a button hole in a leather belt or apron. *42/7*, sf539

Pendants

(Fig 4.12)

65 Small, plain oval pendant with a hanging loop and a small knobbed terminal. It has a small centre hole and two more at a higher level near the edges presumably for hanging small secondary pendants. It is a common type with similar examples from Colchester (Crummy 1983, fig 157, no 4241), *Novaesium* (Lehner 1904, Taf xxxiv, nos 22 and 36), South Shields (Allason-Jones and Miket 1984, cat no 3.661). *84/341*, sf6176

(Fig 4.13)

66 Small lunate pendant with conjoined knobbed terminals and an indication of a hook for attachment. It was probably part of a larger pendant. Such composite pendants are well exemplified by a remarkable find of an officer's belt from Tokije (Mano-Zisi 1957, Tab xiv and xvii). There is also an example from *Vindonissa* (Unz 1972, Abb 5, no

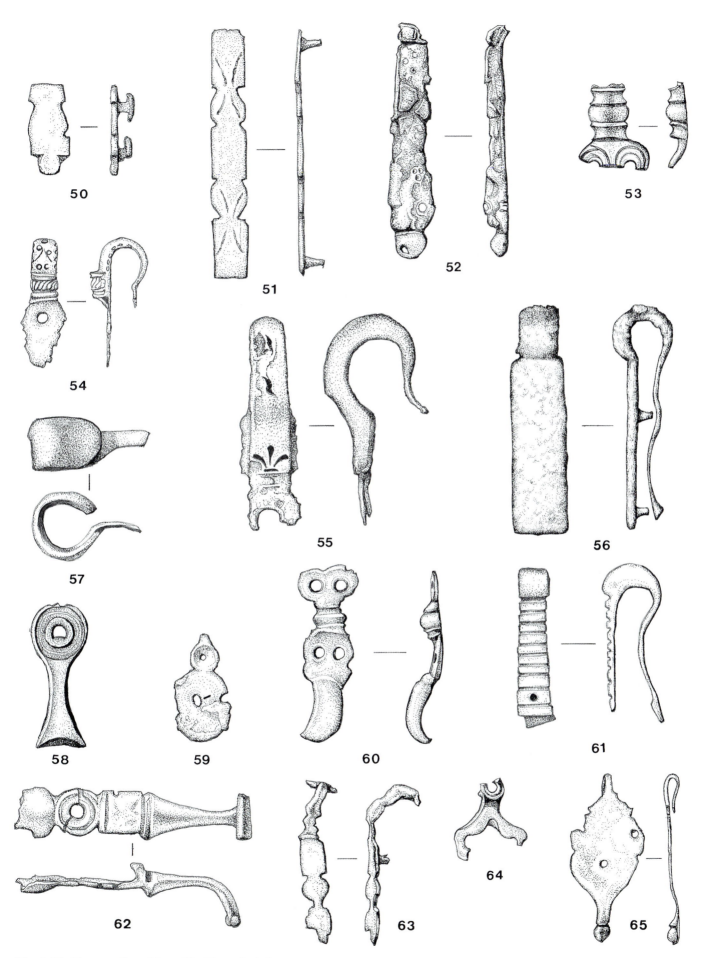

Fig 4.12 Copper alloy objects 50–65; scale 1:1

48), and a very fine one from Caerleon with three subsidiary pendants (Zienkiewicz 1986, 181, fig 60, no 132). But the commonest form is Bishop's type G (1988, figs 47 and 48). Although all these have lost their secondary pendants, the central rivet holes indicate their original presence. *6/-*, sf157

67 Pendant of a common form (Bishop 1988, type 1) with a scroll and leaf pattern in niello.

68 Small lunate pendant with a simple pattern of punched scroll decoration. It is of Bishop type 9 and has a suspension hole for a small circular pendant to hang within the lunate horns. The closest parallel is an apparently plain one from *Cunetio*, Wiltshire (Griffiths 1982, no 8, pl xiv).

69 Base of a leaf pendant with a small terminal knob and incised radial lines. It is a debased variant of Bishop type 4. A residual military piece in a post-military deposit. *90/56*, sf4827

70 Pendant of an unusual type divided into two parts by a medial moulding. The upper half has two lobes with two semi-circular openings and incised lines round the edges and a wolf's head decoration on the suspension loop, similar to three examples from Kingsholm, Gloucester (Hurst 1985, fig 11, nos 1 and 3, and pl 8c). The lower half is semi-circular with a lunate opening and wavy line edges, and a small round terminal. *73/2*, sf1600

71 Lower part of a pendant very similar to no 70, but with a heavier terminal knob and very faint punched decoration round the edge and an incised line forming a heart shape, but slightly off-centre. The upper half could be no 73, as they were found close together, but there is no fit between the two pieces. *78/33*, sf1820

72 Upper part of a small pendant with a finely moulded wolf-head terminal, almost identical with no 70, but with a more delicate punched decoration around the edge (cf also no 71, which may have been the lower half). *78/11*, sf1801

73 Lunate terminal, any decoration on which has been totally obscured by corrosion. There is a suspension hole at the top of the inner lunate for a small secondary pendant (cf no 68). *92/71*, sf3834

74 Heart-shaped pendant with four incised concentric circles and a small central hole is indicative of a circular mount having been fixed there. A semi-circular extension at the base has a serrated edge and a pair of lunate openings. It belongs to Bishop's type 3c (Bishop 1988, fig 44). *80/169*, sf4492

75 Part of a pendant with vine scroll decoration in niello and belongs to Bishop type 11 (Bishop 1988, fig 43), and is very similar to one from Wiesbadan (Ritterling 1915, Taf x, no 22). *90/224*, sf6203

76 Small leaf-shaped pendant with a plain surface and slightly knobbed terminal of common type (cf Crummy 1983, no 4241, fig 157; Ulbert 1959, Taf 51, no 12). *98/143*, sf5994

77 Small leaf pendant which would have been hung from a larger one (cf no 76, and Down 1978, fig 10.49 (published upside down)). For the general type, often with a knobbed terminal, see one from Risstissen (Ulbert 1959, Taf 63, no 15) *Novaesium* (Lehner 1904, Taf xxxiv, nos 387 and 388), Colchester (Crummy 1983, fig 157, no 4241). *81/15*, sf1817

Copper alloy mounts, fasteners, studs and pins

(Fig 4.13)

78 Small phallic mount with a thick tang for fastening to a leather belt or strap and would be added for its apotropaic power. Such amulets are very common on military sites, including Wall, Staffordshire (Webster 1957, nos 4255 and 4257), Ausrüstung (Oldenstein 1976, Taf 42, no 410), and South Shields (Allason-Jones and Miket 1984, 188, cat 3.588). *90/51*, sf5252

79 An unusual form of cloak-fastener with a bust instead of a disc (for the usual type see Wild 1970). The bust is supported by an acanthus leaf with a central concave roundel. As the ears are covered by the hair, it seems probable that a female is represented. The only other example of a bust type cloak-fastener known to Wild is one from Chester and listed by him (ibid, 54, no 54). This has a similar hair style, but the triangular shank projects in the opposite direction. *70/51*, sf1743

(Fig 4.14)

80 Small cloak-fastener with a circular face which appears to be plain except for a deep recess in the centre for holding enamel or a coloured stone or glass (Wild 1970, type VIIIb). *98/61*, sf5451

81 Small cloak-fastener probably plain. Corrosion has removed any trace of decoration, but it may have been silvered, see Wild's type VIII (Wild 1970, fig 2): they are very common in the first century AD at *Vindonissa* (ibid, 143). *92/65*, sf3769

82 Flat circular mount, 47mm diam, with four tangs with washers on the back. Corrosion has removed any traces of decoration, but there are four circular holes, diam 5mm, probably for showing the coloured material onto which the mount was attached. This is an unusual piece, anticipating the open-work of later equipment (cf Oldenstein 1976, Taf 51, no 6001, Taf 88, nos 1138–40). *42/6*, sf528

83 Circular plain mount, *c* 19mm diam, with a serrated edge and raised cordon and a tang 9mm long. A similar edging on a plain mount is seen on a Colchester example (Crummy 1983, fig 151, no 4204). *84/106*, sf4747

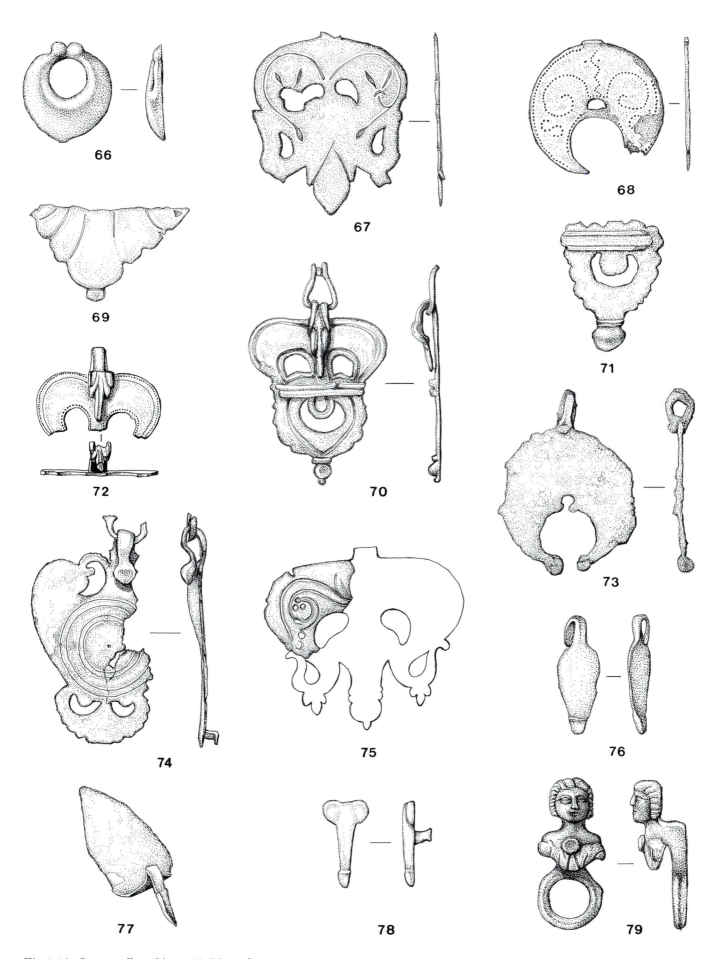

Fig 4.13 Copper alloy objects 66–79; scale 1:1

84 Small fragment of a moulded circular mount, *c* 35mm diam. *91/233*, sf5638

85 Circular plain mount, *c* 19mm diam, with a serrated edge and raised cordon and a tang 9mm long. A similar edging on a plain mount is seen on a Colchester example (Crummy 1983, fig 151, no 4204). *84/106*, sf4747

86 Slightly dome-headed pin with traces of gilding and a long thick tang, 18mm long, for nailing to wood for decoration. They are common on military sites, as at Hofheim (Ritterling 1913, Taf xv, nos 39–41 and 63–5). *7/56*, sf1282

87 One of five domed and flanged studs, between 18 and 20mm diam, the corrosion products have obscured any decoration (cf no 86). *6/46*, sf169

88 Small plain flat circular stud, 11mm diam. *41/6*, sf1344

89 Plain circular stud, very slightly domed and the edge turned down. It has the stump of a centre tang (cf Ulbert 1965, Taf 29, nos 27–34). *90/204*, sf5782

90 Circular mount, 27mm diam, with a dished centre with a rivet hole for a detached mount. *78/11*, sf1797

91 Small slightly domed stud, 8mm diam, with a cross in niello. *90/106*, sf5227

92 Flat circular stud, 15mm diam, decorated with typical crosslet pattern in niello (cf no 85). There is also a cross pattern on the back. The bent tang shows that the thickness of the leather belt or strap, was *c* 3–4mm. *72/71*, sf1799

93 Slightly domed stud, 13mm diam, decorated with niello in the typical crosslet pattern with a thick tang (cf nos 91, 92 and 96). sf5729

94 Flat circular stud, 14mm diam, decorated with a crosslet pattern of crudely executed niello inlay (cf nos 91–3 and 95). *92/22*, sf3370

95 Small circular stud, the flat face decorated with niello with a six-armed crosslet in the centre and crude circles with dotted centres round the edges, probably a degeneration of the stylised floral, pattern, as on a Hod Hill stud (Brailsford 1962, A126, fig 5). *98/173*, sf6310

96 Flat circular stud, 17mm diam, decorated with niello in the form of a crosslet of leaves. It is a fine example of a well known type and the nearest parallels are from Colchester (Crummy 1983, fig 144, no 4175 and fig 151, no 4218). *81/15*, sf1769

97 Flat circular stud, 20mm diam, with a crosslet pattern of leaves in niello. *73/44*, sf1731

98 Flat circular stud, 19mm diam, with an incised figure-of-eight pattern (cf Ritterling 1913, Taf xii, nos 35, 36, 41, and 42). *75/2*, sf1607

99 Circular decorated stud with quarter panels filled with blue and green enamel. Studs of this type are rare (cf Schumacher 1929, Taf vi, nos 44 and 45): there is a domed example from Chichester (Down and Rule 1971, fig 3.18). They presumably have become detached from belt mounts.

100 Part of a plain circular mount, 24mm diam, with three rivets for attachment, two of which survive. Any decoration has been removed by corrosion, but there are traces of silvering. *42/8*, sf532

101 Sheath for a *dolabra*, used for carrying the axe slung from the hip (cf Brailsford 1962, fig 5, A 137; Ulbert 1969, Taf 31, no 191; Crummy 1983, fig 148, no 4198; Down 1978, fig 10.31, no 55; Webster 1960, no 243; Curle 1911, 279, fig 39 illustrates two complete examples from *Vindonissa*). *3/20*, sf114

102 Sheath for a *dolabra* (cf no 101). *7/60*, sf1298

(Fig 4.15)

103 Sheath for a *dolabra* (cf nos 101 and 102). *84/339*, sf5381

104 Part of a *dolabra* sheath, similar to nos 101–103.

105 Part of a *dolabra* sheath with an unusually long attachment arm.

106 Round-headed pin with 15mm long tang for decorating a wooden object. These pins are very common on military sites (cf Ulbert 1969, Taf 44, nos 1–6; Ulbert 1959, Taf 24, no 10). *84/335*, sf5530

107 Pin with a round head with a tang 20mm long, similar to no 106. *98/149*, sf6037

108 Large bronze pin with a round head, 8mm diam, and slightly square, bent shank 36mm long. *80/189*, sf4911

109 Dome-headed tack with a tang 15mm long. *98/145*, sf6025

110 Large dome-shaped headed pin with a 32mm tang suitable for decorating a wooden box or vehicle. *12/44*, sf698

111 Part of a round-headed pin similar to no 107. *92/61*, sf3604

112 Small, flat, circular headed tack with a tang 8mm long. *84/330*, sf5831

113 Long shanked silver pin with a head in the shape of an insect with folded wings, possibly representing a bee, a symbol of richness and plenty. *80/197*, sf4898

114 Moulded ring, 32mm diam, attached to a staple for attachment to a wooden post or similar feature. *92/63*, sf3812

115 Plain ring, 22mm diam. *80/207*, sf5158

116 Moulded ring, 28mm outer diam. These vary in size but are quite common and probably from a scabbard (cf Ulbert 1969, Taf 41, nos 1 and 2; Ulbert 1959, Taf 26, nos 14–20). *84/49*, sf3362

117 Small bronze loop or split pin (cf Frere 1972, no 81, fig 81). *51/18*, sf764

118 Heavy piece of bronze, 2mm thick, with a rounded end. It is difficult to identify such a fragment, it could be part of a box fitting similar to one from Risstissen (Ulbert 1970, Taf 25, no 405). *80/207*, sf5093

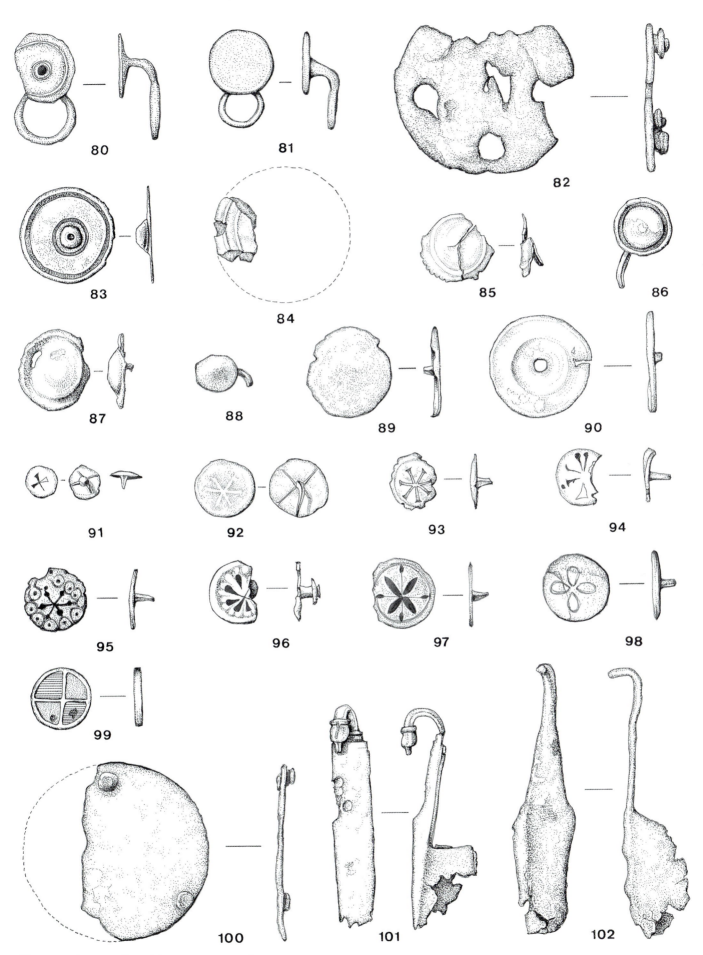

Fig 4.14 Copper alloy objects 80–102; scale 1:1

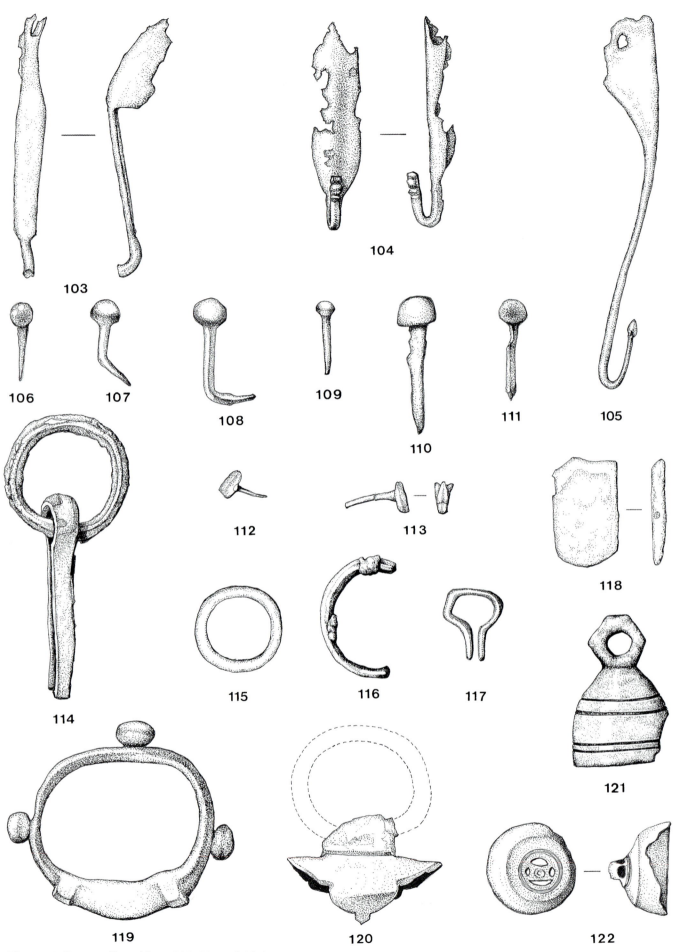

Fig 4.15 Copper alloy objects 103–22; scale 1:1

119 Three knobbed terret of a very common form (MacGregor 1976, nos 78, 80, 86, 88, 89, 92–5, 103, 108). *90/163*, sf5331

120 Harness ring on a masked secondary ring similar to a complete example also from Wroxeter (cf Atkinson 1942, pl 48A, no 6; cf also Webster 1960, fig 8, no 252), and another from *Margidunum* (ibid, no 175). It is a type which had a long life and has been found on the Antonine sites Kastell Feldberg (*ORL*, 20, Taf vi, nos 4 and 6), and Saalburg (Jacobi 1897, Taf lix, nos 1–3). This object was found in the 1952–3 excavations in Insula 9 by K M Kenyon, but escaped inclusion in the report Kenyon 1976. *TR 1 E/PA 5.12*, sf106

121 Small bell of typical military form decorated with incised lines and with a pentagonal suspension loop for attachment to harness and an internal V-shaped iron loop for suspending the clapper (cf Ulbert 1959, Taf 52, no 4). *74/5*, sf1603

122 Small bell with a vented loop top to which is fixed a small piece of iron for suspension and internally for hanging the clapper. Alternatively, a ring could have been attached through the opposed vents. *7/55*, sf13303

(Fig 4.16)

123 Part of a harness bell, of which there are two types, one with four 'corners' at the base and the other, like this, fully rounded with a base diameter of 53mm. It compares with examples from Hod Hill (Brailsford 1962, fig 2, 2 and A33); Hofheim (Ritterling 1913, Taf liv, no 14), Colchester (Crummy 1983, fig 143, no 4165), Risstissen (Ulbert 1970, Taf 26, no 414), Aislingen (Ulbert 1959, Taf 52, no 4), Oberstimm (Ulbert 1978, Taf 30, B438). *91/108*, sf4509

124 Silvered scabbard mount decorated with notches on the front face and moulded ring loops. This is a type associated with the *gladius* scabbard and is found widely, cf examples from Mainz (Behrens 1918, Abb 6, 175), *Novaesium* (Lehner 1904, Taf xxx, no 36), Broxtowe (Webster 1960, fig 5, no 7), Colchester (Crummy 1983, 130–2, no 4194, fig 148). *78/9*, sf1811

125 Thin scabbard mount strip with moulded decoration (cf no 126). *83/66*, sf3856

126 Bronze strip with moulded decoration for a scabbard mount (cf nos 124 and 125). *72/53*, sf1652

127 Staff terminal with a deeply cut spiral groove with the appearance of a screw thread. This unusual pattern derived from the horizontal groove is often found on heads of pins, as on some examples from South Shields (Allason-Jones and Miket 1984, cat 2.523 and 2.534). On the last of these the grooves are at an inclined angle, suggesting the spiral and, of course, the twisted bracelet. *80/192*, sf4984

128 Ferrule, decorated with raised cordons, with an enlarged terminal to provide seating for a coloured stone or similar decoration. *50/83*, sf1710

129 Decorated heads of an iron key of *fleur-de-lys* pattern, often found on early military sites, including Colchester (Crummy 1983, 126, no 4161, fig 142); South Shields (Allason-Jones and Miket 1984, 144–5, cat 3.346); Richborough (Bushe-Fox 1949, 125, pl xxxiv, no 86, in bronze); Wroxeter (Bushe-Fox 1913a, pl x, 29, fig 1, nos 1 and 2); Saalburg (Jacobi 1897, Taf xliv, 477, no 19, fig 76, nos 43–5 and 479). *98/2*, sf4118

130 Bronze collar for attachment to a staff, 18mm diam. *35/15*, sf525

131 Conical hollowed lead weight which could have been a plumb-bob, or attached to a steelyard. It has traces of a collar, possibly for a wood plate into which a hook was attached. The classical examples are a little different from modern ones (British Museum 1929, fig 175; 1951, fig 40, no 11). *84/82*, sf3865

132 Sharp conical point with a moulded base and a long flat shank, slightly bent. The object has the appearance of a plumb-bob for suspension on a *groma* (cf no 131). *97/206*, sf6154

133 Small thick bronze flat ring with a medial line round the circumference. Such rings are fairly common (cf Ulbert 1969, Taf 44, no 39), and it may be part of a composite knife handle. *41/6*, sf526

134 Small casket key-ring with a T-shaped ward. It is unusual to find this type of key and ring, but it is common as a normal lever key (Wheeler 1930, pl xxx, nos 9–12), similar examples have been published from Colchester (Crummy 1983, fig 89, nos 2168 and 2170). *50/31*, sf1578

135 Iron ring with a large oval bezel for an intaglio. *14/37*, sf1156

136 Two pieces of the rim of a large bowl or platter with an ovolo decoration imitating silver (cf La Baume 1964, Abb 87 and 291). A good bronze example is a skillet from Faversham in the British Museum (British Museum 1951, fig 18, no 5). There are crude examples of a bowl with this type of decoration (cf Willers 1907, Abb 41, no 9; Boesterd 1956, no 198 A, pl xv and ix). It could also possibly be an edge from a mirror. *70/77*, sf1675

137 Circular decorated cup-shaped terminals for disguising an iron nail-head of which there are examples for decorating vehicles and furniture. They are common on military sites, including Wall (Webster 1960, 94, 227 fig 8), Colchester (Crummy 1983, fig 204, nos 4640 and 4650), *Novaesium* (Lehner 1904, Taf xxx, nos 39 and 41), Zugmentel (*ORL*, 8, Taf XIII, nos 67, 68 and 71). *90/-*, sf3268

138 Plain bronze domed mask for a large nail head, it was filled with lead for secure attachment. *70/16*, sf1511

139 Circular casing or terminal possibly from a knife handle, or like an example from *Verulamium*, as a lead weight (Frere 1972, 124, fig 37, no 90). *30/53*, sf1898

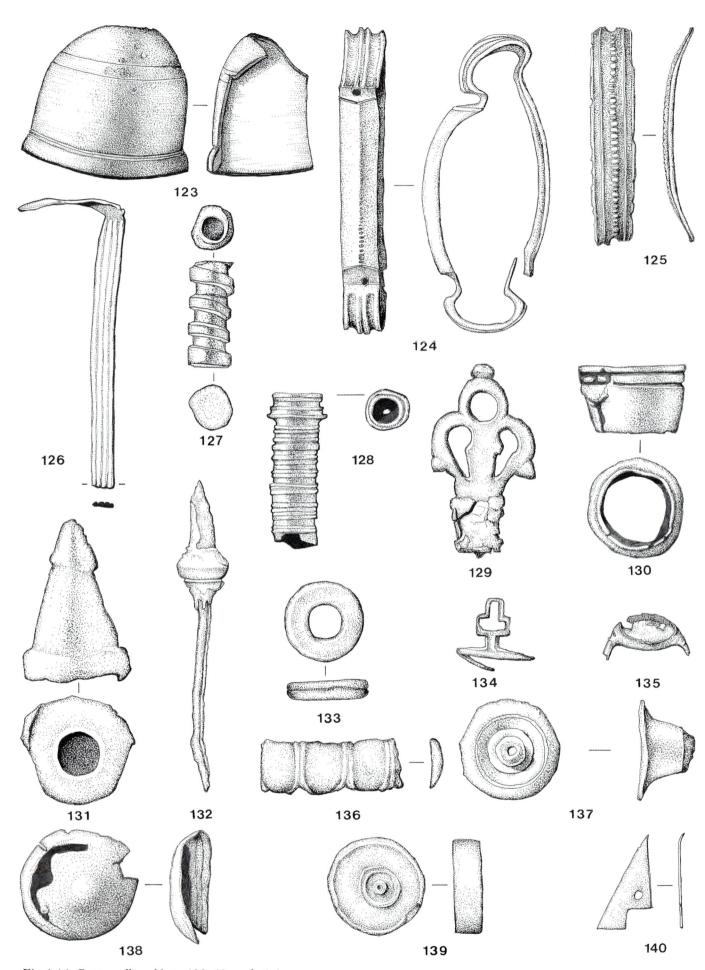

Fig 4.16 Copper alloy objects 123–40; scale 1:1

140 Thin bronze sheet carefully cut to a shape with a small rivet hole. It is probably a piece of inlay or decoration for a wood box. *50/12*, sf705

(Fig 4.17)

141 Heavy staff terminal with an internal hollow for fastening a decorative top or coloured stone or glass. Similar examples are from Hofheim (Ritterling 1913, Taf xvi, no 29, 35 and 37, cf no 128). *77/9*, sf1700

142 Heavy bronze stopper with a moulded circular top from which projects a small loop for attaching a chain. A shallow channel is cut into the bottom face of the stopper. A similar type of object from Aislingen has been identified as an inkpot lid, but is actually the lid of an oil flask (cf Cagnat and Chapot 1920, fig 590). The chain could then have attached it to the rest of the bath equipment (British Museum 1929, fig 118). *80/207*, sf5044

143 a) Decorated bolt terminal to disguise the rivet head. They usually take this dished form with central projections and are presumably used for carts and other vehicles (cf no 137).
b) Circular bronze cover for a lead filling over a nail or bolt head, a similar function to (a). *90/17*, sf3207

144 Lower part of a long-handled unguent spoon. The presence of such objects on a military site may be surprising, but some ointments were used for healing and officers had their families with them. They occur widely (cf Ulbert 1969, Taf 42, nos 5, 11 and 12; Ulbert 1959, Taf 24, no 13). *84/403*, sf6248

145 Bronze ointment scoop in the form of a long pin, necessary for the extraction of ointment from long-necked glass vials. *78/12*, sf1749

146 Long-handled ointment scoop (cf nos 144 and 145). *84/71*, sf3588

147 Ointment probe with a swollen terminal for mixing ointment and a diamond-shaped decoration at the broken end, where there may have been a scoop (cf Ulbert 1969, Taf 42, no 8). *63/5*, sf1147

148 Terminal with a rounded end, probably from an ointment scoop (Ulbert 1969, Taf 42, nos 11–18). *70/75*, sf1742

149 Bronze scoop with a circular bowl and traces of silvering. *72/63*, sf1653

150 Seal box with a plain lid and three holes in the base, similar to three examples illustrated from Rheingönheim (Ulbert 1969, Taf 41, nos 21–3). *91/279*, sf6016

151 Silvered seal box top with moulded repoussé decoration. 84/107, sf4058

152 Seal box lid (cf no 150). 98/229, sf6270

153 Small bronze bar bent at a right angle, probably part of a box fitting. *87/115*, sf6287

154 Head of a silver pin in the form of a clenched fist, below which is a circular hole, 0.05mm diam. Pins pierced in or near the head occur widely, although they are a minority form. Examples occur at Colchester (Crummy 1983, 505, fig 31, no 30), South Shields (Allason-Jones and Miket 1984, 176, cat 3.493), where it is identified as a needle, yet has a circular hole. These small holes are probably for thin chains linked together as part of hair ornaments. The terminal decoration is more difficult to understand. Many features are found on terminals and they often have an amuletic function. It is possible this very small terminal, apparently shaped into a clenched fist, was intended to represent what the Italians call the *mano fica*, thought to prevent the effects of the evil eye. It is known to the Romans as *manus obscaena* (Ovid, *Fasti* V, 333, see also Elworthy 1895, 243–8, and Schmidt 1956, 238). *84/253*, sf5073

155 Small rectangular mount from a box or casket. It has repoussé figures in a moulded surround. In the centre is a double-handled cantharus, flanked by two winged gryphons. This is a theme associated with the Bacchic cult, and a very similar one is on a small gold lunate earring from Colchester (Crummy 1983, 168, fig 205, no 4659; cf also Hutchinson 1986, 525, Gl–167). *78/12*, sf1888

(Fig 4.18)

156 Drop handle with a small centre terminal knob and one at each end of the arms, from a box or casket, similar to the reconstruction from Dunapentele, Hungary (illustrated in Bushe-Fox 1949, pl xlviii). *73/23*, sf1627

157 Edging from a leather or wooden object, from a later deposit, but probably a residual military object. *98/138*, sf5924

158 Finely made medical spatula (cf no 160). *91/71*, sf3816

159 Bronze needle *c* 125mm long (cf no 160, and Crummy 1983, 65, no 1977, fig 70). *91/71*, sf3811

160 Finely made medical spatula, 92.5mm long, with a small rectangular slot at the spatulate end. It was probably used as a needle for stitching wounds (cf nos 158 and 159). *84/71*, sf3594

161 Small bronze pin with rounded, flattened knob, although normally associated with female needs, pins are often found on military sites (cf Ulbert 1959, Taf 24, nos 8–11). *35/14*, sf506

162 Bronze pin, 69mm long. *77/2*, sf1591

163 Lead cube with a bronze casing, only part of which survives. This was probably a weight and allowing for the loss of part of the casing could have been intended for 2 *unciae* (*c* 54g) as the present actual weight is 48.3g and it could have had a suspension ring on the face where there is no longer any casing. *72/67*, sf1884

164 Fragment of bronze casing, one panel has an incised cross. It was probably from a knife handle, similar to another from Wroxeter (Webster 1962b, 37, fig 5, no 13). *41/6*, sf1366

165 Flattened piece of bronze casing, probably scrap. *53/9*, sf550

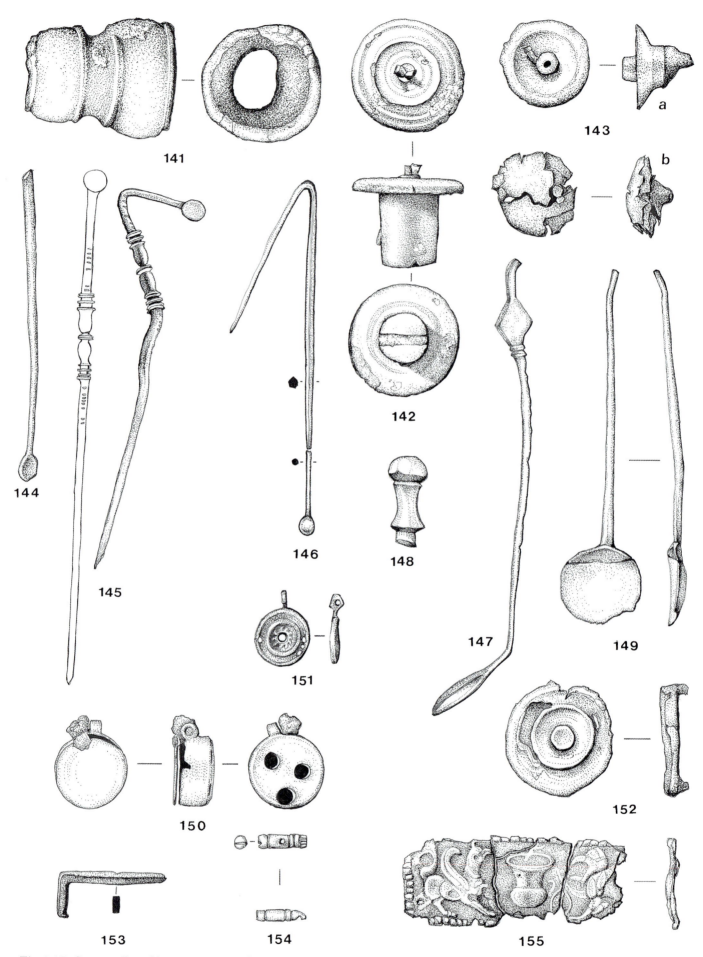

Fig 4.17 Copper alloy objects 141–55; scale 1:1

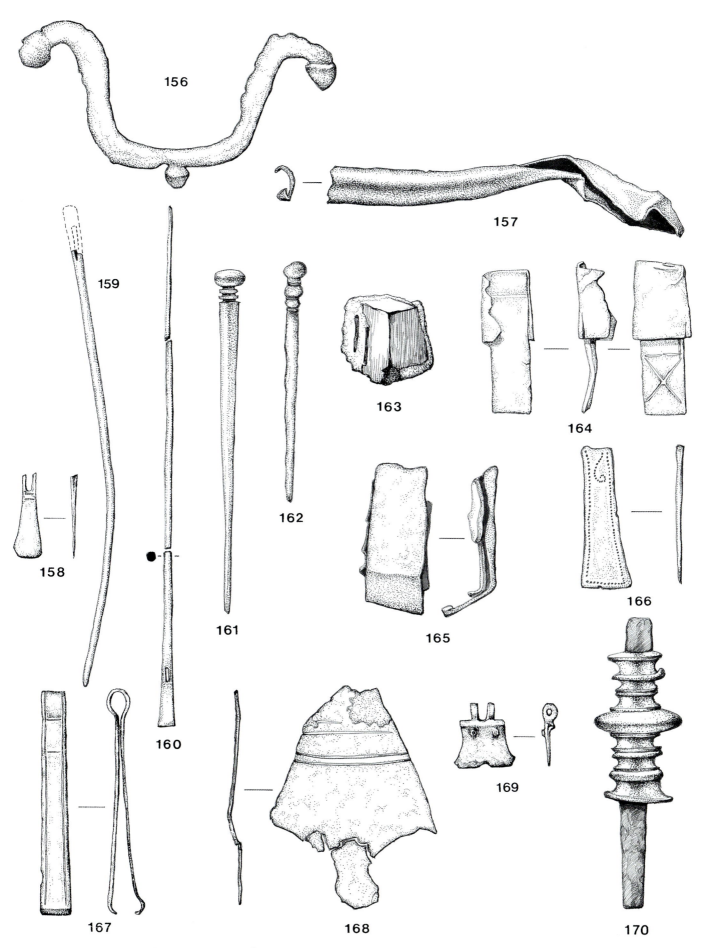

Fig 4.18 Copper alloy objects 156–70; scale 1:1

166 Small tapering metal strip with punched decoration. Traces of iron corrosion at the broken end suggest that it was part of a knife handle. *45/15*, sf502

167 Pair of tweezers from a chatelaine. *43/12*, sf497

168 Fragment of thin bronze plate with a pair of two incised concentric circles. The complete piece, which is unfinished on the underside, is at least 240mm diam. While rejecting this as a possible mirror, Glenys Lloyd-Morgan suggests that it might be part of a decorative mount for a box or piece of furniture similar to the lid plate from *Verulamium* (Frere 1972, 138 and fig 27, no 152). *92/65*, sf4088

169 Small but stout pair of box or casket hinges with a splayed plate with two tang stubs on the inner side for attachment. *77/9*, sf1695

170 Turned and finely decorated bronze attachment to an iron bar, 10mm diam. This is a cross-piece for a folding stool (*sella castrensis*). The quality of the metalwork reflects the importance of the stool as a symbol of office and authority (Salomonsen 1956). A close parallel from a military site comes from Newstead, where Curle found a pit filled with a large collection of ironmongery. This, he concluded, had come from a blacksmith's smithy. Among the piece were five lengths of iron bar very similarly decorated (Curle 1911, pl lxiv, 286–7 and nos 1, 2, 4, and 5). Curle correctly identified these as cross-bars connecting the folding legs of a stool. A complete, but not so elaborately decorated example was found at the legionary fortress at Nijmegen (cf Liversidge 1955, fig 40, and a modern reconstruction in the Nijmegen Museum, fig 41). *50/52*, sf1589

(Fig 4.19)

171 Small bronze skillet, bowl 53mm diam, 32.5mm deep. Handle 55mm long with the usual necked shape and rounded end, pierced by a 6mm diam hole for suspension. Skillets normally issued to legionaries were much heavier, like the examples from Gloucester (Webster 1960, 79 and pl ixb), Caves Inn (Webster 1966, 143–4, pl 30), and Nijmegen (Boesterd 1956, 7–8, nos 14–19, pl i). This fine metalware was produced in north Italy (Willers 1907, Taf vii, 76–9). This is, however, of thinner metal, not so well made and lacks a maker's stamp. *9/22*, sf469

(Fig 4.20)

172 Large circular flat lid, *c* 110mm diam, with a bevelled edge and projecting knob. It is an interesting coincidence that it fits the small skillet (no 171). Bronze lids are not common.

(Fig 4.21)

173 Twisted bronze bracelet, the present diameter, *c* 45mm, is too small for use and is presumably scrap.

Bone objects

(Fig 4.21)

174 Small disc with a non-central hole for suspension, probably a bead for a necklace, or a crude earring. *46/7*, sf889

175 Squared piece with sides of 55mm, probably intended as an inlay but left unfinished. These are usually decorated, like smaller examples from Aislingen (Ulbert 1959, Taf 26, no 23). *84/253*, sf5108

176 Object of uncertain shape and function with a 4mm hole and a groove. *67/22*, sf1472

177 Small toggle of a dumb-bell shape. There is a close parallel from an Antonine deposit at *Verulamium* (Frere 1972, 150, fig 54, no 195). There are other similar unpublished examples from Corbridge and Chester (S Greep pers comm). *73/24*, sf1697

178 Toggle with a phallus at one end and at the other, the clenched fist with the protruding thumb, making the *manus obscaena*, to ward off the evil eye (cf no 154). In these three Wroxeter examples the shaping of the fist has been very perfunctory. There are better examples from Colchester (Crummy 1983, 139–40 with references and fig 164, nos 4258 and 4259). *50/52*, sf1580

179 Toggle, similar to no 180. *70/16*, sf1521

180 Toggle, similar to no 179. *50/52*, sf1581

181 Rough-out for a small pin. *81/89*, sf1957

182 Rough-out of a tapering square-cut length bone for fashioning into a pin. *67/22*, sf1470

183 Rough-out tapering length of bone with two unequal faces intended for fashioning into a pin (cf nos 182 and 184). *67/22*, sf1475

184 Knife handle with a small piece of the knife still attached. *73/25*, sf1725

Objects of iron

(Fig 4.22)

185 Spear-head with a slight medial ridge, similar to examples from Kingsholm, Gloucester (Manning 1985, 161, V31 and 32, pl 76). *90/184*, sf5764

186 Socketed ballista bolt-head, compare with examples from Hod Hill (Brailsford 1962, pl vi, B182 and 183), and Newstead (Curle 1911, pl xxxvii, nos 8, 9, 11, 12 and 16–21, identified as arrow-heads). *78/9*, sf1844

187 Pointed butt-end of a lance (cf Ulbert 1969, Taf 46, nos 32–7). *90/213*, sf6280

188 Square tapering open-ended sheath of metal of varying thickness between 2 and 3mm. It is part of the ferrule of a *pilum* with a solid pointed terminal. This weight probably assisted the flight pattern (cf Ulbert 1969, Taf 47, 52, nos 5 and 6; Ritterling 1914, Taf xvii, no 71, where the

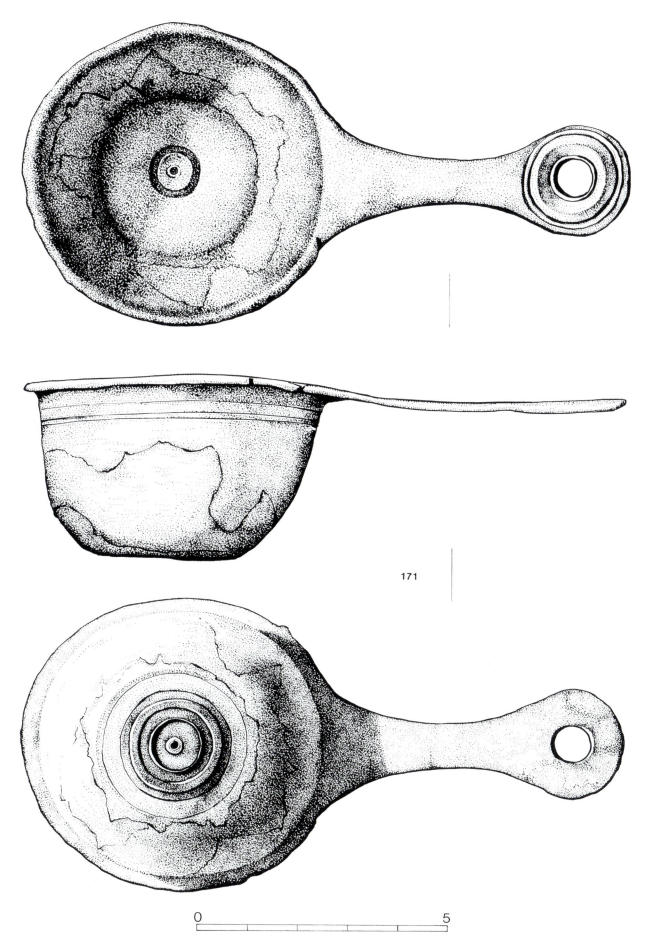

Fig 4.19 Copper alloy object 171; scale as shown

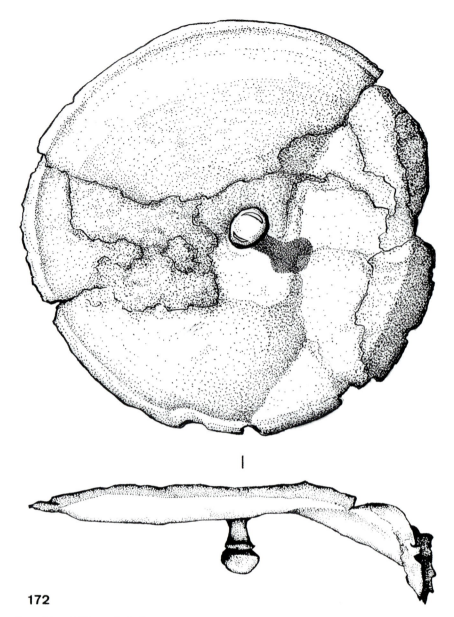

172

Fig 4.20 Copper alloy object 172; scale 1:1

terminal is in a single piece), see also a piece from Hod Hill (Manning 1985, 160, V25a and b, pl 76). *72/120*, sf1806

189 Calthrop, probably military, cf several from Wroxeter (Bushe-Fox 1914, 16, fig 8, no 30; Nash-Williams 1932, 71, fig 22). *83/-*, sf2017

190 Small knife, or chopper, with a solid round handle. It is clear from the section across the blade that the cutting edge has corroded away. *46/7*, sf887

191 Knife with curved blade sharpened on both edges, a shape common to razors, but the type of handle is uncertain where the metal thickens at the broken end. A handle could have been attached, as suggested on the drawing. *70/18*, sf1718

192 Part of a tool with a tang for a wood handle and flat blade 4mm thick, thinning at the end, it is probably a small chisel (cf Jacobi 1897, Taf xxxiv, nos 14 and 22, pl vii, nos 18–22; Brailsford 1962, 14, G24, fig 13). *6/46*, sf176

(Fig 4.23)

193 Punch, cf one from Newstead (Curle 1911, 288, pl lxvi no 10). *84/251*, sf5083

194 Punch with a long square tapered shaft, compare with one from the Carlingwark Loch hoard (Piggott 1973, fig 10, no 64; Brailsford 1962, 14, fig 13, G45). *73/45*, sf1738

195 Rectangular flat piece of iron with a hammered top and thinning at the end, possibly a kind of punch. *78/57*, sf1927

196 Tool with a trowel-like blade and a hooked handle, presumably for suspension. Trowels are not unknown, although not common on Roman military sites, compare with Saalburg (Jacobi 1897, 219, fig 32 nos 12–17). *92/88*, sf4176

197 Tapering blade, thin at the broad end and thicker at the tang. It could be part of a large knife or chisel. *72/79*, sf1772

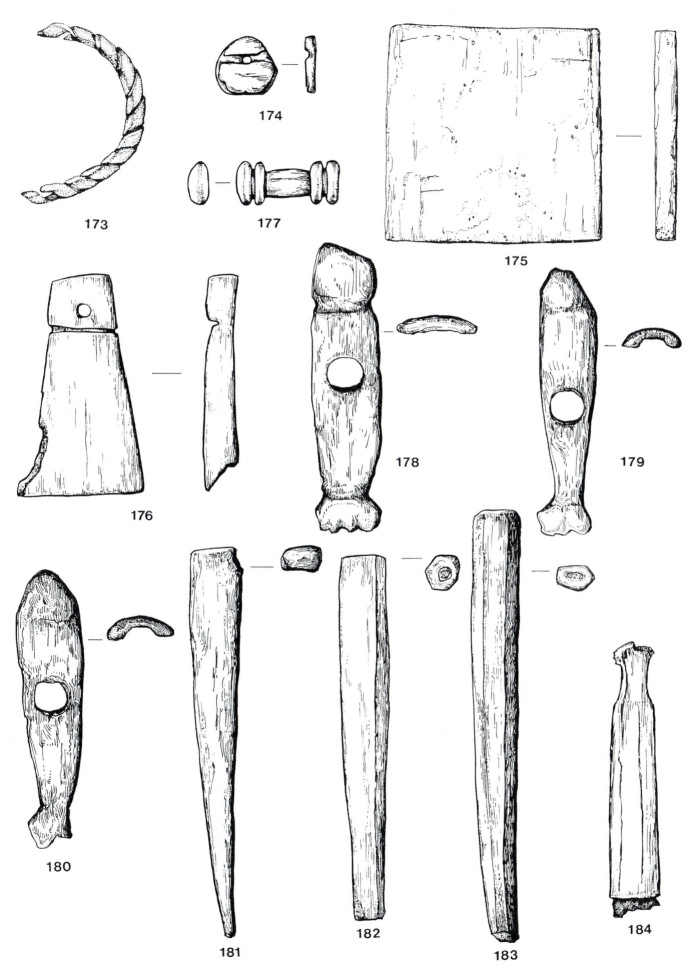

Fig 4.21 Copper alloy object 173; bone objects 174–84; scale 1:1

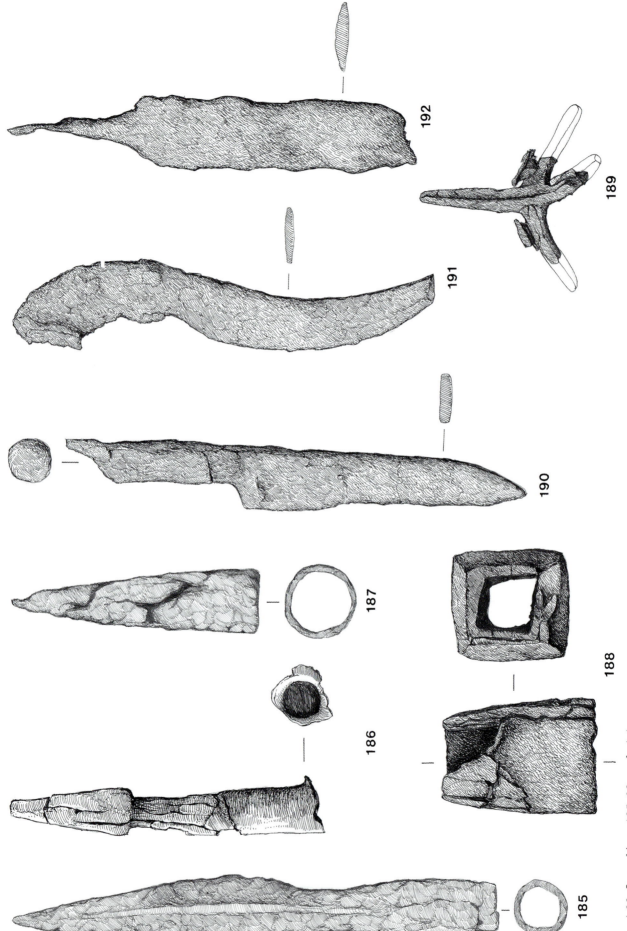

Fig 4.22 Iron objects 185–92; scale 1:1

198 Tool with a thick tang for a wood handle and a broad slightly curved shaft, 4–5mm thick. It is probably a broad chisel or wedge (cf Curle 1911, pl lix, no 1). *72/67*, sf1896

(Fig 4.24; reconstruction Fig 4.25)
199 Folding tripod stand for supporting a large vessel for cooking or heating water. The normal cooking grill is square or rectangular, well exemplified at Newstead (Curle 1931/2, 311–13, fig 20), and there is a smaller circular ring on a tripod from the Carlingwark Loch hoard (Piggott 1973, fig 10, C7), also Brading, Isle of Wight (Cleere 1958, 67 and fig 11a), and Icklingham, Suffolk (Manning 1985, 100, pl xiii). *92/61*, sf–

(Fig 4.25)
200 Small open lamp with traces of an extension at the back. This could either have been a horizontal handle or a vertical hanger with a loop at the top for suspension (cf Manning 1985, 99, pl 3 for the former type, pl 5 for the latter, cf also fig 26). *41/6*, sf1353
201 Small shallow iron lamp-holder with the broken end of a vertical hanger (cf no 202). *6/46*, sf168

(Fig 4.26)
202 Curved horseshoe-shaped object with expanded terminals for thick rivets for attachment to a timber beam or plank, 13mm thick. From the base extend two curved hooks with knobbed terminals. This is clearly for suspending a heavy weight connected by an iron ring. See those attached to cauldron-chains, like the one from the Great Chesterford hoard (Manning 1985, 101, pl 46 and fig 27, types P9 and 10). But the thickness of the wood to which it was fitted is not compatible with roof timbers. An alternative suggestion is that it could have been a cart or vehicle fitting. *80/215*, sf5088
203 Slide-key with a suspension ring, Z-shaped but with five teeth, compare with examples from London and Colchester (Manning 1985, 93, fig 25, no 5). *84/329*, sf5865
204 Suspension or handle loop for attaching to a bowl or cauldron. *84/421*, sf6278
205 Broken end of a wall hook, see also an example from Hod Hill (Manning 1985, 129, pl 59, R24 and 25. *98/193*, sf6208
206 Broad iron ring, 16mm wide, diam 50mm. Thicker rings have been identified as door pivots (Manning 1976, 40, no 152), and on this analogy the thin variety may have been as door hinges on cupboards, like their bone counterparts (Frere 1972, 149–50, fig 53, referring to Fremersdorf 1937/40, 321–37). *70/27*, sf1901

(Fig. 4.27)
207 Heavy pair of hinges with two straps connected by a loop, suitable for a door or a large chest. *6/76*, sf1190
208 Tapered iron butt-end for a staff or spear for a weapon, *c* 21mm diam at the base. The actual butt-end or spear has become detached. *92/91*, sf4131
209 Large, carefully shaped, dome-headed bolt with a round shaft 13mm diam, although square in section below the head. Other examples are cruder (Ulbert 1969, Taf 52, no 34; Curle 1911, pl lxvii, no 15). *84/244*, sf5368
210 Nail, when complete *c* 198mm long (around 4 *unciae*) with a flattened pyramidal head. It conforms to Inchtuthil Group A, but is of the size of Group B (Pitts and St Joseph 1985, 289–90, fig 86). *98/236*, sf6326
211 Similar nail, when complete *c* 150mm long. *90/251*, sf6339

Stone objects

212 Ram's horn carved in amber, a highly prized material considered to have magical properties (for other Romano-British amber items see Henig 1984). This could have been for an earring or a bead, as at South Shields (Allason-Jones and Miket 1984, 34 and pl 1). An amber head drilled for suspension was found at Colchester (Henig 1984, fig 4; Crummy 1983, 51, fig 54, no 1802). *90/24*, sf6241

(not illus)
213 Pebble honestone of dark grey indurated mudstone, roughly rectangular in section, 110mm long, slightly tapered, and possibly of carboniferous origin. It was probably longer in its original form but had been broken to its present size. This would make it suitable only for sharpening knives and razors. One face has been partly cut down, leaving a raised end piece and this may have been done to facilitate it being held on a bench when using the reverse face. This and one of the edge faces gives clear indication of having being used. *84/405*, sf6032

(Fig. 4.28)
214 Small mortar in white marble with projecting lip, not in the form of a normal spout, below which is a slightly raised shield-shaped panel. It is very similar to one from Richborough (Cunliffe 1968, 114, pl lxvii, no 11). A blackening on the lip and part of the rim suggests that it may have been used as a lamp with a floating wick. *92/20*, sf3316

(not illus)
215 Flake of marble from a statue or relief; could be part of a thigh. *98/196*, sf6260

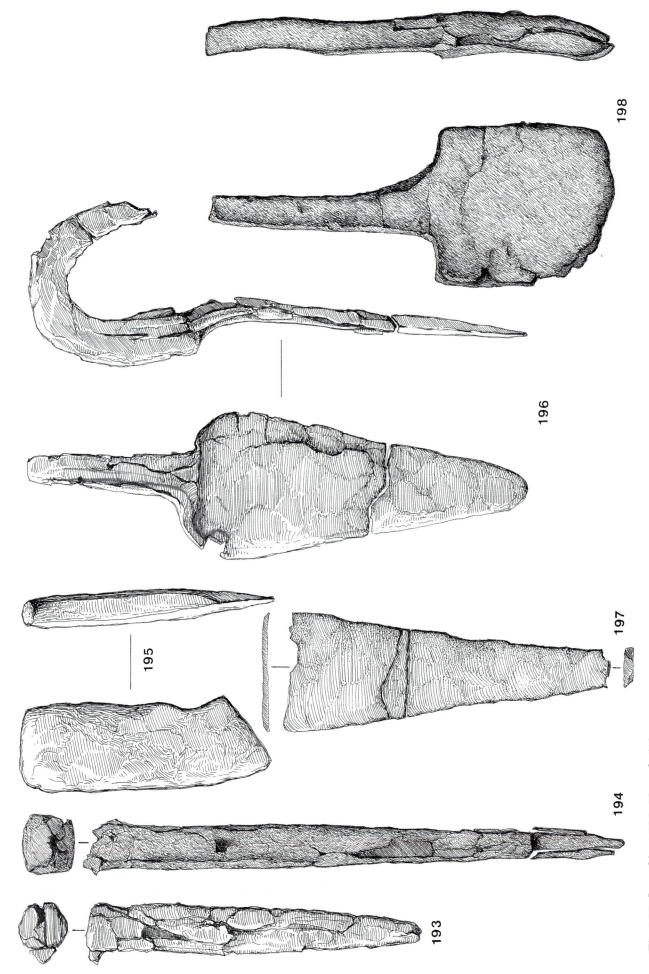

198

196

197

195

194

193

Fig 4.23 Iron objects 193–98; scale 1:1

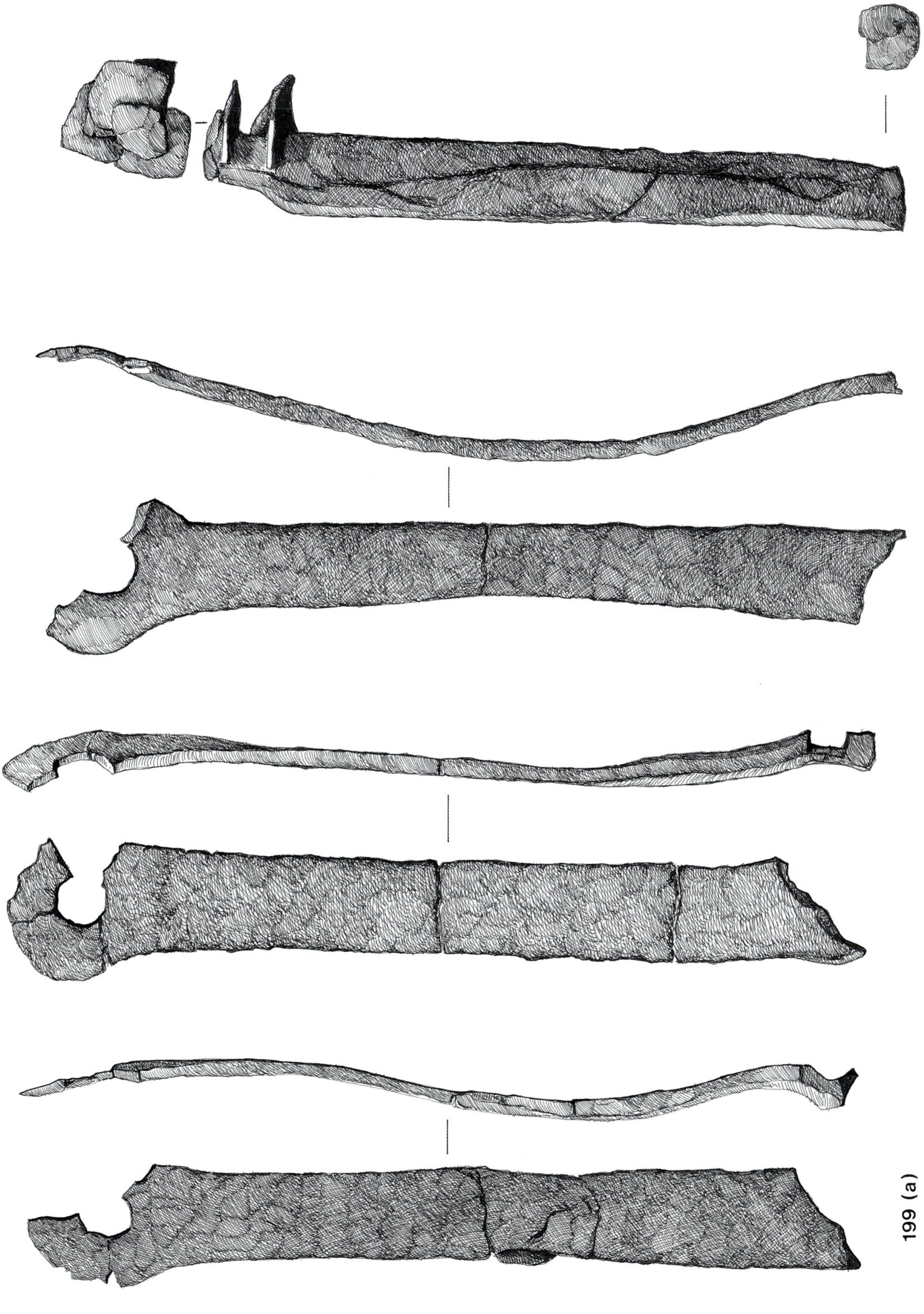

199 (a)

Fig 4.24 Iron object 199; scale 1:1

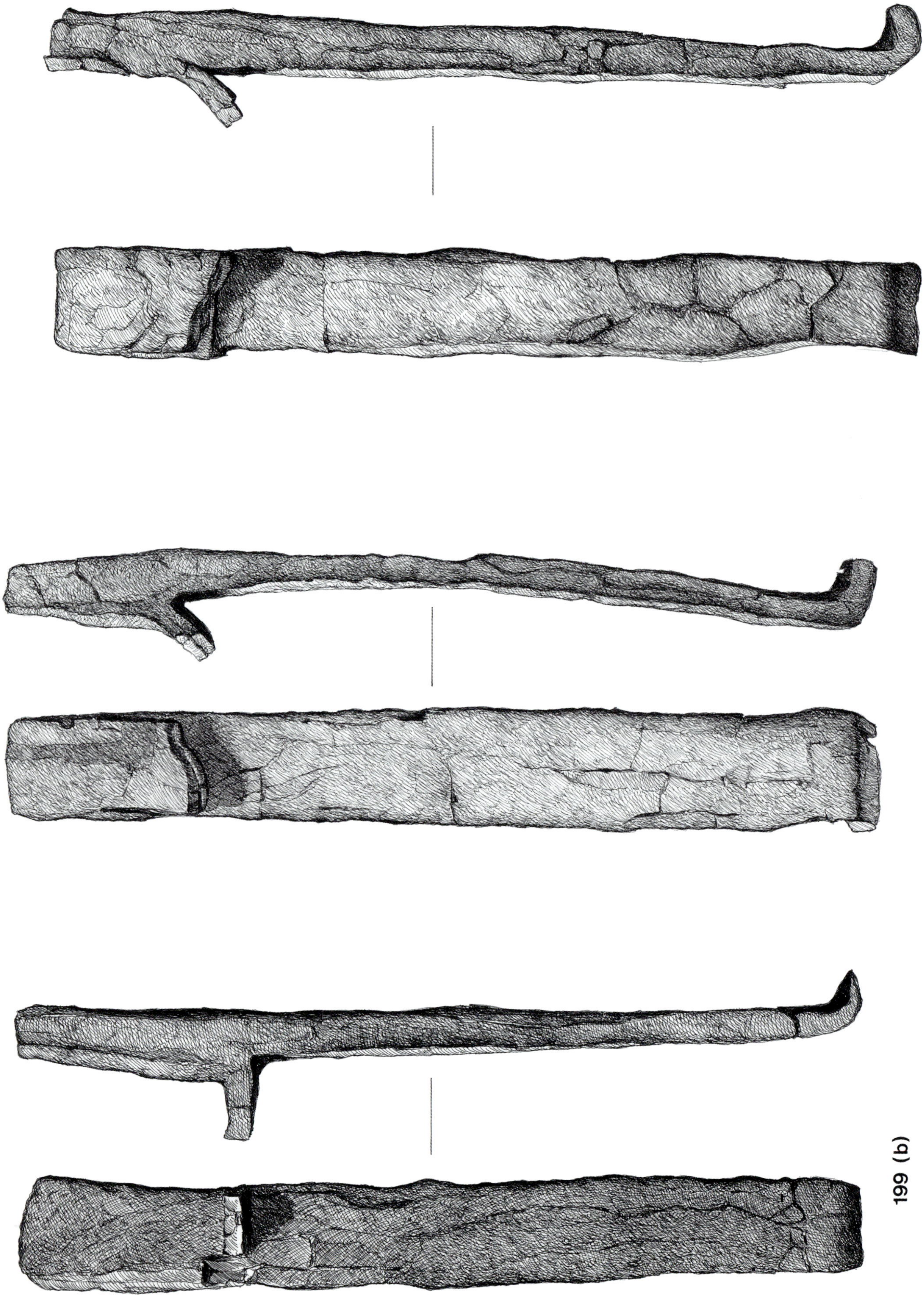

Fig 4.24 Iron object 199 (continued)

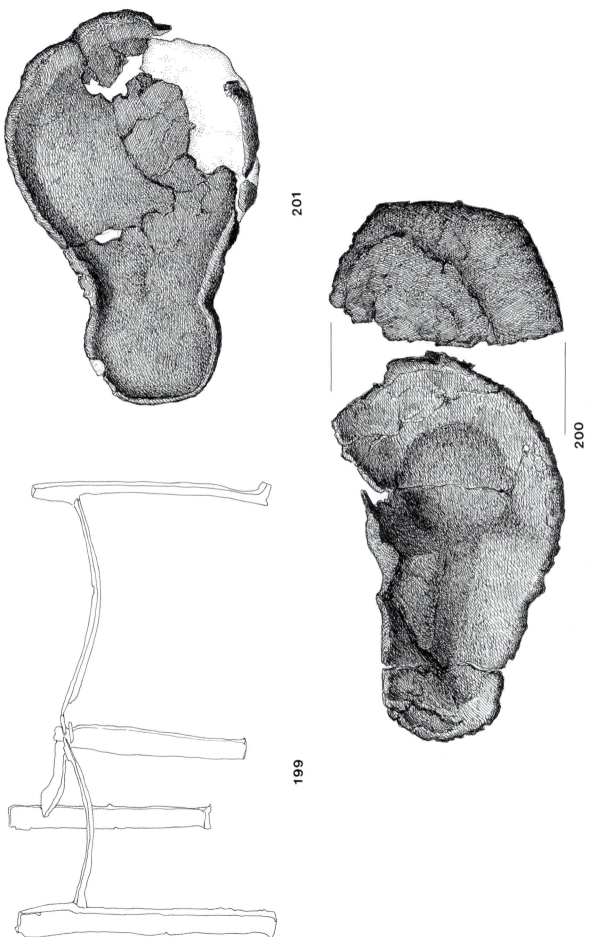

201

200

199

Fig 4.25 Iron object 199 (reconstruction); 200–201; scale 1:1

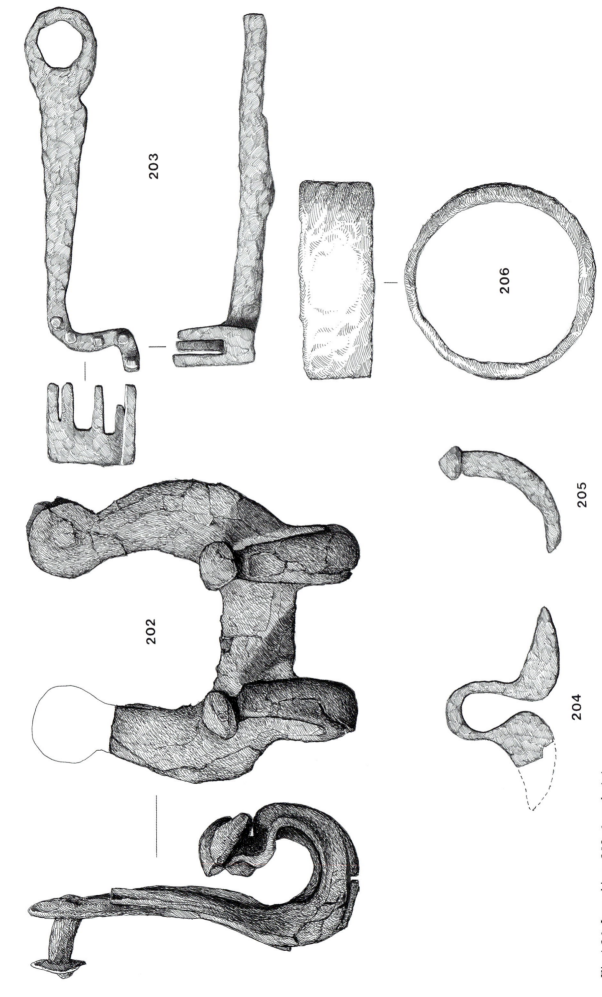

Fig 4.26 Iron objects 202–6; scale 1:1

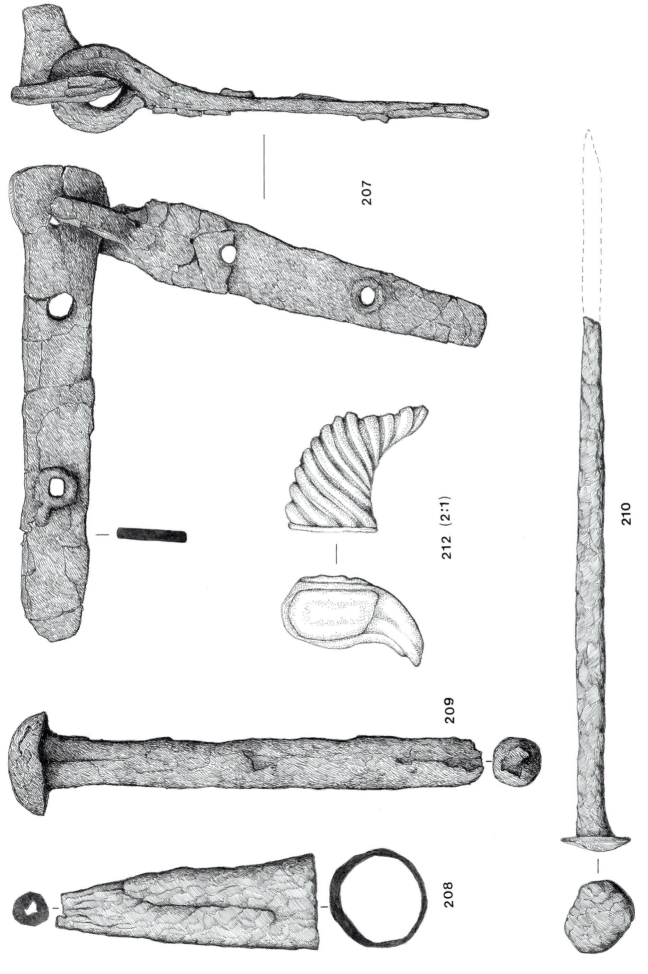

Fig 4.27 Iron objects 207–10; scale 1:1, amber object 212; scale 2:1

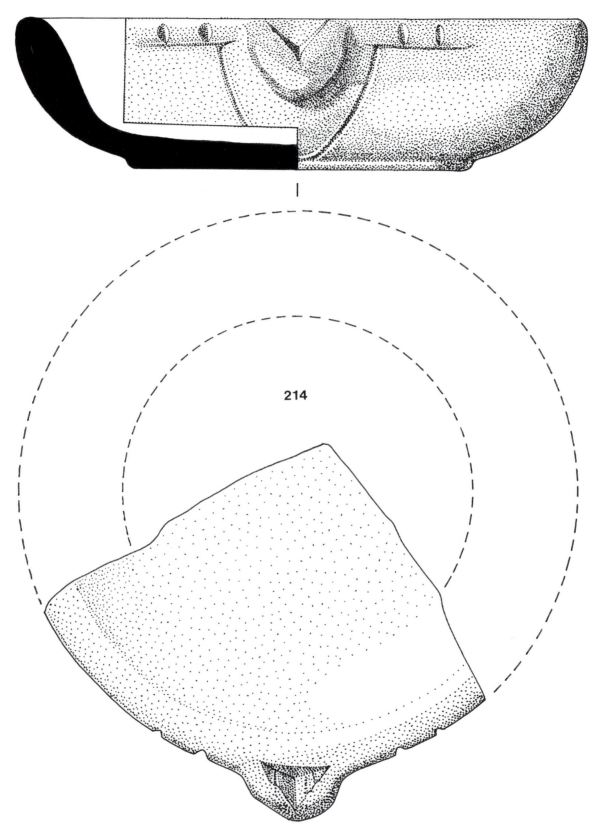

Fig 4.28 Worked stone object 214; scale 1:1

Fig 4.29 The Ptolemaic portrait intaglio and the lion intaglio

The intaglios

by Martin Henig

(Fig 4.29)

1 Sardonyx intaglio depicting, in profile to the left (to the right on an impression) the draped bust of Ptolemy XII (*Auletes* – 'the flute-player') who ruled from 80 to 51 BC. The intaglio is fully discussed elsewhere (Henig and Webster 1983, see also Henig 1991, 50). It was probably lost in military levels and redeposited, though it is possibly an heirloom mislaid at a later date. Two other Wroxeter gems depict Egyptian deities, Isis and Serapis (Henig 1978, nos 355 and 359; Boon 1982b). Dimensions: 14 x 11 x 4 mm. *90/116*, sf5117 Early civilian settlement

2 Intaglio, material identified by M E Hutchinson (1994) as chrome green chalcedony, possibly from Russia or India. The subject is a lion shown seated in profile to the left (to the right on an impression). It has an animal head between its paws and a tree on the right arches over the beast.

   The gem is of Augustan date; a similar intaglio may have inspired a coin of Cunobelin (see Henig 1978, frontispiece and 319 no App 220). Like the Ptolemaic gem, above, it was an heirloom at the time of loss (Henig 1991, 52 fig 11): the context dates from the final military clearance of the site (*c* AD 90). Dimensions 12.5 × 9.5 × 3mm. *84/109*, sf4064 Phase 7i

The Venus (or nymph) of the fountain

by Martin Henig and Graham Webster

(Figs 4.30 and 4.31)

Two fragments of sculpture in a fine-grained sandstone were among the Hadrianic build-up in the south portico. Surviving height 0.635m. Statue of Venus (Fig 4.30), or a nymph, the upper part of her torso nude apart from a necklace and the end of a fillet which bound her hair. Around her loins a mantle is loosely gathered. The figure suffered damage following the demolition of the fountain, so that the head and limbs are missing. Furthermore her right side shows signs of heavy wear, suggestive of the torso having been used as a threshold in the early civilian period.

   Associated with the figure is an urn (Fig 4.31) decorated at its base with a frieze of leaves and with a simple ovolo moulding towards its rim. The concentric grooves on the underside of the foot suggest that it was

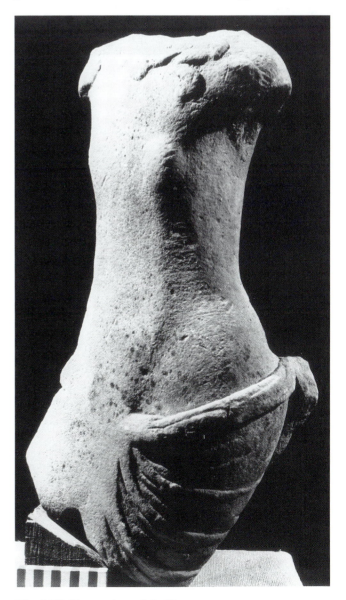

Fig 4.30 Front view of the Venus statue

Fig 4.31 Stone vessel associated with the Venus or nymph

intended to imitate a bronze vessel. A channel cut obliquely through it shows that it was the outlet of a fountain. Height 0.285m. *Area 98*

These items have been published previously (Frere 1984b, 291, 293, and fig 12; Webster 1988, 142, illus 6.18 and 6.19; Henig 1995, 84 and 86, illus 54). The iconographic type is well known, of Hellenistic origin and frequently used for fountains: Balázs Kapossy cites a number of examples, and illustrates one from Viterbo, now in the National Museum, Copenhagen (Kapossy 1969, 14–15, Abb 4). Where water flows from a vase this is generally placed on a column, but a different arrangement may have been followed at Wroxeter. An important factor here would have been the water level, the supply being a leat from the Bell Brook, or a suitable spring near the base of the Wrekin. The foundation graced by Venus must have been a sunken pool so the level of the outlet from the pot would have been that of the water in the gravity-fed channel.

A semi-draped reclining nymph, her left forearm over a water vessel, was found at the Claudian legionary fortress at Risstissen on the Danube (Espérandieu 1931, 419, no 664). Closer to home, the dolphin fountain-spout from the fountain house attached to the *natatio* attached to the *palaestra* of the fortress baths at Caerleon is thought to have accompanied a statue of Venus (Zienkiewicz 1986, 146–7 and, especially, 277–80). Like the Wroxeter urn, the dolphin here was separate and close to the water level. The statue was probably set up in its final arrangement in the mid-second century AD but could have been part of earlier, Flavian, arrangements.

The quality of the carving of the Wroxeter Venus may indicate that it was commissioned by the legionary commander for the garden of the *praetorium* rather than the public courtyard of the *principia*.

5 Pottery

by M J Darling

Military period pottery

The earlier phases of Wroxeter produced 20,206 sherds, 278 estimated vessel equivalents (EVEs), weighing 301kg. Of this material 80% was attributed to the military period. The remainder came from Period 1, early civilian occupation preceding the construction of the buildings in the baths complex. The small quantity of pottery from Period 1 is published with the site evidence for the Roman baths (Darling 2000), but figures relating to the Period 1 group are quoted where they seemed relevant to set the military pottery in context. The excavation evidence suggests that the army remained in occupation in one form or another over the period *c* AD 56–90, some 35 years, the equivalent of a generation. The circumstances which dictated their pottery supply on arrival changed radically over that period; among other factors, changes in garrison between legions and in size would have affected their supply arrangements.

Initially the quartermasters would have had to make provision to supply a garrison of at least a legion, probably garrisoned with auxiliaries on campaign, in an area which was virtually aceramic in terms of native pottery, and far removed from areas where native pottery supplies were readily available. There seems, therefore, to have been little choice but to engage directly in the manufacture of pottery to meet the garrison's needs at that time. Some ten years later, Nero withdrew *Legio XIV*, considered to be the Wroxeter garrison, for an eastern campaign. If the potters were attached to that legion, as seems likely, the question remains as to whether they moved with the legion or remained to serve whichever legion or mixed force took over the fortress. New building work may indicate this changeover of garrisons, and the stratified pottery, particularly from pits, has been examined with this question in mind.

The earliest phase of the Wroxeter fortress may have lasted no more than a decade or so; the succeeding phases, continuing to *c* AD 90, covered over two decades. The assemblage is therefore biased towards the later period, and complicated by the problem of residual pottery. A further major factor to take into account is the relative isolation of Wroxeter both as a fortress and a city, particularly in the early stages. Any local pottery production, especially one originally based on the presence of the army, is unlikely to have been subjected to influences from outside much before the second century, and quite probably not until the major expansion in marketing of Black Burnished Ware 1 (BB1). Any apprentice potters are likely to have been trained in the traditions of the original potters. It is argued that any mechanism or stimuli for stylistic change by such potters, producing cooking and other vessels for the local community, whether military or civilian, would have been unlikely to occur until the latest military period or early in the succeeding civilian occupation.

The replacement of the garrison might possibly have seen some change, but is this probable given that *Legio XIV* left to go on active campaign? Moreover, if the replacement legion was *Legio XX*, which came from an area where native pottery was, by that time, more readily available, and thus with little need for pottery expertise within or attached to the legion, an abrupt change might have been expected. Yet the fabrics indicate continuing local production and changes in vessel types appear minimal.

Reduction of the garrison size is perhaps a more likely stimulus to change, assuming adequate pottery supplies could be obtained from elsewhere. Again the isolation of Wroxeter from the main area of the province is relevant. How large a market to attract new potters would the *canabae* of the fortress have provided, given that the bulk of the forces would be away on campaign? Two models can be postulated. First, that there was a defined 'military' pottery tradition during the military period which ceased with the departure of the army. Second, that military pottery assemblage changed according to circumstances during the military occupation and continued to evolve in the early civilian period. Obtaining the solution to this problem is gravely hampered by the small quantity of pottery from Period 1 contexts and its uneven spatial distribution. For this reason the pottery assemblages from both the military period and Period 1 are presented together so that comparisons across the phases may be made.

There is the further problem of residuality. The timespan is too short for significant changes in pottery types to be recognised and used to assess levels of residuality. Since there is no evidence to suggest any significant level of Iron Age pottery in the area, the earliest deposits, unfortunately the smallest, are the only ones likely to be free from the residuality problem. As the residual content builds up, so our view of the assemblage becomes fogged. The only recourse is to the samian, itself a special type of pottery likely to have a relatively longer life than contemporary cooking vessels. When the samian is considered, the level of residual pottery in both the later military and the earliest civilian periods is high, so that the samian assemblage of Period 1 contains over 60% from the preceding occupation. This apparent high residual content, must, however, be viewed in the light of the known reduction in supplies in the early second century (Marsh 1978), quite apart from the distance between Wroxeter and the entry ports.

With these factors in mind the evidence from the excavations can be examined: the site evidence, the size of the relevant phased assemblages, their spatial distribution, and character. The pottery comes from a relatively small area which extends from the defences into the interior of the fortress, and the use of the inner area changed during the military period. The differing functions of the two main areas would affect the deposition of rubbish, and the courtyard is further complicated by the change of use. The excavated area has been split into three zones to enable examination of the evidence spatially:

- the defences: from the defences eastward to, and including, the *intervallum* road, with Area 98,
- the central area, the main interior area to the east (the location of barracks initially),
- the south, areas to the south of this, north of the assumed line of the *via praetoria*.

Site evidence

The central and south areas produced the largest quantity of pottery for the military period, and also the principal groups from cut features. The nature of the stratigraphy is important for any consideration of the pottery evidence. Below the military demolition layer vertical stratigraphy existed only within features cut into the natural sand, the phasing of which has had to rely on horizontal stratigraphy. In the absence of stratigraphic relationships between features, their phasing relies on an evaluation of the nature of their fill and contents, often only pottery. The structure of the later *macellum* made excavation of the deeply stratified military deposits problematical, particularly in cross-site stratification, quite apart from the disturbances caused by the masonry structure. Often the decision as to whether a context was military or not has had to rely upon the pottery. This is a heavy burden for the pottery, since the quantity from such a long occupation is not large, and changes in the type of assemblage would be expected, quite apart from the differing usage of the excavated areas. The possibility of circular arguments has been ever present.

The minuscule quantity of pottery associated with the earliest barracks provides no real evidence for the definition of an assemblage. Inevitably, much reliance has had to be placed upon the contents of various pits in the central and south areas to define what might have been the primary assemblage. Few of the pits contained any quantity of pottery, pit F2807 being a notable exception, and a few in the same southern part of the site, particularly in Area 72. Bearing in mind that much rubbish was probably disposed of outside the fortress, the context of these pits needs consideration. Many cut wall lines of the barrack-type buildings, but how much later is questionable. Pit digging, with minor exceptions, occurs in areas of non-use, and two occasions seem feasible: the change from barrack-type structures

to the later large building, and the departure of the army. The position is further complicated by later pits dug through the demolition layer, some of which may not have been identified as later, particularly due to the small size of the pottery groups from most of the pits.

Ceramic groups

Where there has been sufficient doubt about the phasing on the basis of fabrics and forms, the contexts have been excluded from analysis. The pits assigned to Phase 4b, the end of the second barracks phase preceding the large building, contribute the first reasonable sample of material. This has been amalgamated with the preceding groups, which separately are too small for reliable assessment, to form the earliest assemblage, termed *Leg*. This is not ideal, since some of these pits could be late in the occupation, and this should be remembered when considering the evidence for this earliest phase. A further complication is the presence of a single large pit group in the southern part of the courtyard area, F2807, which produced an extraordinary assemblage. This had no cutting relationships to aid its phasing, and there is minor contamination from later contexts. The contents are mostly locally made vessels, intermediate between being 'wasters' or 'seconds'. Whatever the interpretation of the pit, its size (representing over 20% on EVEs of all the military pottery), coupled with the highly biased assemblage of vessel types, left no choice but to keep it separate from the other phased groups. To trace any development in the military period assemblage and still achieve realistic samples, the remaining material has had to be simply split between *Late* and *Demolition*, the latter containing 45% (on EVEs and excluding amphorae) of all the military period pottery. The *Late* group comprises all pottery phased to Phases 5–7iii, while the *Demolition* consists of that phased as 7iv only. *Contam* consists of pottery from contexts, mostly in the later phase, which are considered to have been contaminated by later pottery.

The pottery, including samian, from the resulting military ceramic phases and Period 1 is detailed in Table 5.1, with information on fragmentation as sherd/weight and brokenness measure (Orton *et al* 1993, 169, 178). The table excludes amphorae, since a change in collection policy during the excavation complicates the evidence. The amphorae quantities are detailed below.

Thus only 10–12% of the pottery derives from the earliest military occupation, the bulk of the stratified military period pottery coming from deposits after the changes to the internal buildings, and the demolition contexts. Only 16–19% comes from stratified Period 1 contexts, the individual phases producing small samples.

The quality of the evidence for each phase is best measured by EVEs, representing the more diagnostic sherds, as shown in Figure 5.1 which emphasises not only the predominance of the pottery from the demolition, but also the quantity from the pit F2807.

Table 5.1 Pottery: quantities by ceramic group and phase, excluding amphorae

	phase	sherds	%	EVEs	%	weight (g)	%	sh/wt	broken
Leg	0–4b	1867	10.3	2885	10.7	23215	12.5	12.4	0.65
F2807	F2807	1686	9.3	4402	16.3	18047	9.7	10.7	0.38
Late	5–7iii	2838	15.6	3348	12.4	28621	15.4	10.1	0.85
Demo	7iv	7309	40.2	10215	37.9	71174	38.2	9.7	0.72
Contam	Contam	1079	5.9	1898	7.0	11857	6.4		
Period 1	1.1	492	2.7	536	2.0	4139	2.2	8.4	0.92
	1.2	1279	7.0	1048	3.9	10442	5.6	8.2	1.22
	1.3	1593	8.8	2454	9.1	17966	9.6	11.3	0.65
	Contam	45	0.3	183	0.7	912	0.5		
Totals		18188	100	26969	100	186373	100		

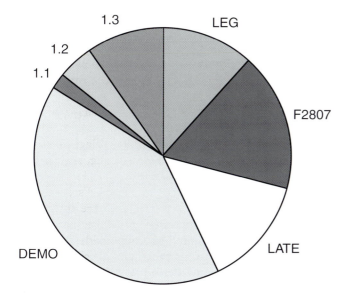

Fig 5.1 Pottery: estimated vessel equivalents (EVEs) by Phase

Spatial distribution

There is also the question of the spatial distribution: Figure 5.2 shows the percentages based on EVEs of each phase by area. This excludes pit F2807 from the central area.

The bulk of the evidence for the main military occupation and the demolition period comes from the south area, while that for the late military comes from the defences zone, which unfortunately has the lowest sherd weights and the highest level of brokenness. The spatial distribution of Period 1 pottery is very uneven, with the bulk from the fragmented defences zone. Full details of the quantities by phase and spatial distribution are in Appendix 3.1.

Fragmentation

Fragmentation with low average sherd weights and high levels of brokenness is highest in the defences area (Fig 5.3), largely due to the nature of deposits. The area had the lowest percentage of cut features, whereas the pottery from the south area is mainly from features and has less brokenness and higher sherd weight, particularly for the *Leg* and *Late* phases. The central area is more variable, with sherds from the *Late* phase being more fragmented, while those from Period 1 pits have higher sherd weights. It is notable that much higher brokenness occurs in the *Leg* phase in the defences area than the average sherd weight would indicate, suggesting secondary rubbish. The brokenness measure emphasises the fragmentary nature of the pottery from the defences area, which produced the bulk of the pottery for both the *Late* phase and Period 1.

Provenance by context type

Another factor affecting the potential value of the pottery is the type of context, examined here spatially by period as a simple division between cut features, pits etc, which are likely to produce less fragmented pottery with a probable lower residuality, and spreading layers. The highest concentration of cut features was in the south area, where 85% (on EVEs) of the features were pits, closely followed by the central area at 66%. Only 33% of the features in the defences area were pits, with an exceptionally high fragmentation and brokenness measure. The measure for brokenness for the pits alone in the defences area reached a high 1.31, compared with 0.41 and 0.46 from the south and central areas.

Figure 5.4 gives the EVEs for the military period and Period 1 according to derivation from features or layers by area. This shows the major contribution of the features in the south area for the military period, mainly derived from pits, whereas the pottery from the central area is almost equally divided between the two types of context. The more diagnostic pottery for Period 1 derived largely from pits and features in the central area. Most of the pottery from the defences zone came from layers rather than features for both periods.

The relative sizes of the more diagnostic groups of pottery from the military phase is clearly shown, the earliest phase having less than half that from the demolition period, with a relatively small quantity coming from the intervening period. The bulk of the pottery from features of Period 1 came from the last phase, and the quantity available from the earlier phases is too small to allow any assessment of the development of the assemblage within the period. Coupled with the

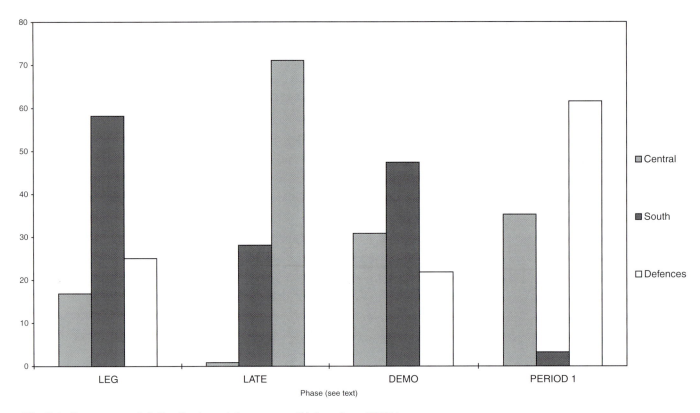

Fig 5.2 Pottery: spatial distribution of the pottery (% based on EVEs)

very uneven spatial distribution, the relatively small quantity, and the residuality problem, the difficulties of Period 1 are made apparent.

Methods

Limited site evidence available when the pottery was being processed led to full quantification of sherd counts, estimated vessel equivalents (EVEs), and weights being applied to the complete assemblage. The recording fields for the basic pottery database, in addition to the quantification fields are:

- fabric
- form
- decoration
- sherd links
- drawing number
- comments

Individual records cover single vessels where identifiable. The same fields were used for the specialist samian database, with additional fields for pottery source, potter's name and die for stamps, date, and reference to specialist reports. The basic database includes the relevant fields from the specialist samian file merged with the coarse pottery.

All the pottery was entered into a computer database (UNIX, transferable to MS-DOS), and merged with a separate phasing database. The specialist pottery (samian, fine wares, amphorae, and mortaria) is boxed separately, as are the drawn sherds.

The pottery is presented as a type series of locally produced vessels covering the main identified vessel types from military and Period 1 deposits, the type numbering being related to the original recording codes to retain the integrity of the database and allow extraction of the incidence of the various types across the phases. This is supplemented by the separate illustration of the F2807 pit group and the non-locally produced vessels from the military phase. Separate sections cover the fine wares either stratified in early contexts or of definitely early date, the non-local mortaria, and amphorae. To integrate with the type series formulated to cover all periods of pottery at Wroxeter (Ellis 2000, 195–257), the catalogue cross-refers to that type series.

Fabric definitions

Local wares

Percentages are based on weight for the stratified assemblage excluding amphorae.

WWO	Normal oxidised fabric, 39%
WWOF	Finer oxidised fabric, 5.3%. As WWO but finer texture
WWR	Normal reduced fabric, 36%. As WWO but reduced firing
WWRF	Finer reduced fabric, under 1%. As WWR but finer texture
WWCR	Normal oxidised fabric with a white to cream slip, 1.7%

a)

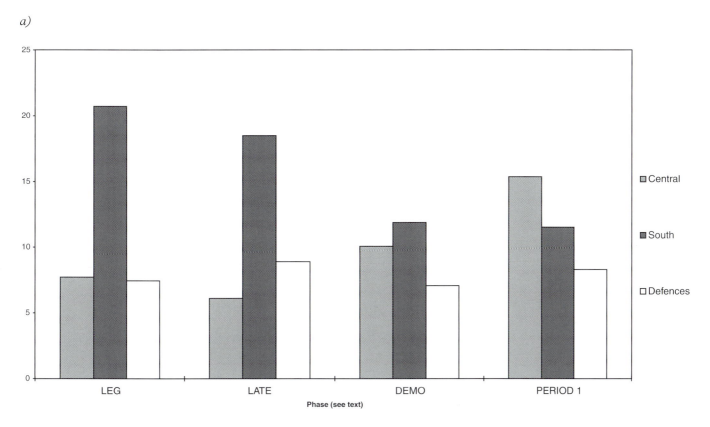

b)

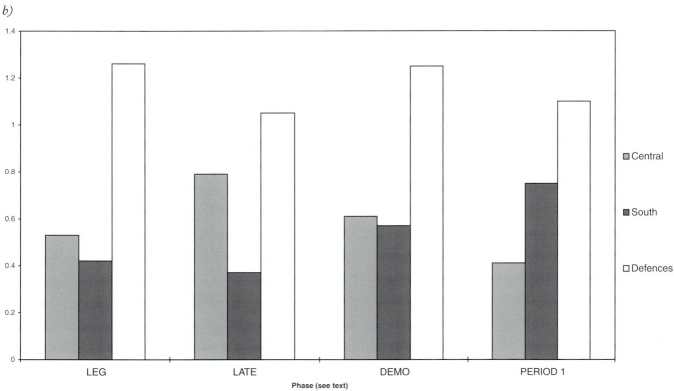

Fig 5.3 Pottery: a) sherd weight by area; b) brokenness measure by area

MWWO	Mortaria, 1.6%. As WWO
MWWOF	Mortaria, under 1%. As WWOF
MWWR	Mortaria, under 1%. As WWR
MWWRF	Mortaria, under 1%. As WWRF
MWWCR	Mortaria, 1.2%. As WWCR

The local fabric varies in its content of quartz inclusions from a relatively fine fabric with sparse inclusions of small size, through differing grades to one with abundant quartz inclusions. The hardness of the fabric varies according to the level of inclusions, and whether

a)

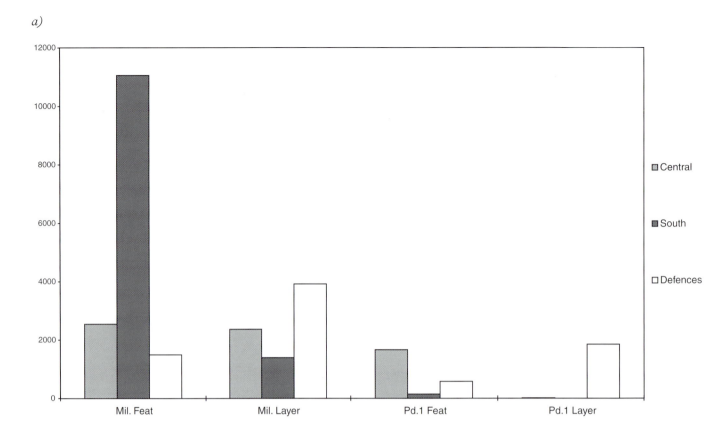

b)

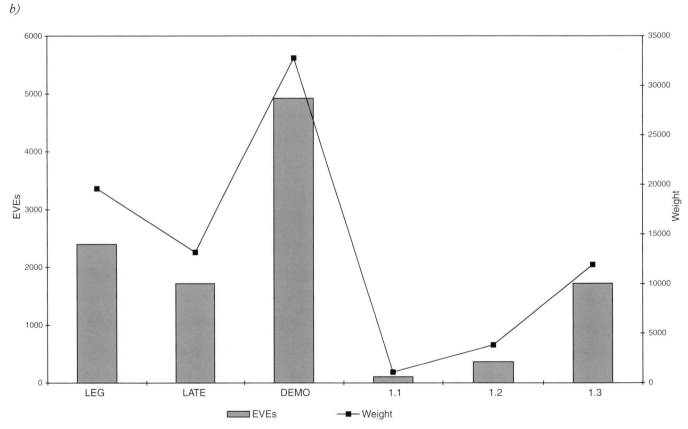

Fig 5.4 Pottery: a) EVEs from features and layers by Period and Area; b) EVEs and weight from cut features by Phase

it is oxidised or reduced, the latter usually being harder fired, sometimes over-fired to the point of being virtually stoneware; generally the vessels are thin-walled, and relatively hard. The basic division of the fabric is between oxidised and reduced, with a normal and a finer version of each. The oxidised normal fabric is also white-slipped. The same variations occur in the mortaria. The reduced version of the fabric often has a partial oxidised core.

The fabric can usually be distinguished from other fabrics, although vessels probably made within the area in a Severn Valley tradition in the second century can pose problems with identification. A routine description of the fabric would fit many others, and identification relies upon the nature of the clay matrix, which has a dense 'porridgy' texture, impossible to describe adequately, with a scatter of quartz grains visible in the hand specimen. The surfaces are normally untreated, burnishing is rare and usually only as occasional burnished lines rather than zones on vessels such as jars, and knife-trimming of the basal zone on jars, bowls, and platters is a common feature. The finer versions of the fabric naturally lead to a smooth surfaced fabric, which may have been smoothed.

Three sherds were examined in thin section by D P S Peacock and revealed grains (<0.2–0.5mm) of quartz, quartzite, and black iron ore set in a matrix of optically isotropic fired clay. Occasional grains of quartzite, sandstone, and possibly chert could be seen. Most of the grains were sub-rounded but a few of the larger ones were very well rounded. In Peacock's opinion the petrology does not permit confident identification of geological origin, but there is no evidence against local production. The well rounded grains suggested a desert environment and could well have derived from the local Triassic beds.

While the same vessel forms occur in both the normal and finer versions of the fabric, there is a level of linkage between fabric and vessel type, as can be seen from Figure 5.5. This is based on EVEs and includes sherds allocated to vessel classes as well as to individual types, eg jar as opposed to a specific jar type. The most striking specific use of a fabric type is WWCR, the cream slipped oxidised fabric, used mostly for flagons, some jars and bowls and, not included in the chart, mortaria. The reduced version, WWR, comprises predominantly jars; it is rarely used for flagons but is common for beakers, bowls, cups etc. The rarest fabric type, WWRF, fine reduced, concentrates primarily on beakers, jars, and cups. Apart from WWCR, the finer oxidised WWOF is used least for jars, but commonly for platters, and almost exclusively for such vessels as lamps, tazze, and less common types, such as triple vases.

Regional wares

SV

Severn Valley wares. Under 1%. Virtually all sherds are standard Severn Valley vesicular fine fabric, grey cored, light red-brown surfaces, some of which appear to have charcoal and/or vegetable tempering. A few do not have the vesicular trait and may be a later variety or from a different kiln. Forms include butt/girth beaker types such as type nos 211 and 212 (Fig 5.37) (a rim fragment resembled a butt-beaker type), tankards, nos 217–19 (Fig 5.37), and jars, none illustrated, but rim fragments were all from simple curved rims. Two sherds came from the *Late* phase, and 18 from the *Demo* phase.

SVR

Severn Valley reduced wares. Under 1%. Fabric as SV but reduced to light to mid-grey; mostly vesicular with charcoal/vegetable tempering. Two thick body

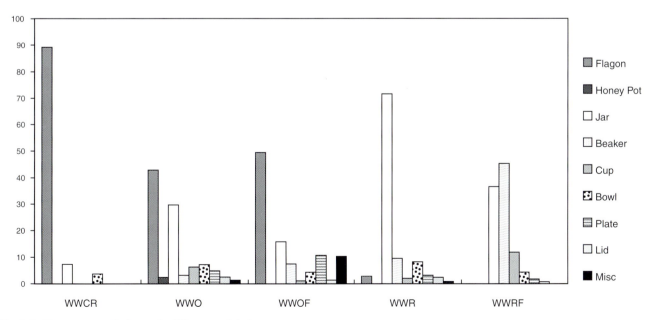

Fig 5.5 Pottery: vessel classes in Wroxeter fabrics

sherds came from *Leg* phase, seven from *Late*, including the jar, no 201 (Fig 5.37), and 14 from *Demo*, including the carinated beaker or tankard, no 220 (Fig 5.37), both vessels handmade. The most unusual vessel is a wheelthrown jar with rustication, no 199 (Fig 5.37), from a contaminated *Late* context. Apart from sherds likely to be from jars, mostly large, a small rim sherd was probably from a platter form of type 105 (Fig 5.33).

MALV

Malvernian, handmade. Under 1%. (Peacock 1968, 415–21, Group A). A single sherd occurred in the *Late* phase, and two further sherds in the *Demo* phase. These are probably intrusive. Not illustrated.

SHEL

Shell-tempered. Under 1%. Just a single sherd from a *Demo* context, possibly intrusive, and not identifiable for source. Not illustrated.

NATIVE WARES

Under 1%. All hand-made unless stated otherwise. The few sherds clearly came from different sources, and apart from a single sherd from a *Leg* context, six sherds came from the *Late* phase and eight from the *Demo* phase. Only two vessels are illustrated, nos 206 and 207 (Fig 5.37). Details of the fabrics are:

Main fabric All sherds in a very similar calcite gritted dark grey fabric, usually with oxidised exterior surfaces, including two curved jar rim fragments (*Demo* and contaminated context), and a neck fragment from a large jar (Period 1). The cooking pot no 206 is probably the same fabric, given burning, and the loss of calcite from the exterior, giving it a vesicular appearance. There is no evidence for burnishing or decoration.

Oxidised native Coarse oxidised fabric with calcareous inclusions, some evidence for smoothing/burnishing. Only a large jar rim fragment, simple curved rim from a probable *Leg* context, and a single body sherd from the *Late* phase.

Fabric with flint and grog Coarse fabric with flint and grog, oxidised one surface; chip only from the *Late* phase.

Sand tempered coarse Just two joining body sherds, coarse dark grey sand tempered fabric; insufficient to be certain whether handmade or wheelthrown, from the *Late* phase.

Coarse fabric with some calcite A fragment of a plain base, and body sherd, probably same vessel; coarse dark grey fabric with some calcareous inclusions, limescale internally, with some burnishing, including possible wide burnish line decoration. Possibly a Malvernian fabric. From Period 1.

Fine textured vesicular with mica Cooking pot rim fragment, no 207, fine textured light grey fabric, light red-brown cortex, grey to brown surfaces; some mica, vesicular; burnished externally. Not certainly handmade.

Traded wares

CREAM

Miscellaneous cream fabrics. 1.6%. This is a fabric group rather than a discrete fabric, the sources unknown. Most of the sherds were fine fabrics, but some with high proportions of quartz inclusions verged on *Verulamium* region white ware. A notable small group which appeared to be confined to military contexts were all from flagons, was a fine fabric with internal grey slip or coating. Similar flagons occur widely on southern sites, as Lake Farm – Wimborne, Cirencester, Exeter, *Clausentum*, and others, and are unlikely to be made locally. The use of white slip on the locally made flagons and mortaria suggests that iron-free clay was not readily available during the military period, although a cup type 75.2 (Fig 5.31) and perhaps the beaker, no 208 (Fig 5.37) might be local products. Where identifiable for vessel form, the majority of sherds were from flagons (as nos 187–9; Fig 5.37); a few were from beakers, with a small group of sherds from the *Demo* phase with painted decoration, mostly circles. Individual vessels included a honey pot (no 191; Fig 5.37), a tazza (no 222; Fig 5.37), a jar (no 194; Fig 5.37), a beaker (no 185; Fig 5.36), a rouletted beaker (no 208; Fig 5.37), and the cup type 75.2 (Fig 5.31), and there were fragments from possibly two platters of the Pompeian red ware form.

Only two sherds occurred in the *Leg* phase, one of which is possibly a chip of a Gauloise amphora, and the other from a flagon with the grey internal coating. Thirty-one sherds came from the *Late* phase, and the quantity leapt to 325 sherds in the *Demo* phase. These are individually described.

GREY

Miscellaneous grey fabrics. Under 1%. A fabric group, including all reduced vessels not certainly assignable to the local WWR fabric or any identifiable source. Illustrated: nos 186 (Fig 5.36), 192, 195–198, 200, 203–205, 209, 213–16 (Fig 5.37). Few of the fabrics are distinctive; individually described.

VRW

Verulamium region white ware. Under 1% (see Tyers 1983 for fabric and types). No vessels are illustrated, and where identifiable for vessel form, virtually all appeared to be from flagons apart from fragments of two lids, one from a *Leg* context. Apart from a fragment possibly from a two-handled flagon, the only type identified was the ring-necked type, the commonest type produced. Three sherds came from the *Leg* phase, and 53 sherds from the *Demo* phase, although 42 of these were probably from a single vessel.

BB1

Dorset Black-Burnished ware, Category 1 (Williams 1977, 163–220). The only sherds occurred as contaminants. Not illustrated.

Table 5.2 Pottery: fabrics by broad phase (excluding amphorae), % of assemblages

I. EVEs, percentages of phased assemblages

	LEG	F2807	LATE	DEMO	CONT	1.1	1.2	1.3
SAMSG	10.2	0.6	8.6	18.9	13.6	18.3	15.6	19.7
SAMCG	0	0.1	0	0	0.8	0	0.3	0
MORV	0.2	0	0	0.1	0	0	0	1.4
MONG	0	0	0	0	0	0	0	0.2
MOCRA	0	0	0	0.1	0.6	0	0	0
MORT1	0	0	0	0	0	0	0	0
MORT2	0	0	0	0.2	0	0	0	0
MORT3	0	0	0	0	0	0	0	0
MOVR	0	0	0	0.3	0.5	0	1.3	0.7
MWWO	1.6	0	0	0.3	0	0	0	1.3
MWWOF	0	0	0	0.2	0.3	0	0	1.8
MWWR	0	0	0	0	0.5	0	0	0
MWWRF	0	0	0	0	0	0	0	0
MWWCR	0	0	0.5	0	1.4	0	0	0.4
WWO	27.1	32.7	40.6	25.6	20.8	22.0	20.1	21.5
WWOF	9.0	0	17.1	5.1	5	1.9	6.7	5.9
WWR	49.2	63.7	26.9	40.2	45.9	20.2	38.7	34.3
WWRF	0	0	1.1	1.4	2.8	0	9.4	2.7
WWCR	0	0	0	2.0	0.8	0	0	2.2
LYON	1.1	0	0.8	0.8	1.4	5.6	1.7	0
CGCC	0	0	0	0	1.0	1.9	0	2.9
CGWH	0	0	0	0	0	0	0	0
CGGW	0	0	0	0.1	0	0	0	0
LRCC	0	0	0	0	0	0	0	0
NIEG	0	0	0	0	0	0	0	0
MICA1	0	0	0	0	0	0	0	0
TN	0	0	0	0	0.4	0	0	0
BLEG	0	0	0	0	0	0	0	0
GBWW	0	0	0	0	0	3.0	0	0.8
CC	0	0	0	0	0	0	0	0
CGBL	0	0	0	0	0	0	0	0
CGWH	0	0	0	0.2	0	0	0	0
PRW2	0	0	0	0.4	0	0	0	0
PRW3	1.1	0	0.2	0.1	0	0	0	0
CREAM	0	0.5	1.1	1.3	0	21.1	0	0.6
VRW	0.4	0	0	0.1	0	0	1.1	0
MICA2	0	0	0	0	0	0	0	0
OXID	0	2.3	0	0.8	2.5	0	0.6	1.2
SV	0	0	0	0.7	0	0	0	0.5
SVR	0	0	0.5	0.1	0.6	2.2	1.1	0
BB1	0	0	0	0	0	0	0	0
BLSF	0	0	0	0	0	0	0	0
GREY	0	0.1	2.6	0.8	0.7	3.9	2.3	2.0
MALV	0	0	0	0.1	0	0	1.1	0
NAT	0.2	0	0	0.3	0.4	0	0	0
SHEL	0	0	0	0	0	0	0	0
Total	100	100	100	100	100	100	100	100
Sample	2885	4402	3348	10215	1898	536	1048	2454

ii Weight, percentages of phased assemblages (*=presence under 0.1%)

	LEG	F2807	LATE	DEMO	CONT	1.1	1.2	1.3
SAMSG	4.3	0.5	3.6	8.3	10.8	8.4	4.8	8.1
SAMCG	0	0.2	*	*	1.0	0	*	0.1
MORV	0.5	0	0.5	0.8	0.1	0	2.4	7.8
MONG	0	0	0	0.2	0	1.4	0.1	0.6
MOCRA	0	0	0	0.2	1.9	0	0	0
MORT1	0	0	0	0	1.6	0	0	0
MORT2	0	0	0	0.3	0	0	0	0
MORT3	0	0	0	0	0	0	0	0.3
MOVR	0	0	0	1.2	2.1	0	1.0	2.0
MWWO	5.5	0	2.2	0.8	0.5	0	1.2	0
MWWOF	0	0	0	0.9	0.6	0	0	7.1
MWWR	0	0	0	*	0.8	0	0	3.3
MWWRF	0	0.2	0	0	0	0	0	0
MWWCR	0	0	2.8	0.5	5.7	0	0	0.3
WWO	41.7	38.7	51.4	35.0	29.0	40.5	27.7	28.9
WWOF	3.8	*	11.6	4.6	4.9	2.9	4.7	1.6
WWR	33.3	58.5	24.0	36.6	33.3	24.6	35.3	29.6
WWRF	0	0	0.4	0.7	2.0	0	0.9	0.8
WWCR	*	0	0.3	3.4	1.6	9.4	6.0	2.6
LYON	0.4	0.1	0.5	0.3	0.5	0.3	0.3	0.2
CGCC	0	0	0	*	0.1	0.1	0.1	0.2
CHWH	0	0	0	0	0	0	0	0
CGGW	0	0	0	*	0	0	0.1	0
LRCC	0	0	0	0	*	0	0	0
NIEG	0	*	0	0	0	0	0	0
MICA1	0	0	0	0	0	0	0	0
TN	0	0	0	0	0.1	0	0	0
BLEG	0	0	0	*	0	0	0	0
GBWW	0.2	*	0	*	0	0.7	0.1	0.2
CC	0	0	0	*	0	0	0.2	0
CGBL	0	0	0	0	*	0	0	0
CGWH	0	0	0	*	0	0	0	0
PRW2	0	0	0	0.6	0	0.4	0	0
PRW3	0.3	0	0.2	*	*	0	0.2	0
CREAM	0.1	0.6	0.7	2.8	0.4	5.0	1.7	1.1
VRW	0.2	0	0	0.3	0.4	0.6	1.7	0.6
MICA2	0	0	0	*	0	0	0	0
OXID	9.3	1.0	0	0.2	0.4	0.1	0.9	0.9
SV	0	0	0.1	0.4	0.3	0.2	4.7	0.5
SVR	0.3	0	0.5	0.4	0.3	2.1	0.6	0.1
BB1	0	0.1	0	0	0.5	0	0	0
BLSF	*	0	0	0.1	0	0	0	0
GREY	0.1	0.1	1.0	1.1	1.2	3.4	4.8	2.0
MALV	0	0	*	*	0	0	0.4	0
NAT	0.1	0	0.2	0.2	0.2	0	0	0.4
SHEL	0	0	0	*	0	0	*	0
Total	100	100	100	100	100	100	100	100
Sample	23215	18047	28621	71174	11857	4139	10442	17966

OXID

Miscellaneous oxidised wares, a fabric group, sources unknown. 1.6%. Where certain identification of the fabric, as WWO or SV was impossible, sherds were coded as OXID. Only two vessels came from the *Leg* phase, the large handmade jar, no 202 (Fig 5.37), and a small body sherd perhaps from a bowl with a cordon on a carination, the fabric resembling Severn Valley ware. A base, no 221 (Fig 5.37), also resembled Severn Valley ware. Just three flagons occurred, no 184, from F2807 (Fig 5.36), a fragment of a ring-necked type with a predominant top-ring from the *Demo* phase,

probably intrusive, and no 190 (Fig 5.37) from a contaminated late context. The only other vessel forms identified were jars, narrow-necked and everted rim types. Individually described.

FINE WARES
All under 1%. See below for full discussion.

CGCC
Central Gaul colour-coated (Greene 1979, 43). Cup (no 232; Fig 5.38); beakers (nos 236, 237; Fig 5.38). Possibly lamps (nos 248, 249; Fig 5.38).

CGWH
Central Gaul colour-coated, white fabric (Greene 1979, 43). Two sherds only from *Demo* phase, intrusive. Not illustrated.

CGGW
Central Gaul glazed ware (Greene 1979, 87). Beaker (no 238; Fig 5.38).

GBWW
Gallo-Belgic white wares. Beaker (no 210; Fig 5.37).

LRCC
Lower Rhineland colour-coated (Greene 1979, 56). Cup (no 233; Fig 5.38).

LYON
Lyon ware (Greene 1979, 13). Cups (nos 223–31; Fig 5.38); beakers nos 234 and 235 (Fig 5.38).

MICA1
Mica dusted, imported bobble beaker (Greene 1979, 129). Beaker (no 240; Fig 5.38).

MICA2
Mica dusted, coarser. A single sherd from a closed form, perhaps a beaker or flagon, came from the *Demo* phase, probably intrusive from Period 2. Probably a local product. Not illustrated.

NIEG
North Italian eggshell (Greene 1979, 75). This is a red cored dark grey fabric with dark grey surfaces, and occurred as a single sherd from F2807 pit from a cup. Not illustrated.

PRW
Pompeian red ware, undifferentiated. Just two platters, nos 243 and 244 (Fig 5.38), source unknown, but possibly local. Individually described.

PRW2
Pompeian red ware, Peacock Fabric 2 (Peacock 1977a, 153). Platter (no 242; Fig 5.38).

PRW3
Pompeian red ware, Peacock Fabric 3 (Peacock 1977a, 154). Platter (no 241; Fig 5.38) and lid (no 245; Fig 5.38).

TN
Terra Nigra (Rigby 1973). Two plates (nos 246 and 247; Fig 5.38).

BLEG
Gallo-Belgic black 'eggshell' ware (Greene 1979, 120). Not illustrated, just two sherds from beakers of the *Camulodunum* (Cam) 120 type. Light red-brown fabric with grey cortex, mid-grey surfaces, highly burnished externally. Very fine tiny quartz inclusions and some red/black specks, fairly micaceous.

BLSF
Black-surfaced Gallo-Belgic types, ?SE England source

Just two vessels, a tiny sherd probably from a beaker of the (Cam) 120 type, and narrow-necked jar (no 193; Fig 5.37). Fine-grained slightly laminar dark grey fabric with scatter of tiny quartz grains, black surfaces, finely burnished to a polish externally. The decorated jar, no 192 (Fig 5.37), although superficially similar, has a coarser fabric, although this could simply be a variant.

MORTARIA
All under 1%. See below for full discussion.

MORV
Rhone Valley mortaria. Very fine textured cream to pale brown fabric, sometimes with a pink core; scattered ill-sorted sharply angular quartz inclusions, also feldspar and biotite. Trituration probably quartz, as in fabric. Nos 250–52 (Fig 5.38).

MONG
North Gaulish mortaria. Fine textured cream fabric with a powdery surface, very rare inclusions, including red-brown and tiny blackish particles. Flint and quartz trituration, extending over the rim, and combined with concentric scoring internally. Hooked rims of Hartley Group 1. Not illustrated.

MOASTE
Mortaria from the workshop of the Atisii brothers at Aoste, Isere, *Gallia Narbonnensis*. Fine textured, micaceous, cream to pale brown, occasionally with a pink core; sparse inclusions of quartz, opaque white and red-brown. Trituration quartz. A sherd occurred residually in a post-military deposit (Period 2.3) Not illustrated.

MORH
Mortaria from the Rhineland. Pale brown fabric with sparse to common angular quartz, scatter of gold mica. Fragment of rim only from *85/112*, Post-military Period 2. Not illustrated.

MOCRA
Cream mortaria, source unknown. Fine textured, powdery, cream fabric with few quartz, red-brown and black inclusions; creamy brown slip. Much of the trituration is lost but it included quartz, opaque soft white and rare black material. The grits are also scattered on top of the rim, and there is rough concentric scoring on the interior and on the rim. The interior surface of no 256 (Fig 5.39) is totally unworn, many of the grits still covered by slip. The basal zone has been knife trimmed, creating shallow grooves. Hartley comments that the fabric is reminiscent of that used in the second-

century potteries at Wroxeter by potters using illegible stamps, but it lacks the heavy tempering often associated with those. The combination of grit and scoring inside and on top of the rim was a common, although not universal, first-century practice.

MORT1

Unknown source mortaria. Pink fabric fired to near cream at the surface, with brownish slip; frequent quartz inclusions. Some quartz on top of the flange and unusual tiny quartz trituration embedded on internal surface. Fragment only from *12/42* military pit F2228, with contamination.

MORT2

Possible early Rhineland mortarium. Fine textured, pink-brown fabric with very few inclusions, sparse small quartz and some red particles. Trituration was probably quartz but only one fragment survives. The only example is burnt. Smoothly finished with furrowed exterior. Hartley considers it probably a pre-Flavian import from the Rhineland. No 253 (Fig 5.38).

MOVR

Verulamium region mortaria. See Tyers 1983 for fabric. Nos 254 and 255 (Fig 5.38).

AMPHORAE

See Peacock and Williams 1986, and the discussion below.

Composition of the phased assemblages

Table 5.2 shows the development of the assemblage chronologically, and to a lesser extent the peculiarity of the pit F2807, which should be disregarded so far as the development is concerned. The unusual character of the pit group arises more from the vessel types, discussed below. Quantities of fabrics by period are presented in Appendix 3.2.

Local wares

The dominance of the local fabrics can be seen in Figure 5.6. This shows a decline in the local fabrics in the *demolition* phase which in view of the obviously high residuality to be anticipated in these contexts is quite marked. While the abrupt decline in the first phase of Period 1 is probably related to the small sample, the final Phase 1.3 is significant. The main occurrence of the cream-slipped local fabric in the *demolition* contexts is noteworthy, and this seems likely to have been an addition to the range later in the occupation. The earliest occurrence was in a building slot of Phase 4b, where it could easily have been intrusive. This fabric is much commoner in the post-military periods, particularly for flagons.

The general occurrence of all WW fabrics and the cream slipped in particular are shown on Figure 5.7, which shows WW fabrics as a percentage of all pottery (excluding amphorae), and the slipped fabric as a percentage of WW fabrics. This shows the broad

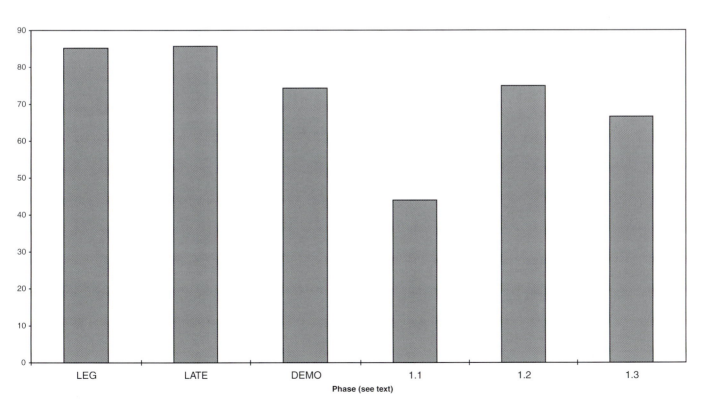

Fig 5.6 Pottery: % EVEs Wroxeter ware (excluding mortaria) by Phase

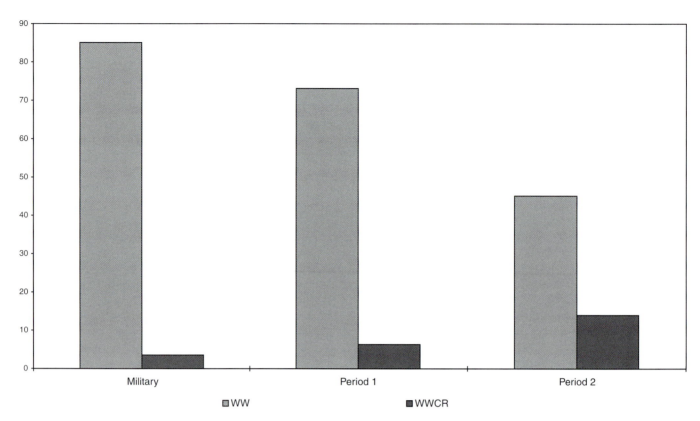

Fig 5.7 Pottery: % Wroxeter fabric by Period, with WWCR as % of all Wroxeter ware (based on weight)

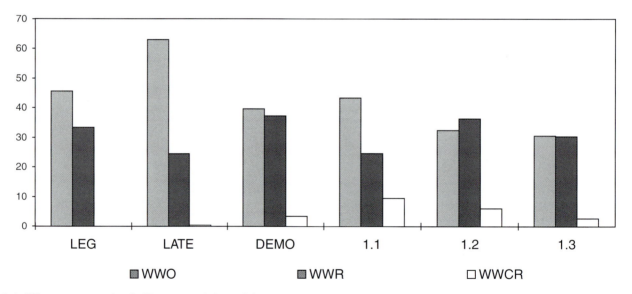

Fig 5.8 Wroxeter ware (excluding mortaria), weight percentages by Phase

decline of Wroxeter wares in the assemblages, and the increasing importance of the cream-slipped version.

The ratio between oxidised and reduced versions of the local fabric appears to remain fairly constant, although it is possible that the reduced version became marginally commoner later (Fig 5.8). The small quantity of pottery from Period 1 provides little evidence for change in this ratio, but it seems clear that within Period 2 the ratio of oxidised to reduced local wares is probably closer to 2:3.

The unusual figures for the *Late* contexts are almost certainly related to the composition of the assemblage in terms of vessel classes, discussed below, with a high proportion of flagons, which would also account for the significantly higher quantity of the finer oxidised fabric.

The highest incidence of decoration on local Wroxeter fabric vessels during the military period occurs in the *demolition* period, when 3% of the sherds were decorated, and approximately that proportion or a little higher occurs in Period 1. This figure includes rouletting, which occurs pre-demolition, and rough-casting, imitating Lyon ware. Rustication and applied barbotine blobs or dots account for 2% in the *demolition* period, and earlier occurrences are confined to the *Late* period, a total of 12 sherds, 0.52%, all deriving from the difficult Area 84 in the defences area, where there is only a single layer with pottery phased to the succeeding Period 1. There is therefore little strong evidence to suggest that rusticated and barbotine decorated wares appeared before the latest military phase.

Non-local wares

The dominance of the local fabrics leaves little room for other fabrics, few of them accounting for more than 1% of the assemblage (Tables 5.2 and 5.3). Two that appear to be of increasing importance, both fabric groups covering more than one discrete fabric, are CREAM, predominantly used for flagons, and GREY. It is possible that the latter is underestimated due to the difficulty in distinguishing between WWR and some similar GREY fabrics macroscopically.

Only two sherds of CREAM occur in the earliest period, one of which is a scrap which could be from a Gailes 4 amphora; the other resembles early flagons found on military sites in the south, for example at Lake Farm, Wimborne. It is also probable that the sparse imports from the *Verulamium* region belong to the later rather than earlier period, although the occasional vessel may have been brought to the site earlier as baggage, along with perhaps the black-surfaced fabric (BLSF) and the Gallo-Belgic white-wares (almost all a single butt-beaker), probably from south-eastern Britain rather than an import. The earliest occurrence of VRW is in Phase 4b, the demolition of the barracks.

A single sherd of GREY occurred in the earliest period, in Area 85 pit F270. The occurrence of Severn Valley wares in the early period is confined to two sherds of the reduced organic-tempered fabric. Two sherds of oxidised Severn Valley ware occur in the *Late* phase, but its main appearance is in the demolition contexts. More appears in Period 1, some of which could be residual, but the wares only become more common in Period 2.

The only mortaria from elsewhere to occur before the demolition period are those from the Rhone Valley, and it is likely that mortaria from the only other significant suppliers, the North Gaulish and *Verulamium* region potters, only appeared late in the military period.

Table 5.3 Pottery: summary of significant other fabrics, percentages based on weight

	LEG	LATE	DEMO	1.1	1.2	1.3
CREAM	0.1	0.7	2.8	5.0	1.7	1.1
GREY	0.1	1.0	1.1	3.4	4.8	2.0
VRW	0.2	–	0.3	0.6	1.7	0.6
MOVR	–	–	1.2	0	1.0	2.0
SV	0.3	0.6	0.8	2.3	5.3	0.6

Summary

The phased distribution of fabrics leaves little doubt that the earlier occupation was supplied almost exclusively by the local potters, and a characteristic of the later assemblages is the diversification of supplies from other sources. The sheer quantity, even allowing for considerable residual material, of local fabrics in the later contexts, and in the post-military periods, indicates that local production continued. Although some decline in the local potting is probable, it appears to have remained as a major supplier until the advent of BB1.

The phased occurrence of South Gaulish samian shows a decline in the *late* period, but the considerable quantities in the *demolition* contexts may give an indication of the residual content of the last phase. The quantity of Flavian samian nearly doubles between the *Late* contexts and those of the *Demo*, but the largest group even in the *demolition* contexts is still the pre-Flavian vessels except in the defences zone. This is discussed below. Since the sample sizes of both all pottery and samian, specifically in the earlier and *Late* period, are broadly similar, this decline is noteworthy.

The samian

Detailed analysis of the samian to relate the military assemblage to the succeeding phases and to assess residuality has been restricted to the first three periods, the military period followed by Periods 1 and 2, corresponding to the early civilian occupation and the construction of the baths and *macellum*. This section seeks to relate the samian and particularly its dating evidence to the site, both stratigraphically and spatially.

The samian from these long excavations has suffered during storage moves, so that some already reported sherds were missing when the quantification records were prepared. The quantity missing, based on individual records, accounted for 6.8% from the military contexts, 5.3% from Period 2, and (unfortunately) 15.5% from Period 1. A notional one sherd, weight 5g, has been included for the missing records (based on the fact that 75% of the records relate to single sherds and the average sherd weight is 6g), except in the case of stamps, normally heavier, where an average weight for the vessel type has been used.

Catalogue of South Gaulish samian stamps

by Brenda Dickinson

Each entry gives: potter (i, ii, etc., where homonyms are involved), die number, form, reading of the stamp, pottery of origin, date, excavation code and phase.

Superscripts indicate:

a   Stamp attested at the pottery in question.

b   Potter, but not the particular stamp, attested at the pottery in question.

c   Assigned to the pottery on the evidence of fabric, distribution and, or, form.

Underlined letters in stamps are ligatured.

1   Abitus 9a 24? ꓱABIT[Ⅎ] La Graufesenque[a]. This was nearly always used on cups, including the pre-Flavian forms 24 and Ritt 9. The die deteriorated, so that some examples, including the Wroxeter one, appear to read - ꓱABDIꓱ. c A.D. 55–70. *78/57*. M7iv.

3   Acutus i 10a 27 ꝪAC La Graufesenque[a]. A stamp nearly always found on form 24, though one example has been noted on form Ritt 8. Other stamps of this potter occur at Velsen (before AD 47), in a Claudio-Neronian group at Narbonne and on Tiberian form 29s. c AD 35–60. *98/186*. 1.2.

11   Albus i 3b 27g OFAꞭBI (Ettlinger 1978, Taf 1, 1) La Graufesenque[a]. Some of the stamps from this die are recorded from Flavian foundations, such as Castleford, Chester (2), the Nijmegen fortress and York, but there are several examples on very small dishes, which seem to be mainly pre-Flavian. Albus was certainly at work in the Neronian period, on the evidence of decoration on form 29s stamped by him. c AD 50–70. *9/30*. 1.1.

13–4   Amandus ii 4a 27g; 27 OFAMAN La Graufesenque.[a] A stamp recorded from the Cirencester Fort Ditch deposit of c AD 55–65 (Hartley and Dickinson 1982, 120, no 1). It is usually on form 27, but occasionally appears on the pre-Flavian cups, forms 24 and Ritterling 8. The site record includes Camulodunum, Fishbourne (Period 1B) and Hofheim, and there is another example from Wroxeter (Site Museum A677 T.T.) c AD 50–65. *92/18; 91/55*. 2.1; 3.3.

15   Amandus iii 1a 37, from a mould stamped below the decoration, O(FAMAN)D(I) retr. (Laubenheimer 1979, 106, fig. 3) La Graufesenque[a]. The die for this was used on Flavian-Trajanic decorated bowls and on dishes of forms 18/31 and 18/31R, rather than 18 and 18R. This makes him one of the latest potters of La Graufesenque to have exported to Britain. c AD 85–110. *92/4* (Probably). 2.4.

19   Aquitanus Incomplete 2 15/17 or 18 OFAQ[La Graufesenque[b]. Aquitanus was basically a Claudio-Neronian potter, who may have started work by AD 40. His stamps occur at Velsen (before AD 47), in the pottery shops at Colchester destroyed in the Boudiccan burning, and on decorated ware which does not look later than the middle of the Neronian period. c AD 45–60. *80/172*. 2.3.

27   Bassus iii 2b 15/17 or 18/31 OF.BAS[SI] La Graufesenque[a]. A stamp of the later South Gaulish Bassus, who worked at La Graufesenque in the Flavian-Trajanic period. His stamps occur at Butzbach (3), Saalburg and the main site at Corbridge. c AD 90–110. *84/45*. 4.0.

32   Calvica 1b 27g CΛLVICΛ La Graufesenque[c]. This may be a stamp of Calvus i, in association with a potter whose name begins in Ca.., but its use on form Ritt 8 makes this unlikely. A stamp with the same reading, but from a different die, occurs at Valkenburg ZH, from the Woerd (mid first-century). c AD 50–65. *84/250*. M7iv.

33   Calvus i 2a 33? [O]FIꝪALVI La Graufesenque[a]. The earliest vessel on which this stamp has been recorded is from Risstissen (before c AD 75) and the latest comes from Newstead c AD 70–95. *91/94*. 2.3

34   Calvus i 5r 15/17 or 18 OF(C)ALVI La Graufesenque[b]. Not one of Calvus's commoner stamps. It has been noted from the Nijmegen fortress (2) and Ulpia Noviomagus sites. There are no examples from pre-Flavian contexts. c AD 70–90. *84/205, joining 84/137*. M7iv; 2.1

35   Carus i 11a 18 KARV[ꙅF] La Graufesenque[a]. Decorated ware stamped by this potter is Neronian-Flavian, but this particular stamp is more likely to be entirely Flavian. It is known from Brecon, Caerleon and the main site at Corbridge c AD 70–90. *80/22, joining 81/69*. 3.4; 3.3

38   Ce- i 2a Ritt. 9 OFCE (in double impression) La Graufesenque[c]. Not recorded before. Neronian, on the evidence of fabric and glaze. *70/16*. 1.1

40   Celsus ii 8b 27 CELSI (Hermet 1934, pl 110, 32) La Graufesenque[a]. The lettering of South Gaulish Celsus stamps divides into two distinct styles, one pre-Flavian, the other almost certainly after AD 70 and certainly in use until the 90s, at least. This belongs stylistically to the later group, and there are two examples from the Ulpia Noviomagus site at Nijmegen. c AD 75–95. *83/536*. 2.1

42   Censor i 2a 15/17 or 18 OFCENS (Laubenheimer 1979, no 38) La Graufesenque[b]. Censor i may have started work c AD 65, but there is no evidence that this stamp was used in the pre-Flavian period. Examples have been noted from the fortress and Ulpia Noviomagus sites at Nijmegen and at Ilkley and Chester. c AD 70–95. *92/17*. 2.3

54 (A.?) Cosius Iucundus 1a' 18 <ƆFCO•IV<C> (Vanderhoeven 1975, 51, no 182) La Graufesenque[a]. All the dating evidence for this potter points to Flavian-Trajanaic activity. The stamp, from a broken die, occurs at Catterick, while the complete version is attested at Newstead. c AD 80–110. *85/127*. 2.1

55 Cosius Rufinus 5a 18 COSIR[VFI] La Graufesenque[a]. The whole of this potter's output is Flavian and his latest stamps, from other dies, are known from Camelon and Newstead. This is from an earlier die, used on form 29. c AD 75–90. *85/105*. 2.3

56 Crestio? 5a? 15/17 or 18 [OF>CREST]IO (Dickinson 1984, S3) La Graufesenque[a]. This appears as an internal stamp on form 29s from La Graufesenque and the Gloucester Kingshom site, both from moulds signed Mod (presumably by Modestus i). It is also in Period I at Verulamium. However, it is not unknown at Flavian foundations, such as Chester (2), the Nijmegen fortress (3) and York (2). c AD 55–70. *83/+*. Unstratified.

59 Damonus 1c 15/17R or 18R OF•DΛMO[NI•] La Graufesenque[a]. No other examples of this stamp have been noted by us so far. Damonus's other stamps occur in Claudio-Neronian groups from La Graufesenque and Narbonne and there is one from Hod Hill. He occasionally stamped early forms, such as 16, 17 and Ritt 1. c AD 35–55. *63/5*. 1.1

66 Ego 1a 27g EGOFE, in a frame with swallow-tail ends, La Graufesenque[c]. This stamp was presumably meant as a joke, ego fe(ci), or just possibly an abbreviated name in Ego. Some examples, including one from Newstead, seem almost to have lost the swallow-tail ends, but here they are pronounced. Flavian. *84/100*. 2.2

68 Fabus 5a' 15/17 or 18 <F>ABVSFE (Hartley 1972, S117) La Graufesenque[a]. A stamp from a broken die, used on the pre-Flavian cups, forms Ritt. 8 and 9. This version occurs in the Cirencester Fort Ditch of c AD 55–65 (Hartley and Dickinson 1982, 121, S.10), while a stamp from the complete die turns up in Period IA (c AD 40/47) at Valkenburg ZH. c AD 55–65. *98/52*. 2.3

69 Felicio iii 5a 46? CEFLICIO retr. Montans[a]. This stamp, though misspelt, is certainly from a die of the Felicio who worked at Montans in the second century. His stamps are quite common in Antonine Scotland, and this particular one is known from Balmuildy and Old Kilpatrick. Others appear in a group of burnt samian from St Cathcrinc Coleman, London, which was probably part of the debris of the Second Fire. c AD 125–145/150. *69/26*. 3.1

70 Felix i 6b 27g OFFEIC (Hull 1958, fig. 9, 6) La Graufesenque[a]. This is a stamp noted from one of the Colchester pottery shops destroyed in the Boudiccan burning, in AD 60/61. It is always on cups, usually form 27, though it was also used on form 24. c AD 50–65. *67/16*. M7v

71 Firmo iii 3a or a' cup [OFIR]MON[IS] or [OFIR]MON La Graufesenque[a]. A stamp from the original die occurs in a group of burnt samian from a pottery shop at Oberwinterthur, Switzerland, which was burnt down in the early 60s. Stamps which cannot be assigned to one version or the other, but which are more likely to be from the broken die, occur at Newstead and Malton. c AD 60–85. *98/83*. 2.3

72 Flavius Germanus 9t 18/31 OF•FL•GER (Dannell 1971, no 33) La Graufesenque[b]. One of the potter's less-common stamps. His wares occur repeatedly at Domitianic foundations both in Britain and Upper Germany, and examples have been noted from sites such as Chesterholm, Malton, Butzbach and Saalburg. He should have been at work by the early 80s, in view of his occasional use of form 29, but this particular stamp is only on plain ware. c AD 85–110. *98/20*. 3.4

73 Florus ii 3a' (possibly), 27g FLO<RI>] La Graufesenque[b]. If correctly identified, this stamp is from a broken die, the original of which was used to stamp a pre-Flavian form 29. A vessel stamped with the broken die (3a') occurs in an early-Flavian context at the Caerleon fortress. c AD 50–65. *98/61*. 2.3

80 Iovius 4c 27 IOVI[I] La Graufesenque[c]. From the general absence of pre-Flavian forms, apart from one cup of form 24, it seems that most of Iovius's output was after c AD 70. c AD 65–90. *1/55*. 1.1

84 Lentu- 1a 18 [LEΛ]TVF (*Mainzer Zeitschrift* 73/74) (1979), 352) La Graufesenque[a]. The footring is heavily worn. The stamp is in a grave at Mainz with stamps of several Claudio-Neronian potters. Elsewhere it occurs on form Ritt. 8 and on form 29 in Neronian syle. c AD 50–65. *78/15*. M5

85 Licinus 7b 29 (LICI[NIANAO] (Fiches *et al* 1978, no 61) La Graufesenque[a]. The decoration of the bowls carrying this stamp is typical of the period c AD 40–60. *17/41*. 3.1

86 Lucceius i 6a 24 (with footring completely unworn) OF.LV[CC] La Graufesenque[b]. The die was applied off-centre and has slipped, giving a double impression. Lucceius's activity was entirely pre-Flavian. Stamps from several of his dies occur at Camulodunum, and his forms include Ritt. 8.

His decorated ware suggests that he began work under Claudius. *c* AD 45–65. *80/192.* M4a

87   Lupus ii 3a' 15/17 or 15 LVPI<u>MA</u> (Dannell 1971, no 59) La Graufesenque[a]. 3a has a frame with swallow-tail ends; the frame of 3a' has had the ends rounded off. Lupus ii's output seems to be entirely pre-Flavian and, although this particular version of the stamp occurs at the Nijmegen fortress, an even later version is known from Risstissen, a site which seems to have been evacuated in the early 70s. *c* AD 50–65. *46/+.* Unstratified

88   Lupus ii 6a 18 LVPVS (Glasbergen 1955, nos 224–5) La Graufesenque[a]. There is no site dating for this stamp, but it was used on the pre-Flavian cups, forms 24, Ritt. 8 and Ritt. 9. A graffito,]an[or]nu[is inscribed on the lower wall, after firing. *c* AD 45–65. *3/13.* 3.2

96   Modestus i 4d 18 OFM<u>ODES</u> La Graufesenque[a]. A stamp noted in a Claudio-Neronian group at Narbonne (Fiches *et al* 1978, no 57), and on the pre-Flavian cup, form Ritt. 8. *c* AD 50–65. *92/65.* M7iv

97   Modestus 9a' 27g OFMOI (from a die originally giving OFMOD) (Laubenheimer 1979, no 135) La Graufesenque[a]. Both versions of the die were used in the pre-Flavian period, but the later one, 9a', must have continued in use into the 70s or even later, on the evidence of sites such as Ebchester and Broomholm. By this time the die must surely have passed from Modestus to another potter. *c* AD 60–75/80. *98/141.* 1.3

98   Modestus i 9b 27g OFMOD (Ulbert 1969, no 44) La Graufesenque[a]. There is no site dating for this stamp, but its use on form 24 and, probably, Ritt. 9 confirms its pre-Flavian date. *c* AD 45–65. *3/20.* 2.1

99   Mommo 9c'' 15/17 or 18 (almost certainly) ƆFMON (from a die originally giving OFMOΛ) La Graufesenque[a]. Stamps from the original die occur on form 24, but also at Rottweil and the main site at Corbridge, the last certainly a survival. The two subsequent versions of the die are not precisely dated, but the final version probably falls within the range *c* AD 75–85. *98/194.* 1.2

100   Mommo 9i 15/17 or 18 [OI[I]Λ]OΛ La Graufesenque[a]. An earlier stamp than the last, noted on pre-Flavian forms (24 and Ritt. 1) and in a group of burnt samian from a pottery shop at Oberwinterthur, Switzerland, destroyed by fire in the early 60s. *c* AD 60–80. *98/52.* 2.3

101   Montanus i 7c or c' 15/17 or 18 ΜOИT[ΛNI] or ΜOИT[ΛN] (Glasbergen 1955, no 277 or 278) La Graufesenque[a]. The original die was used to stamp the pre-Flavian dish, form

16. The broken version was also used in the pre-Flavian period, on the evidence of a stamp from the Gloucester Kingsholm site, and it was still in use in the early 70s, with stamps occurring at Caerleon and Chester. *c* AD 55–75. *85/32.* 2.3

103   Murranus 8f 15/17 or 18 OF.<u>MVRRAN</u> La Graufesenque[a]. This is known from Camulodunum and from Period I at Verulamium (Hartley 1972, S3) *c* AD 50–65. *98/233.* M7iv

104   Murranus 9a 27g OF<u>MVR</u> ΛИ (in double impression. MVR and AN ligatured (Tilhard 1988, 170) La Graufesenque[b]. Like several of Murranus's stamps, this is noted at Flavian foundations (Rottweil and the Nijmegen fortress), though most of his output is pre-Flavian. The full reading of the stamp is OFMVRAN, with MVR and AN ligatured, but on some examples, like the Wroxeter one, the final stroke of the N does not register. The potter's thumb-print is visible on the base, where he pushed down the slight central boss before applying the stamp. *c* AD 55–70. *84/215.* M7iv

105   Murranus 10d' 27g OF<u>MVR</u>R/(from a die originally giving OF<u>MVR</u>RΛ) La Graufesenque[a]. Both versions of the die were used on the pre-Flavian cup, form Ritt. 8. The broken version, as here, occurs in a group of samian from a pottery store at Oberwinterthur, Swtizerland, destroyed by fire in the early 60s. *c* AD 50–65. *98/49.* 3.2

106   C. N- Celsus 3a 27 [OF•C•]N•CE La Graufesenque[b]. All the examples noted so far have been on form 27. Stamps from other dies of this potter come from Chesterholm, Wilderspool and at Nijmegen (in a burial with an *as* of Nerva of AD 97). *c* AD 80–110. *98/33.* 3.2

110   Niger ii 2a 29 O(FNIG)RI (Hartley and Dickinson 1993, fig 104) La Graufesenque[a]. The die was used exclusively on bowls of form 29. All appear to be Neronian, but a few have been noted in Flavian contexts. See fig 5.21 no 31. *c* AD 50–65. *2/36.* 1.1

111–13 Niger ii 3a 27?; 27g (2) OFNGRI;]GRI; OFNGRI (Hermet 1934, no 113) La Graufesenque[a]. The die was reserved for cups, including the pre-Flavian forms 24 and Ritt. 8 and 9. There is one example from Chester. *c* AD 55–70. *3/14; 14 32; 85/105.* 2.2; 1.3; 2.3

115   Pass(i)enus 5a 29 OFP(Λ)ƧƧENI (Durand-Lefebvre 1963, no 547) La Graufesenque[a]. This stamp, used only on form 29, is one of Pass(i)enus's latest. All the bowls concerned are early-Flavian, and there are

examples from Caerleon (2), Carlisle (2) and the main site at Corbridge. c AD 70–80. *97/133.* 2.3

116 Pass(i)enus 50a 24 OP[ASSIE] (Hartley and Dickinson 1982, S33) La Graufesenque[a]. One of the potter's earlier stamps, recorded in the Cirencester Fort Ditch deposit of c AD 55–65 and one of the pottery shops at Colchester destroyed in AD 60/61. c AD 50–65. *78/5.* 1.1

125 Patricius i 3h 15/17 or 18 [OFP]ATRIC(I) (Laubenheimer 1979, no 170) La Graufesenque[a]. The earliest example of this stamp noted by this writer is from the Burghöfe Geschirrdepot of AD 69. The latest ones come from Camelon and Oakwood. c AD 65–95. *84/100.* 2.2

126–7 Patricius i 4c 15/17 or 18 (2) [OF]PATRIC,]ATRIC (Laubenheimer 1979, no 171) La Graufesenque[b]. Most of this potter's output is Flavian, and there is no evidence that this stamp was in use before c AD 70. It has been noted once on an early-Flavian bowl of form 29. c AD 70–90. *92/18, 98/100.* 2.1; 3.1

128 Patricius i 13j 24? [PATR]ICI La Graufesenque[b]. If the form is correctly identified, this must be from one of Patricius's earlier dies, which would have first been used in the pre-Flavian period. c AD 65–75. *84/137.* 2.1

131 Primus iii 12d 29 (OFPRI)MI (Hartley and Dickinson 1982, 120, no 36) La Graufesenque[a]. Kiln-grit survives inside the base, but the footring is moderately worn. The stamp, which is known only on form 29s, occurs in the Cirencester Fort Ditch filling of c AD 55–65. c AD 50–65. *85/II 255.* M3

132 Primus iii 12r 15/17 or 18 [OFPRI]MI (Nieto Prieto *et al* 1989, no 39.1) La Graufesenque[a]. The lettering of this stamp leves no doubt that it comes from a die of Primus iii, in spite of the vertical stroke in the first part of the M, which could be taken to represent AM ligatured. The site record includes Colchester (unburnt, but with burnt material from the Boudiccan destruction), Verulamium (Period II, in a pit filled by c AD 75), Caerleon and a wreck of c AD 75 or slightly later, recovered off Cala Culip, southern Spain. c AD 60–75/80. *16/153.* 2.3

133 Primus iii 12v 18 OFPRIM(I) La Graufesenque[a]. The style of the letters on this stamp suggests Neronian date, though one example comes from the Nijmegen fortress. It also occurs in one of the Colchester pottery shops destroyed in AD 60/61 (Hull 1958, 198, no 15). c AD 50–65. *98/83.* 2.3

134 Primus iii 18b 18 OFPRIM (Hartley 1972, S4) La Graufesenque[a]. Footring slightly worn. This stamp is known both from Period I at Verulamium and from the two pottery shops at Colchester destroyed in AD 60/61. It was used on the pre-Flavian cups, forms 24 and Ritt. 8. c AD 55–65. *63/15.* 1.3

144 Rufinus iii 4c 27 [O]FRVFIN (Durand-Lefebvre 1963, no 634) La Graufesenque[a]. This stamp is known from early-Flavian foundations, such as Caerleon, Carlisle, and the Nijmegen fortress. c AD 70–90. *78/5.* 1.1

151 Saciro i 2a dish, slightly burnt, SACIROF Espalion[c]. A large dish, with base and footring like 15/17R and 18R, but without rouletting. There is a central ring on the base, perhaps round a stamp, and a wide ring above the footring, across which the stamp is placed, at about 45° to it. Stamps of Primulus and Primus are similarly placed on dishes from Espalion, which are thought to have originated there, rather than at La Graufesenque (M. J-L Tilhard, unpub thesis). Saciro used a different die to stamp form 29. Neronian-Flavian? *91/72 + 91/85.* 2.3; 1.3

153 G. Salarius Aptus 1a 29 OF•G•SAL•AP+ (Hermet 1934, no 148) La Graufesenque[a]. Footring scarcely worn. The die was used exclusively on bowls of form 29, one of which, at La Graufesenque, is from the same mould as a bowl stamped by the Claudio-Neronian potter, Lucceius i. c AD 50–65. Unstratified

155 Secundinus i 1a 18/31R [SECVNDI]NIMA La Graufesenque[a]. This occurs in a predominantly Favian-Trajanic group at La Graufesenque (Vernhet 1981, 34, no 19). Other examples come from Dambach, Ober Florstadt and Saalburg (3). Graffito X inscribed under the base, after firing. c AD 85–110. *84/49.* 2.3

156 Secundus ii 11b 27 OFSEC[V] La Graufesenque[a]. Most of Secundus ii's output is early-Flavian. Some of his dies, though not this one, were used to stamp pre-Flavian cups, such as forms 24 and Ritt. 8. c AD 70–90. *86/21.* 4.0

159 Senicio 6a' 29 <S>ENIC(I)<O> (Nieto Prieto *et al* 1989, no 15.1) La Graufesenque[a]. The original version of this stamp occurs in the Cirencester Fort Ditch group of c AD 55–65 and on forms 24 and Ritt. 9. Stamps from 6a', the broken die, while noted once on forms 24 and, probably, Ritt. 8, are much commoner on form 27. Examples are recorded from a wreck of the early 70s off Cala Culip (Spain) c AD 65–80. *98/178.* 1.3

161   Severus iii 28b 27 SEVE La Graufesenque [a]. One of the potter's less-common stamps. An example from Hofheim will be before *c* AD 75, *c* AD 65–95. *77/9.* 1.1

166   C. Silvius Patricius 12a 15/17 or 18 [CSI]LVIP (Laubenheimer 1979, no 264) La Graufesenque[b]. This potter is probably the man who more often stamped only with his *cognomen* (see nos 125–8). His work occurs in Flavian contexts and he occasionally stamped bowls of form 29. One of these, with the same stamp as here, is from a stamped mould of Severus iii (from Strasbourg). *c* AD 70–90. *7/41.* 1.1

167   Silvinus i 7a 27g SILVINIC (from a die sometimes giving SILVINIO) La Graufesenque[a]. A stamp from a die which was used on the pre-Flavian cups, forms 24 and Ritt. 8. The potter's career continued into the early-Flavian period. *c* AD 60–75. *34/20.* 1.1

181   Vanderio 1a 29 VΔΛ [DERIo] (Knorr 1919, Taf 80A) La Graufesenque[a]. A stamp used in the Neronian-Flavian period, mainly on bowls of form 29. It occurs in a group of samian of the 70s at Nijmegen, probably from a pottery shop (Morren 1966, 229, 7, 8). There is also an example on form 18 from Binchester. *c* AD 65–80. *88/6.* 4.0

183   Virthus 9a 15/17 or 18 VIRTHV La Graufesenque[a]. Virthus began work under Claudius, but the bulk of his output is Neronian and a few of his stamps have been noted in Flavian contexts. This particular stamp occurs at York and so is likely to be one of his later ones. Others are known from Castleford and the Nijmegen fortress. *c* AD 55–75. *84/109.* M7iv

184   Vitalis i 1c 18 OFVITALIS La Graufesenque[a]. This stamp of the earlier South Gaulish Vitalis occurs in a burial at Mainz with other stamped samian belonging to the period *c* AD 50–65 (*Mainzer Zeitschrift* 73/74 (1979), 252, no 19. Unstratified

185   Vitalis ii 4b or b' 29 [OF]VIT[ΛLIS] or [OF]VIT[ΛL] La Graufesenque[a]. Graffito IV[? inscribed under the base, after firing. Both the original die and the broken version were used mainly on early-Flavian form 29s. Stamps from the broken die, which are much commoner, occur at Caerleon, Rottweil, and the Nijmegen fortress. *c* AD 70–85. *92/20.* 2.1

186   Vitalis ii 8h'' 33 (burnt) OF.VITA La Graufesenque[a]. This is from the final version of a die which was modified when it was damaged. The original die was in use before AD 75, on the evidence of a stamp from Risstissen. Stamps from the earlier modification come from Ribchester and the Domitianic fort at

Butzbach. There is no internal dating yet for the latest die, but it will almost certainly fall within the period *c* AD 80–95. *84/158.* 2.3

189   O[or]O on form 15/17 or 18, South Gaulish. Neronian. *83/+.* Unstratified

190   ⱶV[or form 15/17R or 18R, South Gaulish. Neronian. *12/42.* M4b

191   ]/CI? on form 24, South Gaulish. Neronian. *9/17.* 2.2

192   MVR...? on form 27, burnt, South Gaulish. Neronian. *51/21.* 1.3

193   ..V..M? on form 29, South Gaulish. Neronian. *83/530.* 2.3

194   Illegible stamp on form 27g, South Gaulish. Neronian. *98/84.* 2.1

195   PRI[? or ⱶICI[, retr., on form 15/17 or 18, South Gaulish. Neronian. *98/131.* M7iv

196   ]ΔΛ IO on form 24, South Gaulish. Neronian. *63/+.* Unstratified

197   O[or]O on form 27g, South Gaulish. Neronian. *63/8.* 1.3

198   IICΛ or IICV retrograde on form 24, marbled, South Gaulish. Neronian. *91/93.* 2.3

199   GERM[?? on form 15/17 or 18, South Gaulish. Neronian or early-Flavian. *29/17.* 2.1

200   ΛΛFIⅨI on form 15/17 or 18, South Gaulish. Neronian. One of the commoner illiterate stamps, already known from Wroxeter (Rowley House Museum, E1285). Examples are noted from Flavian foundations, such as Carlisle and Castleford, but the die may have been made slightly earlier. This is Neronian or early-Flavian, to judge by the fabric and glaze. *91/93.* 2.3

201   ]OƧ? on form 15/17 or 18, South Gaulish. Neronian or early-Flavian. *98/33.* 3.2

202   D[on form 15/17R or 18R, South Gaulish. Neronian or early-Flavian. *97/137.* 2.2

203   ΛVN on form 27g, South Gaulish. Neronian or early-Flavian. *93/2.* 2.3

204   VIΛC on form 27g, South Gaulish. Neronian or early-Flavian. *92/20.* 2.1

205   OFI/I on form 27g, South Gaulish. Neronian or early-Flavian. *92/20.* 2.1

206   ..NIAS•I...(?) on form 27g, South Gaulish. Neronian or early-Flavian. *98/52.* 2.3

207   C[on form 27g, South Gaulish. Neronian or early-Flavian. *98/61.* 2.3

208   OF.VII or OΓΛTI retr., on form 27, South Gaulish. Neronian or early-Flavian. *92/+.* Unstratified

209   ]XI on form 27, South Gaulish. Neronian or early-Flavian. *92/4.* 2.4

210   Illegible, on form 27g, South Gaulish. Neronian or early-Flavian. *98/52.* 2.3

211   ]ΛΛ[or]VV[on form 27 or 33a, South Gaulish. Neronian or early-Flavian. *72/50.* M4b

212   ] on form 29, South Gaulish. Neronian or early-Flavian. *6/1.* 4.0

213 MVC•X•\: on form 27g, South Gaulish. Pre-Flavian. *92/61*. 1.1

214]NΛ[on form 27g, South Gaulish. Pre-Flavian. *93/6*. M7iv

215 [O]IIIⅤ XI on a cup, South Gaulish. An illiterate stamp, previously noted at the Gloucester Kingsholm site and on forms 27 and Ritt. 8. Pre-Flavian. *85/61*. 1.3

216 ..EN.C.. on form 29, South Gaulish. Pre-Flavian. *98/178*. 1.3

217]I\IRV[? on a cup, South Gaulish. Pre-Flavian. *98/205*. M7i

218 OF..[? on form 15/17 or 18, South Gaulish. Probably pre-Flavian. *84/182*. 2.1

219]CIIIV[? on a cup, South Gaulish. Probably pre-Flavian. *98/200*. M7iv

220]V or Λ[on form 27, South Gaulish. Early-Flavian. *98/4*. 3.4

221 VΛ[or]VΛ on form 15/17 or 18, South Gaulish. Flavian. *98/33*. 3.2

222 OXI....X[on form 27g, South Gaulish. Flavian. *85/227*. 2.1

223 IⅤ III[on form 27g, South Gaulish. Flavian. *88/3*. 4.0

224 NII on form 27g, South Gaulish. Flavian. *93/2*. 2.3

225 OF•[on form 27, South Gaulish. Flavian. *90/101*. 3.2

226 OFF[(?) on form 18, South Gaulish. Flavian or Flavian-Trajanic. *86/3*. 4.0

227 ..IⅯ.. on form 27, slightly burnt, South Gaulish. Flavian or Flavian-Trajanic. *51/21*. 1.3

228]OⅮ? on form 27, South Gaulish. Flavian or Flavian-Trajanic. *85/224*. 2.3

229 I\[or]\I on form 27, South Gaulish. Flavian or Flavian-Trajanic. *22/46*. 2.2

230]ASC? on form 27, South Gaulish. Perhaps a stamp of L Tr-Masculus, for whom the date would fit. Flavian-Trajanic. *83/530*. 2.3

231]H\VI on form 27, South Gaulish. Flavian-Trajanic. *86/21*. 4.0

232]VI on form 15/17 or 18, South Gaulish. First-century. *81/15*. 1.1

233 C[, O[or]O on form 15/17 or 18, South Gaulish. First-century. *88/7*. 4.0

Overview of the samian

by G B Dannell

The total distributions of first-century samian from first-century deposits measured by EVE and weight are basically in agreement: 54–59% pre-Flavian, 8–12% Nero-Vespasian, 25–26% Flavian, and 4–12% 'first century'. The evidence is clearly weighted in favour of a preponderance of pre-Flavian material and this is confirmed by the stamps, where it appears that some 70% of first-century stamps are pre-Flavian. This age distribution of the material is not normal for a civilian site in Roman Britain, where the largest absolute delivery and breakage tends to be in the Flavian period and the pre-Flavian content would normally be smaller. Typically, maximum breakage appears to occur *c* AD 75–80.

Two conclusions may be reached: first, the site was established in the pre-Flavian period, secondly, there was a marked decline in samian use during the Flavian period. The date at which the site was first occupied is more difficult to assess. The most exact dating comes from the stamps. However, the method used to produce the histograms (Figs 5.9–5.18) tends to exaggerate both the earliest and latest dates because the spread takes the earliest dates back before AD 43, and forward beyond the final deliveries from the varying production centres. For instance 'Tiberian-Claudian' stamps are most unlikely to have entered the British context before *c* AD 43. Accordingly, entries for *c* AD 35–40 (derived from the samian jargon for Tiberian-Claudian) must belong to the entries post-AD 43, except in the peculiar circumstances where the army might have taken over an existing supply from native sources, not known to be the case at Wroxeter. However, a similar phenomenon might occur later, if, say, a legionary fortress succeeded an auxiliary fort, and the stores were amalgamated, leading to earlier material appearing genuinely in a later context.

The decorated ware provides similar evidence. There is very little to compare with the earliest military material from sites such as Colchester, Lake Farm, or Richborough. However, there is solid evidence for potters who made bowls *c* AD 50–65 and who seem to have provided the majority of the decorated wares found on British military sites of the Neronian period. Potters like Aquitanus, Licinus, and Senicio fall into the earlier group, whereas Mommo and Niger and his associates, like Bassus and Coelus, fall typically into the later one.

The most likely construction date falls in the years *c* AD 55–65. Unfortunately, this straddles the most crucial political and military period of the Boudiccan revolt. It is not possible at this stage of samian research to decide whether or not the evidence is sufficient to distinguish between sites founded either just before, or just after, AD 61.

The earliest groups, ie those dated conventionally to the Claudian or Claudian/Neronian periods, do seem to show a spatially preferential distribution in favour of the south area. The finds come from areas 10, 34, 53, 70, 72, 78, 83, and 98. Whether or not this has any archaeological significance is another matter.

The reduced counts in the Flavian material suggest a lesser intensity of occupation (or supply), in turn hinting at the absence of some or all of the legion for substantial periods, if indeed it was not withdrawn altogether at some time in the later Flavian period. The deposits of samian which fill the gap in the Trajanic period might well represent *vicus* activity. This view is reinforced (on the evidence of the stamps) by a curiosity in the distribution *c* AD 100–120.

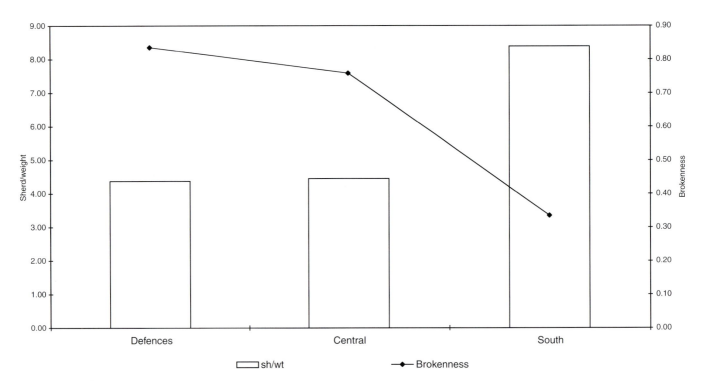

Fig 5.9 Pottery: military samian, sherd/weight and brokenness spatially

It is known that deliveries of samian were in sharp decline at the end of the first century AD. On both military and civilian sites a plethora of imitations (such as 'London ware' and products from the works depot of *Legio XX* at Holt) fill what can only have been a reduction in supply. There is normally a slow recovery in the supply of samian, based upon pottery from Les Martres-de-Veyre, between *c* AD 100 and 120, and then increasing amounts in the Hadrianic period, from Lezoux. At Wroxeter there is almost an equal amount of material from Les Martres-de-Veyre, compared to that of the Flavian period (based on the stamp count), but proportionately it is about normal compared to the quantity for the second century from Lezoux and elsewhere. This again suggests that it is the Flavian material which is scant, but that civilian occupation was picking up from *c* AD 100.

Discussion
by M J Darling

Condition

Fragmentation of the samian was generally high. The lowest average sherd weights occurred in the early military period (up to Phase 4b) and in Period 1.1 (4.3 and 4.6g respectively), both of which registered the highest level of brokenness (sherds/EVEs of 0.77). Discounting abnormal groups, the least fragmented assemblages were from the final phases for all three periods, the military demolition, Period 1.3 and Period 2.3. The area with the lowest fragmentation was the south area, while the highest

fragmentation in military contexts occurred in the defences area. The samian sherds from Period 2 contexts were least fragmented also in the south area (Fig 5.9).

Methods

All the samian has been quantified for sherd count, estimated vessel equivalent (EVEs) and weight, and is merged with the main pottery database. The specialist samian computer database includes details of fabric, form, potter's name, die reference, and date. Period dates such as Neronian and Antonine have been converted to numeric dates for some analyses (details of the equivalent applied are in the archive). The resulting numeric dates have been charted using a Plotdate program which spreads the values, or their percentages, evenly (Tyers 1993). Weight has been used for analysis by date and area as providing a larger more comprehensive sample, while the use of EVEs has been restricted to analysis by vessel type, to which it is most suited. Most figures were extracted for both weight and EVEs, and the difference between the two measures seems fairly minimal.

An overview of the quantity of samian

The sources for the total samian archived for the Military period through to Period 2, which includes a small quantity from areas outside the main excavated area, are shown in Table 5.4. The quantities by period and figures relating to fragmentation are given in Table 5.5. This is the samian from the main excavations, excluding contaminated contexts. Quantities by area and period with details of fragmentation are given in Appendix 3.3.

Table 5.4 Pottery: samian quantities by source

source	sherds	EVEs	weight (g)
South Gaulish	4807	8134	26608
Central Gaulish	1245	3330	10597
East Gaulish	4	5	17
Total	6056	11469	37222

Table 5.5 Pottery: samian quantities by period

period	sherds	EVEs	weight (g)	sh/wt	broken
Military	1459	2543	8085	5.5	0.57
Period 1	461	756	2371	5.1	0.61
Period 2	3785	7607	23952	6.3	0.5
Totals	5705	10906	34408		

Stratified occurrence

The earliest sherds are two vessels dated to the Tiberian-Claudian period, a Dr 27 from a slot of phase 4b (*78/26*) in the south area, and a Dr 17 from a demolition period context (*84/207*) in the defences area. These are followed in date by two stamps, cat no 59 of Damonus from a demolition layer (*63/5*) in the central courtyard, and one of Acutus I from a Period 1.2 context (*98/186*; cat no 3) in the defences area.

The spatial distribution of Tiberian-Claudian samian is shown in Table 5.6. While this shows a concentration in the south area, this mostly arises from a single vessel, and the spread when measured by the number of records is even across the areas. An examination of the spatial distribution of the earliest samian up to AD 70, however, showed some evidence for concentration in the south area, and less fragmentation.

Turning to the later military period, details of the stratified occurrence of Flavian samian in deposits predating the demolition period are given in Appendix 3.4. There is a small concentration in the southern part of the courtyard, from pits in Areas 72 and 77, but the main occurrence is in the defences area. The pits in Areas 72 and 77 also have sherd links with demolition contexts, but it is impossible to tell whether these and the later samian came from the upper layers which may have been contaminated by the demolition layer. The earliest context for these pits would appear to be the demolition of the barracks, but they could be of a later phase. Several pits in Area 72 were associated by sherd

Table 5.6 Pottery: spatial distribution of Tiberian-Claudian samian

area	sherds	%	EVEs	%	weight (g)	%
Central	20	31.3	44	13.3	118	15.8
South	26	40.6	176	53.2	388	52.0
Defences	18	28.1	111	33.5	240	32.2
Total	64	100	331	100	746	100

links, and one of the pits F2894 contained an unworn coin of Nero. While the pit in Area 77 lies in the area of the south range of the large late building, the pits in Area 72 are outside the building to the south-east.

Area 92 was subject to much disturbance and is of dubious reliability, and the stratigraphy of Area 85, which has produced the only evidence for Flavian samian before the demolition phase of 4b, divided into three separate areas due to the *macellum* structure, was particularly difficult to disentangle. All the remaining Flavian samian from the military period came from demolition contexts.

Late Flavian samian, *c* AD 90–100, occurred as a chip of a Dr 33 in *91/193* (Defences area). Flavian to Trajanic samian occurred in *14/37* in the courtyard, from immediately below the demolition layer. Both were probably due to contamination.

Dating

The assessment of the chronological range for a site or part of a site can be approached on several different levels using a computer program to spread the dated values of the pottery. The following distinctions can be made: all the pottery, both coarse and samian; coarse pottery alone; all samian; samian stamps alone; and decorated samian alone.

In the case of Wroxeter, only samian can be used since the dating of the coarse pottery cannot be sufficiently refined for the date range involved, and it is necessary therefore to examine the complexities of the samian dating. All the samian from military contexts has been plotted (Fig 5.10), showing it peaking in the decades AD 50–70, while that from Period 2, the largest group, has its first peak in the decade AD 70–80. The AD 70 peaks appear to arise mainly from Flavian samian, while the secondary peak of Period 2 coincides with the Trajanic period. If all the samian from the military period through to Period 2 is plotted, due to the large residual content of Period 2, the peak for all South Gaulish samian occurs in the decade AD 70–80.

When the more closely dated decorated and stamped vessels (irrespective of site phasing) are plotted for their dated occurrence (here using a five-year interval for greater detail), the profiles are found to diverge, the stamps (Fig 5.11) producing a significantly earlier peak around AD 55–65, while the decorated vessels peak at around AD 75–80. It therefore seems that the dating profile produced by the decorated vessels is similar to that produced by all the samian; it is not, however, identical. Excluding vessels or stamps broadly dated to the first century only reduces the decorated peak slightly. Neither does the exclusion of decorated forms 67, 78, etc, make any substantial difference in the profile.

Analysis of the stamps for vessel form shows only 10.5% are decorated (all Dr 29 except one Dr 37), and apart from two later vessel types, the cup 33 and bowl 18/31 (two examples of each), the stamps are dominated

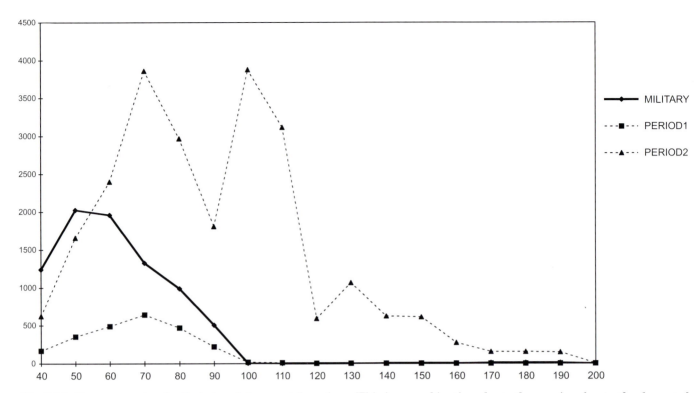

Fig 5.10 Pottery: samian by Period and date, weight values. This is a combination chart, the x axis refers to the decorated bowls plotted by sherds and by records (to relate the decorated more closely with the stamps, records being the 'sherd family' here using a five-year interval for greater detail, the decorated bowls plotted by records representing the 'sherd family' and sherd count), and the y axis is for individal stamps

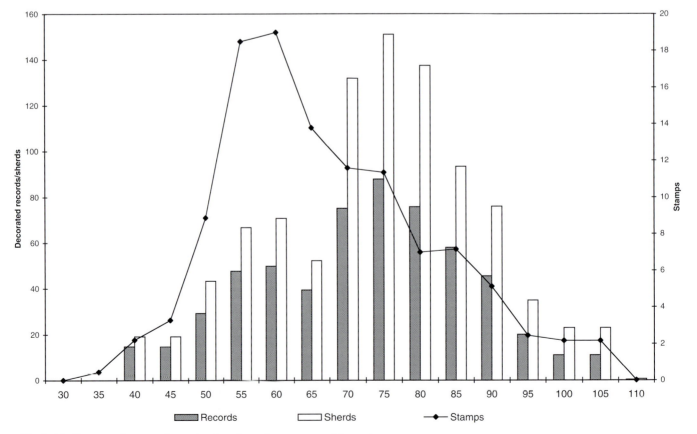

Fig 5.11 Pottery: decorated samian bowls and stamps, weight values

by cups at 51.3% and plates at 33.9%. Over 69% of the plates cannot be differentiated for types between 15/17 and 18, although 26% are form 18s. Eighty per cent of the cups are form 27, 12% form 24, the remainder being a single Ritterling 9 and undifferentiated cups, mostly dated to the pre-Flavian period. The charts in Figure 5.12 show the principal forms as raw values, which emphasise the quantity of cups, and as percentages to evaluate any differences in the dating.

The dating spread of the decorated 29s, the plates, and the cups broadly coincides with about 50% of each type occurring in the period up to around AD 65 (54% Dr 29; 48% plates; 46% cups), although the plates and cups have an overall wider span into the later first century. Whereas overall 45% of all the stamps occur in the period to AD 65, only 27% of the decorated bowls records occur in the same period.

The difference between the dating profiles of the stamps and the decorated wares appears to lie entirely with the almost total exclusion of stamps on Dr 37 and Dr 30 bowls. Of 580 records of decorated vessels, only 271 (47%) refer to the Dr 29 form, 214 (37%) are Dr 37 form, and 47 (8%) are Dr 30 form, the remainder (48) being mixed forms, 29s or 30s or 37s (8%). The possibility that spatial differences might be concerned has been investigated, and the quantities of both stamps and decorated vessels were found to have been equally represented in each area, the defences area dominating both. This dislocation of the dating profiles of stamps and decorated wares is not a specific problem related to Wroxeter, but has also been noted at Lincoln, and seems to be a national trend.

Examination of the samian dating evidence is therefore more complex, depending very largely upon the proportions of Dr 37 bowls in any group. The combination chart below (Fig 5.13) compares the dating profiles produced by an amalgamation of decorated wares (based on records) with the individual stamps (as columns, left axis), and the total samian (line graph, right axis), based on weight. Weight has been chosen for analysis of the samian by area since this includes all finds and is not biased by different fragmentation. This indicates that any assemblage with a quantity of Dr 37 bowls may produce a different dating profile in the overall weight analysis than would be revealed by an analysis of the decorated and stamps alone. Interestingly, the comparison between stamps/decorated sherds and all South Gaulish sherds showed a closer match, with both peaking at AD 75–80. Analysis by weight of all samian is, however, used below on the basis that decorated vessels account for only 20–25% of all the samian records/weight, and bearing in mind the paucity of decorated vessels in stratified military contexts, and fragmentation differences.

Spatial distribution

The spatial distribution of quantities by weight and date is plotted in Figure 5.14. The spatial distributions are important for the information they provide

for the assessment of possible levels of residuality, particularly of military period pottery in later contexts. The quantified figures for each area are given in Appendix 3.3. Figure 5.14a shows the samian from military contexts only, and Figure 5.14b the Period 2 samian (the sample from Period 1 is too small).

These charts again use the raw weight values to show the spatial emphasis. The largest group of stratified military samian came from the south area (43%), followed by the fragmented defences area (34%). Seventy per cent of the small group of samian from Period 1 came from the defences area, followed by 23% from the central area. Over 74% of Period 2 came from the defences area with smaller groups from the central and south areas.

Analysis by area and phase

The central area (Fig 5.15a) produced the smallest spatial group of samian (4.8kg), and had marginally higher fragmentation than in the defences area. Only two military period phases were represented in this area, and the second, the demolition period, contained the bulk of the early samian from the area as a whole. This is reflected in the fragmentation, since the military period had the lowest sherd weight and highest brokenness. The second largest phase group of samian came from Period 2, Phase 2.2, and had a lower peak at AD 60, while Period 2, Phase 2.3, showed a very different dating profile, with very little before a peak at AD 100.

The southern part of the area (Fig 5.15b) produced a slightly larger quantity of samian (7.4kg), with the demolition phase again predominating in the military period, and peaking at AD 50. Period 1 was barely represented, with material from AD 70–90. This area had the least fragmentation, the military having the highest sherd weight and lowest brokenness, while that from Period 2 was similarly less fragmented than in the same period elsewhere. The 3.7kg of Period 2 has a high residual content, peaking at AD 70.

The defences area (Fig 5.15c) produced the largest spatial group from the site (22.2kg) and is dominated by the quantity from Period 2 (17.8kg), and specifically from the last phase, 2.3, peaking at AD 100, but with an earlier and lower peak at AD 70. The quantity from military phases is minimal (2.7kg), the largest group being from the demolition phase, and Period 1 mirrors the earlier Period 2, Phase 2.1 and 2.2, peaking at AD 70. That from Period 1 contexts is marginally less fragmented, the freshest sherds coming from Period 2 contexts. The bulk of the Period 2 pottery is therefore coming from an area which produced relatively sparse military period pottery, mostly belonging to the final phase.

The samian from the military contexts has the highest fragmentation in this area, and is higher than elsewhere on the site. This is the only area where the military samian peaks at AD 70 and it has the highest values for the succeeding decades, and it is notable

a)

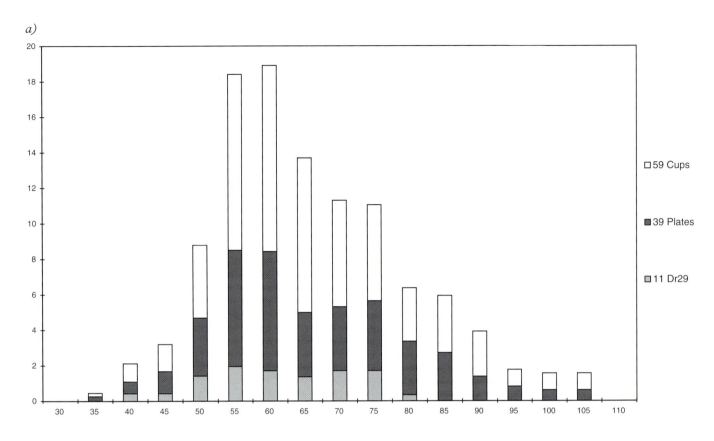

b)

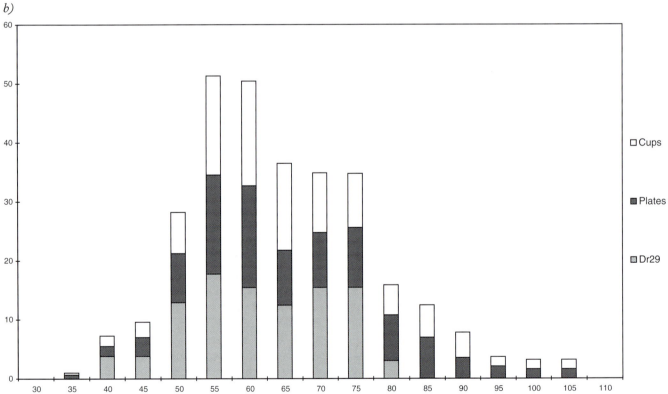

Fig 5.12 Pottery: a) first-century stamps, values of principal forms; b) first-century stamps, principal forms, % by date

that this late samian is only in the last demolition phase, the earlier phases peaking at AD 60. This last group, the latest pottery from military contexts, comes from contexts postdating the demolition of the defences in this area.

In summary, the highest proportion of early samian occurred throughout the phases in the south area. The central area has a relatively high percentage of Flavian in the earliest phase, but this is conditioned by the small size of the sample. Also notable in the early period

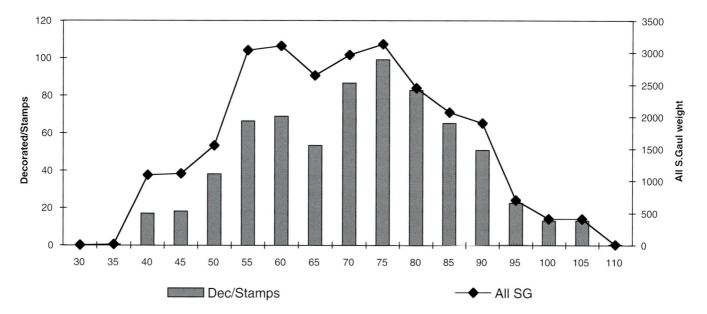

Fig 5.13 Pottery: comparison between decorated samian (580) and stamps (115) and weight (266 kg) of all South Gaulish samian

and later is the high percentage of sherds datable only as first-century from the defences area, largely arising from the greater fragmentation there. The late phase contexts occur only in the south area and defences area, the latter showing a substantially different later assemblage. Once into the demolition phase, the predominance of Flavian in the defences zone is striking, and presents virtually the opposite picture to that prevailing in the south area. A large proportion of the defences area Flavian sherds came from the single area 84, where only a single pot-bearing context of Period 1 intervenes between the military and Period 2 deposits. The significantly higher quantities of Flavian samian continue in the defences area into the later phases of Periods 1 and 2.

Stamps: dating implications

The study used 115 stamps extending to around AD 110 to examine the military period. All are from South Gaul except one early Central Gaulish vessel stamped by Severus v.

Of the 115 stamps (Fig 5.16), only 29 were stratified in military contexts (25%), and the highest percentage occurred residually in Period 2 (40%). The main excavated areas producing military period material yielded 109 stamps, with a heavy concentration (61%) in the defences area, with 22% from the south area, and 17% from the central area. Although the individual spatial samples are obviously small, it is notable that over 51% of the stamps from the defences area were Flavian and Flavian-Trajanic. No Flavian-Trajanic stamps were stratified in military contexts. The highest percentage of pre-Flavian stamps came from the interior, and when analysed spatially within that area, the early stamps clustered in the main central part, with more later stamps in the southern part.

The notable decline to *c* AD 65–70 coincides with the withdrawal of *Legio XIV* by Nero, and it could be argued that the subsequent low numbers appear to indicate a very much reduced garrison, with a further drop in the period *c* AD 80–90 when the number of samian stamps had dropped to about a third of those datable to the initial occupation of *c* AD 55–65. This needs, however, to be considered in relation to the dating profile produced by the rest of the samian, particularly the decorated vessels. The decline *c* AD 65–70 also occurs in the profiles of all samian and the decorated wares, although there is a subsequent rise to a peak *c* AD 75–80.

The sites of Usk, Exeter, Colchester and Lincoln have been used comparatively. The data for Exeter and Usk comes from databases prepared from the published stamp reports (respectively Dickinson 1991, 125 stamps; Hartley and Dickinson 1993, 159 stamps); the data for Colchester has been kindly supplied by Geoff Dannell and that for Lincoln comes from the City of Lincoln Archaeology Unit archive. All emperor or period dates have been converted on an identical basis; the chronological range is identical. An analysis using identified potters only was also prepared which showed the same broad pattern. All non-numeric dates have been converted to equivalent numeric dates, the stamps totalled for each date range, and their value spread over it (ie five stamps of AD 50–70 would have a value of 1.25 for each five-year span), and percentages calculated on the resulting totals to minimise the effects of the differing sample sizes (Fig 5.17).

All sites appear to start in a similar fashion, but it is noticeable that initially the Wroxeter series is weaker and similar to that from Lincoln. The peaks of the dated distribution occur at the same point, namely AD 55–65. All sites decline in AD 65–70, but while the western sites continue downwards, Colchester and Lincoln both show slight rises *c* AD 70–75. Analysis to establish the percentage

a)

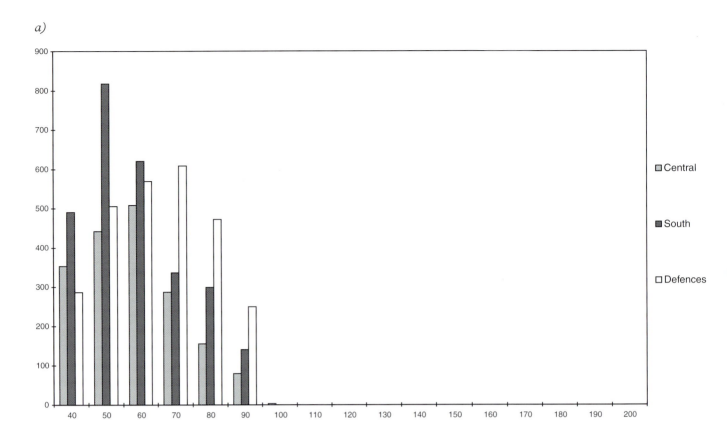

b)

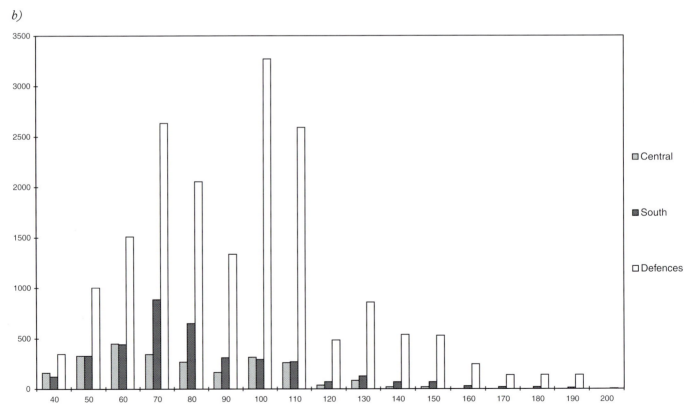

Fig 5.14 Pottery: a) spatial dated distribution of military samian; b) spatial dated distribution of Period 2 samian

a)

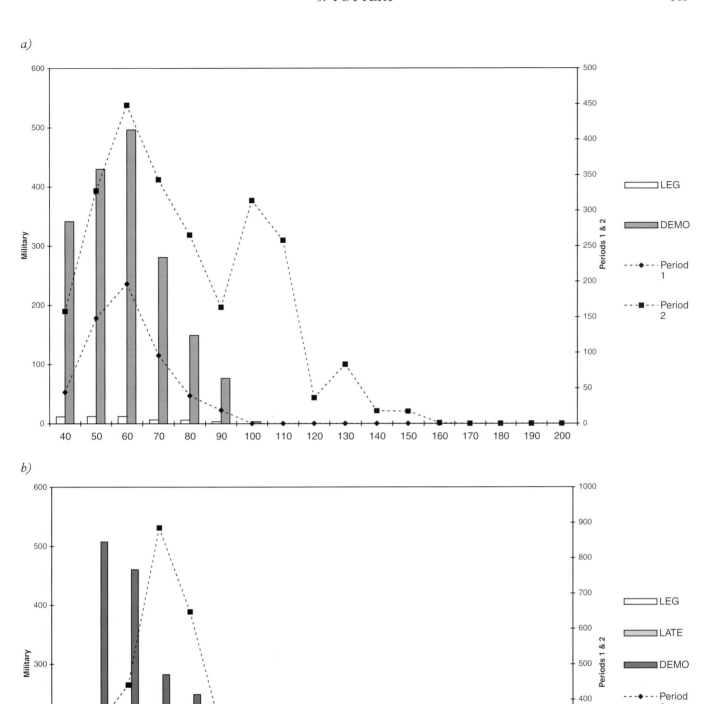

Fig 5.15 Pottery: samian phased by date (weight values) a) central area; b) south area

c)

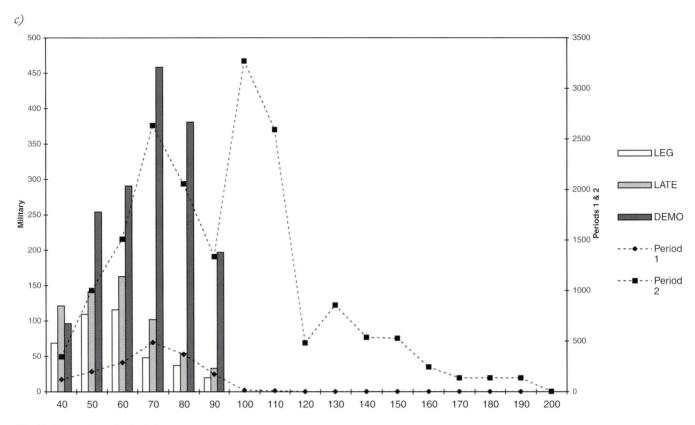

Fig 5.15 continued c) defences area

a) *b)*

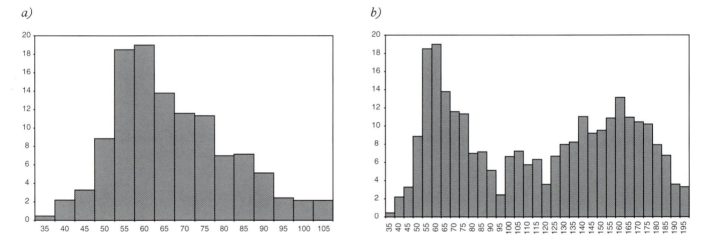

Fig 5.16 Pottery: a) Wroxeter samian stamps dating up to c AD 110; b) all samian stamps from Wroxeter excavations to AD 200

of the samian assemblage represented by stamped vessels shows that stamps account for a maximum of 4.7% in the period *c* AD 50–60, and decline thereafter, slightly in the next decade, but more substantially *c* AD 70–80. The paucity of stamped Dr 37s is certainly a factor in the decline. Although the main drop occurs when the XIVth legion was withdrawn from Wroxeter and a further 8000 British troops were on the continent fighting on the Vitellian side in the Year of the Four Emperors (Tacitus, *Histories* ii, 57), changes in the nature of samian supplies appear to be the cause of this downward movement.

The subsequent steep decline at Usk reflects the withdrawal from that fortress, and while Exeter declines less, Wroxeter stabilises for the period AD 85–90, and aligns more with the eastern sites of Colchester and Lincoln. This leads into a generally and, perhaps unusually, strong early second-century sample, as in Figure 5.16b, which shows all 270 stamps from the excavations, spread by date.

Vessel types

The occurrence of samian vessel types is detailed in Table 5.7 by period, including contaminated contexts (see also Appendix 3.7). While EVEs are apparently the most statistically viable measure to use for vessel types,

Table 5.7 Pottery: occurrence of samian types by period, EVEs and % (★ = below 0.1% presence)

	Military %	EVEs	Period 1 %	EVEs	Period 2 %	EVEs
Decorated bowls						
29	7.8	219	9.4	71	2.1	163
30	0.9	26	2.3	17	0.5	36
37	1.2	33	5.3	40	7.4	586
Dec	–	–	–	–	1.4	110
Dishes						
Ritt 1	2.5	69	0.7	5	–	–
15	–	–	–	–	–	–
15/17	5.5	154	4.2	32	2.3	185
15/17R	0.9	26	–	–	0.4	28
16	–	–	–	–	–	–
17	0.3	8	0.4	3	–	–
18	15.1	424	23.7	179	14	1106
18 or 18R	0.6	18	0.5	4	0.1	9
18R	4.1	115	–	–	1.1	85
18/31	–	–	–	–	11.3	893
18/31R	–	–	–	–	1.3	103
22	1.1	31	–	–	–	–
36	0.1	4	–	–	4.6	363
36 or Curle11	–	–	–	–	★	3
42	0.1	3	–	–	0.7	53
42R	–	–	–	–	0.1	10
79	–	–	–	–	–	–
Curle 15	–	–	–	–	0.1	10
Curle 15 or 23	–	–	–	–	–	–
Curle 23	–	–	–	–	★	3
Ludowici Tg	–	–	0.4	3	–	–
Dishes	–	–	–	–	0.2	13
Cups						
Ritt 5	0.3	8	–	–	–	–
Ritt 8	1.2	35	0.4	3	0.1	11
Ritt 9	0.4	11	–	–	0.4	31
24	13.2	372	8.2	62	2.6	205
25	0.5	13	–	–	–	–
27	35.0	986	33.7	255	31.3	2471
33	0.7	19	–	–	2.4	187
35	0.6	17	4.0	30	3.4	269
78	1.0	29	–	–	★	3
46	–	–	–	–	0.6	49
80	–	–	–	–	0.2	15
Cups	–	–	–	–	0.2	13
Bowls						
Ritt 12	4.0	113	3.8	29	1.1	86
Ritt12 or Curle11	0.8	22	–	–	0.4	29
Curle11	1.3	36	1.5	11	2.2	174
31	0.1	4	–	–	0.3	27
31R	–	–	–	–	★	3
38	–	–	–	–	★	5
44	–	–	–	–	0.3	25
81	–	–	–	–	0.1	10
81R	–	–	–	–	–	–
Bowls	–	–	–	–	3.5	275
Mixed forms						
Cup or Bowl	0.7	19	1.6	12	1.6	126
Bowl or Dish	0.1	2	–	–	0.1	6
Closed forms						
67	–	–	–	–	0.5	40
72	–	–	–	–	–	–
Closed	–	–	–	–	0.2	19
Mortaria						
43	–	–	–	–	–	–
45	–	–	–	–	★	3
Inkwells						
Ritt 13	–	–	–	–	0.3	27
Untyped						
–	–	–	–	–	0.4	29
Total	100	2816	100	756	100	7897

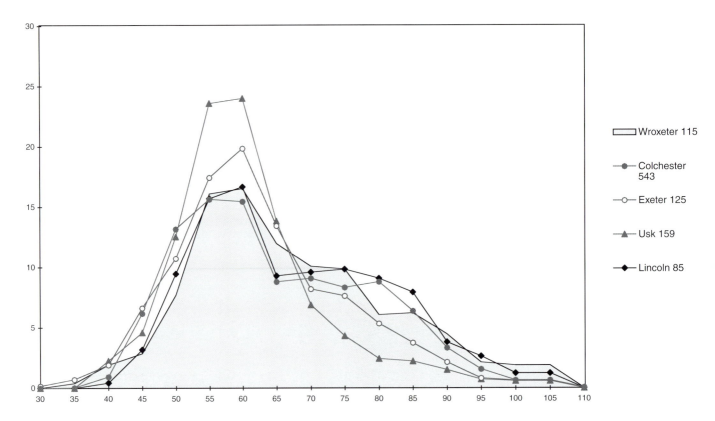

Fig 5.17 Pottery: samian stamps from Wroxeter, Usk, and Exeter (%)

it should be noted that an overall analysis of all the South Gaulish samian indicates that cup forms score highly as EVEs in relation to the measures of sherd count and weight, while decorated vessels score low. The percentage of cups derived from the EVEs measure is roughly double the percentages from count and weight; the percentage of decorated bowls from EVEs is approximately half that from count and weight. The analysis of all South Gaulish samian by vessel type is given in Appendix 3.5, measured by count, EVEs and weight.

The percentage of decorated vessels at Usk is considered to be about 30%, but is based on 'minimum vessels', and no figures are available based on EVEs or any other measure (Tyers 1993, 127). Samian stratified in fortress deposits at Exeter (presumably based on minimum vessels) contains 27.9% decorated vessels (Holbrook and Bidwell 1991, 287, appendix II). A similar percentage of decorated vessels at *Verulamium, Insula* XIV is quoted by Tyers (ibid) but it should be noted that any figures from this site would include the probable pottery shop with a high proportion of decorated ware (Frere 1972, 28). The percentages from Wroxeter are much lower, and Table 5.8 shows these based on EVEs, the number of records (the closest measure to 'minimum vessels' since most records refer to single vessels), and weight. The lower figures for weight and records are based on all samian, the upper on identified forms only. The sample from Period 1 is too small to be reliable. But whatever measure is used, the military period has a relatively low percentage of decorated vessels. This may be due to the location of the rubbish since it has been shown at Usk that the forms

represented differed between areas of the fortress. The Wroxeter samian comes from areas used initially for barracks and may reflect the samian available to ordinary soldiers rather than officers.

In view of the high residual content of the post-military periods, it should be emphasised that the percentage of decorated vessels of all South Gaulish samian from the three periods has been checked, and is 19.8–23.4% on sherd count, 26.6–27.6% on weight and 12.5% on EVEs (the first percentage for records and weight is based on all samian, the second on identified forms only).

The same difficulties of comparison with other quoted figures arises with the ratios of significant types, usually based on 'minimum vessels', those prepared by samian specialists taking into account all sherds, whereas those detailed by Tyers for Usk were based on rim families only. Figure 5.18 shows all three available measures, by sherds, EVEs and weight, and show the ratios between the three significant groups, the decorated 29 to 37, the plate 18 relative to 15/17, and the cup 27 to 24.

Given that the small sample from Period 1 is unreliable, all three measures show the expected increase in

Table 5.8 Pottery: % decorated samian by period

	Military	*Period 1*	*Period 2*
EVEs	9.9	16.9	11.3
Records	17.3 – 18.3	26.4 – 28.0	20.1 – 21.7
Weight	15.9 – 16.2	39.1 – 40.0	27.6 – 28.8

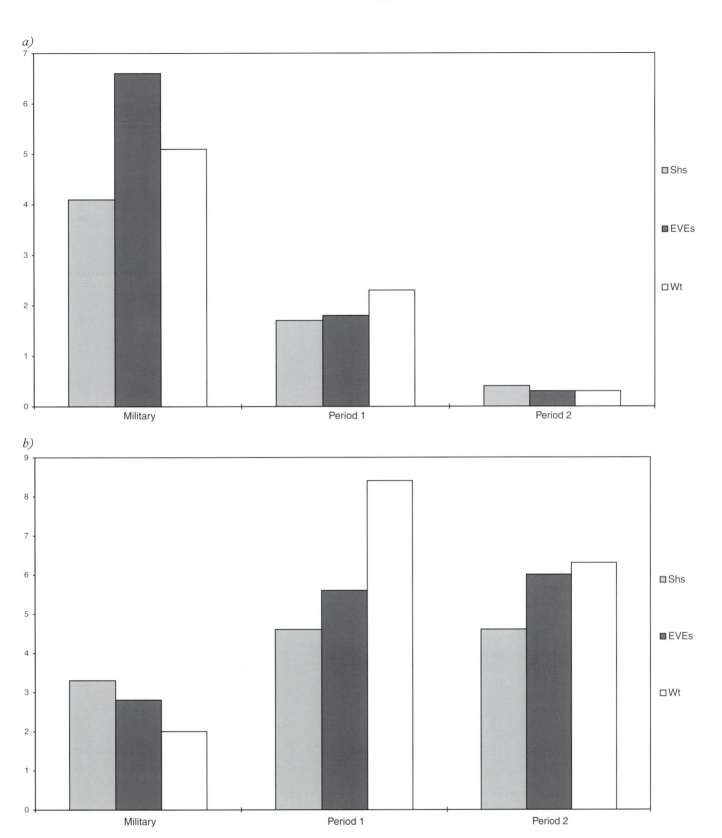

Fig 5.18 Pottery: ratios of samian forms by Period a) forms 29:37; b) forms 18:15/17

the later vessel types, 18, 27 and 37, the latter only exceeding form 29 in Period 2 by 2.2:1 to 3.6:1 (on sherds and EVEs).

Unfortunately very little samian is published in sufficient detail to provide comparative data, although the phase 1 samian from Usk is obviously relevant to any consideration of the Wroxeter assemblage. Here the data only cover the plain wares, and the ratio of decorated bowls of 29 to 37 is unknown. The ratio derived from EVEs at Usk for 15/17 to 18 of 1:2 is broadly similar to that from Wroxeter, but the Usk ratio for cups 24 to 27 of 1:5.6 is much higher than the figure of 1:2.7 on both EVEs and weight at Wroxeter, where more cups of form 24 occur. Despite this difference, the

c)

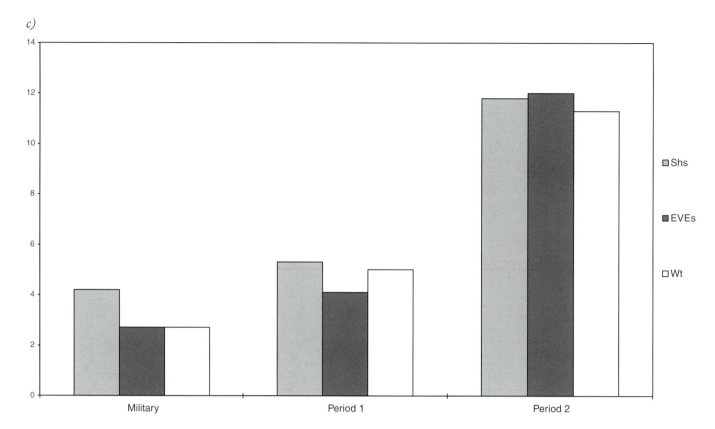

Fig 5.18 continued c) forms 27:24

overall ratio of plate to cup forms at Usk of 1:2 also occurs at Wroxeter.

Of the less common types of dating significance, Wroxeter has both Ritterling 12 and Curle 11 bowls, and these show the expected reversal, with the Curle 11 type becoming commoner in the Period 2 deposits. There are also plates of form 15/17R and 18R and their ratio varies from 1:2.5 to 1:4.4 (weight and EVEs respectively). Only the occasional rouletted plate is recorded from Usk, but this may be due to the concentration on recording rims rather than all sherds.

Until more comparative figures are available from other sites, the significance of higher incidence of the cup form 24 and the occurrence of the rouletted dishes at Wroxeter is uncertain. Whether this is simply a question of the vagaries of samian supply or some other factor is unclear.

Catalogue of South Gaulish samian

by G B Dannell

O = figure type in Oswald 1936–7
H = figure type in Hermet 1934

(Fig 5.19)

1   SG. Form 29. CELADVS style: he shared moulds with the MVRRANVS workshop, (cf Knorr 1952, Taf 15C). It is not clear whether all, or just the majority of his moulds came from MVRRANVS, and the rosette (Knorr 1919, Taf 21, detail 2), does appear on designs particularly grouped with the CELADVS internal stamp. The small four-pronged motif was shared, *ibid* B, and the upper zone rosette is on a bowl in the MVRRANVS style from Lake Farm, Dorset (PM14/HPS), together with the binding. In the lower zone, the medallion and rosette are on a stamped CELADVS bowl from Richborough (D25/78304981); the larger frond is on a MVRRANVS style bowl from Fishbourne (Dannell 1971, fig 126.1) and is with the hare on a bowl from London (ML ex. GH S442). *c* AD 50–65 *41/6; 50/52; 50/68; 53/11; 73/1; 74/6; 75/2.* M7iv; 2.1.

2   SG. Form 29. The leaf was used by the GALLI-CANVS group at La Graufesenque (Fosse Malaval) and then devolved to, or was copied by, other potters, cf Asciburgium (Vanderhoeven 1975, Taf 44.326), stamped by NIGER as with a similar infill leaf (Mus Fenaille, Rodez). *c* AD 55–70 *75/2.* 2.1.

3   SG. Form 29. Pair of opposed stipulated cordate leaves. This shape was used on a number of differently stamped bowls, on Mary (1967, Taf 11.16), by AQVITANVS (who almost certainly bought-in the design), and by ARDACVS (cf Pryce 1947, pl xxiv.14) and in the Fosse Malaval. The small four-pronged motif is similar to that on No 1, but smaller as far as can be presently determined. *c* AD 50–65 *77/3.* 2.1.

Fig 5.19 Pottery: samian 1–11; scale 1:1

4　SG. Form 29. Motifs of this type are common in the Neronian period (there are a number in the Fosse Malaval), and the blurring defies ascription. *c* AD 50–70 *98/+*. Unstratified

5　SG. Form 29. The rosette appears on work stamped by SENICIO (Knorr 1919, Taf 75, detail 49), and the bud is probably on a form 29 from Narbonne, signed below the decoration by SIINICIO, who may or may not be the same man. *c* AD 50–65. *70/18; 70/85; 78/5*. M7iv-v.

6　SG. Form 29. This is a very unusual design and looks more archaic than it is. The bottle-shaped bud is closest to one of a form 29 stamped by SVLINVS from Lake Farm, Dorset (PM14 HPS). That is from what appears to be a Claudian mould, but other bowls have Neronian designs. The cordate bud is similar to, but different from the ones used by AQVITANVS, GENIALIS (cf Knorr 1919, Textbild 10), and SENICIO (cf Glasbergen 1940–4, Afb 56.2), all of which have the same shape but are larger. *c* AD 50–65? *70/18; 70/85*. M7iv.

7　SG. Form 30. The frond and poppy-heads are very similar to those on the form 29 from Colchester (Hull 1958, fig 100.2B), stamped by MARINVS. He appears to have bought in moulds, and has connections with the MODESTVS workshop. The infill leaf resembles that used on the bowl in the CALVVS style (cf Knorr 1919, Taf 96C) *c* AD 50–65 *70/16*. 1.1

8　SG. Form 29. The vine leaf in this size appears on bowls stamped by DARRA, about whom little is known (cf Knorr 1919, Taf 32). *c* AD 45–60? *98/+*. Unstratified

9　SG. Form 30. The heavy wreath appears on a form 30 stamped in the mould by GERMANVS, (cf Hermet 1934, Pl 74.14). The leaf is similar to that shown from La Graufesenque, (cf Hermet 1934, Pl 8.39). *c* AD 65–80? *13/44*. 4.0.

10　SG. Form 29. Oak leaves used by M CRESTIO and other Flavian potters (cf Knorr 1919, Taf 28, detail 26). *c* AD 75–90 *77/2*. 2.2.

11　SG. Form 29. *c* AD 60–75? *80/132*. 3.1.

(Fig 5.20)

12　SG. Form 29. This bowl is in the style of the MVRRANVS workshop, but subtly different in detail. The candelabrum with pendant leaves is known from a signed bowl (ML ex. GH S440), and the poppy-head wreath probably that from the mould-stamped bowl (Knorr 1952, Taf 44A). The frond is not entirely clear, but is similar to that used in the MODESTVS workshop, while the leaf is on bowls in the MASCLVS style (cf Knorr 1952, Tafs 43F and 36A). *c* AD 50–65 *72/19; 72/67*. M4b.

13　SG. Form 29. The upper zone frond was used on bowls signed by MVRRANVS (cf ML ex. GH S442). The goat is O.1828. The large bud in the lower zone was also used by MVRRANVS (cf Knorr 1952, Taf 44B), but the wreath is closer to that on stamped bowls of LABIO (cf Knorr 1919, Taf 44C). The pinnate leaf is on a bowl in the MASCLVS style (cf Pryce 1947, pl xxxiii.19). *c* AD 50–65 *50/52; 78/5; 84/247*. M7iv.

14　SG. Form 29. The pendant in this size was used on a form 29 stamped by VA[N]DERIO (cf Knorr 1919, Taf 80B, note the backing beads). *c* AD 65–80 *73/24*. M7iv.

15　SG. Form 37. Ovolo associated with decoration which normally appears with a different ovolo, signed variously by ALBANVS iii, BASS[INVS, LITVGENVS ii, and G. AT PAS. *c* AD 85–110. *90/179*. 2.2.

16　SG. Form 37. Fan-like ornament, used by potters like M CRESTIO (cf Knorr 1912, Taf V11.1, for a form 29 in the style). *c* AD 75–90 *90/179*. 2.2.

17　SG. Form 37?. Flavian? *90/179*. 2.2.

18　SG. Form 37. Basal wreath with five lobes, the outer two are serrated. It appears with a rare ovolo (known from London, ML 5948G) and at Colchester. *c* AD 75–95? *90/179*. 2.2.

19　SG. Form 29. The lozenge is shown by Hermet (1934, pl 17.16). *c* AD 55–70 *95/226*. 4.0.

20　SG. Form 29. Not enough for ascription, but the square beads and the rosette placed beneath the bird are similar to designs from the Fosse Malaval (La Graufesenque), and suggests a Claudio/Neronian date. *c* AD 50–65 *86/42; 93/12*. 2.1; M7iv.

21　SG. Form 29. The trifid leaf ornament was used on a bowl stamped by PASSIENVS (Moulins Mus). *c* AD 65–80? *97/213*. M7iv.

22　SG. Form 29. Eagle, O.2166a. *c* AD 70–85? *91/23*. 3.0.

23　SG. Form 37. The MEMOR ovolo in one of its imprints (numerous examples from London, ML), the figure is unclear. *c* AD 70–85 *78/5; 91/12*. M7v; 4.0.

24　SG. Form 37. The wreath appears on the work of M CRESTIO (Gloucester, GL 137), and the ovolo is the one he shares with C VAL[ERIVS] ALB[ANVS] (cf Hull 1958, fig 48.3). *c* AD 75–90 *25/43; 84/76; 92/3*. 2.2; 2.3.

25　SG. Form 37. This blurred ovolo does appear to have a trident tip, and as such is almost certainly that of the M CRESTIO/MERCATOR group (cf Knorr 1919, Textbild 36). *c* AD 75–90 *91/105*. 1.3.

26　SG. Form 37. Ovolo with small rosette, associated with bowls in the CALVVS style; the wreath is frequently found with it (ML 4453G). The motifs are also used in a style attributed to BASSVS and COELVS. *c* AD 70–85 *34/14*. 2.4.

27　SG. Form 29. Alternate gadroons and striated rods. The small beads were often used from the late Neronian period. *c* AD 60–75 *85II/241*. M4b.

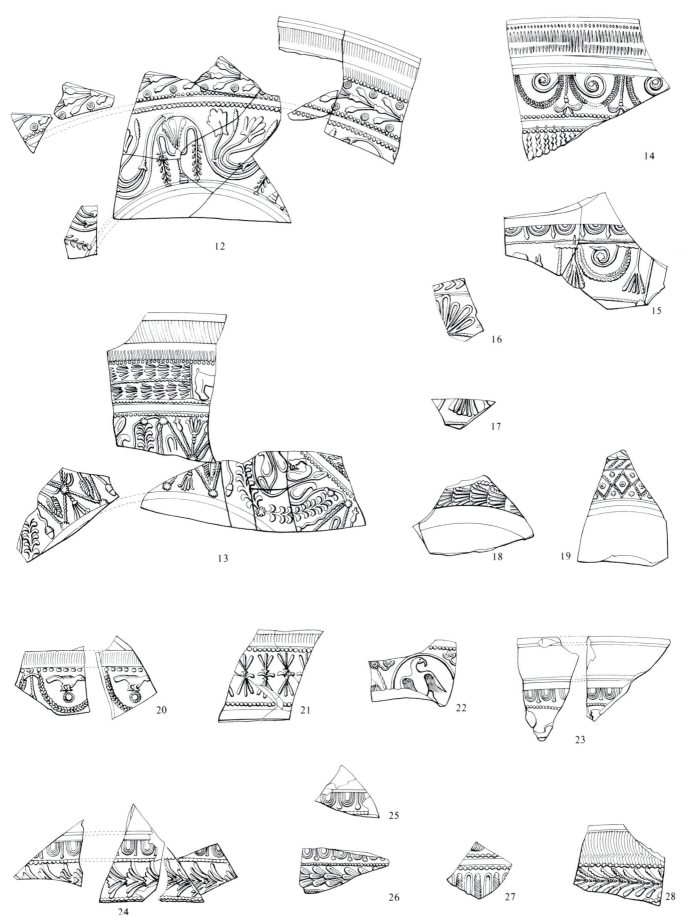

Fig 5.20 Pottery: samian 12–28; scale 1:1

28   SG. Form 29. This wreath looks similar to that on a form 29 stamped by SCOTNVS (cf Pryce 1947, pl xxxv.7+). *c* AD 50–65 *85II/241*. M7iv.

(Fig 5.21)

29   SG. Form 29. Probably from the MODESTVS workshop (cf Knorr 1952, Taf 39F). The tendril binding is used as a basal wreath. *c* AD 50–65 *72/7; 84/5*. M4b; 4.0.

30   SG. Form 29. The putto O.463 is shown in a reduced format here, and since it appears to have been a Flavian type, must be at the end of its range. The frond to the left is found on a form 29 stamped by IVCVNDVS (ML ex. LM A2732Y/2), and for his use of this style cf Knorr (1919, Taf 44J), the lanceolate leaves are bisected. *c* AD 75–90 *84/100; 98/87*. 2.2; 2.3.

31   SG. Form 29. Stamped OF NIGRI, stamp no 110. *c* AD 55–70 *2/36; 10/24; 1.1*.

32   SG. Form 78. IVSTVS ovolo (Framlingham, Ipswich Mus. 1948.146) with chase scene of dog, O.1968, and hares O.2079 and uncatalogued. *c* AD 70–85 *A/16*. M4b.

33   SG. Form 37. Stag of the O.1734 type, although the potters cited would be too early for this piece. *c* AD 75–90? *84/120*. 2.1.

34   SG. Form 29. Perhaps by VITALIS; he stamped bowls with the five-lobed leaf in the lower zone (cf Knorr 1952, Taf 83), and the frond in the upper zone, (cf Knorr 1919, Taf 83, detail 11). He also used the demi-medallion, and astragalus (Rodez, Mus Fenaille), but the hare, does not show two ears as there. *c* AD 70–85 *63/5; 63/19*. 1.1

35. Sg. Form 29. The wreath is very similar to one known to appear on form 37s with single-bordered ovolo (Leicester, 1969 164.11 (4)S; Richborough, 78305588, and Verulamium, M 8 (2)). The birds are O.2248 and 2202 types. The frond is unclear, but appears to have three beads backing it, and is on form 37 with the CRVCVRO ovolo at Caerwent. *c* AD 70–85? *16/135*. 2.2.

36   SG. Form 29. This panel of animals was used widely among the Neronian workshops, and without more decoration is unascribable cf Knorr (1952, Taf 44C) by MVRRANVS, with a different rosette. *c* AD 50–65 *98/52*. 2.3.

37   SG. Form 30. The figure is the complete version of H.50, showing that it is fully clothed. *c* AD 70–85. *10/25*. 1.1

38   SG. Form 29. Dog or small lioness, and large upright twisted rods. *c* AD 60–75? *74/5*. 1.1

39   SG. Form 37. Perhaps from a workshop stamping SABINVS; the birds and wreath known (cf Knorr 1919, Taf 69, details 8, 17 & 18). AD 75–90 *9/30*. 1.1

40   SG. Form 37. Very small leaping bear with trainer?; apparently not catalogued. Flavian? *84/109*. M7iv.

41   SG. Form 37. FRONTINVS style; his ovolo (cf May 1916, pl xxv 33). The figure is restored as an eagle, but may be a putto. The medallion is shown from La Graufesenque (cf Hermet 1934, Pl 85.2), together with the frond. FRONTINVS signed moulds, and stamped them. Some signatures are inscribed after firing, and the moulds may not all be his own manufacture. *c* AD 70–85 *84/100*. 2.2.

42   SG. Form 67. As on most vessels of this form, the detail is often individualistic. Here, the only certain similarity is the bird, O.2288A, used in the CABVCATVS/REGENVS series (cf Hermet 1934, pls 103–5). *c* AD 60–75? *97/142; 97/144; 97/156*. 2.1; 1.3.

43   SG. Form 37. The gladiator is O.1013F, but the bestiarius is not catalogued. The gladiator, from La Graufesenque, is shown with an overlapping ovolo similar to one used by FRONTINVS, and it also appears with an ovolo used by MOMMO (Caerleon, Museum Gardens 1983). The bestiarius in both of these cases is O.1043. *c* AD 75–90 *97/192*. 2.1.

44   SG. Form 37. Ovolo of the FRONTINVS type, but smaller rosette, perhaps the variant used by PAVLLVS (cf Knorr 1919, Taf 65, detail 9). The lion is O.1497T. *c* AD 75–90? *84/100*. 2.2.

45   SG. Form 37 or 29. A similar fan to that on no 16, neither the bird nor bud is clear. *c* AD 75–90 *97/148*. 2.1.

(Fig 5.22)

46   SG. Form 29. The lower zone is very similar to one from Tongres, cf de Schaetzen and Vanderhoeven (1955, pl V111.1), which has both leaves. Here, the bird and large leaf are similar to those used on a bowl stamped CABIATVS from London (ML), although in both of these cases the grapes are the more normal shape. The upper zone trifid motif resembles one used on bowls stamped by BASSVS and COELVS, and COELVS (cf Knorr 1919, Tafs 13B & 24D). *c* AD 55–70 *51/13; 80/123*. 2.2; 2.3.

47   SG. Form 37. Hind, O.1755, probably by CRVCVRO judging from the shape of the bole of the tree (ML 4384G and 4379G, with his ovolo). *c* AD 85–110. *12/27*. 2.2.

48   SG. Form 37. Lion and hound, as at Rottweil, stamped by GERMANVS (cf Knorr 1919, Taf 36B). *c* AD 65–80 *98/+*, Unstratified.

49   SG. Form 37. The frond was widely used on bowls stamped by potters like SEVERVS, and a similar basal leaf on one by IVSTVS (Scarborough, 1023.38, his ovolo). *c* AD 70–90 *84/100*. 2.2.

50   SG. Form 29. Hare with trilobe leaf wreath; too little for ascription, but potters like PASSIENVS stamped form 29 with these details (cf Knorr 1919, Taf 62, 12 and 34). *c* AD 65–80 *84/100*. 2.2.

51   Not used.

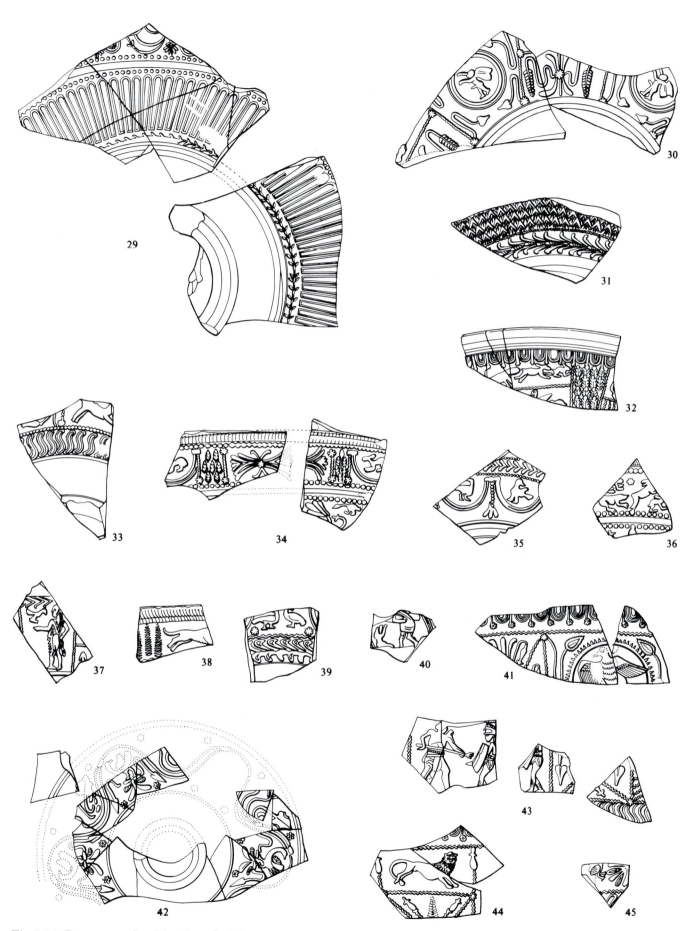

Fig 5.21 Pottery: samian 29–45; scale 1:1

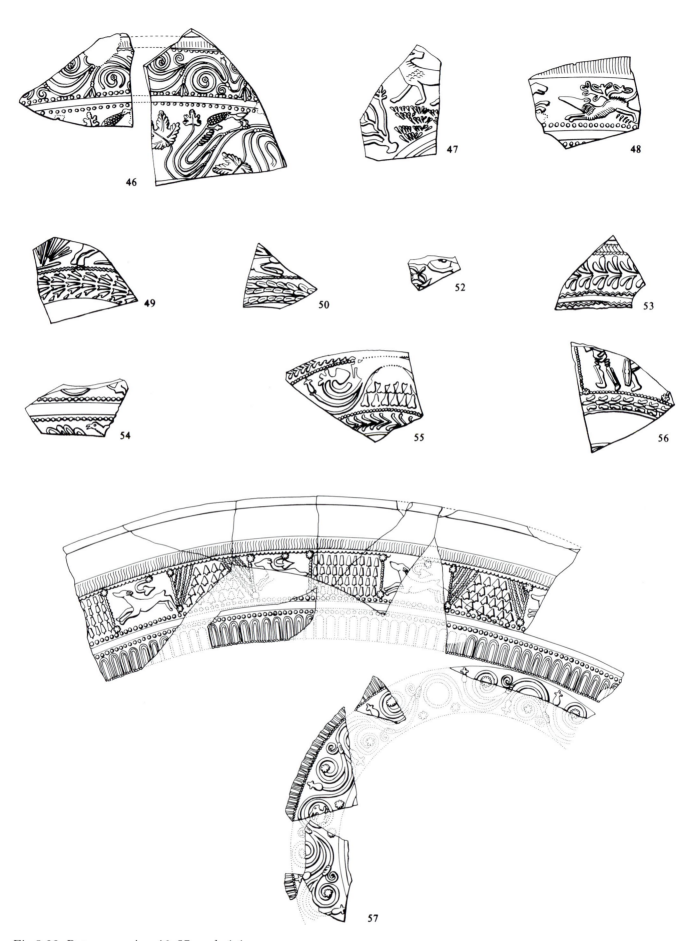

Fig 5.22 Pottery: samian 46–57; scale 1:1

52 SG. Form 29? A very small version of the archer H264. *c* AD 75–90? *92/4*. 2.4.

53 SG. Form 29. The frond is known from bowls stamped by LVCCEIVS and NIGER (Rodez, Mus Fenaille), and note the use of the wavy line in place of the normal beaded border. It also appears on a form 37 from La Graufesenque in the GERMANVS style (cf Hermet 1934, pl 80.8). *c* AD 55–70 *98/172*. 1.1.

54 SG. Form 29. Insufficient for ascription; the dog is O.1968, and the bird, an O.2271 type. Very similar types come from the Fosse Malaval. *c* AD 50–65 *9/17*. 2.2.

55 SG. Form 29. Probably by the IVSTVS workshop; the details all appear on bowls stamped in the mould, all three together on a form 29 from Koenigshöffen (B Dickinson pers comm). *c* AD 70–85 *98/141*. 1.3.

56 SG. Form 37. The gladiator to the left is a version of O.1013H, that to the right, uncatalogued. *c* AD 75–90? *49/65*. 4.0.

57 SG. Form 29. The elements individually belong to a large group of early Flavian potters; the dog O.2017, which Oswald ascribes to Lezoux was used by FRONTINVS (cf Knorr 1952, Taf 25A), and appears on a bowl with the MERCATOR ovolo from London (ML 4340G). The small hare, O.2045 was used on bowls stamped by PASSIEN-VS (cf Knorr 1919, Taf 62, detail 5), and he used the bottle-shaped bud (*ibid*, detail 47), and both infill leaves. There are links to work stamped by CALVVS, IVCVNDVS, SEVERVS and VITAL-IS, and shared mould-makers must be involved. *92/4; 98/111; 98/124; 98/148*. 2.4; 1.2; 1.1.

(Fig 5.23)

58 SG. Form 29. A very odd design, with a V-shaped wreath, usually used as a basal wreath, on form 37, below the central moulding. The figures are a lion, O.1417 used by numerous stamping potters, a boar, O.1682 type, and a hound. The shape of the boar is very similar to one used on a bowl stamped by RVFINVS (cf Knorr 1919, Taf 68A), together with the lion, and bear. The narrow frond is on a stamped bowl from London (ML ex. GH). However, this should not be taken as an attribution. *c* AD 65–80 *92/61; 98/135*. 1.1.

59 SG. Form 37. The ovolo appears on mould-stamped bowls of SEVERVS (Nettleton Shrub and Ilchester). The geese are O.2320, 2312 and 2220 types, the boar is O.1695A. The basal wreath and infill are frequently found on form 37 with the ovolo. *c* AD 75–90 *98/87; 98/141; 98/142*. 2.3; 1.3; 3.3.

60 SG. Form 29. Designs of this type fit best with the stamped work of BASSVS and COELVS. This firm had a long life and seems to have been a genuine partnership, with a fusion of detail appearing on bowls stamped by the potters separately. The cogged medallion is on a stamped form 29 from La

Graufesenque, but note the form 30 with the small rosette ovolo of CALVVS (cf Knorr 1952, Taf 10G). The trifid wreath motif is shown from Rheingoheim (cf Knorr 1952, Taf 9C). The geese, O.2220 and 2257 (with raised wing) are on a stamped form 29 from Moulins. They also appear with the trifid on bowls with the OFVITA [LIS] stamp from La Graufesenque. The pigeon is an O.2247 type. All three birds appear in the work of CALVVS, who also had connections with the BASSVS and COELVS workshop. *c* AD 60–75 *16/163*. 4.0.

61 SG. Form 37. GERMANVS ovolo (cf Hermet 1934, P2 99.37). *c* AD 70–85 *90/197*. 1.2.

62 SG. Form 29. A number of bowl makers could have produced this, cf Knorr (1919, Taf 43F), stamped by IVCVNDVS ii. The gadroon appears frequently on form 37s with a single bordered ovolo (cf May 1916, pl xvii.12), which has not yet been attributed. *c* AD 75–90 *83/57*. M7iii.

63 SG. Form 37. The tail of the boar resembles one on a form 29 with the PASSENVS stamp (cf Knorr 1919, Taf 63B), and the infilled panel is similar to one in the same style from Exeter (1972, level 113A). *c* AD 65–80 *97/156*. 1.3.

64 SG. Form 29. The figure is O.666, and the small leaf was used on a bowl stamped by LVCCEIVS (cf Knorr 1919, Taf 48, detail 3) and on one by BASSVS and COELVS *ibid*, Taf 13, detail 9 to whom, on the basis of the medallion (detail 34), this probably should be associated. *c* AD 60–75 *7/54*. M4b.

65 SG. Form 37. All of the details appear in work associated with stamps of the CALVVS workshop. The palm leaf wreath is on a form 29 from La Graufesenque (Rodez, Mus Fenaille),together with the small leaf below. The sparrow is recorded by Knorr (Knorr 1919, Taf 17, detail 34), and the goose, O.2244 type, appears on form 37 with his ovolo (ML). *c* AD 70–85 *85/217*. 2.3.

66 SG. Form 29. Probably by SEVERVS; the five-lobed leaf wreath is on a form 37 with his ovolo from Carlisle (1982, B 1232/1276). The figure is O.1493, a lion eating a man, which is on another bowl with the ovolo (ML 5139G). *c* AD 75–90 *92/3*. 2.3.

67 SG. Form 29. Not possible to ascribe; the eagle is O.2175, but the sparrow is too incomplete to identify. *c* AD 50–65? *86/40*. 2.1.

68 SG. Form 29. Not enough for ascription; the hare is an O.2107 type. *c* AD 70–85 *91/72*. 2.3.

69 SG. Form 37. This basal wreath was used by a number of Flavian potters (cf Knorr 1919, Textbild 12). *c* AD 75–95 *98/117*. 1.2.

70 SG. Form 29. The very narrow moulding and wavy line indicates a later version of form 29. *c* AD 75–90 *9/27*. 1.1.

71 SG. Form 29. Small segmental leaf used by many Neronian potters, including the group from the Fosse Malaval. *c* AD 50–65? *91/71*. 2.3.

72 SG. Form 67. Small detached berry clusters. *c* AD 65–80? *98/159*. 1.2.

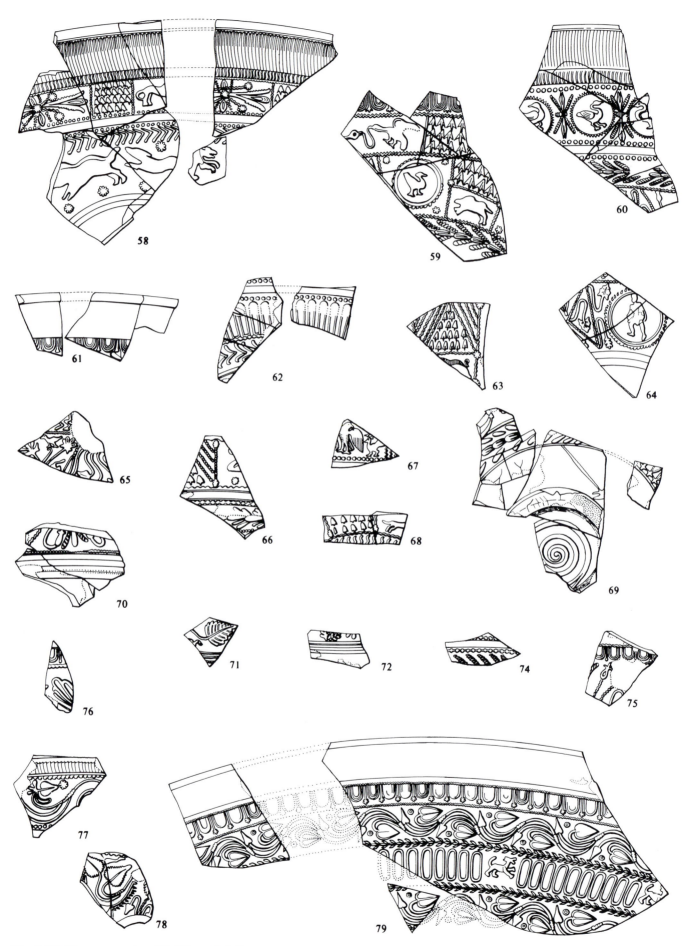

Fig 5.23 Pottery: samian 58–79; scale 1:1

73 Not used.

74 SG. Form 29. Very difficult to even see the scale of this; it is either a bifid, or more likely a trifid leaf motif, cf generally, Knorr (1919, Taf 16) by CABVCATVS. c AD 65–80? *85III/67*. M6.

75 SG. Form 30. Ovolo, and generally similar saltire to a form 30 stamped in the mould by MARTIALIS (Boon 1962, fig 1). The ovolo seems indistinguishable from one which appears on bowls signed by MASCLVS (cf Knorr 1952, Taf 36A) although the spacing varies, so perhaps a number of rollers were impressed from a single die. c AD 50–65 *a/8*. M4b.

76 SG. Form 37. Ovolo used by M CRESTIO and C. VAL[ERIVS] ALB[ANVS], the fan frequently appearing with it. c AD 75–90 *91/72*. 2.3.

77 SG. Form 29. Cordate stipulated leaves of this type occur from the early Neronian period onwards (Southwark, Borough High St with a stamp of AQVITANVS). c AD 50–70? *92/14*. 2.3.

78 SG. Form 29. The festoon was used particularly on bowls stamped by BASSVS and COELVS (cf Knorr 1919, Taf 13 detail 24) and on those stamped by MEDDILLVS (*ibid*, Taf 55K). The leaf appears on a bowl which looks stylistically earlier, but probably is not (cf Ulbert 1959, Taf 34.10). c AD 55–70 *80/181*. 2.1.

79 SG. Form 37. A small bowl in the style associated with CALVVS through common details which appear on form 37s signed in the mould, and stamped from 29s. The ovolo is the one with the smaller of the rosette tips. This bowl has the small lanceolate leaf which appears on a stamped form 29 from Bonn (cf Knorr 1919, Taf 17B; Pryce 1949, lxxix.39). The cordate leaf appears widely on both form 29 and form 30. (CALVVS depotoire, La Graufesenque, form 29 – cf Pryce 1932, pl xxxi.2, form 30). It appears to come from a set of at least three similar leaves differentiated by size. The small gadroon appears with the ovolo from London (ML 5860G, 5876G), and the dog, a reduced version of O.1970, is on a form 37 from London (ML 5858G/5859G), which has medallions similar to those on the Richborough form 30. The small trifid leaf wreath seems to be associated with form 37 (depotoire, La Graufesenque, Catterick, Scarborough).

The style is exemplified in the series of bowls attributed to the 'Potter of the large rosette' from Pompeii (cf Atkinson 1914, pls vii/x). Two bowls with a similar scroll come from London (Walbrook 268B, with handles), and Leicester (2966, 11A.38). c AD 70–85 *92/20*. 2.1.

(Fig 5.24)

80 SG. Form 29. Too little for ascription, cf Hermet (1934, Pl 45.6) for a similar wreath, and another appears in the style of bowls stamped by BASSVS COELVS from Colchester. c AD 50–65? *92/8*. 2.1.

81 SG. Form 29. This little leaf motif is similar to one used on a form 29 stamped by IVCVNDVS i (cf Knorr 1952, Taf 31), which seems rather earlier, but a similar leaf appears in the Flavian period on form 37, with an ovolo attributed to FLORVS and FRONTINVS (ML 3736G). Small rings or roulettes were used on form 29s stamped by ARDACVS, ibid, 2C. c AD 50–65 *86/41*. 2.1.

82 SG. Form 37. Not enough for ascription, but the basal wreath was used widely at Pompeii (cf Atkinson 1914). The bifid is unusual at this date, the figure may be a gryphon. c AD 70–85 *82/33*. 4.0.

83 SG. Form 29. Not enough for ascription, but the triangular leaves are a Flavian detail. c AD 70–90 *92/20*. 2.1.

84 SG. Form 37. This single-bordered ovolo with rosette tip (often blurred to a blob) is unattributed as yet; it goes with a wide range of decorative designs and detail (cf Oswald 1948, pl xiv.2; Dannell 1971, fig 128.19). There are numerous examples from London and the leaf here appears on one (ML 4510G). The ovolo is also used on form 30 (cf May 1916, pl xvii.12). It can be distinguished from similar ones by the slight 'waisting' or incurving of the egg towards the top. c AD 70–85 *92/18*. 2.1.

85 SG. Form 37. This may be the BIRAGILLVS ovolo, with its squared trident tips (cf Knorr 1919, Taf 16, detail 16). c AD 80–100 *92/18*. 2.1.

86 SG. Form 37. This ovolo was used by MEMOR (cf Atkinson 1914, pl xiv.73/74), and another with the same signature from London (ML). IVSTVS also stamped moulds and used the same or a very similar ovolo (Framlingham, Ipswich Mus. 1948.146). c AD 70–85 *86/42*. 2.1.

87 SG. Form 30. The nearest ovolo to this is one with an applied 37 rosette tip from London (ML, ex. 17.825). The decoration has a curved cordate leaf similar to those used on bowls signed by MASCLVS, but no ascription can be made. c AD 50–65 *92/18*. 2.1.

88 SG. Form 30 This ovolo is well known from Claudio-Neronian deposits (cf Knorr 1919, Taf 95D) and a recent form 30 with it from Colchester is stamped in the mould by LVPVS. The trifid leaf motif is on a form 29 from Camulodunum, cf Pryce (1947 pl xxvii.1b/c), which has a leopard used on bowls signed by SABINVS (cf La Nautique, Fiches *et al* 1978, fig 14.2). c AD 50–65 *85/226*. 1.1.

Fine wares: military period and later

Site activities, particularly the building of the baths and *macellum*, led to the dispersal of pre-Flavian fine wares throughout the stratigraphy. Where possible,

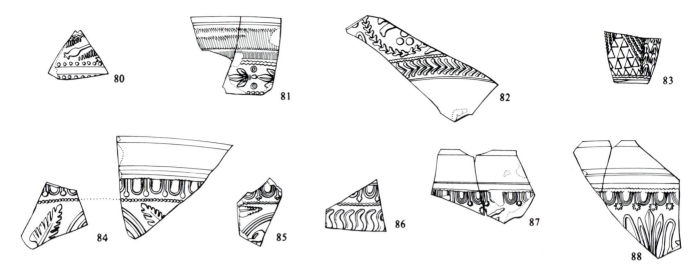

Fig 5.24 Pottery: samian 80–88; scale 1:1

Lyon ware

The main fine ware apart from samian in the military contexts was Lyon ware, the forms (based on Greene 1979) of which are detailed in Table 5.9. Lyon ware was distributed through the stratification; the total quantity from the site, by form, is given in Table 5.10. Much of this consisted of very crushed sherds and, unless definitely a cup sherd, roughcast body sherds have been attributed to beakers, as being the commonest type. The proportion of the earlier cups to the longer-lasting beakers appears to be fairly high, reflecting the Neronian foundation of the site. These can be tentatively compared with the Lyon ware from Usk on the only basis possible, the number of rims. The total

from Wroxeter number 19 beakers and 16 cups, 54% and 46% respectively, against Usk with 31 beakers and 35 cups, 47% and 53% respectively. This seems entirely consistent with the longer occupation of Wroxeter. The ratio of cups to beakers, however, gives a general guide only to the chronological emphasis of a group.

Apart from the above, there are further vessels from Wroxeter, from earlier excavations and from the cemetery, at present in Rowley's House Museum, Shrewsbury (RHM). Details of the Lyon ware are:

Type	Details
1.4	Roughcast cup. RHM E.171. Cemetery
2.4	Rusticated cup. RHM E.168. Marked 'West Room 3'

Table 5.9 Pottery: Lyon ware forms from military period contexts only

form	sherds	%	EVEs	%	weight (g)	%
20	71	46.1	5	2.9	233	49.2
20.4	2	1.3	16	9.4	5	1.1
20.4?	12	7.8	27	15.8	12	2.5
20.5	16	10.4	38	22.2	65	13.7
21	1	0.7	0	0	1	0.2
26	2	1.3	0	0	10	2.1
Beakers	*104*	*67.5*	*86*	*50.3*	*326*	*68.8*
1	2	1.3	0	0	1	0.2
1.3?	1	0.7	0	0	5	1.1
1.4?	1	0.7	8	4.7	1	0.2
1.5	1	0.7	3	1.8	5	1.1
2.4	1	0.7	0	0	5	1.1
3	10	6.5	14	8.2	47	9.9
4.1	15	9.7	51	29.8	46	9.7
5.1	2	1.3	0	0	2	0.4
6	2	1.3	0	0	10	2.1
10	1	0.7	0	0	1	0.2
Cup	6	3.9	0	0	9	1.9
Cups	*42*	*27.3*	*76*	*44.4*	*132*	*27.8*
LAMPS	*8*	*5.2*	*9*	*5.3*	*16*	*3.4*

Table 5.10 Pottery: all Lyon ware, including military and post-military contexts

form	sherds	%	EVEs	%	weight (g)	%
20	170	59.7	51	13.8	573	62.5
20.2	1	0.4	0	0	1	0.1
20.3	1	0.4	8	2.2	5	0.5
20.4	17	6.0	79	21.3	28	3.1
20.5	21	7.4	60	16.2	76	8.3
21	3	1.1	0	0	7	0.8
26	2	0.7	0	0	10	1.1
Beakers	*215*	*75.4*	*198*	*53.4*	*700*	*76.3*
1	1	0.4	0	0	1	0.1
1.1	1	0.4	9	2.4	5	0.5
1.3?	1	0.4	0	0	5	0.5
1.4	3	1.1	28	7.6	11	1.2
1.5	4	1.4	26	7.0	7	0.8
2.4	1	0.4	0	0	5	0.5
3	11	3.9	14	3.8	48	5.2
4.1	16	5.6	51	13.8	47	5.1
5.1	4	1.4	0	0	8	0.9
5.2	1	0.4	0	0	1	0.1
5.4?	1	0.4	0	0	5	0.5
6	3	1.1	16	4.3	20	2.2
10	1	0.4	0	0	1	0.1
Cup	7	2.5	0	0	10	1.1
Cups	*56*	*19.7*	*144*	*38.8*	*174*	*18.9*
LAMPS	*14*	*4.9*	*29*	*7.8*	*43*	*4.7*

3.1	Scale decorated cup (Bushe-Fox 1916, no 73).
5.1	Raspberry cup (Bushe-Fox 1916, no 74).
6	Ribbed cup. RHM Marked 'round room, lowest level'.
8	Latticed cup (Atkinson 1942, fig 44, no A26).
10	Rouletted cup. RHM E.173. Courtyard, north-west.
20.1	Roughcast beaker. RHM Probably from the cemetery.
21	Roughcast folded beaker. RHM E.280.

Unfortunately the museum accession numbers provide virtually no information as to the provenances of these vessels, but apart from those published by Bushe-Fox and Atkinson, it is possible that types 2.4, 6, 10 derived from Atkinson's excavations on the forum site.

Lower Rhineland and colour-coated ware

A single body sherd occurs from a cup, no 233 (Fig 5.38), of the form of Greene's type 4 (1979, fig 24, no 4). Only two other vessels are known from Britain, from Colchester and Richborough.

Central Gaulish colour-coated ware

The earliest occurrence of Central Gaulish colour-coated ware was in the *Demo* deposits. Beakers were the only vessels represented in military contexts, mostly of undefined type, the only type identified being a single beaker of Greene's (1979) type 3. Two lamp fragments are possibly from Central Gaul, but in view of their atypical fabric and the number identified as being from Italy, an Italian source may be more probable (see below). There are, however, larger quantities from Period 2 deposits, probably from more than one source. Of these, only six appeared to be from three cups, with a single rim. An example of the rarer indented beaker type also occurred. Very few of the roughcast beakers had internal roughcasting.

Central Gaulish glazed wares

All the known sherds from the site (total 27, some of them flakes) came from later military or post-military contexts. All were tiny sherds, making form identification hazardous, but most appeared to be from beakers, two from military contexts being probably from a single beaker with vertical ribs, Greene's (1979) type 13, of which a further sherd came from a later layer. One sherd had a single barbotine dot. Only two tiny rim sherds were found, probably representing a single cup of Greene's type 9.

Other glazed vessels from Wroxeter, in Rowley's House Museum, are as follows:

Handled carinated cup, as Greene (1979, fig 41, no 10). Wroxeter site museum, no provenance. Straight-sided beaker, as Greene (1979, fig 41, no 11). RHM E.155, marked 'Tr. W below pavement'. Beakers with barbotine dots, as Greene (1979, fig 41, no 12). Two examples in RHM E.162, with stickers 102 and 103, both from the north-west cemetery. One is published (see Greene 1979 and Bushe-Fox, 1913a, fig 7). Beaker with barbotine 'hairpin' decoration. RHM E.156, marked 'Courtyard W of Ent. Room A, low'. Type as Greene (1979, fig 42, no 13).

The museum accession numbers do not provide provenances but the Central Gaulish glazed beaker with 'hairpin' decoration derived from Atkinson's excavations on the forum site.

Italian colour-coated ware

A rare and more exotic vessel from Wroxeter is in the British Museum (Acc 1871.7–14.8), from the Cato Collection. This is a two-handled Italian cup, from south and central Italy, and is published by Greene (1979, fig 34, no 4). It has proved impossible to obtain more information about the security of the provenance of this cup, although it is marked as 'Observed. Wroxeter 1858'. The possibility remains that this might be a modern import, sold to the Cato Collection with a Wroxeter provenance at a time when Wright's excavations both in the city and in the cemetery would have been current news. Equally, this could have arrived on the site in an officer's baggage (as could be the case with the Lower Rhineland cup), and was perhaps buried with him. The only other vessels from the same area of Italy occur at Colchester and Skeleton Green.

North Italian eggshell ware

Only a single small sherd was found of the commonest form, the cup (as Greene 1979, fig 34, nos 1, 2), in a red-cored dark grey fabric. These cups achieved a widespread if thin distribution, the best known examples from Britain occurring in the grave of M. Favonius Facilis at Colchester (May 1930, pl lxxi).

Gallo-Belgic eggshell *terra nigra*

Only two sherds from beakers of the Cam 120A type were found in military contexts, the earliest being from pit F2908 of phase 4b. A single sherd occurred in Period 1 (in pit F2990), and five further sherds were scattered through later site phases, all of the same vessel type where identifiable. The only exceptional sherds were from post-military contexts, the plain inturned rim (no 239; Fig 5.38), with a very slight groove around the rim, and an offset a short distance down from the rim. No parallels have been traced for this vessel, probably a type of beaker, which appears to derive from the same source on the basis of fabric and finish. A further beaker of the Cam 120A type was found by Atkinson on the forum site, stamped MEDILVE, and another with an illegible stamp (Atkinson 1942, 278), both now in the Rowley's House Museum.

A possibly related although thicker-walled vessel is the fragmentary neck and shoulder, no 193 (Fig 5.37), also in a fine almost grit free fabric with finely polished black surfaces, and decorated with combed lines. A flask in a similar fabric and with the same decorative technique was found at Usk (Greene 1979, fig 52, no 11). The form and decoration of no 192 (Fig 5.37) are also similar, although this differs in fabric and seems less likely to be an import.

Terra nigra

Only one definite sherd of mainstream *terra nigra* was found in military contexts, a fragmentary rim from a Cam 16 plate, no 246 (Fig 5.38). This is was the latest type of *terra nigra* plate, and shares with the cup Cam 58 an unusual distribution related to military sites in the west (Rigby 1977). The only other possible sherd was a slightly abraded rim from a post-military context, which resembles Cam type 4A, no 247 (Fig 5.38). The rim form is, however, one that was also used for 'London ware' (Marsh 1978, type 28). The fabric is finely granular, and the black surfaces have specks of mica. The evidence is equivocal.

Gallo-Belgic white wares

This was rare, all sherds being from closed forms, and probably mostly butt-beakers of the type of no 210 (Fig 5.37), which single vessel accounted for 16 of the 20 sherds from military contexts. A further concentration of sherds from probably a single vessel occurred in area 98 mostly in Period 1 contexts, with oddments displaced into Period 2. The undistinctive fabric and lack of rim details makes it difficult to determine whether these are imports or products of the south-east of England; the latter is suspected. Some of the black-surfaced butt-beakers (as nos 213, 214; Fig 5.37) could be parallelled in Essex and area. The earliest occurrence was the beaker no 210 (Fig 5.37), sherds of which came from pits of phase 4b.

Mica-dusted wares

The only import is the beaker with bosses, no 240 (Fig 5.38), from a demolition context. This is burnt, but is almost certainly of the same type as those from Usk (Greene 1979, fig 53, nos 4–7), with gold mica-dusting, and also the beakers from Lincoln stamped by CAMARO (Webster 1949, 69, fig 11, no 19 and unpublished), Richborough (Bushe-Fox 1932, pl xxxviii, no 286). The source of these beakers is unknown, but is suspected to be northern Gaul, and a Neronian–Flavian date is probable. A fine example from Inchtuthil with complex decoration (Darling 1985, fig 100, no 65), and perhaps also the number found in London (Marsh 1978, type 20) indicate their continuation into the Flavian period.

Only one other mica-dusted sherd was found in military or Period 1 contexts, a body sherd from a closed form from the military demolition phase. This was a coarser fabric, very similar to the local Wroxeter oxidised ware, which has a mica-dusted version in Period 2 deposits, from where this sherd could have intruded.

Pompeian red ware

The rarity of imported Pompeian red ware platters and lids may be the reason for the quantity of local copies. Two imported fabrics are represented, Peacock's fabrics 2 and 3 (1977a); the latter is from Central Gaul, while the former may derive from Gaul or the Mediterranean. No vessels occur in the Italian fabric 1. The unclassified Pompeian red ware sherds appear to be copies, including the internal coating (not found on the local Wroxeter copies). Two vessels only occur, one (no 244; Fig 5.38), from a post-military context but probably residual, having a coarse grey fabric with red cortex and internal slip, the other (no 243; Fig 5.38, unstratified) with a cream fabric and internal slip. Neither is likely to be an import, but their source is unknown.

Painted wares

Painted vessels are extremely rare, and only occur in military demolition contexts and later. All the sherds from military demolition layers were body sherds, and were in cream (7 sherds), grey (1 sherd), and some local oxidised fabrics (6 sherds). The commonest motif appears to be intersecting painted circles. All appeared to be from closed forms, probably beakers or small jars. Two sherds came from Period 1 contexts. All the sherds from the military period were from layers rather than features, mostly unsealed and open to intrusions.

The painted vessels appear to derive from more than one source, and some were probably made locally. Similar sherds have been found in the Midlands, and two sites are of interest. Seven sherds have been found at Baginton (Hobley 1969, nos 132–36; 1972, nos 137, 177), all of which appear to be of cream fabric with red painted decoration, the motifs being mostly fragments of circles; some have dots inside, one sherd having touching circles, but plant-type motifs also occur (Hobley 1969, no 132), and one sherd has traces of rouletting.

More evidence derives from the site at Wall, where numerous sherds have been found, the best group occurring in Gould's excavations of 1961–3 (Gould 1964, nos 125, 126, 150, 151 and 162–70). Apart from a single sherd (Gould 1964, no 168), these are all in cream fabrics with varying designs, mostly circles, and sometimes coupled with rouletting. Most of these appear to be from beakers, some of butt-beaker type, but other more probably from girth-beakers. In Gould's excavations of 1964–6, a further painted sherd was found in a rubbish dump dated by samian to the Neronian period, but in a grey fabric with a painted white lattice design (Gould 1967, fig 12, no 45).

A butt beaker with similar painted circles was found at *Margidunum* in a ditch dated to the late Flavian period (Oswald 1948, pl xvi, no 6). Painting does not appear to be a common characteristic of the Colchester potters, and while a south-eastern source may be suspected, proof is lacking.

Lamps

A number of first-century lamps by-passed the pottery archive and are reported by D Bailey in Chapter 6. Three were stratified in military contexts, one from a Period 1 context, and the rest occurred in Periods 2 and 3 or were unstratified. Of these lamps, Bailey considers only two to be of post-military manufacture, although these are dated by him as Flavian-Trajanic and were both imported, one from North Italy and the other from Italy or Gaul. A single lamp made in Britain of certain second-century date is also in his report. The sources of the 18 first-century lamps studied by Bailey can be summarised: Italy (8 examples), nos 2, 3, 5, 7, 8, 11, 14, 17; Gaul (6), nos 1, 4, 6, 9, 13, 15; Italy or Gaul (3), nos10, 12, 16. The high proportion he identifies as being from Italy suggests that the two lamps recorded with the main assemblage and assigned to Central Gaul (rather than Lyon) may in fact be north Italian, since both are in atypical fabrics.

The total number of lamps in the pottery archive including some from post-military contexts is shown in Table 5.11. Most are tiny body sherds for which the precise type of enclosed lamp cannot be identified. There are 23 individual records, only two of which appear to be the same vessel, so a maximum count would be 22 which, added to Bailey's report, gives a total of 40 lamps. This is a considerable number of lamps, far in excess of the 29 recorded from the Usk fortress, of which only 4 were imported lamps, and where most were locally made open-lamps or cruses (Usk type 27), the count also including lamp fillers (Usk type 16). The spatial distribution of the lamps showed that 24 came from the eastern area (10 from central and 14 from the south) which produced the bulk of the military period pottery, 14 from the defences zone and 2 from areas to the east of the baths.

Mortaria

The early mortaria from both military and Period 1 contexts are related due to the disturbance of many of the military period vessels into later contexts and the small size of both samples, particularly that from Period 1, and are examined for evidence for changing patterns of supply. Table 5.12 details the quantities by fabric from military contexts. Full details of mortaria from Period 1 are reported upon elsewhere (Ellis 2000, 261).

Mortaria from Period 1 totalled only 39 sherds, 1.57 EVEs and 4.387kg. Over 50% on EVEs and weight were locally produced, and the main outside suppliers were potters in the Rhone Valley and the *Verulamium* region (Darling 2000).

The small size of both samples restricts the conclusions which can be drawn. It is, however, clear that locally made mortaria predominated in the military period. The very small quantity of mortaria stratified in Period 1 deposits makes it difficult to assess whether local production continued right to the end of the military period or beyond into the early civilian phase. While over 50% were local products, the high level of residual pottery is relevant, particularly taking into account the fact that 22% were from the Rhone Valley. The types of locally made mortaria remain the same as those in the military contexts, suggesting that these are residual vessels, but the occurrence of locally made mortaria in Period 2 contexts, many dated to the broad period of late first to mid-second century, indicates continuing local production.

The only significant continental suppliers were the potters of the Rhone Valley, and the relatively small quantity from stratified military contexts should be viewed in the light of the higher proportion occurring residually in the Period 1 deposits. The North Gaulish potters do not seem to have supplied many vessels, and, since no sherds occur until the later military phases, may have been competing with the *Verulamium* potters. There was a complete vessel from North Gaul stamped by CASSARIVS from the pit F2990 of Period 1, now missing. This could have arrived at Wroxeter before the end of the military occupation, being dated by Hartley as *c* AD 65–100, though found in Period 1.

The fabric of MORT2, no 253 (Fig 5.38), cannot be certainly attributed to source, although it is possibly an early import from the Rhineland (K Hartley pers comm). A fragment of a mortarium attributable to the

Table 5.11 Pottery: lamps by source

source	sherds	EVEs	weight	type
Lyon	14	29	43	
CGCC?	10	95	21	Fig 5.38, 248, 249
WWOF	2	75	40	Fig 5.33, 126
Open lamps	9	60	192	Fig 5.33, 127

Table 5.12 Pottery: mortaria from military contexts

fabric	sherds	%	EVEs	%	weight (g)	%
MWWO	20	18.5	60	24.7	2300	28.5
MWWO?	1	0.9	17	7.0	215	2.7
MWWOF	2	1.9	25	10.3	740	9.2
MWWR	2	1.9	9	3.7	100	1.2
MWWRF	1	0.9	0	0	40	0.5
MWWCR	41	38.0	42	17.3	1840	22.8
	67	*62.02*	*153*	*63.0*	*5235*	*64.8*
MORV	16	14.8	17	7.0	820	10.1
MONG	5	4.6	0	0	109	1.4
MOVR	12	11.1	37	15.2	1130	14.0
MOCRA	3	2.8	21	8.6	365	4.5
MORT1	1	0.9	0	0	190	2.4
MORT2	4	3.7	15	6.2	235	2.9
Total	*108*		*243*		*8084*	

pottery of the Atisii at Aoste, Isère, *Gallia Narbonensis* (Hartley 1973, 46), normally dated *c* AD 50–85, was found residually in post-military contexts.

Identifiable British suppliers in the early period are limited to the potters working in the *Verulamium* region. These first appear in the later military contexts, and mark the start of a period of trade from that area, increasing in Period 1, and continuing into Period 2. Their occurrence in the late military phase demonstrates a change in supplies within the military period. A similar pattern appears at the fortress at Usk where, although again locally made mortaria predominate, the fortress was relatively close to a possible source of mortaria from Gloucester, and supplies from the *Verulamium* region are considered to belong to the later phase of occupation. Wroxeter would have been more isolated in this respect.

The mortaria in MOCRA fabric (no 256; Fig 5.39) occur only in the demolition period deposits. The fabric is reminiscent of that used for the second-century mortaria made at Wroxeter, but lacks the heavy tempering often associated with those. The combination of grit and scoring inside and on top of the rim was a common first-century practice. If not intrusive into the military deposits, this appears to be part of the diversification of supplies seen in the later phases. MORT1 only occurred as a single body sherd, from an unknown source. MORT3 from Period 1 context was again a single sherd, source unknown.

Amphorae: military period and Period 1

The following incorporates information kindly supplied by David Williams: his report on a proportion of the amphorae is in the pottery archive.

Consideration of the amphorae from the military contexts must bear in mind the change in the collection policy during the excavations, particularly since such a large proportion of the military period pottery came from the central and south areas, the focus of the earlier excavations. This would clearly depress the main amphora, Dressel 20, and we cannot be certain that the 59% weight is a true reflection of the quantity, and its position relative to Cam 186s and other types may be subject to bias. The figures are therefore considered alongside those from Period 1, where most of the amphorae are probably residual from the military phase, and mainly come from the areas excavated later. The spatial divisions used for the later civilian structures are followed to set the military period in context with the later finds.

Table 5.13 sets the amphorae from the military period into the context of the site, showing the differing proportions of the respective assemblages taken by amphorae. The quantity of amphorae from Period 1 may give the clue to a truer view of the military period, although when examined in detail, there are significant decreases in the quantities of Cam 186s and Gauloise

4s (Table 5.15). The Dressel 20s not only increase proportionately in Period 1, but their average sherd weight is triple that from the military contexts; this is probably related to a single context (see below). The figures, however, have to be used with caution and viewed in relation to the site evidence since the bulk of the amphorae overall came from the post-military West Range area (83% in the military period, dropping to 56% in Period 1) and Porticos (9% military, 37% Period 1), both areas with more complete collection policies (broadly equivalent to the defences area). More significantly 81% of the total amphorae stratified in military contexts came from Area 84, in which only a single context with pottery was attributed to Period 1; no contexts from Areas 83 or 92 were phased to Period 1. The individual areas containing the largest groups of amphorae for each period are detailed in Table 5.14.

The largest groups of amphorae from single contexts were *84/244*, a pot and tile surface spread assigned to the military demolition period, with some 58kg, and *91/85*, a Period 1 demolition phase 1.3 context with a minimum of 13kg, representing over 47% of all Period 1 amphorae. This latter context probably contained substantially more amphorae, virtually all Dressel 20s, as the contexts are noted as samples. Since Period 1 is not represented in Areas 83, 84, and 92, the probability that many of the amphorae in those areas in Period 2 are residual from the military period is stronger.

In addition, the rubbish deposited on those areas can be shown to differ in the content of vessel types from that in the central and south area, and the occurrence of amphorae sherds is likely not only to have been governed by the use of individual areas and rubbish disposal methods, but also by secondary use. This is particularly relevant for any consideration of the spatial distribution of amphorae in the military period, since 67% on weight of all amphorae came from a single context, *84/244*, the pot and tile spread noted above, apparently laid as a rough surface, of no relevance to rubbish disposal or use of the area beyond the fact that a hard surface was required. There is, however, no reason to believe it does not represent a true sample of the amphorae in use up to that period.

The wide range of types and sources of amphorae from military contexts (Table 5.15) is notable. As usual the Spanish amphorae predominate, and the main wine amphorae appear to be those from Gaul, the Rhodian types, and a range of Koan types, although the latter could contain a range of products; for example, analysis of one from King Harry Lane, St Albans, identified olive oil as the original contents (Williams 1989). The Rhodian vessels are predominantly in Peacock's fabric 2 (Peacock 1977b), fabric 1 being only 22% on weight, and both fabrics almost certainly originating from the Rhodian Peraea area (see also Empereur and Tuna 1989).

Amphorae of Cam 186 spp form the second largest category. Only a single Cam 186C/Beltran IIA occurred (in *84/205*, a trample layer in the demolition phase 7iv). It is difficult to say whether the rest belong to the Cam 186A or 186C, or even Beltran IIB (Peacock and Williams 1986, classes 17–19). The fabric is typical of amphorae from the southern Spanish coastal regions. Six sherds attributed to a south Spanish origin might also belong to the Cam 186 sp, or alternatively they may come from other fish-produce-bearing amphorae from the same region. The two sherds of unspecified Spanish origin may come from a group of typologically linked ovoid amphorae (Peacock and Williams 1986, class 16, Dressel 7–11).

The flat-bottomed wine amphorae of Gauloise 4 form from southern France (Laubenheimer 1985) make up a significant part of the assemblage, and a fragment of damaged rim possibly belongs to the Gauloise 5 form,

a relatively rare find in Britain. One of the two sherds attributed to the Dressel 28 form may be a French fabric from the same area, while the illustrated no 263 (Fig 5.39) is less certain, and could be a Spanish product.

Dressel 2–4 amphorae came from a variety of sources. The Catalan vessels are all in a reddish granitic fabric, to be equated with Williams's Fabric 1 (Peacock and Williams 1986, 94 and 106). The black sand Dressel 2–4 are in the distinctive 'black sand' fabric, which is characteristic of the region of Campania around the Bay of Naples. Four sherds of Dressel 2–4 form most probably came from Italy on the basis of fabric, while two sherds were in a fabric reminiscent of that normally associated with Dressel 20 amphorae from the Guadalquivir region of *Baetica*. The highest number of Dressel 2–4 sherds are loosely attributed to the eastern Mediterranean region.

A fragment of amphora body with a steeply arched bifid handle attached but lacking the rim, no 260, from a Period 3 context (*90/156*), is quite likely to be from a Koan or even pseudo-Koan amphora (see Peacock and Williams 1986, class 11, where a photograph of an example of a pseudo-Koan from York appears quite similar). Williams reports that a thin-section of the Wroxeter example shows a mixed range of inclusions, with pieces of volcanic glass and rock and metamorphic phyllite. Also present are discrete grains of sanidine and plagioclase feldspar, flecks of mica, and iron oxides. The petrology points to a volcanic origin, most probably in the eastern Mediterranean region, with Kos itself a possible contender.

The less common vessels of the same type as Fishbourne 148.3 form a significant part of the amphorae assemblage (nos 268–71; Fig 5.39), but the source and contents are both unknown. The quantity of these from military contexts may be underestimated,

Table 5.13 Pottery: percentages of amphorae by period

period	EVEs%	weight (%)	wt/sh
Military	2.7	36.2	49.5g
Period 1	4.4	45.5	103.6g
Period 2	1.8	18.7	35.8g

Table 5.14 Pottery: concentrations of amphorae by period and excavation area, based on weight

	Defences area						South	
Period	83	84	85	91	90	97	98	92
Military	–	80.8	*	1.1	*	–	6.1	4.1
Period 1	–	–	–	55.2	3.0	*	33.9	-
Period 2	4.1	24.2	1.6	18.3	10.4	6.7	13.2	14.8

(* = under 1%)

Table 5.15 Pottery: amphorae from military contexts

form	sherds	%	EVEs	%	weight (g)	%
Dressel 20	798	45.6	217	35.0	50770	58.6
Cam186spp	340	19.4	68	11.0	17510	20.2
Dressel 7-11	2	0.1	0	0	235	0.3
S.Spanish	6	0.3	0	0	370	0.4
Haltern 70	28	1.6	0	0	2180	2.5
	1174	67.1	285	46.0	71065	82.1
Fishbourne 148spp	118	6.7	35	5.6	1644	1.9
Gauloise 4	257	14.7	110	17.7	7902	9.1
Gauloise 5?	1	0.1	9	1.5	35	0.*
Dressel 28	2	0.1	7	1.1	210	0.2
	260	14.9	126	20.3	8147	9.4
Rhodian	100	5.7	0	0.	3098	3.6
Italian Dr 2-4	4	0.2	0	0.	120	0.1
Black sand Dr 2-4	3	0.2	0	0.	270	0.3
Catalan Dr 2-4	4	0.2	0	0.	245	0.3
E.Medit. Dr 2-4	13	0.7	0	0.	450	0.5
S.Spanish Dr 2-4	2	0.1	30	4.8	90	0.10
	126	7.2	30	4.8	4273	4.9
Cam. 189	40	2.3	30	4.8	555	0.7
Stoppers	13	0.7	114	18.4	55	0.1
Unidentified	18	1.0	0	0.00	843	1.0
Total	1749		620		86,582	

as it is suspected that some were missing when the archive was prepared (from *84/109* of Phase 7iv, possibly another 1.31kg, which would increase the weight percentage to 3.4%). Apart from their occurrence in the earliest phase at Fishbourne (Cunliffe 1971, fig 100, no 148.3), this type of amphorae is rare. It is known from Lincoln (Darling 1984, fig 18, no 152; others unpublished), Leicester (Hebditch and Mellor 1973, fig 28, no 18, and unpublished R Pollard pers comm), and occurs at York (Monaghan 1993, fig 288, no 2825) and in a post-fortress context at Usk (Webster 1993, fig 178, no 33), although the identification as amphorae of the latter two is queried. A closely similar if not exactly the same type occurs at Kingsholm (Hurst 1985, fig 28, nos 123–5). Its earliest occurrence is in a sandstone layer of phase 4b (*85/248*), which could suggest a Flavian *terminus post quem* based on samian. The dating evidence from York is important since at least three of these amphorae were found in a pit containing a large homogeneous group of samian dating between AD 65–75 (Monaghan 1993, 685; Dickinson and Hartley 1993, 722).

The shape of this amphora is not certainly known, but if the sherds have been correctly identified as belonging to this type, a cylindrical body with oval handles is indicated, as reconstructed at York (Monaghan 1993, fig 288, no 2825). The fabric is very hard, rough and sandy with occasional limestone and some flecks of mica; the colour is normally a light red to red-brown or red-buff. The sandy fabric is relatively distinctive in the Wroxeter assemblage, but it is possible that more than one type is represented in the sherdage, some having a white to cream surface colouration (resulting from the use of saline water), but such colouration does not always cover the complete vessel. The rim, body shape and type of handles are all reminiscent of Tripolitanian and Punic amphorae, particularly Tripolitanian II (Peacock and Williams 1986, class 37). The fabric differs, however, from the Tripolitanian fabrics, and it is only possible to speculate that the source lies either in another area of North Africa or in the East Mediterranean, the origin of the Phoenician tradition.

Although this accounts for only a relatively small proportion of the amphorae from military and Period 1 contexts, there is a considerable quantity (17% on weight) from Period 2. Most of the sherds stratified in military and Period 1 contexts came from Area 84, which is significantly the same area that produced 77% of the sherds in Period 2 contexts, suggesting that these are residual from the military, given that only a single context was phased to Period 1 in this area.

Ribbed sandy red-brown amphorae of the Cam 189 species were most common in the military contexts, although they represented a high percentage of the sherds from Period 1, and still occurred in similar proportions to the military in Period 2. It is clear that the wider variety, Kingsholm 117, is also represented as no 264 (Fig 5.39) and probably the handle, no 265 (Fig 5.39), but the fragmentary nature of the sherdage precludes estimating the division between that and the Cam 189 carrot type, nos 266 and 267 (Fig 5.39). An origin in the area of Egypt seems probable, and a depinto on a 'carrot' amphora from Carlisle indicates that the contents were dates (Tomlin 1991, 301, fig 7; Hird 1992, 61, fig 8, no 12), while the evidence from wrecks indicates similar contents for the Kingsholm 117.

It is likely, taking into account the proportions from the later civilian periods and the probability noted above that many were residual from the military, that the level of amphorae coming into Wroxeter declined significantly after the military withdrawal. There are no directly comparable figures from Usk, but the quantification based on minimum vessels (rims) shows amphorae to have accounted for 5.4% of Phase I, dropping to only 1.7% in Phase II. Amphorae as a proportion of the military period assemblage at 36% weight is obviously lower than the true figure had all sherds been retained, so that comparison with other sites can only be tentative. It is worth noting, however, that the early contexts at Kingsholm (Hurst 1985) produced 56% amphorae on weight, not far below the figure from Lake Farm, Wimborne (unpublished) at 61%, whereas Exeter (confined to Periods 1–1b, Bidwell 1979, table 9) weighed in at 39%. However, Kingsholm is a highly peculiar small assemblage, Lake Farm possibly functioned as a supply base on the south coast, and the area excavated at Exeter (from the legionary bath-house succeeded by the basilica and forum) may not have produced a typical sample of pottery upon which to judge the proportions taken by amphorae.

Moving to the northern frontier in search of comparative material, *Vindolanda* (Bidwell 1985, 173, table vii) provides two figures for amphorae: as a proportion of all pottery over the whole site at 32% (based on 103kg amphorae to total 326kg), and on stratified deposits at 39% (based on 63kg amphorae to total 162kg). There is no way of knowing to what extent the proportion of amphorae at Wroxeter is depressed due to the discard policy, and it is clear from the site evidence that the figures from the western part of the site cannot be extrapolated to estimate the total quantity. Until further comparative figures are available, it seems likely that we can conclude that Wroxeter had adequate supplies of amphorae-borne products during the military period despite the distance from importation ports.

Most of the amphorae from Period 1 (Table 5.16) are probably residual from the underlying military deposits. It is impossible to determine if any of the Cam 186s are of the later type due to the absence of rims. All the Dressel 20 sherds are of comparable fabric to those from military contexts and 68% (by weight) came from a single context 91/85 of the demolition phase 1.3, which also produced a stamp dated *c* AD 50–100. There is no certain evidence that any of this material represented new imports in the early civilian period.

Only one stamp on a Dressel 20 amphora was stratified in a military context; the other was residual in Period 1.3.

Table 5.16 Pottery: amphorae from Period 1 contexts

form	sherds	%	EVEs	%	weight (g)	%
Dressel 20	103	38.3	113	58.0	19447	69.8
Cam. 186 spp	30	11.2	0	0	3529	12.7
S.Spanish	2	0.7	0	0	131	0.5
	135	*50.2*	*113*	*58.0*	*23107*	*82.9*
Fishbourne 148 spp	15	5.6	0	0	572	2.1
Gauloise 4	43	16.0	0	0	1130	4.1
Rhodian	6	2.2	15	7.7	643	2.3
E.Medit. Dr 2-4 spp	3	1.1	13	6.7	358	1.3
Italian Dr 2-4	6	2.2	0	0	75	0.3
Cam. 189 spp	32	11.9	0	0	448	1.6
Stoppers	8	3.0	54	27.7	21	0.1
Unidentified	21	7.8	0	0	1524	5.5
Total	*269*		*195*		*27878*	

(Fig 5.39).

273   The poor impression could be read as PAM (or ATM)C (Callender 1965, no 1279, fig 12, no 26) of which a single example is recorded from Geneva, or less likely as P.ATV IC. Callender (*ibid*, no 1293, fig 12, no 37) notes two examples from Richborough and Trion as P.ATV ( ) IC(eli)?). *84/263*, military demolition, phase 7iv.

POR.PS   Callender no 1370 (25), fig 13, 36–8. Possibly the same die as found at Autun and Port-sur-Saone. The prefix 'POR' almost certainly indicates 'from the warehouse of'. There are many stamps with this prefix; this group of stamps POR.PS or P.S.A may be linked to no 1395, P.S.A deriving from the estates of P S Avitus, broadly dated to the second half of the first century, although the absence of the terminal 'a' and the style of the stamp cast doubt in this case. *91/85*, Period 1.3 (= Ellis 2000, 260, no 1).

The assemblage: vessel classes and functions

Vessel classes by phase

The most unequivocal definition of vessels in an assemblage is by the class of vessel, ie, bowl, flagon, jar, etc. The assemblages including samian from each phase are detailed in Table 5.17 as percentages of EVEs and weight. Analysis of the contaminated contexts is included. The quantities are given in Appendix 3.6 (summary) and 3.7. Period 1 pottery has been excluded due to the small quantity, but is included in the section dealing with functions. Table 5.17 shows the changing composition of the assemblages and, as with the fabrics table, the pit F2807 should be disregarded in assessing the chronological differences.

The most notable feature lies in the *Late* phase, with a marked increase in the quantity of flagons, and a related decrease in the jars category. This seems likely to arise, at least in the EVEs measure, from the strong rim form, resulting in less breakage. Since samian is included, it is perhaps noteworthy that although cups and beakers increase in this phase, it is not of the same order as the flagons.

Vessel functions

The higher proportion of bowls, dishes, and cups in the demolition contexts is directly related to the increased proportion of samian. To examine the composition of the groups more closely, all the vessel types have been individually assigned to functions. Clearly this involves modern assumptions, but the typology of vessels is sufficiently detailed to aid assignation to function. The functions identified are as those used in the Usk report (Greene 1993) to facilitate comparison, and are relatively straightforward. The difficult area is inevitably the 'table/kitchen' category; reeded rim bowls and lids have been allocated to cooking, and some other bowls and dishes have been placed in the 'table/kitchen' group on the basis of their coarser finish, together with Pompeian red ware dishes and their copies. Amphorae are excluded, liquid holders being confined to flagons, jugs, and rare narrow-necked jars. Table 5.18 shows all the pottery, including samian, to give a total overview, while Table 5.19 excludes the samian in order to facilitate as direct a comparison as possible with the assemblage from the fortress at Usk.

This is best viewed graphically in Fig 5.25a. This makes clear the individual peculiarities of the pottery from the pit F2807 and the *Late* group, and the two more 'normal' groups from the earliest and demolition phases can be compared. It also shows even more clearly the astonishing increase in the number of flagons in the *Late* contexts, with only a small rise in the number of drinking vessels, and a decline in both kitchen and table vessels. To examine the possibility that this is due to the spatial distribution, vessels have been analysed for function by area, the main functions shown in Figure 5.25b.

A marked concentration of liquid holders occurs in the defences area, and also relatively low figures for both drinking vessels and table ware. The spatial distribution

a)

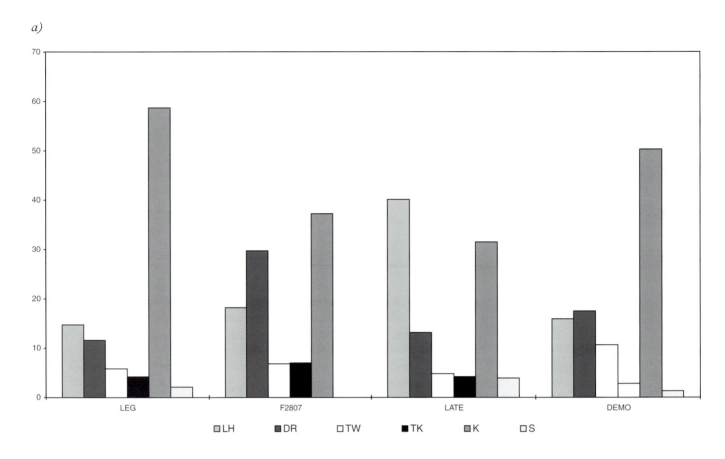

b)

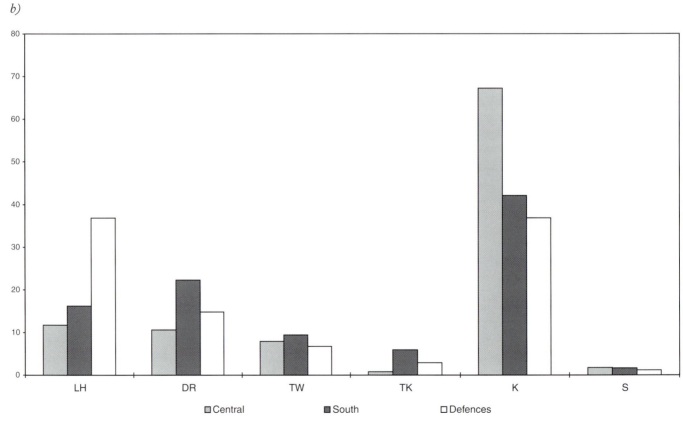

Fig 5.25 Pottery: functions a) main functions, Military period based on EVEs; b) % based on EVEs by area

c)

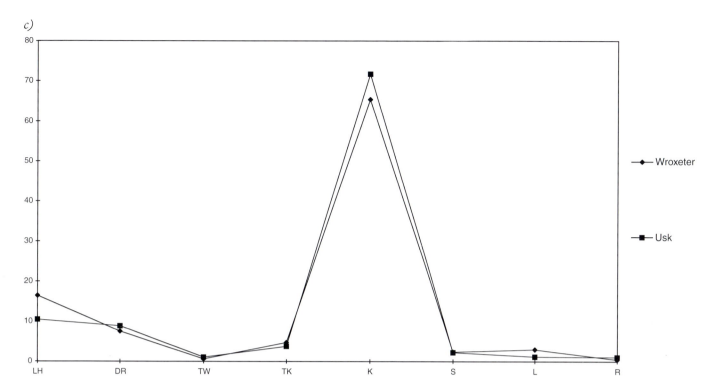

Fig 5.25 continued c) Wroxeter early phase EVEs, Usk phase 1 minimum vessels

of vessels by function has been analysed further to exclude the samian, and this predictably showed a marked decrease in tableware and drinking vessels, less marked for the latter in the courtyard. The abnormally high proportion of drinking vessels in the courtyard comes partly from the inclusion of the pit F2807.

The differences between the two main areas, the defences area and the interior, are marked. The sample sizes, however, differ substantially as does the level of fragmentation, both of which argue for caution. Kitchen vessels are commonest in the central and south areas (the percentages for the latter being affected by the high proportion of drinking vessels from pit F2807), whereas liquid holders are prevalent in the defences area. While it might be tempting to speculate on the basis of the phased figures that the military occupation declined in an orgy of drunkenness, the spatial distribution suggests that these differences arise essentially from the nature of the occupation of the two areas. Examination of the detailed phasing and spatial distribution shows that over half the quantity of liquid holders in the phase occurred in Area 98 and to a lesser extent Area 90, in Phase 7i, with nearly all the remainder deriving from Phases 5 and 6, mostly from Area 84. At least four came from the fill of the fortress ditch, but the largest concentration was from *98/205*, a loam layer, and most were from layers rather than features. While rubbish deposited anywhere is likely to be mixed, the emphasis on liquid holders, specifically flagons, may suggest that nearby buildings were areas for off-duty relaxation.

The increased amount of samian in the later phases is notable. Comparison with the figures based on EVEs excluding samian across the phases shows that although

there are some increases in the proportions in the demolition period, the figures overall are not widely disparate, except in the idiosyncratic *Late* phase. Of the lesser functional categories, lamps occurred only in the interior of the fortress, mostly from the south area, while ritual vessels, tazze, came from the south and defences areas.

Functional comparison with Usk fortress assemblage

To examine the contribution of the coarse pottery alone, and to enable a comparison to be made with the assemblage from the fortress at Usk, analysis for function excluding samian is detailed in Table 5.19.

The only site providing relevant information for any functional analysis of the early Wroxeter pottery is the fortress at Usk. There is clearly a danger in comparing results obtained by differing quantification methods, and a further problem arises with the inclusion of samian in the Wroxeter figures. This is most obvious in the higher proportion of table wares from Wroxeter which would in turn depress the main functional group, kitchen wares.

Using the early period only from Wroxeter and Phase I of Usk, the figures excluding samian tend to suggest that the two assemblages are very similar (Fig 5.25c), since where the Wroxeter figures are appreciably higher, in the category of liquid holders, is precisely the point where EVEs tend to exaggerate, because the strength of the strongly curved flagon neck frequently leads to a complete rim survival. The only appreciable differences, those on flagons and kitchen vessels, are of the same order, and had the Wroxeter pottery been quantified as minimum vessels to facilitate a direct comparison, it is conceivable that the

Table 5.17 Pottery: classes of vessel by phase, based on percentages of assemblages

i EVEs %

	LEG	F2807	LATE	DEMO	CONTAM
Bowl	5.4	6.6	6.3	11.4	4.6
Dish	7.1	7.8	7.9	7.3	12.7
Bowl/Dish	0	0	0	*	0
Cup	5.9	15.2	7.1	12.6	4.4
Cup/Bowl	0	0	0	0.2	0
Lid	0.6	0	1.8	1.8	4.2
Flagon	12.0	18.2	40.1	14.9	14.5
Jar	57.2	36.7	27.3	43.2	48.4
Cooking Pot	0	0	0	0	0.4
Honey Pot	1.4	0	0.5	1.0	0
Jar/Beaker	0	0	0.2	0	0
Beaker	5.7	14.5	6.1	4.9	7.1
Mortaria	1.7	0	0.6	1.1	3.3
Lamp	2.6	0	0	0.6	0.5
Unclassif.	0.4	1.1	2.4	0.9	0
Sample	*2885*	*4402*	*3348*	*10215*	*1898*

ii Weight

	LEG	F2807	LATE	DEMO	CONTAM
Bowl	3.4	8.3	5.0	7.5	4.5
Dish	6.7	5.2	6.0	4.3	13.2
Bowl/Dish	0	0	0	0.1	*
Cup	0.9	5.0	1.7	2.9	1.4
Cup/Bowl	0	0	0.1	0.1	*
Lid	0.1	*	1.1	0.6	1.4
Flagon	15.7	16.8	22.0	15.3	12.9
Jar	33.0	14.3	15.0	16.1	14.2
Cooking Pot	0	0.1	0	*	0.3
Honey Pot	1.2	0	0.3	1.1	0
Jar/Beaker	0	0	*	0	0
Beaker	0.9	3.1	2.8	1.4	1.3
Closed	0	0.7	0.8	1.2	0.8
Mortaria	6.0	0.2	5.4	5.0	13.2
Lamp	0.2	·0	0	0.2	*
Unclassif.	0.1	1.5	0.4	0.6	0.3
-	31.8	44.8	39.5	43.6	36.5
Sample	*23215*	*18047*	*28621*	*71174*	*11857*

(= presence below 0.10%)*

Table 5.18 Pottery: vessel functions, coarse wares and samian based on percentages

	EVEs					Weight				
	LEG	F2807	LATE	DEMO	CONTAM	LEG	F2807	LATE	DEMO	CONTAM
LH	14.7	18.2	40.1	15.9	14.8	16.0	16.8	22.0	16.1	12.9
DR	11.6	29.7	13.1	17.5	11.5	1.8	8.1	4.5	4.3	2.7
TW	5.8	6.8	4.8	10.6	11.2	3.4	8.4	2.6	6.5	11.2
TK										
	4.2	7.0	4.2	2.8	3.6	4.5	4.4	3.9	1.3	2.6
K	58.7	37.2	31.5	50.3	57.5	31.1	15.2	17.9	24.2	30.5
S	2.1	0	3.9	1.3	0.8	10.7	0	8.1	1.2	0.3
L	2.6	0	0	0.6	0.5	0.2	0	0	0.2	*
R	0.4	1.1	2.4	0.9	0	*	1.5	0.4	0.5	0.3
-	0	0	0	0.1	0	32.3	45.6	40.6	45.7	39.4
Sample	*2885*	*4402*	*3348*	*10215*	*1898*	*23215*	*18047*	*28621*	*71174*	*11857*

[Key: LH Liquid Holders; DR Drinking vessels; TW Table Ware; TK Table or Kitchen; K Kitchen; S Storage; L Lighting; R Ritual]

Table 5.19 Pottery: functions excluding samian based on percentages of EVEs and weight

	Eves				Weight			
	LEG	F2807	LATE	DEMO	LEG	F2807	LATE	DEMO
LH	16.4	18.3	43.9	19.6	16.7	16.9	22.9	17.5
DR	7.5	29.9	9.5	8.0	1.2	8.0	3.7	2.1
TW	0.6	6.2	0.7	3.4	0.3	7.9	0.3	1.1
TK	4.6	7	4.6	3.5	4.7	4.4	4.0	1.4
K	65.4	37.5	34.4	62.0	32.5	15.4	18.6	26.4
S	2.3	0	4.3	1.7	11.2	0	8.4	1.3
L	2.9	0	0	0.7	0.2	0	0	0.2
R	0.4	1.1	2.6	1.1	*	1.5	0.4	0.6
-	0	0	0	0.1	33.2	45.9	41.8	49.4
Sample	2591	4370	3059	8287	22228	17916	27591	65237

[Key: LH Liquid Holders; DR Drinking vessels; TW Table Ware; TK Table or Kitchen; K Kitchen; S Storage; L Lighting; R Ritual]

results would have been very close to the Usk figures The samples used are Wroxeter *Leg* phase, 2591 EVEs, Usk Phase 1, 2456 vessels.

Finally, there is the question of any changes seen in the succeeding Period 1 assemblage. Full details are published elsewhere (Darling 2000). There is a high proportion of drinking vessels in phase 1.1, but this has to be viewed in the light of both the relatively small sample, and the high percentage of samian from that phase. Liquid holders decrease from the levels seen in the military contexts, but it is notable that otherwise the assemblage from the last phase (containing the bulk of the pottery) is otherwise relatively similar to that from the military demolition contexts. This, however, has to be viewed in the light of the fact that 66% on EVEs of phase 1.3 came from the Courtyard area (see Ellis 2000), and much of it could be residual.

Non-local vessels: military period

As noted above, the occurrence of non-local vessels other than fine wares is rare in the earliest period, and increases in the late and more particularly the demolition deposits, a trend which continues into Period 1 and later. The main non-local fabrics are the fabric groups of cream and grey wares, *Verulamium* region white wares, including mortaria, and Severn Valley wares.

Cream (Fig 5.37)

The vessels concerned are all types such as flagons and beakers which tend to travel widely. The ring-neck flagons, nos 188 and 189, are both first-century types. The unusual vessel, no 191, perhaps a type of honey pot although no suitable handles were found, is unparalleled, but the beaker, no 208, is a common type. The cordoning of the narrow-necked jar, no 194, suggests a Gallo-Belgic derivation. The tazza, no 222, has a curious frilled flange with a sharp carination below. An example from Richborough from a pit with early pottery (although probably open until the end of the first century) is similar in fabric type and rim form, but does not have the carination

(Bushe-Fox 1926, no 44). The tazze from Fishbourne (types 29.1–2) are similar, one having the same carination below the rim, and the other rim being very close to this example (Cunliffe 1971). A source in southern Britain is possible for all these vessels, but cannot be further narrowed.

Grey (Fig 5.37)

One of the most unusual vessels is the cup no 216, an imitation of a *terra nigra* cup copying the Arretine form, Loeschcke 7, or perhaps the samian form, Ritterling 14. Cam 54 is similar although finer, while Cam 57 is the only local copy. Fishbourne has copies of Loeschcke forms 7 and 8 in local fabric, and types 47.1 and 47.2 are in a fine grey ware with a black micaceous surface (Cunliffe 1971). These are again much finer thinner-walled vessels. Copies of *terra nigra* vessels are common well into the Flavian period, and the source of this vessel is unknown.

The beaker no 209 is from a similar Gallo-Belgic tradition, probably of the general form of Cam 120B, but is far removed from the original in having a relatively sandy fabric, the dark grey surface showing a considerable amount of mica. The copying of the form continues well into the Flavian period, and at Fishbourne copies appear more frequently in Periods 2 and 3, demonstrating the long life of this beaker.

The two fragments of rouletted beakers, nos 213 and 214, are in similar fabrics, although the decoration is slightly different. The fragmentary nature precludes comment beyond the fact that similar vessels are common in the south-east. The same applies to the two narrow necked vessels, nos 192 and 193, both in a Gallo-Belgic tradition.

None of the jar types is particularly distinctive, although it is worth noting that the thick-curved rims of nos 195 and 196, with which the decorated body sherds nos 203 and 204 may be associated on the basis of the fabrics, are similar to jars illustrated by Bushe-Fox (1913a, nos 31, 33, and 34) from pit X, 'low level by Watling Street'. It has not been possible to trace the Bushe-Fox vessels to check their fabrics.

Oxidised fabrics (Fig 5.37)

Non-local oxidised sherds are very rare. The fragment of a flagon top, no 190, is paralleled by vessels from Period 2, and may be intrusive. The most unusual vessel is the large jar, no 202. This came from two pits in Area 72 associated by other sherd links with various other pits and features in that area, phased to phase 4b; sherd links with the demolition layer in the area could come from the layer sinking into features or may indicate a later context for the pits. The original type is impossible to determine in the absence of the rim, and the neck fracture has been trimmed and smoothed to allow reuse of the jar. The unevenness of the wall of this vessel suggests it was partly handmade and finished on a wheel, the shoulder burnished, and the rest of the exterior coarsely smoothed. The fabric is coarse-textured grey, with a brown exterior surface. About two-thirds of the vessel survives, and it is interesting that this is virtually the only jar that could be termed a storage jar. Storage jars are similarly rare at Usk, with only four jars of type 17 occurring in Phase I.

Native wares (Fig 5.37)

Only 16 sherds were recorded as of native origin or tradition. Vessels such as nos 206 and 207 are very rare, as is Malvernian ware, no 258, from a Period 1 context. The earliest occurrence was a fragment of a large simple curved jar rim in a coarse oxidised fabric with calcareous inclusions, and with some evidence for smoothing or burnishing, from a posthole (F2764) in phase 3. Only one other body sherd of this fabric occurred. The main fabric was calcite-gritted, coarse, and dark grey, usually with oxidised surfaces, and included two curved rim jar fragments and a neck from a similar large jar, and the cooking pot, no 206, which has a more vesicular appearance. There is no evidence for decoration or burnishing. One cooking pot rim came from a contaminated earlier military context, a single body sherd from Phase 5, and the rest from the demolition period. The remaining sherds were all individual fabrics and body sherds, apart from cooking pot no 207. This was in a fine textured vesicular light grey fabric with a light red-brown cortex and grey to brown surfaces, with some mica. It was burnished externally, and was not certainly handmade.

Only three sherds of Malvernian ware were apparently stratified in military contexts (all from area 84 where only a single context with pottery is phased to the following Period 1), one a cooking pot, as no 258 (Fig 5.39), from Period 1.2. The stratified occurrence is not strong and only two sherds occurred in Period 1. The main occurrence of the ware in Wroxeter is in Period 2, and even there it is a very minor part of the assemblage.

Severn Valley ware (Fig 5.37)

The earliest occurrence of Severn Valley ware is two sherds of the reduced organic tempered fabric in the early period, both thick sherds possibly from a large jar, while most, in both oxidised and reduced fabrics, came from the demolition contexts.

The fragments from two beaker forms, nos 211 and 212, could be versions of Severn Valley ware, but do not strongly resemble the fabrics of the tankards. Since the ware was made at so many small kilns over a wide area, and in view of their fabric and burnished finish, they have been classified as Severn Valley. No 212 appears to be a butt beaker type (cf Kingsholm, Hurst 1985, fig 31, no 215). The three rims, nos 217–9, all appear to be from tankards, although no handles were found, and it is impossible to be certain whether the early carinated cup is represented by any of these rims. No 220, body sherd in the reduced fabric, is definitely carinated, and appears to have been handmade and perhaps finished on a wheel. A similar but wheelthrown vessel in oxidised fabric occurs at Kingsholm (Hurst 1985, fig 31, no 224). The large jar rim, no 201, is a common Severn Valley type, again in reduced fabric. Some of the fabrics resemble the local Wroxeter fabrics, although their vesicular nature and technical finish distinguish them; an early kiln in the area seems a distinct probability due to the common occurrence of the ware in Period 2. The most unusual vessel attributed to Severn Valley ware is the jar no 199 in reduced fabric with rustication, not a normal technique for these potters, but clearly copying the rusticated wares which start to appear in the late military, and are more common in Period 2, many probably residual from Period 1.

Locally made vessel types

This section examines the incidence of the locally made Wroxeter fabric vessel types in the military period and the following civilian Period 1. The military period is split into the main identified phases, including contaminated to provide unequivocal information on the phased incidence. Unfortunately the quantity from Period 1 is comparatively small and mostly concentrated in the last phase, 1.3, and is therefore presented as a single period. While much of the Period 1 pottery is likely to be residual from the military period, the incidence of some types either exclusively or predominantly in Period 1 helps to identify later types.

Flagons (Figs 5.26 and 5.27)

Flagons form a relatively small site sample, totalling, including identified body sherds, 1444 sherds, 4578 EVEs weighing 274kg. The incidence of the identified types across the phases is shown in Table 5.20

The military period is hampered by the small sample from the earliest contexts. The commonest type is without question type 4 with the flange rim and cordon, to which may be linked variants such as types 5 (Fig 5.26) and 17 (Fig 5.27). This is exceptionally difficult to parallel, and it seems likely that it

Table 5.20 Pottery: locally made vessel types, incidence of flagon types, percentages on EVEs

types	LEG	F2807	LATE	DEMO	CONT	PERIOD 1	overall
1	17.3	0	17.8	13.6	40	5.2	15.6
2	0	0	0	12.4	0	6.2	3.1
3	0	0	7.6	4.1	0	0	1.9
4	48.0	48.6	18.1	21.4	10	37.1	30.5
5	0	9.2	0	0	0	0	1.5
6	0	0	9.5	0	0	0	1.6
7	0	0	0	0	38	0	6.3
8	0	0	5.3	8.1	0	0	2.2
9	0	8.6	1.3	9.2	0	2.1	3.5
10	5.8	25.0	10.0	8.3	6	0	9.2
11	5.8	0	9.8	5.1	0	20.6	6.9
12	0	0	2.6	2.4	0	0	0.8
13	0	8.6	0	0	0	0	1.4
14	0	0	0	0	6	0	1.0
15	11.6	0	7.6	0	0	0	3.2
16	0	0	0	3.5	0	0	0.6
17	0	0	0	0.7	0	0	0.1
18	0	0	0.7	1.0	0	0	0.3
19	0	0	0	3.1	0	23.7	4.5
20	0	0	2.6	0	0	0	0.4
21	11.6	0	7.2	6.8	0	0	4.3
Untyped	0	0	0	0.6	0	5.2	1.0
EVEs	346	699	1323	1475	250	485	4578
Sherds	98	137	449	474	86	200	1444
Weight (g)	3635	2750	6225	9490	1490	3799	27389

is a variant contemporary with the classic collared Hofheim of types 1 and 2. It may be likened to examples from Hofheim (Ritterling 1913, Abb 62, no 1, a variant of type 50) and Neuss (Filtzinger 1972, Taf 18, no 14). Occasional similar flagons are found on the continent but they are as infrequent as in Britain (Lorenzberg: Ulbert 1965, Taf 19, nos 3 and 11; Augst: Ettlinger 1949, Taf 24, no 9; *Vindonissa*: Ettlinger and Simonett 1952, Taf 19, no 429; Neuss: Filtzinger 1972, Taf 18, nos 12, 13; Bad Nauheim: Simon 1960, Abb 14, no 26 from the Domitianic fort). One example was found at Fishbourne (Cunliffe 1971, type 116.1) and another at *Verulamium* (Frere 1972, fig 101, no 56), while some of the Eccles flagons verge on the type (Detsicas 1977, fig 3.2). The variant type 5 is an oddity, and it may be significant that its rim type resembles glass bottle rims (Isings 1957, type 50a).

One parallel for type 4 is of more interest since it occurs at Mancetter, considered to be a possible earlier base for *Legio XIV* (Scott 1981, fig 11, no 8). This was associated with a group of amphorae on a site with samian of exclusively pre-Flavian samian. No close parallels have been traced on other military sites, and their common occurrence at Wroxeter contrasts with all other early military sites, as for example Usk with its predominance of Hofheim types, and many other sites where ring-necked types are more common.

Types 1 and 2 are broadly Hofheim types 50A and 50B, Usk types 1 and 2, and are the most frequent types on military sites on the continent, occurring throughout the Rhine and Danube frontiers (the continental evidence is fully discussed in Greene 1993, 11). At *Camulodunum* they are types 136 and 140, the latter being the most common

flagon on the site. The Hofheim type occurs widely but not necessarily commonly on early military sites up to and including the Flavian period, but while it continues as a dominant type on the Rhineland, it is broadly replaced in Britain by the ring-necked type which is rare at both Wroxeter and Usk, but seemingly common at Exeter and Lake Farm. The overtaking of the Hofheim type by the ring-necked types in Britain in contrast to the Rhineland may be connected with the development of civilian as opposed to military orientated pottery production, as with the early kilns south of *Verulamium* (Richardson 1948, fig 6; Castle 1974, fig 3) and at Colchester (kilns 23 and 26, Hawkes and Hull 1947, 281, fig 58). Types 3 and 22 are clearly related to the basic Hofheim range, the latter with a pronounced undercutting of the rim collar. Only two examples were found, both from the same context.

Ring-necked flagons like type 9 are confined to a few examples from pit F2807 and from the late and demolition phases, and appear to be even rarer than at Usk where they account for only 3.6% of the flagons. The ring-necked type, however, became the commonest type later, judging from the quantity occurring in Period 2 deposits, often in local fabric with white slip.

Parallels occur at Usk for the small cup-mouthed flask of type 15, the disc-rimmed type 8, the two-handled flagons types 10 and 11, and probably also the jugs of type 21 (Fig 5.27). These types have been recently discussed in detail by Greene (1993, 18). These all have widespread geographical distributions, and it is significant that the rim type of type 8 is probably derived from the glass type (Isings 1957, type 50), while jugs as type 54 at Hofheim (Ritterling 1913, Taf xxxiv) imitate bronze jugs, particularly noticeable on the Wroxeter example 21.1. Only two jugs were found at Usk, and an approximate vessel count at Wroxeter of a possible eight simply highlights the vagaries of samples. The two-handled type 10 is closely paralleled by an extraordinary deposit of seven such flagons in a latrine at Mancetter (Scott 1981, figs 13, 14), the deposit also including a jug of Wroxeter type 21. Again the associated samian was Claudian to Neronian.

The distinctive flagon type 7 can be easily paralleled on the continent at Hofheim (Ritterling 1913, Abb 64, nos 4, 6, and 7), Haltern (Loeschcke 1909, Taf xii, no 48), and Vetera (Hagen 1912, Taf lii, no 22). The only examples with a single handle noted in Britain are from Kingsholm (Hurst 1985, fig 24, no 11) and Cirencester (Rigby 1982, fig 61, no 390). The two-handled version is much commoner, and examples occur at the Neronian kiln at Sutri in Italy (Duncan 1964, fig 14, no 156 etc, his form 37), Hofheim (Ritterling 1913, Abb 68, nos 4, 6, 8, and 9), and Neuss (Filtzinger 1972, Taf 22, no 6). They also appear at *Camulodunum* where the form is rare despite examples found associated with kiln 26 (Hawkes and Hull 1947, fig 52, no 5, a variant of form 170; Hull 1963, fig 91, nos 20 and 21), and it is interesting to note that it figures among the products of the kilns at both Brockley Hill (Richardson 1948, fig 7, nos 43 and 45; Castle 1974, 261) and Eccles (Detsicas 1977, figs 3.3 and 3.4).

The flask type 19 occurred in a context phased to Period 1.3, but was probably residual. This has a close resemblance to Ritterling's type figure for his type 55, although he combines several disc-rimmed vessels under this type (Ritterling 1913, Taf xxxiv). Disc-

rimmed flagons occur widely, but it is interesting that small flasks of this type are among the product of the Eccles potters (Detsicas 1977, fig 3.3, nos 65 and 66).

Types 14 and 16 are both single examples, both in the white slipped local fabric, 16 from a demolition context, while 14 was from a contaminated context. Flagons with white slip appear to be common in Period 2 contexts. Given the probable high residual context of many of these contexts, it seems likely that this technique started either in the late military period when the pottery assemblage was becoming much more diverse in both fabric and type, or in the early civilian Period 1.

Jars (Figs 5.28–5.30)

Jars normally account for 50% or more of an assemblage, a sample suitable for detailed examination, particularly to define the earliest military types. The jars have a wide diversity of rim form, and do not form homogeneous groups as at Usk, as might be anticipated from the smaller assemblage spanning a longer period. The stratigraphic occurrence of the main identified jar types in Wroxeter fabrics is shown in Table 5.21, as percentages based on EVEs of the phased assemblages.

The size of the samples from the *Late* phase and Period 1 are unfortunately too small to be significantly useful, but, based on stratigraphic occurrence, jar types 27 and 29–31 are the main early jar types, accounting for 82% of jars, all of which decline appreciably in the later contexts. It should be noted that the simple rounded rim of type 27 lacks distinction, and classification

Table 5.21 Pottery: locally made vessel types, incidence of jar types, percentages on EVEs

Types	LEG	F2807	LATE	DEMO	CONT	PERIOD 1	overall
24	0	6.2	0	0	0	0	1.0
25	4.7	0	0	0	0	0	0.8
26	0	0	0	0.6	0.6	0.9	0.4
27	33.3	36.5	20.0	17.8	28.3	9.8	24.3
28	0.4	1.7	2.5	10.9	13.3	11.9	6.8
29	20.5	22.6	19.7	5.8	0	3.1	11.9
30	25.6	0	9.5	17.1	16.1	13.7	13.7
31	2.1	0	0	4.1	2.2	0.8	1.5
32	0	10.1	1.1	3.2	2.2	2.4	3.2
33	7.2	19.7	22.4	10.5	4.8	15.0	13.3
34	1.6	0	6.8	3.4	3.7	6.1	3.6
35	2.0	1	1.1	7.8	8.1	8.8	4.8
36	0	0	0	5.5	0	0.5	1.0
37	0	0	0	3.2	7.8	2.2	2.2
38	0	0	0	0.9	0	2.9	0.7
40	0	0	0	0	3.3	1.9	0.9
41	0	0	0.8	1.8	0	0.7	0.6
42	0	0	1.3	1.6	3.4	0	1.0
43	0	2.2	0	1.4	1.6	5.3	1.7
44	0	0	0	0.4	0	0	0.1
45	0	0	1.1	0	0	4.1	0.9
46	0	0	0	1.3	0	2.5	0.6
47	0	0	0	0.8	0	0	0.1
48	0	0	0	0	1.0	0	0.2
49	1.2	0	12.7	0.8	1.8	1.6	3.0
Untyped	1.3	0	1.0	1.2	1.8	5.9	1.9
EVEs	1644	1608	907	4258	893	1603	10913
Sherds	375	153	264	805	158	238	1993
Weight (g)	5480	2580	4260	10700	1620	2615	27245

based necessarily on rims may have over-estimated the later occurrence; equally such a simple rim could have a long life. Some versions of this type (as no 144 from F2807 pit; Fig 5.35) are very close to Usk types 11.1 and 11.2, but the classic version with a less pronounced neck (as with type 29) is significantly different. The main early types 27 and 29 are not closely similar to Cam 266 (Haltern 57); the slope of the neck differs, and the classic Wroxeter jars are barely necked. The form is closer to Cam 267 (Hofheim, Ritterling 87).

Although the square rimmed type 28, closely similar to Usk types 11.3 and 11.4, is represented by a possible rim in early contexts (pit F2065), it is more frequent in demolition contexts. Also paralleled at Usk is type 32 (Usk type 13, known in both Danubian and Rhineland zones), but the earliest example is stratified in the late period (phase 5), and others occur in the demolition period contexts. Some rims of type 28 occur in early contexts considered to be contaminated, so that the evidence of its first appearance is equivocal, while there is no evidence to suggest type 32 formed part of the original repertoire, although this may be due to a rarity.

While types 27, 28, and 32 can be broadly paralleled by Usk types, types 29–31 are more individual, type 29 having a less marked neck, and types 30 and 31 being notably more delicate and angular. No close parallels have been traced, although it is clear that they share the same continental derivation as types 27 and 28, discussed by Greene (1993, 22), and may be the products of just one or two potters.

Jar types 33 and 34 occur to a lesser degree in early contexts, and also examples of the everted type 35 (only four vessels, two from pits in Area 72, F2868 and a possible example from F2916, and two from slot F374 in Area 92 of less certain stratification). All of these are commoner in later contexts, and it is debatable that these belong with the early assemblage. The leaf-shape rimmed type 33 is a fairly common type; type 34 is much rarer and more difficult to evaluate (only a single rim occurs in the early period, in the road ditch F948). The variant of type 29 with a notable thickening below the rim (as types 29.3–5) is relatively rare, and first occurs in the later period (phase 5) and in the pit F2807 (nos 149 and 150).

The only type 24, a narrow-necked jar in Wroxeter fabric, came from the F2807 pit. This is a singleton,

clearly copying the Belgic flasks, well illustrated at Nijmegen (Holwerda 1941, pl v, particularly no 185). The form is similar to Cam 231, but is otherwise rare in Britain. The form with decoration occurs at Usk but in a *terra nigra* type of fabric (Greene 1979, 108, type 1). It is more prevalent on the continent, particularly on the Lower Rhine (as Ritterling 1913, Taf xxxvii, no 120A) but also occurs at Rheingonheim (Ulbert 1969, taf 13, no 4).

The narrow-necked jar type 25 was both rare and less well defined, occurring only a fragmentary rims, and it is possible that some of these were fragments from two-handled flagons rather than narrow-necked jars.

The small sample from the late period preceding demolition is unfortunately an inadequate bridge between the early group and the very large sample from the demolition phase, which is characterised by the variety of types represented, many of them as single vessels. Jars of types 27 and 28 continue strongly, and are types that appear on the Northern Frontier (as Gillam 1957, 106–8). The significant difference between the main phases illustrated by the summary Table 5.22 lies in the proliferation of types in the later phases, probably starting in the late military phase (although the sample is perhaps too small to judge).

Notable features of the early jars are the common presence of trimming of the basal zones and the absence of burnishing on the rims or shoulders, although horizontal burnished lines in the area of the girth are quite common, as is the absence of applied decoration. Rouletted decoration occurs on the narrow-necked flask type 24 from the pit F2807, a singleton on the site. Rustication does not occur until the late phase, a few sherds occurring in phases 5 and 6, all in the defences area. The only jar types which could be associated with rustication were types 35 and 37. Burnish inside and on rims and shoulders occurs on types 35, 37, and 42, and all noted examples are from the demolition phase or later. This is often on rusticated vessels and it is worth noting that at sites like Lincoln, where rustication starts early in the sequence, the early vessels are not burnished, and burnishing associated with rustication is usually much later, Trajanic at the earliest. This aspect of rusticated ware needs more research, and could prove to be a dating aid.

Table 5.22 Pottery: locally made vessel types, summary of jar types, percentages on EVEs

Types	LEG	F2807	LATE	DEMO	CONT	PERIOD 1	overall
24-5	4.7	6.2	0	0	0	0	1.8
27-8	33.7	38.2	22.5	28.7	41.6	21.7	31.1
29	20.5	22.6	19.7	5.8	0	3.1	11.9
30-31	27.7	0	9.5	21.2	18.3	14.5	15.2
32	0	10.1	1.1	3.2	2.2	2.4	3.2
33-34	8.8	19.7	29.2	13.9	8.5	21.1	16.9
49	1.2	0	12.7	0.8	1.8	1.6	3.0
Main types	96.6	96.8	94.7	73.6	72.4	64.4	83.1
Minor types	3.3	3.2	5.3	26.5	27.6	35.7	17.1

Beakers (Fig 5.30)

Despite their apparent ubiquity at Wroxeter, beakers produce small samples, the largest being from the pit F2807, a characteristic of which was the high proportion of beakers and cups. The incidence by phase can be assessed from Table 5.23.

The bulk of the beakers were stratified in military contexts, and it is difficult to be certain that the small samples from Period 1 are representative, especially since 43% of the beakers from military contexts derive from the single pit F2807. Seventy four per cent of the beakers from military contexts fit broadly into the category of everted rim beakers. Many of the various subtypes distinguished in recording subsequently turned out to be singletons, and slight variations are of debatable significance, particularly in the eversion or slightly vertical nature of the rim.

There is, however, a clear sub-group, type 55, from the F2807 pit, characterised by their thin walls, fine potting technique, delicate rims, and, where bases have survived, moulded bases. Some are over- or under-fired, and most could be regarded at best as 'seconds'. They were all in normal reduced Wroxeter fabric, and had no decoration. Type 56 has a more upright rim, often stubbier profile and includes examples from F2807. This type includes some exceptionally small examples, such as types 56.10–12 (in fine reduced fabric) and two beakers with varying rouletted decoration, from demolition and post-military contexts, types 56.8–9; at least two are in oxidised fabrics. Type 59 includes larger beakers, all from demolition contexts, of which two are rouletted. Type 57 is a singleton in the fine oxidised fabric, burnished on the shoulder and with a notably delicate rim. Type 60 in oxidised fabric with a more elaborate rim type came from a contaminated military context. A similar vessel occurred in Period 1 (Darling 2000, type BK7.12), and is notable

for having burnishing on both the inside of the rim and on the shoulder, and the oxidised Wroxeter fabric example is closely mirrored by one in a grey fabric from another source.

The only early sites in Britain producing a significant number of similar beakers are Fishbourne (Cunliffe 1971, type 79) and Longthorpe (from the local kilns; Dannell 1987, fig 39). These beakers appear to copy the Lyon beaker, Greene's type 20, and do not closely parallel the Wroxeter series. Beakers with simple rims occur at Usk (Greene 1993, type 14), although the type includes larger vessels verging on jars. Closer parallels occur in the interesting early London fabric, SLOW, Sugar Loaf Court ware (Chadburn and Tyers 1984, particularly nos 33022 and 33023), part of the repertoire of a continental potter. Coarse beakers are relatively rare on the continent, presumably because adequate supplies of the fine wares would have been available, and hardly any close parallels to the Wroxeter everted beakers can be traced, although the basic form is widely distributed both geographically and chronologically.

The widest variety of beakers in coarse ware derives from the Magdalensberg, where beakers with everted rims broadly similar to the Wroxeter examples appear in several fabrics, including Fabric A of the Augustan period (Schindler-Kaudelka 1975, Tafn 4, 5, 8, 12, and 15). The rim form and profile of these beakers is echoed at the Neronian kiln at Sutri by Duncan's form 1 (Duncan 1964, fig 7, particularly no 20), although he considers this form normally to have had handles. It is worth noting that a handled roughcast beaker from Caerleon (Nash-Williams 1932, fig 60, no 304) can be paralleled with Duncan's type 1 (Duncan 1964, fig 7, nos 3 and 4), which emphasises the widespread influence of pottery styles from Italy found particularly in the pottery from military sites. While some of the Wroxeter beakers superficially resemble Lyon ware

Table 5.23 Pottery: locally made vessel types, incidence of beaker types, percentages on EVEs

Types	LEG	F2807	LATE	DEMO	CONT	PERIOD 1	Overall
50	11.2	0	0	2.5	35.2	0	8.2
51	0	0	43.4	2.8	0	0	7.7
52	0	6.5	4.1	0	0	0	1.8
53	0	7.9	0	0	0	0	1.3
54	0	0	0	2.3	0	0	0.4
55	9.0	72.3	12.1	22.7	9.3	0	20.9
56	51.5	10.9	20.2	25.4	0	34.7	23.8
57	0	0	0	1.5	0	0	0.3
58	0	2.4	0	0	0	0	0.4
59	22.4	0	0	37.8	0	0	10.0
60	0	0	0	0	17.6	6.1	4.0
61	0	0	4.1	0	18.5	19.2	7.0
62	6.0	0	7.5	2.5	0	0	2.7
63	0	0	0	0	10.2	8.2	3.1
64	0	0	0	2.5	0	0	0.4
67	0	0	8.7	0	0	0	1.5
Untyped	0	0	0	0	9.3	31.8	6.9
EVEs	134	617	173	397	108	245	1674
Sherds	17	97	54	72	44	57	341
Weight (g)	80	540	650	595	100	268	2233

type 20, the bases are quite different. There is, however, evidence from body sherds to suggest that the occasional attempt was made by the Wroxeter potters to imitate rough-casting, not only on cups (as type 72.1; Fig 5.30) but possibly also on beakers.

The barrel-shaped beakers of type 50 resemble some of the Hofheim vessels, but the closest parallels occur at Neuss (Filtzinger 1972, Taf 5, nos 5 and 14, and from the kilns, Taf 81, no 11). The type 51 can be widely paralleled on the continent at the Magdalensberg, Hofheim, Kempten, Neuss, Koln, and Nijmegen (Hofheim: Ritterling 1913, Taf xxxiii, no 85B; Kempten: Fischer 1957, Taf 3, no 4; Taf 5, nos 5 and 7; Neuss: Filtzinger 1972, Taf 5, no 7; Taf 61, no 10; Taf 81, no 13, the last two from the kilns; Koln: Hagen 1906, Taf xxii, Grab 15; Nijmegen: Vermeulen 1932, pl x, no 93; Stuart 1962, pl 20, no 328). The earliest example in Britain occurs at Longthorpe, a product of the local kilns (Frere and St Joseph 1974, fig 53, no 50). The form, however, continues in use by military potters, as an example was found at Holt (Grimes 1930, fig 64, no 78), and even later at Balmuildy (Miller 1922, pl xlvi, no 10). Examples of both types 50 and 51 have been also found in London although no details of the provenances are known (Marsh and Tyers 1976, fig 12; Anderson 1981, fig 6.2, nos 7 and 11). Whether these are imports from the Rhineland or locally made is not clear; either is possible, and there is evidence for early pottery of continental type being made in London, as cups and beakers noted above (Chadburn and Tyers 1984).

No close parallels have been found for type 52 in Britain, although two distorted fragments from what may have been a similar beaker were found at Cirencester (unpublished). The best continental parallels come from the series of beakers at the Magdalensberg, where examples occur in two fabrics (a form of *terra nigra*, current *c* AD 20–35 (Schindler-Kaudelka 1975, Taf 18, no 93)), and a red fabric with colour-coating of *c* AD 25 (*ibid*, Taf 25, no 117c; Taf 23, no 127b). These beakers are, however, merging with the more shouldered version of type 51, as close parallels for this beaker also occur on the site (particularly obvious in the illustrations, *ibid*, Taf 23, form 127), in the new colour-coated fabrics arriving there *c* AD 20–25. The same merging of the two forms is apparent at Hofheim in Ritterling's form 85 (1913, Taf xxxiii).

Type 53 shows a certain resemblance to types 51 and 52, and may be likened to the example from Hofheim quoted in connection with type 51. This type can also be closely paralleled at Neuss and Nijmegen (Neuss: Filtzinger 1972, Taf 5, nos 5, 9; Nijmegen: Stuart 1962, pl 20, no 327), but no beakers of this form have been traced in Britain.

Of similar continental derivation are the beakers of type 58, both examples occurring residually in post-military contexts. The everted rim and straight shoulder ending in a cordoned carination appear to be of the same type as vessels from the Neuss kilns (Filtzinger 1972, Taf 77, no 9; Taf 78, no 7).

Type 54 is a singleton from the demolition phase, and as a fragment is difficult to parallel, although it seems most likely that this derives from the continent, and more probably from the Danubian area than further north.

A few local copies of Gallo-Belgic beakers of the type of Cam 120 occur as type 62, some fragments suggesting that these were available by phase 4b. The most notable copy of a Gallo-Belgic form, however, is the butt-beaker, type 67, which came from a context associated with phase 7i, the demolition of the defences. This appears to be in a local reduced fabric. As a singleton, its significance is uncertain, but it may be noted that a similar copy beaker occurred at Mancetter (Scott 1981, fig 11, no 7, found with pre-Flavian samian and fragments of *lorica segmentata*). The earliest sherds of the non-local butt beaker, probably from the south-east, were stratified in phase 4b, while the grey and probably Severn Valley ware beakers (nos 211–14; Fig 5.37) were all from the demolition phase.

An unstratified enigmatic sherd in the local fine reduced fabric (WWRF), marked WB S12 (11), cannot be securely typed or illustrated, but is from a thin-walled handled vessel decorated with rouletting. Only a portion of wall with a fragment of upward curving handle (three-ribs) survives. Slight working lines on the interior suggest the wall curves outwards, and it could be from a handled beaker type similar to one from Hofheim (Ritterling 1913, taf xxxiii, no 30B) or, alternatively, from a handled cup, both equally rare in Britain.

Cups (Figs 5.30 and 5.31)

Virtually all the commonest cups, type 68 imitating the samian Dr 27, came from the pit F2807, as did the illustrated examples of the undecorated types 70, 73, and one of the type 75. Cups that clearly belong to the military although occurring in later or unstratified contexts have also been included (Table 5.24). All except a single cup of type 72 above came from military contexts. The cups therefore broadly divide into three categories: imitations of samian cup Dr 27 and 24, cups of the same form as pre-Flavian fine wares, and tripod cups.

Table 5.24 Pottery: locally made vessel types, cup types, quantities

type	Sherds	%	EVEs	%	Weight (g)	%
68	66	49.2	563	71.5	725	68.3
69	3	2.3	20	2.5	30	2.8
70	16	12.0	52	6.6	66	6.2
71	1	0.8	3	0.4	5	0.5
72	3	2.3	18	2.3	11	1.0
73	23	17.3	77	9.8	90	8.5
74	12	9.0	28	3.6	70	6.6
75	6	4.5	26	3.3	20	1.9
Untyped	3	2.3	0	0	45	4.2
	133	100	787	100	1062	100

A possible twelve imitation Dr 27 cups of type 68 came from the pit F2807, and a probable further four occurred in other contexts, the earliest being from phase 5, the rest from the demolition phase. Copies of this samian form are relatively common in Britain, but mainly on sites starting in the Flavian period or later. The form does not occur at Usk, Kingsholm, Gloucester or Exeter. The only other site with possible early production of this form is Fishbourne (form 50) where, out of 26 examples, only 3 are dated to the period after AD 75 (Cunliffe 1971, fig 87). There is considerable variation in form and detail in the copies of this form, the Wroxeter examples being arguably closer to the samian originals that many, as at Fishbourne, Caerleon, Colchester, Richborough, London, Holt, Templeborough, Brough-on-Humber, and Silchester. This list is not exhaustive but indicates that any attempt to date these cups on typological grounds is doomed.

Copies are infrequent on the continent, and while rare examples occur at Holdeurn, in Switzerland and on the Danube, none occur in the large assemblage at Neuss. As with many samian imitations, these cups are copied in types of *terra nigra* at Aislingen and Burghofe as well as at Nijmegen. Why this form was chosen at Wroxeter rather than the Dr 24 copied at Usk, Lincoln, and Longthorpe is important to gauge for the interpretation of the assemblage from the pit F2807, and the individual pottery types, many of which are associated by fabric, technique, and condition. Since the samian form Dr 24 seems unlikely to have survived long after the Neronian period, the copies of Dr 27 may indicate a Flavian date for the group.

Type 69, imitating the samian Dr 24, is also copied at Usk, where it is the only imitation of a samian cup, and at Longthorpe (Dannell 1987, fig 41, no 61 unslipped) and Lincoln (Darling 1981, fig. 23.2, nos 24 and 5, in local red slipped fabric). Otherwise copies are rare, both in Britain, one occurring at Caerleon (Nash-Williams 1929, fig 31, no 58; see also Nash-Williams 1932, fig 58, nos 175 and 176 for examples far removed from the samian form), at York (Monaghan 1993, fig 289, no 2855), and on the continent (Drack 1945, Taf viii, nos 16, 20, of Neronian-Flavian date). All examples of the form at Wroxeter are in the finer oxidised fabric. That the later samian cup Dr 27 was more widely copied is chronologically significant for development of civilian potting.

A possible Flavian date has obvious implications for the other cups in the pit, types 70 and 73. Similar cups made in Britain are those from the kilns 23 and 26 at Colchester (Hawkes and Hull 1947, fig 58, no 12; Hull 1963, fig 91, no 23), the kilns outside the fortress at Longthorpe (Dannell 1987, fig 41, types 59 and 60), at Usk (Greene 1993, type 25), Kingsholm (Hurst 1985, fig 30, no 165, a blown 'waster'), and Lincoln (Darling 1981, 402, fig 23.3, nos 26 and 27). Most of these, however, appear to closely copy Lyon ware types. An exception is the type 60 from Longthorpe (Dannell

1987, fig 41), and it is possible that some of the Lincoln cups in fabrics other than the early red-slipped ware will tie in more closely to the Wroxeter series. Also of interest are cups from a Neronian assemblage at 5–12 Fenchurch Street, London, made in Sugar Loaf Court ware, considered to be a local early London ware (Chadburn and Tyers 1984, particularly no 36005). The more angular profile of the Wroxeter cups is notable, and perhaps significantly similar to Italian cups. Few military sites on the continent have copies of fine ware cups, although a few examples were made at Neuss (Filtzinger 1972, Taf 94, nos 7 and 12 from the kilns). Evidence for decoration is limited to fragmentary examples, but type 70.2 has traces of what appears to be applied scale decoration, while types 70.3 and 70.4 are rouletted.

Two continental sites do, however, suggest a possible derivation for the Wroxeter cups. The first is the Magdalensberg in Austria (occupied *c* 25 BC to AD 45), from which an extensive range of cups and beakers has been published (Schindler-Kaudelka 1975). The fine-walled cups and beakers from the site in *Noricum* all appear to be imported via the trading-centre of *Aquileia*, most coming from Italy (*ibid*, 172), only three vessels deriving from other fine ware production centres (Spain, South Gaul, and Lyon). The Magdalensberg's geographical position and close trading connections with Italy isolate it from the Rhineland, but there can be little doubt that merchants there were trading in *Noricum*. The interest of this site lies in the evidence it provides about the independent development of fine wares in Italy, and it is thus of significance that the Wroxeter cups can be closely paralleled by examples found there. While the closest parallels are in a form of *terra nigra* fabric (*ibid*, Taf 17, no 84), they are part of a long tradition in Italy arising from early coarse ware versions without any form of slip-coating (*ibid*, Taf 35, group 6 for typological range of cups in varying fabrics). That this tradition continued through the first century in Italy is illustrated by the kiln at Sutri (Duncan 1964) where the main period of production was between AD 60 and AD 70. Duncan's form 5 is this type of cup, which he states to be rare on the site. Only one was colour-coated and most were in grey fabric (most of the cups and fine beakers made at Wroxeter are in reduced fabric, oxidised vessels being rare). The evidence suggests that fine vessels in Italy developed independently of those made at Lyon, in Spain and in the Lower Rhineland, and it is to the Italian forms that the Wroxeter cups are related. The implications of this are discussed below.

The cup type 72 appears to be a clear copy of a Lyon ware vessel, with a notable attempt at reproducing the roughcasting on type 72.1, while type 72.2 is rouletted. The tripod cups of type 74 bear a slight resemblance to the Lyon tripod vessels, which would appear to be the inspiration behind the rare copies in Britain (at Usk, Greene 1993, type 24, 11 examples) although these usually have a more rounded profile (but see Kingsholm,

Hurst 1985, fig 26, no 52). The type in coarse ware does not occur at the Magdalensberg or Sutri, although the angular wall suggests Italian influence. No parallels have been traced for the single fragment of the cup type 71 with rouletted decoration, but technically it aligns with the other decorated cups of types 70.3 and 70.4. A further body sherd with similar rouletting seemed likely to be from a cup.

Bowls (Figs 5.31 and 5.32)

The only viable samples for bowls come from the abnormal pit F2807, where the sample is likely to be distorted by near-complete vessels, and the military demolition contexts. The incidence of the various types can be seen in Table 5.25. The only type occurring in the earliest contexts not represented by a rim measurement is type 77, the undecorated carinated bowl of Dr 29 type.

Due to the small sample sizes, the stratified occurrence of bowl types provides little information beyond the fact that the commonest type, the reeded rim bowl type 88, was in use from the beginning, and judging from the quantity in Period 2, continued through until displaced by the advent of BB1 vessels. Bowls of this type are extremely diverse, and display most of the common variations, the flanges varying in angle, most walls being nearer the rounded than the carinated version. The angle of the wall may yet provide a dating clue to the type, but with so few stratified in the earlier contexts there is no basis for clearly defining early and later types. Variant types (as types 89–93) are, however,

consistently later in their stratified appearance, type 92 only occurring in post-military contexts. Also notable is the use of the finer fabric for some of the variants, particularly type 92, suggesting that the function of some of these vessels may have changed.

The general type starts in the Mediterranean and is common in the Rhineland from the Augustan period onwards, and examples still appear in third-century contexts. The different development of pottery in Britain led to its decline by the time of Trajan, and it is probably commonest in the Flavian–Trajanic period. It is, however, notable that examples are scarce on early military sites in the Midlands, such as Wall, Baginton, and Metchley, although one came from the pit at Mancetter which contained the group of two-handled flagons (Scott 1981, fig 13, no 30).

Three samian bowls were copied at Wroxeter, Dr 29 being the most frequent, the bowl or cup Dr 24 (discussed above), and a single example of a Ritterling 12. Copies of Dr 29 bowls are common and continue into the second century, many of the later examples, for instance at Caerleon and in Period 2 at Wroxeter, bearing little resemblance to their prototypes. All the Wroxeter examples appear to copy vessels of Neronian-Flavian date, so far as such copies can be assessed, and there is evidence for one example being stratified in early contexts. The decorated types 78.1–2 and the plain type 77 are closest, while those such as types 78.3–5 should perhaps be regarded as decorated carinated bowls rather than imitations of the samian form. This view is perhaps reinforced by the fact that many occurring in Period 2 contexts are in the cream-slipped

Table 5.25 Pottery: locally made vessel types, incidence of bowl types, percentages on EVEs

Types	LEG	F2807	LATE	DEMO	CONT	PERIOD 1	Overall
77	★	0	0	3.1	0	0	0.5
78	0	0	10.9	9.0	0	0	3.3
79	0	15.2	0	0	0	0	2.5
80	11.2	0	0	3.1	0	0	2.4
81	5.6	76.1	0	0	0	3.0	14.1
82	0	0	0	7.1	0	7.9	2.5
83	0	0	0	0.4	0	15.8	2.7
85	0	0	0	3.4	0	0	0.6
86	0	0	0	3.1	9.5	0	2.1
87	0	0	0	2.0	17.5	2.0	3.6
88	83.2	8.7	64.7	45.8	41.3	43.1	47.6
89	0	0	15.2	3.0	0	0	3.0
90	0	0	0	3.6	0	0	0.6
91	0	0	0	1.1	31.8	5.0	6.3
92	0	0	0	0	0	12.9	2.2
93	0	0	0	0.7	0	0	0.1
94	0	0	6.5	3.0	0	0	1.6
95	0	0	0	0	0	5.4	0.9
96	0	0	0	3.4	0	0	0.6
97	0	0	0	3.0	0	0	0.5
98	0	0	2.7	0	0	0	0.5
99	0	0	0	4.0	0	0	0.7
100	0	0	0	1.3	0	0	0.2
101	0	0	0	0	0	5.0	0.8
Total							
Eves	89	276	184	743	63	202	1577
Sherds	22	85	46	214	33	37	440
Weight (g)	460	1440	1230	3045	371	1094	7670

fabric; one example occurs in a demolition layer, while the fine reduced fabric is used for type 78.3, also from the demolition. The closest parallels in Britain come from Usk (Greene 1993, type 21), Kingsholm (Hurst 1985, fig 25, no 40), and Fishbourne (Cunliffe 1971, type 32). Copies of the samian form occur on continental sites but are relatively infrequent, either because adequate supplies of the samian vessels were easily obtainable, or the pottery of the area already had a tradition of carinated bowls (as in the Danubian area).

Copies of the Ritterling 12 rather than Curle 11 form are very rare in Britain, although distinguishing between the two is hazardous. Despite the distortion of type 79, the flange resembles that of a Ritterling 12 rather than that of a Curle 11, which was copied extensively, appearing at Holt, Chester, and Caerleon. *Camulodunum* form 46 may also be viewed as a copy of a Ritterling 12, but closer copies occur at Lincoln in an early local red-slipped fabric (unpublished), and at York (Monaghan 1993, fig 288, no 2824). This type of bowl is common on the continent in *terra nigra* fabrics and, while it appears in the Rhineland forts, its principal concentration seems to be in Switzerland, the Danube, and Rhaetian forts, where it occurs in both *terra nigra* and coarse red fabrics (Hofheim: Ritterling 1913, Taf xxxvii, 129; Bad Nauheim: Simon 1960, Abb 12, no 35; Neuss: Filtzinger 1972, Taf 36, no 4; Bonn: Barfield *et al* 1963, Abb 9, no 3; Nijmegen: Stuart 1962, pl 24, no 408; Rheingonheim: Ulbert 1969, Taf 11, no 23; Aislingen: Ulbert 1959, Taf 5, no 8; Burghofe: Ulbert 1959, Taf 44, no 8; *Vindonissa*: Tomasevic 1970, Taf 6, no 1; Ettlinger and Simonett 1952, Taf 4, no 68; Taf 9, nos 147, 148, 150; Augst: Ettlinger 1949, Taf 19, nos 16–33, wide variety; Kempten: Fischer 1957, Taf 9, nos 2–5; Taf 13, no 4).

The most interesting bowls at Wroxeter are the carinated types. The type 81 is known solely from the pit group F2807 and in the early contexts. No close parallels can be traced in Britain. Carinated bowls occur at Caerleon (Nash-Williams 1929, fig 36, no 120; 1932, fig 63, nos 445 and 446) and in the phase II pottery at Usk (Greene 1979, fig 46, type 6), but these are either in a *terra nigra* fabric or in the same tradition. Examples occur in the Rhineland forts, but are more common in the Danubian area and in Switzerland, but these are not close in type to the Wroxeter bowls. The vessels closest in form come from the Danubian fort at Aislingen where the bowl in question was in ordinary coarse ware and presumably copied the *terra nigra* versions also appearing on the site (Ulbert 1959, Taf 6, nos 2–4 in coarse ware, and in *terra nigra*, nos 12 and 13). The type has no roots in the native tradition in Britain, and seems most likely to be derived from the continent, perhaps the Danubian area.

The fragmentary down-turned flange with evidence for a spout of type 80 is rare both in Britain and on the continent. Mica-coated versions are known (Marsh 1978, type 34, particularly 34.14). Many vessels in *terra nigra* fabrics occur on the continent with similar flanges, and some with spouts, given that evidence for spouts may be elusive on rim fragments (as from the *Vindonissa* Schuthugel, Ettlinger and Simonett 1952, Taf 4, no 66 in *terra nigra*, and Taf 9, no 149; also from Nijmegen, Stuart 1962, pl 2, no 51).

The bowls of type 82, all probably carinated types, are distinct from type 81, but may well have a similar background. No parallels have been traced for type 83; an example occurred in the demolition phase, and another is known from a Period 2 context. The fragmentary type 86 vessels may also be carinated vessels, and there are certainly similar rims from Danubian sites. A bowl closely similar to type 86.2 was found at *Camulodunum* (Hawkes and Hull 1947, fig 48, no 16), and continental parallels appear to be confined to the Danubian area (Aislingen: Ulbert 1959, Taf 6, no 17; Burghofe: Ulbert 1959, Taf 44, no 11; Lorenzberg: Ulbert 1965, Taf 16, no 11). It is not certain that type 86.3 was carinated, and this belongs to the later pottery and a different tradition with its burnished surfaces. The only example is in the military demolition phase, and may be a contaminant. Little comment is possible on the unusual bowl or dish type 87 which, despite a resemblance to the dish type 110, appears distinct; another similar small bowl came from a Period 2 context.

The bowl type 85 is the only vessel in Wroxeter fabric for which a native British derivation might be claimed. It is closely similar to one from *Camulodunum* but this was an isolated unstratified find (Hawkes and Hull 1947, pl lii, A). Its angular appearance suggests the imitation of a metal form, and similar vessels occur in the Aylesford-Swarling culture, but with pedestal bases. The form may be expected to occur in late La Tène contexts in Gaul, and the significance of a single vessel for the Wroxeter assemblage is uncertain.

No clear parallels for the bowl type 94 have been found in Britain, but it resembles the shouldered jars found in Switzerland and the Danube area, for instance at *Vindonissa* (Tomasevic 1970, Taf 10, no 2), Aislingen (Ulbert 1959, Taf 4, no 15), and Kempten (Fischer 1957, Taf 5, nos 5 and 7). No parallels have been found in the Rhineland.

Type 96 with its heavy rim thickened on the interior is an unusual vessel; another example occurs in the unpublished pottery from Bushe-Fox's excavations, confirming the vertical wall. Although tempting to associate this with Iron Age pottery in Britain, it is more likely to derive from the many La Tène forms with thickened inturning rims found on continental sites such as Oberaden of Augustan date and Haltern (Loeschcke 1909, particularly type 98A). Variations on the same basic form appear on widely scattered sites such as Neuss (where they were made in the kilns, Filtzinger 1972, Tafn 64 and 65), *Vindonissa*, Augst, Lorenzberg, Kempten, Aislingen, Holdern (kiln products, Holwerda 1944, pl iii, nos 249–53), and Mainz.

No parallels on other British sites have been traced, and the continental La Tène repertoire seems its most likely origin.

As with other vessel forms, the demolition phase sees the greatest diversity of bowls, some of which could clearly be intrusive, such as perhaps types 97 and 99, while simple hemispherical bowls such as types 100 and 101 seem to be characteristic of the Flavian-Trajanic period and later. Type 83 is represented in the demolition phase, but is commonest in Period 1, and types 92 and 95 only occur in Period 1.

Plates and dishes (Fig 5.33)

The commonest dish type was type 105 which, together with variant types 104 (distinguished by their more pronounced moulding at the junction of wall and base internally) and 106, account for 78% (on EVEs) of all dishes from the military and Period 1. As with Usk type 29, this copies the form of the Pompeian red ware platter (Table 5.26). None of the examples in standard Wroxeter fabrics had any visible attempt at the internal slip which occurred on some from Usk. Most of the dishes of this type had relatively small diameters, and some were relatively far removed from the prototype, as for instance type 106.

The single example of type 102 from the pit F2807 appears to copy an early samian Dr 18 or a Ritterling 1. No parallels have been traced for the copying of this form in coarse ware. The *terra nigra* plate Cam 16 appears to be the inspiration for type 103 of which only a single complete profile occurs. This type is also copied at Usk, and, clearly, attribution of rim sherds to type 103 rather than 105 is hazardous (103.2 was identified on the basis of fabric and finish).

The curious dish type 107 with a pronounced internal moulding at the internal junction of wall and base cannot be classified as a copy of a definite type, whether samian or otherwise, but fits into the same broad type. But the straight-sided dish type 109, distinguished from the rest due to type and its internal and external burnishing, occurs as a single vessel in the demolition period, and is either late or intrusive.

The grooved rim dish of type 110 first occurs in phase 7i, considered to be the demolition of the rampart, and seemed to be more common in Period 1. As with the copies of Pompeian red ware and other platters, surface finish is limited to knife trimming of the basal area and little else, and again the rim diameters are small. The rim form is similar to Camulodunum 44A but there is no evidence for footrings on the Wroxeter dishes. A similar dish although of larger diameter occurs at York (Monaghan 1993, fig 293, no 2919 from Period 3 of AD 100–140/160). The type is known on Rhineland sites (Neuss: Filtzinger 1972, Taf 37, nos 3, 4; from the kilns, Taf 93, nos 6, 9), and continues to the later first century as at Domitianic Bad Nauheim (Simon 1960, Abb 15, nos 7, 8).

The extraordinary bead and flange dish type 111 came from a context phased to Period 2.1 but was probably residual. This shares many of the characteristics of the earlier military pottery, particularly the knife trimming of the basal zone, and is very similar to an unusual vessel at Hofheim which appears to be part of a 'casserole set' (Ritterling 1913, Taf xxxv, nos 94A and B).

It is uncertain whether the type 108 is a dish or bowl, but seemed more likely to be the former. The use of the finer oxidised fabric for this unique vessel seems to be a later trait for several of the bowls and dishes.

Mortaria (Fig 5.34)

The locally produced mortaria are detailed as part of the mortarium assemblage, discussed above. The local potters contributed 63–65% of the mortaria found in military contexts, and while residual sherds cloud the figures from the very small quantity from Period 1, it seems probable that some local production continued, supplementing an increasing number of vessels brought from elsewhere.

The local mortaria occur in both oxidised and reduced fabrics, the latter apparently deliberate rather than over-firing or subsequent burning, in both normal and finer versions. These divide into two broad types, hook-rimmed and wall-sided, each having variants. The commonest is represented by type 128, with a rim more

Table 5.26 Pottery: locally made vessel types, incidence of plates, percentages on EVEs

types	LEG	F2807	LATE	DEMO	CONT	PERIOD 1	overall
102	0	3.1	0	0	0	0	0.5
103	0	0	0	9.9	0	0	1.7
104	0	25.7	0	12.8	0	0	6.4
105	95.4	71.2	86.8	54.7	100	18.0	71.0
106	0	0	3.9	0	0	0	0.7
107	4.6	0	0	0	0	0	0.8
108	0	0	0	2.1	0	0	0.3
109	0	0	0	1.7	0	0	0.3
110	0	0	9.3	18.9	0	82.0	18.4
EVEs	87	323	129	243	58	61	901
Sherds	17	53	37	38	6	13	164
Weight (g)	1045	885	1090	615	390	152	4177

(* = presence non-rim)

like a curved flange than a strong hook. Only a single example of this type had quartz trituration grit, and the internal finishing particularly of types 128.1–2 make it clear that these were not gritted, a feature of early mortaria. Type 128.5 from a Period 2 deposit has a much more stumpy rim but is basically of the same type. None of this type was in the cream slipped fabric. These form a distinctive group, for which close parallels are very rare. One appears to be a single vessel from Usk (Hartley 1993, fig 190, no 33) in fabric 26, considered to be a locally made vessel, while another is in the interesting early fabric in London (Chadburn and Tyers 1984, no 37011). Also from London is another mortarium of broadly similar type in a fabric considered to probably derive from the early kilns at Eccles (Chadburn and Tyers, 1984, no 37009; Detsicas 1977, fig 3.4–6). The Usk example is typologically dissimilar to the commoner Usk local type with a thicker hook-flange, although it has a poorly finished base, seemingly a characteristic of both Usk and Kingsholm potters, also seen on the Wroxeter bases of types 128.3 and 129.2.

A continental origin for the type seems assured but identification of its location will have to await further publication and research, possibly in south-eastern France, adjacent to Switzerland. No examples have been traced in the Rhineland or on the Danube frontier.

Type 129.1 has similarities to the preceding type, despite the more hooked rim. The hook rim of type 129.2 in the cream-slipped fabric is much easier to parallel, being strongly in the Rhone Valley tradition with the ledge on the top of the rim next to the bead. Although this has trituration grits, it shares with the previous ungritted type a clumsily finished base. This feature also occurs on the mortaria from Kingsholm (cf Hurst 1985, fig 27, no 101), and on mortaria from Usk of the same type (Hartley 1993, fig 190, nos 27, 28) in fabrics probably produced at both Usk and Kingsholm.

The other illustrated cream slipped mortarium, type 131, is a singleton with its bead below the level of the rim; this came from a context believed to be contaminated by later material, and could therefore be a second-century vessel. This is also differentiated from the other vessels by being the only mortarium with sandstone trituration. Only one other example of the use of sandstone occurred, and then mixed with flint, on a body sherd in Period 2 in the unslipped oxidised fabric.

The final hook-rimmed type is type 132, and its identification as a local vessel is tentative on the basis that the fabric appears similar but atypical of the local oxidised fabric. This came from a pit assigned to the demolition period.

More unusual are the wall-sided vessels, of which there are two broad types, 133 and 134, the latter being the only wall-sided example with trituration, in this case fine quartz sand. The dating of wall-sided mortaria is confined to the Claudio-Neronian period, mostly Claudian, and is relatively rare outside the south-east and south coast. Many of those known in

fine cream fabrics without gritting are probably imports and may derive from the Rhineland (as at Neuss, Filtzinger 1972, Tafn 32, 3, and 74 from the kilns), although the quantity at Colchester (Hartley 1985, figs 49, 50; Cam 191) suggests manufacture there. The Wroxeter vessels are, however, in the local oxidised fabric. Examples in the Midlands are very rare; two occurred at Metchley (unpublished) in a light red-brown fabric but were otherwise dissimilar to the Wroxeter examples in form and fabric, while another mended with rivets was found at Mancetter (Scott 1981, fig 13, no 35), in a dark cream fabric, probably an import or from the south-east. An imported vessel occurred at Usk (Hartley 1993, fig 185, no 1).

The paucity of trituration grits appears to be a feature of the early locally-made mortaria. Based on weight, and taking into account the fact that 15% of the sherdage contributed no evidence either way (isolated rims), 34% definitely had no trituration, and a further 14% were probably ungritted. Forty per cent, largely from the cream-slipped vessels, had quartz particles, quartz sand occurred on a maximum of three vessels (7%), one not certainly a mortarium, and sandstone was confined to two vessels only, one mixed with flint, and neither being certainly of the military period.

Feature F2807, pit

Site evidence and finds

This pit was situated in the south-east of the excavated area, immediately adjacent to the later baths walls. It was cut into the natural sand, sealed by the military demolition layer, and lies within a structure, cutting and being cut by no other feature. A site notebook plan, probably at an early stage of definition of the pit, shows it as contiguous with the adjacent construction trench for the baths. Three layers were recorded but there are joining sherds between them, indicating the fill was a single operation. The topmost layer has joining sherds with the demolition layer and other similarly isolated pits in the immediate area. There is some definite contamination evidenced by Central Gaulish samian and a single sherd of BB1. There was no evidence to suggest it was a latrine pit, and while the joining sherds from other contexts may be due to a sinkage over the original pit rather than its true fill, the demolition period seems the most probable occasion for the digging of this pit.

The large quantity of pottery from the pit is unusual for Wroxeter where most pit groups are small, and the analysis of fabrics and vessel classes, types and functions show the extraordinary nature of the assemblage. The contents are exceptional due to the number of vessels showing either over- or under-firing, several certainly being poor 'seconds' if not 'wasters', and the bias of the assemblage of vessel types. A number of vessels in the pit had a distinctive surface discoloration, suggesting that they formed a separate group within the pit (Fig 5.35, nos 137, 149, 145, 150, and Fig 5.36, no 183). A similar discoloration occurs on two copies of Dr 29 bowls (type 77; Fig 5.31) from an adjacent pit, F2806, with sherd links into F2807 and the demolition layer in the area. While the sherdage suggests that many of the poorly fired vessels were substantially complete (usually impossible to reconstruct due to the condition of the sherds), only a few can be proven to have been complete when deposited. The other contents of the pit were a large number of nails and a military pendant. The absence of any bones may be significant.

Six coins were found (SF1821–2, 1869, 1875, 1878 from the main pit fill, SF 1785 from the top fill); all were Claudian, one *dupondius* and five *asses*, all copies; one of the *asses* from the main fill had a hole drilled at the edge which would seem to suggest a date at earliest towards the end of the reign of Nero if not, more probably, later.

Pottery (Figs 5.35 and 5.36)

Four vessels are not of local Wroxeter fabric, namely the flagon, no 184, the beaker probably of the type of Cam 120B, no 185, a body sherd from a probable copy of a glass pillar-moulded bowl, no 186, and a Lyon ware cup rim. These came from the upper fill, and included a sherd link to the adjoining pit F2806.

The remaining contents were all in Wroxeter fabrics. The platter, no 182 was a definite waster, being split across the base, over- and under-fired on the two sides. Tiny holes caused during firing occurred in the bases of the copy Dr 27 cup, no 162, and the beaker, no 152 (type 53). The distortion of several of the vessels, particularly nos 138 (type 9.1), 148, 149, 154 (type 55.1), 164, 165, 173 (type 79), 181, and 182 is considerable, and while some of the vessels appear superficially usable, the assemblage seems to be mainly a dump of rejects. Other oddments of rubbish (as the discoloured vessels) occur, including a fragment of a mortarium of the ungritted flange rim type in local reduced fabric.

Several of the vessels are unique on the site, including the plate, no 176 (type 102), the bowl copying Ritterling 12, no 173 (type 79), beakers, nos 152 (type 53) and 153 (type 52), and the Gallo-Belgic style flask, no 143 (type 24). The precise forms of the bowls, nos 170 and 171 (type 81), the cups, nos 167 and 168 (types 70 and 73), and the delicacy of the everted rimmed beakers are similarly unparalleled. The reeded rimmed bowls are of the usual basic type, but no close parallels occur for the depth of the grooving and rim type. The jar, no 151 (type 32), with its carinated shoulder like the Usk type 13, occurs elsewhere on the site, but this was certainly part of the dump. The cups copying the samian Dr 27 (type 68) are a major part of the group, but only five sherds of the form occur elsewhere on the site.

Thus we have a rubbish pit containing a dump of reject pottery, with a relatively small quantity of other rubbish, coins to provide a *terminus post quem*, and nails suggesting demolition work. It seems clear that the adjacent structure was either already gone or in the process of being demolished. Since the Claudian coins would have continued in use until the bronze issues by Nero of AD 64, and one was pierced, suggesting it was no longer legal tender, a late military date seems indicated, certainly Flavian. Corrosion made any estimate of wear impossible.

The typology of the vessels presents some curiosities, with the juxtaposition of copies of Dr 27, unusual before the Flavian period and later, with what appear to be copies of pre-Flavian fine cups and beakers, bowls of a type rare in Britain but with parallels in the Upper Rhine to Danube area and a jar from the same regional tradition. The only certainty is that these vessels were deposited together, and it does not necessarily follow that they were made at the same point in time or likely to have been in contemporary use. A feasible theory is that these represent the clearing out of a store, although the obvious wasters could suggest that the storekeeper was hoodwinked by the potters off-loading unsaleable vessels, perhaps in the bottom of a crate. If from a store, a mixture of the old with more recent vessels could be expected.

On the other hand, the technical skill exhibited by the copy Dr 27s is of the same order as shown by the fine beakers and cups, and all could have been made by the same potter. This could suggest a potter from the Upper Rhine or Danubian area where the North Italian influence was stronger particularly in the continued use of coarse ware cups, and such an area could also account for the bowls and jar. Proof for neither theory is possible, but together with the other evidence from the site, it strongly suggests a potter or potters working in the pottery tradition of the area broadly from Switzerland to Noricum or Raetia being attached to the army at Wroxeter.

'Military pottery'

Three legionary fortresses in Britain have evidence for the army being substantially involved in pottery manufacture: Usk, Wroxeter, and Inchtuthil. These three sites may be further connected by being the assumed successive fortresses for *Legio XX*. When the individual assemblages are examined, there is no discernible ceramic connection. The pottery from Usk has a distinctive character; that from Wroxeter may be less clear due to the smaller sample and longer occupation, but has equally individual traits, while Inchtuthil vessel types could be lost without trace on many Flavian sites, the early characteristics deriving from perhaps one or two potters having been lost.

The question of the supply of pottery to the army has been well aired (Darling 1977; Breeze 1977; Greene 1977; 1993), and the basic principle that the Roman army was only involved in pottery manufacture under certain circumstances is clear. The continental background to set British sites in their context has been admirably expounded by Greene (1993). Suffice to say that both Wroxeter and Usk fit into the same situation, frontier fortresses established in areas with inadequate or virtually non-existent local pottery, very similar in many respects to the Lower Rhineland in the Augustan-Tiberian period. Both fortresses were in hostile territory; the *Ordovices* were still militant as late as Agricola's campaign of AD 78, and the *Silures* were not finally subdued until the governorship of Frontinus. Wroxeter was even less well located for imports from the continent than Usk. It was these factors which led to the involvement of the army in pottery manufacture.

Local manufacture

Greene's experiments with clay from Usk showed that it fired with little preparation to a fabric very close to that of the fortress pottery. Thin-sections of Wroxeter sherds by David Peacock indicate that the clay could be of local origin, substantiated by the continued appearance of similar fabric in vessels of clearly post-military date and the presence of kilns of later date in the area (Houghton 1961; 1964). Above all, it is the sheer dominance of a single basic fabric and the presence of wasters at both sites which argues most convincingly for local manufacture (wasters at Wroxeter mostly derive from the pit F2807). A particularly interesting waster from Usk is the mortarium inscribed before firing *Pe]lveis contub(e)rnio*; not only was it made specifically for a particular barrack room, but the potter was literate (Greene 1993, 8).

The pottery tradition

The pottery from both sites was entirely continental in form and technique, with no trace of any native pottery influence. It is clear that the potters were working in a continental tradition. Who were they, and what was their relationship to the respective legions? Most of the vessel types can be paralleled at military sites on the Lower Rhine, but a significant number appear to derive from pottery traditions to the south, loosely located in the Upper Rhine to *Raetia* area, with a westward extension into Central Gaul. For Usk, the important vessels are the jars of Greene's types 12 and 13, while Wroxeter has the peculiarity of common cups and beakers, more easily paralleled in this southern area, drawing on North Italian traditions.

Military potters

These widely spaced parallels suggest that the potters were closely attached to the legions. The increase in the number of legionaries epigraphically attested as coming from the provinces of *Noricum*, *Dalmatia* and *Raetia* in the Claudio-Neronian period may be a relevant factor (Webster 1985), in view of the parallels of the Usk jars (Greene 1993, 25, figs 11–13), and the connections of the fine cups and beakers at Wroxeter with the north

Italian tradition, seen particularly at the Magdalensberg. There is no evidence to suggest that the supply of either Lyon ware or samian to Wroxeter was restricted, and these vessels seem likely to have been made by a potter working in the tradition of his homeland, where the manufacture of thin-walled drinking vessels continued much later than elsewhere. The carinated bowls of Wroxeter type 81 (Fig 5.31) also indicate this broad area stretching into *Raetia*.

The contributions to the assemblages of such widely distributed pottery traditions seem more likely to arise if the potters were legionaries. If it is supposed that civilian potters were recruited by *Legio XX* and *XIV* when the absence of adequate pottery supplies in the areas of their proposed fortresses was realised, it would surely have been from south-eastern Britain, and their origin would have been apparent in the pottery types. The probable presence of continental potters at centres such as *Camulodunum* and London is largely irrelevant since these major early centres would have been expanding markets, attractive to enterprising foreign potters. The obvious conclusion is that the legions at Wroxeter and Usk continued the normal practice already established on the Rhine frontier, and that potters were available within the legions.

There is no documentary information about the craftsmen attached to legions until the late second century, to which period the list of *immunes* compiled by Tarruntenus Paternus belongs (*Digest* 50, 6, 7). The term *scandularii* has been translated as 'roof-tile-markers' by Watson (1969, 76), and in view of the strong connection between the manufacture of tiles and pottery at Holt (Grimes 1930) and other military establishments, this may suggest that potters in an earlier period had been included in the legion as craftsmen (although *immunes* are not epigraphically attested until AD 134). This translation is perhaps debatable since the term *tegularii* would be more appropriate to the makers of ceramic roof-files, and Davies's translation as shinglers may be nearer the true meaning (1974, 306). This list was obviously not exhaustive any more than was that of Vegetius (*De re militari* 2, 7), and the exclusion of potters may simply be indicative of their minor status and infrequent occurrence.

It seems likely that the work undertaken by legionaries in the pre-Flavian period, sometimes on an *ad hoc* basis, was more varied, and reorganisation under the Flavian and later emperors resulted in tasks of a non-military nature being undertaken by civilian contractors. Additionally legions on campaign in hostile territory would inevitably have to be more self-sufficient. The potteries postulated for Wroxeter and Usk belong to a different context from the later legionary depots, best known at Holt but presumably also occurring at Caerleon and York.

There is evidence from other sites for potters who were probably army personnel. Much of the pottery at Kingsholm (Hurst 1985, 78) was probably made by the army, and distributed to the fort at Cirencester, and it is notable that some of the jars are strongly reminiscent of jars from Longthorpe (cf Dannell 1987, fig 42, type 76; Hurst 1985, fig 25, nos 23, 24, etc) where potters of diverse traditions were working, the continental element appearing particularly in the 'Roman' vessels such as flagons and mortaria and table wares. This same situation occurs at Lincoln, although jars do not appear to be part of the 'continental' production, but where some of the cups are notably of the North Italian type. The military occupation of Kingsholm and Cirencester would be early for the ready availability of civilian pottery in that area, while *Legio IX* at Lincoln, although not in such a ceramically impoverished area as Usk and Wroxeter, would have found difficulty obtaining supplies of flagons, table ware, and mortaria from local potters.

The extent of military involvement in pottery manufacture

The question of military potting necessarily bulks large, but the involvement should be set in context. The larger area excavated and the size of the sample of pottery at Usk gave Greene a better basis for guessing the manpower requirements than occurs at Wroxeter, and on the assumption that the sample represented 10% he calculated using the fortress area and estimated occupation period that only four potters would have been required (1993, 43). This would have allowed each legionary to break four or five pots each year. Bearing in mind that rubbish distribution in a fortress is unlikely to be even, with probably the bulk being disposed of outside the defences, and that much of that found at both Wroxeter and Usk can be shown to be related to the final demolition phase, any estimate is pure guesswork, but the manpower needed seems negligible. There is also the question of the garrison being away from the fortress on campaign for long periods. A single potter at either site could have produced the vessels with parallels outside the normal Lower Rhine repertoire.

Neither fortress was involved in tile production so no large works-depot as at Holt would have been needed. Later pottery kilns are known by the Severn where suitable clay occurs, and military kilns may have been similarly located. Whether any of the pottery from Wroxeter went to other military sites in the area is unknown. The auxiliary fort to the south may have been occupied contemporaneously, but the quantity of pottery found mostly from field-walking is too small to base conclusions on. The pottery from the fort at Whitchurch does not appear to contain any Wroxeter fabric vessels, but very little was recovered from the early occupation. It is not impossible that forts in Wales, such as Caersws, may have received some pottery from Wroxeter, whether or not it was being made under military control. If so, this would not necessarily be proof of military control of the potting since Wroxeter could have been simply the closest source.

Military potting at Wroxeter

That pottery was made locally by the army, probably by legionaries, has been argued above. It remains to set this into the context of the military occupation. As at Usk, there is evidence to suggest that as the situation changed both with regard to the availability of other pottery and the size of the garrison, so the pottery supply altered. This is further complicated at Wroxeter by the withdrawal of *Legio XIV* by Nero around AD 66/7, so that it may be supposed that the potters, if they were legionaries, left with the legion. The usual assumption, since the area was still a frontier zone, is that *Legio XX* was moved from Usk to Wroxeter. If so, and again assuming the potters were legionaries, did they continue potting at Wroxeter, and can we identify their pottery?

The short answer is that with the relatively small sample, heavily weighted towards the demolition period, our chances of finding secure evidence of *Legio XX* potters are remote. The more remarkable types at Usk were relatively uncommon (jars 13 and 14 accounted for 23% of the jars from the site). Jars of Usk type 13 occur at Wroxeter, and it is notable that most of the jars equivalent to Usk type 11.3 and 11.4 came from demolition or late contexts. The use of a white slip appears to be a later feature of the Wroxeter pottery, but this occurs on flagons and mortaria which were unslipped at Usk. Another possible feature of the later pottery at Wroxeter is the appearance of applied decoration, which is unknown at Usk and seems more likely to be derived from the Midlands.

Another possibility may be suggested. The potters of *Legio XIV* had been working at Wroxeter for some ten years. In this period, it is not inconceivable that they may have trained civilians, and the continued local production may have already passed into civilian hands. What is clear from the pottery is that the same clays were being exploited, and the same or closely similar vessel types continued to be made. The army's preference not to be involved in pottery manufacture may be borne in mind. The large quantities of residual military pottery in the small sample of pottery from Period 1 and that from Period 2 makes it difficult to assess the post-military local production, but various slight nuances and changes in vessel types can be tentatively viewed as indicating a continuum of local production, potters working in much the same tradition as earlier. Unlike Usk, Wroxeter was not close to developing civilian pottery enterprises, so that local manufacture retained a greater importance. Moreover, occupation of the fortress continued, with the attendant demand for pottery from the *canabae* providing a market for enterprising potters.

There is also the fact that as well as being in a state of mutiny at this period (Tacitus *Histories* i, 60), *Legio XX*, the assumed new garrison, would have been depleted by sending a vexillation to support Vitellius in AD 69, and under the Flavian governors they would have been away on active campaign, ultimately leading to their assumed transfer to the fortress at Inchtuthil. The quantity of pottery required by the army would have decreased considerably. The fact that there is no ceramic connection between Wroxeter and Inchtuthil may further indicate the changing response by the army to the pottery supply question, although in fairness it is worth noting that our hypothetical potter producing vessels in a North Italian tradition would be either fairly elderly or dead by this time!

Conclusions

The evidence indicates that Wroxeter, like Usk, fits into the usual pattern of the response of the Roman army when garrisoning a large force in a hostile area with non-existent or inadequate pottery supplies, namely the local manufacture of pottery. Furthermore, the continental parallels indicate potters drawing upon geographically widespread traditions, and the most likely explanation is that they were soldiers. The involvement of the legions in making pottery appears to have been dictated by circumstances, so that as these changed, so the pottery supply situation was adapted. Campaign commitments would have lessened the need for quantities of pottery. More peaceful settled conditions in the area and the presence of the *canabae* would have been likely to have attracted civilian potters. Some civilians may have been trained by the army potters. The work of making pottery is likely to have moved into civilian hands during the military period. This situation, with increasing quantities coming from non-local sources, such as mortaria from the *Verulamium* region, probably continued due to the relative isolation of Wroxeter from any major pottery producers until the advent of BB1, and increased trading from the Severn Valley potters, some of whom set up workshops in the vicinity.

The earliest pottery at Wroxeter would therefore have been made by potters attached to *Legio XIV*, and it is possible that manufacture moved to civilian potters after their departure *c* AD 66/7. If *Legio XX* was the replacement garrison, there is no certain evidence that their potters worked at Wroxeter.

Pottery catalogue

The illustrations (Figs 5.26–5.39) are presented in type order.

The pottery is presented as:
Local fabric type series (Figs 5.26–5.33)
Pottery from pit F2807 (Figs 5.35, 5.36)
Non-local coarse ware vessels (Fig 5.37)
Fine wares (Fig 5.38)
Wroxeter Mortaria (Fig 5.34)
Mortaria of non-local origin (Fig 5.38)
Amphorae (Fig 5.39)

The sequence of the catalogue is: illustration number; its equivalent in the type series used for the entire Wroxeter assemblage as presented in Ellis (2000, 195–257); fabric code; any notable features of the

vessel; context/s; Phase (military phases prefixed 'M', post-military by period); feature numbers, if applicable. Vessels known to be from the large demolition spread are denoted as phase M7v. Where there has been reason to suspect some contamination, an exclamation mark has been added to the phase to indicate this uncertainty. Some vessels have been illustrated from post-military contexts; these were clearly residual from the military period and provide better illustrations of more fragmentary examples stratified in military contexts.

Due to a combination of the important types found in the pit F2807, and the unusual character of the pottery from that pit, some occur twice in the illustrations, to ensure the type series of locally made vessels is comprehensive on the one hand, and to illustrate fully the contents of the pit. Thus, type 4.6 = no 135 in the pit group, etc.

type	Ellis type	fabric	details-context-phase-Feature No
(Fig 5.26)			
1.1	F1.12	WWOF?	41/6 M7v
1.2	F1.11	WWO	knife-trimmed basal zone; some distortion 14/42 1.3 2260
1.3	F1.14	WWO	trimmed basal zone 84/328 M4b! 770
1.4	F1.13	WWOF	87/115 M6
2.1	F1.22	WWO	over-fired 67/17 M7iv
2.2	F1.21	WWCR	80/201 M7iv 654
3	F1.31	WWOF	handle probably three-ribbed 78/5 M7v
4.1	F2.12	WWO	cream slip? 91/247 M6 948
4.2	F2.11	WWO	84/393 M2
4.3	F2.22	WWO	possibly three-ribbed handle 50/31 M7v
4.4	F2.21	WWO	slightly over-fired 50/52 M7iv 2511
4.5	–	WWO	probably three-ribbed handle 73/27 M7iv 2663
4.6	F2.32	WWO	78/57 M7iv 2807
4.7	F2.31	WWO	soft 78/57 M7iv 2807
5	F2.41	WWO	soft;discoloured;unusual handle 78/57 M7iv 2807
6.1	F1.41	WWOF	98/205 M7i
6.2	F1.42	WWOF	98/205; 233 M7i; M7iv
7	F5.31	WWOF	handle probably two-ribbed 7/41 M5i 2276
8.1	F6.23	WWR	over-fired dark grey with red-brown core 7/35 M7v
8.2	F6.21	WWO	98/205 M7i
8.3	F6.22	WWO	handle probably two-ribbed 34/29 M7iv 2312
9.1	F4.11	WWO	over-fired; distorted 51/21; 70/16; 85; 78/11; 33; 57 1.3; M7v; M7iv 2990/3009; 2713; 2807
9.2	F4.12	WWO	handle probably two-ribbed 78/10;11 M7iv 2806/2807
(Fig 5.27)			
10	F8.11	WWO	smoothed girth to base 34/45 M7iv 2322
11.1	F8.21	WWO	98/205 M7i

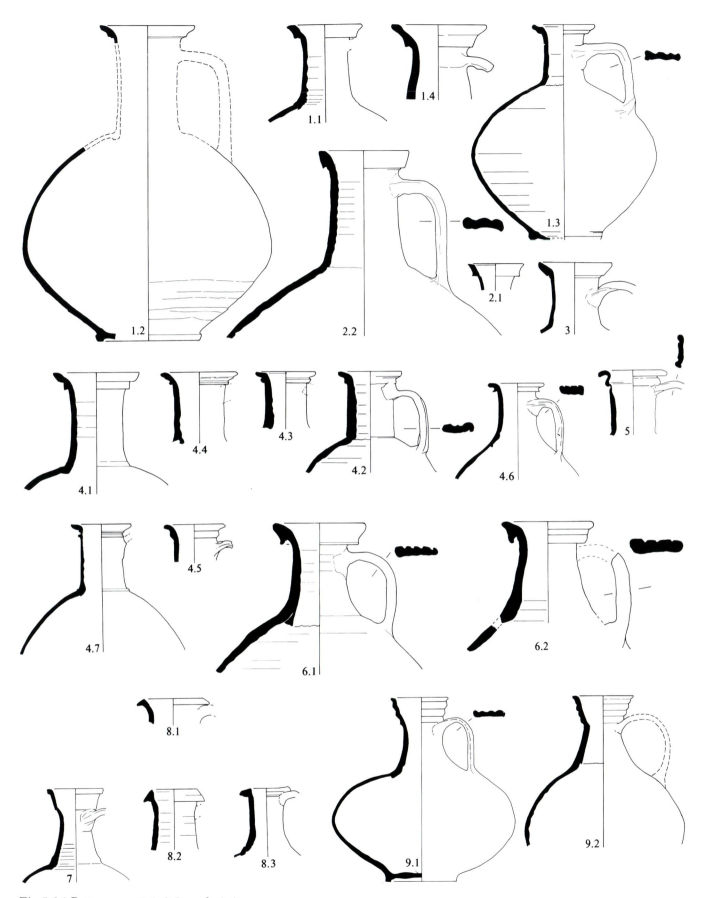

Fig 5.26 Pottery: nos 1.1–9.2; scale 1:4

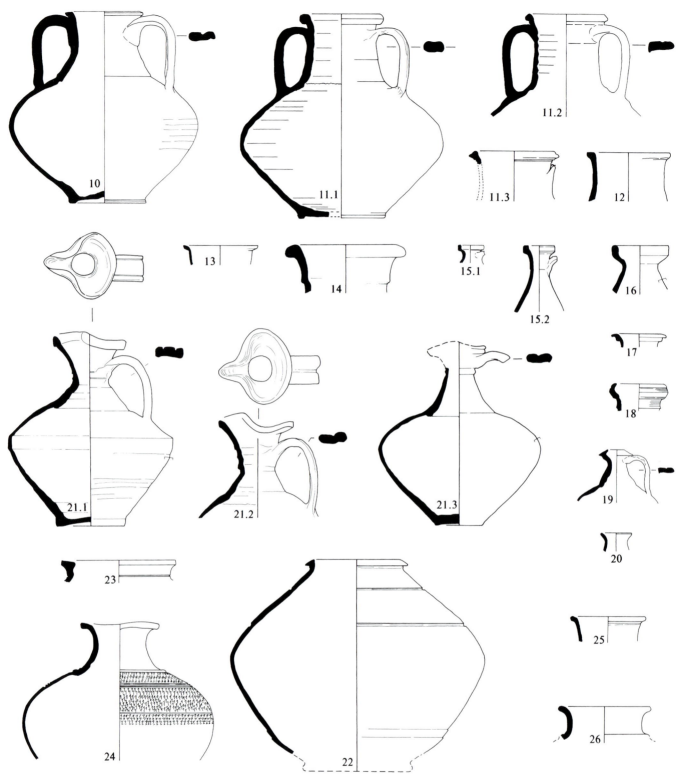

Fig 5.27 Pottery: nos 10–26; scale 1:4

11.2	–	WWO	72/63 and 19 M4b 2905 and 2868
11.3	–	WWR	burnt; handle probably two-ribbed 52/14 M7iv 2247
12		WWO	98/205 M7i
13	F5.51	WWO	soft;discoloured 78/57 M7iv 2807
14	F5.61	WWCR	2/36 M pre-leg 2025
15.1	–	WWO	50/87 M4b 2534

15.2	F5.22	WWOF	84/339 M5
16	F5.23	WWCR	84/125;217 M7iv
17	F1.51	WWO	12/30 M7v
18	F5.11	WWO	groove on neck 78/15 M5 2811
19	F6.11	WWR	14/32 1.3 2246
20	F9.11	WWO	84/251 M7ii
21.1	F10.11	WWR	trimmed basal zone 80/201 M7iv 654
21.2	F10.12	WWO	90/247 M7i 3093

21.3	–	WWO	trimmed basal zone 80/201 M7iv 654
22	JH1.21	WWO	knife-trimmed basal zone 1/59 and 9.31 M7v and M7iv
23	JH3.11	WWO	41/29 M7iv
24	JN1.11	WWR	rouletted; slightly distorted 70/16; 78/11; 33; 37 M7v; M7iv 2807
25	JN1.12	WWO	72/14 M4b 2863
26	JN3.11	WWO	fabric similar SV 12/39 1.3 2229

(Fig 5.28)

27.1	JM7.53	WWR	near complete; irregular burnished lines in basal zone 72/19 M4b 2868
27.2	JM7.56	WWO	39/20 M4b 2289
27.3	JM7.94	WWR	near complete; irregular burnished lines and knife-trimming 72/19 M4b 2868
27.4	JM7.59	WWR	trimmed basal zone 80/201 M7iv 654
27.5	JM7.51	WWR	near complete; irregular burnished lines 72/67; 69; 96 M4b 2908; 2910; 2903
27.6	JM9.21	WWR	irregular burnished lines; knife trimmed 78/16 M7iv 2812
27.7	–	WWR	72/67 M4b 2908
28.1	JM6.22	WWO	70/16 M7v
28.2	JM6.21	WWO	67/21 and 28 M7v and 2.2
28.3	–	WWR	14/31 and 41/6 M7v
29.1	JM7.91	WWR	near complete; basal zone smoothed/trimmed 72/14; 67; 114; 120 M4b 2863; 2908; 2898
29.2	JM3.64	WWR	50/52 M7iv 2511
29.3	JM3.63	WWR	77/2 2.2
29.4	–	WWR	70/51 M7iv
29.5	–	WWR	73/45 M5 2662
29.6	JM7.95	WWR	73/45 M5 2662
29.7	JM7.93	WWR	80/201 M7iv 654
30.1	JM7.82	WWO	smoothed basal zone 44/32 M7iv
30.2	JM7.81	WWR	fine working lines; blob of ?slip 72/48 and 67 M4b 2894; 2908
30.3	JM7.83	WWR	39/22 M7iv 2291
30.4	JM7.84	WWR	irregular burnished lines; smoothed basal zone 39/20 M4b 2289
30.5	JM7.87	WWO	string-marked base 39/20 M4b 2289
30.6	–	WWO	35/45 M7iv 2334
30.7	–	WWR	39/22 M7iv 2291
30.8	–	WWO	7/58 M7iv 2265
31.1	JM8.12	WWR	burnished lines on body 39/26 M3 2293
31.2	JM8.11	WWR	14/37 M7iv
31.3	JM8.13	WWO	7/54 M4bi 2278
31.4	JM8.15	WWR	rim rolled over 70/85 M7iv 2713
31.5	JM8.14	WWO	rim rolled over 45/15 M7v
31.6	JM7.88	WWR	67/22 M7iv

(Fig 5.29)

| 32.1 | JM6.41 | WWR | thin wall; burnish on shoulder 35/15; 19 1.3 2260 |
| 32.2 | JM6.42 | WWR | diagonal burnish lines 92/62 M7v |

32.3	JM6.44	WWR/O	91/193 M7iv
32.4	JM6.43	WWO	91/94 2.3 551
32.5	JM6.48	WWR	91/240 M6i
32.6	JM6.46	WWR	9/30 and 31 M7v; M7iv
32.7	JM6.45	WWR	burnish on shoulder and rim 35/48 M7v
32.8	–	WWO	84/79 M7iv 261/278
33.1	JM7.61	WWO	knife-trimmed basal zone 77/9 M5 2598
33.2	JM7.62	WWO	72/19 M4b 2868
33.3	JM7.64	WWR	77/9 M5 2598
33.4	JM7.63	WWR?	burnt WWO? 77/9 M5 2598
33.5	–	WWR	very hard-fired 50/87 M4b 2534
34.1	JM7.23	WWR	batch-mark? three slashes on rim; burnished lines on body 50/15 M7iv 2488
34.2	JM3.53	WWR	7/58 M7iv 2265
34.3	JM3.51	WWR	12/42 M4b! 2228
35.1	JM3.71	WWR	irregular burnish line; knife-trimmed basal 80/245 M7iv 751
35.2	JM9.31	WWR	12/42 M4bi 2228
35.3	JM3.31	WWR	fine working lines on rim and exterior 75/2 2.1
35.4	–	WWR	84/237 1.?
35.5	JM2.23	WWRF	burnished rim and exterior 41/6 M7v
36.1	JM4.23	WWO	84/79 M7iv 261/278
36.2	JM4.25	WWO	84/79 M7iv 261/278
36.3	JM4.22	WWR	44/14 M7v
37.1	JM2.12	WWRF	fine working lines on exterior 92/61; 72 M7v; M7iv 255; 447
37.2	JM2.11	WWR?	more quartz than usual; burnished shoulder 35/48 M7v
37.3	JM9.41	WWR	50/52 M7iv 2511
37.4	JH4.51	WWR	30/18 M4bi 2020
38.1	JM9.33	WWOF	98/137 1.3
38.2	JM9.34	WWOF	smoothed shoulder 98/171 1.2
38.3	JM9.35	WWR	91/94 2.3 551
39	JM2.41	WWR	91/94 2.3 551
40.1	JM4.31	WWO?	laminated fracture 12/42 M4b! 2228
40.2	JM3.81	WWRF	burnished shoulder 92/72 M7iv! 447
40.3	JM3.55	WWRF	fine working lines externally 6/73 and 12/42 1.3; M4b! 2208; 2228
41	JM5.31	WWO	81/15 M7v
42.1	JM6.33	WWO	7/54; 59 M4b; M7iv 2278; 2284
42.2	JM6.31	WWR	81/15 M7v
42.3	JM6.32	WWR	burnished rim top and neck 70/16 and 72/34 M7v; M4b! 2883
43	JM4.41	WWO	90/253 1.2
44	JH5.11	WWO	possibly a honey pot 34/47 and 63/20 M7iv; 1.3 2325; 2287
45	JM6.24	WWR	90/247 M7i 3093
46.1	JM7.21	WWR	84/230 M7iv 611
46.2	JM6.13	WWR?	10/24 M7v
47	JM5.11	WWR	73/24 M7iv 2662

(Fig 5.30)

| 48 | – | WWR | 30/52 M4b! 2031 |
| 49.1 | JM7.31 | WWO | 73/25; 45 M5 2662 |

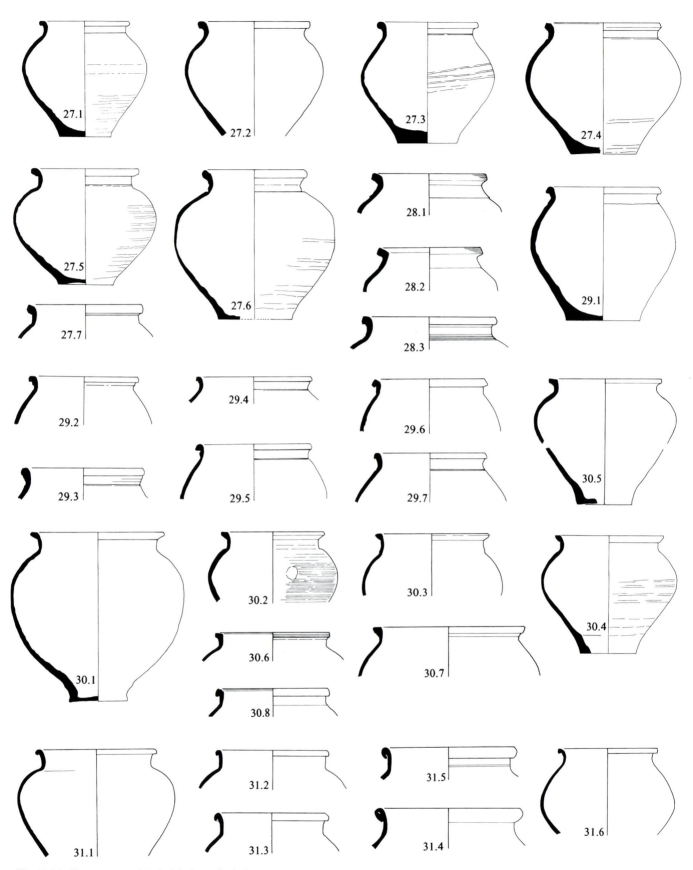

Fig 5.28 Pottery: nos 27.1–31.6; scale 1:4

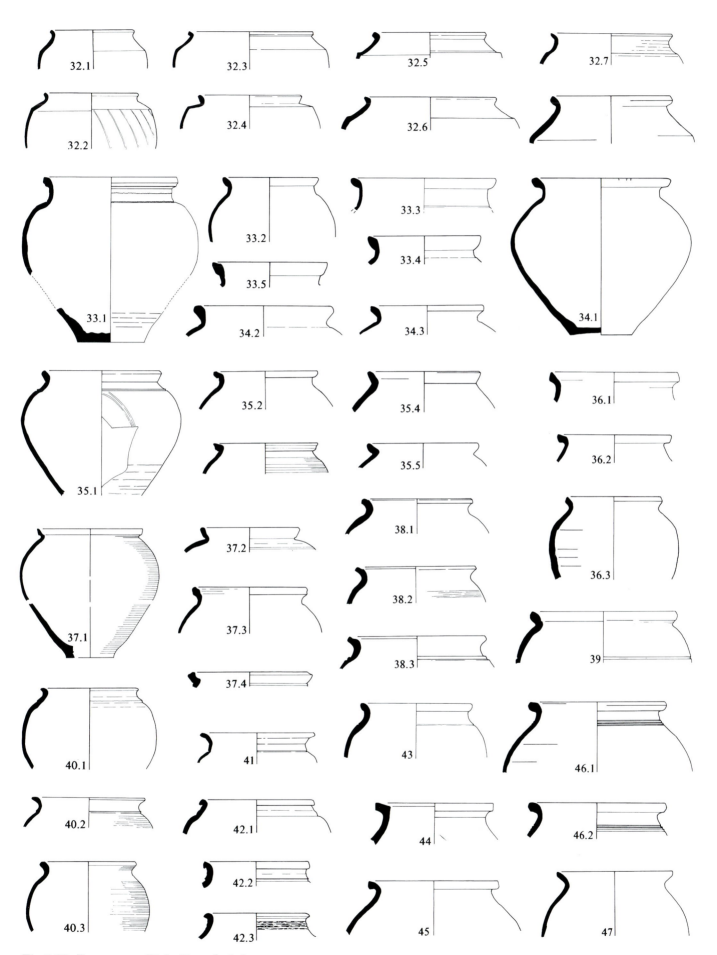

Fig 5.29 Pottery: nos 32.1–47; scale 1:4

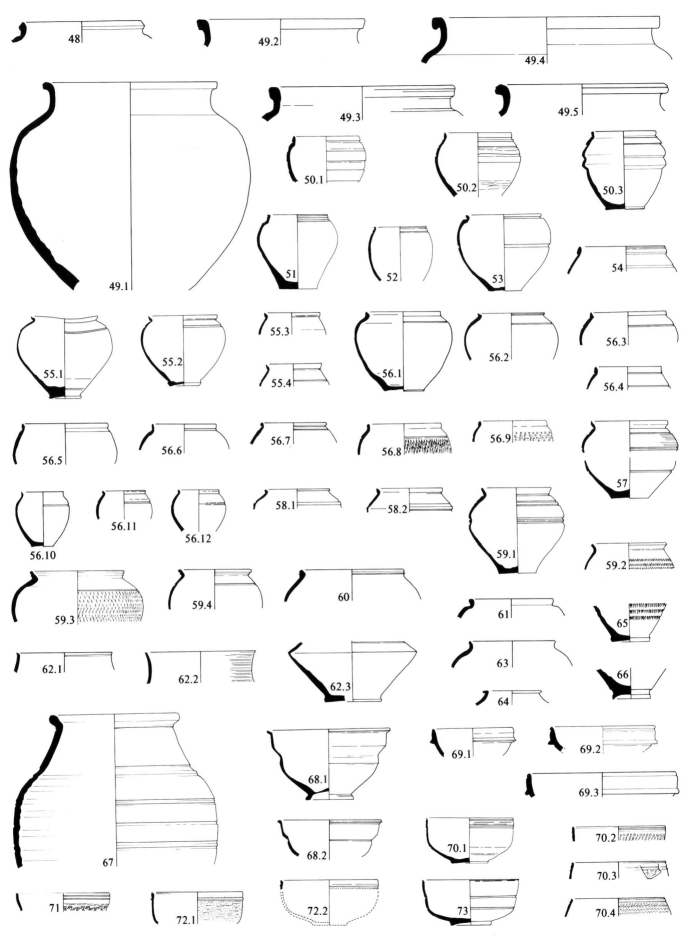

Fig 5.30 Pottery: Nos 48–73; scale 1:4

49.2	JM7.33	WWR	75/16 M4a 2534
49.3	JM7.32	WWO	84/251 M7ii
49.4	–	WWO	92/61; 65; 88; 89 M7v; M7iv; M5 255; 504; 489; 490
49.5	–	WWO	grooved on exterior of rim 50/31 and 73/2 M7v; M7iv 2644
50.1	BK4.52	WWR	traces of burnishing externally 78/9 M7iv! 2805
50.2	BK4.51	WWR	irregular burnished lines below girth 72/114; 48 M4b 2908; 2894
50.3	BK4.57	WWR	occasional burnished line near trimmed base 80/201 M7iv 654
51	BK4.41	WWR	irregular burnishing in basal zone 77/9 M5 2598
52	BK5.11	WWR	78/57 M7iv 2807
53	BK4.61	WWR	light knife-trimming on base 78/11; 33; 57 M7iv 2807
54	BK4.55	WWR	98/179 M7iv
55.1	BK6.15	WWR	over-fired and mis-shapen 78/57 M7iv 2807
55.2	BK6.14	WWR	knife-trimmed base 78/57 M7iv 2807
55.3	BK6.11	WWRF	72/24 M4b 2872
55.4	BK6.12	WWR	73/44 M7iv 2676
56.1	BK4.17	WWO	finely finished; base only trimmed 89/1; 95/1 4.0
56.2	BK4.15	WWO	84/181 M7iv
56.3	–	WWR	44/35 M5 3016
56.4	BK4.54	WWRF	smooth exterior 78/26 M4b 2820
56.5	BK4.53	WWR	72/67 M4b 2908
56.6	–	WWR	smoothed externally 77/9 M5 2598
56.7	–	WWR	groove immediately below rim 73/27 M7iv 2663
56.8	BK4.32	WWR	dark surface; smooth shoulder; incised decoration 50/52 M7iv 2511
56.9	BK4.56	WWRF	distinctive triangular stabs/ rouletting 75/2 2.1
56.10	BK4.23	WWRF	98/234 1.2 2005
56.11	BK4.21	WWRF	80/191 M4b 632
56.12	BK4.22	WWRF	84/110 M7iv 492/496/550
57	BK6.17	WWOF	smooth; non-joining 7/55; 59 M7iv 2247; 2284
58.1	BK12.13	WWO	cordon on shoulder 92/18 2.1
58.2	BK12.11	WWRF	hollow cordon/carination 83/ 536 2.1
59.1	BK3.15	WWO	smoothed basal zone 67/22 M7iv
59.2	BK3.17	WWRF	lightly rouletted 14/43 M7iv 2261
59.3	BK7.16	WWRF?	smoothed shoulder and rim; rouletted 84/261 M7iv
59.4	BK7.11	WWR	grooved exterior rim 72/79 M4b 2916
60	BK7.13	WWO	ragged groove below rim 30/23 M4b! 2020
61	–	WWOF	smoothed exterior and top of rim 63/15 1.3 2287
62.1	BK10.12	WWRF	smoothed exterior 77/9 M5 2598
62.2	BK10.13	WWRF	finely polished darker exterior 98/205 M7i
62.3	BK10.1	WWR	98/205 M7i
63	BK3.22	WWR	highly fired 7/41 M5! 2276

64	–	WWOF	14/37 M7iv
65	–	WWR	light rouletting and base knife-trimmed 50/52 M7iv 2511
66	–	WWRF	smoothed exterior; neat footring 7/55 M7iv 2247
67	BK1.11	WWR	90/247 M7i 3093
68.1	C1.15	WWO	over-fired and distorted; pin-hole in base 78/57 M7iv 2807
68.2	C1.31	WWRF	7/57 M5 277
69.1	B12.61	WWOF	smooth interior 53/11 M7v
69.2	B12.62	WWOF	smooth surfaces 34/29 M7iv 2312
69.3	B12.63	WWOF	burnished interior 34/37 M7iv 2312
70.1	C3.11	WWR	smoothed basal zone; neat footring 78/57 M7iv 2807
70.2	C3.13	WWRF	fragment of barbotine scale decoration 98/145 3.1 1017
70.3	C3.12	WWRF	rouletted 98/196 M7iv
70.4	C3.14	WWOF	rouletted 91/307 M5 1080
71	C5.11	WWRF	impressed decoration 39/18 M4b 2303
72.1	C7.11	WWRF	sandy slip externally imitating roughcast 67/22 M7iv
72.2	–	WWRF	rouletted 6/51 1.3 205
73	C3.21	WWR	smoothed basal zone below groove 78/57 M7iv 2807

(Fig 5.31)

74.1	C4.11	WWRF	smoothed below groove 72/16; 21 M4b 2865; 2870
74.2	C4.21	WWOF	definitely tripod type 67/17 M7iv
74.3	–	WWOF	smooth exterior finish 73/24; 45 M7iv; M5 2662
75.1	C4.25	WWR	93/3 M7iv
75.2	C4.22	CREAM	hard cream ?WW 4.0
75.3	C4.23	WWR	hard coarseish 4.0
75.4	C4.24	WWOF	80/198 M4b 644
75.5	C6.11	WWR	firing ring colour-change Wbg34 4.0
76	–	WWO	92/61 M7v 255
77	B1.22	WWO	discoloured; finely moulded 70/16; 72/9 M7v; M4b 2860
78.1	B1.11	WWO	rouletted 78/17; 10; 15; 6/73; 70/16 M7iv; 1.3!; M7v; M5 2208; 2806; 2811
78.2	B1.12	WWO	rouletted grooved rim 73/44 M7iv 2676
78.3	B2.12	WWRF?	rouletted 92/+; 74/6; 12/27 4.0; M7iv; 2.2 2691
78.4	B2.13	WWO	rouletted 84/78; 142; 206; 209 M7iv
78.5	B2.11	WWO	rouletted 98/131 M7iv
79	B11.11	WWO	mis-shapen; soft ?under-fired 78/57 M7iv 2807
80	–	WWOF	fine working lines; part of a knife-cut spout 67/26; 70/16 2.1; M7v 3244
81.1	B4.13	WWR	soft; smoothed basal zone and ?crack in base 78/57 M7iv 2807
81.2	B4.14	WWR	variable hardness; slightly mis-shapen 78/57 M7iv 2807
81.3	B4.11	WWR	72/19 M4b 2868

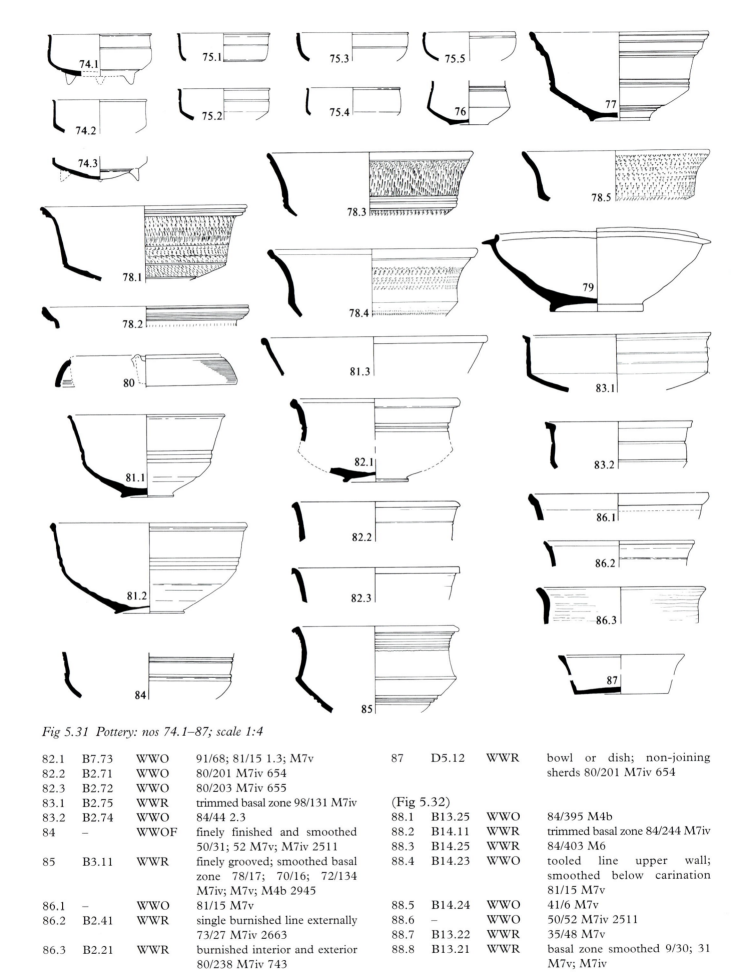

Fig 5.31 Pottery: nos 74.1–87; scale 1:4

82.1	B7.73	WWO	91/68; 81/15 1.3; M7v
82.2	B2.71	WWO	80/201 M7iv 654
82.3	B2.72	WWO	80/203 M7iv 655
83.1	B2.75	WWR	trimmed basal zone 98/131 M7iv
83.2	B2.74	WWO	84/44 2.3
84	–	WWOF	finely finished and smoothed 50/31; 52 M7v; M7iv 2511
85	B3.11	WWR	finely grooved; smoothed basal zone 78/17; 70/16; 72/134 M7iv; M7v; M4b 2945
86.1	–	WWO	81/15 M7v
86.2	B2.41	WWR	single burnished line externally 73/27 M7iv 2663
86.3	B2.21	WWR	burnished interior and exterior 80/238 M7iv 743

| 87 | D5.12 | WWR | bowl or dish; non-joining sherds 80/201 M7iv 654 |

(Fig 5.32)

88.1	B13.25	WWO	84/395 M4b
88.2	B14.11	WWR	trimmed basal zone 84/244 M7iv
88.3	B14.25	WWR	84/403 M6
88.4	B14.23	WWO	tooled line upper wall; smoothed below carination 81/15 M7v
88.5	B14.24	WWO	41/6 M7v
88.6	–	WWO	50/52 M7iv 2511
88.7	B13.22	WWR	35/48 M7v
88.8	B13.21	WWR	basal zone smoothed 9/30; 31 M7v; M7iv

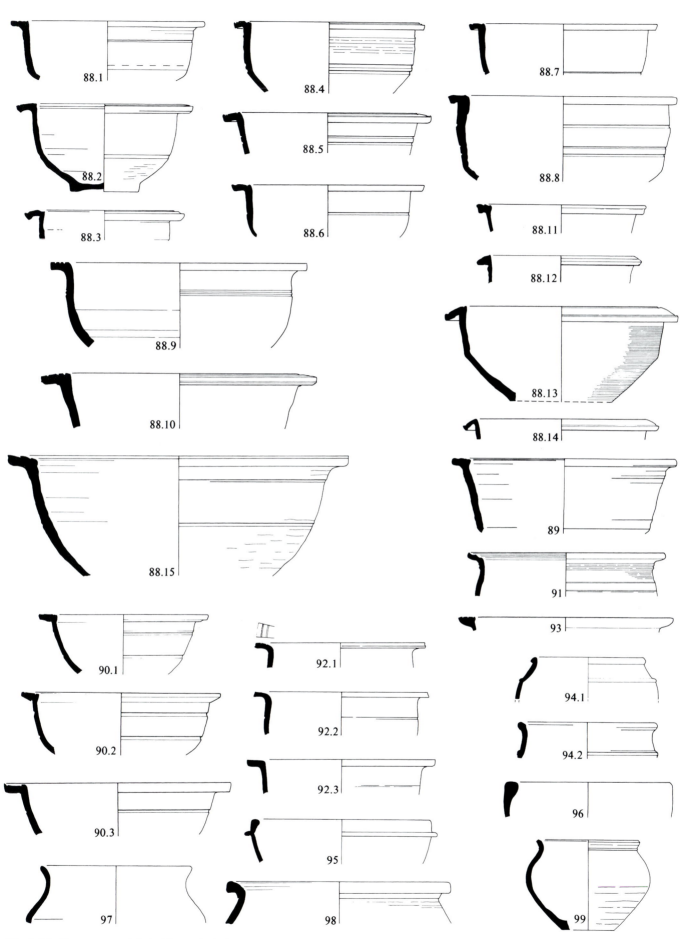

Fig 5.32 Pottery: nos 88.1–99; scale 1:4

88.9	B13.61	WWR	knife trimmed basal zone 80/224 M4b 707
88.10	B14.32	WWO	70/16 M7v
88.11	B13.31	WWR	52/24 M7iv 2401
88.12	–	WWR	14/37 M7iv
88.13	B14.26	WWR	fine tooled lines on exterior 50/87; 75/2 M4b; 2.1 2534
88.14	B14.13	WWR	51/21 1.3 2990/3009
88.15	B15.11	WWR	trimmed basal zone 84/251; 252; 85/68; 69 M7ii; M7iv; M6
89	B13.33	WWR	trimmed base 84/255; 339; 342 M7iv; M5; M6
90.1	B15.12	WWO	90/220 M7i 2079
90.2	B15.13	WWO	85/105 2.3
90.3	B15.14	WWO	14/47; 7/61 M7iv; M4b! 2266
91	B17.21	WWOF	fine working lines; smoothed surfaces 70/16 M7v
92.1	B17.33	WWOF	98/130 1.2
92.2	B17.32	WWOF	98/130 1.2
92.3	B17.31	WWOF	98/130 1.2
93	B13.51	WWO	traces of a cream slip? 7/35 M7v
94.1	B21.13	WWRF?	atypical WWRF; fine working lines exterior 77/2 2.2
94.2	B21.12	WWR	smoothed exterior 84/278 M7iv
95	B12.11	WWR	63/19 1.3 2287
96	JC1.15	WWR	very hard fired 1/38; 9/30; 29/17 M7v; 2.1
97	JW3.21	WWO	84/79 M7iv 261/278
98	JLS2.31	WWR	bowl or jar? 90/220 M7i 2079
99	B22.11	WWR	trimmed basal zone 92/61 M7v 255

(Fig 5.33)

100	–	WWRF	80/207 M7iv 661
101	B7.11	WWOF	knife trimmed basal zone 97/212 1.1 956
102	P1.11	WWR	soft fabric 78/57 M7iv 2807
103.1	P2.12	WWOF	finely smoothed; grooved internally at junction base/wall and centre base 9/30; 22; 29 M7v; M7v!; 2.2
103.2	P2.13	WWO	finely burnished 84/216; 248 M7iv
104.1	P3.11	WWR	soft fabric 78/57 M7iv 2807
104.2	P3.13	WWOF	knife trimmed basal; slight grooves below rim 9/31 M7iv
104.3	P5.11	WWR	variable fabric colours between sherds 78/57 M7iv 2807
104.4	P3.12	WWO	98/196 M7iv
105.1	P4.11	WWOF	offset immediately above smoothed basal zone 1/59 M7v
105.2	P5.14	WWR	trimmed basal zone 91/247 M6 948
105.3	P5.33	WWO	discontinuous grooving; smoothed basal zone 72/14; 24; 34; 67; 75/14 M4b; M4b! 2863; 2872; 2883; 2908; 2630
105.4	P5.15	WWO	nearly complete; knife trimmed basal zone 77/9 M5 2598
105.5	P5.34	WWR	nearly complete; trimmed basal zone 92/18; 22 2.1; M7iv! 161
106	P7.11	WWO	traces slip externally? 77/9 M5 2598
107	P8.11	WWO	trimmed basal zone 72/63 M4b 2905

108	D6.31	WWOF	burnished internally and smoothed exterior 34/37; 63/18 M7iv; 1.3 2312; 2287
109	P10.11	WWOF	burnished interior and exterior; pronounced facets externally 91/230 M7iv
110.1	D5.25	WWR	knife trimmed basal 98/222 1.2 1097
110.2	D5.24	WWO	knife trimmed basal 98/141 1.3
110.3	D5.26	WWR	knife trimmed 98/131 M7iv
110.4	D5.22	WWR	knife trimmed 98/131 M7iv
111	–	WWO	heavily burnt; knife trimmed 91/94 2.3 551
112.1	L3.11	WWO	41/6 M7v
112.2	L3.31	WWR	slightly mis-shapen 72/79; 74/3 M4b; M7v 2916
112.3	L2.12	WWR	81/15 M7v
112.4	L3.32	WWR	very mis-shapen and poorly finished 63/18; 6/73; 12/42 1.3; M4b! 2287; 2208; 2228
113	L2.21	WWR	45/15 M7v
114	L6.51	WWO	91/108 1.3
115.1	L2.17	WWOF	98/180 M7iv
115.2	L2.16	WWO	12/30 M7v
115.3	L5.11	WWO	burnished internally 41/6 M7v
116	L5.21	WWR	98/233 M7iv
117	L6.11	WWR	63/15 1.3 2287
118.1	TZ2.12	WWO	soft discoloured 78/57 M7iv 2807
118.2	TZ2.11	WWOF	traces internal burning 77/9 M5 2598
119	TZ3.11	WWO	notched rim 3/21 2.1
120	TZ5.11	WWO	fingered frilling 98/208 M7iv
121	TZ1.11	WWR	notched rim 77/9; 50/52 M5; M7iv 2598; 2511
122	–	WWR	tazza base? string-marked 78/5 M7v
123	MTV1.11	WWOF	92/61; 63 M7v; M7iv 255; 253
124	–	WWO	?unguent pot base 10/11 M7v
125	–	WWO	ribbed basal zone 50/17; 52 M3; M7iv 2490; 2511
126	ML1.12	WWOF	burnt at spout; SF1894 72/67 M4b 2908
127	ML2.11	WWR	burnt at spout 78/16 M7iv 2812

(Fig 5.34)

128.1	M5.23	MWWOF	no trituration; faint horizontal and diagonal lines on interior 7/38 1.3 2280
128.2	M5.25	MWWOF	no trituration; multiple horizontal/diagonal lines on interior 2/36; 5/15 M0!; 2.1 2025
128.3	M5.21	MWWO	no trituration; clumsily finished base 14/32 1.3 2246
128.4	M5.24	MWWO	no trituration 92/18 2.1
128.5	M5.22	MWWO	no trituration 90/216 2.2
129.1	M5.12	MWWR	quartz trituration 92/18 2.1
129.2	M5.11	MWWCR	quartz trituration 84/301; 321 M6; M7ii 755; 758
130	–	MWWR	quartz trituration 91/210 M5! 1015
131	M5.41	MWWCR	trituration red sandstone 52/22 M4b! 2371
132	M5.51	MWWO?	not definitely WW 78/8 M7iv 2804

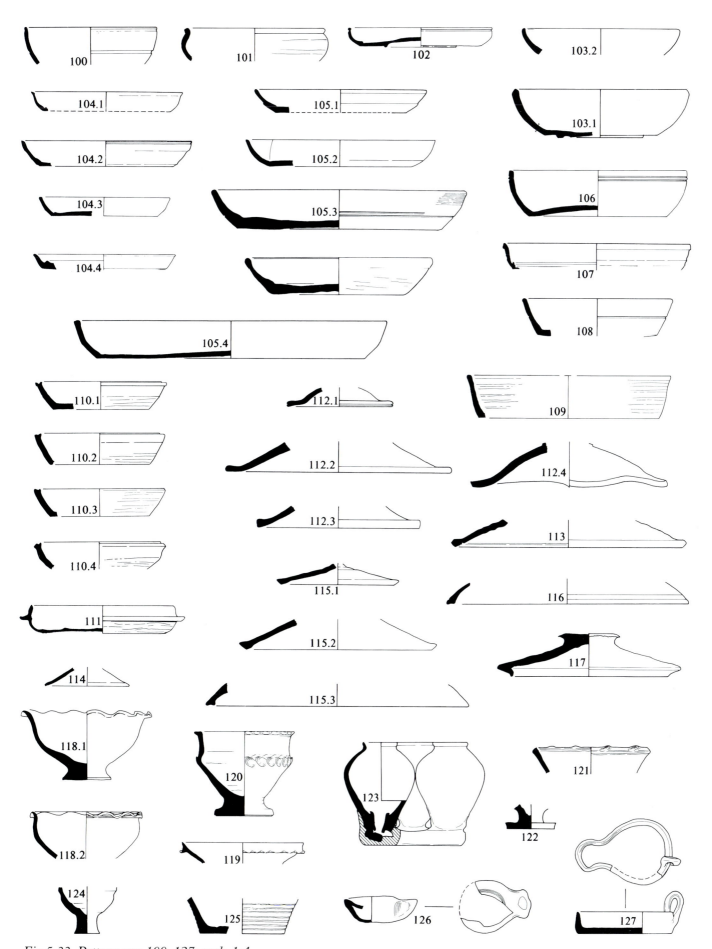

Fig 5.33 Pottery: nos 100–127; scale 1:4

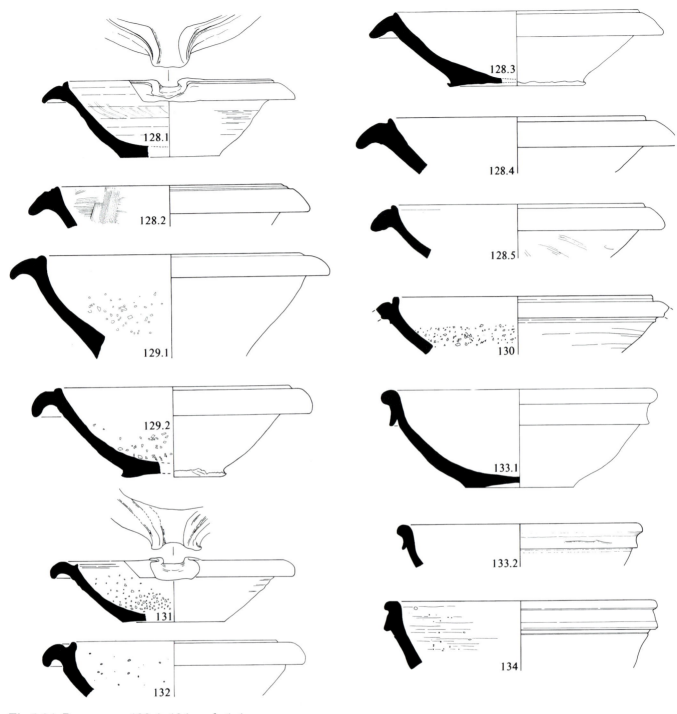

Fig 5.34 Pottery: nos 128.1–134; scale 1:4

133.1	M4.13	MWWO	no trituration; string-marked base 72/19 M4b 2868
133.2	M4.11	MWWO	no trituration 98/52 2.3
134	M4.12	MWWO	fine quartz sand internally 85/248 M4b

(Fig 5.35)

135	F2.32	WWO	well fired 78/57 M7iv 2807
136	F2.31	WWO	soft fabric 78/57 M7iv 2807
137	F2.41	WWO	soft; stained; unusual handle 78/57 M7iv 2807
138	F4.11	WWO	over-fired; mis-shapen 51/21; 70/16; 85; 78/11; 33; 57 1.3; M7v; M7iv 2990/3009; 2713; 2807

139	F4.12	WWO	probably two-ribbed handle 78/10; 11 M7iv 2806/2807
140	F5.51	WWO	soft; discoloured 78/57 M7iv 2807
141	F8.12	WWO	soft fabric; ?discoloured 78/57 M7iv 2807
142	–	WWO	most of body; trimmed base 78/10; 11; 33; 57 M7iv 2806; 2807
143	JN1.11	WWR	rouletted; slightly mis-shapen 70/16; 78/11; 33; 37 M7v; M7iv 2807
144	JM7.55	WWR	knife-trimmed basal zone; blackened rim 78/10; 11; 33 M7iv 2806; 2807

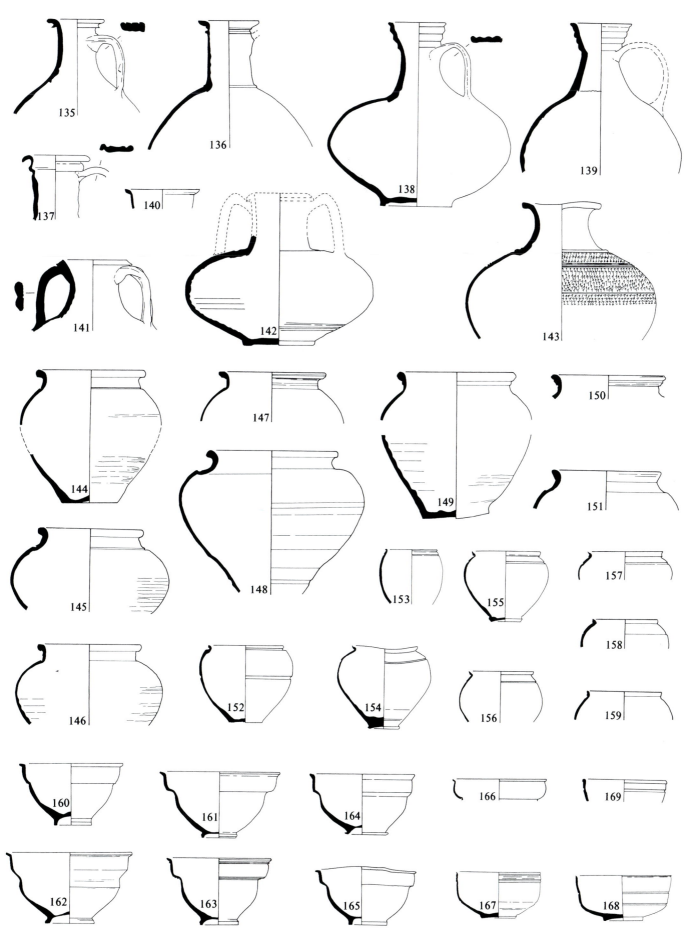

Fig 5.35 Pottery: nos 135–169; scale 1:4

145	JM7.57	WWR	discoloured; irregular burnished lines around girth 78/57 M7iv 2807
146	JM7.54	WWR	over-fired; possibly distorted 78/57 M7iv 2807
147	JM5.52	WWR	soft fabric; ?unused 78/57 M7iv 2807
148	JM7.58	WWR	very over-fired; distorted 78/57 M7iv 2807
149	JM3.66	WWR	discoloured; mis-shapen base 78/57 M7iv 2807
150	JM3.54	WWR	soft discoloured 78/57 M7iv 2807
151	–	WWR	78/57 M7iv 2807
152	BK4.61	WWR	coarser fabric; slight trimming at base 78/11; 33; 57 M7iv 2807
153	BK5.11	WWR	78/57 M7iv 2807
154	BK6.15	WWR	over-fired; mis-shapen; trimmed base 78/57 M7iv 2807
155	BK6.14	WWR	knife-trimmed base 78/57 M7iv 2807
156	BK6.13	WWR	78/57 M7iv 2807
157	BK6.16	WWR	78/57 M7iv 2807
158	BK4.16	WWR	slightly over-fired 78/57 M7iv 2807
159	BK4.44	WWR	less fresh sherd? 78/57 M7iv 2807
160	C1.12	WWO	over-fired; ?distorted 78/57 M7iv 2807
161	C1.14	WWO	over-fired; ?distorted 78/57 M7iv 2807
162	C1.15	WWO	over-fired; distorted; pinhole base 78/57 M7iv 2807
163	C1.32	WWO	78/57 M7iv 2807
164	C1.21	WWO	over-fired; distorted; near complete 78/33; 57 M7iv 2807
165	C1.11	WWO	complete; over-fired; distorted 78/57 M7iv 2807
166	C1.13	WWR	78/57 M7iv 2807
167	C3.11	WWR	smoothed basal zone 78/57 M7iv 2807
168	C3.21	WWR	smoothed basal zone 78/57 M7iv 2807
169	C4.26	WWR	slightly distorted 78/57 M7iv 2807

(Fig 5.36)

170	B4.13	WWR	trimmed base; ?crack in base 78/57 M7iv 2807
171	B4.14	WWR	slightly mis-shapen; variable hardness; trimmed 78/57 M7iv 2807
172	B4.12	WWR	darkened surface; sherds have variable fabric colours 78/57 M7iv 2807
173	B11.11	WWO	mis-shapen; soft fabric; smoothed basal 78/57 M7iv 2807
174	B14.22	WWR	deeply cut grooves 78/57 M7iv 2807
175	B14.27	WWR	78/57 M7iv 2807
176	P1.11	WWR	fairly soft fabric 78/57 M7iv 2807
177	P3.11	WWR	fairly soft fabric 78/57 M7iv 2807
178	P5.13	WWO	fairly soft; smoothed basal zone 78/57 M7iv 2807
179	P5.11	WWR	sherds have variable fabric colours; smoothed base 78/57 M7iv 2807
180	P5.12	WWR	over-fired; ?mis-shapen; differing fabric colours between joins 78/57 M7iv 2807
181	P5.31	WWR?	over-fired; distorted; oxidized exterior/reduced interior 78/57 M7iv 2807
182	P5.41	WWO?	over-fired; distorted; half oxidized/reduced 78/11; 57 M7iv 2807
183	TZ2.12	WWO	soft discoloured 78/57 M7iv 2807
184	F6.12	OXID	light brown fine fabric; burnished vertical on neck and horizontally on body 78/11; 57 M7iv 2807
185	BK10.11	CREAM	white to light grey fine fabric; finely burnished externally and inside rim 78/11 M7iv 2807
186	–	GREY	body sherd from a copy of a glass pillar-moulded bowl; dense sandy fabric; burnish exterior 78/33 M7iv 2807

(Fig 5.37)

187	F2.62	CREAM	hard fine cream fabric; scatter ill-sorted quartz 92/61 M7v 255
188	F4.21	CREAM	cream hard fine fabric 34/20 M7v
189	–	CREAM	cream hard dense fabric 14/37 M7iv
190	F3.44	OX	light red-brown fabric; sparse to common ill-sorted subround quartz; traces lighter slip? 87/114 M6!
191	JH2.11	CREAM	hard fine laminar pinkish fabric; few visible inclusions except red specks 92/65; 77 M7iv 504; 381
192	–	GREY	grey/black fairly fine fabric sparse quartz up to 4mm; vertical incised lines cut by horizontal grooves; burnished and trimmed above and below decoration 77/8 M7iv 2595–7
193	–	BLSF	grey/black fine fabric some mica; combed vertical lines; polished above decoration 50/52; 83 M7iv 2511; 2531
194	JN1.21	CREAM	Pinkish fabric; darker cream exterior surface; smoothed exteror; scatter quartz and red inclusions; near local fabric 84/216; 244 M7iv
195	JM6.12	GREY	dark grey dense fabric sparse quartz 78/5 M7v
196	JM6.11	GREY?	similar fabric to 196 light brown surfaces 50/52 M7iv 2511

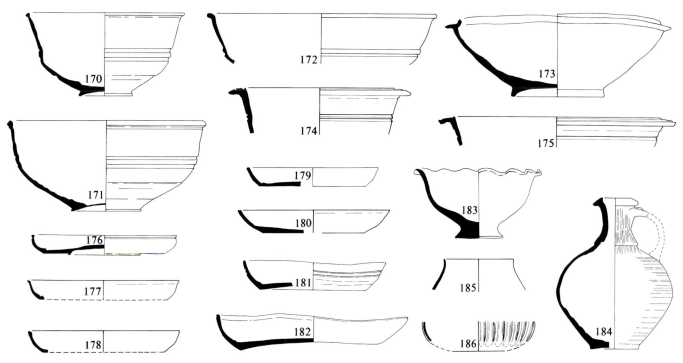

Fig 5.36 Pottery: nos 170–186; scale 1:4

197	JW3.11	GREY	light grey granular open textured fabric; burnished shoulder and inside rim; decorated burnished diagonal lines 78/16 M7iv 2812
198	JM2.24	GREY	burnished shoulder and interior rim; zone stabbed decoration 84/292 M7iv
199	JM2.31	SVR	vesicular with nodular rustication 91/210 M5! 1015
200	–	GREY	dark grey very gritty fabric; burnished rim and lines below 67/17 M7iv
201	JLS2.11	SVR	hand-made 90/232 M7i
202	–	OX	light grey hard coarse textured fabric abundant quartz; brown exterior surface; shoulder burnished; otherwise smoothed externally; fracture at neck smoothed to form a new rim; probably partly hand-made 72/19; 67 M4b 2868; 2908
203	–	GREY	light grey fabric with darker surfaces; sparse quartz; incised lines; ?jar 78/5 M7v
204	–	GREY	light grey fabric with abundant quartz; combed vertical lines between grooves; ?jar 78/5 M7v
205	–	GREY	grey laminar fabric; sparse ill-sorted quartz; not certainly WW 34/20 M7v
206	JC2.11	NAT	grey/black coarse textured fabric with vesicular surfaces; white calcareous inclusions; rilled exterior; soot encrusted 50/52 M7iv 2511
207	JC1.11	NAT	fine textured light grey fabric; light red-brown cortex; grey-brown vesicular surfaces; some mica; burnished externally; not certainly hand-made 91/193 M7iv
208	BK6.31	CREAM	hard fine cream with slight grey core; scatter ill-sorted sub-angular quartz; pimply surface; rouletted lines 98/141; 164; 183; 222 1.3; 1.1; 1.2 1097
209	BK10.14	GREY	light grey dense fabric with common small quartz; dark grey surfaces; exterior surface and inside rim smoothed 73/45 M5 2662
210	BK1	GBWW	cream; exterior cream to light brown/grey; hard fine fabric very sparse quartz; lower zone finely rouletted; upper decorated with deeply incised lines 70/16; 18; 72/16; 21; 25; 67 M7v; M7iv; M4b 2713; 2865; 2870; 2873; 2908
211	–	SV?	red-brown fabric grey core; hard fine texture with few visible iron-ore grits; exterior burnished; zone decorated faintly incised zig-zag 9/31 M7iv
212	–	SV?	red-brown fabric grey core; hard fine fabric with few visible inclusions quartz and iron-ore; highly burnished exterior; cordon unburnished and notched with light vertical lines 30/44 M4b! 2023
213	–	GREY	dark grey fabric with grey/black surfaces; fine hard with common quartz; decorated

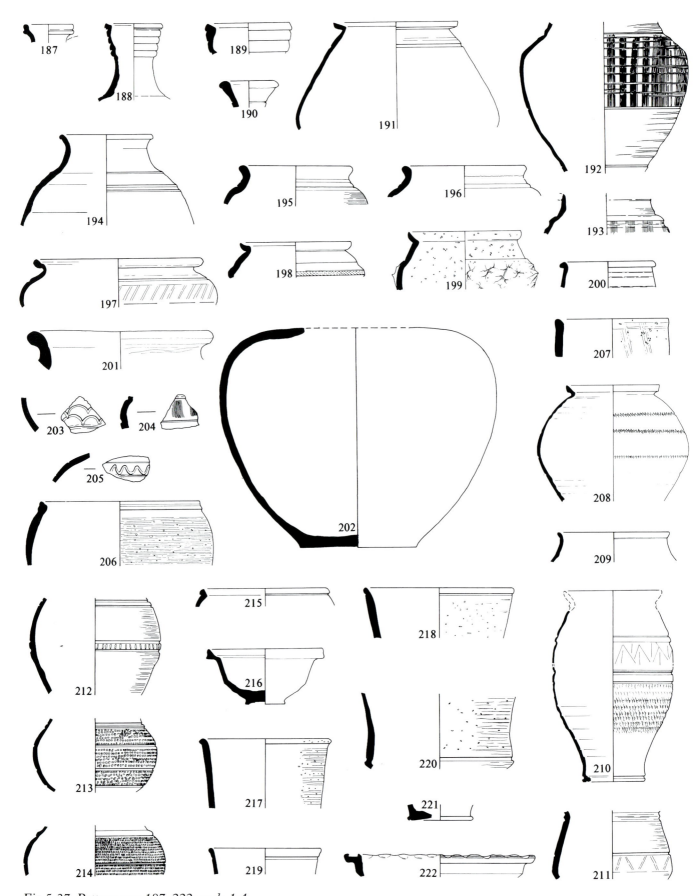

Fig 5.37 Pottery: nos 187–222; scale 1:4

214	–	GREY	punched square impressions in zones demarcated by grooves; burnished above and below decoration 81/11; 15; 51 2.1; M7v; 3.2
			dark grey fabric with dark grey/brown surfaces; fine hard with common quartz; rouletting dissimilar to no 213; finely burnished externally 2/59 M7v 2130/31
215	JM3.11	GREY	84/296 M6 356
216	C2.11	GREY	light grey fabric; grey/black surfaces; very fine hard fabric with very sparse inclusions ?iron-ore; exterior surface burnished extending over rim; interior occasional burnished lines 77/9 M5 2598
217	TK2.11	SV	vesicular grey-cored fabric; burnished exterior 78/5 M7v
218	TK2.13	SV	vesicular grey-cored fabric; smoothed exterior 12/30 M7v
219	TK2.12	SV	vesicular grey-cored fabric 12/30 M7v
220	–	SVR	grey vesicular hand-made fabric; exterior irregularly burnished 9/31 M7iv
221	–	OX	light brown fabric/interior; exterior burnt dark brown-grey; hard gritty fabric smoothed exterior; slight groove underneath footring; possibly a tankard base 81/15 M7v
222	TZ6.11	CREAM	cream hard fairly dense fabric sparse quartz and red inclusions; smoothed exterior; both sides of rim thumbed inwards 78/15 M5 2811

(Fig 5.38)

223	C8.12	LYON	Greene type 1.1 4/33 2.2 2062
224	C8.13	LYON	Greene type 1.5 6/31 2.2
225	–	LYON	Greene type 2.4 12/42 M4b! 2228
226	C8.14	LYON	Greene type 3 78/9 M7iv! 2805
227	C8.16	LYON	Greene type 4.1 92/65; 77 M7iv 504; 381
228	–	LYON	Greene type 4.1 41/6; 70/22 M7v; M7iv 2716
229	C8.17	LYON	Greene type 5.1 12/27 2.2
230	–	LYON	Greene type 6 72/19 M4b 2868
231	C8.15	LYON	Greene type 6 +/+ 4.0
232	C8.11	CGCC	Greene type 1 98/172 1.1
233	–	LRCC	Greene type 4 5/38 M7v!
234	BK3.16	LYON	Greene type 20.5 78/12 M5 2808
235	BK3.11	LYON?	98/137; 154 1.3; 1.1
236	BK8.13	CGCC	Greene type 3 39/12 M7iv! 2301
237	BK9.12	CGCC	Greene type 21 63/10; 15 1.3 2287
238	BK3.12	CGGW	78/12 M5 2808

239	BK12.21	BLEG	83/530 2.3
240	BK3.18	MICA	dark grey fabric ?burnt 72/63; 78/+ M4b; 4 2905
241	P6.11	PRW3	84/377 M2 771
242	P6.13	PRW2	92/18; 61 2.1; M7v 255
243	P5.21	PRW	Hard cream fabric; sparse quartz and red inclusions; slipped interior and just over rim; burnt G/30 4
244	P5.22	PRW	dark grey fabric; red-brown cortex/surfaces; interior/exterior coated dark red; open textured fabric with sparse quartz and more common iron-ore; coating thicker in interior 85/29; 92/20; 98/87 2.3; 2.1 154
245	I.2.18	PRW3	84/404 M6
246	P2.11	TN	91/210 M5! 1015
247	–	TN?	98/48 3.3 678
248	ML1.11	CGCC?	7/38; 77/8 1.3; M7iv 2280; 2595
249	ML1.13	CGCC?	70/17 2.2 2712
250	M1.12	MORV	7/36; 14/37 M4b!; M7iv 2278
251	M1.14	MORV	39/13 1.3 2299
252	M1.11	MORV	35/61 1.3 2299
253	M2.12	MORT2	Rhineland? red-brown fabric; surfaces partially discoloured by burning to drab brown; fine hard fabric with few quartz and red inclusions; no visible trituration; smoothly finished and exterior furrowed 42/14; 52/24 M7v; M7iv 2247; 2401
254	M7.13	MOVR	14/31; 37; 35/27 M7v; M7iv; M3! 2343/4
255	M7.12	MOCR	14/31; 37 M7v; M7iv
256	M11.21	MOCRA	cream fabric coated with yellow-brown slip; sparse quartz; some iron-ore; trituration clay particles some still covered by slip and extending onto rim; basal zone knife-trimmed 39/28; 84/215; 92/20 M4b!; M7iv; 2.1 2292; 154

(Fig 5.39)

257	–	DR20	84/244 M7iv
258	–	DR20	84/244 M7iv
259	–	RHOD	Peacock fabric 1 98/212 1.2 1091
260	–	RHOD	missing 70/16; 73/16 M7v; M7iv 2656
261	–	EM24?	Dr 2–4 E. Medit or Italy 98/143 1.2
262	–	PE47	Gauloise 4 84/423 M5
263	–	DR28	perhaps Spanish 91/193 M7iv
264	–	C189	KH 117 form 92/65 M7iv 504
265	–	C189	handle KH 117 form 98/124 1.2
266	–	C189	92/77 M7iv 381
267	–	C189	handle C189 97/182 1.3
268	–	F148	Fishbourne 148.2 variant type 84/109 M7iv
269	–	F148	Fishbourne 148.2 88/- 4.0

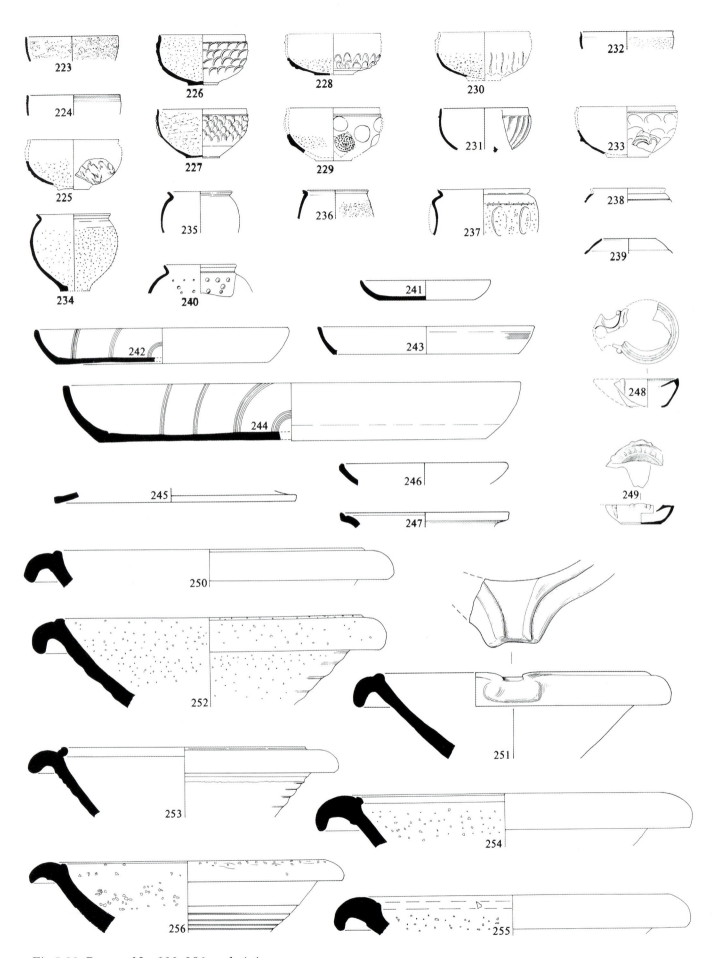

Fig 5.38 Pottery: Nos 223–256; scale 1:4

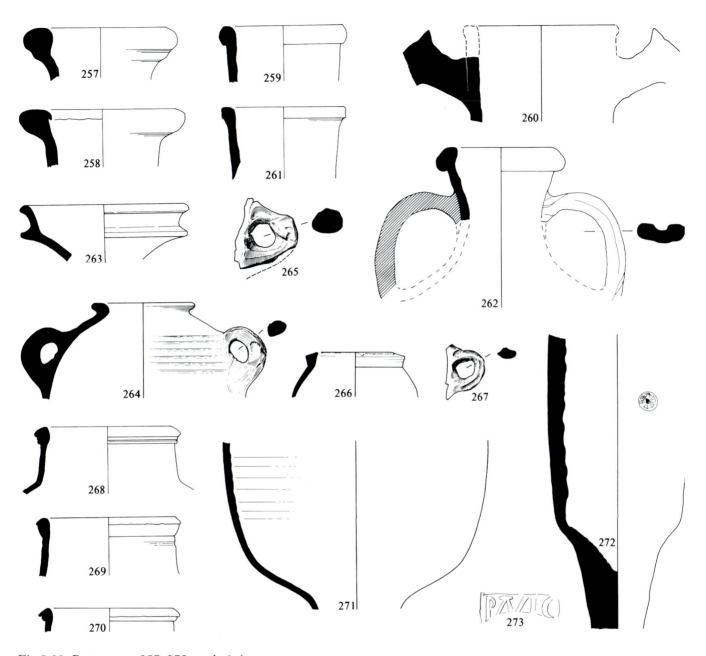

Fig 5.39 Pottery: nos 257–273; scale 1:4

270	–	F148	Fishbourne 148.2 84/122 2.1
271	–	F148?	sandy red-brown with partial salt treated exterior; possibly Fishbourne 148.2 35/61 1.3 2299
272	–	AMPH	unknown source; red-brown fabric light pink-cream surfaces

externally; fine textured sparse white inclusions; hole pierced through wall 51/21 1.3 2990/3009

| 273 | – | DR20 | stamped 84/263 M7iv |

6 Lamps, tile and glass

Catalogue of lamps
by D M Bailey

All are mould-made unless otherwise stated. Although the *Firmalampen* 16 and 17 may be of post-military manufacture, of all the lamps recovered from the excavations of the baths and *macellum*, only one appears to be of certain second-century date, reported on elsewhere (Ellis 2000, 245). Typology follows Loeschcke (1919).

1   Discus and shoulder sherd of a volute-lamp (Loeschcke type IA, shoulder-form IIb). The discus scene is undetermined. Made in Gaul. Mid-first century AD. *92/3* Period 2.3

2   Body and shoulder sherd of a volute-lamp (Loeschcke type IA or IB, shoulder-form IIa, III, or IV). Made in Italy. Mid-first century AD. *91/93* Period 2.3

3   Body and shoulder sherd of a volute-lamp (Loeschcke type IA or IB, shoulder-form IIa, IIIa, or IV). Made in Italy. Mid-first century AD. *92/30* Period 2?

4   Nozzle, shoulder and discus fragment of a volute-lamp (Loeschcke type IB, shoulder-form IIIa). Discus scene: Victoria standing on a globe (figure type as Loeschcke 389). Made in Gaul. Middle years of the first century AD. *98/196* Phase M7iv

5   Rim and volute sherd (Loeschcke type I or IV), made in Italy. First century AD. *6/47* Phase M4b

6   Body and base sherd of a volute-lamp (Loeschcke type I or IV), made in Gaul. First century AD. *37/-* Unstrat

7   Base sherd of a volute-lamp (Loeschcke type I or IV), made in Italy. First century AD. *48/49* Period 3.1

8   Body sherd of a volute-lamp (Loeschcke type I or IV), made in Italy. First century AD. *?84/137* Period 2.1

9   Discus sherd of a volute-lamp (Loeschcke type I or IV). The discus-scene is not determined. Probably made in Gaul. First century AD. *84/258* Phase M7iv

10   Body sherd of a volute-lamp (Loeschcke type I or IV), made in Gaul or Italy. First century AD. *84/292* Phase M7iv

11   Shoulder sherd of a volute-lamp (Loeschcke type I or IV, shoulder-form IVa). Made in Italy. First century. *98/77* Period 3.2

12   Body and base sherd of a volute-lamp (Loeschcke type I or IV), made in Italy or Gaul. First century AD. *98/184* Period 2.1

13   Under-nozzle sherd of a volute-lamp (Loeschcke type I or IV), made in Gaul. First century AD. *98/191* Period 1.1

14   Shoulder sherd of a volute-lamp (Loeschcke type IV, shoulder-form VIa), made in Italy. Second half of the first century AD. *80/64* Period 3.3

15   Shoulder and discus sherd of a lamp (Loeschcke type VIII or V, shoulder-form VIIIb with impressed ovules; compare with Goethert-Polaschek 1985, 712, and Loeschcke 693). Made in Gaul. Second half of the first century. *92/18* Period 2.1

16   Nozzle sherd of a lamp (Loeschcke type IX or X), made in Italy or Gaul. Flavian/Trajanic. *59/8* Period 3.2

17   Sherd of a lamp (Loeschcke type IX or X, shoulder-form IX), made in north Italy. Flavian/Trajanic. *83/-* Unstrat

18   Wheel-made lamp, with applied nozzle. Made in Britain. *80/189* Period 3?

Military tile production
by Graham Webster

At Wroxeter only one fragment of tile recovered from the military deposits was clearly identified as part of a roof tile. Military tile production was well established at this period, although mainly for bath-house construction, where tiles were an essential element, as demonstrated at Exeter (Bidwell 1979, 148). Tiles were made for the heated rooms and also for the roof, and included *ante-fixa*. This shows that the full range of tile products was being produced by the army or by civilian contractors in the mid-first century AD. Nevertheless, it is surprising that at Wroxeter and on the other fortresses in Britain of this period, excavations have revealed a dearth of tiles. Inchtuthil produced a few fragments, but although a sample was examined petrologically, there is no indication in the report of the type of tile represented (Pitts and St Joseph 1985, 339). Longthorpe produced no tile fragments, but a fragment of mortar-flashing was thought to have come from a tiled roof (Frere and St Joseph 1974, 19). It has been generally assumed that the absence of roof tiles indicated the use of thatch or shingles for roofing. But a factor to be considered is that all these buildings were carefully demolished for the reuse of building materials elsewhere. Tiles would, therefore, have been removed and only the broken fragments remain.

Vessel glass associated with the military occupation
By H E M Cool and Jennifer Price

The 1955–85 excavations at Wroxeter produced, in total, 2707 fragments of glass of which only 12.5% were found in military levels. It is likely, however, that many of the fragments found in later contexts were connected with the early occupation because they are mid-first century or Flavian forms. For example, only 50% of pillar-moulded bowl (Isings 1957, form 3, hereafter Isings) fragments were found in military contexts, although the presence of this first-century form at Wroxeter must largely be connected with the military occupation. This report, therefore, has reviewed all of the glass recovered during the excavations likely to have been in use during the Neronian and early Flavian period, regardless of its context. The opportunity has also been taken to include hitherto unpublished material of similar date found during Kenyon's excavations in 1952–53, as only a small part of the assemblage from those excavations was submitted to Dr Harden for comment and publication (Harden 1976).

There were many changes in the types of glass vessels in use in the first century AD. Many of the forms in use when the military occupation at Wroxeter began are easy to identify because they are rare by the early Flavian period. The difficulties of identification are greater for the vessels which might have belonged to the later stages of the military occupation. A number of types that became very common during the Flavian period continued in use into the second century and the fragments from these could have belonged either to the military or the later civilian occupations. Given the amount of first-century material in later contexts the stratigraphical position of the fragments from vessels like this is not necessarily indicative of their period of use.

The first two sections of this report deal with all of the undoubtedly first-century AD glass that was found during the excavations. The first deals with the forms in use in the middle third of the first century which become rare after the early Flavian period. The second section deals with those that were commonest during the Flavian period. The third section discusses those fragments of forms continuing in use into the second century or later which were found in the military levels. These will be dealt with more briefly, as most of the examples of such forms were found in later contexts and for the reason given above it was thought more appropriate to include the full discussion of the types in the report on the glass from the later periods (Cool 2000).

Glass of the mid-first century AD

A minimum of 53 vessels represented by 134 fragments may be securely identified as belonging to the early years of the military occupation. They are all forms that were common during the middle third of the first century AD but which become much rarer on sites first occupied after the early Flavian period. These include polychrome and strongly-coloured pillar-moulded bowls and other cast vessels, mould-blown and free-blown drinking vessels, and containers such as unguent bottles and, possibly, amphorisks. There are also various other vessels whose form cannot be identified but

which can be dated to this period because of the type of glass used.

The composition of the pillar-moulded bowl (Isings form 3) assemblage from these excavations is typical of that on sites where occupation started in the Neronian period or earlier. Polychrome and strongly-coloured pillar-moulded bowls went out of production during the middle part of the first century AD, whereas the production of blue/green ones continued into the Flavian period (Berger 1960, 10, 19; Price 1985a, 304–5; Cool and Price 1995, 15). In Britain polychrome and strongly-coloured pillar-moulded bowls are relatively common only on sites occupied during the Claudian and/or early Neronian periods. On sites which were not occupied until the Flavian period they become much rarer. During the Wroxeter excavations under discussion 19 fragments from a minimum of 11 polychrome and strongly-coloured bowls were found which may be securely placed in the group of glass associated with the early years of the occupation (cat nos 1–15; Figs 6.1 and 6.2). In addition there were also 39 fragments from a minimum of 16 blue/green bowls (nos 16–41; Fig 6.2). Thus 33% of all pillar-moulded bowl fragments in the assemblage are polychrome or strongly coloured. This is the same as the proportion in the assemblage at Sheepen, Colchester associated with the pre-Boudiccan occupation (Harden 1947; Charlesworth 1985), and in stark contrast to that for Chester where the foundation of the legionary fortress does not appear to have taken place until the late 70s AD (Carrington 1986, 18). There only 5% of the pillar-moulded bowl fragments were polychrome or strongly coloured (Cool and Price 1989, fig 19).

The minimum of five polychrome bowls found here include two yellow/brown bowls with opaque white spirals and marbling (nos 1 and 2; Fig 6.1), one of which (no 1) also has deep blue marbling, one yellow/brown bowl with opaque yellow marbling (no 3; Fig 6.1), at least one deep blue bowl with opaque white and some opaque yellow marbling (nos 4–6) and one purple bowl with opaque white specks (no 7). Brown and deep blue pillar-moulded bowls with opaque white marbling are the commonest two-coloured combinations found in Roman Britain (Cool and Price 1995, 17). The inclusion of some opaque yellow in the deep blue and white bowls, as on no 4, is also often found though it is difficult to judge how common the blue, white, and yellow ones were compared with the blue and white ones. This is because the yellow element in the former generally only occurs as isolated patches and broken fragments need not retain any indication that they came from a three-coloured rather than a two-coloured bowl. The addition of blue to the yellow/brown and white bowl (no 1) is much rarer. A similar colour combination occurred on a bowl from Sheepen, Colchester in a Claudio-Neronian context (Harden 1947, 294, no 8, pl lxxxvii), and at *Vindonissa* a yellow/brown bowl with blue, white, and yellow marbling and another of amber glass with white and blue marbling have also been recorded (Berger 1960, 15, no 16 Taf 1;

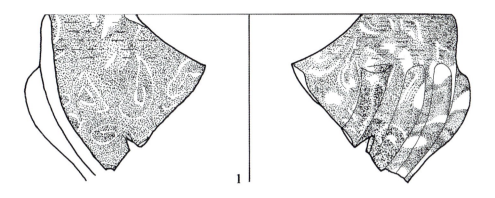

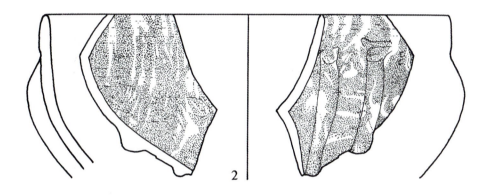

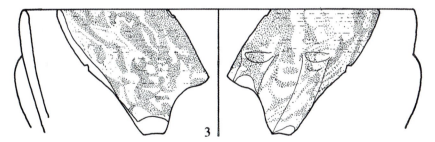

Fig 6.1 Glass vessels: nos 1–3; scale 1:1

17). Purple and white bowls such as no 7 are also not uncommon on Romano-British sites (Price and Cool 1985, 42, 45, no 1, fig 17; Cool and Price 1995, no 4). The combination of yellow/brown with opaque yellow marbling (no 3) is much rarer and in Britain only appears to have been recorded from Traprain Law (Curle 1931–2, 291).

The eight fragments from a minimum of six strongly-coloured bowls also show the same combination of very common colours with much rarer ones. Deep blue

bowls (nos 9 and 10) and yellow/brown ones (nos 11–13; Fig 6.2) are the commonest types of mono-chrome strongly-coloured bowls from Roman Britain (Cool and Price 1995, 18) and both colours have been found during previous excavations at Wroxeter (Rowleys House Museum RHF 54). Number 11 is an example of a small sub-set of bowls which are all made in very dark brown glass and which are all very poorly finished on the exterior. Other examples are known from Kingsholm (Price and Cool 1985, no 3, fig 19),

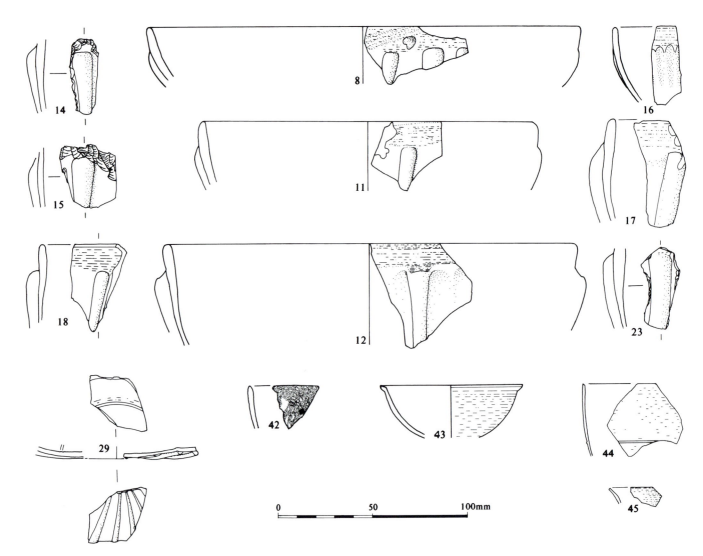

Fig 6.2 Glass vessels: nos 8–45; scale 1:2

Sea Mills, Avon (Cool and Price 1987, 95, 97 no 1, fig 1), Castle Street, Carlisle (Cool and Price 1991, 169 no 622, fig. 152), Colchester (Cool and Price 1995, 18, no 171), and Usk (Price 1995a, 146 no 6, fig 42) and it is possible that these may be the products of one particular glass house. Mid-blue pillar-moulded bowls like no 8 (Fig 6.2) are very rare on British sites and the only other examples appear to be the ones from Balkerne Lane, Colchester (Cool and Price 1995, 18, no 20) and Usk (Price 1995a, 146, 148 no 12, fig 42). Yellow/green bowls such as nos 14 and 15 (Fig 6.2) are also very rare but a few more have been recorded from Britain. Skeleton Green, Hertfordshire (Charlesworth 1981, 119, no 4, fig 64) and Sheepen, Colchester (Charlesworth 1985, mf 3.F7, no 47) have both produced one fragment and there are also three fragments from other sites in Colchester (Cool and Price 1995, 18, nos 22–4). A body fragment of this colour was also recovered during excavations in 1937 at Wroxeter (Rowleys House Museum).

Many blue/green pillar-moulded bowls cannot be closely dated within the first half of the first century AD but some of the examples from Wroxeter have fea-

tures that do allow this. Number 16 (Fig 6.2), for example, comes from a shallow bowl with ribs only on the sides (Isings form 3c) which is a variant generally found in early to mid first-century contexts (Cool and Price 1995, 18, no 25). In Britain this is a very rare form and is only known from Sheepen (Harden 1947, 302, nos 61–61ac, pl lxxxviii), Gilberd Street School, Colchester (Cool and Price 1995, 18, no 25) and Gracechurch Street, London (London Museum). Number 17 (Fig 6.2), by contrast, probably belongs to the later production of blue/green bowls. It comes from a deep bowl with very prominent ribs, a type which is characteristic of the Flavian period in the north-western provinces as can be seen in those from Nida-Heddernheim, a site not occupied until c AD 75–85 (Welker 1974, 23, nos 11–19, Tafn 1 and 2).

The general comments made about the dating of the polychrome and strongly-coloured pillar-moulded bowls, that is that they only commonly occur on site occupied in the Claudian and early Neronian periods, also apply to the polychrome and strong-coloured monochrome cast vessels. In this assemblage there are three monochrome and one polychrome vessels.

Number 42 (Fig 6.2) is from a segmental millefiori bowl (Isings form 1) with the flowers formed by two rings of yellow specks arranged around a central red dot in an emerald green ground. Millefiori glass is never very common even on early sites in Britain, but this colour combination is the one most frequently found. Bowls very similar in shape, colour combination, and pattern to the one found at Wroxeter have been found at Sheepen (Harden 1947, 294, nos 4 and 4a; also body fragments – Charlesworth 1985, mf 3:F2, no 7) and Culver Street, Colchester, which was also from a pre-Boudiccan context (Cool and Price 1995, 28, with references to other body fragments possibly from similar bowls).

Emerald green glass is the commonest colour used for the monochrome cast vessels found in Britain and nos 43 and 44 (Fig 6.2) are made from it. Number 43 consists of a large fragment from a small hemispherical cup with a lip and (probably) a low foot-ring (Isings form 20) like the dark green ones from *Herculaneum* (Scatözza-Höricht 1986, 32 no 18, Taf xii) and Trier (Goethert-Polaschek 1977, 34, no 88, Taf 33). These were in use during the first half of the first century AD and are rare on Romano-British sites, though another emerald green one has been found at Sheepen (Harden 1947, 301, no 59, pl lxxxviii). The other emerald green cast vessel (no 44) was either a segmental or hemispherical bowl with a ground-out rib on the exterior, perhaps like the emerald green hemispherical bowl from a Neronian cremation burial at Sheepen (Charlesworth 1985, mf 1:A6, fig 15, no 6). This is also a rare form in Roman Britain.

The fourth cast vessel (no 45; Fig 6.2) is represented by a small green/blue (peacock) rim fragment. It may have come from a bowl like no 43, but is too small to identify with certainty. This colour is much less common than emerald green, and only a small number of peacock blue cast vessels have been recorded from Roman Britain (Price 1989a, 77). Where it has been possible to identify the vessel type these fragments have either been from hemispherical bowls like no 44, or from bowls with a wide rim and overhang such as no 49 (Fig 6.4) (see below), and not from vessels with a small lip such as no 45.

Nos 59 and 60 (Fig 6.4), from two mould-blown hemispherical ribbed bowls (Cool and Price 1995, 51), may also belong to this early group of glass. These vessels occur in the Tiberian/early Claudian period, as is shown by examples from contexts of that date at *Vindonissa* (Berger 1960, 55) and Fréjus (Price 1988, 30, figs 24–6), and their continuation into the Flavian period is demonstrated by the presence of fragments on Flavian sites in northern Britain such as *Vindolanda* (Chesterholm; Price 1985b, 206, no 1) or Blackfriars St, Carlisle (Price 1990, 166, fig 159.6), as well as Castleford (Cool and Price 1998, 154, nos 38–40, 252), York (Cool 1998, 303, fig 2.4, and Binchester (unpublished).

Mould-blown hemispherical ribbed bowls are not uncommon on early Romano-British sites and all of them have a cracked-off and ground rim, an undeco-rated zone below the rim, a convex side with vertical ribs terminating above two close-set horizontal mouldings on the lower body, and a concave base with raised concentric mouldings. Two slightly different groups have been distinguished. One has an everted rim, a concave zone below the rim, and comparatively widely spaced ribbing which either terminates a little way above the horizontal mouldings or extends to the top of them. The other has a vertical rim and zone below the rim, and closely set ribs. One of the Wroxeter pieces (no 59, Fig 6.4), has short ribs and belongs to the first group. Other examples are known from London (Wheeler 1930, 122, fig 42, 5), Colchester (Harden 1947, 300, pls 86–7, 48; Cool and Price 1995, 53), and Blackfriars St, Carlisle (Price 1990, 166, fig 159.6), while the pieces from pit 7, *Insula XIV, Verulamium* (Charlesworth 1972, 196, fig 74, 2) and Hales Roman villa, Staffordshire (Goodyear 1974, 18, fig 6D) have longer ribs. The second group has a vertical rim and zone below the rim, and closely set ribs. Examples from the second group have not often been recognised; they are known from Hallaton, Leicestershire (Page and Keate 1907, 212 and line drawing) and Usk, Gwent (Taylor 1979, fig 1; Price 1995a, 150, 152–3 no 25, fig 43, pl xii) and the fragment from *Insula XXVII, Verulamium* (Charlesworth 1984, 150, 32, fig 61.18) may also belong to this group.

The straight-sided blue/green fragments with widely spaced vertical ribs, no 61 (Fig 6.4), probably also came from a bowl or cup, which is likely to have been a tall straight-sided or ovoid, rather than a hemispherical, vessel. A similar tall ribbed cup is known from Caerleon (unpublished), and others have sometimes been noted on sites in the western provinces (Price 1991, 67), as at *Aquileia* (Calvi 1968, 101–2, 105, no 250, pl 16, 2), Baden (*Aquae Helveticae*) (Funfschilling 1985, 118, pl 12, 127), and Spiesergasse, Köln (Fremersdorf 1958, 32, pl 34), though they are much rarer than hemispherical bowls. Two dated example are known, the one from Köln came from a cremation burial containing a coin of Nero, and the example from Caerleon was found in a Flavian rubbish-dump below the parade ground.

It is noteworthy that a fragment from another Claudio-Neronian mould blown vessel, a blue/green cylindrical cup with parts of two named gladiators ... *COLVMBVSCAlamus* ..., was found below the *Forum* pavement in earlier excavations at Wroxeter (Atkinson 1942, 195). Cylindrical mould-blown cups with scenes of chariot racing, gladiatorial combat or athletic contests are found in the western provinces in contexts dated to the third quarter of the first century AD, and in Britain and the Rhineland they are frequently associated with military sites (Price 1991, 67).

Hofheim cups (Isings form 12; Cool and Price 1995, 64) are the commonest type of free-blown drinking vessel found on Romano-British sites up to the late Neronian/early Flavian period. At least 13 are represented in this assemblage. One is light yellow/brown (no 103; Fig 6.5) and the rest (nos 164–78; Fig 6.6) are blue/green. These cups can either have small concave bases, such as no 178, or bases with high kicks, and it is probable that a blue/green base fragment with a high kick (no 219; Fig 6.7) also came from a cup like this. Another virtually complete blue/green Hofheim cup with high kicked base has been found at Wroxeter during rescue excavations (Site 1011, unpublished).

Cylindrical and conical beakers with cracked off rims and wheel-cut and abraded decoration similar to those of the Hofheim cups (Cool and Price 1995, 68) were also in use contemporaneously but they never occur in such large numbers. This is reflected in this assemblage, where there is only a minimum of four of these beakers, two in pale green glass (nos 122–4; Fig 6.5), and two blue/green ones (nos 179–81; Fig 6.6), compared with at least three Hofheim cups. A straight-sided yellow/green body fragment with wheel-cut and abraded decoration (no 119) might have come from one of these beakers but the identification is far from secure. These beakers may have concave bases, but a very distinctive form which is internally domed with a flat underside and thick, horizontally outsplayed rounded edge also occurs, see for example one from Sheepen (Harden 1947, 303 no 77, pl lxxxviii). None of the beakers found at Wroxeter retained their bases but the lower body fragment, no 181 (Fig 6.6), is broken at the edge of the base and as the glass seems to be expanding both outward and inward it is very likely that it came from a beaker with the thickened base and outsplayed base-ring.

In addition to these two very common forms of blown mid first-century drinking vessels, there are also two much rarer ones. Number 163 (Fig 6.6) is a blue/green cup with a horizontally out-turned, fire-founded rim, an applied true base-ring, and two elegantly curved handles. It is broken but virtually complete and it is exceptional to find such a well-preserved glass vessel on a habitation site. Unfortunately no details are known of the context in which it was found. The vessel may be dated to the middle of the first century because a similar blue/green cup was found with a female inhumation burial richly furnished with glass vessels of Claudian and early Neronian date at Saintes, Charente Inférieure (Grasilier 1873, 225, no 8, fig 22 bis). This is not a common form and no other examples have been identified from Roman Britain. It is interesting to note that, though superficially no 163 has an elegant appearance, in several respects it is not of very high quality. The glass is relatively bubbly and there are black impurities in the handle, while the applied true base ring is rather heavy and clumsy in appearance.

The yellow/green stepped rim fragment with a fire rounded edge (no 111; Fig 6.5) may also have come from a two-handled drinking cup as the rim formation is frequently used on the stemmed cups often called *cantheroi* (Isings form 38a; Cool and Price 1995, 56 and 100), such as the deep blue one decorated with opaque white rods from Bonnerstrasse, Köln (Harden *et al* 1987, 109, no 42). Again, this form was in use in

the Claudian and early Neronian period and is consequently found only in small quantities on sites in southern Britain. An earlier find from Wroxeter of a very similar rim fragment of deep blue glass with opaque white marvered trails may also have come from a cup of this type (Rowleys House Museum).

Far fewer containers than drinking vessels belonging to this early period can be identified. The most numerous variety is the tubular unguent bottle with a sheared rim (Isings form 8, Cool and Price 1995, 159). One example is mid-blue (no 100; Fig 6.5) and the blue/green fragments (nos 201–8; Fig 6.6) probably represent at least eight more. The form went out of use during the Flavian period and has been found in relatively large numbers on some mid-first century Romano-British sites. At Kingsholm, for example, at least 18 were found (Price and Cool 1985, 44); and in addition to the nine examples found during these excavations, three other blue/green ones have also been found during earlier excavations at Wroxeter (Harden 1976, 41 no 8; Rowleys House Museum F27).

The blue/green rim and handle fragment, no 200 (Fig 6.6), came from an amphorisk (Isings form 60; Cool and Price 1995, 148). Another may be represented by the yellow/green neck and handle fragments, no 114 (Fig 6.5), but here the identification is less secure because of the size of the fragment and it may have come from a jug. Amphorisks are being recognised increasingly often on mid-first century sites in the south of Britain (Price 1987a, 73), but they disappear by the time the sites associated with the Flavian advance to the north were occupied.

In addition to the fragments already discussed, a number of vessels that would have been in use during the mid-first century are represented by fragments. These include eleven fragments from a minimum of five blown polychrome vessels. All of the vessels are decorated with opaque white marvered blobs and trails, a style of decoration characteristic of the mid-first century and earlier which goes out of use by the early Flavian period (Berger 1960, 34). Two of the vessels found at Wroxeter are jugs or flasks. Number 80 (Fig 6.5) is a light yellow/brown folded and flattened rim and cylindrical neck fragment with opaque white marvered trails and no 81 (Fig 6.5) is a light green cylindrical neck fragment, similarly decorated. These could have come from, for example, flasks such as a wide-necked, yellow/green conical one with looped trails from Bond Street, London (Wheeler 1930, 121 no 64, fig 40), or from jugs such as those from Locarno, Italy (Carazzetti and Biaggio Simona 1988, 71, nos 62 and 64, tav ix). Jugs and flasks decorated with marvered trails have not often been recorded from Roman Britain but there is a deep blue with opaque white fragment from Sheepen (Harden 1947, 295, no 22), and two vessels are represented by a yellow with white fragment and a pale green with white conical body from Fishbourne (Harden and Price 1971, 350–1 nos 64 and 65, fig 140). At least one other vessel decorated with marvered trails is represented in this assemblage by the deep blue with white fragment, no 85 (Fig 6.5), but the vessel form cannot be identified.

At least one deep blue vessel decorated with opaque white marvered blobs is represented by nos 86–8, and a yellow/green and white vessel, no 82, may also have had blobbed rather than trailed decoration, though this is less certain. Marvered blob decoration has been recorded on a variety of vessel forms from Roman Britain including Hofheim cups (Eastgate Street, Gloucester, unpublished), a bath flask (Harden *et al* 1968, 58 no 70), and probably also globular ribbed jugs or jars (Price 1983, 168). Normally, however, vessels decorated in this way are only represented by small undiagnostic body fragments and the types of vessels cannot be identified. Fragments with marvered blobs and streaks are much commoner finds on Romano-British sites than those with marvered trails (see Cool and Price 1995, 58–60 for references), so it is interesting that marvered trails are better represented than marvered blobs in this assemblage.

Two opaque blown vessels are also represented by the pale blue fragments nos 89–90 and the white fragment, no 91. Blown opaque vessels are extremely rare on Romano-British sites. Opaque sky blue and jade green fragments were found at Sheepen (Harden 1947, 298–99, nos 43, 44, 46, 47), one of which came from a Period I pit and is thus one of the very small corpus of Roman vessel glass fragments from pre-conquest contexts in Britain. Opaque mid-blue fragments were found at the Cattlemarket, Chichester (Price and Cool 1989, 137 nos 9b–d), and opaque turquoise fragments came from the *vicus* at Caersws (Cool and Price 1989, 38, no 21). An opaque white Hofheim cup has also been identified from London (British Museum).

Nos 185 and 186 (Fig 6.6) may also be associated with this early phase of military activity. They are moulded face masks originally applied to the side of a jug at the bottom of the handle (Cool and Price 1995, 118). These face masks were used on a variety of jugs, but many of the examples found in Roman Britain are similar to no 185 in that the glass from the side of the jug and most of the handle has been grozed away in antiquity to leave the face mask as an object in its own right, as some form of keepsake. With such objects the possibility always exists that they could have been in use long after they were originally made as part of the jug. Thus although nos 185 and 186 were undoubtedly in existence when Wroxeter was first occupied, there can be no certainty as to when they arrived and were deposited on the site.

Masks representing a variety of different gods and mythological beings are found in mid first-century to Flavian contexts. On no 185 the face is rounded, has wavy, centrally parted hair with ringlets on either side of the face, and a band across the forehead. It may represent Bacchus, as on some examples it is possible to see faint vine leaves on either side of the head. This is the fifth example of this mask type to have been found

in Britain. Two other blue/green ones have been found at Mancetter (Scott 1981, 8) and Abergavenny (Price 1993, 217 no 13), and one from Warwick Lane, London (British Museum Acc no 75.2–22) is yellow/brown. All three have been grozed like no 185. Another from Leadenhall Street, London (Roach Smith 1842, 153) is deep blue and retains part of the curved body of the jug which is also deep blue and is decorated with opaque white marvered splashes. Only the examples from Abergavenny and Mancetter came from dated contexts. The former was found in a pre-Flavian context within a rampart, the latter was recovered from a pit with Neronian samian on a site probably occupied between *c* AD 45 and 55, but could already have been old by the time it was discarded, as an identical mask was found at *Vindonissa* in a Tiberian context (Berger 1960, 42, Taf 6.90). This mask pattern thus appears to be one of the earliest in use in Roman Britain. It has been suggested that *Legio XIV* was based at Mancetter before transferring to Wroxeter (Webster 1988, 123), so the discovery of this mask type at both sites may have some significance.

The second blue/green moulded face mask, no 186 only retains the edge of two mouldings, one of which has a pointed tip. Two other moulded face masks were found at Wroxeter during earlier excavations (Atkinson 1942, 233 nos 2 and 3). One of these (*ibid*, pl 62A, no 4) probably represents Bacchus and has a cluster of pointed leaves on either side of the head. Number 186 might have come from a similar mask type but insufficient is preserved for a secure identification to be made.

Flavian vessels

The forms discussed in this section all had their main period of use within the Flavian period and the material consists of 56 fragments from a minimum of 21 vessels. Several of these forms, however, continued to be used into the second century, so it is possible that some could have been associated with the early civilian occupation. Of these, 35% of the fragments were stratified in the military levels, but it is likely that a much greater percentage was in use during the later part of the military occupation.

In addition to the ribbed bowls already discussed there are a further 20 mould-blown fragments from a minimum of six or seven vessels. Three of the fragments, nos 62–4 (Fig 6.4), come from at least two deep blue, truncated conical beakers with almond-shaped bosses (Isings form 31). Number 62 comes from a beaker with large bosses surrounded by a raised rib and set in a diamond-shaped lattice. This belongs to Berger's variant c (Berger 1960, 52), which appears to be the commonest variant in Roman Britain. Fragments have been noted from pit 7, *Insula XIV* at *Verulamium*, a deposit dated to AD 60–75 (Charlesworth 1972, 196, no 2, fig 74.3), Ilchester (Price 1982, 227, no 2, fig 112), and Caersws (Cool and Price 1989, 38, no 15, fig 20), with unpublished examples from Gloucester

(Berkeley Street), Bath, and Chester (Goss Street and Abbey Green). Number 63 is a small fragment from another beaker which also had bosses outlined with a rib, but is too small for any part of the lattice to be preserved, if one existed. Number 64, by contrast, preserves part of the lattice, which is hexagonal and quite unusual, but the fragment is not large enough to show the precise formation of the bosses. Mould-blown, truncated conical beakers decorated with almond-shaped bosses and other decorative elements are not found before the late Neronian period and are primarily a Flavian form (Price 1991, 70). Many of the pieces with almond-shaped bosses were made in strongly coloured glass, such as the deep blue fragments, nos 62–4, and these are interesting because the use of strongly coloured glass was diminishing in the late Neronian and early Flavian period.

The colourless fragments nos 73–7 (Fig 6.4) also come from truncated conical beakers (Isings form 31); these are decorated with different combinations of meanders, shells, rings, ovals, peltas, and foliage. Beakers with these decorative motifs have been studied in recent years by Isings (1975; 1979, 101–3; 1980, 281–2, 291–4, 324, 328, 330–1), Berger (1981), and Harden (Harden *et al* 1987, no 79), among others. Although most early Imperial mould-blown glass was produced in brightly coloured or blue-green glass, these vessels are not usually found in strong colours, and several were made in very pale greenish or colourless glass.

The Flavian date of the truncated conical beakers decorated with these and similar raised motifs is well established. An example from *Vindonissa* with curved horizontal bosses came from a Flavian context (Berger 1981, 23), another with round-ended arcading and vertical spirals was found still packed in a shop in Herculaneum, suggesting that it was in current production in AD 79 (de Franciscis 1963, 138, fig 2.3; Scatözza Höricht 1986, 39–40, no 66, pls vii, xviii), small pieces with various design elements have been found at York (Price 1995b, 347, 355 no 13, fig 142) and Binchester (unpublished) in northern Britain, sites not occupied until the Flavian period, and a large number of these mould-blown fragments were among the glass deposited in pits in the *canabae legionis* at Nijmegen around the end of the first century AD (Isings 1980). In addition, the use of colourless glass for some of these vessels is a chronological indicator, as vessels made of colourless glass do not begin to appear in appreciable numbers until *c* AD 65 and 75 (Harden and Price 1971, 330–1). Colourless glass was increasingly preferred to strongly coloured or polychrome glass from then onwards, especially for drinking cups and other tablewares. It is very probable that the colourless and near-colourless mould-blown beakers with decoration in high relief (Price 1991, 70) were made in imitation of late Neronian or early Flavian colourless blown vessels with relief-cut designs.

Seven colourless fragments were found at Wroxeter, probably representing two or three beakers. The mouldings in very low relief on no 74 (Fig 6.4), which may be part of a shell-shaped or shield-shaped motif, and the well-defined ivy leaf on no 75 (Fig 6.4) have not been recorded on other examples, but the pattern of oval ring-mouldings inside an angular meander on nos 76–8 (Fig 6.4) are well-known. They occur on numerous vessels and fragments bearing meanders, shells, rings, ovals, peltas, and foliage and are found in Italy and the western provinces at sites such as Pompeii (Eisen 1927, pl 63, fig 130), Herculaneum (Scatozza Höricht 1986, pl 1), Rubi, near Barcelona (Gudiol Ricart 1936, fig 5), Oberwinterthur (Rütti 1988, 37, nos 666–7, pls 8 and 33), Augst, Nijmegen (Isings 1975; 1980), *Verulamium* (Charlesworth 1984, 150, 29, fig 61, 15), Usk (Price 1995a, 152–3, 155 no 27 fig 43), York (Price 1995b, 347, 355 no 13 fig 142) and Winchester (unpublished). In addition a pale yellow–green beaker with these motifs, reputedly from Syria, is now in the Römisch-Germanische Museum, Köln (Harden *et al* 1987, 157 no 79).

Number 73 (Fig 6.4) comes from an unusual vessel: it is the rim fragment of a beaker with the outside surface ground away in a zone below the rim to produce an upper body very similar to that found on facet-cut beakers (see below). Below this it retains part of a mould-blown pattern consisting of a rib surrounding the top of an oval indent. A few similar pieces have been noted. Tall colourless conical beakers with long vertical indents outlined by raised ridges are known in Spain, and a piece from an indented cup with much of the surface ground away found at Sidi Khrebish, Benghazi, and two fragments of similar tall indented cups with shallow facet cutting on the outside surfaces from London and *Verulamium* provide further links with the colourless facet-cut beakers produced in the late first century AD (Price 1981, 290–1). The rim and body of a beaker very similar to the Wroxeter piece was found at the Gilberd School site, Colchester (Cool and Price 1995, 54). This had a small cut facet in addition to the mould-blown depression. Number 73 did not come from a dated context, but the combination of colourless glass, mould-blown decoration and ground rim mouldings strongly suggests that it is of Flavian date.

Seven small yellow–green fragments, nos 65–70 (Fig 6.4), are decorated with spiral mouldings and parts of stems and leaves and probably come from one or more open convex-bodied vessels, perhaps bowls. The various vegetal motifs include a horizontal wreath of olive leaves and fruit. The small blue/green body fragment, no 71, may also have come from a vessel decorated in this manner. Little is known as yet about the precise form of these vessels, but similarly decorated fragments have been noted from Colchester (Cool and Price 1995, 50), Caersws (Cool and Price 1989, 38, no 18, fig 20), London, Gloucester, Chester, and Whitton Roman villa, South Glamorgan (all unpublished).

Facet-cut beakers (Isings form 21; Cool and Price 1995, 71) are the first common form of blown drinking vessels in Britain to be made from colourless glass.

They came into use by the late Neronian or very early Flavian period and are common on Flavian sites. They are likely to be well represented in this assemblage as they generally are in those of Flavian to early Trajanic military sites in Roman Britain (*ibid*, 73, nos 395–401) and the other north-western provinces (Welker 1974, 59). It is unlikely that the form continued to be used much into the second century. These beakers occur in both tall and squat varieties. Some have a ridge ground out above and below the faceted zone while others do not. The most recent study of the form (Oliver 1984) has used this feature to divide them into two groups, those without the ridge forming group 1 and those with one, group 2. At present the significance of these variations is not understood. The form is represented in this assemblage by 19 fragments from a minimum of 7 beakers (nos 140–55; Fig 6.5). Approximately one-third of the fragments was found in the military layers. There are two examples of Oliver group 1 beakers, nos 145 and 146, and at least two examples of Oliver group 2, nos 140–44. The other fragments, nos 147–55, must come from at least three different beakers but do not retain any indication concerning the presence or absence of ridges above and below the faceted area.

In this assemblage two tall beakers, one of Oliver group 1, no 145, and one of group 2, no 142, can be identified. A squat beaker is represented by the body fragment no 151. Several other body fragments, nos 152–5, are most likely to come from tall beakers because the facets are long and narrow. Previously in Roman Britain tall beakers of group 1 have been recorded at Cardean, Angus (Wilson 1969, 202, pl xix, no 1; Oliver 1984, 46, no 1) and Fishbourne (Harden and Price 1971, 342, no 41, fig 139). Probable tall group 2 beakers have been found at Caerleon (Nash-Williams 1929, 257, no 2, fig 18; Oliver 1984, 50, no 35), London (Oliver 1984, 50–1, nos 33, 37, and 91), and Strageath (Price 1989b, 197, no 2, fig 100). This apparent scarcity is probably the result of the frequent inability to determine whether a tall or a squat beaker is represented by small fragments. The facet-cutting on most of the fragments from Wroxeter is of good quality with carefully cut, deep facets worked on thick blanks and in two cases, nos 140 and 151, the upper row of the faceted zone formed of alternate full-size and half-size facets to provide a neat edge. In only one case, no 148, are the facets shallow and the blank thin.

The assemblage also contains fragments from a minimum of six colourless cups, beakers, and bowls, made in the same way as facet-cut beakers where the exterior of a blown blank has been completely ground to shape and polished. These vessels were in use from the late first century AD into the second century. None of the fragments from these excavations was found in military layers and only two were found securely stratified in civilian contexts (Cool 2000, nos 703 and 1002). Their presence at Wroxeter needs to be noted, however, because the possibility exists that some may be connected with the military occupation.

Numbers 128 (light green; Fig 6.5), 156 (yellowish tinged colourless; Fig 6.5), and 157 (colourless; Fig 6.5) come from three indented beakers (Cool and Price 1995, 69), and it is possible that the indented body fragments, nos 120 (yellow/green) and no 225 (blue/green; Fig 6.7) may have come from two others. These beakers are commonest in the Flavian period, although they came into use during the second quarter or middle of the first century AD and may not have disappeared until the early years of the second century. Of the fragments found here, nos 120 and 156 were found in the military or military destruction layers, and no 225 came from a main construction layer. The other fragments do not come from dated contexts.

Indented beakers have simple concave bases or domed ones with tubular base-rings. The width of the indents also varies. In most cases the beakers from Wroxeter are too fragmentary for the precise shape to be identified, but no 128 appears to have come from a beaker with a concave base and wide indents, similar to one found in a latrine deposit which contained Flavian pottery at Red House, Corbridge (Charlesworth 1959a, 166, fig 22.2). An almost complete yellow/green tinged colourless example with similar indents and base has also been recovered from Wroxeter during rescue excavations (Site 1011, Price and Cottam 1998, Fig 28b). This most unusual vessel is decorated with small, self-coloured unmarvered specks. By contrast, no 157 came from a beaker decorated with much narrower indents.

Number 158 (Fig 6.5) is a colourless rim fragment from an arcaded beaker (Isings form 33; Cool and Price 1995, 71). These were in use contemporaneously with indented beakers but are much rarer than that form in the north-western provinces. Three examples are now known from Wroxeter, no 158 and two colourless examples, one being virtually complete with diagonal arcading (Site 1011, Price and Cottam 1998, fig 27a–b). Elsewhere in Britain, however, they have been recorded at South Shields (Charlesworth 1979, 166, no 4, fig 84), Caerleon (Nash-Williams 1929, 257, no 4, fig 18), and Colchester (Cool and Price 1995, 71), with unpublished examples from Gloucester (Berkeley Street) and Elginhaugh.

Number 125 (Fig 6.5), from a military layer, is a light greenish/colourless, slightly pear-shaped beaker with a tubular base-ring and wheel-cut decoration. This is not a common Flavian form though its colour and base formation often occur on other Flavian beaker forms such as the indented and arcaded beakers already discussed. The wheel-cut decoration is very similar to that on the colourless beakers which were the commonest drinking vessels of the early and mid-second century (Price 1987b, 188, 202, nos 8–14, fig 2; Cool and Price, 1995, 79). These are most numerous and varied during the middle second century, but it is clear that cylindrical ones with tubular pushed-in base rings were in use at the end of the first century or early in the second; for example, one with a slightly S-shaped profile like no 125 was found in a pit of that date during earlier excavations at Wroxeter (Bushe-Fox 1916, 34, pl xxiii, fig 1). Number 125 thus appears to be a transitional form, combining the colour and some details of shape often seen on Flavian beakers with the shape and decoration of the late first and second century form. These comparisons and its context suggest that a mid- to late Flavian date for it would be appropriate.

In addition to the vessels already discussed, 29 other fragments probably come from first-century vessels, though for various reasons they cannot be as closely dated as the ones already discussed. These, too, are likely to be connected with the military occupation though less than a third were found in military contexts.

Two vessels are represented by the rim and upper body fragments, nos 92 (deep blue; Fig 6.5) and 184 (blue/green; Fig 6.6). Both of these are thin-walled, have out-turned, fire-rounded rims and straight sides and it seems probably that they came from either cylindrical or slightly conical beakers. Such vessels have not often been recognised, though a very similar blue/green rim fragment was found at the Gilberd Street School site, Colchester (Cool and Price 1995, 101, no 701). Rim edges finished by fire-rounding are uncommon on first century AD drinking vessels, but there can be no doubt that these are first-century vessels as no 184, came from a military context and no 92 came from one of the interface phases.

The assemblage also contains seven fragments of tubular pushed-in base-rings: no 112 (yellow/green), nos 129–31 (light green; Fig 6.5), and nos 159–61 (colourless; Fig 6.5), and there is evidence that the base was domed on nos 129 and, possibly, nos 159–61. This type of base is not uncommon on Flavian beaker forms such as the indented and arcaded beakers already discussed, though it also occurs on later forms such as the colourless, wheel-cut beakers noted in connection with no 125. None of these fragments was found in the military levels, but there is a strong possibility that at least the yellow/green and light green examples could have come from first-century vessels.

The identification of no 93 (Fig 6.5) has to be tentative because it is a small fragment. It is deep blue and has a fire-rounded, out-turned rim with the outer edge of a handle attached to it. The handle appears to be horizontal. If this is correct no 93 may have come from a horizontally-handled bowl resembling a saucepan, like the example from an inhumation at Losone, Arcegno (Switzerland), dated to AD 80–120 (Carazzetti and Biaggio Simona 1988, 107, no 127). This type of vessel is sometimes called a *trulla* (Isings form 75b). It was in use during the first century AD but is not a common form. Very few other blown examples have been recorded from Roman Britain, a dark blue one originally discussed as a *skyphos* was found at Fishbourne (Harden and Price 1971, 353, no 67, fig 140), and a dark green one is recorded from Usk (Price 1995a, 164, 167, nos 55 and 56, fig 44).

The deep blue rim fragments, no 94 (Fig 6.5), come from a vessel with a fire-rounded, horizontally out-bent rim. It is not possible to identify the form but the rim diameter suggests it was likely to have been some form of bowl or jar. The wear scratches around the inner edge of the upper face of the rim suggest that this vessel was used with some form of lid.

There are long, cylindrical neck fragments from three blue/green vessels with marked constrictions at the base of the neck, nos 211–13 (Fig 6.7), two of which, nos 211 and 213, were in military or military-destruction layers. Cylindrical necks with marked constrictions at their bases occurred on various type of jugs and flasks in the first and earlier second centuries. One of the fragments, no 211, came from a wide-bodied flask, as part of the upper body was also found, but the vessel type of the other two cannot be identified. Somewhat similar flasks to no 211 have been found at Colchester. The rim, neck, and upper body of a blue flask with a rolled-in rim edge was found at Sheepen (Charlesworth 1985, mf 3:F7, no 53, fig 81) and the upper part of a blue/green one with an out-turned rim with sheared edge like those found on tubular unguent bottles (see nos 100 and 201–8) was found at Maldon Road, Colchester (Cool and Price 1995, 149, no 1170). Neither of these was found in stratified contexts, but both may be of early or pre-Flavian date, as the former was found on a site where the overwhelming majority of material was pre-Boudiccan, and sheared rim edges like that on the latter are much more common during the mid-first century than at any other time.

A number of other fragments may also belong to first century AD jugs or flasks. They are not diagnostic enough for the precise form to be identified but they are made of strongly-coloured glass which was going out of use during the Flavian period. Into this category fall the handle fragments nos 97 (deep blue), 104 and 105 (dark yellow/brown) and possibly 113 (yellow/green), and the rim and/or neck fragments nos 106 (dark yellow/brown; Fig 6.5) and possibly 116–18 (yellow/green; Fig 6.5). Of these only nos 104 and 105 were found in military contexts. The concave base fragment, no 99 (Fig 6.5), may be dated to the first century on similar grounds because it is made of dark blue glass.

Blue/green fragments from jugs or bottles not precisely identified, but definitely or probably in use during the military period, include nos 192, 194 (Fig 6.6), 179 (Fig 6.6), 215, and 216 (Fig 6.7). Number 194 was found in a military context and is a lower handle attachment with a pinched projection from a jug. Whether similar handle fragments, nos 193, 195 and 196 (Fig 6.6), were also in use during the military period is open to question as both are from unstratified contexts. The two blue/green jug, flask, or bottle rims, nos 215 and 216, were not found in dated contexts but are likely to come from early or pre-Flavian vessels because they have the small, folded rims with triangular profile which are common at that period (see for example the pair of blue/green wheel-cut flasks from a Neronian cremation at Sheepen; Charlesworth 1985, mf 1:A8, b and c, fig 17.1 and 2), but much rarer later.

Strongly-coloured glass largely went out of use during the Flavian period so it is highly likely that the deep blue body fragments, no 101, the wine coloured ribbed body fragment, no 102, and the emerald green wheel-cut and undecorated fragments nos 109 (Fig 6.5) and 110, were also in use during the military occupation.

The later first- and second-century forms

The vessel forms in use from the first to second centuries are considered in this section even though some examples have been found in military contexts on the site. Various types of bowls, jars, jugs, and bottles fall into this category. These forms are represented by 710 fragments in the assemblage, but of these only 57 fragments were found in military contexts. With the exception of the cast colourless vessels (nos 47–58, Figs 6.3 and 6.4), only those fragments found in military contexts and the other fragments independently dated to the first century will be discussed here.

As already noted, high-quality, colourless vessels first begin to occur in large numbers in contexts dated to between *c* AD 65 and 75, and it is likely that cast colourless bowls with a wide rim and foot-ring (Charlesworth 1974, 75, no 4, fig 29; Cool and Price 1995, 36), represented here by nos 47–53, came into use about that period or soon after. A rim fragment from Fishbourne, for example, was found in an occupation level dating to the last quarter of the first century AD (Harden and Price 1971, 332, no 26, fig 138). Fragments are quite frequently found in early second century contexts and there are also two from Cramond that must belong at the earliest to the Antonine phase of occupation (Maxwell 1974, 198, nos 6 and 7, fig 16), which suggests that these bowls continued in use in the first half of the second century. The form was certainly present at Wroxeter during the military occupation, as is shown by the base fragment, no 52, and the body fragment, no 53, but some of the other pieces could equally have been in use during the early civilian period or even later in the first half of the second century.

The assemblage contains at least three bowls with a wide rim and overhang, nos 47–9 (Figs 6.3; 6.4). Number 49 comes from the undecorated variety which is not uncommon on Romano-British sites. This is a rather carelessly made example as the width of the rim varies. The other two bowls are much rarer variants which have been decorated by facet-cutting. A variety of patterns were used to decorate the bowls ranging from egg and dart cutting confined to the rim overhang, as on two bowls from Fishbourne (Harden and Price 1971, 334, 336, nos 33 and 34, fig 138), to facet-cutting on all the outside surfaces. The Wroxeter examples show two different styles.

Unlike nos 48 and 49, where only the rim was preserved so the depth of the bowl is unknown, sufficient of no 47 exists to show that it was a shallow bowl entirely covered by facet-cutting. It was found in the sandy make-up below the floors of the *macellum* which gives it a *terminus ante quem* of *c* AD 120. A preliminary note on this vessel was published by Charlesworth (1975, 404–6), at which time only three of the rim fragments had been found. The subsequent discovery of three further rim fragments has shown that no 47 is a bowl with horizontal handles. More fragments of the body and base have also been found which enables more of the facet-cutting on the underside of the base to be seen. The evidence for the handle consists of a small part of the side of the handle projecting out from the rim and two fragments from the interior of the handle. Both of the handle fragments have part of curved ground edges and the larger of the two also has part of a circular perforation. The handles are, therefore, likely to be very similar in shape to those on the oval plate from Zara, Croatia (Mariacher 1966, 22, no 14, fig 25), the circular plate from Adria, Italy (Fogolari and Scarfi 1970, 61), and one described as oval, which may in fact be from a circular plate, from Trier, Germany (Goethert Polaschek 1977, 25, no 55, Taf 30). These have wide curved handles with scalloped and spurred outer edges and a central, broad, arrow-shaped perforation with a circular one on either side. Another handle from a circular plate which has a similar overall plan but only one large central perforation and no facet cutting on the underside is known from Herculaneum (Scatozza Höricht 1986, 32, no 16, pls v2 and xxv).

The upper face and overhang of no 47 are decorated with egg and dart cutting and the exterior is covered by vertical oval facet-cutting, either as a single row on the underside of the rim, or on the handle, side, and base as multiple rows set in quincunx. There is also a row of horizontal oval facets along the lower edge of the facets on the side and a similar row around the edge of the facets on the base. In general the cutting is deep and regular although the horizontal facets are not always regularly spaced and sometimes overlap untidily. The facets on the underside of the rim and, intermittently, on the base ring are much shallower than the other facets and may have been formed accidentally when the deeper facets on the side and base were formed.

Similar oval and circular bowls with this particular pattern of all-over cutting are not uncommon and have been found widely scattered through the western Empire, with examples from Croatia, north-east Italy, Algeria, Spain, and Germany (Price 1987c, 75–7). In Britain other fragments have also been found in London (*ibid*, 77, fn 56), and from Culver Street, Colchester (Cool and Price 1995, 37). In overall appearance these vessels are all very similar to each other, though there are variations in the cutting. It is debatable whether they were all the products of one workshop or whether the blanks were made at more than one centre. It is also unclear whether the different features of the facet-cutting represent more than one workshop, and if so whether the blanks were produced and then traded for cutting (Price 1987c, 79). Perhaps these questions could be investigated by the detailed examination of all the known pieces. In a study of this kind, the apparently accidental facets on the underside of the rim and on the base ring of no 47 might become significant indications of workshop practice. In this respect it is interesting to

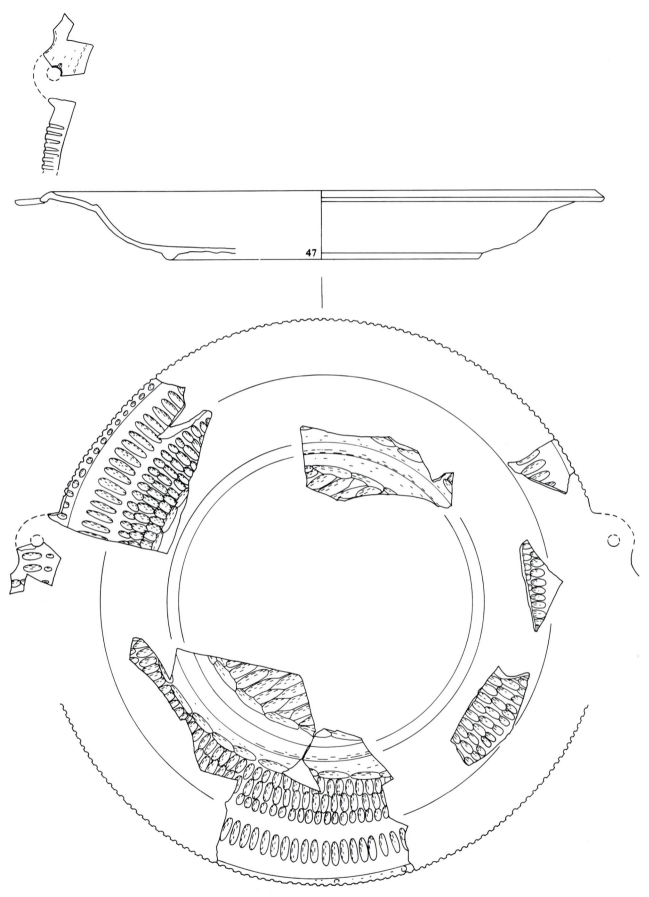

Fig 6.3 Glass vessels: no 47; scale 1:2

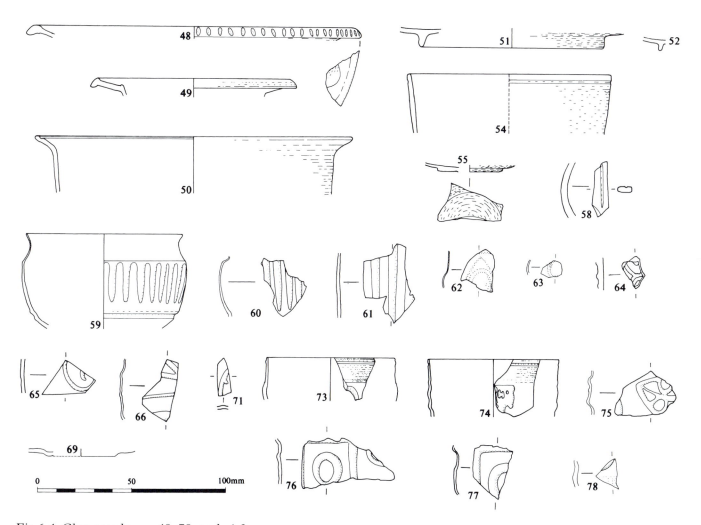

Fig 6.4 Glass vessels: nos 48–78; scale 1:2

note that a circular bowl with this pattern of cutting from the province of Palencia, Spain (Price 1987c, fig 4.1), also had a small number of facets on the base ring similar to those seen on no 47.

Bowls with this style of cutting have not often been found in closely dated contexts. Number 47 provides a *terminus ante quem* of c AD 120 for the style and the example from Culver Street, Colchester, came from a context dated to AD 75/125–150. One was found in a grave dated to the second century at Frixheim-Anstel, Krs Grevenbroich, Germany (Müller 1959, 407, Abb 39, no 9) and another came from a burial chamber at Tipasa, Algeria, which contained multiple inhumations apparently dating from the beginning of the second century to the Antonine period (Lancel 1967, 95, no 198, pl ix.3). Thus the bowls with this style of cutting were clearly in use during the early second century. At present there is no evidence for any earlier use in the first century, though the style of the cutting, which has many similarities with that on facet-cut beakers, strongly suggests that these bowls were in use during the later first century.

The other decorated bowl, no 48, has evenly spaced oval facets on the upper side of the overhang and part of a large, possibly circular, facet on the underside of the rim. This may have come from a bowl where the cut decoration was restricted to the rim and base. The best known and only intact example of this pattern is the circular bowl found in the Cave of the Letters, Israel, where it must have been deposited in the period AD 132–5 (Barag 1963, fig 40, pl 29). This has sharp egg and dart cutting on the overhang and a pattern of alternating large, circular facets and pairs of vertical cuts on the underside of the rim and in a ring on the underside of the base. The cutting of no 48 is clearly of lower quality than on the Cave of the Letters bowl and other more fragmentary pieces decorated in a similar manner, such as the circular, handled bowl from Crain, Yonne, France (Bonneau 1977, 128, no 78, fig 11), and fragments from York Minster (Price 1995b, 355, no 8, fig 142). Instead of the sharp egg and dart cutting on the overhang there is only a row of relatively shallow, widely-spaced oval facets. Other rim fragments with cutting on the overhang edge and circular facets are known from Britain. The piece from Richborough (Barag 1963, 107, fig 40a) has sharp egg and dart cutting, whereas a fragment from Castleford (Cool and Price 1998, 154, no 28, fig 51) has cutting very similar to no 48.

Bowls with wide overhanging rims, wide lower bodies, and base-rings like nos 47–9 were the commonest type of cast colourless bowls in use in Roman Britain during the later first and early second centuries, and examples with a narrow, everted rim without an over-hang, like no 50 were much rarer. Number 50 is, how-ever, the second example to have been found at Wroxeter. A complete example from earlier excava-tions was found in a context dated to 'probably not later than the middle of the second century' (Bushe-Fox 1914, 20, fig 12). Bowls of this shape were some-times decorated with facet-cutting (see for example the bowl with circular facets on the rim and a duck and foliage pattern on the base from a cremation bur-ial at Girton College, Cambridge, which also contained samian dated to between AD 135 and AD 180; Hollingworth and O'Reilly 1925, 32, pl xi; *Fitzwilliam* 46, no 86); a more common form of dec-oration consists of wheel-cut grooves on the upper face of the rim and parallel with the rim edge. Number 50 has one groove on the rim, as does one from Caerhun (Baillie Reynolds 1936, 228, no 4, fig 54), which was found in a context dated AD 80–110. Others from York (Harden 1962, 136, fig 88, HG 218), and Corbridge (Charlesworth 1959b, 40, fig 3.4) have two grooves. Plain bowls of this type have also been found at Chilgrove, West Sussex (Down 1979, 163, no 8, fig 57), and Castle Street, Carlisle (Cool and Price 1991, 169 no 625, fig. 152) and York Minster (Price 1995b, 355, no 10, fig 142) with an unpublished example from Catterick, North Yorkshire (Site 433). The dating evidence of the ear-lier Wroxeter find and the bowls from Caerhun and Girton suggests that the form was broadly contem-porary with the commoner cast colourless bowls with wide overhanging rims.

The fifth colourless cast bowl, no 54 (Fig 6.4), comes from a rarely-recorded form. The rim and side slopes in and the bowl may have been a wide conical one like the example from South Shields (Charlesworth 1979, 167, no 30, fig 48), although that is described as blown and wheel-polished, not cast. A similar cast colourless rim fragment has also been found at *Verulamium* in a context dated to AD 140–55 (Charlesworth 1984, 149, no 16, fig 61.10 – illustrated upside down). That has a groove below the rim on the interior instead of on the exterior as in the case of no 54. An example with a slightly everted rim came from Park Street, Towcester, Northamptonshire (Price 1980, 68, no 1, fig 17). On the general grounds of colour and manufacturing technique a date in the later first or ear-lier second century can be suggested for no 54.

The lower body and base fragments, no 55 (Fig 6.4), also come from a relatively uncommon form of cast colourless vessel. The body is convex-curved and the base flat with a raised disc centrally. A very similar lower body and base fragment was found in a period 2 con-struction deposit, *c* AD 75, at Fishbourne (Harden and Price 1971, 332, no 24, fig 137). Number 58 (Fig 6.4) is a fragment from a colourless curved handle with a small, vertical, wheel-cut on the exterior. Both of the outer edges of the handle are flat which suggests that it has come from a cast vessel which has been ground to

shape, though no polishing marks can be seen. If the fragment does come from a cast vessel this was probably from some form of cup and of first century AD date, and is residual in a bath's construction context. Examples of first-century colourless cast cups with handles include a pair of shallow cups with decoration in high relief from Pompeii (von Saldern 1985, 32, no 6, Abb 5; Ward-Perkins and Claridge 1977, no 116), one decorated with vertical wheel-cut grooves from a period 3 occupation context (AD 100–270) at Fishbourne (Harden and Price 1971, 336, no 32, fig 138) and a *skyphos* with grooved handles from a rubbish pit dated to AD 60–80 at Walbrook, London (Harden 1970, 75, pl x A; Price and Cottam 1998, fig 11).

The complete assemblage of glass from Wroxeter includes 11 fragments from a minimum of nine tubu-lar-rimmed bowls (Isings forms 44–5; Cool and Price 1995, 94). These are common finds on Romano-British sites and were in use between the mid-first and mid-second centuries. A rim fragment from a pale green bowl, no 132 (Fig 6.5), found in an interface layer, may have been connected with the military occu-pation. A ribbed, carinated, pale green body fragment, no 136 (Fig 6.5), from a military destruction layer may have come either from this type of bowl or from ribbed jug of the Ising forms 52/55 range discussed below. Number 108 (Fig 6.5) did not come from a military context but almost certainly was in use during the first century as it is made of emerald green glass which was going out of use during the Flavian period. The depth of the tubular rim on no 108 is relatively shallow and this may suggest that it came from a shallow rather than a deep bowl, perhaps like the emerald green example from Sheepen, Colchester (Charlesworth 1985, mf 3:F5, no 37, fig 80). The assemblage also includes two fragments from applied true base-rings (no 135, pale green, Fig 6.5; no 221, blue/green, Fig 6.7). These may perhaps have come from tubular-rimmed bowls as applied true base-rings are the com-monest base type on these vessels.

Other types in common mid-first to mid-second century use are globular and conical jugs (Isings forms 52 and 55; Cool and Price 1995, 120). In total 46 frag-ments have been identified as coming from a minimum of 12 jugs. Relatively few fragments, however, were found in the military levels: nos 98, 134 (Fig 6.5) and 187–90 (Fig 6.6). The deep blue handle fragment, no 96 (Fig 6.5), is also likely to have been in use during the military occupation as this and other strong colours were going out of use during the Flavian period.

The fragments from the military levels include one light green handle and body fragment from a globular jug with a pinched extension trail on the lower handle attach-ment, no 134, and one deep blue concave base fragment, no 98, which might be from a conical jug of the same shape as one found in a late Flavian inhumation at Grange Road, Winchester (Harden 1967, 238, no 17, fig 7). The other fragments are less diagnostic. The dark blue fragment, no 96, and the blue/green fragments,

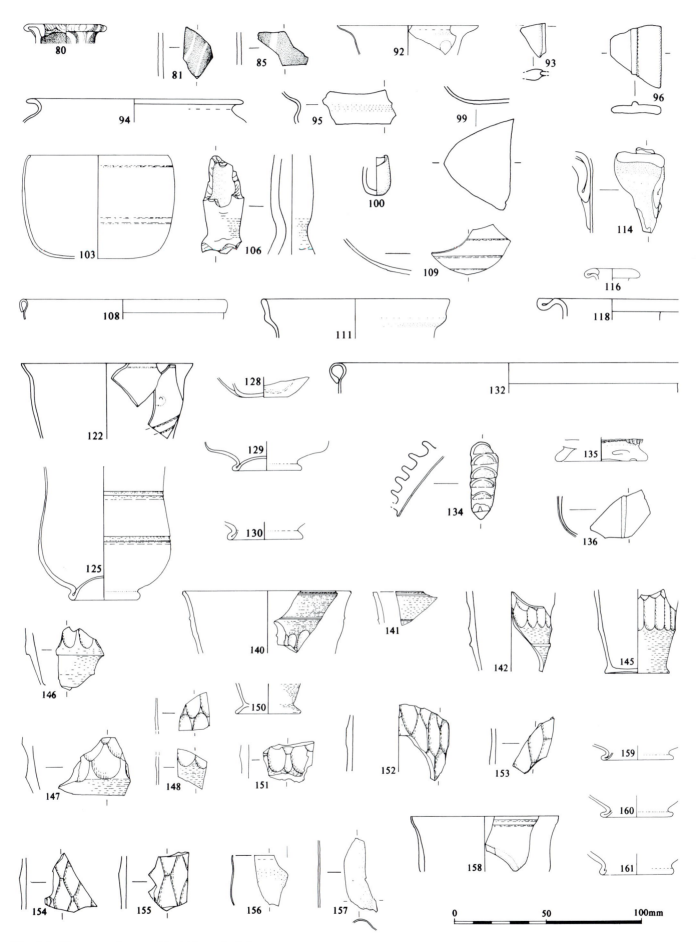

Fig 6.5 Glass vessels: nos 80–161; scale 1:2

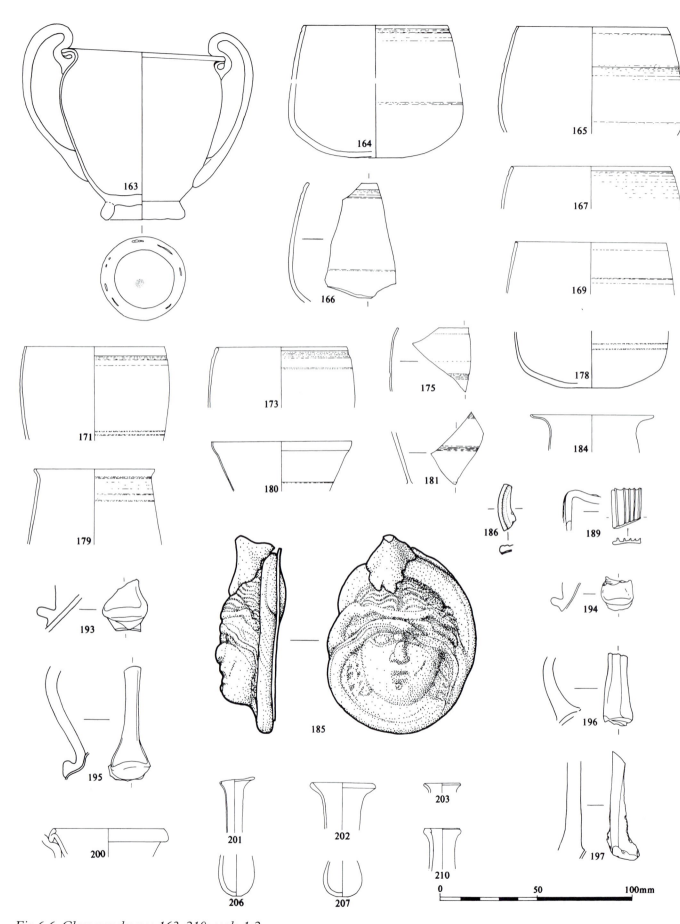

Fig 6.6 Glass vessels: nos 163–210; scale 1:2

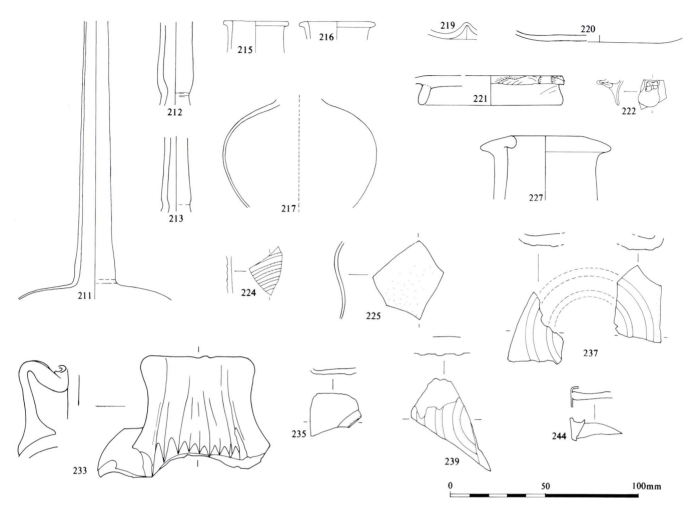

Fig 6.7 Glass vessels: nos 211–244; scale 1:2

nos 187 and 188, come from angular ribbon handles with a central rib. This type of handle was used most commonly on conical jugs but also occurs on some globular ones; it is likely, for example, that the globular jug represented by no 134 would have had a handle of this sort. The blue/green fragments, nos 189 and 190, come from handles with multiple prominent ribs, a handle type used on many of the globular jugs. See, for example, the pale yellowish–green ribbed jug from a cremation burial at Baldock which also contained two samian dishes dated to AD 65–85 (Price 1986, 61, fig 27.2).

Twenty-four percent of the total assemblage (664 fragments) came from blue/green cylindrical or prismatic bottles (Isings forms 50, 51; Cool and Price 1995, 179). These came into use during the Claudian period but do not become common until the Flavian period. Thereafter they are very common and make up a large part of the glass assemblages from sites occupied during the later first and second centuries. The use of cylindrical bottles appears to have ceased early in the second century, whereas that of prismatic square bottles continued as least until the late second century. From the base fragments a minimum of a single hexagonal, four cylindrical, 14 square, and 16 other prismatic bottles are represented in total. From rim and body

fragments it is possible to state that a single rectangular bottle (Isings form 90; Cool 2000, no 481) is also present.

Only 45 bottle fragments (7%) were found in the military levels. Of these four fragments came from square bottles (nos 235 (Fig 6.7) and 241), one from a hexagonal bottle (no 240), 34 from prismatic bottles (nos 232, 233 (Fig 6.7), 236, 237 (Fig 6.7), and 242), four from cylindrical bottles (no 243), and two were rim, neck, or handle fragments which could come from either prismatic or cylindrical bottles (nos 231 and 234). These fragments included the bases from a minimum of one square (no 235) and two prismatic bottles (nos 236 and 237). All of these, and two other small base fragments (nos 238 and 239, Fig 6.7), had patterns of one or more moulded concentric circles, which is the commonest type of base found on these bottles. A comparable assemblage of bottle fragments from a late Neronian-early Flavian militay site was found at Usk (Price 1995a, 184–91).

The disturbances on the site have often led to much glass being redeposited in later contexts, but this does not seem to be an adequate explanation for the very small amounts of bottle glass found in the military layers. Examination of the contexts of forms undoubtedly being used during the military occupation shows that a sizeable proportion are always found in the military layers; in the case of pillar-moulded bowl fragments this was 42% and in the case of Hofheim cup fragments, 72%. Even in the case of the facet-cut beaker fragments, which may have continued in use into the Early Civilian period, 30% were found in military contexts. It seems very likely, therefore, that if prismatic and cylindrical bottles had been much in use during the military occupation a higher proportion would occur in military contexts.

The heat-affected blue/green body fragment, no 244 (Fig 6.7), probably comes from a rare bottle form with two or three internal compartments such as that from Heraclion, Crete (Harden *et al* 1968, 62, no 78; see also Cool and Price 1995, 203). If this is correct it may well have been associated with the military occupation as examples have been found in mid-first century AD contexts. Fragments from Kingsholm, for example, were found in Neronian deposits (Price and Cool 1985, 54, no 85, fig 20).

Overview of the glass vessels in use during the military period

Following the discussion of all the individual types likely to have been in use during the military occupation it is useful to summarise the total assemblage of vessel types. These have been divided into two groups: tablewares and more utilitarian containers. Tablewares consist of drinking vessels such as cups and beakers, bowls – some of which may also have been used for drinking, and vessels employed in serving liquids, such as jugs and amphorisks. The more utilitarian containers are vessels likely to have been used for more long term storage, such as bottles, jars, some varieties of flask and so on. The result of dividing the vessels in this way is shown below.

Cups and Beakers

Cast cup; mould-blown cups and beakers; Hofheim cups and wheel-cut beakers; two handled cup; *cantharos*; facet-cut beakers; indented beakers; arcaded beakers; wheel-cut beakers; miscellaneous cups and beakers. Total: 131 fragments from a minimum of 46 vessels.

Bowls

Pillar-moulded bowls; cast shallow bowls and plates; handled bowls; tubular rimmed bowls. Total: 121 fragments from a minimum of 27 vessels.

Vessels for serving liquids

Amphorisks; polychrome jugs or flasks; conical and globular jugs; jug with pinched handle attachments. Total: 14 fragments from a minimum of 8 vessels, also 8 other fragments from first century AD jugs or flasks.

Utilitarian containers

Tubular unguent bottles; flasks; bottles. Total: 67 fragments from a minimum of 17 vessels.

It is notable that most of the vessels identified were tablewares, with a high preponderance of drinking vessels. The only utilitarian vessel to be found in relatively large numbers was the tubular unguent bottle. Mid-first century and early Flavian assemblages of glass from military sites in Roman Britain often have compositions similar to this, as may be seen from the Neronian assemblages at Kingsholm (Price and Cool 1985). It is possible that some of the more utilitarian forms represented in the Wroxeter assemblage, such as ovoid jars, could have been in use during the military occupation though the absence of any fragments from the military contexts and their frequent absence from comparable assemblages elsewhere perhaps suggests that they were not much used at that time. This bias towards tablewares and especially drinking vessels may relate to the status of the sites producing pre- and early Flavian assemblages. In Britain most are military sites, and it is possible that the assemblages only reflect what the soldiers were using, and that comparable civilian domestic assemblages may have a different composition.

As this is a large assemblage from a high status site, where luxury glass as well as the more everyday vessels might be expected, it is interesting to examine the relationships between the different types of drinking vessels. In this assemblage there are at least 13 Hofheim cups but only two handled cups which would have been contemporary with them and probably would have served the same purpose. The latter is rare everywhere in Roman Britain. The relative frequency of the two types is likely to be the result of differentials of manufacture, price, and supply.

Indented and arcaded beakers combined are slightly outnumbered by facet-cut beakers in this assemblage. This is interesting because the amount of time required to produce a facet-cut beaker would have been much greater than that needed for an indented or arcaded beaker, so they may well have commanded a higher price. These and other relationships between types of vessels noted in this assemblage points towards the future study of the relative status of the forms in use on this and other military sites.

This report was written in 1988–89 and submitted in January 1990. The references to work unpublished at that time but published subsequently were updated in May 1995, July 1998 and July 2001, but no other changes have been made.

Catalogue of military glass vessels

The glass vessels are illustrated in catalogue order (Figs 6.1 – 6.6).

Abbreviations for vessel and object catalogues. BD, base diameter; Dim, dimensions; HT, height; L, length; PH, present height; RD, rim diameter; WT, wall thickness; BD, base diameter. All measurements are in millimetres. All items are stratified military, unless otherwise stated.

Pillar-moulded bowls

These fragments are fire-polished externally and wheel-polished internally. When the rim is present it is wheel-polished internally and externally.

(Fig 6.1)
Polychrome
1   Two joining rim and one body frags. Yellow/brown with opaque white spirals and deep blue marbling. Parts of six prominent ribs with slight tooling marks on upper edges. *72/48* and *119*. PH 43, RD 110, RT 3.
2   Rim frag. Yellow/brown with opaque white marbling. Parts of two prominent narrow ribs with tooling marks on upper edges. *72/48* and *119*. PH 43, RD 110, RT 3.
3   Three joining rim frags. Yellow/brown with opaque yellow marbling. Parts of two prominent ribs with tooling marks on upper edges. *98/77* Baths construction. PH 37, RD c 105, RT 3.
4   Upper body frag. Deep blue with opaque white and some opaque yellow marbling. Part of one prominent rib. *98/187*. Dim 35x19.
5   Rim frag. Deep blue with opaque white marbling. *Tr II H Wpc 4.13b*. PH 13, RT 3.
6   Frag from edge of base. Deep blue with opaque white marbling. Parts of two ribs. *78/16*. Dim 23x13.
7   Two joining body frags. Deep purple with opaque white specks. Part of one wide rib. *91/193* (sf5427). Dim 26x14.

(Fig 6.2)
Strong coloured monochrome
8   Rim frag. Streaky mid blue. Parts of three ribs. Tooling mark on exterior of rim. *78/5* PH 34, RD c 230, RT 4.
9   Base frag. Deep blue. Parts of three shallow ribs. *WC1*. Dim 25.
10 Body frag. Deep blue. Edge of one rib. *78/33*.
11 Rim frag. Very dark yellow/brown. Parts of two ribs. Exterior of rim has tooling marks and is only lightly wheel-polished. *Unstratified*. PH 38, RD 180, RT 3.5.
12 Rim frag. Dark yellow/brown. Part of one rib with tooling mark on upper edge. Exterior of rim only lightly wheel-polished. *80/206*. PH 56, RD c 220, Rim thickness 5.
13 Rim frag. Dark yellow/brown. Edge of one rib. *43/4* Hadrianic. PH 41, RT 5.
14 Upper body frag. Yellow/green. Part of one rib. Frag deliberately broken around edge of rib; one side and top grozed to sharp edges. *90/56*. Dim 40x13.
15 Upper body frag. Yellow/green. Part of one rib. Upper edge grozed to sharp edge. *90/204*. Dim 33x29.

Blue/green
16 Rim frag of shallow bowl. Three close-set, shallow ribs on side of bowl only. *Unstratified*. PH 38, RT 3.
17 Rim frag of deep bowl. Part of one very prominent rib with tooling marks on upper edge. *10/25*. PH 57, RT 6.
18 Two joining rim frags. Bevelled outer edge of rim. Part of one narrow rib. *77/2* Early civilian town and *50/31* Hadrianic. PH 47, RT 4.
19 Rim frag. Edge of one rib. *92/75*. PH 18, RD 140, RT 3.5.
20 Rim frag. Broken at upper edge of rib. *88/7* Hadrianic. PH 18, RD c 160–80, RT 4.
21 Rim frag. *85 III/702*. RT 5.
22 Upper body frag. Part of one rib with tooling marks on upper edge remaining. *2/36* Hadrianic. Dim 50x27.
23 Upper body frag. Part of one rib with tooling marks on upper edge. Frag probably grozed on either side of rib. *83/-*. Dim 43x19.
24 Upper body frags each part of one rib. *81/15*.
25 Description as 24. *92/61*.
26 Lower body and base frag. Side sloping into concave base. Parts of six ribs. Interior only lightly wheel-polished. Base worn; distorted by heat. *72/26*. PH 7, BD c 70.
27 Lower body and base frag. Side curving into concave base. Parts of two ribs. *91/23* Hadrianic. Dim. 34x33.
28 Description as 27 retaining parts of four ribs. *9/23*.
29 Lower body and base frag. Side curving into slightly concave base. Parts of five ribs. Two wheel-cut grooves on interior at edge of base. *84/347*. BD c 60.
30 Lower body frag with two wheel-cut grooves on interior, part of one rib. *9/21*.
31 Description as 30. *52/4*.
31 Description as 30. *92/71*.
32 Description as 30. *9/13* Hadrianic.
33 Description as 30. *83/536* Hadrianic.
34 Description as 30. *83/544*.
35 Description as 30. *84/351*.
36 Description as 30, parts of 4 ribs. *84/52*.
37 Lower body frag retaining parts of two ribs with one wheel-cut groove on interior. *Unstratified* .
38 Lower body frag retaining part of one rib with three wheel-cut grooves on interior. *8/18* Hadrianic.
39 Lower body frag. Parts of four ribs remaining. Wheel-cut grooves and abraded band on interior. *86/41*. Dim 58x39.
40 Two lower body frags. Blue/green. One frag retaining part of one rib. Abraded band on interior. *84/235*. Dim (largest) 28x12.

41 Eleven body frags each retaining part of one rib unless otherwise stated. *67/21; 9/22; 78/12; 84/79; 85 III/70; 84/81* Hadrianic*; 84/132* Hadrianic (2 ribs); *Unstratified (1952–3); 91/159* Early civilian town*; 90/133* Late Roman*; 98/33* Late Roman.

Cast

Polychrome

42 Rim frag of segmental bowl. Floral mosaic. Emerald green ground with opaque yellow specks and opaque red spots. Yellow specks arranged in two rings around red spots. Rim edge rounded; slightly convex-curved side. Surfaces ground and wheel-polished. *92/61* PH 21, WT 2.5.

Monochrome

43 Rim frag of small hemispherical bowl or cup. Emerald green. Slightly everted rim with bevelled upper surfaces and rounded outer edge; convex-curved side. Surfaces ground and wheel-polished. *92/61*. PH 29, RD 75, WT 2.

44 Rim frag of hemispherical or segmental bowl. Emerald green; iridescent surfaces. Bevelled rim edge; convex-curved side. Horizontal rib in shallow relief on body. Surfaces ground and wheel-polished. *98/122*. PH 33, WT 1.

45 Rim frag. Green/blue (peacock); iridescent surfaces. Out-turned rim. Surfaces ground and wheel-polished. *90/139*. Dim 14x11, WT 2.

46 One very small deep blue frag, possibly from a cast vessel. *14/37*.

(Fig 6.3)

47 Six rim, ten body and six base frags (many joining) of shallow bowl with handle. Colourless; occasional small bubbles; iridescent surfaces. Wide everted rim with overhang; upper surface of rim ground flat to leave raised ridge by overhang and at rim/body junction; one rim frag retains edge of projecting handle and another retains parts of scalloped outer edge of handle and perforation. Convex-curved body; flat base with shallow base ring. Exterior facet-cut. Egg and dart cutting on upper surface and outer edge of overhang. At least two rows of oval facets set in quincunx on underside of handle. One row of long oval facets on underside of rim. Three rows of oval facets set in quincunx on exterior of body, bordered at lower edge by ring of oval facets parallel to base ring; similar ring of facets inside base ring bordering rows of oval facets set in quincunx on exterior of base. Shallow circular facets intermittently on underside of base ring. All surfaces ground and wheel-polished; facet-cutting deep and carefully executed apart from circular facets on underside of rim overhang and base ring. These correspond to deep facets on underside of rim and base respectively and may have been produced accidentally when those were being cut. *1974 Sandy make-up below floors of macellum.* Height c 40, RD 300, WT 2 – 3.

(Fig 6.4)

48 Rim frag of bowl. Colourless; small bubbles; iridescent surfaces. Part of wide everted rim with overhang, upper surface of rim ground flat to leave slightly raised ridge by overhang. Exterior facet-cut. Upper surface of overhang has short oval facets; underside of rim has part of a large, probably circular, facet. Surfaces ground and wheel-polished. *Unstratified.* RD 170 – 180; WT 2.5.

49 Rim frag of bowl. Colourless; surfaces dulled. Wide everted rim with overhang, upper surface ground flat to leave raised ridge by overhang and at rim/body junction. Surfaces ground and polished. *68/-*. RD *c* 110–20, WT 3.5.

50 Rim frag of deep bowl. Slightly green-tinged colourless; some small bubbles; iridescent surfaces. Everted rim; convex-curved, nearly vertical side. Wide wheel-cut groove on upper surface of rim. Surfaces ground and wheel-polished. *Unstratified.* PH 30, RD 170, WT 2.

51 Lower body and base frag of large bowl or plate. Colourless; some small bubbles; iridescent surfaces. Wide lower body; vertical base ring; base mostly missing. Surfaces ground and wheel-polished. *80/119* Post Hadrianic. BD 100, WT 2.

52 Lower body and base frag. Colourless; clouded surfaces. Wide lower body; low base ring sloping out; base missing. Surfaces ground and polished. *41/6*. Dim 22x13, WT 2.

53 Body frag of bowl. Colourless; dulled surfaces. Slightly convex-curved side bending through angular carination. Surfaces ground and polished. *41/6*. Dim 33x22, WT 1.5.

54 Rim frag of bowl. Colourless; clouded surfaces. Rim edge rounded; slightly convex-curved side sloping in. Wheel-cut line on exterior below rim edge. Surfaces ground and wheel-polished. *19/18*. PH *c* 30, WT 2.

55 24 body and one base frag of cup, beaker or bowl? Colourless; strain cracks. Side sloping in shallowly to vertically-edged, flat base with central raised disc. Surfaces ground and polished. *91/138* Early civilian town. BD 35, WT 1.5.

56 Body frag. Slightly convex-curved colourless body frag with ground and polished surfaces. *92/18* Hadrianic.

57 Body frag. Flat colourless frag with one bevelled edge, surfaces ground and polished *90/100* (F*602*).

58 Handle frag. Colourless; strain crack, dulled surfaces; ? cast. Curved ribbon handle with sides ground flat. Long rice grain facet down centre of handle. *92/9* Hadrianic Section (max) 9x3.5.

Mould-blown

59 One rim and body and one joining body frag of ribbed bowl. Blue/green; occasional small bubbles. Curved rim, edge cracked off and ground (now chipped). Concave-curved upper body with pronounced carination above convex-curved lower body with short vertical ribs above two horizontal rounded ribs with concavity between; parts of 14 ribs remaining. Lower edge broken at edge of base. *51/21.* PH 47, RD *c* 85, WT 1–2.

60 Body frag of ribbed bowl. Pale yellow; some small bubbles. Small part of concave-curved upper body above pronounced carination and ribbed convex-curved upper body; parts of four ribs remaining. *98/52.* Dim 32x22, WT 1.5.

61 Three joining body frags. Blue/green; some small bubbles; flaking iridesence. Slightly convex-curved side with parts of three vertical ribs. *98/87* Early civilian town. Dim 38x29, WT 1.5.

62 Body frag of almond knob beaker. Deep blue; some elongated bubbles and inclusion, Straight side. Upper part of one almond-shaped boss outlined with raised rib set off-centre inside a diamond-shaped lattice. Part of a (?) horizontal rib above. *86/-.* Dim 21x18, WT 1.

63 Body frag of almond knob beaker. Deep blue; occasional small bubbles. Part of one almond knob shaped boss outlined with raised rib. *14/37.* Dim 11x9, WT 1.5.

64 Body frag of almond knob beaker. Deep blue. Straight side. Lower part of one almond-shaped (?) boss and upper tip of second outlined by elongated hexagonal lattice. Vertical mould seam through bosses. *84/244.* Dim 15x10, WT 3.

65 Body frag. Yellow/green; some small bubbles; iridescent surfaces. Convex-curved side. Part of one spiral moulding. *89/62* Hadrianic. Dim 22x20, WT 2.

66 Two body frags. Yellow/green; some small bubbles; iridescent surfaces. Convex-curved side. Large frag has parts of one straight moulding, one elongated boss, and edge of third moulding. *91/23* Hadrianic. Dim 24x20 and 12x9, WT 1.5.

67 Body frag. Yellow/green; some small bubbles; iridescent surfaces. Convex-curved side. Part of base ring and edge of second moulding. *97/201.* Dim 17x15, WT 2.

68 Body frag. Yellow/green; some small bubbles; iridescent surfaces. Convex-curved side. Parts of two slightly curved moulding and edge of third. *98/-.* Dim 22x20, WT 2.

69 Base frag. Yellow/green; some small bubbles; iridescent surfaces. Convex-curved side. Part of base ring. *90/169.* Dim 15x10, WT 2.

70 Body frag. Yellow/green; some small bubbles. Parts of two mouldings. *98/52.* Dim 8x8, WT 2.

Nos. 65–70 could be from the same vessel.

71 Body frag. Blue/green; small bubbles; iridescent surfaces. Convex-curved side. One curved moulding with pointed expansion at one point. *80/181* Early civilian town. Dim 19x7, WT 2.

72 Body frag. Heavily weathered yellowish green/colourless; some black impurities; much strain cracking; iridescent surfaces. Straight side. Parts of two mouldings, one curved, one looped. *98/138.* Dim 24x26, WT 2.

73 Rim frag of beaker. Colourless; dulled surfaces. Vertical rim, edge cracked off and ground; straight side. Upper part of exterior ground and wheel-polished to produce a narrow rib at rim edge and above a wide ground out horizontal band; below part of a curved rib surrounding a mould blown depression. *19/18.* PH 29, RD 70, WT 2.

74 Three rim frags of beaker. Colourless; some small bubbles; clouded iridescent surfaces. Vertical rim, edge cracked off and ground; straight side sloping in slightly. One wheel-cut groove below rim edge; part of moulding on upper body – (?) leaf. *98/102* Early civilian town. PH 30, RD *c* 70, WT 1.

75 Body frag. Colourless; some small bubbles; dulled surfaces. Straight side. Most of leaf-shaped moulding with stem and part of second moulding. Decoration in high relief and well-formed. *41/6.* Dim 31x24, WT 1–2.

76 Body frag. Colourless; clouded surfaces. Parts of two oval ring mouldings inside an angular meander. Distorted by heat. *98/52.* Dim 50x25, WT 2.

77 Body frag. Colourless; occasional small bubles; irridescent surfaces. Straight-side. Part of an oval ring moulding inside an angular meander. Mouldings in high relief. *89/87* Early civilian town. Dim 28x20, WT 2.

78 Body frag. Colourless; some small bubbles; iridescent surfaces. Frag bent through carination. Part of one curved moulding. *98/83* Hadrianic. Dim 14x14, WT 2.5.

Nos. 76–78 are probably from the same vessel

79 Body frag. Colourless; clouded surfaces. Convex-curved side. Faint traces of horizontal ridge and lattice pattern? Vertical mould seam. *98/87* Early civilian town. Dim 31x12, WT 3.

Blown

(Fig 6.5)

Polychrome

80 Rim frag of jug or flask. Light yellow/brown with opaque white marvered trails on surface. Rim bent out, up, in and flattened; cylindrical neck. *93/3* Hadrianic. RD 45, neck thickness 2.5.

81 Neck frag of jug or flask. Light green (with many elongated bubbles) with diagonal opaque white trails marvered smooth. Iridescent surfaces. Cylindrical neck. *90/204.* Dim 26x16, neck thickness 2.

82 Two body frags. Yellow/green with opaque white trails and streaks marvered smooth and running through complete thickness of glass. Straight side. *92/20.* Dim 30x20, 34x32, WT 3.

83 Body frag. Deep blue with opaque white rod marvered smooth and in part overlain with deep blue glass. Concave-sided. *92/71.* Dim 11x10, WT 3.

84 Two body frags. Yellow/green with opaque white streaks marvered smooth. Convex-curved side. *84/244.* Dim 16x14, 15x13, WT 2.5.

85 Body frag. Deep blue with wide opaque white trail marvered smooth. Straight side. *WP A6 (16) Trench 5d (162).* Dim 22x12, WT 2.5.

86 Body frag. Deep blue with opaque white blob marvered smooth. Convex-curved side. 83/*534.* Dim 18x13, WT 1.

87 Body frag. Deep blue with part of opaque white blob or streak marvered smooth. Straight side. *84/400.* Dim 14x10, WT 1.5.

88 Body frag. Deep blue with opaque white streaks marvered smooth. Convex-curved. *81/69.* Dim 19x12, WT 2.

Opaque

89 Body frag. Pale blue. Convex-curved side, (?) curving into neck. Affected by heat. *5/38.* Dim 26x17, WT 1.5

90 Body frag. Pale blue. *63/15.* Early civilian town.

91 Body frag. Opaque white. Convex-curved. *90/168* (sf5433) Hadrianic. Dim 37x19, WT 2.

Deep Blue

92 Rim frag of beaker(?) Occasional small bubbles and one very large one; iridescent surfaces. Outbent, curved rim, edge fire rounded; straight side sloping in s lightly. Applied self-coloured circular boss. *98/196.* PH 16, RD 75, WT 1.

93 Handle and rim frag of bowl. Dulled surfaces. Outbent rim with fire rounded edge; outer edge of attachment of horizontal handle on rim. *98/138.* PH 17x14, WT 2.

94 Two rim frags of jar or bowl. Occasional small bubbles; dulled sufaces. Horizontal out-turned rim, edge fire rounded. Side sloping out. Wear scratches around inner edge of upper face of rim. *92/65* and *Unstratified.* PH 14, RD 115, WT 1.5.

95 Lower body frag of jar or jug. Occasional small bubbles; strain cracks; flaking iridescent surfaces. Lower body sloping in to constriction above open pushed in base ring; lower part of base ring and all of base missing. *91/298.* Dim 36x17, WT 2.

96 Handle frag of jug. Elongated bubbles; flaking iridescent surfaces. Slightly curved ribbon handle with central rib. *2/20.* Length 32, section (excluding rib) 26x4.5.

97 Neck frag with part of upper handle attachment of jug. *90/222* Hadrianic.

98 Base frag of jug? Occasional small bubbles. Concave base. *50/31* Military and Hadrianic. Dim 34x22, WT 1.5.

99 Base frag of cup, jar, jug or flask. Small bubbles; flaking iridescent surfaces. Side curving into slightly concave base. *5/36* Hadrianic. PH 11, WT 2.

100 Lower body and complete base frag of tubular unguent bottle. Mid blue; many bubbles; streaky impurity in base. Tubular body; convex base with central flattening. *Unstratified.* PH 22, Maximum body diameter 15, WT 1.5.

101 28 undecorated deep blue body frags. *9/21; 41/6; 52/17* (Two frags); *70/16; 70/17; 91/246; 92/61; 92/64; 92/72; 92/77; 98/237; 98/178* (Two frags), *50/30* Hadrianic; *98/68* Hadrianic (Two frags); *84/71; 90/161; 98/138; 98/187; 90/-; g 34;* Unstratified (Four frags, one heat affected); *80/181* Early civilian town.

Wine coloured

102 Body frag. Small bubbles; straight side. One optic blown vertical rib. *Unstratified.*

Yellow/Brown

103 Five rim and body frags of cylindrical cup joining in groups of two and three. Light yellow/brown; some small bubbles; dulled iridescent surfaces. Inturned rim, edge cracked off and ground with inward bevel; slightly convex-curved side with lower body curving in. One horizontal abraded band below rim edge with two similar bands on lower body above change of angle. *72/19.* PH 50, RD 75, WT 1.5.

104 Handle frag of jug. Dark yellow/brown; elongated bubbles. Edge of straight ribbon handle. *51/21.* Length 30.

105 Handle and body frag of jug. Dark yellow/brown: clouded iridescent surfaces. Tip of prong from lower handle attachment retaining part of body. *84/216.* Dim 14x10, WT 1.5.

106 Neck and body frag of flask or jug. Dark yellow/brown; flaking iridescent surfaces. Cylindrical neck with constriction and tooling marks at base; side beginning to slope out. Some edges reworked. *WPB6 3b TR IVC Sec B 158.* Neck diameter 22, neck thickness 4.

107 Five light yellow/brown undecorated frags. *41/6; 67/22; 92/20* (two frags); *92/61.*

Emerald Green

108 Rim frag of tubular rimmed bowl. Flaking iridescence. Vertical rim, edge bent over and down. *84/339.* PH 12, RD *c* 110, WT 1.

109 Two body frags. Light emerald green. Some small bubbles; flaking iridescent surfaces. Convex-curved side. Horizontal wheel-cut grooves -three on larger frag and one on smaller. *70/17* and *70/20.* Dim 40x30 and 22x16, WT 1.5.

110 Three undecorated emerald green body frags *75/2; 58/4* Post Hadrianic; *80/179* Late Roman.

Yellow/Green

111 Rim frag of bowl. Some small bubbles; iridescent surfaces. Out-bent stepped rim with fire rounded edge; side sloping in. *30/34.* PH 21, RD 100, WT 2.

112 Base frag of beaker? Iridescent surfaces. Sides loping into tubular pushed-in base ring. *90/184* Early civilian town. PH 7, BD *c* 35, WT 1.

113 Handle frag of jug. Many elongated bubbles; iridescent surfaces. Upper part of angular ribbon handle broken close at attachment to neck. *22/2.* Handle section 24x5.5.

114 Handle and neck frag of jug or amphorisk. Elongated bubbles and small black impurities in handle; iridescent surfaces. Wide cylindrical neck; folded upper attachment of ribbon handle applied under (missing) rim and to neck. Also two body frags one with edge of handle attachment. *91/72* Early civilian town. Section (handle) 26x5, neck thickness 2.

115 Neck frag. Wide cylindrical neck; one edge possible grozed. *90/216* Hadrianic.

116 Rim frag of jug or flask. Flaking iridescent surfaces. Rim folded out, up, in and flattened. *90/207.* RD 30.

117 Rim frag. Outer edge of a rim similar to 116. *90/177.*

118 Rim frag of flask, jug or bottle? Small bubbles; dulled surfaces. Tubular rim folded out, up, in, and flattened. *91/85* Early civilian town. RD 80, neck thickness 2.5.

119 Body frag of beaker or bottle? Iridescent surfaces; occasional small bubbles. Straight side. One wheel-cut line and three horizontal abraded bands. *9/30* Early civilian town. Dim 74x16, WT 2.

120 Two body frags. Occasional small bubbles; flaking iridescent surfaces. Larger frag has part of large indent. *92/61.* Dim 35x23 and 17x8, WT 1.5.

121 Three undecorated yellow/green body frags. *75/2; 81/15; 72/67* (heat affected).

Pale/Light Green

122 One rim and one joining upper body frag of cylindrical beaker. Pale greenish colourless; some small bubbles; dulled surfaces. Curved rim, edge cracked off and ground with inward bevel; straight side with small accidental deformation from inside. Horizontal abraded band on rim below edge; two wheel-cut lines on upper body. *91/94.* PH 40, RD *c* 90, WT 2.

123 One rim and one body frag of beaker. Pale green; some tiny bubbles; iridescent surfaces. Curved rim, edge cracked off and ground; straight side sloping in slightly. Horizontal wheel-cut line below rim edge. *97/179* Early civilian town. PH 15, WT 1.

124 Rim frag. Similar to 123. Heat affected. *90/184* Early civilian town.

125 One body frag and complete base (joining) of beaker. Pale greenish colourless; some small to medium bubbles; iridescent surfaces. Concave-sided upper body, convex-curved lower body sloping into tubular pushed-in base ring; domed base. Two horizontal wheel-cut lines on upper body, two similar lines at carination to lower body. *92/24.* PH 69, BD 38, WT 1.

126 Upper body frag of beaker. One pale green upper body frag with one horizontal wheel-cut line below (missing) rim edge; two similar lines on upper body. *90/167* Hadrianic.

127 Lower body frag. Light green. One wheel-cut line. *90/5.*

128 Lower body and base frag of indented beaker. Light green; small bubbles; iridescent surfaces. Side sloping into slightly convex base. Lower parts of two large indents. *83/114.* PH 11, BD *c* 25, WT 1.

129 Lower body and complete base frag of beaker. Light green; some small bubbles. Body broken above carination to wide lower body sloping into pushed-in base ring; domed base. *83/534* Hadrianic. PH 14, BD 37, WT 1.

130 Base frag of beaker? Light greenish colourless; heavily weathered surfaces. Lower body sloping into solid pushed-in base ring; base missing. *98/61.* PH 10, BD *c* 40, WT 2.

131 Base frag of beaker? Light greenish colourless; flaking iridescence. Tubular base ring; side and base missing. *Unstratified.* BD 30.

132 Rim frag of tubular-rimmed bowl. Pale green; some small bubbles; dulled surfaces. Vertical rim, edge bent out and down; straight side. One end of frag distorted by heat. *91/52.* PH 17, RD 190, WT 1.5.

133 Handle frag. Light green. At least two central ribs. *84/71* Military demolition.

134 Handle and body frag of globular jug. Light green; some black impurities and dulled surfaces. Lower part of vertical pinched extension trail from handle attachment; six pinched projections, lowest one broken. Convex side of jug broken around edge of trail. *30/7.* Dim (of trail) 43x14.

135 Base frag of bowl or jug. Pale green; small bubbles; flaking iridescent surfaces. Flat base mostly missing; applied true base ring with irregular tooling marks. Side grozed. *Unstratified.* BD 50.

136 Two body frags of bowl or jug? Pale green; occasional small bubbles; iridescent surfaces. One frag bends through rounded carination, other convex-curved. Vertical ribs in shallow relief. Also two other body frags. *84/71* Military demolition. Dim (carinated frag) 32x20, WT 1.5.

137 Body frag. Pale green. Two ribs in shallow relief . *91/110.*

138 Body frag. Pale green; occasional small bubbles; dulled surfaces. Convex-curved side. Part of thick trail doubled back on itself, possibly part of a handle attachment. *84/357.* Dim 24x20.

139 Eight undecorated light green and pale greenish body frags. *72/67; 84/410; 85/70 (2 frags); 85/238; 84/71 Military demolition; 92/61; 98/196.*

Colourless

140 Rim frag of facet-cut beaker. Dulled surfaces; strain cracks. Rim edge cracked off and ground; straight side sloping in. Exterior ground and wheel-polished to leave one rib below rim edge and a second above facet-cut zone. Parts of four oval facets in two rows set in quincunx; upper row consists of alternate large and small facets. *91/94.* PH 30, RD 90, WT 3.5–2.5.

141 One rim, one body and one base frag of (probably) facet-cut beaker. Dulled iridescent surfaces; strain crack. Vertical rim, edge cracked off and ground. Exterior ground and wheel-polished to leave one rib below rim edge and a second above (missing) facet-cut zone. Body frag straight-sided, exterior ground and wheel-polished to leave one rib in low relief. Base frag has part of ground-out base ring. *91/44.* PH (rim frag) 17, WT (rim) 3–3.5.
(nos 140 and 141 could be from the same vessel)

142 Body frag of facet-cut beaker. Occasional tiny bubbles; dulled surfaces; strain cracks. Straight-sided facet-cut zone with lower body sloping in. Exterior ground and wheel-polished. Parts of nine oval facets in two rows set in quincunx to form hexagons; ground out rib on lower body. *90/169.* Outer body diameter of facet-cut zone c 45, WT 2–2.5.

143 Lower body frag of (probably) facet-cut beaker. Clouded surfaces. Very slightly convex-curved side sloping in. Exterior ground and wheel-polished to leave one rib. *Unstratified, 1952–3.* Dim 32x20, WT 3–4.

144 Body frag with the exterior ground and wheel-polished to leave one rib in relief. *Unstratified.*

145 Lower body and base frag of facet-cut beaker. Straight sided facet-cut zone with lower body sloping in to flat base with low ground-out base ring. Exterior ground and polished to leave facet-cut zone in relief. Parts of ten long oval facets in two rows set in quincunx to form hexagons. *10/25.* PH 44, BD c 35.

146 Lower body frag of facet-cut beaker. Occasional small bubbles; strain cracks. Straight side retaining small part of inner edge of base. Exterior ground and wheel-polished to leave facet-cut zone in high relief. Parts of four oval facets. *81/15.* Dim 34x25, WT 1.5–3.5.

147 Body frag of facet-cut beaker. Occasional tiny bubbles; dulled iridescent surfaces; strain cracks. Exterior ground and wheel-polished. Straight-sided facet-cut zone with plain lower body sloping in below. Parts of six circular facets in three rows set in quincunx. *91/117 Hadrianic.* Dim 35x30, WT 4–5.

148 Two body frags of facet-cut beaker. Occasional tiny bubbles; iridescent surfaces. Straight side. Exterior ground and wheel-polished to leave facet-cut zone in slight relief. One frag retains parts of two oval facets from bottom row, other frag has parts of four oval facets in two rows set in quincunx to form hexagons. Facet-cutting shallow. *6/37.* Dim 19x17, 16x14, WT 1–2.

149 Body frag of facet-cut beaker. Iridescent surfaces; strain cracks. Exterior ground and wheel-polished to leave facet-cut zone in slight relief. Part of one facet. *90/178.* Dim 15x6, WT 2.5–3.

150 Lower body and base frag of (probably) facet-cut beaker. Dulled surfaces; strain crack. Exterior ground and polished. Straight side sloping into ground out base ring; most of base missing. *43/6 Hadrianic.* PH 16, BD c 35, WT 2.

151 Body frag of facet-cut beaker. Dulled iridescent surfaces; strain crack. Exterior ground and wheel-polished. Parts of seven oval facets set in quincunx forming top or bottom two rows of facet-cut zone; top or bottom row consists of alternate large and small facets. *83/523.* Dim 27x20. WT 3.

152 Body frag of facet-cut beaker. Occasional small bubbles; iridescent surfaces. Straight side. Parts of 13 long oval facets in four rows set in quincunx to form hexagons and diamonds. *53/11.* Inner diameter c 50, WT 3.5–2.5.

153 Body frag of facet-cut beaker. Occasional tiny bubbles; iridescent surfaces. Parts of six long oval facets in four rows set in quincunx to form diamonds. *5/38.* Dim 34x13, WT 2–3.5.

154 Body frag of facet-cut beaker. Occasional tiny bubbles; iridescent surfaces. Straight side. Parts of nine long oval facets in four rows set in quincunx to form diamonds. *Unstratified.* Dim 30x28, WT 3.5–2.5.

155 Body frag of facet-cut beaker. Occasional tiny bubbles; dulled surfaces. Straight side. Parts of six long oval facets in three rows set in quincunx to form diamonds. *WpC137.* Dim 28x20, WT 3.5–2.5.

156 One rim frag of indented beaker. Slightly yellow-tinged colourless; some small bubbles; iridescent surfaces. Curved rim, edge cracked off and ground; vertical side. Parts of two indents. Also six other body frags, one with part of indent. *84/71 Military demolition* PH 27, WT 1.

157 Two body frags of indented beaker? Occasional small bubbles; dulled surfaces. Straight side; parts of two long narrow indents. *98/52.* Dim (largest) 37x15, WT 1.

158 Rim frag of arcaded beaker. Some bubbles; dulled iridescent surfaces. Curved rim, edge cracked off and ground; slightly concave-curved upper body. Two horizontal wheel-cut grooves below rim; upper parts of two trailed arcades below. *85.3/70.* PH 29, RD 80, WT 1.5.

159 Lower body and base frag. Occasional small bubbles; iridescent surfaces. Side sloping in shallowly to solid pushed-in base ring; domed base mostly missing. *Unstratified.* PH 9, BD 39, WT 1.5.

160 Lower body and base frag. Small bubbles; flaking iridescent surfaces; strain cracks. Side sloping in shallowly to solid pushed in base ring; base missing. *Unstratified.* PH 12, RD 39, WT 1.5.

161 Lower body and base frag. Clouded surfaces. Side sloping into tubular pushed-in base ring; base missing, probably domed. *84/103.* PH 14, BD 40, WT 2.5.

162 Five undecorated colourless body frags. *51/21* (two frags); *72/67; 84/145* (heat affected)*; 91/193; 84/235.*

(Fig 6.6)
Blue/Green

163 A two handled cup in missing small parts of rim and body only. Small, occasionally large, bubbles; iridescent surfaces; black impurities in handle. Horizontally out-bent rim with fire thickened edge; convex-curved body with greatest diameter near rim, sloping into convex base with central kick; applied true base ring with post technique scars. 'D'-sectioned rod handles applied to underside of rim and upper body; looped back to rim edge before curving up, back and down to simple attachment on lower body. HT (excluding handles) 88, RD 88, BD 45, WT 1–3.

164 One rim and two lower body and base frags of cylindrical cup. Occasional small bubbles; purple streaks. Slightly inturned rim, edge cracked off and ground; slightly convex-curved side with rounded carination to lower body sloping into small slightly concave base. One wheel-cut groove below rim edge; one horizontal abraded band above carination. Base worn. *73/25.* PH (rim) 30, (base) 42, RD 80, BD 30, WT 2–3.

165 Rim frag of hemispherical cup. Small bubbles; dulled iridescent surfaces. Slightly inturned rim, edge cracked off and ground; slightly convex-curved side expanding out, rounded carination to lower body. One horizontal abraded band below rim edge and one similar band above carination; one wide wheel-cut groove on mid body. *50/18.* PH 59, RD 80, BD 2.

166 Rim frag of hemispherical cup. Occasional small bubbles; dulled surfaces. Slightly inturned rim, edge cracked off with inward bevel and ground; slightly convex-curved side expanding out; rounded carination to lower body. One broad and one narrow wheel-cut grooves below rim edge, one narrow wheel-cut line above carination. *Unstratified.* PH 64, WT 2.

167 Rim frag of cylindrical or hemispherical cup. Some tiny bubbles; dulled surfaces. Slightly in curved rim, edge cracked off and ground; slightly convex-curved upper body expanding out. One horizontal wheel-cut groove below rim edge with abrasions below. *19/18.* PH 23, RD 85, WT 1.5.

168 Rim frag of cylindrical or hemispherical cup. Occasional small bubbles; flaking iridescent surfaces. Slightly inturned rim, edge cracked off and ground. Two horizontal wheel-cut grooves below rim edge, lowest one narrow. *Unstratified.* PH 17, RD 85, WT 2.

169 Rim frag of cylindrical cup. Occasional tiny bubbles; iridescent surfaces. Vertical rim, edge cracked off and ground; slightly convex-curved side. One horizontal abraded band below rim edge and two on upper body. *98/138* PH 28, RD 80, WT 1.5.

170 Rim frag of cylindrical cup. Iridescent surfaces. Slightly inturned rim, edge cracked off and ground. One horizontal abraded band below rim edge. *78/5.* PH 16, RD 80, WT 2.

171 Rim frag of cylindrical cup. Some small bubbles; dulled surfaces. Slightly inturned rim, edge knocked off and ground; convex-curved side expanding out. Broad horizontal wheel-cut groove below rim edge; one narrow abraded band below groove and two similar bands on lower body. *72/48.* PH 49, RD 75, WT 1.

172 Two rim and 11 body frags of cylindrical cup. Occasional small bubbles; iridescent surfaces. Slightly in-curved rim, edge cracked off and ground; straight side. Wide wheel-cut line below rim edge. *84/237* Early civilian town. PH (rim frag) 17, RD *c* 75, WT 2.

173 Rim frag of cylindrical or hemispherical cup. Iridescent surfaces. Inturned rim, edge cracked off and ground; convex-curved side expanding out. One shallow wheel-cut groove below rim edge, one narrow abraded band below groove. *92/20.* PH 31, RD 70, WT 1.

174 Rim frag of cylindrical or hemispherical cup. Occasional small bubbles; iridescent surfaces. Inturned rim, edge cracked off and ground. One horizontal wheel-cut groove below rim edge, one narrow abraded band below groove. *92/61.* PH 20, RD 70, WT 1.

175 Rim frag of cylindrical or hemispherical cup. Occasional small bubbles. Inturned rim, edge cracked off and ground; slightly convex-curved side. One horizontal abraded band below rim and one wheel-cut groove on body. *90/167* Hadrianic. PH 39, WT 1.5.

176 Seven body frags similarly decorated to 175 and probably from a cylindrical or hemispherical cup. *85.2/248.*

177 Four convex-curved body frags probably from similar cups to 164–76 each with a horizontal abraded band above carination. *92/61; 10/21; j 9; Unstratified.*

178 Three joining lower body and base frags of cylindrical cup. Some small bubbles. Slightly convex-curved

body with rounded carination to lower body sloping into edge of small base. Two abraded horizontal bands above carination. Base worn. *85/238.* PH 28, WT 2.

179 Rim frag of cylindrical beaker. Occasional small bubbles; dulled surfaces. Out bent rim, edge cracked off and ground; straight side sloping out slightly. One narrow horizontal abraded band below rim edge, two similar bands on upper body, frag possibly broken at edge of fourth band. *Unstratified.* PH 41, RD 65, WT 1.5.

180 Rim frag of conical beaker. Some tiny bubbles. Curved rim, edge cracked off and ground; straight side sloping in. One narrow wheel-cut line below rim, one similar line on upper body. *Unstratified.* PH 27, RD 75, WT 1.

181 Lower body frag of conical beaker(?) Occasional small bubbles; iridescent surfaces. Straight side broken at edge of base ring. Two horizontal abraded bands on body. *Unstratified.* Dim 38x22, WT 2.

182 Body frag with wheel-cut groove probably from a cylindrical cup or beaker. *92/61.*

183 Six body frags with abraded bands probably from cylindrical cups or beakers. *92/61; 98/138; WPc 142 TrXH (137)* (4 frag); *Unstratified 1952–3.*

184 Rim frag of beaker(?) Occasional small bubbles; iridescent surfaces. Out-turned rim, edge fire rounded; straight side. *51/21.* PH 18, RD 65, WT 1.

185 Complete mask medallion with frag of handle and side of jug. Small bubbles; streaky green and many black impurities in handle. Part of convex-curved side. Applied oval medallion with flat border. Well moulded, rounded face with features in high relief and pointed chin. Hair shown as undulating ridges running across head on either side of a central parting; head band running across forehead between bunches of leaves on either side of head. Pair of diagonally ridged ringlets on either side of the face. Trail from formation of medallion crosses forehead from left to right. Tip of lower handle attachment on top of head, slightly off-centre. Body of jug broken off neatly behind medallion and only visible from front at top right-hand corner. *92/61.* Dim (medallion) 47x41, WT 1.

186 Frag from edge of mask medallion from jug handle attachment. Dulled surfaces. Part of rounded edge with trail from formation of medallion parallel to side. Tip of one pointed moulding and edge of a second moulding preserved. Small part of jug body on underside. *97/121 Late Roman.* Dim 23x8.

187 Handle frag lacking both edges, possibly from handle with a central rib. *41/42.*

188 Handle frag, description as 187. *50/52.*

189 Handle frag of jug. Elongated bubbles; iridescent surfaces. Angular ribbon handle with five narrow prominent ribs. *70/16.* Handle section (excluding ribs) 15x2.5.

190 Handle frag with at least one prominent rib. *78/5.*

191 Base frag. Side of an open pushed-in base ring. *90/247.*

192 Neck and handle frag of jug or bottle. Dulled surfaces. Cylindrical neck; part of folded upper handle attachment. *84/216.* Dim (neck) 32x20, Neck thickness 3.

193 Handle and body frag of jug. Elongated bubbles; flaking iridescent surfaces. Simple lower attachment of (?)rod handle with pinched projection. Straight side. *Unstratified.* Dim 27x25, WT 2.

194 Handle and body frag of jug. Small bubbles; streaky green impurities in handle. Terminal of simple lower attachment of handle with pinched projection. Side grozed around edge of attachment. *91/110.* Dim 19x14.

195 Handle and body frag of jug. Elongated bubbles; dulled iridescent surfaces; orange inclusion in handle. Curved rod handle with simple lower attachment impressed to produce ridge. Also seven convex-curved body frags. *WPC 314A TrIIG (127).* Handle section 7x5.

196 Handle and body frag of jug. Elongated bubbles; dulled iridescent surfaces. Part of short curved rod handle with simple lower attachment. Handle attachment broken, possibly at impressed ridge or pinched projection like nos 286–8 above. *83/-.* Handle section 11x6.

197 Handle and body frags of jug. Elongated bubbles; streaky green impurities; flaking iridescent surfaces. One rib of ribbed handle deliberately broken on either side, with part of lower attachment retaining part of side. Lower edge of handle and side heavily worn. *72/67.* Dim 53x13.

198 Handle and body frag of jug. Elongated bubbles; iridescent surfaces. Prong from claw lower attachment. *78/12.* Dim 26x9.

199 Handle frag of jug. Clouded surfaces. Straight ribbon handle tooled to form two ribs. *80/199.* Handle section 11x4.

200 Rim and handle frag of amphorisk(?) Elongated bubbles in handle; iridescent surfaces. Rim bent down and up and in diagonally to form triangular profile. Part of ribbon handle with small central ridge attached to neck and under side of rim. *7/55.* PH 17, RD *c* 60, handle section 27x6.

201 Complete rim and part of neck of unguent bottle. Elongated bubbles; iridescent surfaces. Asymmetrically out bent rim, edge sheared and rolled in places; cylindrical neck. *98/130 Early civilian town.* PH 28, RD 19x17, WT 0.5.

202 Rim frag of unguent bottle. Small bubbles; streaky green impurities; iridescent surfaces. Out bent rim, edge sheared; cylindrical neck. *Unstratified.* PH 24, RD 35, WT 1.

203 Rim frag of unguent bottle. Elongated bubbles; iridescent surfaces. Out bent rim, edge sheared. *7/57.* PH 5, RD 20, WT 1.5.

204 Rim frag of unguent bottle. Some bubbles; iridescent surfaces. Out bent rim, edge sheared. *75/2*. PH 7, RD 35, WT 1.5.

205 Rim frag of unguent bottle. Elongated bubbles; out bent surfaces. Out bent rim; edge sheared. *51/13* Hadrianic PH 10, RD 35, WT 2.

206 Lower body and base frag of tubular unguent bottle. Small bubbles; iridescent surfaces. Tubular body; convex base with small central flattening. *Unstratified 1952–3*. PH 22, Max body diameter 19, WT 2.

207 Lower body and base frag of tubular unguent bottle. Description as no 206. *WPD2+* PH 21, Max body diameter 20, WT 2.5.

208 Five lower body frags from similar tubular unguent bottles to 206. *78/5; 98/131; 90/82; 98/61; 80/181* Early civilian town.

209 Lower body and edge of base of unguent bottle similar to 206. *80/215*.

210 Rim frag of unguent bottle. Streaky green impurities; dulled surfaces. Out bent rim, edge rolled in cylindrical neck. *50/31*. PH 24, RD 20, WT 2.

(Fig 6.7)

211 One neck and one joining body frag of flask. Occasional bubbles; iridescent surfaces. Long cylindrical neck expanding slightly towards tooled and constricted junction with wide thin-walled convex-curved body. *51/20*. Length of neck 143, upper neck diameter 13, neck thickness 2, WT 1.

212 Neck frag of flask. Small bubbles; iridescent surfaces. Cylindrical neck expanding slightly towards constricted and tooled junction with body. *38/15*. Neck diameter 17, neck thickness 3.

213 Neck frag of flask. Elongated bubbles; streaky green impurities; iridescent surfaces. Cylindrical neck with tooled constriction at junction with body. *84/71* Military demolition. Neck diameter 16, neck thickness 3.

214 Neck frag. *Unstratified*. Neck thickness 1.

215 Rim frag of jug, flask or bottle. Occasional small bubbles; iridescent surfaces. Rim edge bent out, up and in with small triangular profile; cylindrical neck. *7/60*. PH 15, RD 35, neck thickness 2.

216 Rim frag of jug, flask or bottle. Description as no 215 above. *49/-*. PH 10, RD c 40, neck thickness 2.

217 Two joining body frags of flask. Occasional small bubbles; iridescent surfaces. Convex-curved side with wide upper body broken at edge of neck. *51/21*. Dim 65x58, WT 1.5.

218 Body frag with edge of neck possibly from flask. *92/63*.

219 Base frag of cup or flask. Small bubbles; iridescent surfaces. Concave base with high central kick. Base worn. *9/21*. BD 25.

220 Base frag. Some small bubbles; iridescent surfaces. Side curving into very slightly concave base, probably without pontil scar. Base scratched. *92/72*. BD c 70, WT 2.

221 Base frag of bowl or jug. Small bubbles. Applied true base ring with diagonal tooling marks; slightly concave base. Wide lower body grozed; base worn. *88/5* Hadrianic BD 75.

222 Handle and body frag of cup with folded handle. Small bubbles; iridescent surfaces. Convex-curved side. Lower part of handle applied to side with part of pinched projection fold. *76/3*. Dim 17x15, WT 1.

223 Body frag with rib in low relief. *14/31*.

224 Body frag with parts of five close-set diagonal ribs. *84/71* Military demolition.

225 Body frag. Many bubbles; thick flaking iridescence. Convex-curved side. Part of large circular indent. *84/52* Hadrianic. Dim 34x33, WT 1.5.

226 144 undecorated blue/green body frags *30/12; 34/37; 41/6 ; 50/52; 51/21* (2 joining frags)*; 70/16; 70/17; 70/68* (2 joining frags); *72/14* (5 frags); *72/21; 72/67* (31 frags); *74/3* (2 frags); *75/2* (7 frags); *78/10; 78/15; 80/20* (4 frags); *84/84; 84/107; 84/145* (2 frags)*; 84/209* (3 frags, 2 heat affected); *84/379; 84/405; 85/238; 91/110; 91/193* (2 frags)*; 91/210; 92/24* (3 frags); *92/61* (26 frags); *92/71* (8 frags); *92/77; 84/83* Military demolition (2 frags); *84/71* Military demolition (8 frags); *91/210* Military demolition*; 12/30; 98/162* (2 frags)*; 98/178; 80/199; 80/207; 84/244; 84/251* (6 frags); *84/253; 84/254; 84/266* (2 frags)*; 86/207; 92/22*.

227 Rim and neck frag of bottle. Rim bent out, up and in with triangular profile; cylindrical neck. Horizontal wear scratches on neck. *92/4* Hadrianic. PH 38, RD c 70.

228 Rim and neck frag similar to 227; affected by heat. *98/77* Hadrianic.

229 Rim frag. Similar to 227 with triangular profile. *98/13*.

230 Rim frag. Description as 229. *90/177*.

231 Neck frag, probably from a bottle. *50/12*.

232 One shoulder and side frag from prismatic bottle. *92/61*.

233 Complete handle of prismatic bottle. Angular reeded handle with folded upper attachment retaining part of cylindrical neck and frags of rim; simple lower attachment retaining part of shoulder. *92/20*. Handle section 58x7.

234 Reeded handle and shoulder frag from bottle *92/61*.

235 Base frag of probably square bottle. Base design at least one circular moulding. *84/71* Military demolition. Dim 26x23, diameter of outer circle c 60, estimated width of base c 85.

236 Base frag of prismatic bottle. Base design – at least one circular moulding. *84/108*. Dim 30x10.

237 Four base frags (two joining) of prismatic bottle. Base design at least two concentric circular mouldings in very shallow relief. *41/6*. Dim (two joining frags) 38x24, diameter of outer circle 70, estimated width of bottle c 80.

238 Base frag of prismatic bottle. Base design – at least two concentric circular mouldings. *75/2*.

239 Base frag of prismatic bottle. Base design – at least three concentric circular mouldings. *92/20.*

240 Body frag with 120° angle from hexagonal bottle. *84/142* Military Demolition.

241 Three frags with 90° angles from square bottles. *78/16; 91/193; 92/61.*

242 23 flat frags from prismatic bottles. *14/37; 44/14; 50/39; 70/17; 81/15; 84/84; 84/107* (two frags); *84/251* (two frags.); *85.3/70; 92/90; 92/21; 92/61* (two frags); *92/65; 92/71* (4 frags); *84/71* Military Demolition (4 frags); *84/82* Military Demolition (2 frags).

243 Four body frags from cylindrical bottles with vertical scratch marks *41/6; 81/15; 84/360; 92/20.*

244 Body frag of multiple bottle(?) Flaking iridescent surfaces. Heat affected T-shaped frag, possibly part of the internal dividing wall and part of side. *Unstratified.* Dim 27x10.

Glass objects

by H E M Cool and Jennifer Price

The majority of the glass and frit objects found in the military levels were melon beads and plano-convex counters (Table 6.1). Both of these tend to be very common finds on first- and second-century military sites.

A minimum of 29 frit melon beads were found during the excavations, of which seven were found in the military levels (nos 1–7 and frags nos 8–10; Fig 6.8, 1, 2) and two in early civil contexts (nos 11–12). These beads were in use during the first and second centuries but were most numerous during the first century, and so it is possible that many of the ones found in later contexts could have been associated with the military occupation. The same is true of the two large translucent blue glass melon beads which were found in later contexts.

Table 6.1 Glass objects

Fig no	Cat no	phase	dimensions (mm)	Length/height (mm)	Perforation dimensions	Comments
Turquoise frit melon beads						
Fig 6.8, 1	1	*9/31* sf1315 Mil	16 × 15	14	5.5	Complete; ridge inside perforation
	2	*78/5* sf1631 Mil	16.5	14	7.5	Complete; edges worn by perforation
	3	*98/178* sf6331 Mil	17 × 16	14	5.5	Complete, one edge worn by perforation
	4	*9/21* sf335 Mil	c 18	14	—	50% extant in two joining pieces
Fig 6.8, 2	5	*78/17* sf1714 Mil	19 × 16.5	16.5	7	Complete
	6	*10/25* sf1321 Mil	20	18	9.5	75% extant; groove inside perforation
	7	*30/23* sf1321 Mil	—	16	—	12.5% extant; ridge inside perforation
	8	*39/7* sf1175 Mil	—	16.5	—	25% extant
	9	*50/12* sf710 Mil	—	—	—	Small fragment only
	10	*87/113* sf3326 Mil	—	—	—	Three small fragments
	11	*92/50* sf3326 Mil	—	—	—	Small fragment, ridge inside perforation
	12	*98/178* sf6131 Int	19	15	c 8	50% extant, ridge inside perforation
Black Counters						
Fig 6.8, 3	13	*70/33* sf1746 Mil	11 × 11	6		Base pitted
Fig 6.8, 4	14	*78/23* sf1651 Mil	12.5 × 12.5	6		Base pitted, probably made of dark yellow/green glass
Fig 6.8, 5	15	*81/41* sf1814 Mil	13 × 13	6.5		Base pitted
	16	*92/80* sf3880 Mil	13 × 13	6.5		Base pitted. Smoothed
	17	*54/17* sf518 Mil	17.5 × 15	6.5		Concave, base pitted. One end chipped
	18	*75/2* sf3215 Mil	18 × 16	6.5		Smoothed. Tiny opaque red specks; large void on upper surface. Probably made of dark yellow/green glass
White Counters						
Fig 6.8, 6	19	*51/18* sf781 Mil	8 × 8	6		Base pitted
Fig 6.8, 7	20	*75/2* sf1609 Mil	14.5 × 14	6		Base pitted
Fig 6.8, 8	21	*92/61* sf3831 Mil	17 × 15	6		Base pitted
	22	*84/330* sf5857 Mil	16–17	6		Base pitted. Smoothed voids on surface, 75% extant
	23	*92/64* Mil	17+	6.5		Base pitted.33% extant
Other objects						
Fig 6.8, 9	24	*92/61* sf3623 Mil	9.5	5		Setting or small counter. Blue/green; plano-convex with parallel tooling marks across base.
Fig 6.8, 10	25	*92/21* sf—Mil	28	8		Funnel stem? Blue/green; straight-sided cylinder tapering in slightly at one end to cracked off edge; other edge broken

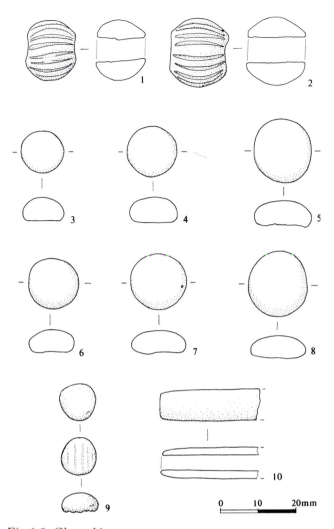

Fig 6.8 Glass objects

Black and white plano-convex counters are found throughout the Roman period but were most numerous during the first and second centuries. For the excavations as a whole 18 black and 11 white counters were found and of these six black (nos 13–8; Fig 6.8, 3–5) and five white (nos 19–23; Fig 6.8, 6–8) were found in the military levels.

The only other glass objects to be found in military contexts are both made of blue/green translucent glass. No 24 (Fig 6.8, 9) is either a very small plano-convex counter or a setting from an object such as a brooch. No 25 (Fig 6.8, 10) is almost certainly the lower end of the stem of a glass funnel (Isings Form 74). These were in use from the Claudian period to the late first century and are not common. In Britain examples have been found at Exeter (Charlesworth 1979a, 229 no 40, fig 71), Shefford, Beds (Kennett 1970, 201), Colchester (Cool and Price 1995, 174), Fingeringhoe, Essex (Colchester Castle Museum), and possibly at Southwark (Townend and Hinton 1978, 151 no 16).

Window glass from the military levels

Although window glass was not an uncommon find on the site as a whole, only two very small frags were found in the military levels (*84/75* and *92/22*). Both were cast blue/green frags with one matt and one glossy surface which was the commonest type of window glass during the first century. The scarcity of window glass from the military levels implies that few windows were being broken, but not necessarily that glazed windows were rare in the military buildings.

7 Faunal remains

by B A Noddle and T O'Connor

The animal bones

by the late B A Noddle

One hundred kilograms of animal bones were presented for analysis, of which 66% by weight proved to be identifiable. This is a low proportion, and is accounted for by the fragmentary nature of the material; most of this fragmentation appeared to be deliberate chopping, carried out before the bone was deposited. The material was presented in a number of grouped layers and some individual layers. These groups were preserved, as they appeared to comprise middens which differed slightly in species and anatomical composition and in the use to which the bone had been put. It was assumed that the contents of the individual layers were straightforward kitchen waste. All the middens except one contained very weathered bones, as if the material on the top had been exposed for some time.

The fragmentation of the groups was of two kinds, either very finely chopped to produce splinters for further working, or more coarsely chopped in the manner described by van Mensch (1974, 159), who suggested the bones had been used for soup-making. Several of the groups contained numbers of bovine scapulae, some of which had been worked by squaring-off the joint end and, in some cases, slicing off the spine. These bones would have been usable as shovels for material such as grain. A similar method of working has been described by Schmid (1972) for the site of *Augusta Raurica*, Switzerland. She suggests that the larger chopped fragments which she also found at this site were for glue boiling.

The midden groups are described under the first layer number comprising them which came to hand. The bone working treatment will be called fine chopping, the 'soup kitchen' method coarse chopping.

1/37	Exposed	Fine chopping	Many sheep and cattle metapodials
85/70	Exposed	Fine chopping	Many worked bovine scapulae
13/88	Exposed	Fine chopping	Many bovine scapulae unworked
65/92	Exposed	Coarse chopping	
66/84	Exposed	Coarse chopping	Worked bovine scapulae
18/92	Not exposed	Fine and coarse chopping	

The species composition of the mammalian bone is set out in Table 7.1. It is expressed in two ways, by fragment count and by minimum number of individuals (MNI). Neither method is very satisfactory for such broken-up material; either many of the bones have been reduced to several identifiable fragments, or individuals cannot be sorted out from the small fragments. The true species composition is probably somewhere between the two percentages. Also, bones from the less common species may have been missed and allotted to the more common species. Thus red deer and horse may have been designated cattle, and roe deer and goat designated sheep. Hence the minimum number of individuals is more reliable for these animals.

From the point of view of meat consumed, there is no doubt that the major constituent of the diet was beef.

Table 7.1 Animal bones: proportions of species present

group		cattle	sheep	pig	goat	red deer	roe deer	horse	dog	hare	total
1/37	a	205 (37)	154 (28)	169 (30)	7 (1)	16 (2)	–	2 (<1)	2 (<1)	–	555
	b	16 (39)	7 (17)	9 (22)	4 (10)	2 (5)	–	2 (5)	1 (1)	–	41
85/70	a	82 (21)	154 (32)	129 (32)	5 (2)	7 (2)	8 (2)	5 (2)	4 (1)	3 (<1)	397
	b	4 (12)	7 (29)	(29)	3 (9)	1 (3)	1 (3)	2 (6)	2 (6)	1 (2)	34
66/84	a	694 (51)	387 (29)	222 (16)	8 (1)	21 (2)	8 (1)	9 (1)	3 (<1)	–	1352
	b	19 (32)	15 (26)	9 (15)	4 (7)	5 (9)	1 (2)	3 (5)	2 (3)	–	58
13/88	a	311 (75)	38 (9)	48 (12)	5 (1)	9 (2)	1 (<1)	1 (<1)	1 (<1)	–	414
	b	12 (35)	7 (21)	7 (21)	3 (9)	2 (6)	1 (3)	1 (3)	1 (3)	–	38
18/92	a	149 (44)	105 (31)	71 (21)	6 (2)	7 (2)	2 (1)	–	1 (<1)	–	341
	b	6 (20)	11 (37)	5 (17)	3 (16)	3 (10)	1 (3)	–	1 (3)	–	30
All other layers	a	398 (48)	155 (19)	251 (31)	4 (<1)	2 (<1)	4 (1)	2 (<1)	–	–	816
	b	54 (38)	35 (25)	43 (30)	4 (3)	2 (1)	2 (1)	2 (1)	–	–	142
Total	a	1839 (47)	993 (26)	890 (23)	35 (1)	62 (2)	23 (1)	19 (<1)	11 (<1)	3 (<1)	3857
	b	111 (33)	85 (25)	83 (24)	21 (6)	15 (4)	6 (2)	10 (3)	7 (2)	1 (<1)	339

a Fragment count (%)
b Minimum number individuals (%)

Table 7.2 Animal bones: anatomical analysis, numbers of cattle bones

group	mandible	vertebrae	upper fore limb	upper hind limb	carpals & tarsals	meta-podials	phalanges	loose teeth
1/37	6	28	22	9	5	5	10	5
85/70	10	9	2	5	5	12	12	29
66/84	5	14	22	16	8	7	13	7
13/88	10	15	17	11	8	7	9	17
18/92	7	13	26	19	7	3	10	7
Other layers	7	21	11	13	8	10	12	12
Average	7	17	18	13	7	8	12	10

The fragment count varies between 21% (85/70) and 75% (13/88), but the average is 47%. Estimation by MNI nearly always gave a lower percentage, but since cattle are so much larger than the other two common species, beef was the main meat. Sheep and pig bones were found in more or less equal quantities, and they comprise about half of the individuals represented. The proportion of one goat to four sheep individuals seems high, but the Welsh Marches are well suited to goat husbandry, which certainly flourished in the later middle ages. There is one red deer to every eight cattle, and one roe deer to every twelve sheep, so hunting seems to have contributed a fair amount to the diet. Several of the pig individuals were wild.

There was one small collection of bones, however, which seems not to have been concerned with either food or boneworking, 48/14. This comprises a large adult and an immature bovine skull, three pairs of mature bovine mandibles, three bones from a young calf, bones from an adult bovine foot, and another bone from a massive bull; one of the horn cores of this animal is also present. There are four sheep bone fragments from two individuals. Two pig bones come from a wild animal and a domestic sow. There is a very large fowl bone and two rabbit bones, probably intrusive. Also present are several fragments from a male human skull. These bones are in various states of preservation, but the human and the bull fragments seemed similar in this respect. Several more bones were found elsewhere which might well have come from the bull, and some sort of disturbed ritual deposit is suggested. Despite its size, this was a domestic bull. The large skull had been cut off by a blow from below.

A further attempt was made to sort out the nature of the bone midden assemblages by carrying out an anatomical analysis of the major divisions of the body among the cattle bones. This is set out in Table 7.2. Two main factors affect the results here, and they cannot be fully separated. One is the differential durability of different bones in the soil, and the other is the deposition of different bones in different areas. The cancellous bones are less durable than the compact, and the teeth more durable than either. Thus vertebrae are usually under-represented, and the hind limb, with less durable ends on more of its long bones, tends to be less well represented than the forelimb. In this particular instance the scapula shovels also made a difference. On the other hand, head and feet bones tend to be concentrated at the point of slaughter unless the metapodials are removed for working and the phalanges with the hide. Carpals and tarsals are grouped separately because they tend to accumulate at the butchery point, the tarsus or hock in particular often being used to suspend the carcass, though this may not have been the case here. Such suspension is often used to split the carcass, and very few of the vertebrae were so split. Rixson (1971) has demonstrated that Roman butchery was often carried out with the carcass lying on its back. Numbers of loose teeth indicate the amount of wear and tear the bone assemblage has suffered in the ground. The joints of the trunk and upper fore and hind limb are the choicest from the point of view of meat. With this in mind the following suggestions are made about the midden groups. 1/37 is mainly kitchen waste apart from the worked material, and is the best preserved group. 85/70 is the worst preserved and has a high proportion of slaughter waste. Long bones seem to have been removed from the small layers to working areas.

Besides being a method of counting species, the MNI can also be used to assess the rough ages of the animals concerned, though many of the individuals cannot be aged, and there is probably a bias in favour of the younger individuals. Chronological ages are not employed. The ages are arrived at from a mixture of dental evidence and epiphysial closure of the bones. The latter is a function of the maturity of the animal and is certainly much earlier in modern animals, from which the only data are available, than in early stock. The age groups used are: newborn, juvenile or partly grown, immature/almost fully grown, and mature. The groupings are remarkably constant for all three of the major species (Table 7.3). Because this is a military encampment, it seems likely that animals were

Table 7.3 Animal bones: age ranges of the major species

age	cattle	sheep	pig
New born	11 13%	9 16%	9 12%
Juvenile	7 9%	7 12%	8 11%
Immature	24 30%	20 36%	28 38%
Mature	37 48%	20 36%	29 39%
Total	79	56	74

bought in, and the age range may represent consumer choice, whereas in a production site many of the bones may be from casualty animals. The soldiers may have purchased potential casualties, however. The mature cattle may have included their own working oxen. Though most of our meat animals today are killed in the juvenile stage, the best carcasses of the slower-maturing animals of the past would derive from immature animals. The number of mature sheep suggests that the local animals were wool producers, as the horn cores suggested a majority of wethers. The number of mature pigs is higher than usual. It suggests the local pigs were kept extensively at pannage.

Besides specific and anatomical identification and age determination, other data concerning the size, sex, and type of the individual can sometimes be obtained. The bones were measured following the method advocated by von den Driesch (1976) with a few modifications. Measurements of whole, and ends of, mature bones give size. Various proportions may give type. Sex is most easily deduced from the horn cores when present, or the canine teeth in the case of horses and pigs. Type is suggested again by the horn core, and sometimes bone proportions. Despite the chopping of much of the bone, there was plenty to measure in the case of cattle and sheep, but suitable pieces were much rarer for the pig, and very few for the other animals. There was only one measurable dog bone, and that was pathological.

Bone measurements for cattle are set out in Tables 7.4 and 7.5. The complete metapodials (Table 7.4) suggest a rather larger animal than was, in fact, the case because many smaller bones have been chopped, as can be seen from the range of proximal widths, which includes the whole bones. In general these animals are typical of the small Iron Age beast, which is no doubt what they were so early in the Roman occupation. The exception is the massive bull found in the *48/14* context with possibly other bones elsewhere. This has an estimated body weight about half as much again as the others. Even in primitive stock this is a large sexual difference, and this animal may have differed genetically from the rest, although its horn core

was not very different in shape. Even so this animal was considerably smaller than the modern animal and indeed than typical fourth-century Roman stock from good agricultural areas.

Table 7.4 Animal bones: cattle bone measurements, whole bones (mm)

bone	length	proximal width	distal width	mid-shaft width
Radius	251	62	47	36
	252	–	–	–
	258	–	–	–
	263	–	–	–
Tibia	300	–	50	–
Metacarpal	156	41	–	24
	160	45	43	24
	163	48	47	27
	165	–	–	–
	167	48	41	26
	167	48	48	27
	170	47	45	26
	170	47	45	27
	170	47	44	28
	172	45	45	27
	174	48	47	26
	175	49	46	26
	175	–	40	27
	177	46	43	24
	177	52	49	28
	179	55	50	30
	180	52	49	31
	180	58	54	32
	185	48	47	26
	190	47	44	29
	198	–	48	32
Metatarsal	193	38	43	24
	200	40	42	24
	202	39	43	23
	203	41	45	24
	205	41	43	23
	208	45	51	28
	212	41	40	22
	213	41	49	25
	217	41	44	24
	220	41	45	24
	222	46	54	27

Table 7.5 Animal bones: cattle bone measurements, ends of mature bones (mm)

bone	position of measurement	measurement (mm)
Lower 3rd molar	maximum length (anterior posterior)	32(2) 33(2) 34(3) 35(3) 36(3) 37(4) 38 39(3)
Scapula	least neck width (anterior posterior)	40 42 43(2) 44(7) 45(2) 46(6) 47(5) 48 49(4) 50(3) 51 54
Humerus	width across distal condyles	52 57 58 61(2) 62 63 65(2) 72
Radius	proximal width maximum	60(2) 64 68 77 85
Metacarpal	proximal width maximum	38(3) 39 40 41 42(4) 43 45(3) 46(3) 47(6) 48(5) 49 52(2) 55 58
	distal width at epiphysial line	40 41 42(3) 44 45(2) 46(6) 47 48(5) 49(2) 50 52 54 60
Tibia	distal width maximum	45 47 52(2) 53(2)
Astragalus	maximum length	56(3) 57(2) 58 59 60(4) 61(2) 72
Metatarsal	proximal width maximum	38(5) 39 40(2) 41(6) 42(4) 43 45(2) 46(3) 47
	distal width at epiphysial line	39 40 41 42(2) 43(44) 43 44(3) 44 45(3) 46(2) 48(2) 49 51 54
1st Phalanx	maximum length	48(2) 49(4) 50(4) 51(5) 52(15) 53(15) 54(12) 55(9) 56(8) 57(5) 58(4) 59 60(4) 61(2) 62 63 64 65

The figure in brackets is the number of bones which were the same size as the preceding measurement

Fig 7.1 Cattle frontal and horn core (cow)

Table 7.6 Animal bones: cattle horn core measurements (mm)

basal circumference	length outer curvature	least basal diameter	greatest basal diameter
100	100	23	35
102	100	24	35
102	97	24	34
108	120	28	38
110	80	27	33
110	105	26	42
112	120	27	38
115	110	30	40
120	110	26	43
125	130	29	43
130	122	31	48
138	130	33	46
140	140	32	51
150	–	37	55
		23	35
		25	32
		26	36
		30	46
		30	46
		30	44
		34	50

Estimated body weight (kg)
Derived from measurements of astragalus, Noddle (1973)
156(2) 158 160 165 169 180 184 192 194 196 280

The cattle were, in general, short-horned, the length along the greater curvature being less than the basal circumference. The greatest and least basal diameters indicate an oval horn, but not so sharply elliptical as the Celtic shorthorn of southern Britain. The shape is very similar for all the horns (Table 7.6), and a scatter plot gives almost a straight line. The frontal bone is high in the centre. A female frontal with horn core is shown in Figure 7.1, and two male horn cores, including the bull discussed above, in Figure 7.2. The other horn in this plate is probably from a castrate male.

The sheep also had small and slender bones, which is again typical of the Iron Age animal (Tables 7.7 and 7.8). They were probably horned in both sexes. Only one complete horn core was found, but there are a number of frontals with broken or chopped horn cores (Table 7.9) and no polled specimens; however, these are more fragile and may not have survived. One feature, however, has not been recorded in such early stock, and this is the projecting orbit of some of the animals (Fig 7.3). This is more typical of the medieval animal (Armitage and Goodall 1977). However, the sheep were probably of the primitive short-tailed kind, although two types may have been present. The shape of the neck of the scapula is a measure of the primitive nature of the sheep, a short thick neck developing with the modern mutton type (Noddle 1978). The scapulae here are of two shapes, both longer than wide but some longer than others. The broken horns on the frontal bones seem to be in two positions, and some have more projecting orbits than others. All these skull fragments seem to come from females or castrate males.

The goats were identified mainly by their metapodials, as is frequently the case with this species. Here, however, these bones are exceptionally short and thick, even in the newborn animal. A selection of them is shown in Figure 7.4 compared with a sheep. This stocky metapodial is typical of many of the flocks of feral goats of Scotland, animals which are supposed to be medieval escapes. These particular robust bones probably come from male animals, which is of interest

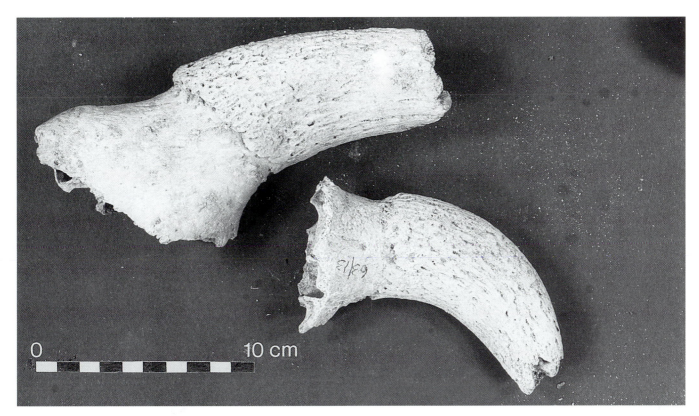

Fig 7.2 Cattle horn core (bull)

Table 7.7 Animal bones: dimensions of sheep and goat bones (mm)

bone	length	proximal width	distal width	mid-shaft width
Metacarpal	*100*	*23*	*27*	*16*
	101	19	20	10
	107	19	21	10
	110	19	22	11
	111	18	-	11
	112	18	21	11
	112	19	21	10
	113	20	22	12
	115	20	21	10
	117	19	21	12
	117	19	22	11
Metatarsal	*106*	*20*	-	*14*
	115	18	19	11
	115	*20*	*23*	*12*
	115	17	20	9
	116	16	19	9
	117	17	20	11
	118	19	22	12
	120	17	19	10
	121	17	19	9
	122	17	21	10
	122	17	21	11
	122	17	-	10
	122	18	20	10
	123	17	20	9
	123	17	20	10
	125	17	19	9
	127	17	20	10
	128	19	20	10
	130	18	21	10
	130	20	21	10
	132	17	20	10
	135	18	20	10

Goat bones in italics

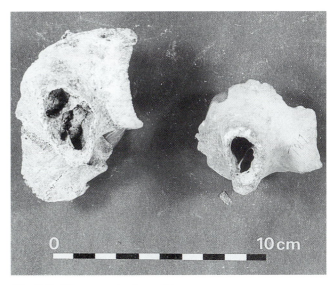

Fig 7.3 Sheep, projecting orbits

in the light of the massive numbers of male goat bones discovered at the West Hill temple, Uley, Gloucestershire (Levitan 1978).

As previously stated, not many pig bone measurements were possible, but those obtained are set out in Table 7.10. As an indicator of size, the most reliable dimension is the length of the lower third molar. This indicates a small animal, again typical of the Iron Age. The larger teeth are most likely to come from wild animals. A massive wild boar canine measures 180 mm along its outer curvature. The metapodials of the domestic pig are fairly slender, which indicates they were kept extensively and not in sties, unlike later Roman pigs.

Table 7.8 Animal bones: dimensions of ends of bones and teeth (mm) of sheep/goats

bone	position of measurement	measurement
Lower 3rd molar	length (anterior posterior)	19 20 21(3) 22(6) 23(3) *24 25*
Humerus	width across distal condyles	24(3) 25(2) 26(4) 27(3) 27(2) *30*
Radius	proximal width maximum	25 26(7) 27 29
	distal width maximum	21 22(5) 23(8) 24(6) 25(4) 26
Metacarpal	proximal width maximum	18(2) 19(8) 20(6) 21 *23 25*
	distal width at epiphysial line	20 21(6) 22(3) *27*
Tibia	distal width maximum	19 21(12) 22(16) 23(5) 24(2) *24 26*
Astragalus	maximum length	21 23(2) 24(8) 25(3)
Metatarsal	proximal width maximum	16(2) 17(15) 18(4) 19(6) 20 *20(2)*
	distal width maximum	12(7) 20(9) 21(4) 22(2) 23 *23*
1st phalanx	maximum length	30(2) 31(2) 32(6) 33(2) 34(4) 35(2)
Scapula	ratio length neck (glenoid-base spine)/minimum neck width	1.06(7) 1.12 1.13 1.14 1.15

The figure in brackets is the number of bones which were the same size as the preceding measurement. Goat bones in italics

Table 7.9 Animal bones: sheep/goat horn core dimensions (mm)

least basal diameter	greatest basal diameter
17	29
17	29
18	30
19	27
20	*30*
22	27
22	36
24	31

Goat bones in italics

The measurements of the bones of the other species are grouped in Table 7.11 and are few in number. There were three partial or complete horse metapodials which are fairly similar in size, which is that of a large pony. Red deer present a problem, because there is such a large difference between the sexes. The few bones here come from an animal rather larger than the present Scottish one, but they are not as large as some Roman specimens. The reduction in size of British deer seems to have taken place during the Saxon period, with the exception of some of the remoter parts of Wales.

The solitary dog bone which could be measured is a metatarsal bearing a healed fracture. However the bone does not seem to have been greatly shortened by this, and comes from an animal about spaniel size. Besides this dog bone, there are a number of other pathological and abnormal specimens, none of them out of the ordinary. The majority of diseases do not show up macroscopically in the bone, and most abnormalities are due to trauma and malnutrition, or are sometimes congenital. Amongst the cattle, three out of twenty-five lower third molars lack the fifth posterior cusp; the mandibles containing two of these also lack the second permanent molar. This is a common abnormality occurring in a normal proportion. Two of the metapodials are asymmetrical and one of these has a lipped distal joint surface on the outside. This is thought to be due to the continued trauma of heavy traction. A mandibular condyle shows signs of arthritis,

Fig 7.4 Comparison between goat and sheep bones

as does a sacroiliac joint. This last may have been the result of an injury partially dislocating this normally fixed joint. Among the sheep there are two defective mandibles. One exhibits mild periodontal disease, which is probably the result of faulty conformation and the other, an immature specimen, has a very uneven bite suggesting that one of the upper opposing molar teeth has been displaced. The posterior tendon sheaths of a metacarpal bone are ossified, but this may be the result of old age. There is a first phalanx with posterior exostoses at the tendon insertion, which may be from the same animal as the metacarpal; the exostoses on both bones would then probably be the result of damaging the tendons. Finally, among the sheep there is a fractured and healed femur, with a certain amount of shortening but very little distortion. Pig pathology is represented by a single abnormal bone, a metacarpal with proximal arthritis. Among the deer bones there is a small antler which appears to have been used as a pick. It has two small anterior projecting tines, which has been noticed in other Wroxeter antlers of a later date. A modern Hebridean animal has a single tine. This specimen is illustrated in Figure 7.5.

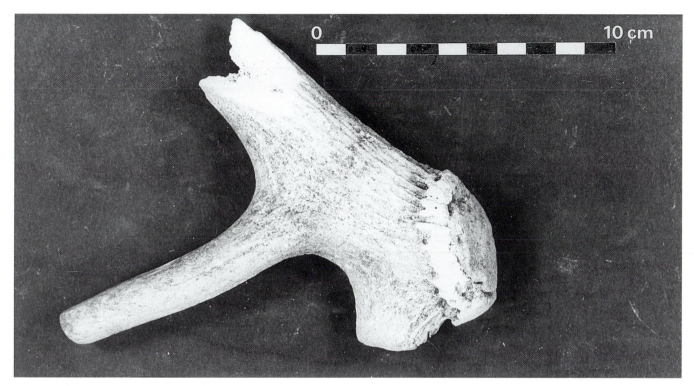

Fig 7.5 Deer antler bone

Table 7.10 Animal bones: pig bone measurements (mm)

bone	position of measurement	measurement
Lower 3rd molar	greatest length (anterior posterior)	31 32(4) 33(4) 35 37
Scapula	least width neck (anterior posterior)	18 19 20(4) 21(6) 22(6) 23(5) 24 *29*
Humerus	Width across distal condyles	27(2) 29 31 32(4) 33 34 36
Radius	proximal width maximum	24 25(3) 26 27(2) 28(2)
Metacarpal	maximum length	67 70 79
Tibia	distal width maximum	26 27 30
Astragalus	maximum length	34 35 37(3) 38 39(2) 40 *43*
Metatarsus	maximum length	76 82
1st phalanx	maximum length	32 33 35 36(2) 39

The figure in brackets is the number of bones which were the same size as the preceding measurement. Wild animal bones in italics

Table 7.11 Animal bones: measurements of bones of other species (mm)

animal	bone	position of measurement	measurement
Horse	Humerus	maximum length	260) same bone
		width distal condyles	65)
	Metatarsal	maximum length	297) same bone
		proximal width	47)
	Metacarpal	distal width maximum	51
Red deer	Scapula	minimum width neck	37
	Metacarpal	maximum length	260)
		proximal width	33) same bone
		distal width	34)
		metatarsal proximal width	38
	Astragalus		53 54 56
	1st phalanx		53 55
Dog	Metatarsal	maximum length	66

In summary, the animal bones from the Wroxeter military settlement consisted principally of cattle, though sheep and pig are well-represented. There is also a fair number of wild animals. Horse bone and dog are very scanty. Most of the large long bones have been chopped either for culinary or industrial purposes, and many bovine scapulae may have been used as shovels. The animals are nearly all small and were probably local Iron Age types, though two varieties of sheep seem to be present. There are a few hints that some of the animals were not slaughtered directly for food. There is no evidence of any unusual pathological conditions.

Bird bones and small mammal bones

by T O'Connor (submitted 1988)

A total of 158 fragments of bird bones was submitted for identification from the military levels at Wroxeter. Table 7.12 lists the relative frequency of species.

Domestic fowl dominates the avifauna, as would be expected on an urban site. The fowl were rather small by modern standards. Measurements of the proximal articular surface of the tarsometatarsus (the most commonly available measurement) gives a mean of 12.92mm (sd = 1.22, n = 11). Of the tarsometatarsi, four bear the spurs characteristic of cockerels, and seven are definitely unspurred. No cases were found with the malformed spurs indicative of capons. This distribution of sexes suggests that a supply of eggs was considered to be at least as important as the availability of cocks for fighting. Almost all the fowl bones are mature.

Two different types of duck were identified. The majority of duck bones are of domesticated duck/mallard (*Anas* sp). Three specimens, however, are of the smaller Aythyinae (eg tufted duck, pochard) although it is not possible to say which of these species is represented. The paucity of goose and swan bones is striking. Maltby observed that, at Exeter, the domestic goose only became a regular and consistent part of the fauna in medieval times (1979, 71). Woodcock are the second commonest species, indicating that hunting of birds was carried on.

The three corvids may be seen as opportunist scavengers, probably living just outside the settlement and moving in by day to feed. That raven is the most frequent of the three contrasts with modern corvid populations and points out the previously greater abundance of this splendid bird.

An assemblage of very small bones from Area 87 was sorted and identified. The species composition of the

Table 7.12 Animal bones: bird species

	no frags	% frags	MNI
Swan (*Cygnus* sp)	1	0.6	1
Goose (*Anser* sp)	2	1.3	1
Duck (*Anas* sp)	5	3.2	1
Small duck (c.f. *Aythya* sp)	3	1.9	1
Buzzard (*Buteo buteo*)	1	0.6	1
Domestic fowl (*Gallus gallus*)	104	65.8	9
Black grouse (*Lyrusus tetrix*)	1	0.6	1
Plover (*Pluvialis* sp)	1	0.6	1
Woodcock (*Scolopax rusticola*)	18	17.4	6
Dove (*Columba* sp)	1	0.6	1
Wood pigeon (*Columba palumbus*)	2	1.3	1
Raven (*Corvius corax*)	4	2.5	1
Crow (*C. Corone*)	3	1.9	1
Jackdaw (*C. monedula*)	1	0.6	1
Unidentified bird	11	7.0	
TOTAL	158		27

Table 7.13 Animal bones: pellet composition

	no frags	% frags	MNI
Common shrew (*Sorex araneus*)	12	20.3	3
Short-tailed vole (*Microtus agrestis*)	16	27.1	4
Wood mouse (*Apodemus* sp)	12	20.3	3
Black rat (*Rattus rattus*)	13	22.0	2
Small bird (cf *Passer* sp)	1	1.7	1
Frog/Toad	5	8.5	
TOTAL	59		13

remains makes it very likely that these bones were deposited as a regurgitated pellet from a carnivorous bird. The bones are well preserved and show little sign of etching by stomach acids. This suggests that the pellet was from an owl, not from a raptor. The following table summarises the composition of the pellet (Table 7.13).

The fauna suggests the presence of pasture rather than woodland in the immediate environs of the site. The most notable feature is the presence of black rat. Although generally believed to have been a medieval introduction into Britain (Corbet and Southern 1977, 237), specimens of black rat from a well at Skeldergate, York, dating from the fourth to eighth centuries AD, have recently been described (Rackham 1979). These specimens from Wroxeter pre-date the Skeldergate rat by at least 300 years, and appear to confirm that black rat was introduced into Britain by the Romans. Armitage (1994) has since reviewed this subject.

Appendix 1: Principal military features by period/phase

All the principal military features (F) illustrated on the feature location plans are listed by Period/Phase. Indeterminate and minor features, such as many of the stake-holes and postholes found within wall trenches, have been omitted from the plans for the sake of clarity. Only those features discussed in the text are numbered on the feature location plans: the complete list of feature numbers for each plan is provided here to aid any further research in the site archive.

Pre-legionary period (Fig 2.1)

Feature No	Type	Area/ Context(s)	Notes
F214	Hearth/clay floor	85.1/153	
F285	Hearth/clay floor	85.2/253	
F349	Sub-rectangular ditch	85.2/256	
F2025	Sub-rectangular ditch	1/42;46;47	
F2025	Sub-rectangular ditch	2/34;35;36	
F2025	Sub-rectangular ditch	9/28	
F2025	Sub-rectangular ditch	30/26;45	
F2409	Drainage? ditch	52/53	
F2735	Drainage? ditch	70/48	
F3251	Sub-rectangular ditch	92/84	

Phase 1 (Fig 2.3)

Feature No	Type	Area/ Context(s)	Notes
F176	Hurdling	85.1/149	
F274	Hurdling	85.2/250	
F444	Hurdling	84/ -	
F1059	Hurdling	84/414	
F3252	Hurdling	91/301	
F3253	Hurdling	84/ -	not numbered
F3254	Hurdling	84/368	

Phase 2 (Fig 2.7)

Feature No	Type	Area/ Context(s)	Notes
F2076	Centre post, gate tower	98/-	
F172	Centurial wall trench	88.3/9	
F175	Centurial wall trench	88.3/10;20	
F178	Rampart	87.1/67	
F204	Centurial wall trench	86/71	
F235	Interval tower brace	84/62	
F244	Centurial wall trench	88.1/12	
F257	Centurial wall trench	86/67	
F281	Transverse rampart timber	84/ -	
F362	Pit	85.2/258	
F433	*Ascensus* remains	84/187	
F434	*Ascensus* turf remains	84/177	
F438	Rampart	84/70;84;177; 187;188	
F440	SE interval tower post	84/70	
F445	*Taberna* N wall trench	92/81	= F448
F447	Centurial wall trench	92/79	
F448	Taberna N wall trench	92/72; 83 45	= F4
F488	*Taberna* wall trench	92/87	
F489	*Taberna* wall trench	92/88	
F511	Rampart	91/115;269;285	
F657	Barrack wall trench	80/204	

Feature No	Type	Area/ Context(s)	Notes
F727	Mess-hall 1, E wall, 1st phase	84/304; 305	F727 to
F728	Mess-hall 1, E wall, 1st phase	84/304; 305	F732 are
F729	Mess-hall 1, E wall, 1st phase	84/304; 305	linked post-
F730	Mess-hall 1, E wall, 1st phase	84/304; 305	holes in the
F731	Mess-hall 1, E wall, 1st phase	84/304; 305	east wall of
F732	Mess-hall 1, E wall, 1st phase	84/304; 305	Mess-hall 1)
F771	Pit	84/374–379; 405;380–381	
F931	Rampart	97/202	= F954
F932	Rampart	90/200;203	
F948	*Intervallum* road ditch	91/254;261	
F953	Inner fortress ditch	97/198;200	
F954	Rampart	97/202	= F931
F976	Mess-hall 2, E wall, 1st phase	84/390	
F995	Centurial wall trench	91/245	
F1000	Lateral rampart timber	91/269	
F1032	Rampart timber corduroy	90/237	
F1048	NW interval tower post	97/248	
F1067	SW interval tower post	97/ - void	
F1072	Rampart timber corduroy	90/237	
F1074	*Taberna* wall trench	98/184	
F1093	*Taberna* wall trench	98/213	
F2003	Oven foundation (cobble & clay)	98/228;240	
F2015	Centurial wall trench	30/9	
F2026	Centurial wall trench	30/47	
F2031	Centurial wall trench	9/34, 30/52	
F2034	Centurial/Barrack? wall trench	30/54	= F2036
F2036	Centurial wall trench	30/57	= F2034
F2053	Barrack wall trench	4/36;60;40; 45,12/47	
F2054	Barrack wall trench	4/39;46;51	
F2061	Barrack wall trench	4/54	
F2075	West post-pit, gate tower	90/259	
F2076	Centre post-pit, gate tower	90/260	
F2077	East post-pit, gate tower	98/243	
F2090	*Intervallum* road ditch	98/218	
F2127	Centurial wall trench	2/33a	
F2128	Centurial wall trench	2/33b	= F2137
F2137	Centurial wall trench	1/23;24; 25:26	= F2128
F2187	Barrack wall trench	5/22	
F2199	Barrack wall trench	6/39;48;49	
F2219	Barrack wall trench	6/79	
F2249	Barrack-block alleyway drain	14/49, 7/64, 39/24	
F2262	Barrack wall trench	14/44, 35/28	
F2266	Barrack wall trench	13/18;28 13/-; 7/61	= F2311
F2278	Barrack wall trench	7/36; 54;54e	
F2282	Barrack wall trench	7/40	
F2289	Indeterminate wall trench	39/20	= F2303
F2292	Barrack wall trench	39/23;28	
F2302	Barrack wall trench	39/16	
F2303	Indeterminate wall trench	39/17;18	= F2289
F2307	Barrack wall trench	39/30	
F2311	Barrack wall trench	34/12;24	= F2262
F2319	Barrack wall trench	33/35;44	
F2333	Barrack wall trench	41/13b;34	
F2336	Barrack wall trench	52/9	
F2354	Barrack wall trench	41/13a	
F2366	Barrack wall trench	41/36	
F2369	Barrack wall trench	53/15	
F2371	Barrack wall trench	42/22, 41/39b, 52/41	
F2408	Barrack wall trench	52/21, 42/23	
F2412	Barrack wall trench	52/42	
F2416	Barrack wall trench	52/46	
F2479	Barrack wall trench	46/9	
F2480	Centurial/barrack wall trench	46/10	= F2565

Feature No	Type	Area/Context(s)	Notes
F2495	Centurial wall trench	50/20	= F2562
F2496	Centurial wall trench	50/23	= F2565
F2541	*Taberna* wall trench	50/95	
F2548	*Taberna* wall trench	50/111	
F2557	*Taberna* wall trench	50/120	
F2562	Taberna N wall trench	76/5;8	= F2495, 77/13;16
F2565	Centurial wall trench	76/9b	= F249, 77/17b
F2602	*Taberna* wall trench	77/66	
F2613	Centurial/Barrack wall trench	76/10, 77/18;60	
F2617	*Taberna* wall trench	77/72	
F2645	*Taberna* wall trench	73/3;6	= F2723
F2664	*Taberna* wall trench	74/28;59	
F2723	Barrack wall trench	70/31	= F2645
F2725	*Taberna* wall trench	70/34	= F2762
F2741	*Taberna* wall trench	70/55	= F2764
F2762	*Taberna* wall trench	70/78	= F2725
F2764	*Taberna* wall trench	70/80	= F2741
F2809	*Taberna* wall trench	78/13;55	
F2816	*Taberna* wall trench	78/21	
F2820	*Taberna* N wall trench	78/26	= F2858
F2858	*Taberna* N wall trench	72/7	= F2820
F2893	*Taberna* wall trench	72/46;86; 117	
F2918	*Taberna* wall trench	72/85	
F2926	*Taberna* wall trench	72/97	
F2937	Taberna wall trench	72/118	
F2978	Centurial wall trench	45/23	
F3013	Centurial wall trench	44/6;8;9	
F3018	Centurial wall trench	44/??	
F3022	Centurial wall trench	44/17;18	
F3062	Barrack wall trench	81/55	
F3093	Inner fortress ditch	90/66;67; 247;248; 250	
F3255	Rampart timber corduroy	97/251	
F3256	Transverse rampart timber	97/-	unexcav
F3257	Transverse rampart timber	97 -	unexcav
F3258	Transverse rampart timber	97/-	unexcav
F3259	Transverse rampart timber	97/-	unexcav
F3260	Transverse rampart timber	97/-	unexcav
F3261	Transverse rampart timber	97/-	unexcav
F3262	Transverse rampart timber	97/-	unexcav
F3263	Transverse rampart timber	97/-	unexcav
F3264	Transverse rampart timber	90/-	unexcav
F3264	Replacement rampart timber	90/-	unexcav
F3265	Transverse rampart timber	90/-	unexcav
F3266	Transverse rampart timber	90/-	unexcav
F3267	Transverse rampart timber	90/-	unexcav
F3268	Transverse rampart timber	90/-	unexcav
F3269	Transverse rampart timber	84/-	unexcav
F3270	Transverse rampart timber	91/-	unexcav
F3271	Lateral rampart timber	84/-	unexcav
F3272	Lateral rampart timber	84/-	unexcav
F3273	End of inner fortress ditch	90/250	
F3274	Four-post structure, gate	98/-	void
F3275	Oven foundation (cobble & clay)	91/249; 250;251; 252;253	
F3276	Mess-hall 3, E wall, 1st phase	91/-	not numbered
F3286	Rampart timber corduroy	97/-	unexcav
F3287	Rampart timber corduroy	97/-	unexcav
F3288	Clay foundation-rampart front	90/-	unexcav
F3292	*Ascensus* post-holes (two)	84/-	voids
F3293	Setting out stake-hole (no. 2)	84/-	void

Phase 3 (Fig 2.24)

Feature No	Type	Area/Context(s)	Notes
F2076	Centre post, gate tower	98/ -	
F2266	Centurial/Barrack wall trench	12/2	
F172	Centurial wall trench	88.3/9	
F175	Centurial wall trench	88.3/10;20	
F178	Rampart	87.1/67	
F204	Centurial wall trench	86/71	
F222	Post hole/pit	86/-	
F235	Interval tower brace	84/62	
F244	Centurial wall trench	88.1/12	
F249	*Taberna*/barrack N wall trench	92/60	
F257	Centurial wall trench	86/67	
F281	Transverse rampart timber	84/??	
F347	Pit (gate?)	85.2/254	
F374	Taberna wall trench	92/64	
F433	*Ascensus* remains	84/187	
F434	*Ascensus* turf remains	84/177	
F438	Rampart	84/70; 84;177; 187;188	
F440	SE interval tower post	84/70	
F445	*Taberna* N wall trench	92/81	= F448
F447	Centurial wall trench	92/79	
F448	*Taberna* N wall trench	92/72;83	= F445
F488	*Taberna* wall trench	92/87	
F489	*Taberna* wall trench	92/88	
F493	*Taberna* wall trench	92/90	
F511	Rampart	91/115; 269;285	
F657	Barrack wall trench	80/204	
F727	Mess-hall 1, E wall, 1st phase	84/304; 305	(F727–
F728	Mess-hall 1, E wall, 1st phase	84/304; 305	F732 are
F729	Mess-hall 1, E wall, 1st phase	84/304; 305	linked post-
F730	Mess-hall 1, E wall, 1st phase	84/304; 305	holes in the
F731	Mess-hall 1, E wall, 1st phase	84/304; 305	east wall of
F732	Mess-hall 1, E wall, 1st phase	84/304; 305	Mess-hall 1)
F770	Pit (mess-hall 1)	84/328	
F931	Rampart	97/202	= F954
F932	Rampart	90/200; 203	
F948	*Intervallum* road ditch	91/254; 261	
F953	Inner fortress ditch	97/198; 200	
F954	Rampart	97/202	= F931
F976	Mess-hall 2, E wall, 1st phase	84/390	
F995	Centurial wall trench	91/245	
F1000	Lateral rampart timber	91/269	
F1032	Rampart timber corduroy	90/237	
F1048	N-W interval tower post	97/248	
F1067	SW interval tower post	97/ -	void
F1072	Rampart timber corduroy	90/237	
F1074	*Taberna* wall trench	98/184	
F1093	*Taberna* wall trench	98/213	
F2015	Centurial wall trench	30/9	
F2026	Centurial wall trench	30/47	
F2032	Centurial/Barrack wall trench	10/17 30/38;53	
F2033	Centurial/Barrack wall trench	30/55	
F2034	Centurial/Barrack? wall trench	30/54	= F2036
F2036	Centurial wall trench	30/57	= F2034
F2038	Centurial/Barrack wall trench	0/32;37	
F2053	Barrack wall trench	4/36;60; 40;45 12/47	
F2054	Barrack wall trench	4/39;46;51	
F2061	Barrack wall trench	4/54	
F2067	Barrack wall trench	4/57 5/40 6/60 12/46	
F2090	*Intervallum* road ditch	98/ -	
F2121	Centurial/Barrack wall trench	2/29	= F2138
F2122	Centurial/Barrack wall trench	2/30;30a; 37;39;42	= F2139
F2127	Centurial wall trench	2/33a	
F2128	Centurial wall trench	2/33b	= F2137
F2137	Centurial wall trench	1/ -	= F2128

Feature No	Type	Area/Context(s)	Notes
F2138	Centurial/Barrack wall trench	1/34;35; 35a;58	= F2121
F2139	Centurial wall trench	1/37;41	= F2122
F2187	Barrack wall trench	5/22	
F2199	Barrack wall trench	6/39;48;49	
F2219	Barrack wall trench	6/79	
F2249	Barrack-block alleyway drain	14/49 7/64 9/24	
F2262	Barrack wall trench	14/44 35/28	
F2266	Barrack wall trench	13/18;28 13/ - 7/61	= F2311
F2278	Barrack wall trench	7/36;54;54e	
F2282	Barrack wall trench	7/40	
F2289	Indeterminate wall trench	39/20	= F2303
F2292	Barrack wall trench	39/23;28	
F2302	Barrack wall trench	39/16	
F2303	Indeterminate wall trench	39/17;18	= F2289
F2307	Barrack wall trench	39/30	
F2311	Barrack wall trench	34/12;24	= F2262
F2319	Barrack wall trench	33/35;44	
F2333	Barrack wall trench	41/13b;34	
F2336	Barrack wall trench	52/9	
F2354	Barrack wall trench	41/13a	
F2366	Barrack wall trench	41/36	
F2369	Barrack wall trench	53/15	
F2371	Barrack wall trench	42/22 41/39b 52/41	
F2408	Barrack wall trench	52/21 42/23	
F2412	Barrack wall trench	52/42	
F2416	Barrack wall trench	52/46	
F2479	Barrack wall trench	46/9	
F2480	Centurial/Barrack? wall trench	46/10	= F2565
F2495	Centurial wall trench	50/20	= F2562
F2496	Centurial wall trench	50/23	= F2565
F2541	*Taberna* wall trench	50/95	
F2548	*Taberna* wall trench	50/111	
F2557	*Taberna* wall trench	50/120	
F2559	*Taberna* wall trench	77/7	
F2562	*Taberna* N wall trench	76/5;8; 77/13;16	= F2495
F2565	Centurial wall trench	76/9b 77/17b	= F2496
F2602	*Taberna* wall trench	77/66	
F2613	Centurial/Barrack wall trench	76/10 77/18;60	
F2617	*Taberna* wall trench	77/ -	
F2645	*Taberna* wall trench	73/3;6	= F2723
F2664	*Taberna* wall trench	74/28;59	
F2721	Barrack wall trench	70/27	
F2723	Barrack wall trench	70/31	= F2645
F2725	*Taberna* wall trench 4	70/3	= F2762
F2734	*Taberna* wall trench 6	70/4	
F2741	*Taberna* wall trench	70/55	= F2764
F2762	*Taberna* wall trench	70/78	= F2725
F2764	*Taberna* wall trench	70/80	= F2741
F2809	*Taberna* wall trench	78/13;55	
F2810	*Taberna* wall trench	78/14	
F2816	*Taberna* wall trench	78/21	
F2817	*Taberna* wall trench	78/22;28	
F2820	*Taberna* /Barrack wall trench 6	78/2	= F2858
F2843	*Taberna* wall trench 4	78/5	
F2858	*Taberna* N wall trench	72/7	= F2820
F2893	*Taberna* wall trench	72/46;86;117	
F2897	Barrack wall trench	72/110;54; 108	
F2918	*Taberna* wall trench	72/85	
F2926	*Taberna* wall trench	72/97	
F2937	*Taberna* wall trench	72/118	
F2978	Centurial wall trench	45/23	
F2987	Centurial wall trench	51/30a	

Feature No	Type	Area/Context(s)	Notes
F2988	Centurial wall trench	51/30b	
F3013	Centurial wall trench	44/6;8;9	
F3018	Centurial wall trench	44/ -	
F3022	Centurial wall trench	44/17;18	
F3062	Barrack wall trench	81/55	
F3063	Barrack wall trench	81/56	
F3075	Barrack wall trench	81/73	
F3076	Barrack wall trench	81/75	
F3093	Inner fortress ditch	90/66;67; 247;248;250	
F3255	Rampart timber corduroy	97/251	
F3256	Transverse rampart timber	97/ -	unexcav
F3257	Transverse rampart timber	97/ -	unexcav
F3258	Transverse rampart timber	97/ -	unexcav
F3259	Transverse rampart timber	97/ -	unexcav
F3260	Transverse rampart timber	97/ -	unexcav
F3261	Transverse rampart timber	97/ -	unexcav
F3262	Transverse rampart timber	97/ -	unexcav
F3263	Transverse rampart timber	97/ -	unexcav
F3264	Transverse rampart timber	90/ -	unexcav
F3264	Replacement rampart timber	90/ -	unexcav
F3265	Transverse rampart timber	90/ -	unexcav
F3266	Transverse rampart timber	90/ -	unexcav
F3267	Transverse rampart timber	90/ -	unexcav
F3268	Transverse rampart timber	90/ -	unexcav
F3269	Transverse rampart timber	84/ -	unexcav
F3270	Transverse rampart timber	91/ -	unexcav
F3271	Lateral rampart timber	84/ -	unexcav
F3272	Lateral rampart timber	84/ -	unexcav
F3273	End of inner fortress ditch	90/250	
F3275	Oven foundation (cobble+clay)	91/249;250; 251;252; 253	
F3276	Mess-hall 3, E wall, 1st phase	91/ -	unexcav
F3286	Rampart timber corduroy	97/ -	unexcav
F3287	Rampart timber corduroy	97/ -	unexcav
F3288	Clay foundation-Rampart front	90/ -	unexcav
F3289	Ditch, W edge of *Intervallum* R	84/ -	not numbered
F3290	Ditch, W edge of *Intervallum* R	91/ -	not numbered
F3292	*Ascensus* post-holes (two)	84/ -	voids
F3293	Setting out stake-hole (no. 2)	84/ -	void
F3297	Centurial wall trench	30/52	

Phase 4a (Fig 2.27)

Feature No	Type	Area/Context(s)	Notes
F2076	Centre post, gate tower	98/??	
F172	Centurial wall trench	88.3/9	
F175	Centurial wall trench	88.3/10;20	
F178	Rampart	87.1/67	
F180	Mess-hall 3, S wall, 2nd phase	87.1/100	= F283
F181	Mess-hall 2, N wall, 2nd phase	87.1/ -	= F289
F184	Mess-hall 2, 2nd phase	87.2/22;23; 24;25 95.2/22	
F186	Mess-hall 3, 2nd phase	87.2/27;28;29 95.2/27	
F222	Post hole/pit	86/ -	
F235	Interval tower brace	84/ -	
F244	Centurial wall trench	88.1/12	
F249	*Taberna*/barrack N wall trench	92/60	
F257	Centurial wall trench	86/67	
F281	Transverse rampart timber	84/ -	= F3284
F283	Mess-hall 3, S wall, 2nd ph	87.1/100	= F180
F289	Mess-hall 2, N wall, 2nd ph	87.1/100	= F181
F374	*Taberna* wall trench	92/64	
F433	*Ascensus* remains	84/187	
F434	*Ascensus* turf remains	84/177	
F438	Rampart	84/70;84;177; 187;188	

Feature No	Type	Area/Context(s)	Notes
F440	SE interval tower post	84/70	
F493	*Taberna* wall trench	92/90	
F511	Rampart	91/115; 269;285	
F753	Mess-hall 1, 2nd ph square PH	84/322	
F754	Mess-hall 1, 2nd ph square PH	84/323	
F770	Pit	84/328	
F786	Mess-hall 2, E wall, 2nd ph	84/331	
F831	Oven foundation (cobble)	84/350	
F931	Rampart	97/202	= F954
F932	Rampart	90/200;203	
F948	*Intervallum* road ditch	91/254;261	
F953	Inner fortress ditch	97/198;200	
F954	Rampart	97/202	= F931
F958	Tile oven	91/263	
F959	Mess-hall 3, E wall, 2nd ph	91/264;280	
F970	Mess-hall 3, N wall, 2nd ph	91/266	
F995	Centurial wall trench	91/245	
F1000	Lateral rampart timber	91/269	
F1032	Rampart timber corduroy	90/237	
F1048	NW interval tower post	97/248	
F1067	SW interval tower post	97/ -	void
F1072	Rampart timber corduroy	90/237	
F1074	*Taberna* wall trench	98/184	
F1093	*Taberna* wall trench	98/213	
F1099	Latrine, mess-hall	91/315	
F2015	Centurial wall trench	30/19	
F2032	Centurial/Barrack wall trench	10/17 30/38;53	
F2033	Centurial/Barrack wall trench	30/55 9/51	
F2038	Centurial/Barrack wall trench	10/32;37	
F2067	Barrack wall trench	4/57 5/40 6/60 12/46	
F2090	*Intervallum* road ditch	98/218	
F2121	Centurial/Barrack wall trench	2/29	= F2138
F2122	Centurial/Barrack wall trench	2/30;30a; 37;39;42	= F2139
F2138	Centurial/Barrack wall trench	1/34;35; 35a;58	= F2121
F2139	Centurial/Barrack wall trench	1/37;41	= F2122
F2249	Barrack-block alleyway drain	14/49 7/64 39/24	
F2262	Barrack wall trench	14/44 35/28	
F2266	Barrack wall trench	13/18;28 13/ - 7/61	= F2311
F2278	Barrack wall trench	7/36;54;54e	
F2292	Barrack wall trench	39/23;28	
F2302	Barrack wall trench	39/16	
F2307	Barrack wall trench	39/30	
F2311	Barrack wall trench	34/12;24	= F2262
F2319	Barrack wall trench	33/35;44	
F2333	Barrack wall trench	41/13b;34	
F2336	Barrack wall trench	52/9	
F2354	Barrack wall trench	41/13a	
F2369	Barrack wall trench	53/15	
F2371	Barrack wall trench	42/22 41/39b 52/41	
F2479	Barrack wall trench	46/9	
F2495	Centurial wall trench	50/20	= F2562
F2559	*Taberna* wall trench	77/7	
F2562	*Taberna*/Barrack wall trench	76/5;8 77/13;16	= F2495
F2645	*Taberna*/Barrack wall trench	73/3;6	= F2723
F2721	*Taberna* wall trench	70/27	
F2723	*Taberna*/Barrack wall trench	70/31	= F2645
F2734	*Taberna* wall trench	70/46	
F2809	*Taberna* wall trench	78/13;55	
F2810	*Taberna* wall trench	78/14	

Feature No	Type	Area/Context(s)	Notes
F2817	*Taberna* wall trench	78/22;28	
F2820	*Taberna*/Barrack wall trench	78/26	= F2858
F2843	*Taberna* wall trench	78/54	
F2858	*Taberna*/Barrack wall trench	72/7	= F2820
F2897	*Taberna* wall trench	72/54; 108;110	
F2987	Centurial wall trench	51/30a	
F2988	Centurial wall trench	51/30b	
F3013	Centurial wall trench	44/6;8;9	
F3018	Centurial wall trench	44/??	
F3063	Barrack wall trench	81/56	
F3075	Barrack wall trench	81/73	
F3076	Barrack wall trench	81/75	
F3093	Inner fortress ditch	90/66;67; 247;248;250	
F3255	Rampart timber corduroy	97/251	
F3256	Transverse rampart timber	97/ -	unexcav
F3257	Transverse rampart timber	97/ -	unexcav
F3258	Transverse rampart timber	97/ -	unexcav
F3259	Transverse rampart timber	97/ -	unexcav
F3260	Transverse rampart timber	97/ -	unexcav
F3261	Transverse rampart timber	97/ -	unexcav
F3262	Transverse rampart timber	97/ -	unexcav
F3263	Transverse rampart timber	97/ -	unexcav
F3264	Transverse rampart timber	90/ -	unexcav
F3264	Replacement rampart timber	90/ -	unexcav
F3265	Transverse rampart timber	90/ -	unexcav
F3266	Transverse rampart timber	90/ -	unexcav
F3267	Transverse rampart timber	90/ -	unexcav
F3268	Transverse rampart timber	90/ -	unexcav
F3269	Transverse rampart timber	84/ -	unexcav
F3270	Transverse rampart timber	91/ -	unexcav
F3271	Lateral rampart timber	84/ -	unexcav
F3272	Lateral rampart timber	84/ -	unexcav
F3273	End of inner fortress ditch	90/250	
F3277	Mess-hall 1, S wall, 2nd phase	84/ -	not numbered
F3278	Mess-hall 1, 2nd phase square PH	84/ -	void
F3286	Rampart timber corduroy	97/ -	unexcav
F3287	Rampart timber corduroy	97/ -	unexcav
F3288	Clay foundation-Rampart front	90/ -	unexcav
F3291	Stone kerb	84/ -	unexcav
F3292	*Ascensus* post-holes (two)	84/ -	voids
F3293	Setting out stake-hole (no. 2)	84/ -	void
F3297	Centurial wall trench	30/52	

Phase 4b (Fig 2.31)

Feature No	Type	Area/Context(s)	Notes
F2076	Centre post, gate tower	98/ -	
F178	Rampart	87.1/67	
F180	Mess-hall 3, S wall, 2nd phase	87.1/100	= F283
F181	Mess-hall 2, N wall, 2nd phase	87.1/-	= F289
F184	Mess-hall 2, 2nd phase	87.1/22; 23;24;25 95.2/22	
F186	Mess-hall 3, 2nd phase	87.2/27; 28;29 95.2/27	
F235	Interval tower brace	84/ -	
F281	Transverse rampart timber	84/ -	
F283	Mess-hall 3, S wall, 2nd phase	87.1/100	= F180
F289	Mess-hall 2, N wall, 2nd phase	87.1/ -	= F181
F403	Indeterminate slot	83/67	
F438	Rampart	84/70;84; 177; 187;188	
F440	SE interval tower post	84/70	
F511	Rampart	91/115; 269;285	

Feature No	Type	Area/Context(s)	Notes
F753	Mess-hall 1, 2nd phase square PH	84/322	
F754	Mess-hall 1, 2nd ph square PH	84/323	
F786	Mess-hall 2, E wall, 2nd phase	84/331	
F831	Oven foundation (cobble)	84/350	
F931	Rampart	97/202	= F954
F932	Rampart	90/200;203	
F953	Inner fortress ditch	97/198;200	
F954	Rampart	97/202	= F931
F958	Tile oven	91/263	
F959	Mess-hall 3, E wall, 2nd phase	91/264;280	
F970	Mess-hall 3, N wall, 2nd phase	91/266	
F1000	Lateral rampart timber	91/269	
F1032	Rampart timber corduroy	90/237	
F1048	NW interval tower post	97/248	
F1067	SW interval tower post	97/ -	void
F1072	Rampart timber corduroy	90/237	
F3093	Inner fortress ditch	90/66;67; 247;248; 250	
F3255	Rampart timber corduroy	97/251	
F3256	Transverse rampart timber	97/ -	unexcav
F3257	Transverse rampart timber	97/ -	unexcav
F3258	Transverse rampart timber	97/ -	unexcav
F3259	Transverse rampart timber	97/ -	unexcav
F3260	Transverse rampart timber	97/ -	unexcav
F3261	Transverse rampart timber	97/ -	unexcav
F3262	Transverse rampart timber	97/ -	unexcav
F3263	Transverse rampart timber	97/ -	unexcav
F3264	Transverse rampart timber	90/ -	unexcav
F3264	Replacement rampart timber	90/ -	unexcav
F3265	Transverse rampart timber	90/ -	unexcav
F3266	Transverse rampart timber	90/ -	unexcav
F3267	Transverse rampart timber	90/ -	unexcav
F3268	Transverse rampart timber	90/ -	unexcav
F3269	Transverse rampart timber	84/ -	unexcav
F3270	Transverse rampart timber	91/ -	unexcav
F3271	Lateral rampart timber	84/ -	unexcav
F3273	End of inner fortress ditch	90/250	
F3277	Mess-hall 1, S wall, 2nd phase	84/ -	not numbered
F3278	Mess-hall 1, 2nd phase square PH	84/ -	void
F3286	Rampart timber corduroy	97/ -	unexcav
F3287	Rampart timber corduroy	97/ -	unexcav
F3288	Clay foundation – Rampart front	90/ -	unexcav

Phase 5 (Fig 2.33)

Feature no.	Type	Area/Context(s)	Notes
F2076	Centre post, gate tower	98/ -	
F178	Rampart	87.1/67	
F180	Mess-hall 3, S wall, 2nd phase	87.1/100	= F283
F181	Mess-hall 2, N wall, 2nd phase	87.1/ -	= F289
F184	Mess-hall 2, 2nd phase	87.2/22; 23;24;25 95.2/22	
F186	Mess-hall 3, 2nd phase?	87.2/27;28;29 95.2/27	
F235	Interval tower brace	84/ -	
F262	Stone building A, E wall	84/337; 371;422	
F277	Stone building A, N wall	84/ -	
F281	Transverse rampart timber	84/ -	= F3284
F283	Mess-hall 3, S wall, 2nd phase	87.1/100	= F180
F289	Mess-hall 2, N wall, 2nd phase	87.1/100	= F181
F356	Latrine pit	84/85	
F417	Stone building A, W wall	84/77	

Feature No	Type	Area/Context(s)	Notes
F438	Rampart	84/70;84; 177;187;188	
F440	SE interval tower post	84/70	= F234
F511	Rampart	91/115; 269;285	
F550	Fire place, stone building A	84/129; 130	
F786	Mess-hall 2, E wall, 2nd phase	84/331	
F831	Oven foundation (cobble)	84/350	
F931	Rampart	97/202	= F954
F932	Rampart	90/200;203	
F953	Inner fortress ditch	97/198;200	
F954	Rampart	97/202	= F931
F958	Tile oven	91/263	
F959	Mess-hall 3, E wall, 2nd phase	91/264;280	
F970	Mess-hall 3, N wall, 2nd phase	91/266	
F1000	Lateral rampart timber	91/269	
F1032	Rampart timber corduroy	90/237	
F1048	NW interval tower post	97/248	
F1067	SW interval tower post	97/ -	void
F1072	Rampart timber corduroy	90/237	
F3093	Inner fortress ditch	90/66;67;247; 248;250	
F3255	Rampart timber corduroy	97/251	
F3256	Transverse rampart timber	97/ -	unexcav
F3257	Transverse rampart timber	97/ -	unexcav
F3258	Transverse rampart timber	97/ -	unexcav
F3259	Transverse rampart timber	97/ -	unexcav
F3260	Transverse rampart timber	97/ -	unexcav
F3261	Transverse rampart timber	97/ -	unexcav
F3262	Transverse rampart timber	97/ -	unexcav
F3263	Transverse rampart timber	97/ -	unexcav
F3264	Transverse rampart timber	90/ -	unexcav
F3264	Replacement rampart timber	90/ -	unexcav
F3265	Transverse rampart timber	90/ -	unexcav
F3266	Transverse rampart timber	90/ -	unexcav
F3267	Transverse rampart timber	90/ -	unexcav
F3268	Transverse rampart timber	90/ -	unexcav
F3269	Transverse rampart timber	84/ -	unexcav
F3270	Transverse rampart timber	91/ -	unexcav
F3271	Lateral rampart timber	84/ -	unexcav
F3272	Lateral rampart timber	84/ -	unexcav
F3273	End of inner fortress ditch	90/250	
F3279	Gulley, W edge, *intervallum* R	84/ -	not numbered
F3286	Rampart timber corduroy	97/ -	unexcav
F3287	Rampart timber corduroy	97/ -	unexcav
F3288	Clay foundation – Rampart front	90/ -	unexcav
F3294	Stone building A, S wall	84/ -	not numbered

Phase 6 (Fig 2.38)

Feature No	Type	Area/Context(s)	Notes
F2076	Centre post, gate tower	98/ -	
F18	Stone building A/B, W wall	87.1/ -	not numbered
F178	Rampart	87.1/67	
F189	Stone building A/B, E wall	87.2/32 95.2/32	
F190	Stone building A/B, E wall	87.2/33 95.2/33	
F192	Stone building A/B, E wall	87.2/37 95.2/37	
F233	Stone building A/B, W wall	84/62	
F235	Interval tower brace	84/ -	
F262	Stone building A, E wall	84/337; 371;422	
F278	Timber vestibule, W wall	84/79	= F261
F280	Store building robber trench	92/71	
F281	Transverse rampart timber	84/ -	= F3284

Feature no.	Type	Area/ Context(s)	Notes
F357	Box drain	84/86	
F417	Stone building A, W wall	84/77	
F438	Rampart	84/70;84; 177;187;188	
F440	SE interval tower post	84/70	
F511	Rampart	91/115; 269;285	
F512	Stone building A/B, W wall	91/97	
F513	Stone building A/B, N wall	91/97	
F550	Fire place, stone building A	84/129;130	
F605	Timber vestibule, S wall	84/148	
F606	Timber vestibule, SW corner	84/208	
F611	Fireplace, stone building A/B	84/230;231	
F612	Timber vestibule, N wall	84/232	
F614	Timber vestibule, W wall	84/??	
F661	Store building robber trench	80/207	
F741	Box drain	91/216 84/316	
F805	Mess-hall 4, SE corner	91/195	
F806	Mess-hall 4, E wall	91/196	
F931	Rampart	97/202	= F954
F932	Rampart	90/200;203	
F953	Inner fortress ditch	97/198;200	
F954	Rampart	97/202	= F931
F1000	Lateral rampart timber	91/269	
F1032	Rampart timber corduroy	90/237	
F1048	NW interval tower post	97/248	
F1067	SW interval tower post	97/ -	void
F1072	Rampart timber corduroy	90/237	
F2000	Box drain	98/227	
F2056	Store building robber trench	5/41 4/50	
F2122	Store building robber trench	1/30 2/37	
F2210	Store building robber trench	6/77	
F2230	Store building robber trench	12/36	
F2247	Store building robber trench	7/55 14/50 35/17;49;66 42/12 52/5;14	
F2312	Store building robber trench	34/29; 37;3041;48	
F2349	Store building robber trench	41/8	
F2373	Store building robber trench	53/14	
F2511	Store building robber trench	50/52	
F2644	Store building robber trench	73/2	
F2713	Store building robber trench	70/85	
F3093	Inner fortress ditch	90/66;67;247; 248;250	
F3255	Rampart timber corduroy	97/251	
F3256	Transverse rampart timber	97/ -	unexcav
F3257	Transverse rampart timber	97/ -	unexcav
F3258	Transverse rampart timber	97/ -	unexcav
F3259	Transverse rampart timber	97/ -	unexcav
F3260	Transverse rampart timber	97/ -	unexcav
F3261	Transverse rampart timber	97/ -	unexcav
F3262	Transverse rampart timber	97/ -	unexcav
F3263	Transverse rampart timber	97/ -	unexcav
F3264	Transverse rampart timber	90/ -	unexcav
F3264	Replacement rampart timber	90/ -	unexcav
F3265	Transverse rampart timber	90/ -	unexcav
F3266	Transverse rampart timber	90/ -	unexcav
F3267	Transverse rampart timber	90/ -	unexcav
F3268	Transverse rampart timber	90/ -	unexcav
F3269	Transverse rampart timber	84/ -	unexcav
F3270	Transverse rampart timber	91/ -	unexcav
F3271	Lateral rampart timber	84/ -	unexcav
F3272	Lateral rampart timber	84/ -	unexcav
F3273	End of inner fortress ditch	90/250	
F3280	Store building robber trench	91/ -	not numbered
F3281	Oven foundation (cobble)	91/ -	not numbered

Feature no.	Type	Area/ Context(s)	Notes
F3286	Rampart timber corduroy	97/ -	unexcav
F3287	Rampart timber corduroy	97/ -	unexcav
F3288	Clay foundation – Rampart front	90/ -	unexcav
F3294	Stone building A, S wall	84/ -	not numbered

Phase 7i (Fig 2.45)

Feature no.	Type	Area/ Context(s)	Notes
F18	Stone building A/B, W wall	87.1/ -	not numbered
F75	Post-hole, building 5	85.3/49	
F121	Building 5, N wall	85.3/65	
F122	Building 5, E wall	85.3/65	
F123	Blocking fence, building 5	85.3/66	= F97
F189	Stone building A/B, E wall	87.2/32 95.2/32	
F190	Stone building A/B, E wall	87.2/33 95.2/33	
F192	Stone building A/B, E wall	87.2/37 95.2/37	
F195	Building 5, W wall and fence	85.2/??	
F233	Stone building A/B, W wall	84/62	
F262	Stone building A, E wall	84/337;371;422	
F278	Timber vestibule, W wall	84/79	= F263
F417	Stone building A, W wall	84/77	
F512	Stone building A/B, W wall	91/97	
F513	Stone building A/B, N wall	91/97	
F550	Fire place, stone building A	84/129;130	
F605	Timber vestibule, S wall	84/148	
F606	Timber vestibule, SW corner	84/208	
F611	Fire place, stone building A/B	84/230;231	
F612	Timber vestibule, N wall	84/232	
F614	Timber vestibule, W wall	84/??	
F805	Mess-hall 4, SE corner	91/195	
F806	Mess-hall 4, E wall	91/196	
F851	Blocking wall	91/223	
F1079	Building 5, S wall	98/203	
F3280	Store building robber trench	91/ -	not numbered
F3281	Oven foundation (cobble)	91/ -	not numbered
F3282	Blocking fence	84/ -	not numbered
F3294	Stone building A, S wall	84/ -	not numbered

Also belonging to this Phase, but not shown on Fig 2.45 are the following: (See Figs 2.38 and 2.54)

Feature no.	Type	Area/ Context(s)	Notes
F280	Store building robber trench	92/71	
F661	Store building robber trench	80/207	
F2056	Store building robber trench	5/41 4/50	
F2122	Store building robber trench	1/30 2/37	
F2210	Store building robber trench	6/77	
F2230	Store building robber trench	12/36	
F2247	Store building robber trench	7/55 14/50 35/17;49;66 42/12 52/5;14	
F2312	Store building robber trench	34/29;37; 3041;48	
F2349	Store building robber trench	41/8	
F2373	Store building robber trench	53/14	
F2511	Store building robber trench	50/52	
F2644	Store building robber trench	73/2	
F2713	Store building robber trench	70/85	

Phase 7ii (Fig 2.48)

Feature no.	Type	Area/ Context(s)	Notes
F18	Stone building A/B, W wall	87.1/ -	not numbered
F75	Post-hole, building 5	85.3/49	
F121	Building 5, N wall	85.3//65	
F122	Building 5, E wall	85.3/65	
F123	Blocking fence, building 5	85.3/66	= F97
F189	Stone building A/B, E wall	87.2/32 95.2/32	
F190	Stone building A/B, E wall	87.2/30 95.2/33	
F192	Stone building A/B, E wall	87.2/37 95.2/37	
F195	Building 5, W wall and fence	85.2/-	= F145
F233	Stone building A/B, W wall	84/62	
F262	Stone building A, E wall	84/337;371; 422	
F278	Timber vestibule, W wall	84/79	= F263
F382	Building 6, N wall	91/80	= F665
F417	Stone building A, W wall	84/77	
F512	Stone building A/B, W wall	91/97	
F513	Stone building A/B, N wall	91/97	
F550	Fire place, stone building A	84/129;130	
F605	Timber vestibule, S wall	84/148	
F606	Timber vestibule, SW corner	84/208	
F611	Fire place, stone building A/B	84/230;231	
F612	Timber vestibule, N wall	84/232	
F614	Timber vestibule, W wall	84/??	
F665	Building 6, N wall	91/146;159	= F382
F666	Threshold, building 6, N wall	91/147	
F715	Building 7, W wall	91/291	
F724	Post-hole, passageway	91/166	
F805	Mess-hall 4, SE corner	91/195	
F806	Mess-hall 4, E wall	91/196	
F1079	Building 5, S wall	98/203	
F3280	Store building robber trench	91/ -	not numbered
F3281	Oven foundation (cobble)	91/ -	not numbered
F3282	Blocking fence	84/ -	not numbered
F3283	Building 7, SW corner	84/ -	not numbered
F3292	Stone building A, S wall	84/ -	not numbered

Also belonging to this Phase, but not shown on Fig 63 are the following: (See Figs 52 and 69)

F280	Store building robber trench	92/71	
F661	Store building robber trench	80/207	
F2056	Store building robber trench	5/41 4/50	
F2122	Store building robber trench	1/30 2/37	
F2210	Store building robber trench	6/77	
F2230	Store building robber trench	12/36	
F2247	Store building robber trench	7/55 14/50 35/17;49;66 42/12 52/5;14	
F2312	Store building robber trench	34/29;37; 3041;48	
F2349	Store building robber trench	41/8	
F2373	Store building robber trench	53/14	
F2511	Store building robber trench	50/52	
F2644	Store building robber trench	73/2	
F2713	Store building robber trench	70/85	

Phase 7iii (Fig 2.50)

Feature no.	Type	Area/ Context(s)	Notes
F18	Stone building A/B, W wall	87.1/ -	not numbered
F75	Post-hole, building	585.3/49	
F121	Building 5, N wall	85.3/65	
F122	Building 5, E wall	85.3/65	
F123	Blocking fence, building 5	85.3/66	= F97
F189	Stone building A/B, E wall	87.2/32 5.2/32	
F190	Stone building A/B, E wall	87.2/30 95.2/33	
F192	Stone building A/B, E wall	87.2/37 95.2/37	
F195	Building 5, W wall and fence	85.2/ -	= F145
F233	Stone building A/B, W wall	84/62	
F262	Stone building A, E wall	84/337;371; 422	
F278	Timber vestibule, W wall	84/79	= F263
F382	Building 6, N wall	91/80	= F665
F417	Stone building A, W wall	84/77	
F509	Building 9, N wall	91/114	
F512	Stone building A/B, W wall	91/97	
F513	Stone building A/B, N wall	91/97	
F550	Fire place, stone building A	84/129;130	
F605	Timber vestibule, S wall	84/148	
F606	Timber vestibule, SW corner	84/208	
F607	Building 8, E wall	84/210;211	
F609	Building 8, E wall	84/214	
F611	Fire place, stone building A/B	84/230;231	
F612	Timber vestibule, N wall	84/232	
F614	Timber vestibule, W wall	84/??	
F627	Building 8, E wall	84/236	
F628	Building 8, S wall	84/241	
F665	Building 6, N wall	91/146;159	
F666	Threshold, building 6, N wall	91/147	
F685	Building 8, E wall	87.3/105	
F724	Post-hole, passageway	91/166	
F738	Building 8, E wall	91/175	
F740	Eaves-drip, building 8	84/315	
F742	Eaves-drip, building 8	87.3/106 84/298	
F803	Building 9, N wall	97/152	
F805	Mess-hall 4, SE corner	91/195	
F806	Mess-hall 4, E wall	91/196	
F814	Building 9, W wall	97/159	
F867	Building 9, W wall	97/188	
F919	Building 9, S wall	90/184	(F919 to
F920	Building 9, S wall	90/184	F929 are
F921	Building 9, S wall	90/184	linked post-
F922	Building 9, S wall	90/184	holes in the
F923	Building 9, S wall	90/184	south wall
F924	Building 9, S wall	90/184	of Building
F925	Building 9, S wall	90/184	9)
F926	Building 9, S wall	90/184	
F927	Building 9, S wall	90/184	
F928	Building 9, S wall	90/184	
F929	Building 9, S wall	90/184	
F939	Building 9, N partition wall	97/196; 197;199	(Ph 1)
F1058	Building 9, S partition wall	90/224	(Ph 1)
F1079	Building 5, S wall	98/203	
F3280	Store building robber trench	91/ -	not numbered
F3281	Oven foundation (cobble)	91/ -	not numbered
F3282	Blocking fence	84/ -	not numbered
F3284	Building 9, S wall	84/ -	not numbered
F3285	Internal structure? Building 9	97/ -	not numbered
F3294	Stone building A, S wall ?	84/ -	not numbered

Also belonging to this Phase, but not shown on Fig 65 are the following:
(See Figs 52 and 69)

Feature no.	Type	Area/ Context(s)	Notes
F280	Store building robber trench	92/71	
F661	Store building robber trench	80/207	
F2056	Store building robber trench	5/41	
		4/50	
F2122	Store building robber trench	1/30	
		2/37	
F2210	Store building robber trench	6/77	
F2230	Store building robber trench	12/36	
F2247	Store building robber trench	7/55	
		14/50	
		35/17;49;66	
		42/12	
		52/5;14	
F2312	Store building robber trench	34/29;37;	
		3041;48	
F2349	Store building robber trench	41/8	
F2373	Store building robber trench	53/14	
F2511	Store building robber trench	50/52	
F2644	Store building robber trench	73/2	
F2713	Store building robber trench	70/85	

Phase 7iv (Fig 2.54)

Feature no.	Type	Area/ Context(s)	Notes
F18	Stone building A/B, W wall	87.1/ -	not numbered
F75	Post-hole, building 5	85.3/49	
F121	Building 5, N wall	85.3/65	
F122	Building 5, E wall	85.3/65	
F123	Blocking fence, building 5	85.3/66	= F97
F189	Stone building A/B, E wall	87.2/32	
		95.2/32	
F190	Stone building A/B, E wall	87.2/33	
		95.2/33	
F192	Stone building A/B, E wall	87.2/ -	
		95.2/37	
F195	Building 5, W wall and fence	85.2/ -	= F145
F233	Stone building A/B, W wall	84/ -	
F262	Stone building A, E wall	84/337;371;	
		422	
F278	Timber vestibule, W wall	84/79	= F263
F280	Store building robber trench	92/71	
F382	Building 6, N wall	91/80	= F665
F417	Stone building A, W wall	84/77	
F509	Building 9, N wall	91/114	
F512	Stone building A/B, W wall	91/97	
F513	Stone building A/B, N wall	91/97	
F550	Fire place, stone building A	84/129;130	
F605	Timber vestibule, S wall	84/148	

Feature no.	Type	Area/ Context(s)	Notes
F606	Timber vestibule, SW corner	84/208	
F607	Building 8, E wall	84/210;211	
F609	Building 8, E wall	84/214	
F611	Fire place, stone building A/B	84/230;231	
F612	Timber vestibule, N wall	84/232	
F614	Timber vestibule, W wall	84/??	
F627	Building 8, E wall	84/236	
F628	Building 8, S wall	84/241	
F661	Store building robber trench	80/207	
F665	Building 6, N wall	91/146;159	= F382
F666	Threshold, building 6, N wall	91/147	
F685	Building 8, E wall	87.3/105	
F738	Building 8, E wall	91/175	
F740	Eaves-drip, building	8 84/315	
F742	Eaves-drip, building 8	87.3/106	
		84/298	
F803	Building 9, N wall	97/152	
F867	Building 9, W wall	97/188	
F919	Building 9, S wall	90/184	(F919 to
F920	Building 9, S wall	90/184	F929 are
F921	Building 9, S wall	90/184	linked post-
F922	Building 9, S wall	90/184	holes in
F923	Building 9, S wall	90/184	the south
F924	Building 9, S wall	90/184	wall of
F925	Building 9, S wall	90/184	Building 9)
F926	Building 9, S wall	90/184	
F927	Building 9, S wall	90/184	
F928	Building 9, S wall	90/184	
F929	Building 9, S wall	90/184	
F938	Building 9, S partition wall	90/–	voids (Ph 2)
F939	Building 9, N partition wall	97/196;	(Ph 2)
		197;199	
F1079	Building 5, S wall	98/203	
F2056	Store building robber trench	5/41	
		4/50	
F2122	Store building robber trench	1/30	
		2/2/37	
F2210	Store building robber trench	6/77	
F2230	Store building robber trench	12/36	
F2247	Store building robber trench	7/55	
		52/5;14	
F2312	Store building robber trench	34/29;37;	
		3041;48	
F2349	Store building robber trench	41/8	
F2373	Store building robber trench	53/14	
F2511	Store building robber trench	50/52	
F2644	Store building robber trench	73/2	
F2713	Store building robber trench	70/85	
F3280	Store building robber trench	91/ -	not numbered
F3282	Blocking fence	84/ -	not numbered
F3284	Building 9, S wall	84/ -	not numbered
F3294	Stone building A, S wall ?	84/ -	not numbered

Appendix 2: Principal military contexts

The following appendix lists, by Area, all the principal military contexts associated with the military features illustrated on the feature location plans. Other contexts, not linked with a particular feature, but representing important archaeological surfaces and horizons, are also included. This is not a comprehensive inventory of all the military contexts excavated on the site, but is intended to provide a summary to assist with any further research that the reader may wish to undertake employing the site archive, and to facilitate cross-referencing between the finds reports and the description of the excavations.

Area/Context	Feature	Phase	Description/Notes
1/30	F2122	6-7iv	Timber wall robber trench fill
2/37	F2122	6-7iv	Timber wall robber trench fill
1/23	F2137	2-4b	Palisade wall trench fill
1/24	F2137	2-4b	Palisade wall trench fill
1/25	F2137	2-4b	Palisade wall trench fill
1/26	F2137	2-4b	Palisade wall trench fill
1/35	F2138	3-4b	Palisade wall trench fill
1/35a	F2138	3-4b	Palisade wall trench fill
13/18	F2266	2-4b	Palisade wall trench fill
13/28	F2266	2-4b	Palisade wall trench fill
14/44	F2262	2-4b	Palisade wall trench fill
14/49	F2249	2-4b	Drainage ditch fill
1/37	F2139	3-4b	Palisade wall trench fill
1/41	F2139	3-4b	Palisade wall trench fill
1/42	F2025	Pre-Leg	Ditch fill
1/46	F2025	Pre-Leg	Ditch fill
1/47	F2025	Pre-Leg	Ditch fill
1/58	F2138	3-4b	Palisade wall trench fill
2/47	F2026	3-4b	Palisade wall trench fill
2/29	F2121	3-4b	Palisade wall trench fill
2/30	F2122	6-7iv	Palisade wall trench fill
2/30a	F2122	6-7iv	Palisade wall trench fill
2/33a	F2127	2-4b	Palisade wall trench fill
2/33b	F2128	2-4b	Palisade wall trench fill
2/34	F2025	Pre-Leg	Ditch fill
2/35	F2025	Pre-Leg	Ditch fill
2/36	F2025	Pre-Leg	Ditch fill
2/37	F2122	6-7iv	Palisade wall trench fill
2/39	F2122	6-7iv	Palisade wall trench fill
2/42	F2122	6-7iv	Palisade wall trench fill
3/55	F2033	3-4b	Palisade wall trench fill
4/36	F2053	2-4b	Palisade wall trench fill
4/39	F2054	2-4b	Palisade wall trench fill
4/46	F2054	2-4b	Palisade wall trench fill
4/51	F2054	2-4b	Palisade wall trench fill
4/40	F2053	2-4b	Palisade wall trench fill
4/45	F2053	2-4b	Palisade wall trench fill
4/46	F2054	2-3	Palisade wall trench fill
4/50	F2056	6-7iv	Timber wall robber trench fill
4/51	F2054	2-4a	Palisade wall trench fill
4/54	F2061	2-4a	Palisade wall trench fill
4/57	F2067	3-4b	Palisade wall trench fill
4/60	F2053	2-4a	Palisade wall trench fill
5/22	F2187	2-4a	Palisade wall trench fill
5/40	F2067	3-4b	Palisade wall trench fill
5/41	F2056	6-7iv	Timber wall robber trench fill
6/39	F2199	2-3	Palisade wall trench fill
6/48	F2199	2-3	Palisade wall trench fill
6/49	F2199	2-3	Palisade wall trench fill
6/60	F2067	3-4b	Palisade wall trench fill
6/77	F2210	6-7iv	Timber wall robber trench fill
6/79	F2219	2-3	Palisade wall trench fill
7/36	F2278	2-4b	Palisade wall trench fill
7/40	F2282	2-3	Palisade wall trench fill

Area/Context	Feature	Phase	Description/Notes
7/54	F2278	2-4b	Palisade wall trench fill
7/54e	F2278	2-4b	Palisade wall trench fill
7/55	F2247	6-7iv	Timber wall robber trench fill
7/61	F2266	2-4b	Palisade wall trench fill
7/64	F2249	2-4b	Drainage ditch fill
9/28	F2025	Pre-Leg	Ditch fill
9/34	F2031	2-3	Palisade wall trench fill
9/51	F2033	3-4b	Palisade wall trench fill
10/17	F2032	3-4b	Palisade wall trench fill
10/32	F2038	3-4b	Palisade wall trench fill
10/37	F2038	3-4b	Palisade wall trench fill
12/36	F2230	6-7iv	Timber wall robber trench fill
12/46	F2067	3-4b	Palisade wall trench fill
12/47	F2053	2-3	Palisade wall trench fill
14/50	F2247	6-7iv	Timber wall robber trench fill
30/19	F2015	2-4b	Palisade wall trench fill
30/26	F2025	Pre-Leg	Ditch fill
30/38	F2032	3-4b	Palisade wall trench fill
30/45	F2025	Pre-Leg	Ditch fill
30/52	F3297	3-4b	Palisade wall trench fill
30/53	F2032	3-4b	Palisade wall trench fill
30/54	F2034	2-3	Palisade wall trench fill
30/57	F2036	2-3	Palisade wall trench fill
33/35	F2319	2-4b	Palisade wall trench fill
33/44	F2319	2-4b	Palisade wall trench fill
34/12	F2311	2-4b	Palisade wall trench fill
34/24	F2311	2-4b	Palisade wall trench fill
34/42	F2312	6-7iv	Timber wall robber trench fill
34/30	F2312	6-7iv	Timber wall robber trench fill
34/37	F2312	6-7iv	Timber wall robber trench fill
34/41	F2312	6-7iv	Timber wall robber trench fill
34/48	F2312	6-7iv	Timber wall robber trench fill
35/17	F2247	6-7iv	Timber wall robber trench fill
35/28	F2262	2-4b	Palisade wall trench fill
35/49	F2247	6-7iv	Timber wall robber trench fill
35/66	F2247	6-7iv	Timber wall robber trench fill
39/16	F2302	2-4b	Palisade wall trench fill
39/17	F2303	2-3	Indeterminate trench fill
39/18	F2303	2-3	Indeterminate trench fill
39/20	F2289	2-3	Indeterminate trench fill
39/23	F2292	2-4b	Palisade wall trench fill
39/24	F2249	2-4b	Drainage ditch fill
39/28	F2292	2-4b	Palisade wall trench fill
39/30	F2307	2-4b	Palisade wall trench fill
41/8	F2349	6-7iv	Timber wall robber trench fill
41/13a	F2354	2-4b	Palisade wall trench fill
41/13b	F2333	2-4b	Palisade wall trench fill
41/34	F2333	2-4b	Palisade wall trench fill
41/36	F2366	2-3	Palisade wall trench fill
41/39b	F2371	2-4b	Palisade wall trench fill
42/12	F2247	6-7iv	Timber wall robber trench fill
42/22	F2371	2-4b	Palisade wall trench fill
42/23	F2408	2-3	Palisade wall trench fill
44/-	F3018	2-4b	Palisade wall trench fill
44/6	F3013	2-4b	Palisade wall trench fill
44/8	F3013	2-4b	Palisade wall trench fill
44/9	F3013	2-4b	Palisade wall trench fill
44/17	F3022	2-3	Palisade wall trench fill
44/18	F3022	2-3	Palisade wall trench fill
45/23	F2978	2-3	Palisade wall trench fill
46/9	F2479	2-4b	Palisade wall trench fill
46/10	F2480	2-3	Palisade wall trench fill
50/20	F2495	2-4b	Palisade wall trench fill
50/23	F2496	2-3	Palisade wall trench fill
50/52	F2511	6-7iv	Timber wall robber trench fill
50/111	F2548	2-3	Palisade wall trench fill
50/120	F2557	2-3	Palisade wall trench fill
51/30a	F2987	3-4b	Palisade wall trench fill
51/30b	F2988	3-4b	Palisade wall trench fill
52/5	F2247	6-7iv	Timber wall robber trench fill
52/9	F2336	2-4b	Palisade wall trench fill

Area/Context	Feature	Phase	Description/Notes
52/14	F2247	6-7iv	Timber wall robber trench fill
52/21	F2408	2-3	Palisade wall trench fill
52/41	F2371	2-4b	Palisade wall trench fill
52/42	F2412	2-3	Palisade wall trench fill
52/46	F2416	2-3	Palisade wall trench fill
52/32	F2409	Pre-Leg	Ditch fill
53/14	F2373	6-7iv	Timber wall robber trench fill
53/15	F2369	2-4b	Palisade wall trench fill
63/18	F2266	2-4b	Palisade wall trench fill
63/28	F2266	2-4b	Palisade wall trench fill
70/27	F2721	3-4b	Palisade wall trench fill
70/31	F2723	2-4b	Palisade wall trench fill
70/34	F2725	2-3	Palisade wall trench fill
70/46	F2734	3-4b	Palisade wall trench fill
70/48	F2735	Pre-Leg	Ditch fill
70/55	F2741	2-3	Palisade wall trench fill
70/78	F2762	2-3	Palisade wall trench fill
70/80	F2764	2-3	Palisade wall trench fill
70/18	F2713	6-7iv	Timber wall robber trench fill
72/110	F2897	3-4b	Palisade wall trench fill
72/7	F2858	2-4b	Palisade wall trench fill
72/46	F2893	2-4b	Palisade wall trench fill
72/86	F2893	2-4b	Palisade wall trench fill
72/85	F2918	2-3	Palisade wall trench fill
72/97	F2926	2-3	Palisade wall trench fill
72/117	F2893	2-4b	Palisade wall trench fill
72/118	F2937	2-3	Palisade wall trench fill
73/2	F2644	6-7iv	Timber wall robber trench fill
73/3	F2645	2-4b	Palisade wall trench fill
73/6	F2645	2-4b	Palisade wall trench fill
74/28	F2664	2-4b	Palisade wall trench fill
74/54	F2664	2-4b	Palisade wall trench fill
76/5	F2562	2-4b	Palisade wall trench fill
76/8	F2562	2-4b	Palisade wall trench fill
76/9b	F2565	2-4b	Palisade wall trench fill
76/10	F2613	2-3	Palisade wall trench fill
77/72	F2617	2-3	Palisade wall trench fill
77/7	F2559	3-4b	Palisade wall trench fill
77/13	F2562	2-4b	Palisade wall trench fill
77/16	F2562	2-4b	Palisade wall trench fill
77/17b	F2565	2-3	Palisade wall trench fill
77/18	F2613	2-4b	Palisade wall trench fill
77/60	F2613	2-4b	Palisade wall trench fill
77/66	F2602	2-3	Palisade wall trench fill
78/13	F2809	2-3	Palisade wall trench fill
78/14	F2810	3-4b	Palisade wall trench fill
78/21	F2816	2-3	Palisade wall trench fill
78/22	F2817	3-4b	Palisade wall trench fill
78/26	F2820	2-4b	Palisade wall trench fill
78/28	F2817	3-4b	Palisade wall trench fill
78/54	F2843	3-4b	Palisade wall trench fill
78/55	F2809	2-3	Palisade wall trench fill
80/204	F657	2-4b	Palisade wall trench fill
80/207	F661	6-7iv	Timber wall robber trench fill
81/55	F3062	2-4b	Palisade wall trench fill
81/56	F3063	3-4b	Palisade wall trench fill
81/73	F3075	3-4b	Palisade wall trench fill
81/75	F3076	3-4b	Palisade wall trench fill
83/67	F403	4b	Indeterminate slot fill
84/62	F233	6-7iv	Building masonry - wall
84/62	F235	2-7i	Interval tower brace
84/ -	F277	5	Building masonry – wall
84/ -	F281	2-6	Transverse rampart timber
84/77	F417	5-7iv	Building masonry
84/187	F433	2-4b	*Ascensus* turf remains
84/177	F434	2-4b	*Ascensus* turf remains
84/70	F440	2-7i	Interval tower post
84/73	F444	1	Hurdling
84/214	F609	7iii-7iv	Timber slot fill
84/232	F614	6-7iv	Timber slot fill
84/331	F786	4a-5	Palisade wall trench
84/70	F438	2-7i	Rampart turves and matrix
84/79	F278	6-7iv	Timber slot fill
84/84	F438	2-7i	Rampart turves and matrix
84/85	F356	5	Latrine pit fill

Area/Context	Feature	Phase	Description/Notes
84/86	F357	6-7iv	Box drain remains
84/129	F550	5-7iv	Fire place fill
84/130	F550	5-7iv	Fire place fill
84/131	F550	5-7iv	Fire place fill
84/148	F605	6-7iv	Timber slot fill
84/177	F438	2-7i	*Ascensus*
84/187	F438	2-7i	*Ascensus*
84/188	F438	2-7i	Rampart turves and matrix
84/208	F606	6-7iv	Timber slot fill
84/210	F607	7iii-7iv	Timber Slot fill
84/211	F607	7iii-7iv	Timber Slot fill
84/230	F611	6-7iv	Fire place fill
84/231	F611	6-7iv	Fire place fill
84/232	F612	6-7iv	Timber slot fill
84/236	F627	7iii-7iv	Timber slot fill
84/237	-	7-7iv	Gravel surface
84/241	F628	7iii-7iv	Timber slot fill
84/244	-	7iv	*Amphora* and samian dump
84/245	-	7iv	Gravel surface
84/247	-	7iii	Gravel surface
84/248	-	7iii	Gravel surface
84/249	-	7iii	Gravel surface make-up
84/251	-	7ii	Gravel surface
84/253	-	7i	Gravel surface
84/298	F742	7iii-7iv	Eaves-drip gully fill
84/304	F727-32	2-3	Palisade wall trench fill
84/305	F727-32	2-3	Palisade wall trench fill
84/315	F740	7iii-7iv	Eaves-drip gully fill
84/316	F741	6	Box drain remains
84/322	F753	4a-5	Square posthole fill
84/323	F754	4a-5	Square posthole fill
84/328	F770	3-4a	Pit fill
84/337	F262	5-7iv	Building masonry
84/340	-	4b	Broken red sandstone layer
84/350	F831	4a-6	Oven foundation (cobble+clay)
84/371	F262	5-7iv	Building masonry
84/374	F771	2	Pit fill
84/375	F771	2	Pit fill
84/376	F771	2	Pit fill
84/377	F771	2	Pit fill
84/378	F771	2	Pit fill
84/379	F771	2	Pit fill
84/380	F771	2	Pit fill
84/381	F771	2	Pit fill
84/390	F976	2-3	Palisade wall trench fill
84/405	F771	2	Pit fill
84/414	F1059	1	Hurdling
84/422	F262	5-7iv	Building masonry
85.1/138	-	7iii	Gravel surface
85.1/149	F176	1	Hurdling
85.1/153	F214	Pre-Leg	Hearth/clay floor
85.2/ -	F195	7i-7iv	Palisade wall trench fill
85.2/226	-	7iv	Gravel surface
85.2/230	-	7iii	Gravel surface
85.2/235	-	7ii	Gravel surface
85.2/242	-	7i	Gravel surface
85.2/250	F274	1	Hurdling
85.2/253	F285	Pre-Leg	Hearth/clay floor
85.2/254	F347	3	Pit fill
85.2/256	F349	Pre-Leg	Ditch fill
85.2/258	F362	2	Pit fill
85.3/64	F121	7i-7iv	Palisade wall trench fill
85.3/65	F122	7i-7iv	Palisade wall trench fill
85.3/49	F75	7i-7iv	Posthole fill
85.3/54	-	7iii	Gravel surface
85.3/66	F123	7i-7iv	Palisade wall trench fill
86/71	F204	2-3	Palisade wall trench fill
86/ -	F222	3-4b	Posthole/pit fill
86/67	F257	2-4b	Palisade wall trench fill
87.2/27	F186	7iv	Building masonry
87.1/67	F178	2-7i	Rampart turves and matrix
87.1/ -	F180	4a-5	Palisade wall trench fill
87.1/ -	F181	4a-5	Palisade wall trench fill
87.1/100	F289	4a-5	Palisade wall trench fill
87.1/100	F283	4a-5	Palisade wall trench fill

Area/Context	Feature	Phase	Description/Notes
87.2/25	F184	4a-5	Palisade wall trench fill
87.2/27	F186	4a-6	Palisade wall trench fill
87.2/43	F189	7iv	Stone wall robber trench fill
87.2/33	F190	7iv	Stone wall robber trench fill
87.2/37	F192	7iv	Stone wall robber trench fill
87.3/105	F685	7iii-7iv	Timber Slot fill
87.3/106	F742	7iii-7iv	Eaves-drip gully fill
88.1/12	F244	2-4b	Palisade wall trench fill
88.3/9	F172	2-4b	Palisade wall trench fill
88.3/10	F175	2-4b	Palisade wall trench fill
90/66	F3093	7i	Ditch fill
90/67	F3093	7i	Ditch fill
90/184	F919-29	7iii-7iv	Palisade wall trench fill
90/200	F932	2-7i	Rampart turves and matrix
90/203	F932	2-7i	Rampart turves and matrix
90/224	F1058	7iii	Palisade wall trench fill
90/237	F1072	2-7i	Timber corduroy
90/247	F3093	7i	Ditch fill
90/248	F3093	7i	Ditch fill
90/250	F3093	7i	Ditch fill
90/250	F3273	7i	Ditch fill
90/259	F2075	2	Post pit fill gate tower
91/80	F382	7ii-7iv	Palisade wall trench fill
91/97	F512	6-7iv	Building masonry
91/97	F513	6-7iv	Building masonry
91/216	F741	6	Box drain remains
91/269	F1000	2-7i	Lateral rampart timber
91/114	F509	7iii-7iv	Palisade wall trench fill
91/115	F511	2-7i	Rampart turves and matrix
91/146	F665	7ii-7iv	Palisade wall trench fill
91/147	F666	7ii-7iv	Door threshold
91/159	F665	7ii-7iv	Palisade wall trench fill
91/166	F724	7ii-7iii	Posthole fill
91/175	F738	7iii-7iv	Timber Slot fill
91/195	F805	6-7iii	Palisade wall trench fill
91/196	F806	6-7iii	Palisade wall trench fill
91/223	F851	7i	Slot fill
91/237	F1072	2-7i	Timber corduroy
91/245	F995	2-4b	Palisade wall trench fill
91/249	F3275	2-3	Oven foundation (cobble+clay)
91/250	F3275	2-3	Oven foundation (cobble+clay)
91/251	F3275	2-3	Oven foundation (cobble+clay)
91/252	F3275	2-3	Oven foundation (cobble+clay)
91/253	F3275	2-3	Oven foundation (cobble+clay)
91/254	F948	2-4b	Ditch fill (Road ditch)
91/261	F948	2-4b	Ditch fill (Road ditch)
91/263	F958	4a-6	Tile oven base
91/264	F959	4a-6	Palisade wall trench fill
91/266	F970	4a-6	Palisade wall trench fill
91/269	F511	2-7i	Rampart turves and matrix
91/280	F959	4a-6	Palisade wall trench fill
91/285	F511	2-7i	Rampart turves and matrix
91/291	F 715	7ii	Slot fill
91/301	F3252	1	Hurdling
91/315	F1099	4a	Latrine fill
92/60	F249	3-4b	Palisade wall trench fill
92/64	F374	3-4b	Palisade wall trench fill
92/71	F280	6-7iv	Timber wall robber trench fill
92/72	F448	2-3	Palisade wall trench fill
92/79	F447	2-3	Palisade wall trench fill
92/81	F445	2-3	Palisade wall trench fill
92/83	F448	2-3	Palisade wall trench fill
92/84	F3251	Pre-Leg	Ditch fill
92/87	F488	2-3	Palisade wall trench fill
92/88	F489	2-3	Palisade wall trench fill
92/90	F493	3-4b	Palisade wall trench fill
95.2/22	F184	4a-6	Palisade wall trench fill
95.2/27	F186	4a-6	Palisade wall trench fill
95.2/43	F189	7iv	Stone wall robber trench fill
95.2/33	F190	7iv	Stone wall robber trench fill
95.2/37	F192	7iv	Stone wall robber trench fill
97/152	F803	7iii-7iv	Palisade wall trench fill
97/188	F867	7ii-iv	Timber slot fill
97/196	F939	7iii-7iv	Palisade wall trench fill
97/197	F939	7iii-7iv	Palisade wall trench fill

Area/Context	Feature	Phase	Description/Notes
97/198	F953	7i	Ditch fill
97/199	F939	7iii-7iv	Palisade wall trench fill
97/200	F953	7i	Ditch fill
97/202	F954	2-7i	Rampart turves and matrix
97/202	F931	2-7i	Rampart turves and matrix
97/248	F1048	2-7i	Interval tower post
97/251	F3253	2-7i	Timber corduroy
98/??	F2090	2-4b	Ditch fill (road ditch)
98/124	-	7iv	Gravel surface
98/175	-	7iii	Gravel surface
98/184	F1074	2-4b	Palisade wall trench fill
98/189	-	7ii	Gravel surface
98/199	-	7i	Gravel surface
98/203	F1079	7i-7iv	Palisade wall trench fill
98/213	F1093	2-4b	Palisade wall trench fill
98/227	F2000	6	Box drain remains
98/228	F2003	2	Oven foundation (cobble+clay)
98/240	F2003	2	Oven foundation (cobble+clay)
98/243	F2077	2	Post pit fill gate tower
98/260	F2076	2-7i	Post gate tower

Features not allocated a context number due to feature being a void; unexcavated; or the context number can no longer be identified. Features are listed in numerical order.

Area/Context	Feature	Phase	Description/Notes
90/voids	F938	7iv	Palisade wall trench fill
97/void	F1067	2-7i	Interval tower post
84/-	F3253	1	Hurdling
84/368	F3254	1	Hurdling
97/-	F3257	2-7i	Transverse rampart timber
97/-	F3258	2-7i	Transverse rampart timber
97/-	F3259	2-7i	Transverse rampart timber
97/-	F3260	2-7i	Transverse rampart timber
97/-	F3261	2-7i	Transverse rampart timber
97/-	F3262	2-7i	Transverse rampart timber
97/-	F3263	2-7i	Transverse rampart timber
90/-	F3264	2-7i	Transverse rampart timber
90/-	F3264	2	Replacement rampart timber
90/-	F3265	2-7i	Transverse rampart timber
90/-	F3266	2-7i	Transverse rampart timber
90/-	F3267	2-7i	Transverse rampart timber
90/-	F3268	2-7i	Transverse rampart timber
84/-	F3269	2-7i	Transverse rampart timber
91/-	F3270	2-7i	Transverse rampart timber
84/-	F3271	2-7i	Lateral rampart timber
84/-	F3272	2-7i	Lateral rampart timber
98/void	F3274	2	Four-post structure gate
91/-	F3276	2-3	Palisade wall trench fill
84/-	F3277	4a-5	Palisade wall trench fill
84/void	F3278	4a-5	Square posthole fill
84/-	F3279	5	Gully fill
91/-	F3280	6-7iv	Timber wall robber trench fill
91/-	F3281	6-7iii	Oven foundation (cobble+clay)
84/-	F3282	7i-7iv	Palisade wall trench fill
84/-	F3283	7ii	Slot fill
84/-	F3284	7iii-7iv	Palisade wall trench fill
97/-	F3285	7iii	Timber Slot? fill
97/-	F3286	2-7i	Timber corduroy
97/-	F3287	2-7i	Timber corduroy
90/-	F3288	2-7i	Clay foundation
84/-	F3289	3	Ditch fill
91/-	F3290	3	Ditch fill
84/-	F3291	4a	Stone kerb?
84/-	F3292	2-4b	*Ascensus* post-hole fills (two)
84/-	F3293	1	Setting-out stake-hole fill
84/-	F3294	5-7iv	Building masonry

Appendix 3 Pottery data

3.1: Quantities of military period and Period 1 pottery by phase and spatial distribution

1) Military period

	LEG	F2807	LATE	DEMO	Contam	Military
Sherds						
Defences	912	0	2452	2490	238	6092
Central	257	0	23	1986	697	2963
South	698	1686	363	2833	144	5724
Total	1867	1686	2838	7309	1079	14,779
EVEs						
Defences	721	0	2325	1987	368	5401
Central	486	0	29	3254	1129	4898
South	1678	4402	994	4974	401	12449
Total	2885	4402	3348	10215	1898	22,748
Weight (g)						
Defences	6772	0	21,774	17,561	2198	48,305
Central	1982	0	140	19,987	7751	29,860
South	14,461	18,047	6707	33,626	1908	74,749
Total	23,215	18,047	28,621	71,174	11,857	152,914

2) Period 1

	Per 1.1	Per 1.2	Per 1.3	Per 1.3 (contam)	Period 1
Sherds					
Defences	487	1279	879	18	2663
Central	5	0	612	27	644
South	0	0	102	0	102
Total	492	1279	1593	45	3409
EVEs					
Defences	526	1048	836	6	2416
Central	10	0	1482	177	1669
South	0	0	136	0	136
Total	536	1048	2454	183	4221
Weight (g)					
Defences	4085	10,442	7372	187	22,086
Central	54	0	9420	725	10,199
South	0	0	1174	0	1174
Total	4139	10,442	17,966	912	33,459

3.2: Military period pottery, quantities of fabrics (excluding amphorae) by phase

1) Sherds

	LEG	F2807	LATE	DEMO	CONTAM	total
SAMSG	225	9	171	1049	111	1565
SAMCG	0	3	1	1	7	12
MORV	4	0	5	6	1	16
MONG	0	0	0	5	0	5
MOCRA	0	0	0	2	1	3
MORT1	0	0	0	0	1	1
MORT2	0	0	0	4	0	4
MOVR	0	0	0	11	1	12
MWWO	5	0	6	8	2	21
MWWOF	0	0	0	1	1	2
MWWR	0	0	0	1	1	2
MWWRF	0	1	0	0	0	1
MWWCR	0	0	23	14	4	41
WWO	886	455	1466	2457	393	5657
WWOF	45	1	227	195	43	511
WWR	622	1193	798	2721	431	5765
WWRF	0	0	23	59	15	97
WWCR	1	0	15	120	11	147
LYON	22	1	33	83	15	154
CGCC	0	0	0	11	2	13
CGGW	0	0	1	8	0	9
LRCC	0	0	0	0	1	1
NIEG	0	1	0	0	0	1
MICA1	1	0	0	0	0	1
TN	0	0	0	0	1	1
BLEG	0	0	0	1	0	1
GBWW	13	1	0	6	0	20
CC	0	0	0	2	0	2
CGBL	0	0	0	0	1	1
CGWH	0	0	0	2	0	2
PRW2	0	0	0	17	0	17
PRW3	6	0	5	1	1	13
CREAM	2	3	31	322	8	366
VRW	3	0	0	53	3	59
MICA2	0	0	0	1	0	1
OXID	26	14	0	17	3	60
SV	0	0	2	18	2	22
SVR	2	0	7	14	6	29
BB1	0	2	0	0	5	7
BLSF	1	0	0	4	0	5
GREY	1	2	13	84	7	107
MALV	0	0	1	2	0	3
NAT	1	0	6	8	1	16
SHEL	0	0	0	1	0	1
–	0	0	4	0	0	4
Total	1867	1686	2838	7309	1079	14,779

2) EVEs

	LEG	F2807	LATE	DEMO	CONTAM	total
SAMSG	294	28	289	1928	258	2797
SAMCG	0	4	0	0	15	19
MORV	5	0	0	12	0	17
MONG	0	0	0	0	0	0
MOCRA	0	0	0	10	11	21
MORT1	0	0	0	0	0	0
MORT2	0	0	0	15	0	15
MOVR	0	0	0	27	10	37
MWWO	45	0	0	32	0	77
MWWOF	0	0	0	20	5	25
MWWR	0	0	0	0	9	9
MWWRF	0	0	0	0	0	0
MWWCR	0	0	15	0	27	42
WWO	781	1441	1358	2616	395	6591
WWOF	259	0	574	520	95	1448
WWR	1420	2803	900	4105	871	10099
WWRF	0	0	36	141	54	231
WWCR	0	0	0	206	15	221
LYON	31	0	28	85	27	171
CGCC	0	0	0	0	18	18
CGGW	0	0	0	5	0	5
LRCC	0	0	0	0	0	0
NIEG	0	0	0	0	0	0
MICA1	0	0	0	0	0	0
TN	0	0	0	0	8	8
BLEG	0	0	0	0	0	0
GBWW	0	0	0	0	0	0
CC	0	0	0	0	0	0
CGBL	0	0	0	0	0	0
CGWH	0	0	0	15	0	15
PRW2	0	0	0	45	0	45
PRW3	33	0	8	10	0	51
CREAM	0	20	36	131	0	187
VRW	10	0	0	10	0	20
MICA2	0	0	0	0	0	0
OXID	0	100	0	80	47	227
SV	0	0	0	75	0	75
SVR	0	0	16	9	12	37
BB1	0	0	0	0	0	0
BLSF	0	0	0	0	0	0
GREY	0	6	88	83	13	190
MALV	0	0	0	5	0	5
NAT	7	0	0	30	8	45
SHEL	0	0	0	0	0	0
-	0	0	0	0	0	0
Total	2885	4402	3348	10,215	1898	22,748

	LEG	F2807	LATE	DEMO	CONTAM	total
CGCC	0	0	0	28	6	34
CGGW	0	0	1	27	0	28
LRCC	0	0	0	0	1	1
NIEG	0	1	0	0	0	1
MICA1	1	0	0	0	0	1
TN	0	0	0	0	10	10
BLEG	0	0	0	5	0	5
GBWW	55	5	0	30	0	90
CC	0	0	0	20	0	20
CGBL	0	0	0	0	4	4
CGWH	0	0	0	5	0	5
PRW2	0	0	0	390	0	390
PRW3	60	0	50	5	5	120
CREAM	15	100	210	2021	45	2391
VRW	35	0	0	190	45	270
MICA2	0	0	0	5	0	5
OXID	2160	185	0	105	45	2495
SV	0	0	15	295	30	340
SVR	75	0	150	300	30	555
BB1	0	20	0	0	55	75
BLSF	5	0	0	40	0	45
GREY	30	10	295	795	140	1270
MALV	0	0	10	25	0	35
NAT	30	0	65	175	20	290
SHEL	0	0	0	5	0	5
-	0	0	25	0	0	25
Total	23,215	18,047	28,621	71,174	11,857	152,914

3.3: Quantities of samian by period and area

area	period	sherds	EVEs	weight (g)	g/sherd	broken
Central	Military	412	543	1832	4.45	0.76
	Period 1	88	191	543	6.17	0.46
	Period 2	387	677	2438	6.3	0.57
	Sub-total	*887*	*1411*	*4813*		
South	Military	417	1246	3498	8.39	0.33
	Period 1	35	76	158	4.51	0.46
	Period 2	528	1369	3696	7.0	0.39
	Sub-total	*980*	*2691*	*7352*		
Defences	Military	630	754	2755	4.37	0.84
	Period 1	338	489	1670	4.94	0.69
	Period 2	2870	5561	17818	6.21	0.52
	Sub-total	*3838*	*6804*	*22243*		
	TOTAL	5705	10906	34408		

3) Weight

	LEG	F2807	LATE	DEMO	CONTAM	total
SAMSG	987	93	1023	5931	1278	9312
SAMCG	0	38	7	6	122	173
MORV	125	0	130	555	10	820
MONG	0	0	0	109	0	109
MOCRA	0	0	0	145	220	365
MORT1	0	0	0	0	190	190
MORT2	0	0	0	235	0	235
MOVR	0	0	0	880	250	1130
MWWO	1265	0	615	575	60	2515
MWWOF	0	0	0	670	70	740
MWWR	0	0	0	10	90	100
MWWRF	0	40	0	0	0	40
MWWCR	0	0	795	370	675	1840
WWO	9680	6990	14,717	24,890	3440	59,717
WWOF	870	5	3316	3265	585	8041
WWR	7730	10,550	6880	26,030	3951	55,141
WWRF	0	0	100	470	240	810
WWCR	5	0	75	2385	185	2650
LYON	85	10	142	182	55	474

3.4: Stratified occurrence of Flavian samian vessels pre-dating the demolition period

Phase	Area	Box/Cxt	Detail	Feature no	Form	Date
3	Defences	85/246	Pit	F270	Dr 29	65-80
3	Defences	85/71	Pebbles		Dr 37	70-95
4b	Defences	85/254	Latrine	F347	Dr 37	70-85
4b	Defences		-do-		Dish	Flavian
4b	Defences		-do-		Dr 18	Flavian?
4b	Defences	85/259	Pit	F361	Dr 27	Flavian
4b	Defences	84/362	Pit/slot	F858/863	Dr 30	75-90
4b	Defences	88/12	Pit/slot	F225/244	Dr 18	Flavian?
4b	South	80/191	Slot	F632	Dr 18 (x 2)	Flavian
4b	Central	a/16			78	70-85
4b	Central	30/43	Latrine	F2022	Dr 18	Flavian
4b	Central	8/21		F3028	Dr 27	Flavian
4b	South	72/9	Posthole	F2860	Dr 36	Flavian
4b	South	72/48	Pit	F2894	Dr 18	Flavian
4b	South	72/19	Pit	F2868	Dr 29	Flavian?
4b	South	72/55	Pit	F2898	15/17-18 & 30	Flavian?
5	Defences	84/266	Rubble		Dr 18	Vespasian
5	Defences	84/83	Const		Dr 27	Flavian
5	Defences	87/47	Robbing	F127	Dr 27	Flavian
5	Defences	84/280	Hearth	F550	Dr 18	Flavian?
5	South	77/9	Pit	F2598	Stamp No 161	65-95
			-do-		Dr 35/36	Flavian?
5	South	92/89	Pit	F490	Dr 18	Flavian
5	South	92/90	Pit	F493/504	Cup/bowl	Flavian?
6	Defences	83/63	Pebble surface		Dr 37	Early Flavian
6	Defences	85/67	Road		Dr 29	65-80
6	Defences	91/308	Pre-stone bldg		Dr 27	Flavian
					Dr 29?	Flavian?
		91/257	Pre-stone bldg		Ritt 12	Flavian?
6	Defences	84/343	Rubble		Dr 18	Flavian
6	Defences	84/319	Trample		Dr 18	Flavian
6	Defences	84/91	Gulley?	F378	Dr 18	Flavian
7i	Defences	90/203	Rampart turves		Dr 37	Flavian
7i	Defences	97/198	Ditch		chip	Flavian?

3.5: Samian vessel types, all South Gaulish wares, irrespective of phasing

Vessel type	Sherds	EVEs	Weight (g)
29	454	448	2987
29 or 30	1	0	1
29 or 37	13	0	111
30	62	74	325
30 or 37	39	82	185
37	384	411	3468
15	1	0	5
15/17	187	371	1325
15/17 or 15/17R	2	0	5
15/17 or 17	4	0	89
15/17or 18	70	3	613
15/17R	37	51	382
15/17R or 18R	30	0	591
16	1	0	3
17	3	11	7
18	749	1694	4587
18 or 18/31	1	0	64
18R	5	0	26
18 or 18R	16	31	78
18/31	6	41	74
18/31R	1	0	20
18R	104	200	1083
18R or 18/31R	2	6	12
22	2	31	50
24	148	652	917
24 or 27	1	0	3
27	851	2907	4086
27 or 35	4	0	6
27 or 42	1	5	2
33	7	10	15
33A	7	18	19
35	51	150	182
35-C	1	0	6
35/36	61	126	214
36	41	102	237
36 or CU11	1	0	10
42	12	50	100
67	34	40	86
72	1	0	1
78	6	32	36
B	49	0	211
BD	25	2	101
BR	1	0	11
C	162	3	405
CB	5	0	11
CD	1	0	3
CLSD	16	0	33
CU11	55	122	416
CU15	1	0	6
D	164	1	611
DR	1	0	2
R1	6	74	186
R12	74	228	704
R12 or CU11	70	51	827
R13	9	3	17
R5	1	8	4
R8	16	49	44
R9	8	42	33
-	742	5	972
Total	4807	8134	26,608

3.6: Pottery vessel classes, occurrences by phase, summary

1) Sherds

	LEG	F2807	LATE	DEMO	CONTAM	Total
B	77	89	71	491	51	779
D	85	58	114	399	74	730
BD	0	0	0	9	1	10
C	44	106	72	388	38	648
CB	0	0	3	12	1	16
L	2	1	17	31	27	78
F	99	153	463	696	88	1499
J	401	154	266	919	166	1906
CP	0	1	0	1	3	5
HP	33	0	11	40	0	84
JBK	0	0	1	0	0	1
BK	46	100	86	188	57	477
CLSD	0	2	35	102	10	149
M	9	1	34	52	12	108
LAMP	3	0	0	11	3	17
Z	2	8	11	30	2	53
-	1066	1013	1654	3940	546	8219
Total	1867	1686	2838	7309	1079	14,779

2) EVEs

	LEG	F2807	LATE	DEMO	CONTAM	Total
B	157	290	212	1169	87	1915
D	204	341	264	746	241	1796
BD	0	0	0	2	0	2
C	170	671	236	1288	83	2448
CB	0	0	0	19	0	19
L	17	0	60	179	79	335
F	346	799	1343	1526	276	4290
J	1651	1614	913	4417	918	9513
CP	0	0	0	0	8	8
HP	40	0	15	105	0	160
JBK	0	0	7	0	0	7
BK	165	637	203	498	135	1638
CLSD	0	0	0	0	0	0
M	50	0	15	116	62	243
LAMP	75	0	0	60	9	144
Z	10	50	80	90	0	230
-	0	0	0	0	0	0
Total	2885	4402	3348	10,215	1898	22,748

3) Weight (g)

	LEG	F2807	LATE	DEMO	CONTAM	Total
B	781	1499	1433	5317	528	9558
D	1564	936	1704	3059	1562	8825
BD	0	0	0	87	5	92
C	210	897	493	2080	167	3847
CB	0	0	14	44	5	63
L	30	5	315	395	165	910
F	3650	3025	6305	10,900	1530	25,410
J	7660	2585	4280	11,485	1680	27,690
CP	0	10	0	5	30	45
HP	285	0	90	775	0	1150
JBK	0	0	5	0	0	5
BK	199	565	801	1007	158	2730
CLSD	0	130	235	881	100	1346
M	1390	40	1540	3549	1565	8084
LAMP	41	0	0	128	3	172
Z	20	270	106	439	30	865
-	7385	8085	11,300	31,023	4329	62,122
Total	23,215	18,047	28,621	71,174	11,857	152,914

3.7: Vessel classes, occurrence by phase

1) based on percentages of EVEs 114.69 EVEs

	LEG	F2807	LATE	DEMO	CONT	1.1	1.2	1.3	2.1	2.2	2.3	2.4
Decorated bowls												
29	9.5	.	.	8.9	7.3	8.2	24.7	4.5	5.3	2.3	0.9	2.3
Dec	.	.	.	.	.	.	.	.	0.6	1.5	1.2	5.0
30	1.0	31.2	.	0.7	.	11.2	0.6	1.0	0.6	.	0.6	.
37	.	.	1.4	1.5	.	4.1	6.0	5.3	6.3	5.7	8.0	10.3
Dishes												
R1	2.4	.	.	0.2	21.2	.	.	1.0	.	.	.	.
15	.	.	.	.	.	.	.	.	.	.	.	.
15/17	2.0	.	5.2	3.2	26.0	.	1.2	6.1	5.2	3.8	0.8	4.2
15/17R	2.4	.	0.7	0.9	.	.	.	.	0.4	1.3	0.1	.
16	.	.	.	.	.	.	.	.	.	.	.	.
17	.	.	.	0.4	.	.	.	0.6	.	.	.	.
18	11.2	56.3	14.5	16.0	8.1	42.9	12.1	23.8	20	24.6	9.9	5.0
18R	.	.	24.2	1.4	6.6	.	.	.	2.2	1.0	0.9	.
18/31	.	.	.	.	.	.	.	.	1.0	5.2	15.3	21.4
18/31R	.	.	.	.	.	.	.	.	.	2.2	1.6	.
22	10.5	.	.	.	.	.	.	.	.	.	.	.
31	.	12.5	.	.	.	.	.	.	.	1.5	.	1.5
36	.	.	.	0.2	.	.	.	.	0.6	0.6	7.5	0.6
42	.	.	.	0.2	.	.	.	.	1.4	0.7	0.5	.
42R	.	.	.	.	.	.	.	.	.	.	0.2	.
79	.	.	.	.	.	.	.	.	.	.	.	.
CU15	.	.	.	.	.	.	.	.	.	0.4	0.1	.
CU15 or 23	.	.	.	.	.	.	.	.	.	.	.	.
CU23	.	.	.	.	.	.	.	.	.	.	0.1	.
Lud Tg	.	.	.	.	.	.	1.8	.	.	.	.	.
D	.	.	.	0.6	2.2	.	.	0.8	0.2	0.1	0.3	0.6
Cups												
R5	.	.	.	.	2.9	.	.	.	.	.	.	.
R8	11.9	.	.	.	.	.	.	0.6	0.2	0.6	.	.
R9	.	.	.	0.6	.	.	.	.	0.6	.	0.5	.
24	7.1	.	35.0	13.0	.	.	3.6	11.4	5.3	3.7	1.5	1.5
25	.	.	4.5	.	.	.	.	.	.	.	.	.
27	19.4	.	11.8	43.8	18.7	12.2	38.0	36.6	41.0	31.4	28.7	26.6
33	.	.	.	0.2	5.5	.	.	.	0.2	2.4	3.0	2.9
35	.	.	.	0.9	.	10.2	.	4.1	0.6	0.5	4.5	10.1
78	9.9	.	.	.	.	.	.	.	.	.	0.1	.
46	.	.	.	.	.	.	.	.	.	0.2	1	.
80	.	.	.	.	.	.	.	.	.	1.1	.	.
C	.	.	.	.	.	.	.	.	0.3	0.4	0.1	.
Bowls												
R12	11.6	.	1.7	3.7	0.7	8.2	10.2	0.8	1.4	1.3	0.8	2.1
R12 or CU11	1.0	.	1.0	0.8	.	.	.	.	0.3	0.4	0.4	.
CU11	.	.	.	1.8	0.7	.	1.8	1.6	1.5	2.3	2.3	3.1
31R	.	.	.	.	.	.	.	.	.	.	0.1	.
38	.	.	.	.	.	.	.	.	.	.	0.1	.
44	.	.	.	.	.	.	.	.	.	.	0.5	.
81	.	.	.	.	.	.	.	.	.	.	0.2	.
B	.	.	.	.	.	.	.	.	.	0.5	5.8	1.1
Mixed forms												
CB	.	.	.	1.0	.	3.1	.	1.8	3.8	0.6	1.2	1.7
BD	.	.	.	0.1	.	.	.	.	.	.	0.1	.
Closed												
67	.	.	.	.	.	.	.	.	0.9	2.0	.	.
CLSD	.	.	.	.	.	.	.	.	.	.	0.4	.
Mortaria												
45	.	.	.	.	.	.	.	.	.	.	0.1	.
Inkwells												
R13	.	.	.	.	.	.	.	.	.	0.2	0.5	.
-	.	.	.	.	.	.	.	.	.	1.5	0.2	.
Total	100	100	100	100	100	100	100	100	100	100	100	100
EVEs	294	32	289	1928	273	98	166	492	1460	1355	4605	477
	LEG	F2807	LATE	DEMO	CONT	1.1	1.2	1.3	2.1	2.2	2.3	2.4

2) based on percentage of weight (g)

	LEG	F2807	LATE	DEMO	CONT	1.1	1.2	1.3	2.1	2.2	2.3	2.4
Decorated bowls												
29	14.2	.	3.5	13.8	8.9	30.4	35.3	21.0	9.1	7.5	3.1	3.9
Dec	.	.	0.3	1.4	.	.	.	0.1	0.8	3.6	2.2	1.8
30	2.0	9.9	.	0.8	.	6.7	5.5	0.5	2.0	0.8	0.6	.
37	1.2	.	1.8	3.1	0.4	3.5	8.3	13.9	18.1	15.9	20.3	29.8
Dishes												
R1	0.3	.	.	0.1	11.9	.	.	0.2	0.1	.	.	.
15	0.5	.	.	.	.	.	.	.	.	.	.	.
15/17	7.1	.	3.4	2.4	45.6	6.4	0.2	1.9	2.7	4.1	0.5	1.2
15/17R	7.5	.	0.6	2.3	.	.	1.6	0.3	0.3	2.8	0.1	.
16	.	.	.	.	.	.	.	.	.	.	0.02	.
17	.	.	.	0.1	.	.	.	0.1	.	.	.	.
18	16.2	37.4	19.8	20.4	8.4	15.9	15.3	20.1	15.7	8.6	9.0	3.4
18R	4.1	.	26.0	2.5	6.1	9.5	0.4	3.2	1.3	2.4	1.9	0.6
18/31	.	.	.	.	.	.	.	.	1.5	3.3	13.2	13.9
18/31R	.	.	.	.	.	.	.	.	0.4	4.5	3.7	2.6
22	4.6	.	.	0.1	.	.	.	.	.	.	.	.
31	.	27.5	.	.	.	.	.	.	.	1.2	1.3	2.8
36	1.0	.	0.2	0.03	.	.	.	.	0.4	1.8	3.3	6.1
42	.	.	.	0.3	.	.	.	.	1.0	0.1	0.2	.
42R	.	.	.	.	.	.	.	.	.	.	0.2	.
79	.	.	.	.	.	.	.	.	.	.	0.7	.
CU15	.	.	.	.	.	.	.	.	.	0.1	0.2	.
CU15 or 23	.	.	.	.	.	.	.	.	0.02	.	0.07	.
CU23	.	.	.	.	.	.	.	.	.	.	0.02	.
Lud Tg	.	.	.	.	.	.	0.2	.	.	.	.	.
Dish	6.3	1.5	7.9	4.1	7.8	0.9	0.8	7.3	9.9	8.5	3.6	10.8
Cups												
R5	.	.	.	.	0.3	.	.	.	.	.	.	.
R8	1.7	.	.	0.1	0.3	.	.	0.2	0.04	0.1	0.04	.
R9	.	.	.	0.2	0.4	.	.	.	0.2	.	0.03	.
24	5.3	14.5	16.0	5.1	.	3.8	2.0	2.8	1.7	1.8	0.9	1.2
25	.	.	1.0	.	.	.	.	.	.	.	.	.
27	4.9	2.3	5.8	22.2	2.7	10.4	10.1	15.8	18.0	12.3	13.4	7.1
33	0.1	.	.	0.03	5	.	.	.	0.1	1.3	2.6	1.4
35	.	.	.	0.5	.	1.4	.	1.4	0.3	0.6	1.6	5.0
78	1.8	.	.	0.1	0.4	.	.	.	.	0.1	0.02	.
46	.	.	.	.	.	.	.	.	.	0.04	0.7	0.3
80	.	.	.	.	.	.	.	.	.	0.5	.	.
C	0.3	6.9	4.4	0.9	0.3	.	0.4	0.9	1.5	2.6	1.6	0.8
Bowls												
R12	10.9	.	1.8	4.7	0.1	4.9	11.5	0.6	1	0.8	0.7	1.9
R12 or CU11	0.6	.	3.8	6.6	.	.	.	3.8	5.1	1.3	0.4	0.2
CU11	0.1	.	.	2.7	0.4	.	1.0	0.9	1.2	2.9	2.2	2.4
31R	.	.	.	.	.	.	.	.	.	.	0.1	.
38	.	.	.	.	.	.	.	.	.	.	0.4	0.3
44	.	.	.	.	.	.	.	.	.	.	0.5	.
81	.	.	.	.	.	.	.	.	.	.	0.1	.
81R	0.1	.	.	0.4	.	.	.	.	.	.	.	.
B	1.3	.	.	1.1	.	2.3	1.2	1.3	1.3	2.0	5.2	0.6
Mixed forms												
CB	.	.	1.4	0.7	0.8	0.3	1.0	0.9	1.1	0.6	0.6	0.6
CD	.	.	.	.	.	.	.	.	.	.	0.02	.
BD	.	.	.	1.3	.	.	.	0.6	0.1	1.0	0.7	.
Closed												
67	.	.	.	0.1	.	.	1.0	1.1	0.7	0.5	0.1	.
72	.	.	.	.	0.1	.	.	.	.	.	0.03	.
CLSD	.	.	.	0.1	.	.	.	0.2	0.2	0.4	0.4	.
Mortaria												
43	.	.	.	.	.	.	.	.	.	.	0.1	.
45	.	.	.	.	.	.	.	.	.	.	0.1	.
Inkwells												
R13	.	.	0.6	0.2	.	.	.	.	0.02	0.02	0.02	.
-	7.9	.	1.8	1.5	0.3	3.8	4.4	1.1	4.4	5.8	3.7	1.3
Total	100	100	100	100	100	100	100	100	100	100	100	100
Wt	987	131	1030	5937	1400	346	505	1520	4486	4606	14804	1470
	LEG	F2807	LATE	DEMO	CONT	1.1	1.2	1.3	2.1	2.2	2.3	2.4

Bibliography

AdT, 1984 *Augusstadt der Treverer*, Exhibition catalogue, Rheinisches Landesmuseum, Trier, Mainz

Allason-Jones, L, and MacKay, B, 1985 *Coventina's Well: a shrine on Hadrian's Wall*, Chesters

Allason-Jones, L, and Miket, R F, 1984 *Catalogue of small finds from South Shields Roman fort*, Newcastle upon Tyne

Almgren, O, 1923 *Studien über Nordeuropäische Fibelformen der ersten nachchristlichen Jahrhunderte mit Berüchtsichtigung der Provinzialrömischen Formen*, Leipzig

Anderson, A C, 1981 Some continental beakers of the first and second centuries AD, in *Roman Pottery Research in Britain and North-West Europe* (eds A C Anderson and A S Anderson), BAR **S123**, 321–48, Oxford

Annable, K, 1976 A bronze military apron mount from *Cunetio, Wiltshire Archaeol Natur Hist Mag*, **69**, 176–9

Armitage, P L, 1994 Unwelcome companions: ancient rats reviewed, *Antiquity* **68**, 231–40

Armitage, P L, and Goodall, J A, 1977 Medieval horned and polled sheep: the archaeological and iconographic evidence, *Antiq J*, **57**, 73–89

Arsdell van, R D, 1989 *Celtic coinage of Britain*, London

Atkinson, D, 1914 A hoard of samian from Pompeii, *J Roman Stud* **4**, 26–64

—, 1916 *The Romano-British site on Lowbury Hill in Berkshire*, Reading

—, 1942 *Report on excavations at Wroxeter (the Roman city of Viroconium) in the county of Salop, 1923–1927*, Oxford

Baillie Reynolds, P K, 1936 Excavations on the site of the Roman fort at Caerhun, seventh interim report, small finds, *Archaeol Cambrensis*, **91**, 210–46

Baker, A, 1969/70 Aerial reconnaissance over Viroconium and military sites in the area 1969, *Trans Shrops Archaeol Soc*, **59**, 24–31

—, 1971 Viroconium: an aerial study of the defences, *Trans Shrops Archaeol Soc*, **58**, 197–219

Ball, F, and Ball, N B, 1988 The Canterbury try and mitre square – an appreciation of its proportions, *Antiq J*, **67**, 294–301

Barag, G, 1963 The glassware, in *The finds from the Bar Kokhba period in the Cave of Letters* (Y Yadin), Jerusalem

Barfield, L H, Wentscher, J, and Wild, J P, 1963 Die Ausgrabungen unter dem Universitätsgebäude Bonn im März 1962, *Bonner Jahrbücher*, **163**, 342–67

Barker, P, 1985 Aspects of the topography of Wroxeter (*Viroconium Cornoviorum*), in *Roman urban topography in Britain and the Western Empire* (eds F Green and B Hobley), CBA Res Rep, **59**, London, 109–17

—, 1993 *Techniques of Archaeological Excavation*, 3rd edn, London

—, 1997 *The Baths Basilica at Wroxeter*, London

Behrens, G, 1918 *Neue und ällere Funde aus dem Legionkastell*, Mainz

Berger, L, 1960 *Römische Gläser aus Vindonissa*, Basel

—, 1981 Neufund eines Glasbechers der Form Isings 31, *Gesellschaft pro Vindonissa Jahresbericht*, 23–8

Bidwell, P T, 1979 *The Legionary Bath-house and Basilica and Forum at Exeter*, Exeter

—, 1985 *The Roman fort of Vindolanda at Chesterholm, Northumberland*, HBMC Archaeol Rep **1**, London

Birley, E, 1939 The Beaumont inscription, the *Notitia Dignitatum*, and the garrison of Hadrian's Wall, *Trans Cumberland Westmorland Antiq Archaeol Soc*, **39**, 190–226

—, 1961 *Research on Hadrian's Wall*, Kendal

Birley, A R, 1981 *The Fasti of Roman Britain (Quintus Veranius)*, Oxford

Bishop, M C, 1988 Cavalry equipment of the Roman army in the first century AD, *Military Equipment and the Identity of Roman Soldiers*, BAR, **S394**, Oxford, 67–196

—, and Dore, J N, 1988 *Corbridge: Excavations of the Roman Fort and Town, 1947–80*, HBMC Archaeol Rep, **8**, London

Boe, G, de, 1981 Hout-en Steenbouw in het Oosten van het Romeinse Tongeren, *Archaeol Belgica*, **238**, 32–6

Boesterd, M H P den, 1956 *Description of the Collections in the Rijksmuseum G M Kam at Nijmegan, 5, The bronze vessels*, Nijmegen

Bogaers, J E, 1974 Troops auxiliaires dans la partie Neerlandaise de la Germania Inferior, *D'Études sur les Frontières Romaine*, 447–63

Böhme, A, 1972 *Die Fibeln der Kastelle Saalburg und Zugmantel*, Saalburg Jahrbuch, Bericht des Saalburg Museums, **29**

Bonneau, M, 1977 Un habitat rural d'époque Gallo-Romaine à Crain Yonne, *Revue archéologique de l'Est et du Centre Est*, **28**, 116–31

Boon, G C, 1962 Remarks on Roman Usk, *Monmouth Antiq*, **1.3**, 28–33

—, 1970 Excavations on the site of the *Basilica Principiorum* at Caerleon, *Archaeol Cambrensis*, **119**, 10–34

—, 1982a The coins, in *Report on the Excavations at Usk, 1965–1976: The Coins, Inscriptions and Graffiti* (ed W H Manning), Cardiff, 3–42

—, 1982b An Isiac intaglio from Wroxeter rediscovered, *Antiq J*, **62**, 356

—, 1988 Counterfeit coins in Roman Britain, in *Coins and the Archaeologist* (eds P J Casey and R Reece), 2nd edn, London, 102–88

Brailsford, J W, 1962 *Hod Hill I: Antiquities from Hod Hill in the Durden Collection*, London

Breeze, D J, 1977 The fort at Bearsden and the supply of pottery to the Roman army, in Dore and Greene 1977, 133–45

British Museum, 1929 *British Museum Guide to Greek and Roman life*, London

—, 1951 *British Museum Guide to the Antiquities of Roman Britain*, London

—, 1958 *British Museum Guide to the Antiquities of Roman Britain*, 2nd edn, London

Buchem, H J H, van, 1941 *De Fibulae van Nijmegen*, Bouwsteenen voor een Geschiedenis van Nijmegem, **3**

Bushe-Fox, J P, 1913a *First report on the Excavations on the Site of the Roman town at Wroxeter, Shropshire*, Soc Antiq Res Rep, **1**, London

—, 1913b The use of samian pottery in dating the early Roman occupation of the north of Britain, *Archaeologia*, **64**, 295–314

—, 1914 *Second report on the Excavations on the Site of the Roman town at Wroxeter, Shropshire*, Soc Antiq Res Rep, **2**, London

—, 1916 *Third Report on the Excavations on the Site of the Roman Town at Wroxeter, Shropshire, in 1914*, Soc Antiq Res Rep, **4**, Oxford

—, 1926 *First Report on the Excavations of the Roman Fort at Richborough, Kent*, Soc Antiq Res Rep, **6**, London

—, 1932 *Third Report on the Excavations of the Roman Fort at Richborough, Kent*, Soc Antiq Res Rep, **10**, London

—, 1949 *Fourth Report on the Excavations of the Roman fort at Richborough, Kent*, Soc Antiq Res Rep, **16**, London

Cagnat, R, and Chapot, V, 1920 *Manuel d'Archéologie, Romaine*, **2**, Paris

Callender, M H, 1965 *Roman Amphorae*, Oxford

Calvi, M C, 1968 *I Vetri Romani del Museo di Aquileia*, Pubblicazioni dell'Associazone Nazionale per Aquileia, 7, Aquileia

Campion, G F, 1938 Excavations at Broxtowe, *Thoroton Soc Annual Rep 1938*

Canti, M, 1988 *Wroxeter baths site, soil report*, Ancient Monuments Lab Rep, **1/88**

Carazzetti, R, and Biaggio Simona, S, 1988 *Vetri Romani del Cantone Ticino*, Locarno

Carey, E, (trans) 1914 *Dio's Roman History*, London

Carrington, P, 1977 The planning and date of the Roman legionary fortress at Chester, *J Chester Archaeol Soc*, **60**, 35–42

—, 1986 The Roman advance into the north western midlands before AD 71, *J Chester Archaeol Soc*, **68**, 5–22

Caruana, I, 1992 Carlisle; Excavation of a section of the Annexe ditch of the first Flavian Fort, 1990, *Britannia*, **23**, 45–109

Casey, P J, 1994 *Roman Coinage in Britain*, 2nd edn, Aylesbury

Castle, S A, 1974 Excavations at Brockley Hill, Middlesex, March–May, 1972, *Trans London Middlesex Archaeol Soc*, **25**, 251–63

Chadburn, A, and Tyers, P 1984 The Roman ceramics from Fenchurch Street, *Early Roman pottery from the City of London*, **5**, Department of Urban Archaeology, London

Charlesworth, D, 1959a The glass, in The Roman bath house at Red House, Beaufront near Corbridge (C Daniels), *Archaeol Aeliana*, 4 ser, **37**, 164–6

—, 1959b Roman glass from northern Britain, *Archaeol Aeliana*, 4 ser, **37**, 33–58

—, 1972 The glass, in Frere 1972, 196–215

—, 1974 Glass vessels, in Excavations at the New Market Hall, Gloucester 1996/7 (M Hassall and J Rhodes), *Transactions of the Bristol and Gloucestershire Archaeological Society* **93**, 75–6

—, 1975 A Roman cut glass plate from Wroxeter, *Antiq J*, **55**, 404–6

—, 1979 Glass from the excavations of 1966, 1967 and 1973, in *The Roman Fort at South Shields* (J Dore and J Gillam), Soc Antiqs Newcastle Upon Tyne Monog, **1**, Newcastle upon Tyne, 166–7

—, 1979 a Glass including material from all other Exeter sites excavated between 1971 and 1976, in Bidwell 1979, 223–31

—, 1981 Glass from the burials, in *Skeleton Green, a late Iron Age and Romano-British site* (C Partridge), Britannia Monograph, **2**, London, 268–71

—, 1984 The glass, in Frere 1984a, 46–73

—, 1985 The glass, in *Sheepen: an Early Roman Industrial Site at Camulodunum* (R Niblett), CBA Res Rep, **57**, London, mf 1:A6–A9; 3:F1–F11

Cleere, H, 1958 Roman domestic iron work, as illustrated by Brading Villa, Isle of Wight, *Bull Inst Archaeol London*, **1**, 55–74

Clifford, E M, 1961 *Bagendon: a Belgic Oppidum, a record of the excavations of 1954–56*, Cambridge

Cool, H E M, 1998 Early occupation at St Mary's Abbey, York: the evidence of the glass, in *Form and Fabric: Studies of Rome's Material Past in honour of B R Hartley* (J Bird ed), Oxbow Monograph 80, 301–5, Oxford

—, 2000 The Roman vessel glass, in Ellis 2000, 162–85

Cool, H E M and Price, J, 1987 The Roman glass, in Sea Mills Bristol: the 1965–1968 excavations in the Roman town of Abonae (P Ellis), *Trans Bristol Gloucester Archaeol Soc*, **105**, 92–9

—, 1989 The glass vessels, in *Caersws Vicus, Powys: Excavations at the Old Primary School* (J Britnell), BAR, **295**, Oxford, 31–43

—, 1991 The Roman vessel and window glass, in The metal-work, glass, and stone objects from Castle Street, Carlisle: excavations 1981–2 (T Padley), *Roman Waterlogged Remains at Castle Street, Carlisle* (ed M McCarthy) Fasc 2, 165–76, Cumberland Westmorland Antiq Archaeol Soc Res Rep, **5**, Kendal

—, 1995 *Roman Vessel Glass from Excavations at Colchester, 1971–85*, Colchester Archaeol Report, **8**, Colchester

Cool, H E M, and Price, J, 1998 The vessels and objects of glass, in *Roman Castleford Excavations 1974–1985, 1: The Small Finds* (H Cool and C Philo), Yorkshire Archaeology 4, 141–94, Wakefield

Cool, H E M, Lloyd-Morgan, G, and Hooley, A D, 1995 *Finds from the Fortress*, Archaeol York, **17/10**, York

Corbet, G B, and Southern, H N, 1977 *The Handbook of British mammals*, 2nd edn, Oxford

Corder, P, 1943 Roman spade-irons from *Verulamium*, with some notes on examples elsewhere, *Archaeol J*, **100**, 224–31

Cotton, M A, 1947 Excavations at Silchester 1938–9, *Archaeologia*, **92**, 121–67

Courtney, T W, 1978 Chesterfield, in Goodburn 1978, 430–2

Cracknell, S, and Mahany, C, 1994 *Roman Alcester: Southern Extramural area, 1964–1966 Excavations. Part 2, Finds and discussion*, Roman Alcester Series, 1, CBA Res Rep, 96, London

Crawford, M, 1974 *Roman Republican Coinage*, Cambridge

Crummy, N, 1983 *The Roman Small Finds from the Excavations in Colchester, 1971–9*, Colchester Archaeol Report, **2**, Colchester

Cunliffe, B W, 1968 *Fifth Report on the Excavations of the Roman fort at Richborough, Kent*, Soc Antiq Res Rep, **23**, London

—, 1971 *Excavations at Fishbourne, 1961–1969, 2: The finds*, Soc Antiq Res Rep, **27**, London

Curle, J, 1911 *A Roman Frontier Post and its People: the fort at Newstead*, Glasgow

—, 1917 Note of additional objects of bronze and iron from Newstead, *Proc Soc Antiq Scotland*, **51**, 231–3

—, 1931/2 An inventory of objects of Roman and provincial Roman origin found on sites in Scotland not definitely associated with Roman constructions, *Proc Soc Antiq Scotland*, **66**, 277–397

Dannell, G B, 1971 Samian pottery, in Cunliffe 1971, 260–316

—, 1987 Coarse pottery, in *Longthorpe II: the Military Works-depot: an episode in landscape history* (G Dannell and J Wild), Britannia Monog, **8**, 133–68

Daniels, C M, 1978 *J Collingwood Bruce: Handbook to the Roman Wall*, 13th edn, Newcastle upon Tyne

Darling, M J, 1977 Pottery from early military sites in Western Britain, in Dore and Greene 1977, 57–100

—, 1981 Early red-slipped ware from Lincoln, in *Roman Pottery Research in Britain and North-West Europe* (eds A C Anderson and A S Anderson), BAR **S123**, Oxford, 397–415

—, 1984 *Roman Pottery from the Upper Defences*, Archaeol Lincoln, **16/2**, Lincoln

—, 1985 The other Roman pottery, in *Inchtuthil: the Roman Legionary Fortress* (L Pittts and J St Joseph), Britannia Monog, **6**, London, 323–38

—, 2000 The Period 1 pottery, in Ellis 2000, 258–63

Davies, J L, and Spratling, M G, 1976 The Seven Sisters hoard: a centenary study, in *Welsh Antiquity* (eds G C Boon and J M Lewis), Cardiff, 121–47

Davies, R W, 1974 The daily life of the Roman soldier under the Principate, in *Aufstieg und Niedergang der Römischen Welt* (ed H Temporini) 2, Berlin, 229–338

Davison B, 1989 *The barracks of the Roman army from the first to the third centuries AD. A comparative study of the barracks from fortresses, forts, and fortlets with an analysis of building types and construction, stabling and granaries*, BAR **S472**, Oxford

Detsicas, A, (ed), 1973 *Recent Research in Romano-British Coarse Pottery*, CBA Res Rep **10**, London

—, 1977 First-century pottery manufacture at Eccles, Kent, in Dore and Greene 1977, 19–36

Dickinson, B, M, 1984 The samian ware in *Verulamium Excavations*, **3** (S Frere), Oxford Univ Comm Archaeol Monog, **1**, 175–97, Oxford

—, 1991 Samian potter's stamps, in *Roman Finds from Exeter* (N Holbrook and P Bidwell), Exeter, 46–55

Dickinson, B M and Hartley, B R, 1993 Samian ware, in Monaghan 1993, 722–5 and 745–69

Dilke, O A W, 1987 *Mathematics and Measurements*, London

Dillon, J, 1989 A Roman timber building from Southwark, *Britannia*, **20**, 229–31

Dollfus, M A, 1975 Catalogue des fibules de bronze Gallo-Romaine de Haute-Normandie, *Mémoires présentés par divers savants à l'Académie des Inscriptions et Belles-Lettres de l'Institut de France*, **16**, 9–261

Dore, J, and Greene, K, (eds) 1977 *Roman Pottery Studies in Britain and Beyond*, BAR **S30**, Oxford

Dorey, T A, 1960 Agricola and Domitian, *Greece and Rome*, 7, 66–77

Down, A, 1978 *Chichester Excavations*, **3**, Chichester

—, 1979 Chichester Excavations 4: *The Roman Villas at Chilgrove and Upmarden*, Chichester

Down, A and Rule, M, 1971 *Chichester Excavations*, **1**, Chichester

Drack, W, 1945 *Die Helvetische Terra Sigilatta-Imitation des 1 Jahrhunderts nChr*, Basel

Driesch, A, von den, 1976 The measurement of animal bones from archaeological sites, *Peabody Museum Bulletin*, **1**

Duncan, G C, 1964 A Roman pottery near Sutri, *Pap Brit School Rome*, **32**, 38–88

Durand-Lefebvre, M, 1963 *Marques de Potiers Gallo-romains trouvées à Paris*, Paris

Eisen, G A, 1927 *Glass: its Origin, History, Technic and Classification to the sixteenth century*, New York

Ellis, P, (ed) 2000 *The Roman Baths and Macellum at Wroxeter, a report on excavations by Graham Webster, 1955–85*, London

Elworthy, F T, 1895 *The Evil Eye*, London

Empereur, J-Y, and Tuna, N, 1989 Hieroteles, potier Rhodien de la Peree, *Bull Corres Hellenique*, **113**, 277–99

Espérandieu, E, 1931, *Recueil Général des Bas Reliefs, Statues et Bustes de la Germanie Romaine*, Paris

Ettlinger, E, 1949 *Die Keramik der Augster Thermen, Ausgrabungen 1937–8*, Monographien Zur ur- und Frühgeschichte der Schweiz, 6, Basel

—, 1973 *Die römischen Fibeln in der Schweiz*, Berne

—, 1978 Stempel auf römischer Keramik von der Engehalbinsel Bern, *Jahrbuch des Bernischen Historischen Museums*, **55–8** (1975–1978), 115–28.

—, and Simonett, C, 1952 *Römische Keramik aus dem Schutthügel von Vindonissa*, Veröffentlichungen der Gessellschaft pro Vindonissa, **3**, Basel

Feugère, M, 1985 *Les fibules en Gaule Méridionale de la conquête à la fin du Ve siècle après J-C*, Revue Archéologique de Narbonnaise, Supplément, **12**, Paris

Filtzinger, P, 1972 *Novaesium V: Die Romische Keramik aus dem Militarbereich von Novaesium*, Limesforschungen, **11**

Fiches, J L, Guy, M, and Poncin, L, 1978 Un lot de vases sigillés des premières années du règne de Néron dans l'un des ports de Narbone, *Archaeonautica*, **2** 185–219

Fischer, U, 1957 *Keramik aus den Holzhausern Zwischen der 1 und 2 Querstrasse*, Cambodunumforschungen, **11**

Fitzwilliam 1978 *Glass of the Fitzwilliam Museum*, Cambridge

Fogolari, G, and Scarfi, B M, 1970 *Adria Antica*, Venice

Forest Products Research Laboratory, 1937 *Growth and Structure of Wood*, London

—, 1941 *A Handbook of Home-grown Timbers*, London

—, 1956 *Reaction Wood*, London

—, 1957 *Identification of Timbers*, London

—, 1960 *A Handbook of Softwoods*, London

—, 1964 *A Handbook of Hardwoods*, London

—, 1965 *The Movement of Timbers*, London

France, N E, and Gobel, B M, 1985 *The Romano-British Temple at Harlow*, Gloucester

Franciscis, A, de, 1963 Vetri antichi scoperti ad Ercolano, *J Glass Stud*, **5**, 137–9

Fremersdorf, F, 1937/40 Römische Scharnierbänder aus Bein, *Vjesnika Hravatskoga Archeoloskoga*, Drustva, 18–21

—, 1958 Römische Bunt glass in Köln, *Die Denkmäler des Römische Köln*, **3**, Köln

Frere, S S, 1972 *Verulamium excavations*, **1**, Soc Antiq Res Rep, **28**, London

—, (ed) 1977 Sites explored: Roman Britain in 1976, *Britannia*, **8**, 356–425

—, 1983 *Verulamium excavations*, **2**, Soc Antiq Res Rep, **41**, London

—, 1984a *Verulamium excavations*, **3**, Oxford Univ Comm Archaeol Monog, **1**, Oxford

—, 1984b Roman Britain in 1983, *Britannia*, **15**, 266–332

Frere, S S and St Joseph, J K, 1974 The Roman fortress at Longthorpe, *Britannia*, **5**, 1–129

—, 1983 *Roman Britain from the air*, Cambridge

Frere, S S, Stow, S, and Bennett, P, 1982 *Excavations on the Roman and Medieval Defences of Canterbury*, Archaeol Canterbury, **2**, Maidstone

Funfschilling, S, 1985 *Römische Gläser aus Baden-Aquae Helveticae aus den Grabungen 1892–1911*, Gesellschaft pro Vindonissa Jahresbericht, 81–160

Gillam, J P 1957 Types of Roman coarse pottery vessels in Northern Britain, *Archaeol Aeliana*, ser 4, **35**, 180–251

Giffen, van A E, 1948 *Opgravingen in de Dorpswierde te Ezinge en de romiense terpen van Utrecht, Valkenburg ZH en Vechten* Jaarverslag van de Vereeniging voor Terpenonderoec

Glasbergen, W, 1940/44 Versiede Claudisch-Neronische Terra Sigillata van Valkenburg, ZH, *Jaarverslay van de Vereeniging voot Terpenendock*, 206–36

—, 1955 Pottenbakkersstempels op Terra Sigillata van Valkenburg ZH (1942), *Jaarverslag van de Vereeniging voor Terpenonderzoek*, **33–37** (1948–1953), 127–48

Goethert-Polaschek, K, 1977 *Katalog der Römischen Gläser des Rheinischen Landesmuseums*, Trier

—, 1985 *Katalog der Römischen Lampen des Rheinischen Landesmuseums*, Trier

Goodburn, R, (ed), 1976 Sites explored: Roman Britain in 1975, *Britannia*, **7**, 291–377

—, 1978 Sites explored: Roman Britain in 1977, *Britannia*, **9**, 404–72

—, 1979 Sites explored: Roman Britain in 1978, *Britannia*, **10**, 268–338

Goodyear, F H, 1974 The Roman villa at Hales, Staffordshire: the final report, *N Staffordshire J Field Stud*, **14**, 1–20

Gould, J, 1964 Excavations at Wall (Staffordshire), 1961–3, on the site of the early Roman forts and of the late Roman defences, *Trans Lichfield S Staffordshire Archaeol Hist Soc*, **5**, 1–50

—, 1967 Excavations at Wall (Staffordshire), 1964–6, on the site of the Roman forts, *Trans Lichfield S Staffordshire Archaeol Hist Soc*, **8**, 1–40

Granger, F, (ed) 1983 *Vitruvius 1: de Architectura*, Books 1–5, London

—, 1985, *Vitruvius 1: de Architectura*, Books 6–10, London

Grasilier, P-Th, 1873 Memoire sur un tombeau Gallo-Romain decouvert à Saintes en Novembre 1871, *Revue Archéologique*, **25**, 217–27

Greene, K, 1977 Legionary pottery, and the significance of Holt, in Dore and Greene 1977, 113–32

—, 1979 *Report on the Excavations at Usk, 1965–1976: The Pre-Flavian Fine Wares*, Cardiff

—, 1993 The fortress coarse ware, in Manning 1993, 3–124

Griffin, M, 1984 *Nero, the End of a Dynasty*, London

Griffiths, N, 1982 Early Roman military metalwork from Wiltshire, *Wiltshire Archaeol Natur Hist Mag*, **77**, 49–59

Grimes, W F, 1930 Holt, Denbighshire: the works-depot of the Twentieth Legion at Castle Lyons, *Y Cymmrodor*, **41**

Groller von, 1901 *Das Stand Lager von Carnuntum*, Der Römische Limes in Österreich, **2**, Berlin

Gudiol Ricart, J, 1936 *Los Vidrios Catalanes*, Monumenta Cataloniae, **3**, Barcelona

Haalebos, J K, 1986 *Fibulae uit Maurik*, Oudheid Kundige Mede Delingen, Supplement 65, Leiden

Hagen, J, 1906 Ausgewählte römische Gräber aus Köln, *Bonner Jahrbücher*, **114–5**, 379–441

—, 1912 Augusteische Töpferei auf dem Fürstenberg, *Bonner Jahrbücher*, **122**, 343–62

Hanson, W S, 1978 The organisation of Roman military timber supply, *Britannia*, **9**, 293–305

—, 1987 *Agricola and the Conquest of the North*, London

Harden, D B, 1947 The glass, in Hawkes and Hull 1947, 287–307

—, 1962 Glass in Roman York, in *An Inventory of the Historical Monuments in the City of York*, **1**, Eburacum Roman York (RCHM), London, 136–41

—, 1967 The glass jug, in Two Flavian burials from Grange Road, Winchester (M Biddle), *Antiq J*, **47**, 238–40

—, 1970 Ancient glass, II: Roman, *Archaeol J*, **126**, 44–77

—, 1976 Fragments of glass, in Kenyon 1976, 41

Harden, D B, and Price, J, 1971 The glass, in Cunliffe 1971, 317–68

Harden, D B, Hellenkemper, H, Painter, K, and Whitehouse, D, 1987 *Glass of the Caesars*, London

Harden, D B, Painter, K S, Pinder-Wilson, R H and Tait, H, 1968 *Masterpieces of glass*, London

Hartley, B R, 1972 The samian ware, in Frere 1972, 216–62

—, and Dickinson, B, 1982 The samian, in *Early Roman occupation at Cirencester* (J Wacher and A McWhirr), Cirencester, 119–46

—, 1993 The samian stamps, in Manning 1993, 207–15

Hartley, K F, 1973 The marketing and distribution of mortaria, in Detsicas 1973, 39–51

—, 1985 The mortaria, in Niblett 1985, **57**, 92–3

—, 1993 The mortaria, in Manning 1993, 390–437

Hattatt, R, 1985 *Iron Age and Roman brooches, a second selection of brooches from the author's collection*, Oxford

Hawkes, C F C, and Hull, M R, 1947 *Camulodunum: First Report on the Excavations at Colchester, 1930–1939*, Soc Antiq Res Rep, **14**, London

Hebditch, M, and Mellor, J, 1973 The forum and basilica of Roman Leicester, *Britannia*, **4**, 1–83

Henderson, C, 1988 Exeter (*Isca Dumnoniorum*), in Webster 1988, 91–119

Henig, M, 1978 *A Corpus of Roman Engraved Gemstones from British Sites*, BAR, 8, 2nd edn, Oxford

—, 1984 Amber amulets, *Britannia*, **15**, 244–6

—, 1991 Antique gems in Roman Britain, *Jewellery Stud*, **5**, 49–54

—, 1995 *The Art of Roman Britain*, London

Henig, M, and Webster, G, 1983 A Ptolemaic portrait, on an intaglio from Wroxeter, *Antiq J*, **63**, 369–71

Henig, M, Webster, G, and Wilkins, R, 1987 A bronze dioscorus from Wroxeter and its fellow from Canterbury, *Antiq J*, **47**, 360–2

Hermet, F, 1934 *La Graufesenque (Condatomage)*, Paris

Hildyard, E J W, 1945 The ancestry of the trumpet fibula, *Antiq J*, **25**, 154–8

Hird, L, 1992 Coarse pottery, in Caruana 1992, 58–62

Hobley, B, 1969 A Neronian-Vespasianic military site at 'The Lunt', Baginton, Warwickshire, *Trans Birmingham Archaeol Soc*, **83**, 65–129

—, 1973 Excavations at 'The Lunt' Roman military site, Baginton, Warwickshire, 1968–71, second interim report, *Trans Birmingham and Warwickshire Archaeol Soc*, **85**, 7–92

—, 1975 *Excavations at the Lunt Roman Fort, Bagington, Warwickshire*. Birmingham and Warwickshire Archaeological Society, **87**

Holbrook, N, and Bidwell, P T, 1991 *Roman Finds from Exeter*, Exeter Archaeol Rep 4, Exeter

Hollingworth, E J, and O'Reilly, M M, 1925 *The Anglo-Saxon Cemetery at Girton College, Cambridge*, Cambridge

Holwerda, H H, 1941 *De Belgische waar in Nijmegen*, Den Hague

—, 1944 Het in de Pottenbackerij van de Holdeurn Gefabriceerde Aardewerk uit de Nejmegsche Grafvelden, Oudhkde. *Meded Rijksmus Oudh Leiden*, **24**, Suppl, Leiden

Hoppus, 1750 *Hoppus's Measurer*, London

Houghton, A W J, 1961 A Roman tilery and brickfield at Ismore Coppice, Wroxeter, *Trans Shropshire Archaeol Soc*, **57**, 7

—, 1964 A Roman pottery factory near Wroxeter, Salop, *Trans Shropshire Archaeol Soc*, **57** (ii), 101

Hull, M R, 1958 *Roman Colchester*, Soc Antiq Res Rep, **20**, London

—, 1963 *The Roman Potters' Kilns at Colchester*, Soc Antiq Res Rep, **21**, London

Hull, M R, and Hawkes, C F C, 1987 *Pre-Roman Bow Brooches*, BAR, **168**, Oxford

Humphrey, J, 1976 *Excavations at Carthage conducted by the University of Michigan,* Tunis

Hurst, H R, 1976 Glevum, a *colonia* in the West Country, in *The Roman West Country* (K Branigan and P Fowler, (eds), Newton Abbot, 63–80

—, 1985 *Kingsholm*, Gloucester Archaeol Rep, **1**, Cambridge

—, 1988 Gloucester (*Glevum*), in Webster 1988, 48–73

Hutchinson, M E, 1994 *Identification of a green stone from Wroxeter Roman city, Shropshire*, Ancient Monuments Lab Rep, **32/94**

Hutchinson, V J, 1986 *Bacchus in Roman Britain*, BAR, **151**, Oxford

ILS Dessau, H, 1916 *Inscriptiones Latinae selectae*, Berlin

Isings, C, 1957 *Roman Glass from Dated Finds*, Groningen

—, 1975 Exchanged for sulphur, in *Festoen opgedrgen aan A N Zadoks-Josephus Jitta bij haar zeventigste verjaardag*, Bussum, 353–6

—, 1979 Roman glass from Nijmegen, in *Recent Finds of Roman Glass from the Netherlands* (S Lith and C Isings), Annales du 8e Congrés de l'Association Internationale pour l'Histoire du Verre, 101–4

—, 1980 Glass from the *canabae legionis* at Nijmegen, *Ber Rijksdienst Oudheidkund Bodenmonderzoek*, **30**, 281–346

Jackson, D A, and Ambrose, T M, 1978 Excavations at Wakerley, Northants, 1972–75, *Britannia*, **9**, 115–242

Jackson, J, 1951 *Tacitus: The Annals*, London

Jacobi, H, 1937 Das Kastell Saalburg, *Der Obergermanishe-Raetische Limes des Romerriches*, **11**

Jacobi, L, 1897 *Das Römerkastell Saalburg bei Homburg von der Höhe*, Homburg von der Höhe

Jobst, W, 1975 *Die Römischen Fibeln aus Lauriacum*, Forschungen in Lauriacum, **10**

Johnson, S, 1976 Wroxeter, *Archaeological excavations 1975*, London

—, 1977 Wroxeter, *Archaeological excavations 1976*, London

Jones, G D B, 1968 The Romans in the north-west, *Northern Hist*, **3**, 1–26

—, 1977 The Roman campaign base, Rhyn Park, near Chirk, *CBA Group 8 West Midlands, Archaeol Newsheet*, **20**, 45–52

—, 1990 Searching for Caradog, in *Conquest, Co-existence and Change* (eds B Burnham and J Davies), Lampeter, 57–64

Jones, M J, 1975 *Roman Fort Defences to AD 117*, BAR, **21**, Oxford, 82–8

—, 1988 Lincoln (*Lindum*), in Webster 1988, 145–66

Kapossy, B, 1969 *Brunnenfiguren der hellenistischen und römischen Zeit*, Zurich

Kennett, D H, 1970 The Shefford burial, *Bedfordshire Mag*, **12**, 201–3

Kenyon, K, 1940 Excavations at *Viroconium*, 1936–37, *Archaeologia*, **88**, 175–227

—, 1943 Excavations at the Wrekin, Shopshire, 1939, *Archaeol J*, **99**, 99–109

—, 1976 Excavations at Viroconium in Insula 9, 1952–3, *Trans Shropshire Archaeol Soc*, **60**, 5–73

Kenyon, R, 1987 The Claudian coinage, in *The Coins from the Excavations in Colchester 971–9*, (N Crummy, ed), Colchester Archaeol Rep, **4**, Colchester, 24–41

Knorr, R, 1912 *Die Terra-Sigillata Gefässe von Aislingen*, Dillingen

—, 1919 *Töpfer und Fabriken Verzierter Terra-Sigillata des ersten Jahrhunderts*, Stuttgart

—, 1952 *Terra-Sigillata Gefässe des Ersten Jahrhunderts mit Topfernamen*, Stuttgart

Kovrig, I, 1937 *Die Haupttypen der Kaiserzeitlichen Fibeln in Pannonien*, Dissertationes Pannonicae ser 2, **4**

La Baume, P, 1964 *Römisches Kunstgewerbe*, Braunschweig

Laubenheimer, F, 1979 La collection de céramiques sigillées gallo-romaines estampillées du Musée de Rabat, *Antiquités Africaines*, **13**, 99–225

—, 1985 La production des amphores en Gaule Narbonnaise, *Centre de Recherches d'Histoire Ancienne*, **66**, Paris

Lancel, S, 1967 *Verrerie Antique de Tipasa*, Paris

Lehner, H, 1904 Die Einzelfunde von Novaesium, in Novaesium, Das im Anftrag des rheinschen Provinzialverbandes von Bonner Provinzialmuseum, 1887–1900, Ausgegrabene Legionslager, *Bonner Jahrbücher*, 111–14

Lenoir, M, 1979 *Pseudo-Hygin, des fortifications du camp*, Paris

Lepper, F, and Frere, S S, 1988 *Trajan's Column*, Gloucester

Lerat, L, 1956 Catalogue des collection archéologique de Besançon, 2: Les Fibules Gallo-Romaines, *Annales Littéraires de l'Université de Besonçon*, **2**, Archéologie, 3, 1–51

—, 1957 Catalogue des collections archéologique de Montbéliard, Historique (et) les fibules Gallo-Romaines de Madeure, *Annales Littéraires de l'Université de Besançon*, **16**, Archéologie 4, 2–26

Levitan, B, 1978 The animal bones, in *Excavations at West Hill, Uley, in 1977: the Romano-British temple* (A Ellison), Comm Rescue Archaeol Avon, Gloucester, Somerset, Bristol

Liversidge, J, 1955 *Furniture in Roman Britain*, Leicester

Loeschcke, S, 1909 Keramische Funde in Haltern, *Mitteilungen der Altertums-Kommission fur Westfalen*, **5**, 103–322

—, 1919 *Lampen aus Vindonissa*, Zürich

MacGregor, M, 1976 *Early Celtic Art in North Britain*, **2**, Leicester

Mack, R.P., 1973 *The Coinage of Ancient Britain*, London

Mackreth, D F, 1985 Brooches from Roman Derby, in Roman Derby: excavations 1968–1983 (J Dool *et al*), *Journ Derby Archaeol Nat Hist Soc*, **105**, 281–99

—, 1986 Brooches, in *Houses in Roman Cirencester* (A McWhirr), 104–6, Cirencester Excavations 3, Cirencester

—, 1994 Copper alloy and iron brooches, in *Roman Alcester: Southern Extramural Area, 1964–1966 Excavations. Part 2, Finds and Discussion* (S Cracknell and C Mahany), 162–77, Roman Alcester Series, **1**, CBA Res Rep, **96**, London

Maltby, M, 1979 *Faunal Studies on Urban Sites: the animal bones from Exeter, 1971–5*, Exeter Archaeology Report **2**, Sheffield

Manning, W H, 1976 *Catalogue of Romano-British ironwork in the Museum of Antiquities*, Newcastle upon Tyne

—, 1981 *Report on the Excavations at Usk 1965–1976: The Fortress Excavations 1968–71*, Cardiff

—, 1985 *Catalogue of the Romano-British iron tools, fittings and weapons in the British Museum*, London

—, (ed), 1993 *Report on the Excavations at Usk 1965–1976: The Roman Pottery*, Cardiff

—, and Scott, I R, 1979 Roman timber military gateways in Britain and on the German frontier, *Britannia*, **10**, 19–61

Mano-Zisi, D, 1957 *Nalaz iz Tekije*, Beograd

Mariacher, G, 1966 I vetri del Museo di Zara restaurati, *Bolletino del Musei Civici Veneziani*, **11**, 1–15

Marsh, G, 1978 Early second century fine wares in the London area, in *Early Fine Wares in Roman Britain* (eds P Arthur and G Marsh), BAR 57, Oxford, 119–223

—, and Tyers, P, 1976 Roman pottery from the City of London, *Trans London Middlesex Archaeol Soc*, **27**, 228–44

Mary, G, 1967 *Novaesium I. Die südgallische aus Neuss*, Limasforschungen 6, Berlin

Mattingly, H, 1965–68 *Coins of the Roman Empire in the British Museum*, *1–6*, London

Mattingly, H, *et al.* 1926 *The Roman Imperial Coinage* Vol 2, London

—, *et al.*, 1984 *The Roman Imperial Coinage* Vol 1, 2nd edn, London

Maxwell, G, 1974 Objects of glass, in The Roman fort at Cramond, Edinburgh, excavations 1954–1966 (A Rae and V Rae), *Britannia*, **5**, 177–9

May, T, 1916 *The Pottery found at Silchester*, Reading

—, 1922 *The Roman Forts at Templebrough, near Rotherham*, Rotherham

—, 1930 *Catalogue of Roman pottery in the Colchester and Essex Museum*, Cambridge

Mensch, E, van, 1974 A Roman soup kitchen at Zwammerdam, *Berichte van de Rijksdienst voor het Oudheidkundig Bodemonderzoek*, **24**, 159–65

Miles, D, 1986 *Archaeology at Barton Court Farm, Abingdon, Oxon*, Oxford Archaeological Unit Rep, **3**, CBA Res Rep, **50**, London

Miller, S N, 1922 *The Roman Fort at Balmuildy*, Glasgow

Monaghan, J, 1993 *Roman Pottery from the Fortress*, Archaeol York, **16/7**, York

Moore, C H, 1925 *Tacitus Histories*, Loeb

Morren, C G A, 1966 Een Terra-sigillata-handelaar te Nijmegen? *Numaga* 13.4, 223–32

Müller, G, 1959 Frixheim-Anstel Kreis Grevenbroich, *Bonner Jahrbücher*, **59**, 401–10

Nash-Williams, V E, 1929 The Roman legionary fortress at Caerleon in Monmouthshire. Report on the excavations carried out in 1922, *Archaeol Cambrensis*, **134**, 237–407

—, 1932 The Roman legionary fortress at Caerleon in Monmouthshire: report on the excavations carried out in the Prysg Field 1927–9, *Archaeol Cambrensis*, **87**, 48–104

Niblett, R, 1985 *Sheepen: an Early Roman industrial site at Camulodunum*, CBA Res Rep, **57**, London

Nieto Prieto, J, *et al*, 1989 *Excavacions arqueologiques subacuatiques a Cala Culip 1*, Girona

Noddle, B A, 1973 Determination of the body weight of cattle from bone measurements, in *Domestikationsforschung und Geschichte der Haustiere* (J Matolcsi, ed), Budapest, 377–89

—, 1978 Some minor skeletal differences in sheep, in *Research Problems in Zooarchaeology* (D Brothwell, J Clutton-Brock and K Thomas, eds) 133–41, Inst Archaeol Lond Occ Pub, **3**, London

Ogilvie, R M, and Richmond, I, (eds) 1967 *Cornelii Taciti, de vita Agicolae*, London

Oldenstein, J, 1976 Zur Ausrüstung römischer Auxiliareinheiten, *Bericht der Romische-Germanischen Kommission*, **57**, 59–284

Oliver, A, 1984 Early Roman faceted glass, *J Glass Stud*, **27**, 35–58

ORL 1894 *Der Obergermanisch-raetische Limes des Römerreiches* (E Fabricus ed)

Orton, C, Tyers, P, and Vince, A, 1993 *Pottery in Archaeology*, Cambridge

Oswald, F, 1936/7 *Index of Figure-Types on Terra Sigillata (Samian Ware)*, Liverpool

—, 1948 *The Commandant's House at Margidunum*, Nottingham

Page, W, (ed) VCH, 1908 *The Victoria County History of Shropshire*, **1**, London

Page, W, and Miss Keate, 1907 Romano-British Leicestershire, *VCH Leicestershire*, **1**, London, 179–219

Paton, W R, (ed) 1969 *Polybius*, London

Peacock, D P S, 1968 A petrological study of certain Iron Age pottery from western Britain, *Proc Prehist Soc*, **34**, 414–27

—, 1977a Pompeian Red Ware, in *Pottery and Early Commerce: characterization and trade in Roman and later ceramics* (D Peacock, ed), London

—, 1977b Roman amphorae: typology, fabric and origin, *Coll de L'École Française de Rome*, **32**, 261–78

Peacock, D P C, and Williams, D F, 1986 *Amphorae and the Roman Economy*, London

Peter, M, 1990 Eine Werkstätte zur Herstellung von subaeraten Denaren in Augusta Raurica, *Studien zu Fundenzen der Antike*, **7**, Berlin

Petersen, E, 1900 Dioskuren in Tarent, *Röm Mitt*, **15**, 3–61

Petrikovits, H, von, 1975 *Die Innenbauten Römischer Legionslager Während der Prinzipatszeit*, Abhandlungen der rheinische-westfälischen Akademie der Wissenscaffen, **56**, Opladen

Phillips, E J, 1977 *Corbridge, Hadrian's Wall, east of the North Tyne*, Corpus Signarum Imperi Romani, Oxford

Piggott, S, 1973 Three metal-work hoards of the Roman period from southern Scotland, *Proc Soc Antiq Scot*, **87**, 1–50

Pitts, L F, and St Joseph, J K, 1985 *Inchtuthil: the Roman Legionary Fortress*, Britannia Monograph, **6**, London

Price, J, 1980 The Roman glass, in Excavations at Park Street, Towcester (G Lambrick), *Northamptonshire Archaeol*, **15**, 63–8

—, 1981 Roman glass in Spain, unpublished PhD thesis, Univ Wales, Cardiff

—, 1982 The Roman glass, in *Ilchester*, **1**: *Excavations 1974–5* (P Leach), Bristol, 227–32

—, 1983 The Roman vessel glass, in *The East and North Gates of Gloucester*, 168–70 (C Heighway), Western Archaeol Trust Excav Monog, **4**, Bristol

—, 1985a The Roman glass, in Pitts and St Joseph 1985, 302–12

—, 1985b The glass, in Bidwell 1985, 206–14

—, 1986 Glass jug, in *Baldock: the excavation of a Roman and pre-Roman settlement 1968–72* (I Stead and V Rigby), Britannia Monograph, 7, London, 61–3

—, 1987a The Roman glass in Brandon Camp, Herefordshire (S Frere), *Britannia*, **18**, 71–6

—, 1987b Glass from Felmongers, Harlow in Essex. A dated deposit of vessel glass found in an Antonine pit, *Annales du 10e Congrés de l'Association Internationale pour l'Histoire du Verre*, Amsterdam, 185–206

—, 1987c Late Hellenistic and early Imperial cast vessel glass in Spain, *Annales du 10e Congrés de l'Association Internationale pour l'Histoire du Verre*, Amsterdam, 61–80

—, 1988 The Aiguières and Argentière sites at Fréjus Forum Julii, *Journées d'étude Association Française pour l'archéologie du Verre*, 2, 24–39

—, 1989a The glass, in *Pentre Farm, Flint 1976–81: an Official Building in the Roman Lead Mining District* (T J O'Leary), BAR, 207, Oxford, 77–86

—, 1989b The Roman glass, in *Strageath: Excavations within the Roman Fort 1973–8* (S Frere and J Wilkes), Britannia Monograph, 9, London, 193–203

—, 1990 Roman vessel and window glass, in *A Roman, Anglian and Medieval site at Blackfriars Street, Carlisle: excavations 1977–9* (M McCarthy, ed), Cumberland Westmorland Antiq Archaeol Soc Res Rep, 4, Kendal, 164–79

—, 1991 Decorated mould blown tablewares in the first century A D, in *Roman Glass: Two Centuries of Art and Invention* (M Newby and K Painter, eds), Soc Antiq London Occas Paper, 13, London, 56–7

—, 1993 The Romano-British glass, in Excavations at the Roman fort at Abergavenny, Orchard Site, 1972–73 (K Blockley, F Ashmore and P Ashmore), *Archaeol J*, 150, 168–242

—, 1995a Glass vessels, in *Report on Excavations at Usk 1965–76: The Roman small finds* (W Manning, J Price and J Webster), Cardiff, 139–91

—, 1995b Roman glass, in *Excavations at York Minster Volume 1 part 2: The Finds* (D Phillips and B Haywood), London, 346–71

Price, J, and Cool, H E M, 1985 Glass including glass from 72 Dean's Way, in Hurst 1985, 41–54

—, 1989 Report on the Roman glass found at the Cattlemarket, County Hall and East Pallant House sites, Chichester, in *Chichester Excavations*, 6 (A Down), Chichester, 132–42

Price, J, and Cottam, S, 1998 *Romano-British Glass Vessels: a Handbook*, Handbook in Archaeology 14, CBA, York

Pryce, T Davies, 1932 Decorated samian, in Bushe-Fox 1932, 94–123

—, 1947 Decorated Terra Sigillata, in Hawkes and Hull 1947, 168–74

—,1949 Decorated samian, in Bushe Fox 1949, 160–85

Rackham, J, 1979 *Rattus rattus*: the introduction of the black rat into Britain, *Antiquity*, 53, 112–20

Radice, B, (ed) 1979 *Polybius, The Rise of the Roman Empire*, London

Rawes, B, 1981 The Romano-British site at Brockworth, Glos, *Britannia*, 12, 45–77

Remesal, J, 1986 *La Annona Militaris y la Exportacion de Aceite a Betico Germania*, Madrid

RIB, Collingwood, R G, and Wright, R P, 1965 *The Roman Inscriptions of Britain*: 1, Inscriptions on Stone, Oxford

Richardson, K M 1948 Report on the excavations at Brockley Hill, Middlesex, August and September 1947, *Trans London Middlesex Archaeol Soc*, 10, 1–23

Richmond, I A, 1935 Trajan's army on Trajan's Column, *Pap Brit School Rome*, 13, 18–23

—, 1947 The Roman city of Lincoln, *Archaeol J*, 103, 48–50

—, 1959 The Agricolan legionary fortress at Inchtuthil, *Limes-Studien 1957*, Basle, 152–5

—, 1968 *Hod Hill II: Excavations Carried out Between 1951 and 1958*, London

Rickman, G E, 1971 *Roman Granaries and Store Buildings*, Cambridge

Rieckhoff, S, 1975 Münzen und Fibeln aus dem Vicus des Kastelle Hüfingen (Schwarzwald-Baar-Kreis), *Saalburg Jahrbuch, Bericht des Saalburg Museums*, 32, 5–104

Rieckhoff-Pauli, S, 1977 Die Fibeln aus dem römischen Vicus von Sulz am Neckar, *Saalburg Jahrbuch, Bericht des Saalburg Museums*, 34, 5–28

Rigby, V, 1973 Potters stamps on terra nigra and terra rubra found in Britain, in Detsicas 1973, 7–21

—, 1977 The Gallo-Belgic pottery from Cirencester, in Dore and Greene 1977, 37–45

—, 1982 The coarse pottery, in *Early Roman Occupation at Cirencester* (J Wacher and A McWhirr), Cirencester Excavations, 1, Cirencester, 153–200

Riha, E, 1979 *Die Römischen Fibeln aus Augst und Kaiseraugst*, Forschungen in Augst, 3, Augst

Ritterling, E, 1913 D*as frührömische Lager bei Hofheim im Taunus*, Annalen des Vereins für Nassauische Altertumskunde und Geschichtsforschung, 40

—, 1915 Das Kastell Wiesbaden, *Der Obergermanische-Raetische Limes des Romerriches*, 31, Heidelberg

Rivet, A L F, and Smith, C, 1979 *The Place-names of Roman Britain*, London

Rixson, D A, 1971 The animal bones, in Excavations at Leferne Rd, Old Ford, E3 (H Sheldon), *Trans London Middlesex Archaeol Soc*, 23, 72–4

Roach Smith, C, 1842 Observations on Roman remains recently found in London, *Archaeologia*, 29, 145–66

Robinson, H R, 1975 *The Armour of Imperial Rome*, London

Rolfe, J C, 1924 *Suetonius, The lives of the Caesars*, London

Rolland, H, 1965 Bronzes antiques de Haute Provence, *Gallia*, supplementary volume, 18, Paris

Rutti, B, 1988, *Die Gläser. Beiträge zum römischen Oberwinterthur Vitudurum 4*, Züricher Denkmalpflege Monographien, 5, Zurich

Saldern, A, von, 1985 *Römische Hochschliffgläser*, Jahrbuch des Museums für Kunst und Gewerbe Hamburg, 4, 27–42

Salomonson, J A, 1956 *Chair, Sceptre and Wreath: historical aspects of their representation on some Roman sepulchral monuments*, Groningen

Scatozza Höricht, L A, 1986 *I Vetri Romani di Ercolano*, Ministero per i beni culturali ed ambientali soprintendenza archeologica di Pompei Cataloghi, 1, Rome

Schaetzen, P de, and Vanderhoeven, M, 1955 La Terra Sigillata a Tongres, *Bulletin de l'Institut archeologie liègeois* 70 (1954–5), 1–284

Scheirmacher, W, 1935 Die Neckarlinie von Wimpfen bis Rottweilund Hüfingen, *Der Obergermanish-Raetische Limes des Romerriches*, 11

Schindler-Kaudelka, E, 1975 *Die Dünnwandige Gebrauchskeramik vom Magdalensberg*, Klagenfurt

Schmid, E, 1972 *Atlas of Animal Bones*, Amsterdam

Schmidt, P, 1956 *Dunkle Mächte von Aberglauben einst Heute*

Schönberger, H, 1969 The Roman frontier in Germany: an archaeological survey, *J Roman Stud*, 59, 144–97

—, 1978 *Kastell Oberstimm; die Grabungen von 1968 bis 1971*, Limesforschungen, 18, Berlin

Schumacher, K, 1929 *Kastell Osterbucken, Der Obergermanish-Raetische Limes des Romerriches*, 40

Scott, K 1981 Mancetter village: a first century fort, *Trans Birmingham Warwickshire Archaeol Soc*, 91, 1–24

Sellwood, D, 1976 Minting, in *Roman Crafts* (D Strong and D Brown, eds), London, 63–74

Simon, H.-G, 1960 Römische Funde aus Bad Nauheim, *Saalburg Jahrbücher*, **18**, 5–34

Squire, R, 1958 *Tacitus*, London

St Joseph, J K S, 1949 Roman Britain in 1948, *J Roman Stud*, **39**, 104–5

—, 1953a Air reconnaissance of southern Britain, *J Roman Stud*, **43**, 81–97

—, 1953b Roman forts on Watling Street near Penkridge and Wroxeter, *Trans Birmingham Archaeol Soc*, **69**, 54–6

—, 1955 Air reconnaissance in Britain, 1951–5, *J Roman Stud*, **45**, 82–91

—, 1959 Air reconnaissance in Britain, 1955–7, *J Roman Stud*, **48**, 86–101

—, 1961 Air reconnaissance in Britain, 1958–60, *J Roman Stud*, **51**, 119–35

—, 1966 Air reconnaissance in Britain, 1961–64, *J Roman Stud*, **55**, 74–89

—, 1973 Air reconnaissance in Roman Britain, *J Roman Stud*, **63**, 234–46

—, 1977 Air reconnaissance in Roman Britain, 1973–76, *J Roman Stud*, **67**, 125–61

Stanford, S C, 1973 The Wrekin, Wellington, CBA Group 8 West Midlands, *Archaeol Newsheet*, **16**, 9–10

Stead, I M, and Rigby, V, 1989 *Verulamium: the King Harry Lane site*, English Heritage Archaeol Rep, **12**, London

Stevens, C E, 1948, Notes on Roman Chester, *Chester Archaeol Soc J*, **35**, 49–52

Strickland, T J, and Davey, P J, 1978 *New Evidence from Roman Chester*, Liverpool Inst Extension Stud Rep, **7**, Liverpool

Stuart, P J J 1962 Gewoon aardewerk uit de Romeinse Lagerplaats en de Bijbehorende Grafvelden te Nijmegen, *Oudheidkunde Mededen Rijksmuseum Oudheid Leiden*, **43**, Suppl, Leiden

Sutherland, C V H, 1935 *Romano-British Imitations of Bronze Coins of Claudius I*, American Numis Soc Numis Notes Monogand, **65**, New York

Swoboda, E, 1964 *Carnuntum: seine Geschichte und seine Denkmäler Römische Forschungen in Niederösterreich*, **1**

Taylor, G, 1979 *Catalogue of the glass exhibition for the 8th Congress of l'Association Internationale pour l'Histoire du Verre*, Oxford

Thackeray, H St J, and Marcus, R, 1960 *The Works of Josephus: The Jewish Wars*, London

Thom, A, 1962 The megalithic unit of length, *J Royal Stat Soc*, ser A, **125**, 243

Thomas, C, 1981 *A Provisonal List of Imported Pottery in Post-Roman Western Britain and Ireland*, Redruth

Tilhard, J-L, 1988 Céramiques à vernis noir et sigillées des fouilles de 'Ma Maison' à Saintes, *Revue Aquitania*, Supplement 3, 85–197

Tilson, P, 1973 A Belgic and Romano-British Site at Bromham, Beds, *Archaeol J*, **8**, 23–66

Todd, M, 1969 Margidunum: excavations 1966–8, *Trans Thoroton Soc*, **73**, 5–104

Tomasevic, T 1970 *Die Keramik der XIII Legion aus Vindonissa, Ausgrabungen Königsfelder 1962–3*, Veröffentlichungen der Gessellschaft pro Vindonissa, **7**, Brugg

Tomlin, R S O, 1991 Roman Britain in 1990, II. Inscriptions, *Britannia*, **22**, 293–311

—, 1992 The twentieth legion at Wroxeter and Carlisle in the first century. The epigraphic evidence *Britannia*, **23**, 141–58

Townend, P and Hinton, P, 1978 Glass objects, in *Southwark Excavations 1972–1974* (H Sheldon), Southwark and Lambeth Archaeol Excav Comm, London

Tyers, P A 1983 *Verulamium region type white-ware fabrics from London, Early roman pottery from the City of London*, **4**, unpubl archive rep, Mus London

Ulbert, G, 1959 *Die römischen Donau-Kastelle Aislingen und Burghöfe*, Limesforschungen, **1**

—, 1965 *Der Lorenzberg bei Epfach*, Munich

—, 1969 *Das Frührömische Kastell Rheingönheim: die Funde aus den Jahren 1912 und 1913*, Limesforschungen, **9**

—, 1970 *Das Römische Donau-Kastell Risstissen, Teil 1: Die Funde aus Metall, Horn und Knochen*, Urkunden zur Vor- und Frühgeschichte aus Südwürttemberg-Hohenzollern, **4**

Unz, C, 1972 Römische militärfunde aus Baden, *Aquae Helveticae, Jahresbericht 1971*, Veröffentlichungen der Gesellschaft pro Vindonissa, **9**, Brugg

Vanderhoeven, M, 1975 *Funde aus Asciburgium*. Heft **5**, Duisburg und Rheinhausen

Vegetius, *Epitoma Rei Militaris*, ed Lang, Teubner 1885

Vermeulen, W, 1932 *Een Romeinsch Grafveld op den Hunnerberg te Nijmegen*, Amsterdam

Vernhet, A, 1981 Un four de La Graufesenque (Aveyron): la cuisson des vases sigillés, *Gallia*, **39**, 26–43

Walthew, C V, 1981 Possible standard units of measurements in Roman military planning, *Britannia*, **12**, 15–35

Ward-Perkins, J, and Claridge, A, 1977 *Pompeii AD 79*, London

Watson, G R, 1969 *The Roman Soldier*, London

Webster, G, 1949 The legionary fortress at Lincoln, *J Roman Stud*, **39**, 57–78

—, 1957 A section through the Romano-British defences at Wall, Staffordshire, 1954–5, *Trans Birmingham Archaeol Soc*, **75**, 24–9

—, 1960 The Roman military advance under Ostorius Scapula, *Archaeol J*, **115**, 49–98

—, 1962a The defences of *Viroconium* (Wroxeter), *Trans Birmingham Archaeol Soc*, **78**, 27–34

—, 1962b Some bronze objects from Wroxeter, *Trans Birmingham Archaeol Soc*, **62**, 35–9

—, 1966 A Roman bronze saucepan from Caves Inn, *Trans Birmingham Archaeol Soc*, **81**, 143–4

—, 1975 *The Cornovii*, London

—, 1978 *Boudicca: the British revolt against Rome AD 60*, London

—, 1981 *Rome against Caratacus*, London

—, 1982 Prehistoric settlement and landuse in the west midlands and the impact of Rome, in *Field and Forest* (T Slater and P Jarvis, eds), Norwich, 47–8

—, 1985 *The Roman Imperial Army*, London

—, 1988 (ed) *Fortress into City: the Consolidation of Roman Britain, first century AD*, London

Webster, G, and Daniels, C, 1970 A street section at Wroxeter, *Trans Shrops Archaeol Soc*, **59**, 15–23

Webster, G, and Stanley, B, 1964 *Viroconium: a study of problems*, *Trans Shrops Archaeol Soc*, **57**, 112–31

Webster, P V, 1993 The post-fortress coarsewares, in Manning 1993, 227–379

Wedlake, W J, 1982 *The Excavation of the Shrine of Apollo at Nettleton, Wiltshire, 1956–1971*, Soc Antiq Res Rep, **40**

Welker, E, 1974 *Die Römischen Gläser von Nida-Heddernheim*, Schriften des Frankfurter Museums für Vor- und Frühgeschichte, **8**, Bonn

Wheeler, R E M, 1930 *London in Roman Times*, London Museum Catalogue, **3**, London

Wheeler, R E M, and Wheeler, T V, 1932 *Report on the Excavation of the Prehistoric, Roman, and post-Roman site in Lydney Park, Gloucestershire*, Soc Antiq Res Rep, **9**, London

—, 1936 *Verulamium, a Belgic and two Roman cities*, Soc Antiq Res Rep, **11**, London

Wild, J P, 1970 Button-and-loop fasteners in the Roman provinces, *Britannia*, **1**, 137–55

Willers, H, 1907 *Neue Untersuchungen über die römische Bronzeindustrie von Capua und von Niedergermanien*

Williams, D F, 1977 The Romano-British Black-Burnished industry: an essay on characterization by heavy mineral analysis, in *Pottery and Early Commerce: Characterization and Trade in Roman and later ceramics* (D Peacock, ed), Sheffield, 163–220

—, 1989 Amphorae, in Stead and Rigby 1989, 115–16

Wilson, D R, (ed) 1969 Roman Britain in 1968, *J Roman Stud*, **59**, 198–234

—, 1974 Sites explored: Roman Britain in 1973, *Britannia*, **5**, 397–460

—, 1984 The plan of *Viroconium Cornoviorum*, *Antiquity*, **58**, 117–20

Wright, R P, and Hassall, M W C, (eds) 1971 Inscriptions: Roman Britain in 1970, *Britannia*, **2**, 289–304

Wright, R P, Hassall, M W C, and Richmond, I A, 1955 *Catalogue of the Roman inscribed and sculptured stone in the Grosvenor Museum*, Chester

Wright, T, 1872 *Uriconium; an Historical Account of the Ancient Roman City and of the excavations made upon its site at Wroxeter in Shropshire*, London

Zienkiewicz, J D, 1986 *The Legionary Fortress Baths at Caerleon, 1: The Buildings*, Cardiff

Index

by Peter Ellis